EARLY ONE MORNING

Barnett Freedman 35.

I have seen
A curious child, who dwelt upon a tract
Of inland ground, applying to his ear
The convolutions of a smooth-lipped shell;
To which, in silence hushed, his very soul
Listened intensely; and his countenance soon
Brightened with joy; for from within were heard
Murmurings . . .

EARLY
ONE MORNING
IN THE SPRING

Chapters
on Children and on Childhood
as it is revealed in particular
in Early Memories
and in Early Writings

by

WALTER
DE LA MARE

OCTAGON BOOKS

A DIVISION OF FARRAR, STRAUS AND GIROUX

New York   1977

Reprinted 1977
by special arrangement with the Macmillan Company

OCTAGON BOOKS
A DIVISION OF FARRAR, STRAUS & GIROUX, INC.
19 Union Square West
New York, N.Y. 10003

Library of Congress Cataloging in Publication Data

De La Mare, Walter John, 1873-1956.
  Early one morning in the spring.

  Reprint of the ed. published by Macmillan, New York.
  Bibliography: p.
  Includes index.
  1. Children.   2. Children—anecdotes and sayings.   3. Children
  as authors.   I. Title.
HQ781.D35   1977   301.43'14   77-22034
ISBN 0-374-92098-2

Manufactured by Braun-Brumfield, Inc.
Ann Arbor, Michigan
Printed in the United States of America

To
GILES and STEPHEN

'Nothing is brought to perfection at first.
We must be children before we grow men.'

'One year is sufficient to behold all the magnificence of nature, nay, even one day and night; for more is but the same brought again. This sun, that moon, these stars, the varying dance of the spring, summer, autumn, winter, is that very same which the Golden Age did see.'

CONTENTS

★

Contents

A star * in the text refers to the Notes, which begin on page 549.

ILLUSTRATIONS

★

Illustrations

Certain of the illustrations in this book are reproduced from photographs supplied by the Rischgitz International Art Agency.

INTRODUCTION

★

There are few things in the world so sure of a welcome in any human mind as a creature brand-new to this life of ours, young in time, and of a brief earthly experience. Its kind matters little: beast, bird, or fish—from the lionet and the infant elephant, by way of the long-tailed lamb, that 'picture of innocence', and the blind blunt-headed kitten, to the newly-hatched alligator and the infinitesimal crab—the human impulse is the same. A peculiar wistfulness is mingled with our pleasure in them. We realize their comparative helplessness, yet marvel at their finish, competence and vigour. They amuse us, yet with a certain pathos. They have what is often an odd, awkward, and even grotesque, yet ravishing beauty of their own. There is a tinge of heavenly foolishness in that beauty; and we accept these young and ardent living things simply for what they are and regardless of their future—the sober actualism, for example, of the farmyard pig, the inanity of the domestic fowl, the cunning of the fox, the ferocity of the panther.

Furthermore, this is a delight shared by the very young with the very old: the young with a more curious zest—their voices soaring into rapturous exclamation at first glimpse of any such novelty; the old with a more ruminative regard, a remote and absent look in the eyes above the smiling mouth.

Human infancy too may be almost as universally beguiling. A little beyond this stage, however, the welcome is not so much assured. Even children (English children, at any rate), however hospitable they may be in other respects, are far less apt to

Introduction

squander their friendly advances on one another—on strange *children*, that is. To their kin, in their own likeness, they may be much less than kind. Nor is the adult attitude to childhood by any means always as friendly and open-hearted as that to calfhood or puppyhood. It may even be hostile, resembling that of the malevolent nobleman I encountered recently in a dream, who at his decease left strict instructions that on no account were his bones to be laid even in the neighbourhood of those of children! Others, plagued by fret and care in the company of the 'wantons', bundle them all into one mental rag-bag and label it 'Nuisance'. Others, though amiably inclined, are ill at ease with children, not entirely at ease even with their own; although there by the grace of God once went they. In sober truth too it must be admitted that if by Circean enchantment *all* their adult acquaintances were transformed into children again, leaving them only their present characters, ways and habits—well, they might still prefer any other room in the house to the nursery.

Most adults, on the other hand, are at least friendly to childhood and to children. With a benevolent eye they watch their gambols, are amused at their primitive oddities, give what they suppose to be the countersign, and depart. A few take children as they take one another, just as they come, welcome them for what they are, refrain from making advances, and are gladly admitted on these terms into the confraternity. The very few—as few in books as in life—have the equivalent of what the born gardener is blessed with—a green thumb. He can pluck up a plant and without the least danger examine its roots. However delicate his specimen may be, his cloistered wizardry will succeed in bringing it into flower. He resembles the solitary occasionally to be encountered in one of the London parks, feeding with minute crumbs a cluster of sparrows that hop about his feet as if he were St. Francis in disguise. *Can* mere crumbs, we ask ourselves, be hypnotic?

Such are the various degrees of approach between the grown-up and the young, from sheer insensitiveness to the rarest insight and understanding. And yet, I believe those who can win nearest to childhood, and be wholly at peace, at liberty, and at ease in its company, would be the first to acknowledge that they can never get nearer than very near, never actually *there*. Why is this? Might it not be assumed that our only need is to recall our own child-

Introduction

hood, to re-enter a more or less remote past, and find our quarry awaiting us. We should then not only forgive everything, if there is any need; we should understand everything. But since at best we can thus recapture only one childhood, is there any other source on which we can trustfully rely? Few human beings are indifferent to their early memories. At mention of them the eye brightens, the voice resounds, the pace of life within quickens; and once the tale is begun, the difficulty is rather to bring the teller of it to a standstill than to spur him on. And this craving is shared to the full by children themselves. Nothing will keep them quieter in the chimney corner than legends beginning, 'When I was young', especially if the Confessor was naughty, unfortunate, in trouble, punished, or uncommonly stupid. They do not realize that *now* is their only chance of ensuring similar treasure of their own.

This being so, the main intention of the pages that follow is to present childhood by way of recollection—early memories gleaned from many witnesses, not always perhaps of a very valuable kind, but chiefly from those who were best able to put them into words, since they were themselves writers. With a few exceptions these witnesses belong to the past, some of them to the distant past. But as, although childhood itself changes little, habits of mind and outlook and the treatment of children vary from one generation to another, this, I think, gives their testimony the greater interest. To make the most of any such memory of childhood we must endeavour, first to enter the mind of the recorder, and next, to enter the mind of the child whom he is telling us about. We can then compare the former with ourselves as we are now, the latter with the self we once were.

Allowance must be made for a natural enthusiasm. Any recollection of childhood, though it is all but invariably endeared to its possessor, is not for that reason alone of any intrinsic value in itself. We speak of some old jobbing gardener whom we hob-nobbed with at the age of five as if he were a grandiose celebrity we were once permitted to shake by the hand at fifty; of an early nurse or governess as if she were as famous, if not as comely, as the Queen of Sheba, or as malignant as Jezebel; of an old tumbledown shed in a small back garden with all the romantic sentiment nowadays bestowed on a locality where some stellar film actress has consented

Introduction

to spend a honeymoon. Such enthusiasm tends to cloy; and especially if it recalls only the ghost of the scent of the flower once so sweet to our own young noses.

But most of the autobiographers quoted in this volume have been men or women of genius, and many of their contributions are of a kind that we should not have foreseen. Since too a man of genius is said to include among his available elements those of a woman and a child, this should give what he tells us a value all its own.

The primary incentive of this book then has been merely a lively interest in children; not any foolish notion to *explain* them; still less to condescend to them—a house might as well condescend to its foundations—or, heaven forfend, to vindicate them. Its method has been the presentation of chosen specimens of children thus viewed in retrospect. It is in the nature of a mosaic, all its brighter and valuable fragments having been borrowed, though it sadly needs a pattern and has no particular design. There cannot but have been a good deal of picking and choosing, and there are no doubt many salient omissions. Repetition was also unavoidable, repetition, that is, of similar experiences and events in childhood. There the similarity ends, for all such experiences and events are coloured and modified according to the temperament, character and circumstances, of their recorder.

Even in respect to so simple a plan as this I am only too conscious of many shortcomings. The course is meandering, the arrangement far from systematic, the field has been only partially explored, and there may, I fear, be many blunders. The voice of the chaffinch, too, the *pink pink* derided by Robert Bridges, will occasionally be heard in the chorus of wood-notes wild, for many of our recorders were poets. But its note is intended only as the compiler's 'Hear, hear!' and may be forgiven on that account. It would, however, be both absurd and ungracious to apologize too much for a piece of literary patchwork that consists in the main of specimens of other men's silks and satins, velvets, taffetas and brocades, so rich, fresh, and various. The design may be poor, the stitching clumsy, and the lining unworthy; but the fabric itself, for those at least who care for childhood at all, is excellent.

Apart from early memories, many examples of writings in childhood, both in prose and in verse—the work chiefly of children

Introduction

who became famous—will be found in the later chapters. They are only gleanings; but no substantial collection of them, so far as I am aware, has been made before. They, also, offer vivid and first-hand evidence concerning the mind, heart, and imagination of childhood; and if allowance be made in them for inexperience and lack of skill, it may be evidence not only intimate but also enlightening and valuable.

The earlier chapters will need a far greater tolerance. Here the author has ventured where even the expert treads, or at any rate should tread, as delicately as King Agag himself. There are few better methods of plumbing the depths of one's own ignorance on any particular subject than by writing a book about it. Needless to say, this hardly warrants the publication of that book. Since, however, a keen interest in all that concerns children (which in the last few months, I confess, has steadily increased rather than diminished), enticed me into attempting to lighten my own darkness by collecting a few relevant facts, data, and even statistics, my hope is that there may be others not much more enlightened who will find them of interest. They too are borrowings, the hardiest venture being a page or two on the legal status of children. Much of this perhaps should be treated as mere digression and ignored, as should also the chapter on Memory, and for the same reason. It is intended merely as a finger-post.

Children suffer from and may be preserved by three handicaps. Compared with their elders they are physically a feeble people; they are at once impounded if found straying; and they seldom have any money. Gullivers in Brobdingnag, they are debarred from many of its inhabitants' social, practical, intellectual and emotional affairs. Its *conventional* language is for the time being beyond their use, if not beyond their understanding, though, as we shall see, they may become deft in translation. To intelligent children, nevertheless, the world of the adult often seems no less 'childish' than that of children seems to the wholly adult. They cannot 'see the necessity'. The estimate in both cases may fall far short of the truth.

Lastly, there has been no intention, even if there should appear to be any inclination, in what follows, to dogmatize about children. Even to generalize about them is well on the way to being lost. Still, early memories, no less than early writings, suggest that

Introduction

to change, apart from inclining, a child's individual nature, to graft faculties that are not innate, to instil what is alien to temperament and personality—that all this lies beyond us. Train up a child in the *way* he should go, said the wisest of the wise; some modern experts prefer to substitute *would* for 'should'. 'For of such is the kingdom of heaven'; some latterday critics of life would prefer a mechanical Utopia or (unlike Marjory Fleming who couldn't abide her eight times eight), a lifeless immensity monarched by a Mathematician. And as we make our universe, so must we abide by it.

That was Swift's conviction; and the theme of childhood reminds me of his Lemuel's first adventure. If, a Lilliputian oneself as regards any personal universe, one ventures down to the sea of childhood, it appears, as did Lilliput's, to be exquisitely shallow. A sky of a blue pale as turquoise arches above it, for the sun's resplendent travelling; look close, and its every drop of water is charged with life. There is a curious minute wildness everywhere. Its tiny ripples, thin as silver, break like the finest of glass upon its sands. One ventures in, and on; the further one wades the greater the danger of drowning, and the more the ocean deepens and widens, spreading out its waters at last towards the illimitable horizon of human life. For Childhood is the name of the world's immediate future; of such, and such alone, is the promise of the kingdom of man.

PART I

*

EARLY LIFE

CHAPTER I

THE SUPPLY

★

1. *'Sorrow doth utter what us still doth grieve,*
But hope forbids us sorrow to beleeve.'

The London street hoardings of fifty years ago, apart
from being usually mud-bespattered, were far from
bountiful in works of art. But because perhaps these were
so few, they were memorable. Even a child took notice.
I recall, for example, two rather primitive shovels, genteelly inviting me in my early youth to call a spade a spade. There was a
beautiful maiden with a goblet smiling up at the abundance of a
vine, and she, I fancy, still smiles on. 'Bubbles' competed with a
human scarecrow in preaching that cleanliness is next to godliness;
and a poet in a simple couplet was already celebrating certain
pens. *Mr. Waukenphast*—is *his* familiar silhouette also a phantasm
of this distant past?

But what set the deepest seal on my young consciousness, and
even sub-consciousness perhaps, was a pictorial parable in black
and white, with the legend, 'What Will He Become?' On its
extreme left was the vignette of a bonny baby boy with a curly
head. Its other panels—six in all, and arranged in triplets—illustrated the lesson insisted on by Solomon, by Dante, by Hogarth,
by the author of that superannuated little masterpiece, *Sandford &
Merton*, and by a thousand tracts—the choice that humanity has to
make between the broad and the narrow roads. Here the broad
led to debauched ruin, the narrow to a smiling, silvery, spruce
prosperity. The intention of the parable was excellent. That of
Dr. Jekyll and Mr. Hyde was as yet in limbo. Nevertheless for
the paragon in the poster—the old gentleman, I mean, whom the
artist had certainly intended to make benign rather than spruce—I

3

Early One Morning

conceived a hatred beyond words. Can this have been because the picture was hinting that even at the age of six or seven years it is impossible to go back and begin again? A third road, it is true, the perilous road that leads on into fair Elfland, which Thomas the Rimer shared with its Queen, was not even hinted at; but of that I had not then heard. Perhaps it was solely the horror of growing old, in *any* direction, that filled me with dismay. Either conclusion to the long journey, at any rate, was disquieting.

Yet another riddle in connection with this parable failed to occur to me. Many years later I was sharing with a small daughter an exhibit in a silversmith's window showing the evolution of a spoon—a tablespoon. In an elegant case lined with cockled blue velvet there lay, first a narrow oblong strip of metal; next to this was another piece of metal, in the shape of a spoon cut out in the flat; and finally, after similar gradations, there was a specimen of the burnished and finished article on which to feast our envious eyes. 'But surely,' said she at last, gazing on through the window-glass at these transmogrifications, 'that can't be the *same* spoon, Daddy!'

So in the poster with the Infant X and his two ultimates. They could not both be the same X. And yet, perhaps if one could scrutinize their hearts as closely as their faces, they somehow might prove to be. Since, too, as seems likely, this presentment of him was by no means a novelty even in 1880, poor X (if, that is, the artist had a model), must be now nearing his seventies, possibly his nineties. And whichever he may have become, pillar of the State or an outcast in its portico, he is not likely to be commended by the swains of the present generation. He was a scion of the old contemptibles, the Victorians, to whose disconsolate sepulchres continual pilgrimage is being made nowadays, not for the purpose of bringing nosegays of rosemary for remembrance or pansies for thoughts, but of scribbling mocking comments beneath their epitaphs. Alas, when yet another seventy years shall have rolled, the infant X's of the present day will themselves have gone on, and this age also will be ripe for indictment.

Indeed, commonplace but sorrowful fact, all the X's who were born in 1918 have by now abandoned the obvious appearances of childhood. Even their young-personhood now is over. A multitude of children have succeeded them, of course; for humanity

4

The Supply

continues to resemble a mysterious lake whose living waters are continually refreshed, and as continually ebbing away. The apprehension none the less which occurred to Thomas Malthus that the supply might become excessive is less urgent than it was. On the other hand, anxiety lest the source should utterly fail; the possibility of a fiery distemper carrying off every living soul on earth above the age of twelve—leaving the children thus spared to their own juvenile devices; the hope that timely help from on high—if only to make amends for the priceless *minds* lost in the war—may endue the next generation with a finer understanding than the best we can now boast of—such alternatives as these can concern only the writer of fantasies. An imaginary world consisting of nothing human except children would at least give him plenty of scope, and perhaps a good deal of pleasure. In *The Goslings* Mr. J. D. Beresford, apart from a few male exceptions, spared only the females of our kind.

Except at any rate by means of some such drastic catastrophe as this, or by some miraculous change in spirit, humanity itself cannot *en masse* begin again, however desirable in our present doubts and difficulties that consummation may appear to be. The fresh and virgin waters are so rapidly and indisseverably involved with the rest.

Moreover, the Garudâ stone is lost, the *elixir vitæ* remains as yet undistilled. We ourselves are therefore compelled to endure the process of growing older. And whatever we may be becoming, and whether individually we were rejoiced or grieved at being allowed to 'get down from the table', childhood is an experience, a kind of life, a condition of being, that in no earthly existence occurs twice. There are beliefs, there are surmises to the contrary, to which reference will be made; but they remain surmises.

Not that the experience of being a child in any human circumstances is all cakes and ale, all magic and merriment. It has one advantage, however; the advantage that children are merely guests at this feast, and are not responsible for what is on the table. In respect to the latest comers, at least, now we *are*. Our aim and desire no doubt, however far this fall short of attainment, is to ensure them a fair field and every conceivable favour; and to make the feast a rather more inviting affair than the tea party to which Alice was invited in Wonderland. There was no jam, there was

5

no cake, and, to judge from the picture, no bread and butter even. The butter had been the best, but may have been used up to make the watch keep time. Two members of the party were out of their wits, though only harmlessly so. The bees in *their* bonnets were honey bees whose tongues were their only sting; the bats in their belfries were not of the vampire species. And last, their bosom friend, whom we may suspect also of being a poor relation, when he was not telling stories flagrantly guileless of a moral, was most of the time asleep. Alice herself was at an enquiring age.

A bright idea came into her head. ' "Is that the reason so many tea-things are put out here?" she asked.

' "Yes, that's it," said the Hatter with a sigh: "it's always tea-time, and we've no time to wash the things between whiles." . . .

' "But what happens when you come to the beginning again?" Alice ventured to ask.

' "Suppose we change the subject," the March Hare interrupted, yawning. . . .'

That is always the danger—changing the subject, and yawning.

2. '*Some hae meat, and canna eat,*
And some wad eat that want it.'

This is uncommonly like the nursery tea-parties in the House of Life. They, at any rate, are always coming to a beginning again. And there is never too much time to wash up. Our chief consideration is, first the fare to be provided; and next, how many 'pretty little clarissimos' and 'clear-minded and clear-hearted children' are to be provided for.

As to the fare, that is largely Mother Nature's concern. Red in tooth and claw she may be, we know that by heart; but her hair (when she is in England at any rate) is the colour of ripe corn, her eyes are as blue as the early speedwell, and when she walks through the fields it is not a reticule she carries but a cornucopia. Her view is that—far from merely 'enough'—only a superabundance is as good as a feast. Inveterately confident, it would seem, of man's common sense, she leaves to him the distribution of that super-abundance, the obligation to share it round as equitably as he can, the decision concerning desirable 'extras', and the duty of keeping an eye on the table manners.

The Supply

Nature indeed is a standing marvel. Apart from her higher mathematics, to which even Everyman is nowadays compelled to listen in, she knows our simple arithmetic—addition, subtraction, multiplication and division—not merely by heart, but after incalculably long practice. Her moulds and patterns and designs are to all appearance as faultless as ever they were. Even with that beauty of the world, and paragon of animals, Man, she seems still to be doing her chequered best. And it is not at *her* decree that the children of England are rapidly dwindling in numbers. So rapidly that it is predicted that for every score of English children—a particularly pleasing variety—who will welcome in this present spring, with

'Sing levy dew, sing levy dew, the water and the wine;
The seven bright gold wires and the bugles that do shine. . . .'

—such is their native jargon—there will be only ten, thirty years hence. The elderly, being a good deal more tenacious of life than they were in my young days, will have increased in proportion. Our green and pleasant land may not prove to be the less green or pleasant for being less populous, but, until the balance between young and old adjusts itself again, there will be many empty cradles, and an increasing demand for 'grandpa's chair'.

The world of the coming 'sixties then will be a more sedate and sober if not necessarily a wiser world, but there will be a good deal less gaiety in it. On the other hand, if children are to be so many fewer in the near future than they are to-day, it is more than ever desirable that they should be of the best attainable quality and thoroughly well nurtured, and that nothing of value inherent in them shall be wasted. The ideal Spartan state which Plato had in mind when he conceived his *Republic* cannot in population have exceeded that of London in the age of Elizabeth. Its scheme allowed for amplification, but not, we may presume, to the degree we ourselves are accustomed to. There is however no reason to suppose that on this account he would have altered his view of children. In what follows, from Benjamin Jowett's translation, Socrates is speaking:

'We may observe in young children', he says, 'that they are full of spirit almost as soon as they are born, whereas some of them never seem to attain to the use of reason, and most of them late

7

enough!' . . . 'We would not have our guardians grow up amid images of moral deformity, as in some noxious pasture, and there browse and feed upon many a baneful herb and flower day by day, little by little, until they silently gather a festering mass of corruption in their own soul. . . . You know also that the beginning is the most important part of any work, especially in the case of a young and tender thing; for that is the time at which the character is being formed and the desired impression is more readily taken. . . . And shall we just carelessly allow children to hear any casual tales which may be devised by casual persons?' . . .

While listening to these serene remarks we may have paused a moment at certain phrases—'images of moral deformity', for example, or 'casual tales', or 'silently', or (not *reason* but) 'use of reason'. Plato's first sentence is the key to the rest—that children are full of spirit almost as soon as they are born. If we give the fullest possible signification to the word 'spirit', is that the prevailing conviction nowadays regarding young children? It seems no more synonymous with 'tiny tots' than with 'Master mischeevious'. Is it too staid and sententious? What follows may illuminate this question a little.

The belief that children are full of spirit was not at any rate the impression that was given me as a child by the most familiar of the hymns that were then, as now, set apart for the young. Mrs. Alexander's are among the best of these, though none that she wrote excels Baring Gould's 'Now the day is over', with its minute but vivid glimpse of man's whole universe. How remotely shrill their strains in memory sound! 'There is a green hill far away', for example. There was always a walled and very beautiful little city in my imagined picture of this hill, in spite of the 'without' in the second line, a word which—to the detriment of the poetry—was afterwards altered to 'outside'!

But, 'We are but little children weak' was perhaps the most popular of Mrs. Alexander's hymns, and these two particular adjectives denote, I think, the general conception of childhood that was current in her time. Moreover she entitled the volume containing this hymn—a collection of which a hundred editions appeared—*Hymns for Little Children*, whereas Jane Taylor had entitled hers, *Hymns for Infant Minds*. Both writers, needless to say, refrained within the limits they set themselves from being 'casual'.

8

The Supply

3. *'When like the early rose*
Beauty in childhood grows.'

Many of Mrs. Alexander's contemporaries not only emphasized both the 'little' and the 'weak', but added a mawkishness
of their own. This literary ill treatment of children is not confined
to writers in verse, though metre appears to sweeten the temptation. Charles Dickens delights in endearing belittlements no less
than Swinburne, who was an idolator of children, and particularly
of infants. Poems like 'Philip my King' and 'Baby Bell' are in this
key, which at its most plangent is responsible for such little delicacies as 'Our wee white Rose', 'Only eight pounds to hold a soul!',
and 'Tiny alabaster girl, Hardly bigger than a pearl'.

English novelists seldom mention the weight, often the height
and bulk of their characters; their habitual insistence on the
stature of children seems to be as instinctive as it is universal. But
what in particular has it to do with the case? They are little only by
comparison—as we are, compared with gorillas. Were not Nelson, Napoleon and Keats, not to mention their remote cousin, that
strong and silent artist, *Homo neanderthalensis*, all of them comparatively little men? Has it not been shown that genius usually
chooses for its physical abode extremes in human magnitude?
Young things, as we shall see, who may look as frail as a harebell,
may not only be of as hardy a habit but also uncommonly free
and vigorous in mind.

To what degree the stature of children, on the other hand, affects adult treatment of them is a pretty problem. The briefest of
visits to a house wherein the occupants of the nursery had mixed
the Food of the Gods with their breakfast porridge would at least
divulge the fact that there is such a problem. Whatever the answer
may be, children, even young children, even stunted children
need, by and large, be no more weak and feeble little sillies than
lambs are not small sheep. And whether or not his own private
view of himself is of any value, a quite ordinary child, I fancy,
would prefer almost any obloquy to that of little *and* weak—in
wits, will, character, or even so much as 'in the chest'.

I remember at any rate one undersized reprobate of over fifty
years ago who, although he was far from being *full* of spirit, and
was certainly not 'born to any high estate', could never whole-

heartedly intone, 'I am a worm and no man'. He shared too Dr. Inge's disapproval of the psalmist's aspiration that the children of the daughter of Babylon should (either be orphaned, since he was fatherless himself, or) be 'taken and dashed against the stones'. Even though the composer of the musical setting to these words in which he raised his youthful voice had squandered on them his aptest *fortissimo*, he could see in mind too clearly perhaps the austere granite courtyard, the blood and the broken skulls. He delighted none the less in the earlier verses of this desolate psalm, in the green still waters, and the wind-swayed gilded triangular harps hooked over the pollard willows. And he vowed to remember Jerusalem so seriously that this may to some extent justify even at this early age his indignation at an eloquent preacher's expounding of the thesis that metaphorical milk—of which we shall hear more later—is for babes and meat only for grown men. Whether, had he known that Dr. Watts once defended his own treatment of the psalmist by remarking that after all he was not a Christian, it would have set this child questioning, I cannot say. Then he had the caution to keep his sentiments to himself.

To discourse on children at all is to be beset with pitfalls, and overwhelmed with 'material'. 'The hum of multitudes is there', and even the least officious of beadles is apt to become confused. To attempt to be exhaustive on any aspect of them would resemble Mrs. Partington's to control the Ocean with a mop. For this reason alone there is no more than occasional mention in this volume of 'child study' and of 'child psychology'. They are in the nature of sciences, and beyond its range; and merely to sip of the well from which that kind of knowledge is drawn may be more dangerous even than remaining thirsty. 'In everything that relates to *science*', said Charles Lamb, 'I am a whole Encyclopædia behind the rest of the world.' And this was a century ago!

Still, even the novice is at liberty to stray at ease and for pleasure into these fresh woods and pastures. The life of childhood, if it is pondered over closely and heedfully, is as wide and various, as strange and mystifying as human nature itself. It is a vast landscape seen at daybreak. And there are plenty of wild flowers, however clumsy the botanist may be in the arrangement of them—flowers too of a lively colour and fragrance that appear to have been hitherto rather oddly neglected. The novice is at least capable of a keen

The Supply

interest—friendly or otherwise—in children and in childhood, since he has not only been a child himself, but may also in part have been responsible for the appearance of other children in this world, including a bevy of the second generation. Indeed, the saddest feature, as it seems to me, of grandfatherhood—both in respect to these hostages and to one's own second childhood—is that it is likely to be brief. So far *this* novice can go, then, but, alas, little further.

Even the narrowest of nurseries, of course—a cage containing maybe only one hopping, chirping inmate—offers a rich opportunity for chastened enquiry, though few adoring mothers, few proud fathers take full advantage of it. They have in their charge, to say the least of it, one of the most delicate and complicated pieces of mechanism in the world, any single organ of which, hand, heart or eye (in spite of Helmholtz's detraction of the last as an optical instrument), infinitely surpasses in craftsmanship, subtlety and operation the domestic mower, motor car or sewing machine. They may spend time, pains, love, life and money in a constant endeavour to keep that specimen in order, and—unless Nature herself is no more than a stepmother—have intuitions to that end. Yet even a good father may know little of how his child 'works', and takes a long time to discover who, and even what *kind* of being, works it. He may, intermittently, exult in his infant and yet seldom scrutinize and ponder. He notices but infrequently notes. The paterfamilias who, in Cowper's words, is not only 'a man of letters, manners, morals, parts' and 'father and friend and tutor all in one', but also a trained and enlightened expert in paidology, probably resides in Utopia—and his children will probably be tempted to emigrate to Erewhon!

How many of us could even declare on what date our all-precious Nathaniel first succeeded in standing *alone*—a completely conscious and radiant triumph of body and mind, as anyone who has witnessed this feat will agree; how far he understood speech and words before he could use them; what was his first articulate sentence; and what the extent of his infant vocabulary when he was three? That, it seems, may have been but twenty words, it may have been 1500. By the age of four it may have expanded to 4000; and that is about two thirds of the vocabulary of the English Bible. And at five? Well, 'a visitor calling on Richard Garnett, the philologist, in 1840, was asked to wait for a few minutes in the study. Hearing a crackling sound, he looked round and saw a crumpled *Times* newspaper on the floor. Presently a child of five emerged from under the newspaper, and fixing the visitor with his eye enquired, "And what is *your* opinion of the Abyssinian question?" The child was Richard the Second, the author of *The Twilight of the Gods*. *Miss* Blue Stocking at the same age may have gone even a step further, and be enquiring, as did Charlotte Yonge, 'Mamma, how do the men that write the newspaper know of all the things that occur?'

The novice too may be fortified, unless he is wholly dismayed, by the fact that of late years the most settled views on children—themselves, their faculties, their culture and training—have been sharply jarred. Even the nursery quota system which promises to affect the future beyond all surmise is only of yesterday. Parents, teachers, pedagogues, philosophers, sociologists, biologists, religionists, politicians and governments appear to be at irreducible odds on these vital questions; and it is a long journey from the conception even of the True-born English child down to the most atrocious of all current phrases, cannon-fodder. Meanwhile, the barometer of human destiny is hardly at *Set Fair*; and the very beings whom this controversy most concerns—the children themselves—can necessarily volunteer but little help. Whatever virgin views they may have are beyond their expression. They wait, and may, in time, see. But when the wherewithal and the opportunity to communicate their views are available, these are no longer virgin, since early childhood then is over.

It is the ideal goal that eludes us—not merely the best way of attaining it. How many of us could describe the paradise we should delight to share—its surroundings, its company? What conditions of mind and being, within earthly view, would ensure our being truly happy, or interested, or interesting, or truly anything, for even a century—let alone 'for ever and ever'? But is it a much easier task to declare clearly and fully the kind of childhood we should have chosen for our own life on earth, for our coming hither? What special faculties of body and mind, and in what proportion; what kind of mother and father, and ancestors; in what country of the world; in which century, past, present or future; and in what ineffable surroundings?

The Supply

It is a peculiarity of human nature that though most men can easily suggest what they assume would be a change for the better in their circumstances—work, leisure, rewards, scope, social advantages and so forth—very few, it appears, would prefer to change themselves to the degree of becoming anybody else. But kind of self and niche in life apart, are we certain even what cultivation and culture would most blessedly have profited us in childhood, and that to our inmost satisfaction in later life? Little or much, home-made or otherwise, cramming or nibbling, learning wide or deep, book-based or nature-fed, self-inspired or imposed from without, chiefly of body, of intellect, of manners or of morals? And this to what precise end: for the betterment of ourselves, or our fellow creatures; during our life on earth, or the life hereafter? If only questions were as easy to answer as they are to ask!

We should modestly of course prefer the best for ourselves, but who could with complete assurance even outline that best, and would then venture to become a child again to justify the choice? Cultivation indeed implies not only a knowledge of climate, seasons, soil and tillage, but of the species of crop. And which of us in his own estimation is nothing more valuable than a specimen of a species of crop? We may at least attempt to conceive the fuller potentialities of the soil, in view of our own limited harvests, and while remaining a little uncertain what *are* the sovereign dews of Heaven and its essential sunshine, endeavour to keep away from our successors the slug, the cabbage butterfly and the aphis; too much lime, or synthetic manure. We want no child to waste its sweetness, nor *merely* to itself to live and die. That being so, all the virtues, or as many of them as *are* educible, we should most of us wish to include in our list of wants. Still, 'You should teach your children', wrote Lady Mary Wortley Montagu to her daughter, the Countess of Bute, in February 1749,
'to confine their desires to probabilities, to be as useful as is possible to themselves, and to think privacy (as it is) the happiest state of life. . . . Sincerity, friendship, piety, disinterestedness, and generosity, are all great virtues; but, pursued without discretion, become criminal. One of your acquaintances made a ball the next day after her mother died, to show she was sincere . . .'

But there is another consideration, at which both the lover of

13

Early One Morning

privacy and the individualist may falter, even though he may agree. In the words of John Morley:—

'What the young need to have taught them . . . is that they are born not mere atoms floating independent and apart . . . but soldiers in a host, citizens in a polity whose boundaries are not set down in maps, members of a Church the handwriting of whose ordinances is not in the hieroglyphs of idle mystery, nor its hope and recompense in the lands beyond death. They need to be taught that they owe a share of their energies to the great struggle which is in ceaseless progress in all societies in an endless variety of forms, between new truth and old prejudice, between love of self or class and solicitous passion for justice, between the obstructive indolence and inertia of the many and the generous mental activity of the few. . . .'

CHAPTER II

SOLITUDE

*

1. *'Companion none is like unto the mind alone.'*

What angel in my own remote childhood, I wonder,
taught me when alone to be happy. What gratitude
could repay such a boon? Of solitude in early childhood there is little for the body, but much for the
mind. Children need not talk, even when they can. Much goes in,
little comes out. We may call but can win few direct answers. We
can at best only interpret. Of answers concerning the state of solitude given in retrospect, however, there are many—allow what
we will for the enchantment afforded by distance and the deceits
of memory.

'Like all children, I began', says Oliver Wendell Holmes, 'to
speculate on the problems of existence at an early age. I remember thinking of myself as afloat—like a balloonist—in the atmosphere of life. I had come there I knew not how, but I knew I had
got to come down sooner or later, and the thought was not
welcome. . . .'

And Anthony Trollope:

'I will mention here another habit which had grown upon me
. . . which I myself often regarded with dismay when I thought of
the hours devoted to it, but which, I suppose, must have tended
to make me what I have been. As a boy, even as a child, I was
thrown much upon myself. . . . I was always going about with some
castle in the air firmly built within my mind. . . . For weeks, for
months, if I remember rightly, from year to year, I would carry
on the same tale, binding myself down to certain laws, to certain
proportions, and proprieties, and unities. Nothing impossible was

15

Early One Morning

ever introduced—nor even anything, which from outward circumstances, would seem to be violently improbable. I myself was of course my own hero. Such is a necessity of castle-building. But I never became a king, or a duke—much less when my height and personal appearance were fixed could I be an Antinous, or six feet high. I never was a learned man, nor even a philosopher. But I was a very clever person, and beautiful young women used to be fond of me. And I strove to be kind of heart, and open of hand, and noble in thought, despising mean things; and altogether I was a very much better fellow than I have ever succeeded in being since. There can, I imagine, hardly be a more dangerous mental practice; but I have often doubted whether, had it not been my practice, I should ever have written a novel. . . .'

Of the solitary dreamers in childhood who only dream on we never hear, and therefore cannot lament over them. Jane Taylor, like Trollope, and to our endless gratitude, also survived these dangers. She was, says her sister and collaborator, Ann, who survived her by forty-two years, a saucy and lively child. At the village baker's shop in Lavenham in Suffolk she used to be perched up on the kneading-board to recite, preach or tell stories to his customers. She shared 'deeply imaginative' plays with her sisters—*Moll and Bet, The Miss Parks, The Miss Sisters, The Miss Bandboxes* and *Aunt and Niece*, with royalties in the minor parts. These plays sufficed her until she was ten or twelve years old. She then began to spend her playtime in one of the three large empty parlours of her father's house at Lavenham, spinning a whip-top (Balzac preferred black coffee and candlelight), while she composed in her head tales and dramas which she afterwards put down on paper. 'She would spend hours in this kind of reverie.' 'She lived in a world wholly of her own creation, with as deep a feeling of reality as life itself could afford.' Indeed, she said, 'I have sometimes lived so much in a *castle*, as almost to forget that I lived in a *house*.' One of her favourite resorts was a disused pigsty!

Emily Brontë also found constant secret delight in her 'Gondal' romance, which continued from childhood even into her twenties, and which she shared only with her sister Anne. Of the literary first-fruits that have been the outcome of such solitary reveries we shall hear much more in a later chapter.

'So', yet again, says Coleridge, 'from being petted and bullied,

ANN AND JANE TAYLOR
From the painting by their father, Isaac Taylor
By permission of the National Portrait Gallery

Solitude

I became fretful and timorous, and a tell-tale; and the schoolboys drove me from play, and were always tormenting me, and hence I took no pleasure in boyish sports, but read incessantly. My father's sister kept an *everything* shop at Crediton, and there I read through all the gilt-cover little books that could be had at that time, and likewise all the uncovered tales of Tom Hickathrift, Jack the Giant-killer, etc., etc., etc., etc. And I used to lie by the wall and *mope*, and my spirits used to come upon me suddenly; and in a flood of them I was accustomed to race up and down the church-yard, and act over all I had been reading, on the docks, the nettles, and the rank grass. . . .'

A brief solitude, much earlier in his life, by nearly depriving him of it, persuaded him to speak:

'. . . In this year [1774] I was carelessly left by my nurse, ran to the fire, and pulled out a live coal—burnt myself dreadfully. While my hand was being dressed by a Mr. Young, I spoke for the first time (so my mother informs me) and said: "nasty Doctor Young!" The snatching at fire, and the circumstance of my first words expressing hatred to professional men—are they at all *ominous*? This year I went to school. . . .'

John Galt tells of another such moment, when he was less than two years old. It was concerned with the birth of a sister.

'I was . . . at the time in the custody of someone, standing on the kitchen dresser, caressed and caressing, when the event was proclaimed to "all the house". Whoever had charge of me forgot I was on the dresser, and leaving me there, ran into the passage to hear the news more particularly. Well do I recollect my horror at being so abandoned; I looked over the edge of the dresser as Shakespeare makes Edgar look over the cliff at Dover, and seeing my perilous height, roared and ramped and stamped "as it were a nightingale" till removed. . . .'

But one must attempt to occupy that small body if one is to share the perilous height.

There is a curious similarity again in the recorded 'earliest' memories of Goethe and of Herbert Spencer. Both are of solitude, to both are attributed enduring emotions, and both are prefaced by warnings which it is advisable to bear in mind in regard to all similar recollections. 'Of incidents in childhood', says Herbert Spencer, 'my remembrances have assumed that secondary form

Early One Morning

which I suspect they mostly do in advanced life—I simply remember that I once remembered.' Provided that any such secondary form is an exact facsimile as far as this is possible, of its first original, it is of course no less trustworthy; and if the *confusion* referred to by Goethe in what follows is a conscious one, it may, conceivably, be resolved. The virgin recollection often, if not always, has a quality, an air, an isolatedness in its aspect that seems to make it recognizable as such.

'When we wish to remember what has befallen us in earliest youth, we often find that we confuse that which we have heard from others with an actual personal experience. Without therefore instituting an exact investigation, which could lead to nothing, I am conscious of our having lived in an old house which consisted of two houses that had been thrown into one. . . . On the second floor there was a room which was called the garden room, because by means of a few plants one had endeavoured to supply the want of a garden. As I grew up, that was my favourite retreat, which filled me not indeed with sadness but with ardent longing. Beyond these gardens, over the walls and ramparts of the city one looked upon a beautiful and fruitful plain—the same which stretches towards Höchst. There in summer-time as a rule I learnt my lessons, waited till the thunderstorms were over, and could never satisfy myself with seeing the sun go down directly opposite our window. But, at the same time, when I saw the neighbours wandering through their gardens, looking after their flowers, the children playing, parties of friends enjoying themselves, and I could hear bowls rolling and skittles falling, there was early awakened in me a feeling of solitude, and resulting from it a vague yearning, which, corresponding with the seriousness and foreboding natural to my temperament, showed its influence at an early age and more distinctly in future years.'

And Herbert Spencer:

'There was a little sister Louisa, a year my junior, who died at two years old; and playing with her in the garden left faint pictures which long survived. There also survived for many years, recollections of getting lost in the town, into which I had wandered to find the house of some friends to whom I was attached; the result being that the crier was sent round to find me. My most vivid childish recollection, however, worth mentioning because

Solitude

of its psychological interest, is that of certain results caused in me by being left alone for the first time. Everyone was out save the nurse, who had been left in charge of me; and she presently seized the occasion to go out too, locking up the house and leaving me to myself. On one evening a week, which happened to be the evening in question, it was the custom to ring a peal on the bells of the chief church in Derby, All Saints'; and while I was suffering the agonies of this first experience of solitude, its bells were merrily going. The effect was to establish in me so strong an association, that all through the earlier part of my life, and even in adult years, I never heard these bells without a feeling of sadness coming over me. . . .'

And here again is the prolific John Galt:

'. . . I was a soft, ailing, and growing boy. I have no remembrance of the enjoyment of perfect health for several years, and yet I was not ill; a sort of "all-overishness" hung about me, and when not engaged with my flowers I lounged on my bed, which gave me a kind of literary predilection: all sorts of ballads and story-books were accumulated by me, and some of them have left impressions that still remain fresh and unfaded. . . .'

2. 'He might have been said to have been . . . Solomon's Old Man.'

In the telling of these vividly sharable experiences no direct hint is given that the writer is actually seeing himself, objectively, as a child. And to what precise extent in imagination he became again the child spoken of, it would be difficult to say. Both Goethe and Spencer are convinced that this acute feeling—'agonies'—of solitude, accentuated in Goethe's case by the hollow rolling of the bowls, and in Spencer's by the pealing of the church bells, was the cause of a 'vague yearning', of a recurrent 'feeling of sadness' in later years. But *why* a child should be tortured by being alone is another question. The sound of bells may itself be a direct and challenging incantation, but of *what* we can tell nothing. We may be similarly 'enchanted' by a certain colour—the remote blue of a stormy sky, the green of verdigris, Chinese vermilion; and this *beyond all reason*.

Nor is enforced solitude to a young child necessarily a torture

Early One Morning

or the cause of melancholy. 'This is the first thing I remember,' says Ellen Terry in her *Memoirs*; and later adds, 'It wasn't long after my birth':—

'In the corner of a lean-to whitewashed attic stood a fine, plain, solid oak bureau. By climbing up on to this bureau I could see from the window the glories of the sunset. My attic was on a hill in a large and busy town, and the smoke of a thousand chimneys hung like a grey veil between me and the fires in the sky. When the sun had set, and the scarlet and gold, violet and primrose, and all those magic colours that have no names, had faded into the dark, there were other fires for me to see. The flaming forges came out and terrified while they fascinated my childish imagination.

'What did it matter to me that I was locked in, and that my father and mother, with my elder sister Kate, were all at the theatre? I had the sunset, the forges, and the oak bureau.' Ellen Terry is in agreement here with Spencer and Goethe. She attributes a deep and permanent influence to these first surroundings, but a kindly influence. Whereas in a child of a less happy disposition the mere grinding of the key in the lock, let alone the lapping flames of the satanic forges, might have proved a reiterated nightmare. 'I hold very strongly that a child's earliest impressions mould its character perhaps more than either heredity or education. I am sure it is true in my case. What first impressed me? An attic, an oak bureau, a lovely face, a bed on the floor. Things have come and gone in my life since then, but they have been powerless to efface those early impressions. I adore pretty faces. I can't keep away from shops where they sell good old furniture like my bureau. I like plain rooms with low ceilings better than any other room; and for my afternoon siesta, which is one of my institutions, I often choose the floor in preference to bed or sofa.' As for the 'glories of the sunset', the footlights were very soon to reveal their influence as clearly as Wordsworth revealed that of the sound of the rivulets in the face of Lucy Gray.

In no case, apparently, was either the woe or the bliss of these early experiences confided to others. Again and again, questions similar to these will present themselves.

Even when, in hope of enlightenment, our direct questions to children are rewarded with intelligible answers, we must be cau-

Solitude

tious. They must be accepted with a grain of salt, or sugar. Children are wary of telling secrets. Full allowance, even when they appear to be candour itself, must be made on the score of fear, vanity or compliance, no less than of consideration, courtesy and tact. It is not merely the resourceful grown-up who is sinuous in his dealings with the young, but also *vice versa*. Children in varying degree know themselves and their own minds, and are skilled spectators; but concerning this knowledge we—even though once it was ours also—chiefly have to guess. We are every one of us, and particularly in childhood, to some extent malleable, guidable, persuadable, and it is possible to cow, suppress, distort, madden, and perhaps all but destroy the active self within. Heathcliff made this attempt on Linton. But to what extent can you *change* that self within? Never surely—glands or no glands, or whatever the number of 'personalities'—to anything like the degree of substituting another self. 'A man', said Bacon, 'that is young in years may be old in hours, if he have lost no time.' So may a child. Children master shared conditions with an amazing rapidity, adapt themselves to their surroundings like sagacious chameleons, dodge pitfalls, evade the crafty, simulate catalepsy, and when pursued, scuttle away into their impregnable burrows. And, even more surprising, they consider the feelings of the adult.

In a book entitled *The One I Knew Best of All*, the author of *That Lass o' Lowries* and the once immensely popular *Little Lord Fauntleroy*—a small boy who, alike in memoried appearance, character, manners, and in his author's treatment of him, suggests the word 'velveteen'—vividly recalls, when she was about three years old, visiting her mother's bedroom for her first private view of an infant sister. Alas, she found a visitor there—herself a mother—seated beside the four-post bed. This lady at once began to be winning.

' "And what is your New Baby's name to be?" she asked.

' "Edith," was the answer.

' "That is a pretty name," said the lady. "I have a new baby, and I have called it Eleanor. Is not that a pretty name?" '

This, confesses Mrs. Hodgson Burnett, was 'an awful problem'. She did *not* think Eleanor a pretty name. She tried to do so, as if by a sheer muscular effort; and failed. To her taste it was an ugly name. 'That was the anguish of it. And here was a lady, a nice lady . . .

Early One Morning

a kind lady, who had had the calamity to have her own newest baby christened by an ugly name!'

The little girl 'positively quaked with misery. She stood quite still and looked'. But the lady persisted—tactless, foolish, normal, nice kind lady. '*Don't* you like it?' she enquired, in a petting coaxing voice. The child yearned at her in vain.

'She could not say a thing she did not mean, but she could not say brutally the unpleasant thing she did mean. She compromised. ' "I don't think," she faltered, "I don't think—it is—as pretty—as Edith." '

How naïve, how simple, how delicious! 'She was kissed and cuddled and petted . . . and nobody suspected.'

Ask any intent small child what he or she is 'thinking' about. An absent yet speculative haze usually creeps into the motionless eyes, followed perhaps by a faltering, flagging, and perhaps exasperating '*I-don't-know*'. Yet, if only we had the ears to hear,

> 'In the swamp in secluded recesses
> A shy bird is warbling a song. . . .'

This is never of course an easy question to answer accurately at any age, for thinking, though we may seldom realize it, is an immensely complex business, and one's inward ruminations may be as rapid and condensed and as delicately filamented as a dream.

And again:

> 'I love a little modest child
> That speaketh quietly,
> That blushes up to its blue eyes,
> And hardly answers me——'

but even if *no* answer come, and the blue eyes remain untenanted, it by no means follows that our little quiet modest child had none to offer—or that the blush-inciter would enjoy being illuminated.

'Out of the darkness of my infancy', says Edmund Gosse in *Father & Son*, 'there comes only one flash of memory. I am seated alone, in my baby-chair, at a dinner table set for several people. Somebody brings in a leg of mutton, puts it down close to me, and goes out. I am again alone, gazing at two low windows, wide open upon a garden. Suddenly, noiselessly, a large, long animal

Solitude

(obviously a greyhound) appears at one window-sill, slips into the room, seizes the leg of mutton and slips out again. When this happened I could not yet talk. . . .' What solitary infantine reverie the entry of the greyhound interrupted is not related.

How far back in the life of this busy-minded and astonished little mute, Edmund Gosse, should we have to penetrate before we arrived at the clean slate, the *tabula rasa*, of his infant mind? Is any human consciousness ever absolutely new to its surroundings? At birth man 'enters a ready-made world of labels and prescriptions', and his 'potentialities are converted to its customs and conventions with far less consideration than screws are fitted to bolts'. And, according to William Bell Scott, it is not until 'we fully attain to conscious volition as a possession, to the antagonism of the *me* and the *not me*, that we suddenly become a rational hide-bound creature'. How early in life this may occur will be found in another chapter. But if these are facts, a new-born baby, given these 'potentialities', may be justly compared with a traveller in a country which to him is as yet unexplored, but one in which the fauna and flora, and every object, or at least every quality of every object, however attractive or strange, displeasing or marvellous, is never completely novel, and never wholly unexpected. 'I have been here before, but when or how I cannot tell.' Is the brain beneath the softly pulsating head a bee's comb of a myriad *empty* cells? Or are they replete with a nectar merely awaiting conversion into terrestrial honey?

3. 'Look, what I lack my mind supplies!'

In sober fact the brain-cells of an infant are mysterious enough. Unlike those of the body which are continually perishing in the process of multiplication, these cells survive until its last breath is out of that body. According to one theory, we are told, brain-cells all appear at a very early age; according to another, they grow in numbers until the organism has reached the age of about twelve. But how they grow and out of *what* they grow remains unknown. No less inscrutable is the precise relation between the brain and the mind. As a creature, at any rate, whose earliest gestures, actions, humours and so forth we vaguely or clearly translate into our own terms, however precarious the operation may be, the youngest

23

Early One Morning

possessor of a mind is a masterpiece of complex life. And what is life? Life, says Herbert Spencer, is a definite combination of heterogeneous changes, both simultaneous and successive, in correspondence with external co-existences and sequences. And that is yet another little masterpiece, a synthetic gem of a synthesis! But though it defines life, it gives no hint of its cause, or its origin.

'*Infancie*', says Jeremy Taylor, 'hath life but *in effigie*, or like a spark dwelling in a pile of wood: the candle is so newly lighted, that every little shaking of the taper, and every ruder breath of air, puts it out, and it dies.' And William Blake:

> '. . . A weeping Babe upon the wild,
> And weeping Woman pale reclin'd,
> And in the outward air again
> I fill'd with woes the passing wind.'

The very title of the poem from which this stanza comes, 'The Crystal Cabinet', is a splinter of genius, if not of a genius of Spencer's order. And was Wordsworth, whom Blake charged with confusing the Vegetable World with that of the Imagination, merely indulging his fancy when he wrote:

> 'Our birth is but a sleep and a forgetting:
> The Soul that rises with us, our life's Star,
> Hath had elsewhere its setting,
> And cometh from afar'?

Coleridge, too, is referring to the præter-sensuous if not to the pre-sensuous in the following:

'I remember that at eight years old I walked with him [his father] one winter evening from a farmer's house . . . and he told me the names of the stars and how Jupiter was a thousand times larger than our world, and that the other twinkling stars were suns that had worlds rolling round them; and when I came home he showed me how they rolled round. I heard him with a profound delight and admiration; but without the least mixture of wonder or incredulity. For from my early reading of fairy tales and genii, etc., etc., my mind had been habituated *to the Vast*, and I never regarded *my senses* in any way as the criteria of my belief. I regulated all my creeds by my conceptions, not by my *sight*, even at that age. Should children be permitted to read romances, and

24

Solitude

relations of giants and magicians and genii? I know all that has been said against it; but I have formed my faith in the affirmative. I know no other way of giving the mind a love of the Great and the Whole. Those who have been led to the same truths step by step, through the constant testimony of their senses, seem to me to want a sense which I possess. They contemplate nothing but *parts,* and all *parts* are necessarily little. And the universe to them is but a mass of *little* things. . . .'

Nor should we have heard but for an accident at what age Herbert Spencer—like a hatched-out duckling to its millpond—took to metaphysics. Among his father's memoranda after his death he found the following note:—

'One day when a very little child, I noticed as he was sitting quietly by the fire, a sudden titter. On saying, Herbert what are you laughing at, he said, "I was thinking how it would have been if there had been nothing besides myself".'

The titter is the more amusing for the fact that it came from a philosopher who in later life laughed heartily at times, but chiefly for the sake of exercise, and who kept little wads of cotton wool in his waistcoat pocket for use when dinner-table talk grew irksome. The recollection of such little domestic events is unlikely; still more so when the amusement is inaudible. Henrik Ibsen as a child, we are told, when sitting quietly by himself, would sometimes break into a prolonged soundless laughter, until he shook. What *he* was laughing at is left a conundrum. His fellow creatures?

William Bell Scott was not content with reverie. His 'very earliest' recollection, he tells us, was that of asking a nursemaid on their daily walk with his little sister: 'If she saw me as I saw her, was I living, and how was it I came to live, and if I did not wish to live what should I do.' He himself heard these questions repeated to his mother, who then sent the girl away and told him to confide his ruminations to nobody but herself. When he was a big boy he would 'know better'!

Lord Herbert of Cherbury, in later years not only a poet and philosopher but also a soldier, declares that as a child he *preferred* to remain tongue-tied until he felt he could speak to some purpose. He then (after how prolonged a silent soliloquy?) asked a question which Herbert Spencer may already have faced before his father broke in upon *his* early musings.

Early One Morning

'I was born in Eyton, in Shropshire, between the hours of twelve and one of the clock in the morning; my infancy was very sickly, my head continually purging itself very much by the ears, whereupon also it was so long before I began to speak, that many thought I should be ever dumb. The very furthest thing I remember is, that when I understood what was said by others, I did yet forbear to speak, lest I should utter something that were imperfect or impertinent. When I came to talk, one of the furthest inquiries I made was, how I came into this world? I told my nurse, keeper, and others, I found myself here indeed, but from what cause or beginning, or by what means, I could not imagine; but for this, as I was laughed at by my nurse and some other women that were then present, so I was wondered at by others, who said, they never heard a child but myself ask that question. . . .'

That 'laughter'—how familiar a ring it has! The groping tentative horns subside; the baffled snail softly retreats into its shell. But by no means necessarily into inactivity. Herbert moreover tells us only the 'furthest' of his inquiries. Even the nearest might have been beguiling!

And so with our own day. 'My life,' says Mr. Forrest Reid in *Apostate*, 'from as far back as I can remember, was never lived wholly in the open. I mean that it had its private side, that there were things I saw, felt, heard, and kept to myself. There were thoughts I kept to myself, too; and above all dreams. Not deliberately, I dare say, but because I had not yet words in which to put them.'

If the first few years' events of our own lives lie hidden in an impenetrable darkness, we may marvel at the retrieval of experiences as remote yet as clear and distinct as these. But that is not to discredit them. We cannot but accept Henry James's statement that he could recall his first impression of Paris—a glimpse of the Place Vendôme—even though his infant eyes surveyed it out of a carriage window 'when he was little more than a year old'. He was not only a supreme observer but so habitual in introspection that a mere glance at the face or attitude or gesture of a fellow-creature must have been all that he needed whereby to divine what they represented of thought, mood or emotion. This must have been a lifelong habit, and his novels are proof of it. Are we justified in any less confidently accepting, then, the testimony of

Solitude

an imagination as exact in its statements as Thomas Traherne's?

'. . . . This, my dear friends, this was my blessed case;
For nothing spoke to me but the fair face
Of Heaven and Earth, before myself could speak,
I then my Bliss did, when my silence, break.
My non-intelligence of human words
Ten thousand pleasures unto me affords;
For while I knew not what they to me said,
Before their souls were into mine conveyed,
Before that living vehicle of wind
Could breathe into me their infected mind. . . .
Then did I dwell within a world of light,
Distinct and separate from all men's sight,
Where I did feel strange thoughts, and such things see
That were, or seemed, only revealed to me,
There I saw all the world enjoyed by one;
There I was in the world myself alone;
No business serious seemed but one; no work
But one was found; and that did in me lurk.
    'D'ye ask me what? It was with clearer eyes
To see all creatures full of Deities;
Especially one's self: And to admire
The satisfaction of all true desire. . . .
To reign in silence, and to sing alone,
To see, love, covet, have, enjoy and praise, in one.'

What wonder if parlour catechisms a little later in the life of a child are often barren? Washed, scrubbed and tidied, and set in the midst of appraising eyes, we are expected in the words of an old epitaph to be 'affable and amiable to all' our 'acquaintance'. We stand mutely surveying father or godfather, aunt, coaxer, briber, well-meaner, Cheshire-Cat smiler, and must submit. And observing our mild, if restrained faces, the visitor enquires: 'Well, my little man, and how are *you?*' or, 'What a big boy you are getting!' or, 'What have *I* got, eh, a ball?' or, 'Now couldn't you spare me *one* of those pretty curls?' or, ' *We* know someone who likes sugar, don't we?' The smiling, indulgent, stooping face is lit with the kindliest intentions. But no oasis shows in the human Sahara. It is we who are old, so old; and, even though we may not

Early One Morning

yet have learned our letters, we can read these inquisitors like a book. Covert scrutiny of a young child's face in the presence of strangers at least suggests that little pitchers with long ears make constant use of them. I have known a child of three return from his usual perambulator walk with his nurse, among similar *cortèges* 'in the Park', and, without the least prompting or obvious purpose, begin mimicking the characteristic Nannie manners, gestures, affectations, and even remarks.

In respect to what most closely concerns them, and in spite of appearances to the contrary, many young children remain aloof, self-contained, shut up—the key ever ready to be turned in the oiled wards of the magic box. And for the most part how fumbling are the fingers that attempt it. The fumblers themselves none the less have all of them been children. They too no doubt cherish their own memories of childhood. Why then have they (and we) so little skill with what they would call the childish? The very word 'childish' indeed is something of a snare, since it has nowadays usurped the place of childlike.[1] Shakespeare never used it except in a depreciatory or unflattering sense. We ourselves are less discriminating, and are apt to apply it to the complete nature of a child. 'What children do is frequently simple or foolish; what infants do is commonly pretty and engaging; therefore *childish* is taken in the bad, and *infantine* in the good sense.' The latter word is becoming a rarity; the former might be reserved for those of a larger growth.

And what, commonly, are the characteristics of a child? 'Innocence, obedience, trustfulness, limited understanding, etc.' says Webster's Dictionary. But even if we accept these qualities, the first-hand testimony already cited suggests what remarkable additions are hidden in that '*etc.*'.

---

[1] It is a little curious too, as well as inconvenient, that we have no common single English word nowadays that signifies a young child of either sex, except girl and boy; which may refer to human beings up to the age of sixteen and over. For girls of, say, twelve years and over we have maid, miss, lass, damsel, but none is now colloquial English. 'Lad' hints at the schoolmaster or an errand-boy, and 'a youth' is tinged with the mawkish. Bairn is a pleasant word, but it has never stayed far south.

CHAPTER III

ASPECTS

*

1. *'The jargon . . . can have no attraction to the tyro of ten years old.'*

The more one observes or reads about children, and the more closely one broods over one's buried past, the more elusive is the term *child* of strict definition. When at haphazard it enters the mind, the relevant image is usually, I suppose, merely that of a human creature of few years and a minute stature. Mine by good fortune happens to be a particularly pleasing specimen, derived probably from the Bible or from Blake. It certainly cannot be anything in the nature of a Narcissus-like conception of myself in infancy! John Earle in his*Microcosmographie* gives *his* miniature: 'A child is a man in a small letter, yet the best copy of Adam before he tasted of Eve or the apple. . . . Could he put off his body with his little coat, he had got eternity without a burden, and exchanged but one heaven for another.' But whatever the precise image may be, how immense a host of children, and a host of what diversity, the word has to *represent*!

Apart from several other characteristics with which we shall presently be concerned, children may be defined with the utmost simplicity as human beings of a certain age—an age, that is, according solely to the calendar. And that in general is the definition now utilized by the State. Until three years ago, for example, it made many distinctions between 'children' under the age of fourteen, and 'young persons' over that age and under sixteen. And although there are still important distinctions between children and young persons over the age of fourteen and under *seventeen*, that barrier was then largely dispensed with. The complete flock within this fold is very numerous—about eleven million strong!

Early One Morning

An adult child in these matters must here tread with extreme caution, trusting that if he slip, it will be forgiven him. Until the beginning of last century, except in relation to apprenticeship, the Legislature little discriminated between children and any other species of human being. The Factory Act of 1802, 'An Act for the Preservation of the Health and Morals of Apprentices and Others, employed in Cotton and other Mills, and Cotton and other Factories', was the first Act with what in a modern sense may be called a humanitarian end in view.[1] Children, of course, have always been forbidden to break any law applicable to them, but since the beginning of last century the chief aim of legislation on their account has been to ensure their well-being. If *they* can be termed *minima*, the Law definitely does now concern itself with them; but, apart from their education, far less in respect to what they do than to how they are to be done by. It is pertinaciously

[1] In 1767 an Act was passed 'for the better Regulation of' certain Parish Poor Children; and in 1793 an Act concerned with the ill usage of apprentices; but it does not appear that either statute was of much effect. Possibly the first specific reference to children in any Act of Parliament occurs in a statute of the reign of Henry VIII: 'Children under fourteen years of age, and above five, that live in idleness and be taken begging, may be put into Service by the Governors of Cities, Towns, Etc. to Husbandry, or other Crafts or Labours.' Children of six, living in idleness!

In subsequent Acts the term child is judicially defined as equivalent to 'infant' —a special period of infancy being referred to. The first Act in which the word was defined in relation to *affinity* was the Fatal Accidents Act of 1846: 'The word "child" shall include Son and Daughter, and Grandson and Granddaughter, and Stepson and Stepdaughter.' The first Act in which it is defined in relation to *age* was the Industrial School Act of 1857: ' "Child" shall include any Boy or Girl who in the opinion of the Justices is above the Age of Seven and under the Age of Fourteen.' The word 'opinion' is suggestive.

In his Commentaries (1769) Sir William Blackstone refers to the fact that 'by the antient Saxon law, the age of twelve years was established for the age of possible discretion, when first the understanding might open'. Under that age a child could not be 'guilty in will'. 'By the law', he continues, 'as it now stands, and has stood at least ever since the time of Edward the Third, the capacity of doing ill, or contracting guilt, is not so much measured by years and days, as by the strength of the delinquent's understanding and judgment. For one lad of eleven years old may have as much cunning as another of fourteen; and in these cases our maxim is, that "malitia supplet ætatem". Under seven years of age, indeed, an infant cannot be guilty of a felony, for then a felonious discretion is almost an impossibility in nature; but at eight years old he may be guilty of a felony.'

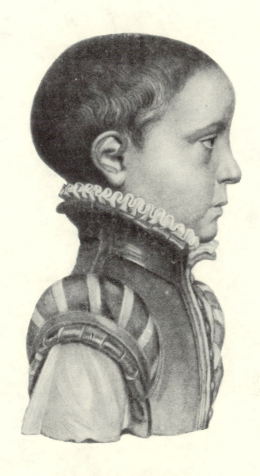

FRANCIS BACON
From an engraving by F. Holl
after a drawing by Arthur Hughes of a
coloured bust that belonged to the Earl of Verulam

Aspects

defensive on their behalf. A few particulars—and only a reading between the lines can give them life—may show to what extent. No child under the age of eight can now be guilty of an 'offence', whereas until 1933 the age of capacity to commit a crime had by the Common Law been seven years. No child or young person may now be sent to penal servitude; but it was not until 1863 that any distinction referring to felony was made between children and their elders. Then, the Garrotters Act stipulated that in the case of an offender under sixteen years of age who had been sentenced to be whipped, the number of strokes should not exceed twenty-five, and the instrument used should be a birch rod.

Special juvenile courts, sitting somewhere apart from the usual courts, or when these are not held, now deal with any child who, because he lacks proper and adequate care and guardianship, is exposed to moral danger, to falling into bad associations, is beyond control, or against whom certain offences have been committed, or who is a member of the household of any such offender. Any such child may be sent to an approved school for a certain number of years, or be entrusted to the care of specified proper persons. Proceedings in these juvenile courts must not be published except by order, and the words 'conviction' and 'sentence' must not be used in connection with children who are dealt with summarily. A child between eight and fourteen may thus be dealt with for indictable offences other than homicide, and a fine may be inflicted. If the child is a boy and between the ages of eight and seventeen, his punishment may be a private whipping with six strokes of a birch rod.

These courts also deal with any petty offences committed by a child, or with any refractory child brought up before a magistrate by a despairing parent or guardian.

Any responsible person above the age of sixteen may be charged with the wilful assault, ill treatment, neglect, or abandonment of anyone *under* that age. There are regulations relating to begging, to exposing a child under seven years old to the risk of burning or scalding, to allowing a child of between four and sixteen to be in a brothel, to encouraging seduction; also with reference to the sale of tobacco to those under sixteen, and of intoxicants to those under eighteen; to the safety of children (who swarm in their thousands) at public entertainments, to their taking part in them,

31

to cleansing them from vermin, to their adoption (in this case the age is raised to twenty-one), and to their employment abroad. No child can be employed in street trading; and there are many further restrictions referring to the age, the days, and the hours when a child may be employed at all, and to what kind of employment; also in respect to dangerous public performances and to his training for them. Moderate chastisement of a child by its father—or by any person, such as a schoolmaster, to whom he delegates his right to chastise—is not regarded as an assault, although a child has no legal right either to hit back, or, like Charles Waterton, to fix his teeth in the disciplinarian's calf, or, as in the case of David Copperfield, in his hand. In the 'bullying' of one child by another the Law is not at present interested. Bullying is an unofficial term which came into the language in 1710; *bullyrag* following it all but a century afterwards. And last, it is a felony to cause a child to die before it has any existence, unless it be to save its mother; and no human being under the age of eighteen can now be sentenced to death.

Instances, hardly credible nowadays, reveal how recent have been the measures to exclude young children from the scaffold and other severities. 'Thus,' says Blackstone, 'a girl of thirteen has been burnt for killing her mistress: and one boy of ten, and another of nine years old, who had killed their companions, have been sentenced to death, and he of ten years actually hanged; because it appeared upon their trials, that the one hid himself, and the other hid the body he had killed, which hiding manifested a consciousness of guilt, and a discretion to discern between good and evil. And there "is" an instance in "our books" where a boy of eight years old was tried at Abingdon for firing two barns: and it appearing that he had malice, revenge, and cunning, he was found guilty, condemned, and hanged accordingly. . . .'

In 1817, a boy of fifteen, the leader of a gang, was whipped at the cart's tail out of Frome for stealing money from a shop; later, three of his companions were transported for seven years.

On August 1, 1831, John Amy Bird, who was then under fourteen years of age, with the hangman's rope around his neck on the gallows, 'exclaimed in a firm and loud tone of voice, "Lord, have mercy on us! . . . All the people before me take warning by me".'

Aspects

2. '*Thwackum was for doing justice, and leaving mercy to heaven.*'

To realize what the above provisions imply, the problems they were intended to solve, and the effects on those concerned, one must imagine or *see* actual cases in terms of flesh and blood. What they denote is a circumspect, considerate and benevolent attitude in the State towards children. One can see forethought and sagacity peeping out through these restrictions like the eyes of a cat shut up in a basket. Fledglings—if a young person of fifteen can be so described—of every species, wren to vulture, are being safe-guarded from birds of prey; the birds themselves in view being frequently those responsible for the fledglings. The State tacitly refuses to presuppose natural affection, maternal love. And rightly: there was a devilish death-rate among children in the middle of last century, owing to facilities for their insurance. And shoeless and famished children in rags, and ailing infants as decoys for compassion were as common in my early days as were 'poor labourers out of work'—who sang for charity to the tune of 'The first good joy that Mary had'.

The meshes of the net are on the large size at times; the rich man's offspring, for example, might face the defencelessness of his sixteenth birthday a moral and physical wreck due in much to over-indulgence, and his parents escape scot free. And there is a dismally wide scope, when a wolf sits at the door, to the terms ill treatment and neglect. The rod, morever, may be spared too much, the tongue too little; and mere lovelessness may entail a tragic setting.

Apart from the advantages of education, the State offers no reward, either to its virtuous or brilliant children or to the parents who have done their best for their own. Nor, oddly enough, is there any domestic festival, day of thanksgiving and gaiety, to celebrate, as it were, a child's national coming-of-age.

3. '*And so Tom awoke; and we rose in the dark.*'

Legislation on behalf of children has been chiefly due to a slow and protracted change of heart or mind. It has rooted out gross abuses; but usually in the face of violent and almost incredible opposition. The vilest of the old evils probably remain unrecorded

33

and are lost in oblivion. Humanity's moral mixens are less conspicuous than its pigsties. But even a glimpse at certain facts suggests their range.

In England in 1817, for example, there were, roughly, a thousand apprenticed chimney sweepers. 'These boys were as a rule children whom nobody wanted.' Some had been sold to their masters for two or three guineas—'the smaller the child the better the price'. 'A few were kidnapped or enticed away.' In age they might be four or five years, most of them were from six to eight. 'Their terror of the pitch-dark and often suffocating passage had to be overcome by—a greater terror below. . . . The more humane masters would threaten to beat them, or perhaps promise' a slice of plum-pudding at the top. 'The less humane would set straw on fire below or thrust pins into their feet.' After a few days of this work, sores formed on knees and elbows. 'Some boys' flesh', said a master in his evidence before a Committee of the House of Commons, 'is far worse than others and it takes more time to harden them off.' Still, as a rule the parts affected even of the least satisfactory children became 'cartilaginous' in six months! 'But you must keep them a little at it even during the sores, or they will never learn their business.'

Their sores cicatriced, their fears at last subdued, they settled down. Occasionally a child was burned or roasted to death, occasionally he perished of suffocation in the chimney among the soot he had himself dislodged. Some might get a washing once a week, some during the summer, others none at all for years. They usually slept in a cellar, with the soot—occasionally on a mattress. Since the chimneys were narrow and tortuous, and time is always precious, *young* children were indispensable, and dwarfish stunted children were a boon. In the small flues the children had to keep their arms straight up above their heads; 'If they slip their arms they get jammed.' Thus a crumpled shirt might be fatal. Up a chimney twelve inches square a boy of seven could climb 'with ease', said a master sweep. But a chimney of 1818 might be made only seven inches square; and, that being so, not only a tiny but a naked child was necessary. A master sweep, Thomas Allen, testified that he had been articled in 1795 at the age of three and a half. 'I have been obliged myself to go up a chimney naked, but I do not like to see my children do so'!

34

Aspects

These particulars are taken from *The Town Labourer*, by G. L Hammond and Barbara Hammond. And when one has digested them, William Blake's poem 'The Chimney-Sweeper' takes on a different colouring, as does Lamb's Essay on the subject. And had Shakespeare anything specific in mind when he referred to chimney-sweepers in 'Fear no more the heat o' the sun'? Similar conditions of body and mind had to be endured by any child of eight working in the mines. Harnessed with a girdle round his (or her) naked waist, from which a chain hooked to it passed between the legs to the coal truck or corve behind, he had to crawl along passages not perhaps exceeding eighteen inches in height. Children were allowed to work in the mines for only thirteen or fourteen hours a day—in 1842. Fifty years before that, children in the mines never perhaps saw daylight from Sunday to Saturday afternoon. Or a younger child might be a trapper —in charge of one of the doors that guided the draught of air through the mine. 'I'm a trapper in the Gamber Pit', attested a child of eight years old in 1842, before the Children's Employment Commission. 'I have to trap without a light, and I'm scared. I go at four and sometimes half past three in the morning and come out at five and half past [P.M.]. I never go to sleep. Sometimes I sing when I've a light, but not in the dark: I daren't sing then.' What wonder these children sometimes took on the appearance of creeping animals, abject and idiotic.

An Act as far back as 1842 prohibited the employment in the mines of boys under the age of ten and of all females; and the Coal Mines' Regulations Act was passed in 1887. Mr. Tom Mann, who was born in 1856, in an account of his early days in Warwickshire, relates that all his family began work early, 'I being rather favoured by not beginning till 9 years of age, whilst an elder brother began at 8, and a younger one at 7.' Before he was eleven he himself started down in the mines—a 'Wind-way man', hauling 'dog and chain fashion', and naked to the waist, 'dons' —wheel-less tubs—along the roadways of the mine, frequently not more than two and a half feet in breadth. On scores of occasions, he tells us, he sank down at this work in complete physical exhaustion.

Conditions in the mills were hardly less blighting. We can guess too what was the condition of children who were blind, or deaf

35

Early One Morning

and dumb, or imbeciles, or 'farmed' out in workhouses, caravans and the canal barges, or those engaged in match-box making, straw-plaiting or in bakeries, before the Law began to interest itself in them. In home labour, 'them that has the most children is the best off, their little fingers is so quick'. Even in 1894, when Miss Gertrude Tuckwell published *The State and Its Children*, 'the Educational test', she tells us, was still so low 'that in certain districts where the old bye-laws are in force, children of 10 years of age are working full-time in employments other than Factories, Workshops and Mines, while such latitude is allowed with regard to half-timers that it is possible for a child to be working at seven years old'.

Since the State in England represents the People of England, it is the public conscience that must be tender and kindly before the State can be protective. The public conscience represents a multitude of private consciences; our chief concern is with our own. Yet we may not even perceive the evils for which posterity will summarily indict us.

How difficult it is to *realize*, for example, that during the year 1933 alone, one thousand and thirty-eight children were killed while they were using our roads. Rather more than half of them were playing in, or were running into the roadway; 163 of them were coming out from behind or in front of stationary vehicles; 190 were merely crossing the road. Only nine of them were deaf, five had bad sight, and two were lame. We must translate these figures into children heard and seen—now alive, now dead—if we wish to be aware of what they signify. 390 of these children were not yet five years old; and 656 of them were boys of under ten years old—many of them, probably, of the more headlong, harum-scarum, venturesome type. And what of the sixty to eighty children who are thus injured or crippled *every day*? Even if we ignore the loss of life, who can compute the grief and misery all this implies? 'In Rama was there a voice heard, lamentation and weeping. . . Rachel weeping for her children. . . .'

This is one notorious fact that may perhaps wear a particularly ugly look in the future. Another is of a very different kind. Of the persons (many of them again, possibly, of the more rash and headlong—and equally wasted—kind of human beings) who were found guilty of housebreaking and kindred offences three years

36

Aspects

ago, nearly three out of five had not yet come of age; and the number of such offences was more than three times that of the annual average between 1910 and 1914. Conditions have been hard; but when full allowance has been made on this score, and for lawless nature, something seems to have been insidiously amiss in a good many childhoods.

It is a hardly less astonishing than joyous fact, moreover, that the Society for the Prevention of Cruelty to Children only recently celebrated its jubilee in England. Like many other invaluable ideas and ideals, this one not only seeded in an individual mind, but as though borne thither on the wings of chance. Both in America first, and in England afterwards, the crusade owed its origin to the initiation of societies bent not on the protection of children but of animals. When a plea on behalf of the former, and one which was entirely out of order, was voiced at a meeting of the S.P.C.A. in Liverpool in 1882, 'I am here', boldly declared its president, 'for the prevention of cruelty, and I cannot draw the line at children.' Nor could the Baroness Burdett-Coutts, Benjamin Waugh and the author of *Jessica's First Prayer*. They worked indefatigably for a flawless cause. The relevant Act was passed in 1889; and in 1895 the Society received its Royal Charter—'to prevent the public and private wrongs of children and the corruption of their morals'. The Act secured the right of entry into any house; allowed the taking of evidence from the child concerned as well as from its father and mother; and the custody of the victim if this were deemed advisable.

When it is realized that the 'smaller cases' dealt with by the Society have included such horrors as leaving a baby unlifted out of its cradle for weeks, till toadstools grew around the child out of the rottenness; keeping a child in a cellar till its flesh became green; breaking both the arms and a thigh-bone of a two-year-old baby, leaving it untended—and worse; we can estimate what suffering its four million cases since its inception have helped to prevent. But the fact that even during the twelve months that ended March 31, 1933, the Society dealt with 43,521 cases, affecting the welfare of 106,382 children (over 12,000 of whom had a 'home' of one room), and prosecuted in 511 cases, shows how nebulous 'the line' drawn at 'cruelty' may still appear—and in what conditions.

37

CHAPTER IV

INTELLIGENCE

★

1. ' "Yes, my simple friend," said Socrates, "but the answer is the reverse of easy." '

If in 1886 Mrs. Hodgson Burnett had decided to choose a bride for the dainty hero in her story, she could have wedded her at twelve years old to a husband of fourteen. Now she would have to wait until they were both of them sixteen. And it is at this age, sixteen, expert psychologists have declared, after a prolonged series of tests, that the human 'intelligence' attains its zenith or maximum. To classify by age is easy, but how declare the status of a child's mind? The chief difficulty has been to agree upon a comprehensive and exact definition of the word intelligence, a difficulty that remained formidable even to a Consultative Committee appointed by the Board of Education in 1924 to consider the use of such tests in education. It appears, says their Report—even to the novice a vividly interesting survey and summary of an intricate problem—'that, though there is considerable difference of opinion among psychologists regarding hypotheses about the nature of general "intelligence", there is nevertheless a large measure of agreement in regard to the connotation of the phrase for practical purposes. It appears to be a general mental ability operating in many different ways, given as part of the child's natural endowment, as distinct from knowledge or skill acquired through teaching or experience, and more concerned with analysing and co-ordinating the data of experience than with mere passive reception of them. . . .'

Professor Thorndike has suggested that there are three main types of inborn intelligence: that for words and ideas, that for manual skill, and the social type—the ability to get on well with one's

38

Intelligence

fellows. 'These three types are positively related, but not necessarily in a high degree.' Other considered definitions of intelligence are the power of abstract thinking; the power of good responses from the point of view of truth; the ability to act effectively under given conditions. But one authority declares that its nature can at present hardly be discussed at all 'owing to the vagueness of the term involved and our paucity of information about the facts'. A further question arises. Unless in some degree an increase of intelligence occurs after the age of sixteen, who is really competent to set the appropriate tests?—a more embarrassing task even than that of passing them. This we may speedily discover if we attempt to test our own.

A definition is important since children and adults are often classified by this means. But intelligence is not our only gift. What tests would enable us to measure, for example, a child's instinct, or intuition, or his sense of beauty, or, no *less* valuable, his sense of duty? Innocence and intelligence may be happily at home in the same child; but how test the former? And last, that sovereign sense of the profound loveliness and significance which imagination gives to the world around us—what yardstick can be devised to measure that?

Millet, says Mr. Laurence Binyon, in *The Followers of Blake*, was haunted by the memory of a line of Virgil that he had learnt in childhood: *Majoresque cadunt altis de montibus umbræ*:—

'It seemed to hold so much more than it said, and to fill the mind with just that breadth and solemnity of significance which he desired for his art. Samuel Palmer was haunted in like manner by something seen—the shadows of the foliage of an elm, cast on a wall by the full moon. It so happened that there were words spoken to drive the memory deep into his mind, for, as he looked on the trembling shadows, his very remarkable young nurse, who was "deeply read" in the Bible and in Milton, murmured the lines,

> Fond man! The vision of a moment made,
> Dream of a dream, and shadow of a shade.

"Vision", "dream", and "shadow"; these were pregnant words, full of the very stuff out of which the young painter's art was to be made. And the light breaking in on the shadows from a hidden source; how often was this to be the main motive of his compositions.'

Understanding, judgement, insight, intellect, and the intelligence to make a full use of them—the well that supplies these sovereign waters is at the world's end, where the fairies that attend a child's cradle reside. We can do much by use and practice, but cannot, it seems, increase our own private supply. If then all the intelligence we have at our disposal was in full flower when we were sixteen, and the State seems inferentially to have concurred in this belief, we may well be a little more modest in our estimate of childhood.

2. *'I mean to make it understood*
That though I'm little I am good.'

Whatever sovereign little treasury of 'intelligence' a child who has attained a third of the age of sixteen may possess, he must nowadays begin—not first to reveal it, of course but—to go to school. Briefly this means that for so many hours every week he becomes one of a party of his coevals under the guidance of 'masters' or 'mistresses', who from being strangers may or may not become his friends. In lieu of doing what they might be doing elsewhere—better or worse—the flock sit or stand in rows and browse chiefly on books. Many children continue this process at home in the evening. In their leisure, nature or some inward inclination is free to give them a quest of their own. All work and no play—even in school hours—would make Jack a dull boy, although one Jack, at least, John Milton, survived even this harsh handicap. Here then is a third aspect of childhood, its docility and lack of 'knowledge'.

In the chapters that follow many comments will be found on the subject of schooling made by those who in the past have been its beneficiaries or victims. But it is not for this reason alone that few will be volunteered. My own schooling, however valuable, having been limited and sadly wasted, there can be no question that on my arrival in Utopia I should be immediately deprived of an inkpot. A few borrowed dates and landmarks, however, may be of very modest service to those readers who may be unfamiliar with them.

Intelligence

It was not until the year 1406 that the 'Statute of Education' established in England the right of freemen to *learn*. Four years after this the Gloucester Grammar School case established the right of freemen to *teach*.

In 1476 Caxton introduced the printing press into England, which I suppose has probably had more influence on the occupation of the human mind than any other device made by man. Nevertheless it is said that two centuries before Shakespeare's boyhood it was dangerous for a villein to be 'knowne for one that was lerned', and fatal, possibly, if he were found with 'a penner and inkhorne'. 'Thou hast most traitorously corrupted the youth of the realm in creating a grammar school,' says Jack Cade in *Henry IV*. Nowadays the *mark* of 'an honest, plain-dealing man' instead of a signature is as rarely encountered as a lutanist at a sherry party or glee-singers at the crossroads. One's backward glance for many reasons may nevertheless rest a little fondly on those Middle Ages when, apart from the bookish learning of abbey and monastery, 'the boy of common birth'—in Professor Adams's words—'but warlike connections received instruction in arms in the castle courtyard', when as page and as squire, 'the well-born were prepared for the duties of knighthood, the apprentice was trained to his craft and the son of the merchant to business'.

Comenius's pictured lesson book for children *Orbis Sensualium Pictus*, was published in 1658, twenty-six years after the birth of John Locke, the author not only of an invaluable treatise on Education, but of the following monition:

'Many children imputing the Pain they endured at School to their Books they were corrected for, so join those *Ideas* together, that a Book becomes their Aversion, and they are never reconciled to the Study and Use of them all their Lives after; and thus Reading becomes a Torment to them, which otherwise possibly they might have made the great Pleasure of their Lives. . . .' Not that Locke approved of cosseting the young. He regarded Æsop's Fables as the master key for them in literature, and recommended that a child should wear very thin shoes and have his feet bathed every day in cold water. If, he argued, we coddled our hands as we do our other extremities, it would be from our hands we should take cold; which recalls a conversation between Montaigne and a peasant in the wintry fields, whom he had found clad

Early One Morning

only in a shirt. He enquired if he was not perishing of cold. 'Is your face cold?' asked the peasant. 'No,' said Montaigne. 'Then imagine', was the reply, 'that I am all face.' I suppose we are all of us in many ways, at least more than we assume, 'all face'.

Helvetius, who regarded a child as in the nature of a machine, died in 1771. This was five years before the birth of Herbart, who based his system of education on the theory that nurture is of no less value than innate endowment. *Emile* was published in 1762. And Froebel, who regarded young children not as machines, not as creatures unique and unpredictable, but as plants to be delicately cultivated, and in the happiest surroundings, died fifty-three years before the first Parliamentary Grant of £20,000 was made in England for the building of schools, and sixty years before another first grant was expended for the founding of training schools for teachers. The National School Society was founded in 1811, the British and Foreign School Society three years afterwards. The 'Sunday Schools' had begun their work towards the close of the eighteenth century. Education in England was made provisionally compulsory in 1870, wholly compulsory in 1918—when the prolonged controversy on the question of religious teaching in schools was hushed rather than resolved.

During the two centuries before 1870 'the grammar-schools of the country were totally inefficient'; education was at a low ebb. Nowadays, unless they are being independently educated, all children five years of age are compelled to attend school, are led, that is, to the waters of learning; and many of them are permitted to sip of this refreshment when they are three. The youngest children and many of them under three years old are taken charge of in the 'Baby Rooms' of certain schools in certain districts. A baby room follows the ideal, not always very closely perhaps, of Froebel or Dr. Montessori. Its all-but-infants are free to move about as they please, they learn by playing, and a few toys are provided. Certain habits of body and mind are instilled, the gods called *meum* and *tuum* appear, and the phantom perhaps even of citizenship. There are also nursery schools, many of the open-air type, equipped with baths, beds, charts, meals and so forth, where the very young are intended to be 'natural, free and happy'. It is pleasanter in the spring time to see young lambs scattered with their dams over the hills and meadows rather than penned in a

42

fold; but there is the weather, the wolf, the wise shepherd to keep in mind. On the other hand, in the year 1927 there were over two million children in England and Wales under the age of three, and only a thousand of them were in nursery schools.

In everything relating to education indeed there is far more difficulty than safety in numbers. As soon as the Elementary Education Act of 1870 had been passed, children at school multiplied like flies—butterflies. In 1818 there were 2124 parishes in England without any school at all. In 1871 the average daily attendance at efficient elementary schools of any description—in the metropolis —was 175,000. Seven years afterwards one in four of the 615,000 London children requiring elementary instruction was attending *Board* Schools—under 3857 teachers, 406 of whom held 'first class certificates'. In 1927—in England and Wales—there were some 5,700,000 children* between the ages of three and fourteen in the elementary schools alone; apart, that is, from secondary, preparatory, and 'private' schools, containing only about 400,000 children. At present, only rather more than two out of seven children continue to attend any school, day or evening, between the ages of fourteen and sixteen, a crucial period of development, and still, as we have seen, in the eyes of the Law one mainly of childhood.

The vast problem of education, then, is bound up with these millions. There are problems in connection with the rest, but of these we shall hear much in a later chapter. And what are the 'elementaries' taught? Their school-time consists of about 27 hours a week for 44 weeks in every year, for nine years. Of these 27 hours, 2½ are spent in Bible instruction, prayers and hymns; rather more than 10 on English (including reading and writing) and arithmetic; 5 on history, geography, singing and drawing; about 5½ on science and practical work (including needlework and domestic economy for girls and woodwork and metal-work for boys); about 1½ on physical education—play intervals accounting for the rest. In round figures, this is about 11,000 hours of schooling in all. Set down in that summary fashion it appears at first sight a long time, 'a weary time'; and often may the children agree. Nevertheless it is a good deal less than one third of a child's nine years of waking life, even if we allow him half the day for slumber. A grown man, if he dutifully devotes only half an hour every day to reading his newspaper, will have spent one sixth of

Early One Morning

this time in so doing in nine years; and not far short of the whole of it on his daily meals if they occupy about three hours. The moral of which is that these millions of children have not *very* much time in which to become richly literate and decently learned.

When a child learns; in what surroundings; from whom; and in what habitual company is not much less important than what he is taught and to what end. Criticism of the national system is neither diffident nor restrained. Even in 1871 certain detractors disapproved of 'elementary school work, nicely executed'. A witness before a Select Committee of the House of Commons hotly objected to the teaching by the London School Board of geography, physiology and grammar. Grammar (which until the sixteenth century meant only Latin grammar), he maintained, is 'an enervating exercise'. 'Extra subjects' tend 'to diminish the fierce virtues of an ancient people'. As for physiology, 'when the Author of the Universe hid the liver of man out of sight he did not want frail human creatures to see how he had done it'. Alas, education or no education, there are still many frail human creatures who have not only never seen or handled this troublesome organ, but are little more than vaguely aware of its habits. According to Mr. Pitmilly, in Mrs. Oliphant's delectable story, 'The Library Window', the ghostly has its origin there: ' "It arises generally, if I may use such words in the presence of ladies, from a liver that is not just in the perfitt order . . . and then you will see things".'

Hannah More, on the other hand, who had pronounced and progressive views on feminine culture, and whose avowed aim in her writings was 'to render piety fashionable and popular', had no misgivings as to the virtues of 'extra subjects', and the following letter to Macaulay when he was six years old far from precludes grammar:

'Though you are a little boy now, you will one day, if it please God, be a man; but long before you are a man I hope you will be a scholar. I therefore wish you to purchase such books as will be useful and agreeable to you *then*. . . . You must go to Hatchard's and choose. I think we have nearly exhausted the Epics. What say you to a little good prose? Johnson's? . . . I want you to become a complete Frenchman, that I may give you Racine. . . . I think you

44

Intelligence

have hit off the Ode very well, and I am much obliged to you for the dedication.'

Seven years afterwards his mother was still egging him on:

'My dear Tom. . . .

'I know you write with great ease to yourself, and would rather write ten poems than prune one: but remember that excellence is not attained at first. . . . Spare no time or trouble to render each piece as perfect as you can, and then leave the event without one anxious thought. . . . You see how ambitious your mother is. She must have the wisdom of her son acknowledged before Angels and an assembled world. My wishes can soar no higher. . . .'

Even these few borrowed data indicate how far from easy it is nowadays for a quite young English child to remain illiterate*, but they give no notion of the problem involved in removing this disability. How often a mother describes her youngest and dearest as a handful, even 'a rare handful': 'That child is more than one person's work to manage!' What then of thirty or forty children, who by a caprice of nature infrequent even in early Victorian families, happen to be all of them under seven years old? In the elementary schools of England and Wales there are now above five million children. They sit under some 170,000 teachers. If we had a flock of two score lambs, or, better, of unequally intelligent and enclosed and vocal kids—little goats—whose powers of speech resembled those of a cross between a parrot and a mockingbird, and we wished to teach them tricks to be performed in which they were but mildly interested, how many skilled trainers should we employ for this purpose? In our elementary schools a teacher who perhaps was a child herself a very few years ago may have a class of well over that number of five- to six-year-old *homines sapientes* to persuade into the paths of learning; and this perhaps in a sunless, stuffy, malodorous schoolroom with not a patch of blue sky or a green leaf in sight. Nor is 'herself' misleading, since three out of four teachers in these schools are women, and many of them have 'growing boys' to control.

The wonder is that in any such circumstances quite young children may have acquired in gifted and devoted hands not only the rudiments of book-learning, but the looks also that betoken happiness, and a courtesy that is beyond price.

Early One Morning

3. *'Learn young, learn fair; learn auld, learn mair.'*

As to the adult, 'what passes for stupidity is much oftener a want of interest'; a remark that can be applied to children with a rather different implication.

'Men and women', says Jowett, 'cannot be brought together in schools or colleges at forty or fifty years of age; and if they could the result would be disappointing. The destination of most men is what Plato would call "the Den" for the whole of life, and with that they are content.' And Plato himself:

'Solon was under a delusion when he said that a man when he grows old may learn many things—for he can no more learn much than he can run much; youth is the time for any extraordinary toil. . . .'

If by learning, learning by rote is intended, this seems to be the general rule. It is more difficult when we are old than when we are young. The acquisition even of a new physical dexterity, or a few names—of wild flowers, for example, or of gadgets in a machine, or of new words, or of new meanings to words, may be humiliatingly arduous. 'Extraordinary toil', however, is no exaggeration when we consider the woeful hours spent in childhood, and the endless repetition that was then involved in getting any lesson word-perfect, in embodying in the mind such conveniences as the alphabet, the tables of weights and measures and of multiplication; historical dates; the arbitrary signs and symbols and the definitions of arithmetic, algebra, geometry, music; geographical lists; rules for genders, declensions, conjugations and so forth.

What nightmares of desperation these involved! I can myself shamefully recall failing on three successive days at the age of eight or nine to have mastered the meaning of *largo, allegro, legato,* and being repeatedly punished for it. I can recall the very spot where five or six years later the acute conviction overcame me that to learn the Greek alphabet was a task beyond human achievement. And I feel a little easier at these confessions after reading of a little episode in the life of Ann Taylor, though she at the time (alas!) was very young. Again and again she had been told, and in the same lesson, that t-h-y spelt *thy*, and as often when she was asked what t-h-y spelt, the *thy* 'unaccountably slipped' out of her memory. Her indulgent mother (who had yet herself been a child) could only

Intelligence

attribute this to 'wilful perversity', and whipped her. The rod was not spared, but an idea of human justice had been perilously jolted. Whether the whipping helped Ann's t-h-y to spell *thy* is not related. That our 'intelligence-age'* on these occasions would have been reckoned, say, at minus six-months, there is little question.

Like the formation of good habits, which William James deemed to be of such sovereign value, this learning by rote may be of the utmost use. How much it varies in efficiency between one adult and another may be seen in the mere addition of a column of figures, the sorting of a pack of cards, or the looking up of a word in a dictionary. But though, in spite of effort, the elderly may find it difficult to learn, it by no means follows that they have no desire to learn. As Christina Rossetti amusedly discovered, one may suddenly acquire or inherit at an advanced age a peculiar avid greed for information, and may even attempt, however forlornly, to satisfy it. There is an encyclopædia habit—the foregoing pages may have more than hinted at its perils—and it usually blossoms late. One may indeed become a childlike victim to the belief that merely to be surrounded by works of reference is tantamount to containing their contents.

It would perhaps be too harsh and merciless to submit the mature to any enforced test of their knowledge and learning, even those of them, I mean, who are truly if belatedly anxious to polish up their own minds. The day may come none the less when adult education of some kind is the rule rather than the exception; when periodical re-examinations in appropriate subjects must be submitted to by parents, the clergy, schoolmasters, doctors, journalists, editors and authors; by all those whose duty, or bias, it is to teach anything to anybody.

Meanwhile, for English children, schooling, whatever its value or effect may be, is universal. It is a boon that may be now as free as the air they breathe. But in countries less blessed than the United Kingdom, France, Germany and the United States, illiteracy is still rampant. During the last decade for example the percentage of illiterates in Turkey was about 92, in India 90, Egypt 86, Brazil 67, the Soviet Union 48, Spain and Greece 43, and Italy 26. How many illiterates there were among her subjects in the spirited age of Queen Elizabeth or the Augustan of Queen Anne would be a difficult figure to track down. But even if the percentage were 99, it

47

Early One Morning

would be absurd to assume that there were then proportionately
fewer gifted, sagacious, active-minded and knowledgeable human
beings, including children, than there are in our own day. Learning
undigested or indigestible is worse than useless. It may conspire
at unlearning and at the neglect or disuse of natural intuitions and
faculties. Even if it be assimilated, it may be a substitution for
something more valuable; and its quality and the power to make
use of it entirely transcend, of course, its mere quantity.

4. 'From beginnings so small.'

Schooling of any kind, we shall be reminded again and again,
is but one means and method of education. When then does
education itself begin? Literally of course ages before a child only
three years old sets off for the first time to its kindergarten, or perhaps, aged two, to join the Babies. A child's body at any rate
began its being in the dark abysm of time. It is the self-proclaimed
outcome of an inscrutably remote ancestry, which must also concern his mind and spirit. As Hardy says:

> 'I am the family face;
> Flesh perishes, I live on,
> Projecting trait and trace
> Through time to times anon,
> And leaping from place to place
> Over oblivion. . . .'

And Dryden:

> '. . . If by traduction came thy mind,
> Our wonder is the less to find
> A soul so charming from a stock so good;
> Thy father was transfused into thy blood. . . .
> But if thy pre-existing soul
> Was form'd, at first, with myriads more,
> It did through all the mighty poets roll,
> Who Greek or Latin laurels wore,
> And was that Sappho last, which once it was before. . . .'

And Blake:

48

Intelligence

... Was Jesus gentle, or did He
Give any marks of gentility?
When twelve years old He ran away,
And left His parents in dismay.
When after three days' sorrow found,
Loud as Sinai's trumpet-sound:
"No earthly parents I confess——
My Heavenly Father's business!
Ye understand not what I say,
And, angry, force Me to obey. . . ." '

Even when an infant is wanted, hoped for, provided for, and actually ordered, no kind of specification is practicable. Both providence and nature as well as the State insist that its parents shall accept what comes. Unlike any mere machine, it cannot be returned to the Works. Missing parts remain missing, and grave defects are extremely difficult to make good. The mutinous and the unhappy may taunt a father with 'I didn't *ask* to come into the world'. The wiser father forbears the obvious retort. Because perhaps love and apprehension are too closely pent up in his heart for utterance, and with all his soul he is sharing at that moment what has been expressed so tenderly by Thomas Hardy :

'. . . Fain would I, dear, find some shut plot
Of earth's wide wold for thee, where not
One tear, one qualm,
Should break the calm.
But I am weak as thou and bare;
No man can change the common lot to rare.

'Must come and bide. And such are we——
Unreasoning, sanguine, visionary——
That I can hope
Health, love, friends, scope
In full for thee; can dream thou wilt find
Joys seldom yet attained by humankind!'

Even the children of one family may be more unlike than like one another. As, too, with the most seemly of hedge sparrows, a cuckoo may sometimes find its way into the human nest; and we cannot foresee what formidable great-aunt or dubious great-

Early One Morning

grand-uncle may not seize an opportunity of reminding well-meaning parents that he or she is not altogether gone.

> 'Behold, my lords,
> Although the print be little, the whole matter
> And copy of the father; eye, nose, lip,
> The trick of's frown, his forehead, nay, the valley,
> The pretty dimples of his chin and cheek, his smiles,
> The very mould and frame of hand, nail, finger. . . .'

There may be clues so tiny as to be almost imperceptible—a mere movement of the hand, or an inherited darker spot on the amber-clear iris of one of the eyes that may not show itself until a child is in its teens. In a chapter in *My Life* on his relatives and forbears, Alfred Russel Wallace refers dutifully to the great Sir William, and to the family crest, but with a more personal accent of satisfaction to a slight peculiarity in one of his own eyebrows, which he thought had been passed on to him by his maternal great-grandfather.

And who can say what influence the parental soul has on a child's conception; though nowadays much more attention is given to the heritage of the body? But any venture into the province of chromosomes and genes (or *gens*) would be an even more precarious expedition for an ignoramus than to lay down the law or to define education. Between a child's 'dusk and its day time' other influences may be at work. This is at least an ancient tradition, and involves the obscure problem of the influences of the mind on the body and *vice versa*, concerning which we have most of us had emphatic experience. Long before the State is even acquainted with its name—or its father has welcomed it if only for the solatium it brings in his Income Tax—an infant comes into the world not merely ready-made, not merely a host of resemblances, but also of a unique pattern.

The miracle of life is now visible, in all its parts and magnitude. It is also audible. An infant's first cry, detectable by a sensitive ear even beneath the roar of Niagara or a morning chorus of birds in a forest, is often called wailing. It is more like an hosanna, a challenge or a dirge. What are this creature's faculties? How far already ajar are those 'five ports of knowledge' which few of us keep either alertly sentinelled or hospitably agape? It can taste and

Intelligence

smell a little, we are told by the expert; and its sense of touch rapidly advances in delicacy. It can see; and though it shuns a strong light, it soon begins to look and watch, to mark and learn. For a few days it cannot hear, but may attempt to localize sound in a fortnight. Its movements are at first random, reflex or instinctive.

'Will comes later'; but this department of child psychology, we are warned, is as yet 'but poorly developed'. In the weakness of an infant's limbs, says St. Augustine, and not in its will, lies its innocency. 'I myself have seen and known an infant to be jealous though it could not speak. It became pale and cast bitter looks on its foster brother, who was sharing its wet-nurse.' That Will manifests itself early every monthly nurse—not excluding Mrs. Gamp or Juliet's, whose charge when asked, 'Wilt thou not, Jule?' stinted and said 'Ay!'—would agree. There may be babes of a halcyon docility, but in most the Old Adam is soon apparent.

In mere appearance indeed an infant but a few hours old can *look* at least a century more antiquated than its own grandmother: that tiny, sage, yet unspeculative visage; the domed brow; the tranquil and sublime self-security. Even in the moment of astonished scrutiny one may become aware of a curious alarm. This sentient image might be the shrunken mummy of the prototype of all the Pharaohs! Innate ideas? Are we not rather confronting a taciturn epitome of all human wisdom?

In sober fact that capacious (and not always toppling) toothless head is in size, stature compared with stature, twice that of an adult's. The brain is 'enormous in proportion to the size of the body'; and is a hive of a myriad mysterious cells. The head—both itself and its contents in constant use—is growing in every direction, millimetre by millimetre, on and on. You can admire, measure, bless or fondle that warm, pulsing, invaluable, gentle and enigmatical dome, thinly flossed with fine hair. But you can guess or discover no more of its inward processes than will make a learned paragraph in a book. The paragraph will embalm knowledge, but it will pass on no vital secret.

Now and then the very self within challenges you from the eyes of a friend or an enemy. An infant's eyes, serenely slow in motion but at times of a marked vivacity though usually agaze, much more seldom disclose any inmate behind the window. It may be searching for secrets but keeps its own. The most casual scrutiny

Early One Morning

of its furrowed countenance, its body, limbs and general 'finish' cannot but reveal that it is fearfully and wonderfully made—the arched five-toed foot, the chill, clasping, lean-fingered hands, the shell-like nails, the small, flat, convoluted ear, the softly sucking mouth, the milk-blue eyes with their delicate brows and fringing lashes, the faint fair down, the silken skin. 'Perfect little body, without fault or stain on thee. . . . Thy mother's treasure wert thou. . . .'

Such once were we, one and all. And if the reader will glance at the copy of *The Times* which appeared on his birthday's eve, it will give him in a fragmentary and perhaps disconcerting fashion something of what the great world looked like a few hours before he made his first, or latest, appearance on its Stage. Also the general scenery, a few of the leading characters and even a glimpse of the plot of the drama, comedy, melodrama or farce for which he had at that moment not the smallest responsibility.

Not that all babies, even in their mothers' eyes, approach perfection. William Hutton relates that he was so remarkably ugly an infant that his mother was 'afraid she should never love' him. 'My mother,' says Robert Southey, 'asking if it [himself] was a boy, was answered by her nurse . . . "Ay, a great ugly boy!" and she added, when she told me this, God forgive me!—when I saw what a great red creature it was, covered with rolls of fat, I thought I should never be able to love him.' Still, both infants were unmistakably alive. Whereas Hardy, at birth, like Aksakoff, was assumed to be dead, until he was rescued by his nurse, who exclaimed to the surgeon: 'Dead! stop a minute; he's alive enough, sure!'

The ugly duckling then, even if he grows up into a goose rather than a swan, may be soon easily loved. And perhaps for this very reason. That at least is the lovely Perdita's account of the matter—unless one heartlessly suspects that she is tipping the scale a little for the sake of contrast. In infancy, she confesses, 'I was swarthy; my eyes were singularly large in proportion to my face, which was small and round, exhibiting features peculiarly marked with the most pensive and melancholy cast.' This lack of personal beauty, however, 'tended much to endear me to my parents, particularly to my father, whom I strongly resembled'! Her mind, no less than her features, she tells us also, early showed

52

Intelligence

a bent towards a life 'marked by the progressive evils of a too acute sensibility'.

5. *'Ah, honey! she said, have you got so far ben as that?'*

But whether an infant is moribund, ugly, or a pygmy prince of beauty, we see only the surface of the miracle and enigma it actually is. Last night, said Swift, I saw a woman flayed, and you would hardly believe how much it altered her for the worse. The mordant cynicism, which is no less true of an infant, is itself a little superficial, though a mere broken nose would not have served Swift's horrific purpose. Beneath that skin lies concealed a complex engine of exquisite ingenuities, which is not only developing moment by moment, and moment by moment converting mere air and milk and the grace of God to its own infinitely various purposes, but is also practising and learning, and is in some degree under conscious control. The engineer too of this extravagantly unmachinelike machine *seems* to be present, whatever his origin or responsibility may be. Even, indeed, if merely growing in bulk like a tree were an infant's sole accomplishment, the acorn would remain no less notable than the oak. And, as Ben Jonson continues:

'A lily of a day .
Is fairer far in May,
Although it fall and die that night——
It was the plant and flower of Light.
In small Proportions we just beauties see,
And in short measures life may perfect be.'

Nor is that perfection at a moment's standstill. Return again in three weeks', a month's time, in six, in a year, in two, to renew acquaintance with this swaddled, passive, speechless, fumbling, groping little atomy; and at every visit compare with your own during the same period its progress and the changes it has undergone, without and within. It is clear at least that its 'cultivation' has waited for no man, whatever the hindrances that may have been put in its way.

Early One Morning

6. *'Who knows the fate of his bones?'*

A fraction of an inch beneath the skin are hidden the bones, and, come to them, we are undoubtedly altered for the worse; though even a child may remain unappalled at the discovery. When Edmund Gosse was 'just four', a lady showed him a large print of a human skeleton. ' "There!" said she, "you don't know what that is, do you?" Upon which, immediately and very archly, I replied: "Isn't it a man with the meat off?" ' He adds, though it is hard indeed to believe it of such a child, that this was his only 'clever' remark in 'an otherwise unillustrious childhood', and even takes the edge off the cleverness by explaining that he had often watched his naturalist father engaged in anatomizing a fish. The motive of the lady, then, in showing him her print is far less intelligible than his own response to it. A child, provided it is full daylight, may be a hardy realist. He has perhaps even 'a natural craving for horrors' and also possesses a funny bone. If so, he may be more curious than terrified at what might daunt the mature. In later life, even though a skeleton is one's chief means of support and one's final legacy to the world of the living, we are apt to shun its *memento mori*. Yet it may be a telling experience to become vividly conscious of its presence within us as, with its exquisite poise, nimbleness and flexures, it gravely, hastily, or daintily descends a staircase. With the fingertips to explore too the projections and hollows concealed beneath the mask forming the tell-tale face which is so tiresomely familiar to others, so infrequently present in one's own consciousness, and which yet to a sharp observer may readily expose what one would much prefer to keep private.

In this a child has the advantage. He too may be the sharpest of observers, but his own young face is usually better company and is less scored with symbols. Even his bones are far more supple. If I slept in oiled blankets and was dosed with gin, I gathered when I was young, I might become an admirable tumbler if not a Human Serpent; and Mr. Hugh Fisher had not then questioned me with,

> 'Are bones less beautiful
> Because they are our own?
> Clothed Venus' body not
> A lovely skeleton?'

54

Intelligence

It is with bones that the anthropologist is largely concerned. According to their evidence, we are told, the human infant is nothing more or less than a big-brained apelet or apeling, since one of its remoter ancestors in darkest Africa some millions of years ago had ascended from a stock which otherwise branched into the once-fabulous gorilla and the chimpanzee. That ancestor's 'distinctive muscular skill' enabled him to acquire speech; and a remarkable joint in his lengthening thumb, to handle the crutch or cudgel which has evolved into pen, scalpel, sceptre, divining-rod and gun. In view of the gun, perhaps, this ancestor may well have become the mythical Satan of the brute creation. On the other hand, whatever may have happened to humanity, the gorilla has more or less persisted in his fidelity to his remote original. His brain, we are told, weighs about 20 ounces and contains between three and four thousand neurons. Man's brain is of an average weight of 49 ounces and contains 9,200,000 neurons. Their two minds we cannot compare. In spite of Lenin's brain having been sliced into 31,000 sections by Professor Vogt, they gave, says Dr. Bernard Hollander, no information of the intellectual abilities, emotions and passions of the living man. The autocrat died; his brains became useless; 'and there an end. . . .'

Not that the physiologists are even yet in complete accord concerning an infant's dark ages. It was not generally agreed until after the middle of the last century that rudimentary humanity existed in a period so distant in time as the Pliocene. Here, in a climate described as, at first, genial and mild, our progenitors had the most various and lively company, including that of the mastodon, four-horned animals of the antelope type, and creatures of all shapes and sizes whose latterday representatives a child is so much at home with when he visits them in the Zoological Gardens in Regent's Park.

How hard it is for an ignoramus to embrace scientific facts at which some inward counsellor falters. When one compares a man-child with an equally young gorilla or chimpanzee, how can one conceive by what inward persuasion or outward influence he has at last become so much pleasanter to look at, and so much more vulnerable and less able to fend for himself? His prolonged helplessness in infancy indeed is said to be one of the chief factors in his evolution into a being so gentle, cunning and wise. That too

Early One Morning

is a hard saying, and fails to explain the process which refined human sensibility, desire and creative delight to a delicacy that bequeathed him his music, his Taj Mahal, his missals, his lenses and his gems.

Mercurial monkey though he frequently is, a young child's grave and serene face with its changing expressions is in aspect the very antithesis of the forlorn or mischievous or ferocious or melancholy countenances of his far-distant hairy cousins. Transported back to the Africa of that remote past, *they* would not, I suppose, be grossly out of keeping with *their* ancestry. If, hand in hand with his mother, little Edgar Allan Poe, in his 'calling' clothes described on a later page, could have returned thither, he would be as alien an object as the Serpent in paradise. Not only too has simian man suffered changes rich and strange, but he imposes them on the nearest and dearest of his four-footed adherents; and yet, no matter what remarkable metamorphoses the human fancier persuades the dog to endure, it still remains in every one of them so radically not a cat.

Moreover, however clearly and truly man's physical past may be conceived, any such conception has no present actuality. It has been built up of relics; it is an imagined thing; and it is the off-spring of a human consciousness and of a mind which then had no local habitation. What *Signor Pongo* 'thought of' his earthly surroundings or his destiny we have not the faintest notion, except only that his survey must have been very different from our own.

Some new discovery, some new angle in our regard of the past, some unforeseeable and profound intuition might alter the whole perspective of man's history. Life is short, and there may yet be awaiting us retrospective views of this strange terrestrial museum when we ourselves have gone on our way. We have to remind ourselves how recent a theory that of evolution, with all its marvels, is. And waste straws may show the way of the wind. In *The Lady's Magazine* of 1829—by no means a flippant periodical, since it was intended to be a mirror of belles-lettres and the fine arts, and children are seldom reflected in it—there is a brief essay on the state of the world before the Deluge:

'Of the antediluvian world . . . we cannot expect to know *much*; but even of the most remote period we may learn *something* from the Scriptures. "In the beginning (we are informed) God created

56

Intelligence

the *heaven* and the *earth*." Omitting the former (however anxiously we look forward to it), we shall only take notice of the latter. . . . Before this signal disaster [the Flood] occurred, above 2300 years are calculated to have passed. During nine centuries of that period, Adam appears to have exercised the chief sway, although his authority was not completely influential over the distant communities of his numerous descendants. . . .'

'Methinks there be not impossibilities enough in Religion for an active faith,' said Sir Thomas Browne; and the same may be said of Science. But Time which antiquates antiquities also has its own picturesque methods of dealing with human 'facts' and ideas.

7. *'The monkeys might with equal justice conclude that . . . we . . . are conveying ideas to one another.'*

D o we, perhaps, too much disparage the faculties of the 'lower creatures'? In regard to speech, for example? It does not *appear* that the son of man alone is possessed of an adequate means of communication with his kind, or that the singing of birds in the dusk of March or at summer daybreak is any more merely the strains of a kind of animated musical box than was the song of Wordsworth's highland reaper. Have the bees and the ants achieved merely a mute civilization? There are other ways of expression than with the tongue.

When recently, I have read, two experimentalists in America, Mr. and Mrs. Kellogg, brought up their infant, Donald, in the close and habitual company of a chimpanzee they called Gua, his junior by two and a half months, they discovered that Gua when she was three years old had a language of her own, which, they declare, they were 'soon able to reduce to a system of perfectly recognizable and significant sounds'. They discovered also that though Donald had a definite advantage in his capacity for development in this respect, the small ape seemed to have the greater power of understanding speech. By far the longer list of simple expressions which child and ape showed themselves able to understand was Gua's.

That 'bones with the meat off' tell a fascinating story even to the novice is beyond question, but the most important feature of a child's past, whatever his physical ancestry may have been, is that

57

Early One Morning

it has led to him and to the present. It is not the roots but the upper twigs and branches of his family tree that are his most anxious concern; to what goal he appears, with or without our assistance, to be bound, rather than where his superbly articulated framework originated. Humanity far transcends the monkey in inquisitiveness, but this has not always been to its own advantage. Any tract of knowledge, whether scientific or otherwise, is of only a relative value. The wise use it best. Blessed alike are man and child that do not 'know too much'. When, then, guileless Miss Curious enquires: 'Mamma, please where do babies come from?' the candid reply, as I suppose, will be none the less enlightening if it begin: 'My dear, babies' *bodies* and *bones*. . . .' For any piece of knowledge is chiefly of relative value; it is but one cube, however lively in hue, in the vast mosaic. And how easy it is to dislocate the fragments, or to keep one in a private fob pocket, unaware of its place in the pattern.

In *Notes of a Son and Brother*, Henry James, speaking of his early years, remarks that he was then under the impression that life and knowledge were 'simply mutual opposites, one inconsistent with the other', and that if one of the two must go to the wall, it should be life. 'There was to come to me of course in time the due perception that neither was of the least use—use to myself—without the other. . . . The conflict and the drama involved in the question . . . was to make consciousness . . . supremely intense and interesting.'

That parenthesis, 'use to myself', whether it imply modesty or egotism, or both, is the paramount incentive of the artist. Whatever joys may come of this scrupulous *use*, his earthly faith rests there. That perhaps is why he may squint at certain aspects and upshots of what is called progress, and revolt at the dissemination of poison-gas.

CHAPTER V

CHANGES

★

1. *'My dear one, my pretty one, it really is the spring time.'*

In human maturity comparatively few radical physical changes take place; during childhood they are continuous. In her *Study of Growth and Development*, published in 1933, Miss R. M. Fleming gives minute particulars, accompanied by numerous graphs and tables, of such changes. All these were based on a periodical examination, extending over some ten years, of fourteen age groups of schoolchildren, 2219 boys and 2073 girls, of whom a large majority were of Welsh stock. When we come to the memories of childhood related in this volume, many of Miss Fleming's conclusions will be of capital interest, though it does her absorbing study small service to detach them from their context.

Changes in the colouring of the hair after birth always, she found, took the form of darkening. A baby's blue eyes may become brown, yet will not, alas, become blue again; but marked change in eye colour, which is rare after the age of nine, occurs in fewer children than may change in the colour of the hair. One of Miss Fleming's examinees, a child eight years of age, had a left eye the inner half of which was blue, the outer brown, and a right eye of a light brown with a darker ring near the pupil. Perhaps her name was 'Betty Martin'?

At every age, the mean of all head measurements is greater in boys than in girls, the difference in cranial breadth between the sexes being less than that in length. The heads of girls seldom show any increase in their breadth after sixteen, while growth in this respect in boys may be continuous. In all physical measurements except stature the boys have an advantage over the girls at every

Early One Morning

age. 'But mere size in brain', says Dr. Bernard Hollander, 'conveys nothing, without a knowledge of the quality of its texture.' A child or a 'man may have a large brain, and yet not manifest much intelligence, but both will exhibit power of some sort or other'. The difference in the mean of *stature* until the age of eleven is trifling, boys being usually very slightly taller. Girls make a spurt between eleven and fourteen, but after this age boys become steadily taller.

But Miss Fleming was not content with mere measurements. She discovered, for example, that in their spare time boys keenly pursue hobbies of a 'much wider range' than girls do. Few girls confided to her that they had any hobbies, apart from needlework, cooking, reading, dancing and walking, though one girl confessed that she kept pets, and one expressed her enjoyment in 'big-game hunting'.

Miss Fleming also classified her children according to their conspicuous characteristics, dividing them into groups. The first of these racial groups consisted of individuals with dark eyes, dark hair and a complexion either dark, with a fresh colour in the cheeks, or of a uniformly rather pale olive. These children revealed interests and abilities æsthetic rather than analytical. Their inclination was towards literature and music rather than towards mathematics and science.

'I so feared', says Henry James, 'and abhorred mathematics that the simplest mathematical operation . . . always found and kept me helpless and blank.' For him, when he was a boy, 'the pang' as well as the marvel was that the 'meanest minds and the vulgarest types approach these matters without a sign of trepidation, even when they approach them, at the worst, without positive appetite'. Daunted by this test, he 'withdrew from the scene . . . a deeply hushed failure'. On the other hand it is on record that a Korean lad of sixteen could add up 'twenty-five items of four figures each in seven seconds by mental calculation'; and that a blind and feeble-minded young man, named Henry, could by the same means give 'the cube root of any number running into four figures in an average of four seconds'.

Some children, Miss Fleming refreshingly attests, thoroughly enjoyed subjects in which 'their school records indicated complete failure'. Others preferred school subjects to games, though they

60

Changes

usually kept this fact to themselves for fear of being considered prigs. The children in her first group had for the most part no pronounced ambition to get on in life, their inward need inciting them to serener scenes than those of Vanity Fair, and, at worst, to 'a dreamy acquiescence'. 'We are the music-makers, we are the dreamers of dreams'. They cared little for strenuous physical exercise, but enjoyed country walks and showed 'a deep awareness of beauty in nature'. Some of them had a 'contagious enthusiasm for literature or poetry or music which attracted their fellows'. If they themselves become teachers, they may deliberately choose a post in an obscure rural school; and their influence on their scholars in 'arousing enthusiasm for learning is great'. We may not perhaps have suspected that the disinclination to field at long stop for torrid hours at a stretch, or to expose one's immature shins to a football boot is largely due to racial influences. But how clearly one sees and salutes the dark-eyed, quiet-minded teacher who can kindle flame even in damp tinder.

Miss Fleming's second group consisted of individuals with blue or light eyes, fair hair, fine and wavy, and a fair fine skin. In much else they showed striking differences from the first group. No fewer than six out of ten of the girls in this, as compared with one out of ten in the other, were eager for games and physical exercise, and especially hockey. The first group enshrined only one hockey *fan*. Several of the boys in this group were reported as having good organizing ability, and in general they had more decided likes and dislikes than the boys in the other group. When asked what they cared for most, some of them confessed instead what they hated. They were active and ambitious. Many wanted to travel, and in their reading preferred tales of adventure.

In spite of these pronounced contrasts in temperament, ability and interest, the children in both groups had one thing in common —long heads. Evidence is accumulating, says Miss Fleming, which suggests that an 'intermediate type' of head 'may have been fundamental in the history of modern man, and the extreme longheads and extreme broadheads may be divergences in different directions of evolution'. Would it be fantastic to say, then, that there is Mind awaiting the opportunities of this human and physical development?

To this chapter of her *Study* Miss Fleming appends a grave

Early One Morning

warning on the perils and pitfalls incident to school examinations, and in particular examinations intent on 'academic subjects'. Alfred Russel Wallace, as will be seen, was no less critical of examinations in natural science. The danger vanishes if every individual child is considered, physically, mentally, and spiritually, on the background of its own development—and not in relation to a general average of what are called 'rules of development'. William Blake, indeed, went so far as to declare that all real *knowledge* even is intuitive, and regarded 'education' as a sin.

A glimpse out of the past of a child who at least suggests fair hair, blue eyes and a long head and who never sat for *any* school examination, may not be inappropriate. In her Memoir of her husband, Sir Richard, written in 1676, Lady Anne Fanshawe tells us of the education given to her in her childhood by her mother. This 'was with all the advantages that time afforded, both for working all sorts of fine works with my needle, and learning French, singing, lute, the virginals, and dancing. Notwithstanding I learned as well as most did, yet was I wild to that degree, that the hours of my beloved recreation took up too much of my time; for I loved riding, in the first place, running, and all active pastimes: in short, I was that which we graver people call a hoyting girl; but, to be just to myself, I never did mischief to myself or people, nor one immodest word or action in my life, though skipping and activity was my delight. . . .'

Years afterwards, on a voyage with her husband, these two—he and his hoyting girl—were in danger of being captured by a Turkish galley and carried away as slaves. The captain of her ship, 'this beast', as she calls him, locked her up in her cabin. With half a crown she bribed the cabin boy who consented to give her the blue thrum cap he wore and his tarred coat. She put them on, and, flinging away her night-clothes, 'crept up softly and stood upon the deck' by her husband's side, 'as free from sickness and fear as, I confess, from discretion; but it was the effect of that passion which I could never master'. Alarmed by the display of force, the Turkish ship-of-war tacked about and left them. 'Good God!' cried her husband, looking upon her and snatching her up in his arms, 'Good God! that love can make this change!'

There is another warning. Boys of from nine to eleven, says Miss Fleming, often go through a phase of 'liking to help' at

Changes

home, and shrink then from rough physical sport. Their parents in consequence may become anxious on their account and be afraid that they will prove 'effeminate'. In fact they are going through 'a curious physical stage when feminine characteristics are dominant', and this stage will pass away. Attempts to force boys out of it by 'mockery or rough means' will result in misery, and possibly 'a permanent nervous complex may be set up'. 'When my father died,' says Philip Hamerton, who was then aged eight, 'I was simply a child though rather a precocious one . . . but between two and three years after that event the child had become a boy.'

But in all generalizations concerning humanity and particularly children, we must, as Miss Fleming counsels us, keep sharply in mind the individual. Norms and averages are a convenient and useful means of information. But no child is in all respects either average or even normal. Moreover, says Dr. Johnson, 'there is no instance of any man, whose history has been minutely related, that did not in every part of life discover the same proportion of intellectual vigour'. And is not that equally true of moral vigour? The great man, said Victor Cousin, 'represents the quintessence of his epoch'. So in his much smaller world must the great child. And all in proportion. He should have also at least as great a flexibility or plasticity of intelligence; and if he have good fortune he may never lose it.

'Late learners', again, said Bacon, 'cannot take the ply; except it be in some minds that have not suffered themselves to fix, but have kept themselves open and prepared to receive continual amendment which is exceeding rare.' Hence the statement, 'Give me a child up to the age of six and you may do what you please with him afterwards', which was quoted by Cicero, but has been, it seems, falsely attributed to Ignatius Loyala. Indeed, as a friend suggests, St. Ignatius was even humbler than St. Francis of Assisi, and therefore is more likely to have said 'Give me *to* a child of six and he will afterwards do what he likes with *me*'.

2. 'Yea, we ourselves were once what these are now.'

It is the endless variety of children—a variety often concealed beneath the surface of the similar—that is most striking even when we compare them with their seniors. And yet when we

Early One Morning

watch these young and noisy barbarians all at play, or, some drowsy summer afternoon, peer in on the rows of stooping tongue-tied heads through the windows of a village schoolroom, how easy it is to smile or shrug, 'Children!' and to leave it at that.

Men in their late thirties, forties, and early fifties are practically contemporaries. They may share much the same tastes, pursuits, outlook and incentives; common sense and worldly wisdom being effective solvents. They mix easily. A little picnic party on the other hand consisting of an infant of two, a girl of about four, a boy of six, a girl of ten and a 'young person' aged fourteen and a quarter, is another matter, even though a French governess of forty, seated on a neighbouring tree-stump and reading a yellow-back, is present to keep the peace. The generations, so to speak, of children are minute.

In their *Psychology of Childhood*, Drs. Naomi Norsworthy and Mary Whitley present a vitalizing 'cross-section of child life at five and at eleven'. 'The facts stated' are 'generalized, and may not fit the mental image one calls up of some particular child in many traits. . . . However, it may serve as a guide.' The children studied were American.

At five years old children in stature, we are told, range from thirty-four to forty-six inches, and grow a little over two inches a year. 'The sitting height is large, relative to the standing height.' Their weight is from thirty-four to forty-six pounds, and this increases by a little more than four pounds in the course of the year. The brain is about eight-ninths of its adult weight. The twenty milk teeth should show as yet no gaps. Relative to their age, they need a larger amount of food, and at more frequent intervals, than an adult; much less meat, half as much *fat*, plenty of air and sunshine and about eleven hours' sleep a day. At this age they are beginning to develop a more independent personality, and one different perhaps from that at the age of three, though their conscience (let us be exceedingly cautious!) is as yet derived wholly from authority. 'They learn to be whatever will secure them the greatest advantage, coy, whining, patient and good-tempered or vociferous and teasing, shy, obedient, polite, bold according to the value in personal returns which such behaviour brings'—subtleties of behaviour no less clearly evident in some crafty young wife out of a play by Congreve. Their 'lies' are often

64

Changes

merely the outcome of imagination, of faulty perception and memory, but at times are told on purpose, to evade punishment, or in hostility to their elders. They should by now—if so taught or not misled—have mastered their bodily functions; be able to blow their own noses; help to keep themselves clean; pipe up aptly 'Please' and 'Thank you', and so forth; use both fork and spoon; cry less when hurt, and yell less when angry. Crossness and sulks should be things of the past!

The chief moral habit needed at this age is obedience—to wise and proper bidding. And as their time-sense is weak they should be rewarded or punished immediately, if desirable; and the punishment, our experts maintain, should fit rather the child than the naughtiness.

All this is but a fraction of what children are 'like' at the age of five—and there are admirable pages on their 'play interests', their prominent instincts and mental inclinations. A minute personal experience may be of interest here—that of overhearing not long ago a talk in the dark after bedtime between a child aged two and a half years and her brother of five. She was enquiring apparently at what age she would be really grown-up, independent, her own mistress. At sixteen? she pleaded. No, not sixteen. At eighteen? Oh, yes, you *might* at eighteen. (This in a rather falsetto, throaty voice.) What shall I do *then*? Oh, then you will be able to do your own hair; and brush it; and get out the tangles. A silence followed; perhaps the serpent-haunted stair had creaked.

This sage counsellor, not long before this talk occurred, had on his mother's behalf succeeded in laying the table for dinner for three, including the arrangement of four kinds of flowers in three vases. Being asked if he knew how to manage the coffee machine, he replied a little scornfully, how could that not be so, as he had himself explained to their late and somewhat artless cook how it worked. His chares finished, he enquired: 'Unless you have anything else for me to do, Mummie, may I please go upstairs again? I don't like hanging about.' Together, no doubt, with millions of other 'blue-eyed banditti', 'when the dark is beginning to lower', he occasionally listens in. But for a large part of one particular Children's Hour he listened in without approval, until it came to a 'talk'. In this he became engrossed. It was about the *World*, he explained. He merely *meant* this; for he is by no means a

Early One Morning

juvenile wiseacre, though, like his sister, he frequently reflects his elders.

Not very long afterwards he spent about three and a half hours one afternoon, with an interval for tea, disentangling and sorting the silks in his mother's work-basket. That will be a no less æsthetic but more fatiguing operation when he is himself a husband. He was then summoned by his nurse. It was on the brink of bedtime; and his usual quiet half-hour over an atlas with his father was in jeopardy. He broke out into angry lamentations and was promised that, if he now behaved himself, he should have a few minutes with the atlas when he was in bed. Otherwise, no father and no maps. For a moment he debated the two procedures, whether to accept this offer or to show his Nannie what he thought of her. He decided against his Nannie, and much too vigorously for a gentleman. When he was undressed his skin was flushed from head to foot. Quietened down and in bed, he was persuaded to apologize to his Nannie, asked for and was refused the atlas, but was given a sheet of paper instead, on which he drew a vindictive caricature of the beloved offender. 'You must go to sleep now, and I'll take that away,' said his mother. 'No,' he said, 'I want to keep it.' 'Why?' 'Because it will make me laugh to look at it.'

On the surface this is a frivolous narrative, but if we translate the three and a half hours spent on the silks; the disappointment, the revenge, the solace, the whole episode, into adult terms, even Napoleon might not pooh-pooh it as a manifestation of human energy. The child concerned cannot yet read, but that his atlas is no mere plaything—his bedroom is hung with maps—is proved by his whispered reply from memory to the question: What is east of Greenland? Iceland. And east of that? England. And west? Oh, Canada, of course! When asked how he knew where Ceylon, Cape Horn, etc., *are*, he replied—thoroughly amused by the simplicity of the question—'Why, by their shapes!' Most of his answers of this kind, when it may seem almost too sanguine to be sure they are correct, are whispered. Hardened grown-ups, when asked for information, may brazenly supply it, right or wrong; but rather seldom resort to a courageous, 'I don't know'. The confession is something of a feat in itself, since to know we do not know is next best to knowing. Or second best, perhaps, if we remember

66

Changes

Dr. Johnson's habit when he found himself in a library unfamiliar to him, of quietly browsing from title page to title page. When his lynx-eyed henchman observed him so engaged, and enquired why, he replied that in future he would know where what he wanted to know would be at his disposal.

The age of six is an immense twelve months beyond that of five in the time-world of a child. And here, for illustration (no less than for warning and encouragement to ambitious parents) is Coleridge:

'At six years old I remember to have read Belisarius, Robinson Crusoe, and *Philip Quarll*; and then I found the Arabian Nights' Entertainments, one tale of which (the tale of a man who was compelled to seek for a pure virgin) made so deep an impression on me (I had read it in the evening while my mother was mending stockings), that I was haunted by spectres, whenever I was in the dark: and I distinctly remember the anxious and fearful eagerness with which I used to watch the window in which the books lay, and whenever the sun lay upon them, I would seize it, carry it by the wall, and bask and read. My father found out the effect which these books had produced, and burnt them.

'So I became a *dreamer*, and acquired an indisposition to all bodily activity; and I was fretful, and inordinately passionate, and as I could not play at anything, and was slothful, I was despised and hated by the boys; and because I could read and spell and had, I may truly say, a memory and understanding forced into almost an unnatural ripeness, I was flattered and wondered at by all the old women. And so I became very vain, and despised most of the boys that were at all near my own age, and before I was eight years old I was a *character*. Sensibility, imagination, vanity, sloth, and feelings of deep and bitter contempt for all who traversed the orbit of my understanding, were even then prominent and manifest. . . .'

By pride fell the angels—but how many 'very vain' *cherubs*, I wonder, keep the fallen ones company? Until reading this confession—not necessarily inaccurate because it was retrospective—one may have assumed that to be crowned a 'character' (the Englishman's glory, though hardly his ambition) is an honour reserved for the elderly. Yet who would have the heart to wrest it from the brows of this infant Samuel, even though, like Napoleon, he set it on his own head?

67

Early One Morning

Eight years after Coleridge turned six, William Hazlitt, whose only recollection in later years of the four he spent as a child in Boston and Philadelphia was the taste of barberries ('still in my mouth after an interval of thirty years'), wrote the following letter to his father. And Cleopatra herself could not have sweetened the unction of its final '*still*'. Has not this letter also a trace of the 'character' the author of the *Liber Amoris* would have confessed himself to be? The writer was eight years old.

'My dear Papa,—I shall never forget that we came to america. If we had not came to america, we should not have been away from one and other, though now it can not be helped. I think for my part that it would have been a great deal better if the white people had not found it out. Let the others have it to themselves, for it was made for them. I have got a little of my grammar; sometimes I get three pages and sometimes but one. I do not sifer any at all. Mamma Peggy and Jacky are all very well, and I am to.—I still remain your most affectionate son, William Hazlitt.'

As for 'sifer any at all', a letter written by Hazlitt to his brother two years after this—and to be found on a later page—suggests first, as with Henry James, that early arithmetic may be an *ignis fatuus*; and next, that quite apart from his looks we should not judge a dunce even by his own admissions. High lights may cast black shadows.

Apart from sarcasm, nothing may wound a child more deeply indeed, whatever the provocation may be, than to be called stupid. It cuts back far too severely the sprouting shrub, and may even for a time succeed in making him so. It would appear that every mind has its own method of dealing with new knowledge. Until that knowledge is expressed in its own terms it cannot be grasped, 'taken in'. Bright minds are the more original and may for this reason appear at times the more dense. That is perhaps why Ann Taylor failed with her t-h-y. At that moment she couldn't see *how* these letters spelt the sound *thy*. Better then never to call a child a dunce until he is dead—if only for the reason that it is galling to be refuted. Besides, the dunce himself may retaliate.

William Bell Scott, when he was a young child, was taken by his father for a walk one morning. They stopped at the gate of an old herbalist Quaker who kept a little day-school attended by

R. H. BARHAM, AS A BOY
'THOMAS INGOLDSBY'
From a miniature

WILLIAM HAZLITT
AGED THIRTEEN YEARS
From a miniature by John Hazlitt

SIR WALTER SCOTT
AS A BOY
From a miniature

Changes

William. On the gate was a brass plate bearing this Dr. Bachelor's name and the words *Hinc Sanitas*. His father, who was with friends, asked William what the words meant; and laughed when he failed to tell him. 'I was so savage at his not knowing his laugh would wound me, that when we reached home I shut myself in my bedroom, got hold of my Bible—it was a Sunday evening and the book was handy—and there I took an oath, as I had been told it was to be done, by holding the Bible straight up in my right hand, that when I was old enough and strong enough I would be the death of him.'

Miss Fleming relates, too, how even the tenderest of tributes, and the gentlest amusement may put a match to an inward bonfire. 'Quite early in my work,' she says, 'I learnt how careful one must be to fall in with the serious view children take. I was in a small school on a remote Welsh moorland. When I'd finished my work I said that any child could stay and talk to me—if they wanted to. A small person of five years, with large dark grey eyes and thick waving black hair, and a delicate pale oval face asked me "Please what type am I?" I smiled and said she would make a lovely moorland fairy. (I had previously told the children the tale of the Lady of Llyn y fan fach.) She stamped her foot angrily and said, "I don't mean nonsense like that. When Dr. Fleure measured my granny she was 'Mid-Mediterranean' and I *did* want to be the same as granny." So I took my instruments, went a mile and a half to a solitary Welsh cottage, measured them both again and talked seriously on the past history of the peoples of the Welsh moorland, explained how the Lady of Llyn y fan fach was real history; and so comforted the anxious little mind—and incidentally made two very good friends who really helped me in my research.'

3. '"*It takes a long time to grow up,*" quoth Eleven.'

At the age of *eleven*, we are told by the authors of *The Psychology of Childhood*, children in height range from fifty-one to fifty-eight inches, in weight from sixty to seventy-eight pounds, boys on the average being four pounds heavier than girls, and gaining four pounds to their six (as the girls overtake them in height), during that year. The brain has now all but ceased to increase either in size or in weight; though, by comparison with that of the

Early One Morning

adult, the heart is still small in relation to the size of the arteries. At this age children need six-tenths as much food as a man 'at moderate work', and nine and a half hours' sleep every day. Their rapacity is such that their diet, while varied and plain, should be 'bulky' rather than concentrated. They are now in a world 'made up mostly of their own kind', and only 'occasionally touched by the orbits' of grown-ups. The latter are tolerated as convenient, but are often incomprehensible; at best foolish, at worst unjust. 'At no time may there be such complete mutual impatience or even misunderstanding.'

The world of the eleven-year-olds is one of vivid action; and of the most varied fauna and flora, real and imaginary. In this world they experiment and investigate beyond caution, defying danger, and to their hearts' content. Adults and their habits may be even rather unseemly mysteries; though the understanding few among them may win whole hearted trust, love and even adoration. 'In general, there is a distinct drawing apart of the sexes' at this age, 'a dislike for each other's ways, a lack of sympathy with each other's interests'. Girls to boys seem silly, boys to girls are rough and 'horrid'. Boys therefore should be led by one of their own sex. Nevertheless, children of this age—in America, at any rate—are rated as 'remarkably good', as compared with young persons of fourteen to fifteen—a complete seventy per cent of them being definitely so. What, I wonder, would be the percentage for adults. Not *so* good, perhaps; but probably 'better' than we commonly suppose. And here, again, for a modest check on the psychologists, is a brief domestic survey of three children round about ten years old.

Towards the conclusion of *The Memoirs of a Highland Lady*, its very vivacious author, Elizabeth Grant, sums up the characters and accomplishments of herself and her two younger sisters when they were children together at Rothiemurchus, an old country house in the Highlands, about a hundred and thirty years ago. She herself, she tells us, was extremely 'plain and shy'—which, after her earlier pages, will come as a surprising confession to any reader of her delightful book, and particularly the 'plain'. She was also flighty and capricious and easily grew tired of any given task. She idled her time away, laughing and chattering. But, though doubtful herself if schooling had done her 'much good', she was a quick learner.

Changes

Jane, she tells us, was conscientious, dutiful, slow and clumsy. 'Her needlework was abominable, her playing dreadful, her writing was wretched, her figures could not be read.' However, she 'overcame all these difficulties' by unfailing industry, was a happy child and none the worse in after life for the discipline involved.

As for Mary, 'the stupidity of that strange heavy child had hitherto rendered every attempt to rouse her vain'. At eight she could not read, was a mere scribbler, and refused even to try to count. Romping and dancing were distasteful to her. She liked to sit quiet, her doll for company, or to cut up cake and apples into dinners for it. But even in doll-economy she was sadly wanting. 'She was tall, large, and fair, as big nearly as Jane, and looked as old. I was excessively fond of her.'

And lo, fifteen years afterwards, when sparkling gossip about Sir Walter Scott (that 'gigantic Jack Horner' as William Bell Scott calls him), and the Ettrick Shepherd and Mrs. Hemans and Lord Jeffrey is adorning her sister's pages, Mary is suddenly referred to as the Beauty of the Northern Meeting! 'She had grown up very handsome, and never lost her looks; she had become lively and, to the amazement of the family, outshone us all. She was in fact a genius and a fine creature—poor Mary!' Since the *Memoirs* leave Mary happily married, 'poor' is a little obscure.

Here then is *one* dunce transmogrified. At some little distance from her in every respect we have Casanova, who asserts that he was an imbecile up to the age of eight and a half, and that he was then cured by 'magical practices'. But all such cures at least seem to be magical. Dr. Samuel Smiles, himself a 'character', who for 'sweeping the streets' of the mighty has earned a good deal more ridicule than he deserves, disarmingly confesses:

'I was only an average boy, distinguished for nothing but my love of play. . . . I could not have been very bright, for one day, when Hardie [a schoolmaster] was in one of his tyrannical humours, he uttered this terrible prophecy in a loud voice: "Smiles! You will never be fit for anything but sweeping the streets of your native borough." A nice encouragement for a little scholar!'

Fanny Burney, because as a child she was 'quiet' and demure, and—far less conspicuously—a perceptive and clever mimic, also had the reputation of being a dunce, though her mother did not share this view. *She* had 'no fear' for Fanny. And Fanny of her

71

Early One Morning

graciousness will return to these pages, together with other 'dunces'.

The mere age of a child can easily deceive us as to the powers of his mind. Children also *look* young, and in much act so similarly that we pay them only a childish attention, and suppose them to be much of one kind. Examine steadily however, intense face by face, any throng of children clustered round a street Punch and Judy Show, and this illusion will vanish for ever. They may be chiefly *Angli*, and they are all of them *children*, but—except in some half-hidden earnestness and in their momentary self-oblivion—they may not suggest *Angeli*. But then, why thus compare them. The angels themselves, including the cherubim, one of whom was 'the mighty winged spirit of the storm', once in human conception had no similitude to children, but, as Donne declared in one of his sermons, were *primogeniti dei*, and impregnably formidable. It was modern sentiment that littled them for the nursery and the churchyard.

Besides, looks may be deceptive. The boy who sat for the youthful Christ in the Temple for William Collins' picture was in great demand, quotes Mr. S. M. Ellis, 'for cupids, angels, and whatever else was lovely and refined'. In private life he was a gambler, a thief, and wore a stiletto when he was twelve.

At least as common a phrase for a child as 'little angel' is little imp, little varmint, little limb and such. Little wretch is not unfamiliar, and little demon not unknown. There are staid children, prim and hoity-toity children. The very word *demure* hints at a sort of permanent stability. The face that by way of his words gazes up at us from out of Lord Herbert of Cherbury's cradle even *looks* to be the philosopher's it actually was. The child whose portrait graces *The Young Visiters* is positively dowageresque. Indeed there is much to suggest that we are born in spirit, if not in mind, of an age, or of no age, which, with variations, we shall continue in until we die. The tranquil bleached blue eyes of a very old woman—as of one of the Ancient Mariner's gentler shipmates—may mirror what is only else to be found in an infant's. The bachelor of forty was once the bachelor of eight, and the spinster of seven is discovered at last to have been always one of those wise, invaluable, self-forgotten ones whom the fortunate are privileged to possess as a counsellor or friend, of any age up to ninety-nine.

72

Changes

But while the greybeard in petticoats awakens compassion, and the matron of six may be both entertaining and amiable company, and the 'knowing', green or dry, are usually odious, the best of all gifts to the beloved of the gods is that of perpetual youth. And just as the artist in any medium tends, after a prolonged and arduous circuit, to return at length to a well-won simplicity again, so those who are born young may inherit another childhood, which far from being a silly, child*ish*, aping, sham affair, resembles a serene St. Martin's Summer, except only that it even more closely resembles a lively St. Nicolas's Spring.

4. 'The unimaginable touch of time.'

'Man's breathing miniature', then, during its first few years of life not only changes more rapidly and radically in certain respects than it will at any time after it ceases at sixteen to be a child in the eyes of the law, but its age at any year is also of many kinds—physical, apparent, comparative (in intelligence tests and so forth), and virtual. Apart from these it has to submit to a general standard of age set by adults, in their conception of, and in their own relation to children. This must affect the children themselves in mind, conduct, in what they attempt, and in their outlook. It is a standard that varies to some extent from century to century. And the tendency nowadays in our conception and treatment of children is to keep them young—and younger perhaps than in fact and faculty they actually are. Of all the saints, Everyman of Protestant England holds dearest St. Nicolas. He may nod to St. Patrick, but is far less familiar even with St. Christopher. And he much prefers St. Nicolas in his German *alias*, Santa Claus. Christmas and Childermas are celebrated as one feast. It would hardly be an exaggeration to say that children, and particularly 'little children' were discovered in the early years of the nineteenth century. Its general attitude to them, which may be compared with Mrs. Alexander's on a previous page, may be seen in a glimpse of two little books intended for their use.

In a tiny volume entitled *Letters to a Child*, written by the author of *Ministering Children*, Letter IV begins, not very winningly: 'Dear Child, Do you know what an Allegory is?' and Letter IX: 'My dear Child, You know that men, and women and children

73

Early One Morning

may be called at any age to leave this world. . . . I will tell you in this Letter of four children who were all called away from one village. . . .' Though Death—and the dread of what may follow him—pertinaciously peers in through the crannies of this hearse-like little *Vade Mecum,* there are also flowers in it and birds and woods and the lazy blue of the sea. But even the sea is introduced in order to lure in a little girl who collects seaweed to sell to make money for the missionaries. The gentle authoress believed that it is imperative to persuade a young child, who may be as eager with life as a dewdrop is with the colours of the rainbow, to brood on its brevity. Almost every sentence of her minute volume is in a hushed, candied, yet faintly menacing strain. It is as though the tender, or hardy, plant must be watered only drop by drop with her own *elixir vitæ,* and even that distilled. Ours nowadays is sterner stuff—from the vats of Hollywood.

It was realized none the less in the nineteenth century that a young child has brains and a sense of humour as well as a soul; and that they need not be at odds. My own scribbled copy of *The Child's Guide to Knowledge* is one of the fifty-fifth edition. Guides not to mere knowledge but to Science have long ago superseded it in the nursery. It begins: What is the World? The earth we live on. Who made it? The great and good God. Are there not many things in it you would like to know about? Yes, very much. Pray, then, what is bread made of? The child in these pages—'A'—is even more real and solid and downright than his questioner 'B', and—Solomon minimus—he already knows all the answers!

'The most commonplace subjects,' runs the introduction, 'and those which occur most frequently in almost every conversation, are, by youth, either totally disregarded, or but imperfectly understood.' The authoress had 'ever found that to produce, encourage, and satisfy an inquisitive curiosity upon every subject, was attended with the double advantage—of information and amusement to her pupils'. This pygmy tome *may*, for the time being, have satisfied Charles Darwin, whose questions, says Galton, were always consummately apt. Its index begins with Acorns and ends with Zinc; and among the *A*'s alone are such seductions to the enquiring mind as adamant, allspice, aloes, ambergris, apples, apricots, arrack and asses' milk—the last a diet by no means out of use in some of our own scholastic establishments.

74

Changes

To feed not the soul, not the desire for knowledge, but the imagination of the young, and still be not unmindful of their morals, Joseph Payne, who (in 1872) was the first professor of education appointed in England by the College of Preceptors, published, about thirty years before this date, his *Select Poetry for Children*. He confesses to having freely adapted and altered his originals 'to the design of his work', and his selection—for children aged between six and twelve—contains plenty of Cowper, Mary Howitt, Jane Taylor and Wordsworth—we should not perhaps expect any Keats or Shelley—and a few specimens from Beaumont and Fletcher; but not a line from Herrick, Vaughan, Blake or William Shakespeare.

Shakespeare's absence is remarkable. Dr. Bowdler's Edition of the Plays had appeared as far back as 1818, and no poet is referred to more often or with more ardour in the memoirs of this time—with which we shall presently be concerned. The briefest comparison of Joseph Payne's selections with those of our own day intended for children will show the change that has occurred in the view.

In Shakespeare's time a man was considered old when he was in his forties—as Montaigne philosophically admitted; and the child beside him kept pace with his pace. In age, *his* nine was, approximately, I suppose, our twelve; his twelve, our fifteen or even later. Students at the Universities were once what we should now call children. In Brooke's poem on the theme of Romeo and Juliet, Juliet is sixteen. In Shakespeare's play 'she is not fourteen', and this child, this 'green-sickness carrion', this baggage and tallow face, greets her Romeo—'Hamlet in love'—in these words:

> 'O! I have bought the mansion of a love,
> But not possess'd it, and, though I am sold,
> Not yet enjoy'd. So tedious is this day
> As is the night before some festival
> To an impatient child that hath new robes
> And may not wear them. . . .'

and,

> 'I am not I, if there be such an "I";
> Or those eyes shut that make thee answer "I".

75

Early One Morning

If he be slain, say "I"; or if not "no":
Brief sounds determine of my weal or woe.'

and,

'Some word there was, worser than Tybalt's death,
That murder'd me: I would forget it fain;
But O! it presses to my memory,
Like damnèd guilty deeds to sinners' minds.
"Tybalt is dead, and Romeo banished!" '

It is a speech so 'grown-up' that it would not be amiss in the mouth of Macbeth! What bearing the fact that in Shakespeare's day no woman was permitted to appear upon the stage of a theatre may have had on the age of his heroines, I do not know. Most of them are mature, Gertrude, Lady Macbeth, Cleopatra; but Marina, like Juliet, is fourteen years old, Miranda fifteen, Perdita sixteen, and Imogen is of about the same age.

5. ' "*I wot that they are lovers dear*" '.

In his *Autobiography* Lord Herbert of Cherbury relates that: 'Passing two or three days here, it happened . . . that a daughter of the Duchess . . . going one evening from the castle to walk in the meadows, myself with divers French gentlemen attended her and some gentlewomen that were with her; this young lady wearing a knot of ribband on her head, a French chevalier took it suddenly and fastened it to his hatband; the young lady, offended, herewith demands her ribband, but he refusing to restore it, the young lady addressing herself to me, said: "Monsieur, I pray get my ribband from that gentleman." Hereupon, going towards him, I courteously, with my hat in my hand, desired him to do me the honour that I may deliver the lady her ribband or bouquet again. . . .'

The chevalier protested, but in vain; and with his usual vanity Lord Herbert, bound, as he says, by the oath taken when he was made Knight of the Bath, all but brought the squabble to a duel, and insisted on taking the glory of it. This daughter of the Duchess was then about ten or eleven years of age, and Juliet was a matron by comparison! What age too would one *guess* was that noble lady, Jane Grey, once proclaimed Queen of England, when

76

Changes

Roger Ascham, come to say good-bye, found her lonely in her chamber at Brodegate, the Duke and Duchess gone hunting, and she herself reading *Phædon Platonis?* The book was a refuge to mind and spirit, she told Ascham. It had been bestowed on her by her tutor, 'who teacheth me so gently, so pleasantly, with such fair allurements to learning'—as compared with the cruel taunts and threats, the nips and bobs and worse ('till I think myself in hell'), preferred by her father and mother. She was then twelve years old.

At fourteen her rival Elizabeth wrote a letter—that will be found on a later page—to the Lord Admiral Seymour, of a kind that, even if it were prompted, few girls of her age to-day would even attempt. A century and a quarter after this, on the 1st of August, 1672, John Evelyn wrote in his Diary:

'I was at the marriage of Lord Arlington's only daughter (a sweet child if ever there was any) to the Duke of Grafton, the King's natural son by the Duchess of Cleveland; the Archbishop of Canterbury officiating, the King and all the grandees being present. I had a favour given me by my Lady; but took no great joy at the thing for many reasons. . . .'

The bride was five years old, her husband nine. This 'sweetest, hopefullest, most beautiful child, and most virtuous too . . . sacrificed to a boy that had been rudely bred,' was remarried seven years afterwards, when she was twelve.

Although, in the early years of the eighteenth century, young misses of birth and breeding, and their elders also, were sadly wanting in the very rudiments of learning, as both Richard Steele and Swift lament, they were precocious enough in their ways and arts and manners. In *Chickens feed Capons*, 'a Dissertation on the Pertness of our Youth in general', of 1731, quoted by Miss Dorothy Gardiner in *English Girlhood at School*, the author protests: 'Instead of Babies, Playthings and other pretty innocencies used of old, our Girls at 10 or 11 years of Age keep their select Companies and treat 'em with as much Solemnity and Expence as their Parents do their own Acquaintance; this prevails not only at Court but in the City . . . there is as much Fuss made at some Houses against such a Miss . . . comes to visit the Daughter as if a Duchess was expected . . . when the visit is returned she must be dressed up to the heighth of the Mode. . . .'

Early One Morning

A girl in the past came of age when she was twelve years old. But prior to this she may have had several matrimonial adventures. Miss Eileen Power in her *Mediæval People* cites the case of Grace de Saleby, an heiress. She had been twice widowed before, at the age of eleven, she was married to a third husband, who paid three hundred marks for the privilege! Elizabeth Ramsbotham at the age of thirteen was married to an eleven-year-old whose name was John Bridge. 'But he never used her lovinglie, insomoche that the first night they were maried, the said John wold eate no meate at supper, and whan hit was bed tyme, the said John did wepe go home with his father'. Such marriages—whether like Grace's or John's—must once have been fairly frequent. Abductions of heiresses of fourteen indeed were more than mere episodes in kitchen romances until recent times.

Again; in 1797, a remote relative of Longfellow's, Eliza Southgate, was writing home to her father and mother in a strain that would suggest to any modern parents either that their young daughter was deranged or was destined to irradiate the pages of *Punch*. She is thirteen.

'Medford, May 25, 1797.

'My dear Parents:

'I hope I am in some measure sensible of the great obligation I am under to you for the inexpressible kindness and attention which I have received of you from the cradle to my present situation in school. Many have been your anxious cares for the welfare of me, your child, at every stage and period of my inexperienced life to the present moment. In my infancy you nursed and reared me up, my inclinations you have indulged and checked my follies —have liberally fed me with the bounty of your table, and from your instructive lips I have been admonished to virtue, morality, and religion. The debt of gratitude I owe you is great, yet I hope to repay you by duly attending to your counsels and to my improvement in useful knowledge.

'My thankful heart with grateful feelings beat,
With filial duty I my Parents greet,
Your fostering care hath reared me from my birth,
And been my Guardians, since I've been on earth,
With love unequalled taught the surest way,

Changes

And Check'd my passions when they went astray.
I wish and trust to glad declining years—
Make each heart gay—each eye refrain from tears.
When days are finished and when time shall cease
May you be wafted to eternal peace

Is the sincere wish of your dutiful Daughter,
                                        'Eliza Southgate.
'Robert Southgate, Esqr. & Lady.

That this cannot have been a set piece is suggested by the fact that her headmistress is left unmentioned, and proved by the prevailing tone of the letters that follow it. It is not merely Eliza's *language* that is elderly.

Here again is a chance sidelight on the theme from the *Manchester Guardian* of December 9, 1815. Its cautious context leaves it a little doubtful whether or not its Mary had been sadly contrary, and had been playing with fire. She couldn't, like foolish Harriett, have been playing with *matches*. In either case, the last few words of the announcement hardly suggest to modern ears a child of seven. It is headed, 'Died': 'On Tuesday, 5th instant, Mary Ann, daughter of John and Mary Weatherall, of this town, aged seven years. The deceased may be enumerated among those who in the dawn of life fall the victims of fire; and her troubled and disconsolate parents, ever tender and affectionate, clearly evince to all their acquaintance that parental love and solicitude should be invariably manifested in watching and reclaiming the giddiness of youth.'

As to imaginary children, since Alice was seven and a half years old when she ventured through the Looking-glass, she cannot have been *older* in Wonderland. And 'dreams' so galumptious and prolonged as were these two are unlikely to occur during one week-end. But if her White Rabbit had taken cover not fifty years ago but yesterday, how old should we *guess* her to be?

The discipline of the first great public schools in England also suggests a change of view. The seventy scholars at Winchester, which was founded in 1378, were between eight and twelve years of age. Work began at half-past five in the morning and there were no regular holidays. Dean Colet, having inherited considerable estates from his father, made his plans for St. Paul's School

Early One Morning

—'153 boys to be taught free'; and he himself loved children so fondly that there are as many 'lytels' in his preface to the grammar he wrote for them as there are currants in a bun. His boys began work at seven; whereas at Harrow, whose scholars were compelled to talk Latin even when at play, work began at six in summer and at dawn in winter. This school was opened in 1611, Macharie Wildblood being the arresting name of its first scholar.

To go back for but a moment to the fourteenth century, Chaucer's 'litel clergeon' or chorister, Hugh of Lincoln, was only seven years old when at risk of being 'beten thryës in an houre' he used to creep away to learn the Latin words of an enchanting song which he had heard, O *Alma Redemptoris Mater*, a song which he himself continued to sing even after his throat had been cut. The treatise on the Astrolabe, which Chaucer wrote under 'ful lighte rewles and naked wordes in English'—'For Latin ne canstow yit but smal, my lyte sone'—was indited especially for the instruction of that son when he was ten. And though Chaucer carries out his own precept, '. . . Sothly me semeth betre to wryten un-to a child twyes a good sentence, than he forgete it ones . . .' it is scarcely the kind of fare that children ten years old are accustomed to in the elementary schools of our own day.

There seems little doubt that earnest parents of the past, whether justly or otherwise, expected more of their young children than they appear to expect in these days; and James Mill—perhaps because he was himself a utilitarian philosopher—expected much more. 'I have no remembrance of the time when I began to learn Greek,' writes his son John Stuart, in his *Autobiography*;
'I have been told that it was when I was three years old. My earliest recollection on the subject, is that of committing to memory what my father termed Vocables . . . I faintly remember going through Æsop's Fables, the first Greek book which I read. The Anabasis, which I remember better, was the second. I learnt no Latin until my eighth year. At that time I had read, under my father's tuition, a number of Greek prose authors, among whom I remember the whole of Herodotus, and of Xenophon's Cyropædia and Memorials of Socrates; some of the lives of the philosophers by Diogenes Laertius; part of Lucian, and Isocrates' *ad Demonicum* and *ad Nicoclem*. . . . What he [my father] was himself willing to undergo for the sake of my instruction, may be judged

Changes

from the fact that I went through the whole process of preparing my Greek lessons in the same room and at the same table at which he was writing; and as in those days Greek and English lexicons were not, and I could make no more use of a Greek and Latin lexicon than could be made without having yet begun to learn Latin, I was forced to have recourse to him for the meaning of every word which I did not know. This incessant interruption, he, one of the most impatient of men, submitted to, and wrote under that interruption several volumes of his History and all else that he had to write during those years.

'The only thing besides Greek, that I learnt as a lesson in this part of my childhood, was arithmetic: this also my father taught me: it was the task of the evenings, and I well remember its disagreeableness.'

And John Milton:

'I had, from my first years, by the ceaseless diligence and care of my father (whom God recompense), been exercised to the tongues and some sciences, as my age would suffer, by sundry masters and teachers both at home and at the schools.' And again:

'My father destined me, while yet a little child, for the study of humane letters, which I seized with such eagerness that from the twelfth year of my age I scarcely ever went from my lessons to bed before midnight; which, indeed, was the first cause of injury to my eyes, to whose natural weakness there were also added frequent headaches.'

As a contrast to this discipline we have that of the fathers and mothers referred to by Robert Burton, such silly mothers as make mincing and smart little manikins or *mannequins* of their children, and give them the appearance of being as vain, worldly, feather-witted and empty-headed as they are themselves. *They* are not yet obsolete.

'So parents often err, many fond mothers especially, doat so much upon their children, like Æsop's ape, till in the end they crush them to death, *Corporum nutrices animarum novercæ*, pampering up their bodies to the undoing of their souls: they will not let them be corrected or controlled, but still soothed up in everything they do, that in conclusion "they bring sorrow, shame, heaviness to their parents . . . become wanton, stubborn, wilful, and disobedient; rude, untaught, headstrong, incorrigible, and graceless";

81

Early One Morning

"they love them so foolishly", saith Cardan, "that they rather seem to hate them. . . ." "I would to God (saith Fabius) we ourselves did not spoil our children's manners, by our overmuch cockering and nice education, and weaken the strength of their bodies and minds. . . ." '

Whether or not over much cockering is still a common thing in the home life of children nowadays, it can hardly be doubted—recent legislation alone would be evidence enough—that childhood is now conceived of as persisting longer by some years than it did in the view of our ancestors. In regard to their physical and mental capabilities we keep children back rather than urge them on, and expect less of them than was once expected of them. The consequence is that—apart from the prematurely old and wordly-wise—who face a grisly actuality in our mean streets and miserable slums—the majority of children enter 'life' later than once they did. Provided that too much or the wrong kind of progress is not demanded of them in their schooldays, this affords them greater peace and quiet for their full and continuous development, and is in much a blessing. Whether it is *wholly* an advantage either to themselves, to their future, or to the world at large is another question, and one to which it may be easier to find an answer at the end of this book. There is at any rate little in favour of positive hindrances to young and ardent minds. In life's long steeplechase the fences have to be faced, and our early years are the least likely to be wanting in nerve, agility and spirit.

CHAPTER VI

CHILDHOOD IN POETRY

★

1. *'And then in Eden's paradise,*
He placèd him to dwell.'

Milton, as we have seen, attributes his headaches and the injury to his eyesight not to his father's 'forcing' but to his own 'impetuosity in learning'. How much his poetic imagination and his poetry itself were affected in later years by this glut of book-learning is clear in a positive sense. It became at last a magic mirror in his hands, reflecting with his own supreme and substantial splendour the gods and goddesses, the demigods and heroes, cities, palaces and classic landscapes that as a child he had imaged in it.

But negatively, who can say? As with Swinburne, whose roses and lilies seldom affect us as things seen vividly and at a certain actual moment in the mind's eye, but rather as abstractions, so too Milton's rathe primrose and pale jessamine, his pansy freaked with jet, his twisted eglantine and daisies pied, even his fresh-blown roses 'washed in dew', do not *appear* to have been derived as directly from nature as—one might hazard—almost invariably do similar and no less lovely references in Shakespeare. *His* and Perdita's daffodils, that come before the swallow dares, and take the winds of March with beauty; their violets dim, and pale primeroses seem to proclaim that at need he himself might even have dated and placed them! He, like Oberon, *knows* a bank whereon the wild thyme grows—even though what in writing he had in mind was only a memoried image of it. Ophelia's pansies and rosemary, Perdita's violets, her streaked gillyvors, hot lavender, and early-bedding marigold, like the 'ruined choirs' of autumn, strutting chanticleer, the icicles that hang by the wall, the frozen

Early One Morning

milk in pail, and the green fields of which Falstaff babbled (if of green fields babble he did), are almost as vivid in the reading of them as are our own remembered, sharp-seen glimpses of the actual and the real. The flowers in the plays are cold with rain, sweet with their nectar, and of the earth earthy. We might at any moment see a butterfly flitting between our eyes and the printed page. Wordsworth's daffodils, too, though less utterly made his own perhaps than Shakespeare's, are scarcely distinguishable from the remembrance of some nodding, multitudinous drift of them such as we have seen for ourselves in an English valley. Milton's 'bells and flowerets' have a beauty all their own—and his; resembling with their 'quaint enamelled eyes' the most delicate embroidery 'inwrought with figures dim'. They are uniquely touched in, made personal—treasure trove. It is their place of origin that differs. And in Shakespeare's case was not this place in his childhood called not 'humane letters', but Out-of-doors?

Similarly with the English poets and the children whom they present to us in their poems. Some of these children are wholly natural. Others are idealisations. Others—viewed in the light of the imagination—are as unique and isolated as

> 'the daisy in Noah's meadow
> On which the foremost drop of rain fell warm
> And soft at afternoon. . . .'

On the whole the poets tend, like the hymn-writers, to emphasise the littleness of childhood, and, following modern views, to 'juvenate' their children. Any attempt to make up—in a story, let us say—apt and natural talk for a child of five or three years old will prove how very easy it is to fall into this trap.

If indeed we compare poems about children written by the poets of the sixteenth and seventeenth centuries—their grave and lovely epitaphs, for example, or for that matter those in prose in the eighteenth, with similar poems written during the last century, the contrast is apparent. There are exceptions. Andrew Marvell's 'nymphs' on the one hand—one might assume from what he tells us of them—resemble children even though they are well into their teens. It is their beauty, however, like that of flowers, that is ageless, rather than themselves. The children of Landor, Whittier, Whitman, Prior, Robert Bridges, are both in looks and character unlittled and natural. Wordsworth swings from one extreme to the other, with 'his sister Emmeline', 'a little prattler among men', his *H.C.*, 'a fairy voyager', the child he seems to refuse to understand in *We are Seven*, and the child in *The Pet Lamb*, in which the evening colours and every syllable are exquisitely in keeping with the youth and innocence of both of them.

'Alice Fell' is another exception; but if anything Wordsworth tends to under-age his children. Another Alice, Lewis Carroll's, is at least as dignified as the queens she meets. But his dedications and some of his poems range from the sentimental even to the mundane. When, on the other hand, in some of his poems Mr. William Davies speaks of a child, a child itself, in its own natural kind, comes to life in his words. He sees what he sees; not merely the 'hell-born childishness' of war, but the half-closed eye of the 'love infant' in 'The Inquest', 'leering' that it may have been murdered. He tells also of

> 'a boundless prairie, when it lay
> So full of flowers it could employ the whole
> World's little ones to pick them in a day. . . .'

and lo, there the world's little ones are: we see them picking the flowers. And these, like the children, seem to have suffered no darkening, no sullying, no loss of beauty and 'virtue'; or greenness, sweetness and life; when he looks, the buttercup looks back, a bird twinkles in the tree, the water sings an instant louder: he and they have been in an immortal conspiracy together for over fifty years. His own poems are his children.

> 'The world may call our children fools,
> Enough for us that we conceive.'

Most modern verse—and this folk-rhymes and proverbs (and Dr. Heinrich Hoffman) all but never do—is apt to prettify its children, dream or real; to patheticize them, scattering its lines with such words as tiny, guileless, girlish, tomboy, tears, angels, death and Heaven. If we attempt to translate, so to speak, their verbal portraits into the pictorial we shall see how widely they differ from the children of Dürer, Velasquez, Botticelli, and even of Gainsborough and other painters of his time. Robinettas, if rare in the nursery, are very welcome, but there are also young

Early One Morning

falcons, butcher-birds, jays. 'She has eyes as blue as damsons, She has pounds of auburn curls.' That is natural; but Longfellow's 'Those heavenly Zingari' is a bad second-best even to his 'blue-eyed banditti'. And the 'heaven' to which these poets so frequently banish the beloved one is apt to *look* as vacant if not as unrealized as the conception of the angel the child has become. It is not at any rate the heaven, vague even though that may be, referred to by John Beaumont in these solemn lines:

> 'Dear Lord, receive my son, whose winning love
> To me was like a friendship, far above
> The course of nature, or his tender age,
> Whose looks could all my bitter griefs assuage.
> Let his pure soul, ordained seven years to be,
> In that frail body, which was part of me,
> Remain my pledge in heaven, as sent to show
> How to this port at every step I go.'

When childhood itself rather than children is the poet's theme, and particularly the poet's own childhood, his outlook and imaginative treatment are seldom sentimental. Such poems as these are usually concerned not with any definite age in childhood, or its physical and intellectual characteristics, or even its earthly surroundings, but with a state of being. How far can we accept their witness? Can we trust the evidence of *any* human creature who has fallen in love? Or may not this be the kind of evidence which, with due provisos, is the most valuable? To describe such poets as mystics is to elude the question. It may isolate their attitude, but hardly explains or justifies it. In any case a freshness and radiance enters their words, as of dew and daybreak in April.

'Happy those early days when I Shined in my angel infancy!' says Vaughan. 'Before I understood this place.' What precise age, ancestry and cultivation does this statement imply? And again:

> 'Were now that Chronicle alive,
> Those white designs which children drive . . .
> Quickly would I make my path even,
> And by meer playing go to Heaven. . . .'

'designs', I gather, meaning aims and intentions; 'drive', pursue; and 'go', go back. With Vaughan's 'meer playing' we shall be

Childhood in Poetry

concerned later. Wordsworth laments not only the loss of childhood but the inward blindness of age: 'The things which I have
seen I now can see no more,' while yet treasuring

> 'those first affections,
> Those shadowy recollections,
> Which, be they what they may,
> Are yet the fountain light of all our day,
> Are yet a master light of all our seeing. . . .'

And again—in *The Excursion*:

> 'thou, who didst wrap the cloud
> Of infancy around us, that thyself,
> Therein, with our simplicity awhile
> Might'st hold, on earth, communion undisturbed. . . .'

How clear-coloured and actual a picture too is that of his 'curious
child', and how like Vaughan's:

> 'I have seen
> A curious child, who dwelt upon a tract
> Of inland ground, applying to his ear
> The convolutions of a smooth-lipped shell;
> To which, in silence hushed, his very soul
> Listened intensely; and his countenance soon
> Brightened with joy; for from within were heard
> Murmurings. . . .'

The mere beauty of this 'curious child', though not a word
definitely refers to it, recalls Coleridge's 'lovely boy':

> 'Encinctured with a twine of leaves,
> That leafy twine his only dress,
> A lovely Boy was plucking fruits,
> By moonlight, in a wilderness.
> The moon was bright, the air was free,
> And fruits and flowers together grew
> On many a shrub and many a tree:
> And all put on a gentle hue,
> Hanging in the shadowy air
> Like a picture rich and rare.

Early One Morning

It was a climate where, they say,
The night is more beloved than day.
But who that beauteous Boy beguiled,
That beauteous Boy to linger here?
Alone, by night, a little child,
In place so silent and so wild——
Has he no friend, no loving mother near?'

This serene light and transparent colour resembles that of the *Songs of Innocence*, even though the beauteous Boy is wandering far from the haunts of the Piper. It may be said that the children in such poems as these are to ordinary children what physically the young horsemen on the frieze of the Parthenon are to ordinary young men. But William Blake was not *only* 'imagining' with the insight that divines the hidden; he was also remembering. As a child himself, he had visions, now of the face of God at a window, filling him with terror; now of the prophet Ezekiel in the fields, for telling of whom he was beaten; now of a tree filled with angels, their wings 'bespangling every bough like stars'. And again, of angelic figures walking among haymakers at their work —who themselves little resemble the haymakers that we ourselves usually observe in our country walks, simply because they shared, like his angelic figures also, Blake's *mind*.

2. '*And how a littling child mote be
Saint er its nativitie.*'

Traherne, too, is recalling not a dream but an actual experience in his 'Meditations' when he says:
'Certainly Adam in paradise had no more sweet and curious apprehensions of the world than I when I was a child. . . . I knew by intuition those things which since my apostasy I collected again by the highest reason. . . . All tears and quarrels were hidden from my eyes. Everything was at rest, free and immortal. . . . So that with much ado I was corrupted, and made to learn the dirty devices of the world, which I now unlearn. . . . The riches of nature are our souls and bodies, with all their faculties, senses and endowments. . . .'
There came a time when he accepted the 'thoughts' of others and forgot his own:

Childhood in Poetry

'So I began among my playfellows to prize a drum, a fine coat, a penny, a gilded book etc. who before never dreamed of such wealth. Goodly objects to drown all the knowledge of Heaven and Earth!'

Lord Herbert of Cherbury in the following argument goes even further afield:

'When I came to riper years, I made this observation, which afterwards a little comforted me, that as I found myself in possession of this life, without knowing any thing of the pangs and throes my mother suffered, when yet doubtless they did not less press and afflict me than her, so I hope my soul shall pass to a better life than this without being sensible of the anguish and pains my body shall feel in death. For as I believe then I shall be transmitted to a more happy estate by God's great grace, I am confident I shall no more know how I came out of this world, than how I came into it. . . .'

He continues this thesis in two Latin poems, *Vita* and *De Vita Coelesti conjectura*, and resumes:

'And certainly, since in my mother's womb this plastica, or formatrix, which formed my eyes, ears, and other senses, did not intend them for that dark and noisome place, but, as being conscious of a better life, made them as fitting organs to apprehend and perceive those things which should occur in this world; so I believe, since my coming into this world my soul hath formed or produced certain faculties which are almost as useless for this life, as the above-named senses were for the mother's womb; and these faculties are hope, faith, love, and joy, since they never rest or fix upon any transitory or perishing object in this world, as extending themselves to something further than can be here given, and indeed acquiesce only in the perfect, eternal, and infinite.

'I confess they are of some use here; yet I appeal to everybody whether any worldly felicity did so satisfy their hope here, that they did not wish and hope for something more excellent; or whether they had ever that faith in their own wisdom, or in the help of man, that they were not constrained to have recourse to some diviner and superior power than they could find on earth, to relieve them in their danger or necessity; whether ever they could place their love on any earthly beauty, that it did not fade and wither, if not frustrate or deceive them; or whether ever their

Early One Morning

joy was so consummate in any thing they delighted in, that they did not want much more than it, or indeed this world can afford, to make them happy. The proper objects of these faculties, therefore, though framed, or at least appearing in this world, is God only, upon whom faith, hope, and love were never placed in vain, or remain long unrequited.'

Blake's visionary angels may have been (no less 'experience' even if they were), a pure fantasy of the imagination, but we can produce no proof of it. And to dismiss or disdain Traherne's 'apprehensions' merely because we have never shared them is rather too easy a way out of a difficulty. It is in unusual minds that we expect unusual events, the fruit of unusual powers of perception. Even when he was a child of four, Traherne tells us, he used to speculate and wonder how 'the earth did end'. With walls or sudden precipices? Or perhaps did the face of Heaven lap down so close upon its margins that a man could 'hardly creep under'? Or was it upheld by pillars or by abysses of dark waters; and, if that were so, what upheld these? It is with conjectures of this *nature* that the modern astronomer is busy, his optic glass ranging stellar universes a myriad light-years away. One 'lowering and sad evening', he being alone in a field, the wildness terrified the child: 'I was a weak and little child and had forgotten there was a man alive in the earth.' And Coleridge's words echo this forlornness: 'It was a climate where, they say, The night is more beloved than day.'

What Thomas Hood tells in rhyme in 'I Remember' Thoreau repeats in prose:

'If thou art a writer, write as if thy time were short, for it is indeed short at the longest. . . . The spring will not last for ever. . . . Again I say, Remember thy Creator in the days of thy youth. Use and commit to life what you cannot commit to memory. Why did I not use my eyes when I stood on Pisgah? . . . Ah, sweet, ineffable reminiscences!'

And John Clare, looking back out of the darkness and misery of his last asylum, becomes a poet in the rarest of senses:

'. . . I long for scenes where man has never trod;
A place where woman never smiled or wept;
There to abide with my Creator, God,
And sleep as I in childhood sweetly slept:

Childhood in Poetry

Untroubling and untroubled where I lie,
    The grass below—above the vaulted sky.'

To be a child, these witnesses gravely declare, is to be an exile,
and an exile haunted with vanishing intimations and relics of
another life and of a far happier state of being—of a lost Jerusalem
to which it is all in vain (by the waters of Babylon) to pine to
return. Consciousness itself, they declare, resembles the awakening out of a dream of innocence, serenity and bliss.

'Father, O Father! what do we here,
In this land of unbelief and fear?
The Land of Dreams is better far
Above the light of the morning star.'

Its very radiance and peace may continue awhile to shine on our
young heads and to transmute the things of a world as yet 'not
realized', but it fades quickly into the light of common day. Every
man, in Jeremy Taylor's words, to take the other side of the
account,
'is born in vanity and sin; he comes into the world like morning
Mushromes, soon thrusting up their heads into the air and con-
versing with their kindred of the same production, and as soon they
turn into dust and forgetfulnesse; some of them without any other
interest in the affairs of the world, but that they made their parents
a little glad, and very sorrowful: others ride longer in the storm;
it may be until seven yeers of Vanity be expired, and then per-
adventure the Sun shines hot upon their heads and they fall into
the shades below, into the cover of death, and darknesse of the
grave to hide them. But if the bubble stands the shock of a bigger
drop, and outlives the chances of a childe, of a carelesse Nurse, of
drowning in a pail of water, of being overlaid by a sleepy servant,
or such little accidents, then the young man dances like a bubble,
empty and gay, and shines like a Dove's neck or the image of a
rainbow, which hath no substance, and whose very imagery and
colours are phantastical; and so he dances out the gayety of his
youth. . . .'
Transitory glimpses of the lost may be recovered:

'. . . I sought no more that after which I strayed
    In face of man or maid;

91

Early One Morning

But still within the little children's eyes
    Seems something, something that replies,
They at least are for me, surely for me!
I turned me to them very wistfully;
But just as their young eyes grew sudden fair
    With dawning answers there,
Their angel plucked them from me by the hair. . . .'

And even the seemingly past-recall, if we accept George Mac-donald's statement, is neither inactive nor beyond a far-deferred recovery:

'. . . I think that nothing made is lost;
That not a moon has ever shone,
That not a cloud my eyes hath crossed
But to my soul is gone.

'That all the lost years garnered lie
In this Thy casket, my dim soul;
And Thou wilt, once, the key apply,
And show the shining whole. . . .'

The mind in the act of creation, said Shelley (who 'never learned to sit with folded wings'), is as a fading coal. So to these poets was the state of early childhood, even although for them its ardour and light had not yet faded wholly out of remembrance. Our days, then, in childhood as in later life, in the words of William Drummond, 'are not to be esteemed after the number of them but after their goodness'. The flowers 'made of light' shine no more in their primal loveliness, though this may be revealed again and again as if by reflection—an experience described by Mr. Frank Kendon in *The Small Years* when he first chanced on the blue succory:—

'The flower was a miracle to me, something rich and strange, and I had to register my discovery (I suppose) on a mind not my own to be sure it was credible. But before I found [this witness] my flower had faded quite out of its beauty by the heat of the summer afternoon. . . .'

That fading reminds me of a similar experience when I was my-self about seven. My flower was not the celestially blue succory, but a colourless convolvulus (a species which Edmund Gosse when

he was six informed his father he was raising in a salt cellar). But its
cool dark heart-shaped leaves and waxen vase-like simplicity
awoke in me a curious wonder and delight, and I remember it as
vividly and with the same peculiar intensity as I remember the
shimmering seeding grasses bowing in the windy sunshine when I
lay rapturously watching them one morning in a later June. I
plucked the flower out of the hedge to take it home to my mother.
But when I came into the house it had wreathed itself into a spiral
as if into a shroud. And when I realized it would never more be
enticed out of it again, I burst into tears!—'burst into my mother's
arms', as a little boy of three the other day described the consequences of seeing in motion at a circus a Mechanical Man!

3. 'In the silence of morning the song of the bird.'

'So the child of whom I am writing', runs Walter Pater's tale
of the hawthorn, 'lived on there quietly; things without thus
ministering to him, as he sat daily at the window with the bird-
cage hanging below it, and his mother taught him to read, wondering at the ease with which he learned, and at the quickness of
his memory. . . . How insignificant, at the moment, seem the
influences of the sensible things which are tossed and fall and lie
about us, so or so, in the environment of early childhood. How
indelibly, as we afterwards discover, they affect us. . . . The realities
and passions, the rumours of the greater world without, steal in
upon us, each by its own special little passage-way, through the
wall of custom about us; and never afterwards quite detach themselves from this or that accident, or trick, in the mode of their first
entrance to us. . . .'

Among the most vivid of these in Mr. Romilly John's early
childhood was a fountain, and the beauty of its falling waters; the
luminous bright red too of a glass of grenadine. But even commonplace objects and very familiar ones have the power to whisper
this secret *Sesame*, and may keep it far beyond the years of childhood—a bird seen very close; or held, its beadlike unspeculative
eyes shining, in the hand; condensed mist on a grass-spider's web,
the cheeping of a midnight mouse in the wainscot, the sickle of
the new moon, the first splinters of ice in winter frost, the first
snow—as in this description of it from *The Small Years*—no less

true to nature than that in Ascham's *Toxophilus*, but filled with a rapture known only to a child:

'. . . If the snow were wet, or still falling, so that we knew we could not go out, we would lean all together on the low nursery window-sill, staring out across the road to the orchard, our eyes made dizzy by the constant slow flakes as they floated down and by to settle. Four pairs of eyes were not enough to notice all, nor four excited voices enough to announce all the novelties, the birds that flew down, the solitary waggon that drew by, the depth of the snow in the wheel-tracks, or in the scoop-shaped laurel leaves immediately underneath us, or how it piled up against the window-glass, or how the millions of grey specks fought one another in the sky above the elm tops. We lived then, except for our mere bodies, in the world outside; games and books and fire were all forgotten while we gave our souls over to the snow. . . . The wonder of it, the nearness now, the whiteness, the brightness, the way you screwed your eyes up, the tidyness of the world! At first it was pleasure enough just to walk on it, feeling your feet sink in, and the squeak and crunch of your steps; then to run, careless whether you were on path or grass, the great delight being to make your tracks in snow that had not been imprinted before, to run scattering and then to stop and look back at the way you had written in the snow. Once, I remember, we looked over a gate with a great sloping field as white as a giant's sheet of notepaper, and we climbed into this field and ran wildly, writing our names with our feet in giant letters for the sky to read. . . .

'The sky was darker than the land; indoors through windows the light struck upwards to the ceiling instead of downwards to the floor; out of doors our hands and faces looked brown and rosy in contrast with the whiteness of the snow; our voices had no echoes, our games, our world, our characters were all necessarily different from those of the ordinary week-day world. There was nothing that the miracle did not change, and nothing, however trivial, which was not impressed with twice its normal significance upon minds intoxicated with the white excitement. So it was then, and so it is to-day; for if the truth be told there is a child in everyone when snow is about, and the word *snow* is richer in youthful associations than almost any other English word. . . .'

And the snow may be London snow, as in Robert Bridges'

Childhood in Poetry

poem, which itself transports memory into the wilds of childhood
again.

'. . . And all woke earlier for the unaccustomed brightness
Of the winter dawning, the strange unheavenly glare:
The eye marvelled—marvelled at the dazzling whiteness;
    The ear hearkened to the stillness of the solemn air;
No sound of wheel rumbling nor of foot falling,
And the busy morning cries came thin and spare.
    Then boys I heard, as they went to school, calling,
They gathered up the crystal manna to freeze
Their tongues with tasting, their hands with snowballing;
    Or rioted in a drift, plunging up to the knees;
Or peering up from under the white-mossed wonder,
"O look at the trees!" they cried, "O look at the trees!" . . .'

To dismiss as pure illusion what poets such as Vaughan and
Traherne and Blake attest because any such experience in childhood as theirs is, we assume, rare and extraordinary is merely to
measure life by a home-made foot-rule. Their poetry is itself rare
and extraordinary. Must that also go by the board? 'For my owne
part,' writes Vaughan, who was by profession a doctor of medicine, 'I honour the truth wherever I find it, whether in an old or
a new Booke, in *Galen*, or in *Paracelsus*; and Antiquity (where I
find it grey with errors), shall have as little reverence from me as
Novelisme.' And where shall we begin and end our incredulity?
    ' "My love," said my mother, looking up from her work . . .
"shan't we call him Augustine?"
    ' "Augustine," said my father dreamily, "why, that name's
mine."
    ' "And you would like your boy's to be the same?"
    ' "No," said my father, rousing himself. "Nobody would know
which was which. I should catch myself learning the Latin accidence or playing at marbles. I should never know my own identity, and Mrs. Primmins would be giving me pap." . . .'
He is eventually given the name of Pisistratus.
    " 'Pisistratus christened! Pisistratus! who lived six hundred years
before Christ was born. Good heavens, madam! you have made
me the father of an Anachronism." '
    Shall we then dismiss these particular poets with their 'golden-

95

Early One Morning

age-of-childhood stuff' as *Anachronisms* and have done with it?

Well and good, but many other poets, who after all are human beings and so as likely to be at odds one with another in other respects as the prosaic and matter-of-fact may be, have volunteered their own variants of the same fantastic legend—Lamb, Lowell, Longfellow, Stevenson, Thomas Moore, Elizabeth Barrett Browning, Tennyson, Father Tabb. To ignore their evidence would fall a good deal short at least of being 'scientific'. Shelley is even persuaded to discover not only innocence and bliss in such recollections, but a goddess full-grown—Intellectual Beauty:

> '. . . While yet a boy I sought for ghosts, and sped
>   Through many a listening chamber, cave and ruin,
>   And starlight wood, with fearful steps pursuing
> Hopes of high talk with the departed dead.
> I called on poisonous names with which our youth is fed;
>   I was not heard—I saw them not——
>   When musing deeply on the lot
> Of life, at that sweet time when winds are wooing
>   All vital things that wake to bring
>   News of birds and blossoming——
>   Sudden, thy shadow fell on me;
> I shrieked, and clasped my hands in ecstasy!

> 'I vowed that I would dedicate my powers
>   To thee and thine—have I not kept the vow? . . .'

and he, ineffectual angel of a remarkable energy of mind, never completely learned

> 'To look on nature, not as in the hour
> Of thoughtless youth; but hearing oftentimes
> The still, sad music of humanity. . . .'

It has been left to our own enlightened day to discover the secret of laughing at *everything* that is tainted with the transcendental—and so doing unto others as they may be tempted to do unto us.

Ah, yes, whispers Common Sense, but wait a little longer until these early ecstasies have ebbed or gone flat or turned cheat, what then? Shelley himself can preach his own funereal sermon on this trite text. When he was twenty-two, and the father of Ianthe, he

SUPPOSED PORTRAIT OF SHELLEY, BY HOPPNER

Childhood in Poetry

writes to Hogg: 'My friend, you are happier than I. You have the pleasures as well as the pains of sensibility. I have sunk into a premature old age of exhaustion, which renders me dead to everything. . . .' This apparently was in part because Harriet, though 'a noble animal', could, like most of Shelley's schoolfellows at Syon House Academy and Eton, neither 'feel poetry' nor understand philosophy. A few months later the sixteen-year-old daughter of William Godwin darted into his life. He caught up a bottle of laudanum, says Peacock, who had come to call on him, and said: 'I never part from this.' And yet, urged Peacock, ' "it always appeared to me that you were very fond of Harriet".' 'Without affirming or denying this he answered: "But you did not know how much I hated her sister." '

And this—written on March 4th, 1812, was what his worldly wise father-in-law thought of him:

'My good friend—I have read all your letters (the first perhaps excepted) with peculiar interest, and I wish it to be understood by you unequivocally that, as far as I can yet penetrate into your character, I conceive it to exhibit an extraordinary assemblage of lovely qualities not without considerable defects. The defects do, and always have arisen chiefly from this source, that you are still very young, and that in certain essential respects you do not sufficiently perceive that you are so. . . .'

Which might have been a still more crushing summary if Godwin had been able to follow it up with a calculation showing how many centuries 'younger' a boy of twenty is than a baby of three.

CHAPTER VII

HAPPINESS

*

1. 'And that as much sun as would gild a daisy.'

How oddly the Slough of Despond referred to by Shelley contrasts with a comment on her life made by Frances Power Cobbe, when she was seventy: 'That it has been *worth living* I distinctly affirm. . . . I would gladly accept the permission to run my earthly race once more from beginning to end.'

If the old serpent could first slough his skin, perhaps; but Frances Cobbe must have been *very* pleasant company to herself. To another way of thinking life seems little more than a sequence of minor deaths; as the youthful progression: cradle—nursery—dame-school—preparatory school—public school—university—the World, may be said to be. And it is from a translation by Henry Vaughan of the sixth book of *De Arte Voluntatis* that the following is taken.

'. . . Though we dye but once, yet do not we dye at once: We may make, yea we do make many assaies or tryals of dying: Death insinuates it selfe, and seizeth upon us by peecemeals; it gives us a tast of it self: It is the Cronie, or Consort of life: So soon as we begin to be, wee begin to wast and vanish; we cannot ascend to life, without descending towards death: Nay we begin to dye before we appeare to live; the perfect shape of the Infant is the death of the *Embryo*, childhood is the death of Infancie, youth of Childhood, Manhood of youth, and old age of Manhood. When we are arrived at this last stage, if we stay any long time in it, and pay not the debt we owe, death requires interest; she takes his hearing from one, his sight from another, and from some she takes

98

Happiness

both: The extent and end of all things touch their beginning, neither doth the last minute of life do any thing else, but finish what the first began. . . . Life is a Terrace-walke with an Arbour at one end, where we repose, and dream over our past perambulations. . . .'

Alexander Pope, and 'tis perhaps his nature to, seats himself with puckish amusement in the middle of this seesaw and ironically comments:

> '. . . . Behold the child, by nature's kindly law,
> Pleased with a rattle, tickled with a straw:
> Some livelier plaything gives his youth delight,
> A little louder, but as empty quite:
> Scarfs, garters, gold, amuse his riper stage,
> And beads and prayer-books are the toys of age:
> Pleased with this bauble still as that before,
> Till tired he sleeps, and life's poor play is o'er. . . .'

The paternal, as distinct from the fatherly, view of children—'certain cares, uncertain comforts'—may be a model of patience and indulgence, but is also apt to be prosaic. Nevertheless, what the author even of 'I Remember' makes of his child in his *Parental Ode* is no more than what with ease the sportive cynic might make of Man in Hamlet's soliloquy—interlard, that is, each sentence of poetic insight with one of actualistic mockery; e.g. *What* a piece of work is a man! . . .

> 'Thou happy, happy elf! . . .
> Thou tiny image of myself! . . .
> Thou merry, laughing sprite!
> With spirits feather-light,
> Untouch'd by sorrow, and unsoil'd by sin. . . .'

This has a faint trace even of Vaughan himself; but not so the three lines that have been omitted:

> 'But stop—first let me kiss away that tear. . . .
> My love, he's poking peas into his ear! . . .
> Good heav'ns! The child is swallowing a pin!'

Truth will out; but such waggery as this wears a little threadbare when it is expanded into six or seven similar stanzas. Every jaded

99

Early One Morning

grown-up has of course shared Hood's despair in the presence of an infant with this insatiable zest to convert the without into the within. And possibly Mr. Bultitude's also, when the limber elf has broken out into a schoolboy, and not yet had time to 'grow heavy'. 'He hated to have a boy about the house, and positively writhed under the irrelevant and irrepressible questions, the unnecessary noises and boisterous high spirits which nothing could subdue.' 'His son's society was to him simply an abominable nuisance, and he pined for a release from it from the day the holidays began.' And presently, enter Dick himself! This *Vice Versa* attitude, however—that of the bell-wether to the new season's lambs—is of no particular period or value. There are fogies so old that they cannot endure the strains of a barrel-organ, even though a tiny gibbering marmoset is perched on its green baize to remind them of their past.

But there is a view precisely the contrary of this. 'Looking back on my days,' writes Richard Middleton, 'I can say that I do not regret a single hour that I have passed in the company of children. It was not that their wayward hands spared my always vulnerable vanity; but they struck without malice, and their blows were as welcome as the rebukes of conscience.'

The chief English poets who have shared a divination of childhood to which the term 'mystical' has been applied, apart from being poets, had little of nurture in common. Henry Vaughan came of an ancient family, Traherne was the son of a shoemaker, William Blake of a hosier, and Wordsworth of a law agent. Their careers were equally dissimilar. Gifted alike with a rare delicacy of sense and sensibility, they declared none the less that early childhood is a state of bliss rather than of simple happiness. But they too must often have been the victims of extremes in mood and feeling—a rapt and timeless peace and wonder; a forlorn and lightless dejection.

The miseries incident to childhood, they themselves would have agreed, are not the less violent and atrocious because they are unsharable and unmanageable, or soon over. Nor am I referring here to the causes of such unhappiness—these will come later—but rather to a general and transitory condition of mind, or poise of feeling, a tone and tenour and look of life that to the youngest of children may be scarcely endurable. The summary 'happy' or

Happiness

'unhappy' is little more than a cloak, gay or dark, to denote the indefinable. It would be no less difficult to find a word that would fit any more precisely even the pervasive mood or emotional poise of the thirties, forties or fifties of maturity.

The spirit in childhood may flag, or conceal itself, or rebel, not necessarily by reason of its own nature and origin, but at having been compelled to accustom itself as best it can to a 'place' as yet not 'understood'; and that whether it is already vaguely familiar or in some directions shatteringly strange. It is as though life had shown a child his new coat, a Joseph's coat of the most diverting colours and pattern, and then had 'forbidden him to wear it'. Mere discipline in itself does not seem to have this effect—not even the discipline of the Cameronian gentleman of Lochiel, mentioned by Galton, who, when bivouacking with his son in the snow, noticed that the boy had rolled up a snowball to make himself a pillow. He rose, kicked it away, sternly ejaculating: 'No effeminacy, boy!'

Since happiness too is an affair of moments more usually than of days or even hours, we seldom with a generous abandonment pay *that* supreme tribute to our destiny; and few people confess to ever having been merely contented. That would be too pretty a compliment to our circumstances, and not pretty enough for ourselves. In recalling our childhood, on the other hand, it may more probably occur to us to declare it to have been a *happy* state than the reverse. Positives are less outstanding than negatives—particularly when one's character is concerned. Or is it easier to forget life's many blessings than its sea of troubles, even though time may succeed in turning the red one green. If so, a little more weight, but not too much, may be given to the evidence for youthful bliss. Not only to the rapture—page after page—of Serge Aksakoff's inexhaustible *Years of Childhood*, but also to the more moderate English and Irish testimony of Charlotte Yonge and Frances Power Cobbe.

'I do not recollect so far back as some people do,' says Charlotte Yonge. 'I can hardly date my earlier recollections. Mine was too happy and too uneventful a childhood to have many epochs, and it has only one sharp line of era in it, namely my brother's birth when I was six and a half. I can remember best by what happened before, and what happened after. . . .'

Early One Morning

2. 'But who can call this dull content
By the sweet name happiness?'

John Ruskin, who from his A B C onwards had been taught to be circumspect in the use of words, describes his childhood as 'serene', rather than happy. He enjoyed his nursery books, and delighted in a Scotch aunt (in spite of the fact that she gave him cold mutton on Sundays), because she had not only a garden full of gooseberry bushes sloping down to the Tay, but a door which opened out on to its clear, brown, swift-eddying pebbled water—'an infinite thing for a child to look down into'. Mutton cold or hot for a child destined some day, it was hoped, to become a bishop, no luxuries, solitude, and a strict discipline were the settled lot.

Verse by verse, patriarch by patriarch, genealogy by genealogy, he was nourished on the English Bible. But even though he was allowed to play with his mother's gold vinaigrette when on a stool beside her he shared the family pew in church on Sundays, he became afflicted with such a horror of the Sabbath that it would come over him as far back in the week as Friday. As for playtime, the garden at Herne Hill, though paradisal in many respects, was unlike the Eden that Cain and Abel never saw, since *all* its fruits were forbidden. His aunt at Croydon, where flowed the Wandle, enriched his 'monastic poverty' on a birthday before he was four with 'the most radiant Punch and Judy she could find in all the Soho bazaar'. It was as big 'as a real Punch and Judy, all dressed in scarlet and gold'. But although this sumptuous birthday present impressed him so much that in old age he could remember not only Mr. Punch himself but also his aunt's looks and gestures as she herself 'exhibited his virtues', and though his mother was obliged to accept the gift, he was afterwards quietly told 'it was not right' that he should have it. It was (an alien but familiar word in my own schooldays) confiscated.

'Nor did I painfully wish, what I was never permitted for an instant to hope, or even imagine, the possession of such things as one saw in toy-shops. I had a bunch of keys to play with, as long as I was capable only of pleasure in what glittered and jingled; as I grew older, I had a cart, and a ball; and when I was five or six years old, two boxes of well-cut wooden bricks [lignum vitæ].'

Happiness

Thus he mastered 'very utterly the laws of practical stability in towers and arches' by the time he was seven or eight years old.

'With these modest, but, I still think, entirely sufficient possessions, and being always summarily whipped if I cried, did not do as I was bid, or tumbled on the stairs, I soon attained serene and secure methods of life and motion; and could pass my days contentedly in tracing the squares and comparing the colours of my carpet; examining the knots in the wood of the floor, or counting the bricks in the opposite houses; with rapturous intervals of excitement during the filling of the water-cart, through its leathern pipe, from the dripping iron post at the pavement edge; or the still more admirable proceedings of the turncock, when he turned and turned till a fountain sprang up in the middle of the street. But the carpet, and what patterns I could find in bed-covers, dresses, or wallpapers to be examined, were my chief resources, and my attention to the particulars in these was soon so accurate that, when at three and a half I was taken to have my portrait painted by Mr. Northcote, I had not been ten minutes alone with him before I asked him why there were holes in his carpet. The portrait in question represents a very pretty child with yellow hair, dressed in a white frock like a girl, with a broad light-blue sash and blue shoes to match; the feet of the child wholesomely large in proportion to its body; and the shoes still more wholesomely large in proportion to the feet. . . .'

What, if he had been able to read and understand it, he would have thought of this account at the age of three and a half—the summary whippings in particular—we can only guess. But he might well have queried that 'contentedly'—'Is this tepid tolerance all that growing old will do for me!' After having 'arrived' in life, we are most of us apt to be a little complacent concerning the hardships of the journey. Benignly eyeing what in part at least he made of himself in his childhood, the sage approves of what may yet in fact have been acute odds against him. Goethe had his toy stage and blessed his destiny for it. Ruskin was compelled to sacrifice his Dog Toby and blessed his. The pangs of the rod, the leaden tedium, if they were not forgotten, he left for the most part unrecorded and forgiven.

'Serene and secure' is in any case an unusual tribute from a man to his early childhood. For few childhoods can have been without

Early One Morning

their wild fits of sulks or passion, their griefs and pangs and stagnant hours of sickness and humiliation. If care killed the cat, too much pampering and clotted cream may stifle a kitten. Even under a loving home-rule and in the sunniest surroundings the young may pine and wilt. There are children timid or tongue-tied or hostile or fearful of rebuff, who having no one in whom to confide their deepest secrets keep them to themselves. It may be growing older that brings *them* ease and lightness, sets them free.

Mary Coleridge—guileless, wise and impetuous in mind and spirit throughout her life—was yet, she confesses, an unhappy child. 'I was such a numb, unliving child, that all that period of my life is vague and twilight, and I can recall scarcely anything except the sharp sensations of fear that broke the dull dream of my days. So soon as I began to awake to life, my childhood fell away from me.' That ogre *fear* alone may take many shapes and disguises, as we shall see—of God, of hell, of punishment, of ridicule, of pain and shame as well as of the ghostly and the dark. As for homesickness, a malady practically unknown to some children, its ravages in early life may be as far beyond our full comprehension as it is beyond cure. And there are minor grievances.

Southey, for example, complains bitterly of his want of playmates and exercise, but not less bitterly of having to share his aunt's bed, to which after having been awakened out of his beauty sleep he was transferred every night when her warming-pan had been taken out. For hours, too, he would lie awake in the early morning not daring to stir lest he should arouse his adult bedfellow. To be able to share this particular memory with him in *any* degree is to be aware of a peculiar kind of infant woe.

Even, then, though the very young may intensely realize the full meaning of the word misery, both of body and mind, it by no means follows that in after years they will remember what it *meant* to them when they were children.

CHAPTER VIII

BOOKS ON CHILDHOOD

★

1. 'Knowledge is folly, except grace guide it.'

Hitherto it is chiefly with children *en masse*, as they have been counted, marshalled and educated, measured, tested and explored, legislated for, poeticized, sorrowed over and divined, that we have been concerned. Of recent years—as even a glance at the catalogue of the Library in the British Museum, or, on a smaller but hardly less intimidating scale, that of the London Library will reveal—there has been an immense increase in the number of books devoted to the subject of children and childhood. And all such books, though it is not always apparent, must have been the work of those who had the advantage of once themselves having *been* children. The knowledge thus amassed—concerning the most complicated and elusive of the mammals—may, like all knowledge, be of value for its own sake. If insight and imagination share the use of it, it may be of infinite practical advantage.

Experts devote themselves to the consideration, with appropriate experiment, of the nature and nurture of children; their faculties—physical, moral and intellectual; their ways and sayings and habits; their intelligence and 'mentality', normal or otherwise; their reading, amusements, and temptations; and their use. And even the best-meaning amateur or quack is austerely warned against trespassing in these preserves. It needs, for example, not only skill and practice but a conscience to make judicious use even of intelligence tests. And if we ourselves were the subjects of such enquiries we should heartily concur. Childhood is now a commodious department of psychology, and enjoys, apart from Pediatrics, a twig of science devoted solely to itself—Paidology.

Early One Morning

Indeed so vast is this field of knowledge and in much even yet so obscure and theoretical, that even the specialist is in danger of failing to detect the child in a wilderness of statistics. The mere parent, in his view, may be of little more importance than to feminine eyes the bridegroom is at a wedding. The family has also fallen into the shade in specialistic esteem. Moreover, the modern father and mother have a narrower range for observing and *learning* children than that enjoyed by their great-grandparents. *Their* respectable quiverful of the dear and the different might run in numbers from, say, seven to forty. An eighteenth-century quiverful even of as many children as there are Articles of Religion, and the boast of one father and one mother, which I could specify, can hardly have been unique. As for a remoter past; on Good Friday in the year 1276, runs the legend, the Countess of Henneberg, then forty-two years of age, who had been cursed by a beggar woman when the lady had railed at her for having twins, gave birth to no fewer than 365 children. It was a righteous judgement on her. The male infants were christened John, and the females Elizabeth—in order presumably to avoid confusion!

Apart from the scores of books published since 1850 with children and childhood for theme—their play, their games; their employment; their health, hygiene, nerves, minds and mortality; their religious instruction, and beyond all, their education; there have been personal and illuminating accounts—by William Canton, Alice Meynell and Lady Grey, for example—of individual children, closely and lovingly observed; their ways and wiles and habits, their dreams, humour, questionings and sagacity. Among the more recent of these are *The Limber Elf* and *One Fair Daughter*.

On the same quest, there is the inexhaustible field of fiction to explore. Not merely story-books *about* children—from *Uncle Tom's Cabin, Little Women* and *Alone in London* to *Dream Days, The Jungle Book* and *A Little Boy Lost*—and a host of others, good, bad and indifferent, written in the hope that bright young eyes or attentive ears will drink them in, but also tales of an endless variety, with a young mind for nucleus or focussing point, from *Huckleberry Finn* and *Masterman Ready* to *What Maisie Knew, The Spring Song* and *Dew on the Grass*. Novels too nowadays, to the disgust of those who find greenhornhood jejune and tedious, are apt more than ever they were to begin with a thinly disguised

106

Books on Childhood

hero or heroine in long-clothes, or, as with Betsy Trotwood's protégé, before that, and to proceed with his weaning and teething and so forth, until dotage returns to nonage again.

When the begetter of Miss Trotwood brings children into his fiction, nature herself is certainly seated at his elbow, or is, a little quizzically perhaps, looking over his shoulder, but they are clearly as much of his own creation as of hers. He gilds their golden hair, polishes their blue eyes, shrills their treble voices. He tends to idolize them. His sentiment has been no less busy with them than his genius, and particularly when they are asleep, or saying their prayers, ill, hungry or miserable. David Copperfield perhaps comes closest to life. The first 'objects' of infancy that assumed a 'distinct presence' for him, we are told, were in human form— his mother 'with her pretty hair and youthful shape, and Peggotty, with no shape at all'—but with cheeks so appetizing that he wondered the birds did not peck at them in preference to apples. After which small gleanings, David's memory proceeds to blossom like a hawthorn in May.

Nowadays the professional man's family is 'up to average' if it can be specified as .9 of an infant. Wage- (as distinct from salary- or fee-) earners may still boldly or blindly venture on a family of four;[1] but nine-tenths of a child is the current fraction among the well-to-do. This is so much better than none at all that one studious hour spent every day in the company even of only nine-tenths of a son or daughter may be full of enlightenment. And the most telling, if not the earliest, discovery is likely to be this—that any child is at least no less of an individual than he will prove to be in after years. He has not yet been broken in, made to fit and conform. Nor has he yet learned, adding art to nature, to conceal himself and his secrets from prying eyes and intrusive questions. However much he may have in common with other children, and may be graphed and tabulated, he remains a child unique.

If divination could win in far enough, we might discover that— apart from physical disabilities, which are chiefly inherited—an

---

[1] The average number of persons in each family of the United Kingdom in 1811 was 4.74, and there were 5.65 persons to each inhabited house. In 1891, the relative figures were 4.73 and 5.32. In 1911, 4.50 and 5.05. The jibe at the prolific Victorians seems to have a slender basis. The average family has now, I think, dropped to about 3.5.

Early One Morning

apparently dull child is in a large degree merely a child mishandled. More easily even than most children too, a highly gifted child can be made less able, less teachable and far less approachable by a blind, fumbling, clumsy, silly, selfish and wrong-motived treatment of it. It is so easy to confuse the child-lover with the lover of childishness, who is apt to sit dandling in the middle of a fence, with sentiment on the one side and a soon-wearied amusement on the other. Literally to 'spoil' a child is very seldom the outcome of deliberate effort. To undervalue one, to shun taking it seriously enough, is rather, surely, the rule than the exception. To humour is much easier than to appraise. But since, as any mother would agree, after a little careful observation, and within a week, a definite advance in the mastery of its surroundings, in skill and assurance, may be detected in an infant of under a year old—an advance not usually so apparent in an adult of between fifty and sixty—a little circumspection will not be amiss.

If, as Galton said of Darwin, a man's understanding and ability are revealed by the aptness and scope of his questions, this is no less true of a child. The child has a far wider scope in ignorance. Indeed, as Samuel Butler says in his *Note-Books*, if he could put questions rightly we should know the answers. The question rightly put contains the answer in itself. But the answer will be quite unlike what we expect. Whether new to the world, or a pilgrim from some unconceived-of region of reality, or a creature destined to pass, like a caterpillar, through a series of mental transformations, he needs time wherein to learn our ways and customs and idioms and laws. To this end he lies meditating in his cradle and struggles doughtily on against a sea of troubles and obstruction. If he is a knowledgeable child he will with his questions of Why and How, chiefly conspicuous at the age of four and five, not only put the most knowledgeable of adults on his mettle, but may quickly exhaust a complete repertory of information. His mere energy of mind, his fickle rapidity of attention and delight in action may weary even the most willing spectator to sheer exhaustion. But he himself will forgive even that!

Any fool, said Cardinal Newman, can ask unanswerable questions. A child, even though he may be ill or peevish or overtired, seldom *intends* to do so. The sharp and clever of course delight in attempting to trap the unwary, to pit wits against wits. In dealing

Books on Childhood

with *them* it is perhaps as well to abandon our own wits for the time being, and to fall back on our wisdom!

'The art of observing children', said Rousseau, in 1762, is 'an art which would be of immense value to us, but of which fathers and schoolmasters have not as yet learnt the first rudiments.' Of recent years as an object of science rather than of art the child has been almost as much observed as he is observant. He has, as we have seen, been examined and classified, compounded and reduced to norms and averages. The norm however, is a rather nebulous entity. In what village, town or city in England shall we find a fellow creature willing to be dismissed as 'the man-in-the-street'? And averages, like all statistics, can be elusive and deluding. The average age of three children who are respectively one, three and fourteen years old is six; but what relation has this figure to the actual trio? There may be many approximate examples of what is deemed an average intelligence or intellect, but where shall we find an average *mind* or personality or soul or self?

If that is our quarry, we might as well lie in wait for the average of nineteen sunsets, or seek for the average pot of gold at the foot of the average rainbow. The only human being competent to reveal what any child is, is that child himself; but even he can only reveal what he is in part, and he cannot share his being. So far as his intellect and feelings and passions are concerned, our only certain truth concerning them is that derived from a comparison of them with our own. This needs a vigilant insight, heaven-sent opportunities, and is acutely fatiguing.

There are however three other obvious methods of learning about children and childhood. First, by way of what the child volunteers concerning himself—in his play, his scribblings and drawings, his music, his writings and so forth. Next, by way of what we can recall and revive of our own childhood, dwindling back in memory for this purpose to the days of our petticoats. And, last, by sharing their actual memories of childhood with others. We can examine what a child does; we can compare him with what we ourselves once were; or with what other men declare that they were when *they* were young.

Examples of the writings of children, restricted with few exceptions to those who have afterwards become well-known authors, will be found in a later chapter. Here and there in what follows

Early One Morning

I shall venture to give a few memories of my own childhood, not for their own sake or because they have any particular value, but as mere comments on those of others. Caution is no less desirable in accepting early recollections than it is in dealing with the results of any direct observation of childhood. But, for the purpose we have in mind, the former have many advantages.

There is not only a multitude of them to share and to choose from, they are also of many kinds and qualities. They can be compared and may be checked one with another. If we dislike children—'mischievous little imps', 'tiresome brats'—on any principle or pretext, we shall then have better and fuller reasons for so doing. And, contrariwise, our interest and pleasure in them can only be given a wider scope. Nor can they fail to recall more clearly, and here and there even to revive what of childhood is left in ourselves. The chief risk, but an easily remedied one, is that we shall quickly weary of their abundance.

One thing is certain, and will at once become evident. However trivial and piecemeal they may appear to be in themselves, they seemed to be deserving of careful record to those whom they solely concerned. We are most of us only too eager to share the garden of memory—the exotics and hybrids of our later years; but the fondest of glances seems usually to alight not merely on the wallflowers and Sweet Williams, the buttercups and wild roses of childhood, but even on its chickweed, eyebright and pimpernel. All such memories should be enjoyed, perhaps, if enjoyable they be, not too many at a time. Many have already been quoted, but before others follow, and in view of Herbert Spencer's warning against mere remembrances of having remembered, it might be as well to consider for a moment what such terms as these signify.

CHAPTER IX

MEMORY

*

1. 'This Ledger book lies in the braine behinde.'

Few words are more often on the tongue than *remember* and *forget*. But it is exceedingly difficult to conclude even to one's own private satisfaction what precisely they imply. Every minute of our lives we are dependent on Memory's bounty. Without its aid even our own faces in the glass would be strange to us. Yet we usually take its enigma for granted, fondly supposing, apart from a humiliating shock on occasion, that we can retrieve as much of it, of a passable quality, as we need. It is a shallow inference. The enchantress is generous, but she is implacable. She will surrender, restore to us, only what she herself has deemed worthy of preservation, and, far worse, only the fraction of a tithe even of that.

What memory *is*, with its methods and workings, its vagaries and diseases, and even more emphatically what it is not, namely the temporarily or permanently unrequired, the partially confused, the latent, the submerged, the irretrievable—all this has been the intense preoccupation of the modern psychologist. How could it be otherwise since it is the only treasury available for the operations of his science? Its survey, quite apart from its aptitude for use, needs the most delicate skill. It is indeed the battle-ground on which rival philosophies meet, and part. The novice's safest attitude perhaps is that of a patient disciple. Still, to ponder a while on the early memories of other men, and particularly if they were men of active minds and keen interests, may be some aid in at least eliciting the complexities of the problem, and may deepen interest in the mysteries of what after all is the most valuable thing a human being possesses—a mind.

III

Early One Morning

It is remarkable, then, that the majority even of memoirists who, one might assume, would be keenly concerned with it, appear to have taken memory and all its ramifications more or less for granted. Sprightly as a pullet returning thanks to Heaven for her first diminutive egg, the explorer of his own past—after a few paragraphs or pages devoted to a cautious survey of the uppermost twigs of his family tree—usually exclaims with a lively and enlivening enthusiasm: 'My earliest memory is. . . .' He then proceeds to relate some faultlessly clear and concise little incident or experience that occurred when—perhaps sixty or seventy years ago—he was two, or four, or even five years old. If it is an early 'first', a tinge of self-congratulation may be apparent; if a late—say six or upwards—shame or even surprise is seldom expressed. All that six years' dark without one single enlightening beam of memory's taper! This, surely, is one of the oddest of the many mysteries with which life is beset. There is another no less so.

We are each one of us at any moment all that our past has made of us, and all that we have made of our past. Poised in the fleeting instant of the present—which, until its very apex, was the future, and which, as soon as its content is registered in thought or action, has become the past—we not only find in that instant an iota of novelty, of life and action hitherto unexperienced in this exact form, but also have included in it an iota, however much condensed or richly referential it may be, of what we call memory. When we have discovered how many angels may be accommodated on the point of a needle, we may also discover how much of memory may be compressed in consciousness into an instant of time.

Bereft of memory even for a few moments we should be at once astray in the wilds of the utterly strange and unrecognizable. Complete loss of memory would reduce us in mental perception to the condition of a new-born infant—self, being and the actuality around us as yet utterly unrealized. However old we might be, the world would then be brand new. We should become nothing more than horrific adult virgin mind-in-body zeroes, though of a myriad intricate potentialities. Were the inanimate wax models in the Marylebone Road suddenly given human life and faculty, their fate would then precisely resemble our own.

Memory is involved even in the minutest of experiences, though

Memory

only the merest fraction of the vast aggregate of experience is active in consciousness at any particular moment. The rest consists of what may be recalled at need, of what is recoverable if the appropriate stimulus is forthcoming, and of the forgotten—a subsided mass which lies, apparently, not beyond the plummet of dream or of hypnosis, and is still active and essential part and parcel of self hood, but is for the most part irretrievably foundered. Even in the event of recovery it might yet remain beyond our definite recognition.

> 'Ah, Memory, thou strange deceiver!——
> Who can trust her? How believe her?
> While she keeps in one same pack
> Dream and real upon her back.
> When I call her, want her most,
> She's gone wandering and is lost.
> Swift, capricious as the wind——
> The wondrous sweets she leaves behind!
> Where—without her—I? for lo,
> When she is gone I too must go!'

And yet how easily we are beguiled into ignoring this comparative impotence of the mind. So constant and abundant and seemingly uncontrolled is the current and perpetual supply of our memories, they can be so various in kind and quality, and so effortlessly combined and dissembled, that we fail to realize how vast a proportion even of the immediately experienced has swiftly and silently drifted beyond recall. We plague ourselves with efforts to recover a word or a name or a date or an experience, as if merely to have mislaid it for a while were a remarkable imbecility. But pause a moment and attempt to revive in memory, without aid or reminder, the experiences even of the last five consecutive minutes in every detail—not merely their sensations and perceptions, sights, sounds, odours, touchings, voices perhaps and words, but the fleeting and inward images, thoughts and emotions that accompanied them. Much may re-present itself, much more will not. What minimum duration of time is necessary to what may be called an act of consciousness is—for the amateur at any rate—puzzle enough. In two or three seconds a greenfinch, a swallow or a yellowhammer has completed its habitual cadenza, and a walking horse has advanced four paces. How many such successive units can we actually recall, how much of each was memory and expectation, and how much of the mind-stuff which filled the interstices between the several notes or hoof-beats is retrievable? In ten seconds a gramophone needle has travelled about twelve yards over the outer surface of a twelve-inch record whether it consisted of jazz or Bach, folk-song or funeral march—analyse precisely what in memory consciousness has left of any single second of that journey.

To recall the content of five minutes' experience fully and *purely* is utterly impossible for another reason, since this would entail not only a precise facsimile of it, but also a complete unconsciousness of our present state and surroundings. *Any* feat of recollection resembles of course a consummate conjuring trick; but the sheer impotence of forgetting is more like black magic. And so with the latest hour that has slipped behind us, or day, or week, or month—a fresh and vernal past replete with the active and the useful. The further its content recedes the less of it we can unaidedly recall, the greater the disproportion between the vanished and the come-again. Even what does return is the equivalent in content only of single, scattered and discrete moments. We recall points of consciousness, so to speak, not periods.

When we turn to the past we find ourselves gazing out as it were across a drift of the invisible; and there may softly make itself perceptible a this or a that which though it be but the minut-est fraction of what were once its immediate surroundings is yet more or less complete in itself. It is what is called a *memory*.

In area, it may be miniature; it may be panoramic. It flowers out as if by chance. But can we recall what we never observed; see again what was visible in the field of the eye but left unfocused; hear again what we failed, if only for the ghost of a moment, to listen to? And if, phantom-wise, we recall sitting down in yesterday's chair, do we, in thus remembering, reoccupy our ghostly bodies or do we observe them?

If merely personal impressions are of any value in this enquiry, it appears that to memorize one must hear *and* listen; see, focus eye, *and* pay heed. What lies at any particular moment either out of focus or unattended to, will not form part of any normal memory. I have frequently sat next to a lady at tea or dinner, and afterwards,

Memory

while recalling the clearness or darkness of her eyes, or the outline of cheek and chin, and perhaps even a fleeting expression, have yet wholly failed to recall even the colour of her clothes. Yet, it seems, of memoried momentary things loose concatenations may be formed; and the inwardly expressed desire or assertion, 'I will remember this', appears to seal the impression more enduringly. We remember too what interests both head *and* heart, intellect *and* feelings; but may not be aware to what profundities some triviality we may recall was actually attached.

Once captured, cautiously kept in mind, quietly watched and waited upon, any memory may woo in, conjure up, in the most wayward and desultory fashion, certain familiars of its own, and then others. And as each in turn appears, the rest slip away—retire into an anteroom. But even so much as a complete minute-full of the past is past regaining, though within the compass of the time spent on a recollection (which, again, cannot but add to itself novelties of the present, active and actual), we can examine it again and again, as if it resembled a picture hung upon the wall of the mind. And there perhaps in due time—a treasured Old Master —it will stay, and we can enjoy it when we wish to.

Indeed the act of recalling and reviving gives to a recollection an entity all its own. Though it is but the reflex of an infinitesimal patch of the never-ceasing woof and weft issuing from the loom we call experience, henceforth it may remain isolated, as though embalmed—a rare, or common, fly in amber. And it is such flies as these, when they are distant enough in time—according to the calendar—we call our first or early memories.

But if what we can retrieve even of yesterday—of a complete twenty-four hours' thinking, talking, doing and dreaming—is by comparison with its sum-total of experience so minute; if of the month before last we may perhaps find it impossible, unaided, to retrieve even as much—how rich or poor a harvest of memories will readily reward us from, say, any period of eight full years of our past? At the first syllable of a decoy how many of *their* infinitely multitudinous and infinitesimal carrier pigeons, neat little messages clipped to coral-coloured leg or wing, will return at once to the dovecote? And how many of these will be birds come back for the first time since their tiny cage of the present released them into the enormous vague of the past?

Early One Morning

Of eight consecutive years of mature life, what full and coherent account could we produce, without any help from reminders—hearsay, letters, calendars, journals, newspapers—of their eight punctual birthdays, their eight ravishing May Days and full-fed Christmases, their thirty-two perfidious quarter-days, their 104 glazed or unglazed crescent moons, and fitful full moons, their 418 British Sabbaths, their accumulated weeks, even months of busy mealtime, their two and a half thousand issues of our morning *Thunderer* or *Whisperer*—radiant with *their* records of yesterday's battles, murders and sudden deaths, not to mention some three complete years of intermittent dreaming?

Any such attempt to recover the past over so wide a range *may* be well rewarded. The prospect of it none the less is usually dismaying. Even if we confined ourselves to the good advice we were responsible for, to a friend's conversation, to the letters we wrote with so much vivacity or repulsion, or to those we thankfully or thanklessly received, not very much scribbling would suffice for a most disorderly total. Pause for a moment to consider what is implied not of the remembered, but of the forgotten, when we use the word *home*, or say, *I*.

2. '*Two sisters keep this little shop—*
Jane Memory, and Ann Reminder:
When Jane's asleep, or not yet up,
Or out, or absent, Ann must find her.'

If indeed we depended solely on a purely spontaneous memory we should be reduced to the barest pittance of the past. But since at every moment of the day our senses and our thoughts revive in us that past—and every perception is largely compounded of recognition—memory *appears* to be all but infinite in its resources. And if we aid the survey of our chosen period with artificial reminders of any kind, our recollection of it, far from being a wilderness, blossoms like the rose—though it may often be a faded rose. Occasional startling breakdowns occur even here—as when two friends, and familiar friends, who are unknown to one another come to see you and, on attempting to introduce them, you fail to recall either's name! A complete bevy of names indeed

116

Memory

—of flowers or what not—may be habitually elusive; in my own case, hydrangea, saxifrage, bergamot, cyclamen, gladiolus. The sight of any one of these almost always evokes a sort of aura where the name should be, and as often as not two or three others of the bevy will politely present themselves instead! Names are merely tags or labels, whatever value we put upon our own; but a failure of this kind, caused probably by some clumsy personal interference in the workings of the mind, had best be forgotten. It is else only too likely to recur. In general, reminders are successful even though moderately so. As Proust discovered by deliberate and ingenious devices—smells and scents, the taste of cake dipped in tea and so forth—there is an immense field of the *revivable* which we seldom make any effort to retrieve. How much of it, and in what proportion that much is to the irrevocable, only the psycho-analyst could declare.

What is needed is a crafty hint, a significant cue, an inviting nucleus. The skein of silk is there, that is certain. We must grope very heedfully for a loose end. The cue must accord in some respect with our need. We must fish with the appropriate fly. The recovery of but a note or two of music, enough to shape an air or melody, may suffice for the wherewithal of a song unheard since infancy. *Sesame!*—it is done. A word or two about a minor character in a novel—say, his long nose, his narrow feet, his hat-band; the briefest hint of some crucial scene or episode—and the 'forgotten' tale itself like a bird's-eye view of a familiar country-side may at once swiftly revive in the mind. Its aura too; what we mean when we say it is a good, or bad, or stupid, or astonishing book.

Or even better, we may dip into childhood; since to salve, with or without any clue, some piece of wreckage of that distant past, jetsam which we supposed had sunk for ever beneath the sea of oblivion, may be a peculiarly pleasing experience. We may ponder for a while on some completely isolated and insulated scrap of memory of these early days; keeping it softly before the inward eye in the surrounding darkness of the mind. And (if the wind is in the South) there may silently appear some one of its fellows of the same time and place. It may have the appearance of being very minute. As we watch, it seems to draw nearer, as if we were attaining an ampler focus. And presently after, in the little theatre of the mind, the stage may be brilliant and lively with a complete scene from the past all but as fresh as when it first met our waking eyes.

Some years ago, a dear and revered friend, then in her eighties, confided to me that without any perceptible cue there had suddenly appeared in her mind the memory of standing one morning, when she was a small child, beside her father while he conversed with the Duke of Wellington then riding in Hyde Park. Indeed it is generally agreed that in advanced age memory may thus retrieve the seemingly lost unaided, and especially the lost from childhood.*

May this not be in part perhaps because then we have more time for quiet musing and reverie? Since the present is less 'with us' and the future is rapidly narrowing in, we can then the more blessedly regale ourselves on the past. The aged distil their memories; or rather they decant the wine in the cobwebbed bottles laid down perhaps fifty, sixty, seventy years ago in the cellarage of the mind. Its bouquet has improved. It is still, but mature. The child, on the other hand, bee-like, is after nectar—heedless of honey. By no means a butterfly either by nature or inclination, he is intent on the now and the new, sucks avidly at the passing moment, his mind the hive.

Our whole life long this recording apparatus, memory—whether it is alert or sluggish, in good order or bad—steadily persists in its labours, continues to *record*; in large part automatically, though it seems we may oil and ease, or neglect, its works. But if consciousness may be crudely compared in its operations to a clock, it is one of many dials. It continues, for example, to assure us who we are, what we are, when we are, and where we are. It reports perpetually on the ease or discomfort of the body, the state of our mood and temper, whether we are alone or companioned—and concerning the mood and temper of that companionship. It may be perpetually reminding us of whence we have come and to some extent whither we are going, though not perhaps why or how we exist. And all this apart from a multitude of other little duties and obligations, the incessant to-and-fro of sensations and perceptions—the frustration or non-performance of any one of which will set off some kind of faint or loud alarum. And every organ, even cell, we possess is said to have a memory

Memory

of its own. At mere thought of one's little finger, it answers 'Here am I!' It need be, then, but a minutely shameful confession to agree, 'Yes, I have a very poor memory—for dates, you know', so long as the clock with all its dials serenely keeps going, expending on our behalf not merely time but what may be called potent self-life-stuff.

Not that any one of the dials is necessarily as accurate as we ourselves may fondly suppose it to be. There is little need to remind ourselves of that! It has been proved for example that no less than half the impressions of colour registered by an ordinary adult are untrustworthy. Here, two kinds of inaccuracy are involved, that of observation and that of recollection. Habit and skill make certain kinds of pure observation impracticable. Is it possible, for instance, to *see* objects as if they were flat surfaces illuminated? We impose habitually a third dimension. So too with a picture, as the smallest experiment will show. Moreover we are most of us so wholly accustomed to what we assume to be the way in which our own clock records the present that we are apt to resent and discredit the evidence for other ways and methods.

This clock is that which, were we mere machines, I suppose, might be called the Self, the Ego. But its dials have an odd habit of fulfilling their duties in accordance with some secret understanding between themselves, like the several instruments in an orchestra obeying some unseen conductor—now the fiddles and now the horns and now the clarionets take precedence. And, since we are not machines, the Self deals with these records in its own capricious fashion, and without maybe our being aware of it.

In some degree we 'set 'that clock, and so manipulate its dials that they shall, we fondly hope, record for us what, when we need it, will be available. And we each one of us not only have our own instinctive method of doing this, but also keep certain of these dials more active than the rest, to accord with our varying aims, schemes, interests, desires, hobbies, temporary obsessions. We thus assimilate most easily what we prefer and require. Our intention is to remember what we surmise will be of use to us, and to our advantage. But, as Thoreau says, 'we hear and apprehend only what we already half know' and spontaneously pay little attention to anything else. 'Every man thus *tracks* himself through life. . . . His observations make a chain'—shackles from which at last he may strive in vain to escape.

Early One Morning

The factors that tend to convert experience into memories appear to be the extent, the sharpness and the profundity of our interest in and attention to that experience. We record automatically the most salient moments of life; the high lights, that is, whatever the depth of the surrounding shadows. What is at the same moment in part familiar and in part acutely strange, as well as emphatic and intense, is likeliest, at the fitting invitation, to be revived again. Beads of matching size and shape and colour make also lasting keepsakes.

And this power, we are told, of 'storing up new impressions reaches its maximum in early youth'.

'With boys the memory for objects is first developed, then words of visual content, words of auditory content, sounds, terms denoting tactual and motor experiences, numbers, abstract conceptions, and, lastly, emotional terms; with girls, the order is words of visual content, objects, sounds, numbers, abstract conceptions, words of auditory content, terms denoting tactual and motor experiences, and emotional terms.'

The authors of *The Psychology of Childhood*, from which this extract is borrowed, point out that children are poorly endowed with words denoting such abstractions as joy, sorrow, hope, care; and that this is not surprising. None the less 'investigators' have actually deduced from this fact that children under fourteen years of age 'possess a very poor memory for emotions'. From which we might ourselves deduce that the investigators themselves must in this respect have completely forgotten what it is to be a child at all.

How many such impressions must a lively child in animating surroundings receive in the course of a single morning? Thus, his every sense busy—and mute or at rest if not required—from countless differing points of view he learns and memorizes his objects, and also acquires his words for them. How so completely familiar an object as his mug or kitten or toy monkey can remain in some degree novel enough to excite his interest or affection is a curious problem. But indeed it is the most familiar objects that hold in reserve for all of us this particular wizardry. Any act of physical or mental skill is the apex, as it were, of an amassed pyramid consisting of hosts of lively impressions. Manners, too, courtesy, tact, sympathy, magnanimity, judgement and even insight—the trend of heart and mind and intellect—are in a large measure outcomes of memoried states and attitudes, and of states and attitudes repeated of set intent.

The chief and prevalent association in all our memories is the association with self. This happened to *me*. Which kind of me is another question. 'A mean action', says Rousseau, 'does not torture us when we have just committed it, but long afterwards when we recall it to mind; for the remembrance of it never dies.' 'My earliest memory of all', says Thomas Carlyle, 'is a mad passion of rage at my elder Brother John (on a visit to us likely from his grandfather's); in which my Father too figures though dimly, as a kind of cheerful comforter and soother. I had broken my little brown stool, by madly throwing it at my brother; and felt for perhaps the first time, the united pangs of Loss and of Remorse. I was perhaps hardly more than two years old; but can get no one to fix the date for me, though all is still quite legible for myself. . . .' When four times older than that (partly perhaps because I was sick for home) I used to tease a little girl a year or two younger than myself. When she cried, her pale face mottled pink and blue. It told tales; and then caution strove with rage! The bleared blue-grey eyes in that mottled face look passively back at me across fifty-two years.

Fortunately or unfortunately, what Rousseau says is true only of *some* of our mean actions. We might otherwise spend all our later days in sackcloth and ashes. But though, it is said, there is an overseer, a controller in the mind, whose office it is to conceal in the limbo of oblivion what it is painful to recall, voluntary effort may be one's utmost hindrance in an attempt not only to remember but also to forget. If too the attention is divided, only the vaguest impression will remain even of what we wish and try to memorize. One can *then* read and re-read a long paragraph in a book, or repeat a lesson or a poem, or appear to be engrossed in the talk of a friend, and yet be able to recall nothing of it all but a vacant haze.

3. *'That great thoroughfare of the brain, the memory.'*

Most of our memories, however, are not the outcome of effort. Every day of our lives is fed by a host of fleeting impressions which we make no attempt whatever to record and

Early One Morning

retain. The vast majority of these are lost beyond definite recall. A few *are* retained. They must then have had some quality or characteristic that distinguished them from the lost. What differentiated them? Since we value so highly what was none the less spontaneously recorded, how precious would be the prescription that would enable us with ease and certainty to select from the present what we should in the future treasure the most. This secret appears to be as difficult of discovery as that of falling asleep; that waft of the enchanter's wand for which we so often pine in vain, and which *may* perhaps be due to so simple a factor as the position of one's eyes.

It may be that any experience thus spontaneously revivable was accompanied by some momentary access of *self*-consciousness— 'This is happening to me!' Or—and this is often volunteered as an explanation—it perhaps concerned more than one layer or stratum of consciousness, more than the superficial self. For although 'the same thoughts do commonly meet us in the same places, as if we had left them there till our return', failures in the recall of complete tracts even of the most personal kinds of experience can be astonishing. After an interval of only a few years, for example, one may read over a piece of one's own composition that must have involved many days of preparation and hard work, and may yet remain a little dubious of its authorship.

The nucleus or germ of a story may be actually noted down on paper, and that note may afterwards refuse to surrender the least hint of what it was intended to convey. It is as if not a plot or character or situation were its true theme, but a certain state of the mind. As for bright ideas, or 'happy thoughts' left unnoted, since their origin is as mysterious as their onset is rapid, it is no wonder perhaps that they may vanish out of remembrance as swiftly and finally as a dream. None the less even though any such bright idea, once lost, may be irrevocable, it need not be moribund: a fish put back into the water may breed.

On the other hand, with an almost magical precision, a vocabulary appropriate only to a certain piece of writing *may* in the act of composition rill on and on without let or hindrance. This no doubt is true of other crafts than authorship, and of all the professions. Memory is the mistress, and at times she is as indulgent as she is seductive. We are in her service. But again and again she will refuse us her best; though it is for her most innocent lapses that we are apt to blame her most!

Nor can we even be certain of the nature of her gifts—of the mind-*stuff* of which recollections are composed. We cannot on the knife-edge of the passing moment at the same time experience anything and analyse that experience. And what assurance have we that the contents of that fleeting moment were actually the same as they appeared to be immediately after the moment was past? Even in appearance that moment's mind-stuff (as may be proved) is an extremely elusive quarry and may consist of a medley of many kinds of images. In a discussion with Professor Max Müller, Francis Galton maintained that he himself 'thought hardest when making no mental use of words'. The Professor, he began to suspect in the course of it, apart from becoming heated, had ceased to be completely ingenuous, and he presently abandoned the argument. But it led him to engage in an experiment which he described in a tract entitled *Arithmetic by Smell*.

When, he says, in general, 'we propose to add, and (in so doing) *hear* the spoken words "two" and "three", we instantly through long habit *say* "five" or if we *see* those figures, we have a mental image and write five'. He hoped to prove that other images may be substituted for both the aural and visual. Leaving aside experiments with Colour, Touch and Taste, he tried Smell-symbols, using peppermint, camphor, carbolic acid, ammonia and aniseed. He made five tubes, one for each odour (sprinkled on cotton wool) and so designed that a squeeze at the end of each produced a scented whiff through its nozzle. He taught himself to associate two whiffs of peppermint with one of camphor, three of peppermint with one of carbolic acid, and so on. He next 'practised little sums in addition', first with the scents, and then with the 'mere imagination' of them, and 'finally succeeded perfectly'.

It was a conclusive triumph of the utmost ingenuity over such tedium and difficulty as even to those who are actively interested in the mysterious operations of the mind might well be insupportable. But then Galton was Galton; and flattery could say no more. Moreover, by similar but instinctive methods of 'imagining' a *child's* mind is registering its experiences the whole day long.

It is memory's diversity of images that vividly animates the passing moment and its objects—images-of-all-work, in Professor

Early One Morning

T. H. Pear's phrase—especially those capable of a diversified host of jobs, as are those of 'geniuses, wits and cranks'. A far richer diversity of images indeed may be present in any recollection than protracted examination may disclose; images we owe not only to our senses of sight and hearing, of smell and taste and touch, but to those also of movement and motion, and some of them in a strangely phantasmal disguise. Indeed it is acutely difficult—at least for the amateur—to observe thought in operation close enough to be able with certainty to sort out its details.

And now and then one is startled by the bizarre. While lying awake one morning, enjoying what appeared to be the wreckage of a dream, there suddenly appeared close under my eyes from out of the 'little Nowhere of the mind' a typed sheet of paper, so clearly discernible and flawless in appearance that I could vow not a comma had gone astray. I examined it closely but could read not a single word. This surprised me, since my dreaming-self often and easily reads in sleep, either print or handwriting. Later I remembered that I was not at that moment wearing my customary reading spectacles. Did this mean that the inward eye of the early and drowsy waker also needs this aid! An answer to the question came to me a night or two afterwards, for then in a dream I found myself reading unspectacled a volume of early memories of engrossing interest, even though it was badly printed on poor paper.

Many years ago too that magician, Hypnos, put into my hand a small thick foxed little tome, the first page of which showed a series of diagrams. Next to a white circle described as 'Reality' was a black representing 'Unconsciousness'. A third completely black except for a minute segment, was designated 'The Consciousness of a Fly'. A fourth with a yet wider segment was for *Man's* consciousness put. These diagrams and the letterpress clearly suggested that when at last the white segment spread until not even the thinnest thread of black remained, Reality and Consciousness became one: Nirvana! Of what kind and order, I wonder, were the remaining propositions in that dingy little dream book?

Memory

4. *'Memory should not be called Knowledge.'*

But apart from personal and spontaneous recollections there is another kind of memory which Bergson dismisses as hardly worthy of the name. It is that which is for the most part due to repetition, is scoffed at as 'parrot' memory, though the process of recording it is called 'learning by heart'. In sober fact, little of the heart is usually concerned in it, and not much even of the head. It has already been referred to as *the* bugbear of childhood.

'Consciousness reveals to us a profound difference, a difference in kind, between the two sorts of recollection [that of reading over a lesson, and that of recalling the lesson learnt]. The memory of a given reading is a representation, and only a representation; it is embraced in an intuition of the mind which I may lengthen or shorten at will; I assign to it any duration I please; there is nothing to prevent my grasping the whole of it instantaneously, as in one picture. On the contrary, the memory of the lesson I have learnt, even if I repeat this lesson only mentally, requires a definite time, the time necessary to develop one by one, were it only in imagination, all the articulatory movements that are necessary: it is no longer a representation, it is an action. And, in fact, the lesson once learnt bears upon it no mark which betrays its origin and classes it in the past; it is part of my present, exactly like my habit of walking or of writing; it is lived and acted, rather than represented: I might believe it innate, if I did not choose to recall at the same time, as so many representations, the successive readings by means of which I learnt it. . . .'

The very word *lessons* at once recalls our youth. Most lessons of this kind indeed are the affliction only of our early days. In later life the term usually signifies *moral* lessons, reiterated by Providence, nature or humanity, abruptly and sharply, and resembling the other kind only in so far as they are both unpleasant and useful. How gladly should we all, and particularly children, welcome facility in this kind of learning which is for obscure reasons denied to us. And especially in view of the fact that we learn so much else— the greater part of our vocabularies, for example, our knowledge of flowers, animals, the seasons and mankind—without this conscious and exacting effort, and yet keep it with comparative ease at our disposal. None the less not only a good deal of our knowledge, but much even of our worldly wisdom, our axioms, our opinions and ideas, are of this nature. Since we swallowed it whole it is apt to remain undigested. Merely to *commit* to memory is often to accept the husk for the sake of a kernel doomed to be infertile.

We need of course for our workaday purposes many precise facts. They should be at hand. But a number even of these might better perhaps have been left, until they are actually wanted, in the lesson books or the encyclopædias from which they were derived. Their revival by this means in their appropriate contexts may bestow a life and meaning on them which otherwise they will not possess. So perhaps with many of the lessons learned in childhood —mainly by rote, and at what expense of spirit, tears and despair.

A friend confided to me not long ago that he had been casually reminded of his Latin conjugations, whereupon he discovered that he could repeat them as accurately as he had ever managed to repeat them in his youth, though they had not recurred to his memory in that form and shape (nor for any purpose!) for over forty years. He could recall even the printed design of the page of the grammar from which he had learned them. Unlike archæological relics such fragments unfortunately are seldom works of art.

Not that even parrot memories are finally secure. There is the frequently cited case of the patient who discovered that he was able to recall of the ten digits only 5 and 7; and another of a 'highly educated' man whose memory had been denuded of all conception of the letter 'F'. There is a form of aphasia that results in printed words being still recognizable, though the individual letters have lost their import; and *vice versa*. Apart too from the problem of dual personality, and that of temporary subsidences of complete drifts of experience, 'there are . . . examples, also, of memory surviving all other faculties . . . amid general darkness and ruin of mind'. If that is so, there may come a moment either when we shall be able to avail ourselves of no future, or be suddenly bereft of the past.

Dr. Bernard Hollander records many cases of loss of memory due to injuries to the forehead: two male patients, for example, who in spite of having been recently married, could remember no events prior to the injury. One of them was positive he had never even met his wife. A workman, again, fell off a scaffolding, only seven feet high, and the right side of his forehead struck an iron screw. When he recovered consciousness he had lost his sense of time, of self-orientation, and the ability to notice things; and frequently afterwards lost also control of his temper. It seems 'he' remained, but in these respects could not 'get through'.

Moreover, though mastered memories of the parrot *kind*—such as our daily habits of body and mind, walking, talking, toileting, our manners and many of our morals—may remain securely imbedded and active, what becomes of the vast quantity of the lessons and reading and precepts that we endeavoured again and again in childhood to get by rote or by heart, though the attempt failed, or only very partially succeeded? How large and lamentable a part of our school work remains in that condition. Incomplete, falsifying and confused memories of this kind are neither personal nor parrot; they are like sullen lumps of coke on a sad fire, not pretty even to look at.

5. 'The past is fled and gone, and gone.'

Prodigies of memory of this purely mechanical order are many. The husband of the author of *The Mysteries of Udolpho*, for example, after listening to a debate in the House of Commons could—inopportune chameleon—repeat it *verbatim* next morning. 'I have more than once', declares the invaluable Dr. Brewer, 'heard Woodham, a fellow of Jesus, repeat a column of *The Times* after a single perusal.' To be more amused and mystified than impressed by accomplishments so remarkable may betoken merely the green eye of jealousy. A 'bad' memory of this kind is a constant humiliation to an adult and may be sheer torture to a child. But it does not necessarily imply stupidity. Among mankind, but very seldom among manikins, creep and flourish human hermit crabs burdened with little mountains of flawless facts and information which even their owner would be none the worse for discarding—tiny pebbles and semi-precious stones, the plain and the highly coloured, but still external, as it were, to the mind and imagination. If not too wantonly paraded, this carapace may give an air and a dignity and a picturesqueness that only the man of silence can rival. Better yet, it makes its possessor exceedingly serviceable when statistics and time-tables, dictionaries, directories, almanacks and blue-books are not at hand. But as with the missing mummy in a pyramid, we may search in vain for the very soul of memory which the erection seems to have been accumulated to conceal.

How great a joy on the other hand it must be to possess such a memory as Cuvier's is said to have been. He had so precise an eye for form that he never forgot the shape of an object he had once seen. Turner too having carefully looked at a ship could go home and draw its details as accurately as if he were still standing in front of it. The famous black boy called Blind Tom, who as an infant was so feeble that he was sold as a makeweight with his mother, and in intelligence never excelled even a child of six, lived none the less in a little paradise of music, never forgetting any composition he had once been able to play.

A valuable but more exhausting activity, dependent no less on memory and resembling blindfold chess, is recorded of Napoleon. Clever, arrogant, hot-tempered, he had as a boy a 'prodigious' memory. In after life he could keep three—or was it five?—secretaries busily employed with pen and ink. Pepys again declares that Fuller, the author of the *Worthies*, could not only tell him more about his own family than he knew himself, but also that he 'did lately (1661) to four eminently great scholars dictate together in Latin, upon different subjects of their proposing, faster than they were able to write, till they were tired'. 'If he should forget the last sentence dictated he could take refuge in an *Utcunque*.'

Utcunque, then; even if such feats as *these* are leagues beyond us (and of what priceless benefit is the faculty for them in examinations), we can remain thankful that, though our minds may be very imperfect catalogues, they can yet acquire a more delectable memory out of one pregnant glance at the west front of Lincoln Cathedral, at the staircase in the Chapter House in Wells, at the library in Merton College, at desolate Stonehenge on a winter's evening, or at a Pembrokeshire seascape, than is manageable perhaps after a discursive survey or protracted study.

Good and poor memories, the psychologists tell us, 'find their ultimate explanation in the plasticity of the synapses in the cortex of the brain'. Even if one eyes a little askance that 'ultimate', children, it appears to have been proved, have a greater retentive power than adults; though this varies at different ages and with the two sexes, and of course between individuals. That being so, what

Memory

very heedful advantage should be taken of this power. For however useful and valuable rote-memories may be, they would, surely, be doubly valuable and far more virtually useful if they did not remain sterile, but in such a state as would continue to enrich the living and active mind.

The mere repetition, again, of a few genuinely personal memories may at last render them less profitable than the learnt-by-rote may be—our oft-repeated private fund, say, of anecdotes and episodes, of coincidences, of dreams, of great occasions. Slender thus indulged himself with his youthful *bona robas*, and Falstaff with his practical jokes. In this way we acquire not only a series of gramophonic memories, but also a machine which will manipulate its own records. Fortunately we fail to realize how much of what we think and converse with, discuss and argue about, is nothing better than a private supply of these stock conveniences. And apart from personal and private collections, every trade, profession, calling and office has its own repertory—scholars, with their obscure authors far more deservedly dead than the language they wrote in; doctors and their cases; sportsmen and their shoots or bags or catches; collectors and their 'finds' and fakes and bargains.

'The life of an individual,' says Oliver Wendell Holmes, 'is in many respects like a child's dissected map. If I could live a hundred years, keeping my intelligence to the last, I feel as if I could put the pieces together until they made a properly connected whole. As it is, I, like all others, find a certain number of connected fragments, and a larger number of disjointed pieces, which I might in time place in their natural connection. Many of these pieces seem fragmentary, but would in time show themselves as essential parts of the whole. What strikes me very forcibly is the arbitrary and as it were accidental way in which the lines of junction appear to run irregularly among the fragments. With every decade I find some new pieces coming into place. Blanks which have been left in former years find their complement among the undistributed fragments. If I could look back on the whole, as we look at the child's map when it is put together, I feel that I should have my whole life intelligently laid out before me. . . .'

And again we are reminded of the treasure beyond price that is sunken beyond salvage in the submarine valleys of the ocean of the forgotten, of which such revivals are merely islanded peaks.

Early One Morning

Beyond unaided salvage, that is. Opium, declares De Quincey, revived for him some of the minutest incidents of his childhood. 'Of this', he says, 'I feel assured, that there is no such thing as *forgetting* possible to the mind. . . . Whether veiled or unveiled, the inscription remains for ever; just as the stars seem to withdraw before the common light of day, whereas, in fact, we all know that it is the light which is drawn over them as a veil.' A near relative of De Quincey's, again, declared to him that when, as a child of nine, she hung on the very verge of death by drowning, she had recalled—'simultaneously as in a mirror'—the complete experiences of her whole small life. And this exquisitely minute and comprehensive diorama, or at least a salient part of it, had been retained in memory for ninety years after the actual event! 'Simultaneously as in a mirror'—it is as if the soul had a consciousness peculiar to itself. Leigh Hunt as a small child had a similar experience. He tumbled into a mill-race, escaped undamaged, but *he* could afterwards recall not a vestige of what passed in his mind.

At the age of nine Darwin went to Dr. Butler's school at Shrewsbury as a boarder, and being fleet of foot would often run home and back between class hours. When he was late, he prayed earnestly to God to help him, and marvelled at this aid. He delighted in long solitary walks, spent in engrossed thought; and once in this half-tranced condition fell seven or eight feet from a public footpath on the old fortifications round Shrewsbury. 'The number of thoughts which passed through my mind during this very short but sudden and wholly unexpected fall, was astonishing.'

But life is brief and leisure is scanty. Even with the future of a Methuselah assured to us, and a Napoleonic memory, how much of the present should we squander in recollection of the past? And how many cronies would be willing to share our mementoes, which however animating to ourselves may for others be no better than dry biscuits without the sherry? Children become only too familiar with *this* edifying variety of Once-upon-a-time.

At what age this habit is apt to seize on its victims, one could only guess; very young children at any rate are immune from its temptations, though within a few summers they may revel in being informative to the younger yet. 'Tell me,' a five-year-old, already mentioned, was overheard addressing his sister of two and a half, 'tell me, what is mortar made of?' 'I *wish*', was the doleful

Memory

reply, 'you wouldn't ask me questions you know I don't know the answers of.' Such 'petties' easily weary us with their firefly chatter, but, except possibly one with another, they seldom 'reminisce'.

To what extent thought, which to a great extent is a sifting and rearranging of memories, is practicable without imagery of any kind, verbal or otherwise, is still apparently an open question: at any rate in the West, where minds are more likely to be vacant by habit than by disciplinary effort. On occasion we certainly *seem* to be entertaining nothing more substantial than the ghosts or phantoms of ideas, which may nevertheless prove almost as serviceable as the ideas themselves. With these a young child's mind must also be freely haunted.

CHAPTER X

MAKING UP

★

1. *'In the time of my childhood 'twas like a sweet dream*
To sit in the roses and hear the birds sing.'

Moreover, needless to say, it is not solely on the traffic of the senses—with their incessant news of the world without—that memory depends for its wherewithal. The mind is not merely a warehouse, it is also a manufactory, never idle and incredibly prolific. If we consider for example how much of what comes into our minds we refrain from using or deliberately discard when we write a letter or talk to a friend, we shall catch a glimpse of memory's enormous slag-heap. All day long we subsist on fantasies of our own contriving, on what we can adapt, combine, modify and re-create out of our experience. It is not only the poet's eye that is capable of dealing with airy nothings, though the faculty for conversion and transmutation varies beyond measure between individuals.

The simplest example will suffice. At the bare hint, we can instantly evoke and contemplate with the inward eye, let us say, a white bowl filled with blue flowers, and the next instant can convert it into a blue bowl filled with white flowers. At the word of command the flowers will as instantly wither in the bowl, or the bowl become empty. We most of us also occupy countless moments of the present imagining purely hypothetical scenes of the future, though usually the imagining bears only the faintest resemblance to the event—even if it ever eventuate! Since man, however sapient he may be, is habitually irrational, experience, it seems, endeavours in vain to teach us how futile for the most part both the pangs and joys of anticipation prove to be. There are dungeons and torture-chambers in Spain as well as 'castles', and a good deal

Making Up

of our waking life is spent in them. Lurid apprehensions of the future—daymares as distinct from daydreams—are assuredly dismally real to a young child. Even in the light of the morning, clouds of gloom may descend on him at the mere thought of going to bed; and a punishment deferred is a punishment abominably multiplied.

All the arts and some of the sciences none the less depend upon this kind of fantastic activity for their very existence. Fiction and drama would be otherwise solely imitative, a series of facsimiles pieced together out of fragments of the past. There is, it appears, nothing imageable in the mind which, however inscrutable the method may be, cannot within certain limits be changed at will. Once the image, for example, of a human is clear to the inward eye, he will submit himself at our caprice to any change of attire or circumstance we care to dictate. At an unwhispered behest he will even remove his own head and place it, smiling, under his arm. None the less although in actuality we could continue to survey his face for minutes together—glance after glance at eye, mouth, brow and hand—we seem to be unable for more than an instant to keep his *image* in view. It will continue to return at intervals perhaps, but (as it seems to one observer) it refuses to linger, to stay. These devices of the mind are familiar enough and have already been referred to; but they profoundly concern memory. Even the casual reading of a newspaper involves us in the most extortionate acrobatics of the fancy, of which we are almost wholly unaware.

The Hindus, I have been told, have a theory that the power of a man's memory depends on the number of incarnations he has endured. With each reincarnation the power of recall increases; and there are seven of these in all. But, ignoring this and similar clarifying theories, what is to be said of the imagination, in Blake's meaning of the word, whereby alone we dimly contemplate the reality of which the world of the actual is no more, as it were, than the scenic curtain? Every fusion of memory, every fancy and fantasy, dream and daydream, subsides into that vast repository designated the 'unconscious', of which we are not *so* unconscious as to be wholly unaware of its contents. And although at night we stop being awake, there seems little reason to doubt that we are engaged in dreaming in some degree the whole day long. There appears to be a perpetual hazelike drift of the visionary in the

Early One Morning

background of consciousness. The self slips from thinking into dreaming without any perceptible jolt or jar. There seems to be no detectable change in the fabric. But waking *breaks* off the dream. Moreover, dreams seem to be catalogued, as it were, in our minds among our memories of actuality and our fantasies, and we may perhaps make undiscriminating use of all three. Sleep has its own private uses for the mind, and however wildly fantastic these may be, the self then accepts them as all in the dark's round. Early in life—though it is very difficult to recall how far—these nocturnal experiences are more likely to frequent the day, the *waking* mind.

The least change of bodily temperature or one due to an infinitesimal quantity of certain drugs, will set fantasy and its minions working like a summer-evening merry-go-round. The brakes are off the wheels of the brain. 'A few years ago,' says Thomas Holcroft, 'having a slight fever, and lying awake in the night, I found I could speak extempore verses on any given subject (for I proposed two or three to myself), many of them approaching excellence, and the others full of high-sounding words, and such as would be thought excellent by some. . . . Have found nearly the same facility occasionally, when actually writing poetry, after having considered my subject a certain time, and made a certain number of verses, or rather, after rousing the faculties. In my sleep I have read many a page of poetry that never was written. Others have told me they have done the same. Mr. N—— says he has several times gone to bed with his mind wearied by considering a question of science which he could not resolve, has slept or dozed, and the resolution has intruded so forcibly upon his thoughts, that it has awaked him. . . .'

This is a tale many times told, and even Influenza may be one of the magicians. One such dream, the fabric of this Demon, in my distant past included not only the effortless composition of verse of a faultlessly Miltonic harmony; but the goddesses in their verdant haunts that were its theme themselves vocalized and dramatized that verse!

All young children of course, particularly imaginative children, immeasurably delight in, and *may* at times be the sport and prey of daydreamings; whether these are of their own weaving or have been imposed on them by books, pictures and so forth. It is all but

134

Making Up

impossible in after life to recall their vividness, frequency and intensity. They are experiences very seldom shared even if words can suffice for the purpose; and they are in consequence usually ignored by the adult.

2. 'Who knows what wells are a child's unthinking eyes?'

It would indeed not be easy to *state* the precise difference, in the effect on one's mind, between (a) a firsthand memory, (b) a memory not firsthand but of some past event in one's life described by others, (c) the recollection of an invented or imagined incident, and (d) a dream. Confusion here seems likelier to occur in childhood, but appears even then to be rare—though again and again children have been impelled actually to put the question whether life itself is not in the nature of a dream. 'When shall I wake up?' But instead, living on sends us to sleep! In maturity we are seldom in much doubt, and can be morally certain of the genuineness even of a very early memory. The only final test however would be to borrow that fascinating device of Mr. Wells's, a Time Machine—one of the most magical objects even to look at in all fiction—and be wafted back to the memoried event's distant moment, and on the journey be transformed into the very infant one then was. Would that be an intensely surprising reunion? All that has happened since has been part and parcel of a continuity of being. Has it not also been a continuity of much the same *kind* of consciousness?

When, as heedfully as I can, I examine the contents of any memory of my own childhood, nothing of importance appears to be wanting that would be present if it referred to an experience of only yesterday. Nothing vital *seems* either to have been lost or added. However difficult it may be to resume in memory one's five-year-old body, little change appears to have taken place in the consciousness of its tenant. The Alice in us may nibble the mushroom, and may dwarf in stature to that degree, yet in mind she is recognizably the same Alice. Gulliver, whether he is amused in Lilliput by pygmy court affairs as futile as those of a doll's house, or confronted in Brobdingnag by affairs gigantic solely in the estimation of the oafs concerned in them, is still the same Gulliver —but then, he embarked, at Bristol, grown up!

Early One Morning

What of the hapless Mr. Bultitude? When in *Vice Versa* he returns to his son Dick's school, he takes him*self* back with him; but even at that the difference between this self and the raucous young barbarians around him is mainly one of habit and taste. He cannot abide their horrid gambols and peppermints; they find *him* insupportable. He is much the same fish, but the water strikes cold. In his character and morals, as compared with his son's, there is a sad falling off. He is a pompous, priggish, unfriendly, isolated, and physically unpleasant little sneak. He cannot have *become* all that, though. Growing old, please Heaven, is not quite so disastrous. He must even as an infant have been that way inclined. Whereas Dick, the noble Dick, who, so far as I can remember, refrains even from grumbling at the deterioration in his own physique, blossoms like the aloe, and pours out money for bunting, chinese lanterns and tipsy cake, in abandoned high spirits and in hatred of elderly and yet not wholly uncondonable cant. Would that there were any hope of meeting him again when age has wreaked its worst on *him*! He had first to live down his father!

Not that if the self of my childhood (mounting the Machine) were transported immediately into my own elderly cranium, and had to share my blunted sensibilities and pandemonium of a mind, *it* would notice no differences. That seems highly improbable. It would be amazed, no doubt, at my stagnant 'reactions'. As we grow older we are apt to fall into the fallacy that by merely naming we explain. *Oh, that? That is so-and-so* lazily suffices us. One eyes for example a certain dazzling complex mystery of colour and design in a perpetually rhythmic and delicate motion. It is, we say, the *fire* in the grate.

Not so with a young child. It cannot feast its wonder at it enough. Its names too for things as well as the things themselves are often vivid novelties. It leaps with joy upon a new one as did Robinson Crusoe on the footprint in the sand. And such novelties, especially perhaps nameless novelties, keep for a while their marvel and magic, their horror or ridiculousness, their loveliness or blessed reminder. Nor may even the wear and tear of a long lifetime obliterate the mystery of a familiar object seen in remote retrospect. How else could Aksakoff, an old man and in the pangs of a mortal illness, have so blessedly exulted in the trees and

136

flowers, the fish and birds and butterflies, and the complete poignant human panorama of *his* early childhood?

If the mind's future can be compared to the dried-up channel of a river, then consciousness will supply the water of many sources that will then flow into it. That water may course full and deep, sparkling and shallow, fresh or stale. At times a mean trickle creeping in sand between bleached and barren rocks will be our sole reward for continuing to live at all. When the stream runs slow but brimming, or tumultuously fast and free, it is a very pleasing experience. But both for quantity and quality the flow or head of water depends not only on the present but chiefly on the past— on memory.

The 'rolling stream' is not the only apt metaphor. When Galton was writing his reminiscences, some of them, he says, became so sharp and vivid that occasionally he lost his sense of time. This is a peculiarly vivid experience. It suggested to him the replacement of what our sense of time usually makes of its phenomena by that of a 'permanent panorama, painted throughout with equal vividness, in which the point to which attention is temporarily directed becomes for that time the present'. This being so, the brightly coloured future is merely latent, veiled; and the 'Cosmos is one perpetual Now'. He adds that 'philosophers have often held this creed intellectually', but that he himself had been initiated. And there are other initiates of similar but deflecting views.

If only, we may sigh, we knew the secret of directing 'attention' on the past, how much richer the future might be. But even when we succeed in focussing a patch of the panorama which, when it was painted or, according to Galton, reviewed, was brilliant with zest and excitement and inordinately precious to us, how often the colours have faded and how inadequate may seem the design. To be in love is a state wherein one memoried image is paramount. Our thoughts and feelings then resemble the petals round the disk of a daisy, a nimbus encircling the moon. This blissful but chequered condition may recur—and even frequently! Or the daisy may be a passion-flower; the nimbus foretell storm. But while the image of each loved one remains in memory, and, though bereft perhaps of the light, with its attendant heat, that never was on sea or land, may still be admired and dear and awaken sentiment, where now are the strangeness and sweetness,

Early One Morning

the pining and foreboding, the despair and rapture, and the thousand and one trivialities which then seemed to be brimming over with meaning and symbol? Memory may be a trained pointer, but she cannot retrieve life itself. Indeed the difference between any act wildly lived and that act recalled, whatever its charms may be, is in general extreme. We may deplore even the antiseptics and narcotics which the mind uses so freely in dealing with the filth and horrors of the past.

Nevertheless, in spite of all its trickeries and limitations, its frailties and shortcomings, and particularly in view of the few wretched little remnants and relics of the years of childhood available to most of us, a wonder of wonders memory remains.

'Memory!' exclaims Bishop Hall, 'the great Keeper or Master of the Rolles of the soule, a power that can make amendes for the speed of time, in causing him to leave behinde those things which else he would so carry away, as if they had not beene'. And St. Augustine:—

'I will soar, then, beyond this power of my nature also [the senses], ascending by degrees unto Him who made me. And I enter the fields and roomy chambers of memory, where are the treasures of countless images. . . . For even while I live in darkness and silence, I can bring out colours in memory if I wish, and discern between black and white, and what others I wish; nor yet do sounds break in and disturb what is drawn in by mine eyes. . . . For these too I can summon if I please, and immediately they appear. And though my tongue be at rest, and my throat silent, yet can I sing as much as I will. . . . I recall at my pleasure. . . . These things do I within, in that vast chamber of my memory. For there are nigh me heaven, earth, sea, and whatever I can think upon in them, besides those which I have forgotten. There also do I meet with myself, and recall myself—what, when, or where I did a thing, and how I was affected when I did it. . . . Great is this power of memory, exceeding great, O my God—an inner chamber large and bound-less! Who has plumbed the depths thereof?'

He is amazed that men should marvel at earth's mountains, seas and rivers, at the stars in their courses—'and omit to wonder at themselves': 'Truly, O Lord, I labour therein, and labour in my-self. . . . But what is nearer to me than myself? And, behold, I am not able to comprehend the force of my own memory, though I cannot name myself without it. . . . Of what nature am I? A life various and manifold, and exceeding vast. . . . Through it all do I run to and fro, and fly; I penetrate on this side and that, so far as I am able, and nowhere is there an end.' The complete passage from the *Confessions* is a tribute to memory as true as it is ardent—and that of a flaming spirit. And, each in our own measure, we can add a *benedicite*.

3. 'That ship of priceless wares, Oblivion.'

But it will not alter the fact that the greater part of what happens to us in life is neither remembered nor worth remembering. So to spend one's time that it will be welcome *if* it is recalled, is no bad maxim and habit, although it is one which might half empty our schools, both of masters and pupils. It sounds as tame as *Safety First*, yet it by no means precludes a variety of experiences which at their onset may be diabolically pungent, provocative and unpleasant. Endured and for the time being done with, they retire into a decent obscurity. When revived, by some strange alchemy of the mind they may appear to have shed the worst of the features that made them so unwelcome. Even in their childhood children might agree to that.

Memory, that is, tends to improve what is left in her charge, if she thinks it worth while. The worst, whether we wish it or not, she may entirely suppress. So at any rate the psychoanalysts affirm. It is even suggested that the experience of the first two years of life are usually submerged beyond all hope of recovery because they were so painful. Still there may be recallable events in life which it would be difficult, surely, to rival—out of *any* forgotten past—for sheer horror and desolation, even if we are ourselves no more responsible for them than we were in childhood. Distance lends them appeasements. We can even be mildly and mockingly amused that we were once so miserable, and particularly perhaps if that once was our childhood.

Our happy moments may also in revival take to themselves an aura unforeseen—though the happiest of all, moments of strange illumination and ecstasy, may be irrevocable. And though shameful acts may, but not apparently must, blacken and worsen in this process, mere silly mishaps and misadventures and events neither

Early One Morning

jubilant nor self-flattering are among the most entertaining we have to look back upon. A complete chapter of accidents is by no means the least diverting to read over again in one's Book of Life. And the recalled caricatures—often the most telling of portraits—which one made of oneself five, ten, thirty, fifty years ago—it had better not be *too* recent—may be among that book's liveliest illustrations.

A good memory, then—any indelible array of dates and names and so forth apart—must be judged not merely by the quantity or even by the variety of its resources, but by their quality and intrinsic value. And *the* paramount question is, *Whose* memory is this? *Ceteris paribus*, and given the opportunity, one might prefer the recollection of a mermaid combing her yellow hair above the surfy billows of her rock to that of shaking hands with William IV; a serene hour of solitude or companionship on the Acropolis in the days of Pericles to a befogged week of Wapping in our own; a witch of the old school to a vamp of the new; one of Schubert's songs heard in childhood to—perhaps—all jazz music. But change places with, say, Chaucer or Defoe or Dickens, and *his* Wapping might be to our Athens as gold is to tinsel. Yet even if we keep for the most part only what is native to us and naturally retained and recalled, a somewhat obscure art may come to the aid of nature and we shall be that much the richer.

There are moments in life too, and particularly in childhood, that may have to wait many years for their realization. And even if the realization is then a little rueful we shall not begrudge it. There need be few tears at the deathbed of an illusion. I recapture, for example, from a morning not far from forty years ago, the vividest glimpse of a bright green and somewhat austere sofa, resembling that in the famous portrait of Madame Récamier. In my open palm lies shining a little Danaë's shower of gold which had descended on me for my first literary contribution to the *Cornhill*. I toss the golden sovereigns in my hand, and remark to myself: 'Well, if authorship is as easy as all that, I shall *soon* be free from care!' When I am a *man* . . . , boasts the child.

Sheer neglect of what may instantly and irretrievably become memory, whether we like it or not, is a curious human shortcoming since we have, strictly speaking, so little else. Nor do we so much value the choicest recollections we actually have, not

THACKERAY, AGED THREE
WITH HIS FATHER AND MOTHER
From a water-colour drawing by George Chinnery

Making Up

even those of childhood, as to be incapable of 'improving' them, and especially when we recount them to others. Deliberate trimming, of course—and quite apart from purposes of deception—is a dangerous luxury, and, as a habit, fatal to any respectable soundness of mind.

For the most apart we spend as little time and trouble in the consideration of *what* in the future might be most richly treasurable in memory as we do of the methods that are most likely to succeed in assuring its remembrance at all. Since the merely habitual tends to fade and die away out of the mind, and an unemotional jog-trot routine leaves little behind it, the lesson is obvious. We must, again, not only lie in wait for the unusual, and it will need a good deal of the usual as background; but must also *desire* to record and remember it. The housebreaker—of both kinds —the deep-sea sailor, the steeplejack, the trapezist, the explorer, the spy, the gangster, the prefect of police—they one and all *daily* experience, and may as punctually forget, events which in the life of a bookworm—who may none the less have adventures and excitements of his own—would remain one of the supreme splendours of his earthly career, and the master jewel of his table talk.

What then of children, and their ruts and routines and precise time-tables; the stolidly good-as-gold compared with the mercurial-as-mercury; their nicest of conduct and their perilous escapades? Any experience that is pure and potent oil to the flame of life *now* may illuminate the future with its own welcome and blessed phantom. That is no less true of childhood. It does not follow however that what may appear of excellence at the moment is of this quality, since experience is of value only in relation to a certain *plus*—the experiencer; and he changes. Whatever happens, each one of us remains, on earth, the centre of his own universe—a universe limited by his own consciousness and comprehension. There are few such universes that might not by effort be extended, or at least more intently explored. And memory may flourish in what superficially might appear to have been a pitifully narrow range of circumference. Still, the better the child, the wider and richer in the memorable his given range will be.

Even at that, once more, he will eventually retrieve out of the quicksands of the past only the most miscellaneous kind of wreckage. Complete tracts of experience are out of the question. If,

Early One Morning

without help, we wish to recall what we believe we should value out of the past, and more especially the distant past, the expedition resembles Robinson Crusoe's to the wreck: a goodly ship once, and crammed from deck to keel with a precious cargo —which is all *there*. But except for an occasional raft-load it is beyond our contrivance and all our ingenuity to recover it. And every tide. . . . And the rainy season. . . . And some outrageous tempest. . . . Like, that is, the most popular item in a seaside concert, the memories we enjoy most consist of Selections—by no means always Played by Request—and seldom those of a skilled musician intent on giving them at least a semblance of a sequence. The key, the time, the balance, the phrasing, the style—all are at odds.

CHAPTER XI

TIME

★

1. *'Time, you old gipsy man,*
   Will you not stay . . . ?'

But even if Memory *is* in much so casual and niggling yet is still a wide gleaner, should not the recollections of a man aged seventy concerning his last sixty years seem at least six times more various, vivid and valuable to him than those of his first ten? The evidence will, I think, suggest otherwise. But, in any case, every child—however narrow his surroundings may be—has at least enough of memory and memories to go on with. His air is quick and dense with reminders, his explorations of the actual keep them company. He lives swiftly in the fleeting moment. In maturity we tend to pay more heed to what is within (and a muddled medley that may be), than to what is without. And much of the time we might spend on observation of the novel and in scrutiny of the familiar, we give—less even to thinking and imagining than—to reading; which, even if it is excellent reading, is at a remove from actuality. Our minds are freely parasitic. And often we merely 'sit'. Children seldom merely sit.

We cannot then assume that either in area or quality the little private universe we each of us have built up and survey has expanded in proportion to the time we have spent in it. The fact is of course that one's interest in life needs incessant revitalization. It may flag and fade and all but perish. As we age, habit may deaden perception, routine dull its edge, convention smother impulse, and small cares, the mere necessity not so much to live as to make a living, may stupefy the imagination and quench the spirit. Human beings can endure and survive tragic grief or loss or disappointment or failure, and even success, no less than they can

143

Early One Morning

flourish on danger, passion and enthusiasm. But little drops of trouble's water, little grains of care's sand, wear away in time the hardest of stones, put out of gear the most delicate machinery!

There are happy people, there are stoics, there are the seemingly contented at every age. But even if in natural high spirits or as the result of a practised philosophy we continue to welcome both the seen and the unseen with a cheer, it does not follow that when we are seventy we shall have at our command twice as extensive a view of life as we had at thirty-five, or seven times that at ten. It is not an arithmetical question. We cannot survey or enjoy in the passing moment more than that moment can give or hold; and this is true at any age. The available quantity of the rememberable —apart, that is, from the revivable—seems to vary from age to age, and in relation to state of mind, health and other circumstances.

It is the pace of life too that counts. In general it is begun at a spirited gallop, slackens into a heady disjointed canter, then to a steady trot or discursive amble, and last—though *en route* to the most restful of stables—to a sedate and leisurely walk. Much depends on pedigree, form and training. And the speed varies at any age between individuals and in accordance with their incentives and incitements. But there is the labyrinthine problem of *time* to consider. Real and personal time, that is, rather than— though it cannot but be in relation with—mere clock-time. Of this—one of their many blessings—young children can have little knowledge, since they cannot 'tell' it.

There is but one *manageable* time of any kind or order—that of the transient moment. And this is gone before we can hail it, 'Here thou art!' Our days are made up of these moments, and we register them in the mind as it were spatially, and in relation to what they hold, cumbrous jars or tapering phials of action, thought and feeling. In general it may be said that the larger the number of experiences of any kind poured into the passing moment, so much the more 'time' will an hour of those moments seem to hold. In other words, it is noticeable, salient, and novel perceptions with their outcome that appear to take up most time—as it flows away. During any absorption of the mind—heedless of external events— the very *sense* of time seems to fall into abeyance. The clock-hours vanish away like morning mist. Extreme happiness none the less

Time

appears to have no concern with mere minutes. And though unusual discomfort of mind or body may slow down the wheels of existence to a sluggardry almost beyond endurance, there are exceptions even to this.

After a local and ineffective injection of cocaine for the extraction of two molar teeth, one of them a wisdom tooth, some years ago, I remarked as politely as possible to the dentist that the experience we had so inequitably shared must have taken 'a long time'. He nodded, forceps in hand. I suggested: 'At least five minutes?' He glanced at his watch—and said: 'Seventeen!' Or was this perhaps an attempt at consolation? Love delayed has the contrary effect. 'For so have I seen', says Jeremy Taylor, 'an amorous person tell the minutes of his absence from his fancied joy, and while he told the sands of his hour-glasse, or the throbs and little beatings of his watch, by dividing an hour into so many members, he spun out its length by number, and so translated a day into the tediousnesse of a month. . . .'

Time closely attended to begins to imitate eternity—as waiting for a temperature in a critical illness or an experiment in holding the breath will prove. The gravest disadvantage of boredom too is that it spends two hours at least on what cheerfulness can manage in ten minutes. A child in the nursery with nothing to do, then, is a Sindbad with an Old Man of the Sea on his shoulders—called Time; a rider, invisible, heavy as lead, but unspurred.

But there are three kinds of personal time, not merely that of the present, but that of the past and of the future. And each one of them has its own hour-glass. What extends time now may seem to contract it in retrospect; and *vice versa*. Next year seems further off than last, whatever the calendar may say. The monotonous as it drears on resembles sterile versts of time—sullen clouds over a sullen sea; but once it is over, it has all but evaporated. It is amusing to watch time's tape-measure at work—by imagining ourselves for example in the dock, attentively listening to the following judicial sentence: 'For each one of your misdeeds during the three weeks of midsummer ten years ago, you will be sent to prison for ten years; the periods to run consecutively. (*A pause; and a glance at the papers*) I should say, *concurrently*. You may now leave the court; but must return in ten years' time to begin your sentence.' Alter the word *misdeeds* to 'acts of grace and virtue', and *prison* to 'Paradise', how rapidly the time-computations will change.

'I can remember', says William Hutton, 'my mother dandling me on the knee, feeding me with the infant spoon, and nursing me in the arms. I also remember the form and colour of my dress. But although eighty-two years have passed by, yet that space of time seems amazingly short; the reason is obvious, memory only brings the two points of *then* and *now* into view, and skips over every incident between the two. But when we look forward, if but for *one* year, the time appears long, because we foresee an infinite number of incidents between the two points.'

How versatile a piece of mechanism again is the hour-glass not merely of sleep, but of daydream—the delight of childhood. A dream itself, though but the workmanship of a moment, as scores of examples attest, may appear to have occupied hours, and even days, of serene or violent, coherent or utterly disordered experience; while yet, between the beginning and end of a void refreshing sleep, not even niche enough in time for a word of gratitude to gracious Morpheus seems to have intervened. Ever and again in the dark hours we may appear to have lain suspended for æons, midway between sleep and wake; like the weed that roots itself in ease on Lethe Wharf; and this, even though not so much clock-time has been involved as will admit of a mouse making its first nightly circuit of the wainscot. And from what may appear to be the profoundest of slumbers we may be roused by the mere stopping of a clock. It is curious too that even in childhood we have little difficulty in joining up at morning the thread that was broken by sleep overnight.

'I pray you, what is't o'clock?' asks Rosalind. 'You should ask me, what time o'day;' says Orlando, 'there's no clock in the forest.' Whereupon Rosalind explains to this eager listener how time travels in divers paces with divers persons. But all her instances refer to present time. It is with the thief to the gallows, she says, that time gallops, 'for though he go as softly as foot can fall he thinks himself too soon there'. And yet, says Dostoievsky somewhere, how observant is a man on his way to his execution. That, one would suppose, would retard the pace. But all such statements are hazardous', and every question pertaining to time seems to be hedged about with paradox and contradiction.

Time

In general—though it is always perilous to generalize—as the pace of life slackens, the capacity of every unit of time has dwindled. The large jars contain but half measure; and yet the milestones are more rapidly left behind. We appear, that is, to have far less time wherein to grow old and wise, than in which to cease to be young. The thoughts of youth are long long thoughts, and the days of childhood are (to *us*, unimaginably) *long* days. 'These winter evenings,' in childhood, writes William Bell Scott, 'lighted by candles and warmed by the tiled fireplace, appear in memory to have lasted for ages, like the period of the Plantagenets or Tudors; yet they must only have continued a very few seasons in perfection.' And yet at neither end of life are we particularly anxious to go to bed! How far the number and clarity of our personal memories, which individually cover so tiny an area, depend on the apparent rapidity or slowness in the time that went to their making is a more difficult question.

'Beyond small portions of time which can be felt as rhythms,' runs *Psychology of Childhood*, 'our very terms are abstract', at any age. But in childhood perception of space develops more swiftly than that of time. A young child is confused even by such terms as yesterday, to-morrow, next week; and even to a six-year-old, phrases like last spring, the day before yesterday, a month ago may be unintelligible. 'Arithmetic books to the contrary, the eight-year-old's day is from waking time till dark', and, as with all of us, contains 'a varying, indefinite number of hours. Not, however, till nine or more birthdays have passed does a child begin to regard a year as other than a wonderfully long period, and to date events in his past either with any great accuracy, or over long intervals'.

'A year'! Who cannot recall the abject fury of resentment aroused by the smiling adult's 'Will you have it now, or wait till you can get it?' To a child a mere twenty-four hours of future time resembles an impermeable sheet of plate glass, severing it from where beyond all words it longs to be. The looking forward to a promised pleasure, the last enormous week before the end of term, even the hour spent in bed in waiting to get up when sleep refuses to return to eager eyes and senses—childhood knows all about that, and Southey, as we have seen, has put it into words. 'Ah yes, "to-morrow",' I hear a small voice out of the past sepulchrally repeating; 'but "to-morrow" never comes!'

147

Early One Morning

A child's day of long languid summer hours or in the darker indoors of winter, however, is not the less brimming with action and interest because so minute a fraction of it will remain in memory or be revivable, when that day is long over. Nor of course is the unremembered afterwards inactive. Largely of this his mind is being made. Does he make any attempt to fix his memories? Frequently, yes, it seems. A child of three (who now is six) used always to spend his last waking minutes in bed telling himself in a very small voice what had happened during the day: *N went here, N saw this, did that*—on and on. As for *dating* events in one's past, one's clock then may be as fatuously slow on some occasions as it is fast on others.

CHAPTER XII

DOINGS

*

1. 'Such is the uneven state of human life.'

Child-time, then, compared with adult-time is pretty much what a child might suppose clock-time to be compared with watch-time—far less condensed. Having so much of it at his disposal, what, and how much, we may enquire, does a child do with it? As regards any twelve-hours' body-work and mind-work and expense of vital energy does that of a father aged, say, forty-two, proportionately exceed that of his six-year-old son?

Were mere age all that is to be taken into account, the paternal product should be, we might assume, seven times as great in quantity, and—after so prolonged a practice—much finer in quality. But is this so? That father, quite naturally, considers his day's work both serious and important. He even dresses, converses and conducts himself in accordance with that conviction. Since it concerns the well-being not only of himself but also of his household (apart from any service he may be rendering society and the State) it *is* of course very serious and important.

A child of six, on his side, may at some chance remark be suddenly moved to enquire what his father actually does in life; and, if encouraged, may follow this polite question up with others—about money and wages and rent and property and so forth; rather as if he had come from another planet and had there, a little tepidly, *heard* of these earthly matters. He pays his parent the compliment of taking him seriously, that is, he wants to be informed, though his desire may wane even before the information begins to wilt.

Early One Morning

His father, contrariwise, though he may be loyally amused to hear of his son's doings during his absence, is unlikely, unless these were also misdoings, to take them very seriously. In Vaughan's words, he regards them as 'meer playing', but is unlikely to connect them with going to Heaven. But even though his son should agree with him, is this quite fair? Compare the one normal day's activities with the other's. In terms of mere nourishment-value of body and mind, which was the more laborious and bountiful? What skill was involved in either case, what attention, what energy?

Hoop, tops, marbles, dice, kite, bow and arrow, pop-gun, bricks, soldiers, trains, chalks, dolls, shops, nurseries, mud-pies or pebbles in a bowl of water—with this kind of thing, in endless variety, apart from any purely mental business or discipline, a child 'plays'. He has his own jargon too. There are literally dozens of words in the English dialects devoted to the game of marbles alone. And though in these games he richly enjoys himself, and though his play is the outcome of pure impulse, it involves skill, knowledge, attention and ingenuity. Translate these objects into their adult equivalents; they involve hard labour, which in the child's case was labour self-imposed. What else he may have done with his time may have been—as we have seen—not only equally skilled busyness, but of use and service to others. Occasionally, in the phrase of a five-year-old, his play is little short of 'penal solitude'.

The pauper apprentices of as tender years in the bad old times worked for a pittance in vile conditions. In his seventh year William Hutton was sent to work in a silk mill from five o'clock in the morning to seven at night (and was whipped for any offences) at a wage of a shilling a week. Yet work of this kind was infinitely less profitable (though not necessarily more active) to these children than is a child's *play* to him. This was at once the evil of the old system, and its fatuity even from a merely utilitarian point of view. But a woman-child of eight or nine, even nowadays, in a household, or room-hold, where every mouth is a problem, does not, when school is over, or during her holidays, merely play at being a grown-up. In mind and responsibility and even at heart to all intents she *is* one. Her dolls are live babies, sisters and brothers, and these lean and shrill young foster-mothers may be met with,

Doings

indomitable souls, by the score in any London park or populous slum. And their reward at the end of their day's toil is seldom to be reckoned in ha'pence.

All this may suggest special pleading, since children for the most part can in much, very fortunately, take care of themselves. Still, in what sense—apart from necessity and financial profit—is speculating on the Stock Exchange, or breeding pigs, or dealing in meat, or prescribing physic, or the writing of books, or the painting of pictures, a more exhausting, instructive, or even worthier occupation than these of children?

Nor does paterfamilias take his own mere 'play' or sport either less seriously, or with more verve, alertness and animation. Indeed he commits himself to far more solemn observances. His sense of rivalry may be almost painful to witness—his chagrin, mortification and despair. Beaten! I have shared a railway carriage (in America) with some fifteen to twenty fellow creatures haggard and deathly and utterly dejected—because of a lost game of football. Half England is in sackcloth when the 'ashes' are in jeopardy. Adult man too revels in paraphernalia, and, if possible, expensive paraphernalia—with his greens and links, his pitches and courses, his fields and moors and shoots and lawns and courts and pools and reaches, his billiard and bridge rooms, casinos and clubs. If money could buy a Sea to swim or fish or sail in, all Seven of them would long since have become private property; and some day he may parcel out the air, and make a country club of Venus. There is no limit to the time and pains, trouble and temper he will squander on amusing himself in austere accordance with the rigour of the game. He may spend on a small steam yacht, a pygmy sports car, or a highly indifferent racing stable, what would clothe and keep a copious little Victorian family for months.[1]

---

[1] In his *Discoveries in England* Mr. Emile Cammaerts has a chapter on games. He refers with the tenderest irony to the unwillingness in Englishmen to grow old, and serious—except in their pleasures. 'The two diminutive figures on the golf course proceeded mechanically, without a gesture and seemingly without a word, on their appointed way. The thirteen white figures on the cricket ground seemed to stand in set attitudes, as if they had shared the fate of Lot's wife. One of them keeps on bowling, and the other keeps on blocking. . . . I remember hearing a schoolmaster shouting to his boys during a football match: "Don't *play* with it!"—it of course meaning the ball—and wondering what such an exclamation could mean. I did not know then that it is only on the Continent

Early One Morning

Whereas, though his son of six uses no less energy in *his* mere play, and may be as deeply engrossed in it, unless he has been surfeited with toys or 'spoilt', he will be perfectly happy—imagination his ritual—with a mound of sand, a penny pail and a wooden spade; a ditch, a twig, a bent pin and a galley pot; a cart made of a packing case, old iron, elbow grease and the sweat of his brow; a little putty, gunpowder or quicksilver. Which of the two evokes the keener eureka in the prowling sportsman's breast—his first cock-sparrow or his hundredth hippopotamus? Which of the two adventurers is likelier to pity his prey, or to abide by self-imposed game laws? 'One day in mistake I shot a robin,' says Mr. Herbert Read of his childhood. Not only did it seem a deadly sin, but it was 'a crime my cousin made more terrible by promising to keep it a secret from the world.'

A child of course delights to mimic his father's graver occupations, but he also has his own. They are not the less onerous because to a grown-up they seem to be only play. By their means he is learning, practising and realizing the use of his body and his brains, and mastering his surroundings. This, concerning all that nature and his mind bestow on him, is meat and drink to a lively child. It not only satisfies an instinct, but is deliberate; and may win rewards of its own, as well as praise, love or a sugarplum.

Positive advance in this mastery is easily detectable even within a fortnight in the life of an infant less than two years old. One of these, tiny doll in fist, paused recently before a polished brass door-handle, having noticed its reflection on the surface. She stayed a moment or two, watching it, then gently moved the doll to and fro, while the tinier reflection in the brass followed suit. Satisfied with this experiment, she drew nearer and steadily scrutinized her own image in the handle. An even younger baby who could no more than crawl on all fours and was still at the dribbling stage of life, noticed a drop of its spittle fall on the carpet, silver an instant in the window light, then darken and vanish. It then dribbled intentionally, watched the silvering, and proceeded to rub in the darkening spot with its forefinger. Out, out, damned

that games are *played*; in England they are *performed*, like a stage drama or some kind of religious rite.' Before deciding whether to welcome or counter this little thrust we had better consider a further comment: 'This craving of English authors for poetry is another consequence of the race's childlike spirit.'

Doings

spot! There could, surely, be no question of the process of mind?

Another child of three (who, before her first birthday, had taught herself to whistle a little twittering stave and had then abandoned the art) began enquiring about words. '*Umbrella, Mummie. Why Um?* Potatoes, why *toes?*' However Lilliputian, this is research-work. On these *lines* the man of science proceeds. On these lines James Watt, who was a weakly and delicate child, had little schooling and was in much self-taught, discovered the locomotive steam engine, whose activities were afterwards so bitterly deplored by John Ruskin.

A child may appear to fail in the easy; but, going his own way, triumph over the difficult. 'I absolutely declined', says Ruskin himself, 'to learn to read by syllables; but would get an entire sentence by heart with great facility, and point with accuracy to every word in the page as I repeated it. As, however, when the words were once displaced, I had no more to say, my mother gave up, for the time, the endeavour to teach me to read, hoping only that I might consent, in process of years, to adopt the popular system of syllabic study. But I went on to amuse myself, in my own way, learnt whole words at a time, as I did patterns; and at five years old was sending for my "second volumes" to the circulating library. . . .' As a later chapter will prove, it is not only love that 'finds out a way'.

It was the enchanting graphic rhythmical patterns on the printed paper of a composition that first wooed Lord Berners to music when he was a child—not the sounds they represented. And what precisely was in Thomas Hardy's consciousness—not merely the instinct of mimicry, perhaps—when 'in play' as a child of six or seven years old, he dipped 'a little wooden sword, which his father had made for him . . . into the blood of a pig which had just been killed, and brandished it as he walked about the garden exclaiming: "Free Trade or blood!" ' We may fail to interpret this heady excitement, but can share in part the rapturous gravity with which at four years old he received from his father the gift of a small accordion, his own name and the date written upon it: Thomas Hardy, 1844.

Early One Morning

2. '*Even such a happy Child of Earth am I.*'

B ut as yet we are still in the natural world. A child may venture far beyond it even when 'at play'. Socrates had his dai-
mon, Henry James his 'genius', Dr. Faustus his familiar, Napoleon
his star, and a child may have 'playmates', not less immaterial than
these, or more dangerous. As for talking to *himself*, or seeing with
his own waking eyes what he could not establish as actual, or make
others perceive or a belief in magic—proclivities of this kind need
hint at not a vestige of that mental insecurity which may accompany them in later life. He is unlikely to confide to others such
experiences as these, unless it be to one or two of those nearest
to him whom he can wholly trust, though he may perhaps, like
Edmund Gosse, at length share them with the world at large.

'Being so restricted . . . and yet so active, my mind took refuge
in an infantile species of natural magic. . . . I formed strange super-
stitions, which I can only render intelligible by naming some
concrete examples. I persuaded myself that, if I could only discover the proper words to say or the proper passes to make, I
could induce the gorgeous birds and butterflies in my Father's
illustrated manuals to come to life, and fly out of the book, leaving
holes behind them. I believed that, when, at the Chapel, we sang,
drearily and slowly, loud hymns of experience and humiliation,
I could boom forth with a sound equal to that of dozens of singers,
if I could only hit upon the formula. During morning and evening
prayers, which were extremely lengthy and fatiguing, I fancied
that one of my two selves could flit up, and sit clinging to the
cornice, and look down on my other self and the rest of us, if I
could only find the key. I laboured for hours in search of these
formulas, thinking to compass my ends by means absolutely irrational. . . . I feel quite sure that nothing external suggested these
ideas of magic, and I think it probable that they approached the
ideas of savages at a very early stage of development. . . . '

And, almost as if in direct challenge of the disparaging 'savages',
William Bell Scott continues the tale. 'The impression', he says in
his *Autobiographical Notes,* which 'I am about to describe remained on my mind for a considerable period of time. My impression or experience was this, that I could transfer myself from
the top to the bottom of the stair, from the upper landing to the

Doings

hall, without the action of going down step by step. I cannot think it was wholly a delusion, because I remember on one occasion standing still for a moment after so descending with a feeling of wonder. Perhaps this may have been the last time I had so descended, or supposed I had so descended; it was my awaking to something. Other impressions of a similar kind I had that I am now unable to describe. . . .'

One of Sir Henry Newbolt's recurrent dreams in childhood was that of 'rising from the ground with a slight effort and floating under the ceiling or down the staircase, until by relaxing my clenched hands I let myself come to earth like an aeronaut with a parachute'. So entrancingly natural is this experience that it seems to suggest a watery past. Indeed the conviction even in age that one could fly if only one knew *how*, fades slowly. The effect in this case was vivid enough to suggest an attempt to actualize it, and he threw himself down a short flight of stairs. . . . The dream still recurred, but 'became less interesting'. After listening to a sermon on St. Peter's ardent attempt to walk on the Sea of Galilee, in all good faith one Sunday evening he followed the Apostle's example, using for this purpose the pigeons' large earthenware basin full of water. Nightmare rather than dream was my experience as a child of repeatedly finding myself in an empty room with colourless floor, walls and ceiling that converged into an infinite distance, at the uttermost extremity of which, I realized, was God. Daylight investigation of *this* dream never occurred to me.

There is yet another activity in which the child of six resembles his father of sixty, that of fancy and invention, of 'making things up'. If that father is a painter or a poet he may prefer the phrase, creative imagination. Even with a child this may be a purposeful, coherent and arranged affair. It is the outcome of a process in the mind, which in much remains mysterious, but which involves apparently more than the faculty to combine and fuse the remembered. When a fine novel, or picture, or building, or symphony is the outcome, we hail it as a revelation of one of man's supreme *kinds* of achievement—a work of art; and Science gladly responds 'Amen'. The attempt in a child is usually dismissed as yet another kind of playing, though—in spite of his limitations—he may have faced it, as we shall see, with complete gravity and with a like

Early One Morning

delight and 'joy in the making'. 'Methinks', wrote Thoreau, 'my present experience is nothing; my past experience is all in all. I think that no experience which I have to-day comes up to or is comparable with, the experiences of my boyhood. . . . In youth, before I lost any of my senses, I can remember that I was all alive, and inhabited my body with inexpressible satisfaction; both its weariness and its refreshment were sweet to me. . . . I wondered if a mortal had ever known what I knew. I looked in books for some recognition of a kindred experience, but, strange to say, I found none. Indeed, I was slow to discover that other men had had this experience. . . . With all your science can you tell how it is, and whence it is, that light comes into the soul?' And is not all true creative experience so illuminated?

And again:

'We seem but to linger in manhood to tell the dreams of our childhood, and they vanish out of memory ere we know the language. . . . There are as many strata at different levels of life as there are leaves in a book. Most men probably have lived in two or three. When on the higher levels we can remember the lower levels, but when on the lower we cannot remember the higher.'

'Very pretty but rather nebulous,' may be the matter-of-fact comment. 'There have always been Peter Pans—children who have never grown up; and Thoreau perhaps was one of these. But it is not the green-room of childhood that is of serious account in this world; only the great stage of Man.' Thoreau, however, has his own defence. The children will soon be given grown-up parts. And are even the matter-of-fact sure of their own 'level'? It must of course be admitted that the value and significance of any particular memory depend not on the age to which it refers, but on whose it is and what it is concerned with. This of course is no less true of early memories. That men of genius have deemed their own not only worth the trouble of recording, but of sovereign interest in themselves has already been made clear. And one of their reasons for this may be that suggested by Mr. Herbert Read in *The Innocent Eye*:

'The echoes of my [later] life which I find in my early child-hood are too many to be dismissed as vain coincidences; but it is perhaps my conscious life which is the echo, the only real experi-

156

Doings

ences in life being those lived with a virgin sensibility—so that we only hear a tone once, only see a colour once, see, hear, touch, taste and smell everything but once, the first time. . . .'

How many 'real experiences'—*onces*—of *this* nature can we ourselves retrieve?—such 'meetings' as our first winter snowdrop or February crocus, the liquid sweetness of wallflowers beneath a sunny window, the touch of linen, silk or velvet, of human hand or breast or cheek; the triumph of mastering even a button—Prythee, let *me* undo this button! Or a sentence of three syllables; the clutch of a coveted object; light, sunbeam, moon-shadow; rebuke, comfort; loved one gone, loved one come back? And what of dread and terror, grief and desolation? A host of such events have been among our earliest experiences. It is the definite placing of them that memory usually forbids. Vanished beyond hope of recovery must remain for all but a very few of us the *first* pure perception of any now-familiar object or feeling, the sheer primal miracle that made it at its moment for the first time ours. Even concerning much later perceptions the most delicate of efforts may be in vain. But now and then, and as if by enchantment, the little theatre of the mind may surrender *the* very image of something—of a vast placid grazing carthorse, let us say, a coarse-ridged oak-bough seen very close, a towering field of buttercups, one's own mother's face or attitude at a particular instant—as one saw it *then*. It is an instantaneous revelation of the abyss that divides us from our childhood.

There are simple onces and complex onces. The convolvulus of my childhood had not the wondrous blue of Mr. Kendon's succory flower. The succory had neither the waxen huelessness nor symmetry of the convolvulus. What the two flowers, apart from their beauty, had in common was a child's instant acceptance, and a delight in them worthy of their marvel. For even if this were my first convolvulus, it must instantly have evoked many memories, and one secret part of its influence was due to its coming upon me in a certain mood. Had I that morning been miserable or running away from home or in a frenzy of fear, how different a 'once' its effect would have been. Such is the sorcery of emotion. One hardly knows which situation is the more inviting to analyse—Titania's infatuation for ass-headed Bully Bottom, or *vice versa*. Comparatively simple '*onces*' even quite late in life can be a reviv-

157

ing reward; and in the ordinary daily round need not be very infrequent. Only this morning, for insignificant example, I noticed for the first time when pouring a little milk into a cup how like the trill of a bird was the noise of the fall of its last interrupted cascade.

The very earliest years of childhood then cannot but have been pressed down and running over with fresh, novel, vivid, sharp, engrossing, dumbfounding sensations, perceptions and imaginings. And the first twelve will deposit perhaps the richest part of that mysterious mental sediment we call the subconscious, whereon the very tap-roots of the judgement and the imagination feed. No wonder then if *memories* of childhood (for the rememberer at any rate) usually have a glint, a glamour, a bright particular sharpness, a reanimation all but peculiar to themselves.

'I know nothing', says Thomas Holcroft, 'that tends so much as the anecdotes of childhood, when faithfully recorded, to guide the philosopher through that very abstruse but important labyrinth, the gradations that lead to the full stature, peculiar form, temperament, character and qualities of the man.'

Such memories afford, says George Crabb, 'the purest of enjoyments and serve the noblest of purposes; the recollection of all the minute incidents of childhood is a more sincere pleasure than any which the present moment can afford'. And George Crabb was the author not of *Tiny Tales for Teeny Tots,* or *Rollicking Rhymes for Rampageous Little Rascals,* or *Sparrow Pasty,* but of that solid and invaluable book, *English Synonyms Explained.* And it is Autobiography, of course, collections of reminiscences, and, less fruitfully, Lives and Memoirs, that are the treasury of such recollections.

PART II

★

EARLY
MEMORIES

CHAPTER XIII

AUTOBIOGRAPHY

★

1. *'Then I turned about and cried, "But who am I?"'*

In *A Tale of Two Cities*, that precise and gentle-minded old man, three years from his eightieth birthday, Jarvis Lorry, returns to *his* childhood:

'Sydney turned his eyes again upon the fire, and, after a silence of a few moments, said:

' "I should like to ask you:—Does your childhood seem far off? Do the days when you sat at your mother's knee seem days of very long ago?"

'Responding to his softened manner, Mr. Lorry answered:

' "Twenty years back, yes; at this time of my life, no. For, as I draw closer and closer to the end, I travel in the circle, nearer and nearer to the beginning. It seems to be one of the kind smoothings and preparings of the way. My heart is touched now by many remembrances that had long fallen asleep, of my pretty young mother (and I so old!), and by many associations of the days when what we call the World was not so real with me, and my faults were not confirmed in me." '

There is a touch of fondness here, but Mr. Lorry's conviction not only that in the minds of the aged memories of childhood are revived, but also that they themselves draw near to the beginning again, is often suggested in autobiography. As soon as we are grown up indeed—whenever that may be—does not our own childhood seem very long ago'? *Memories* of it appear also to be remote, but in a different sense. They, however frequently or seldom recalled, are not affected by the passing of time. The image of 'the house where I was born', that is, if we can remember any

161

part of it, when it is revived in memory at the age of sixty is in appearance precisely the same as when it was recalled at the age of thirty-five. The rememberer changes and decays—or, rather, his body does. Not so the memory—that can only vanish, and may return. Mr. Lorry does not say how he awoke his 'many remembrances' from their sleep. Would that Dickens had enabled him to do so. But in thus awakening them he had become sharply aware at the same time of the 'place' referred to by Vaughan and of the World 'that is too much with us'.

In a critical and comparative study entitled *The Autobiography*, published in 1909, Miss Anna Robeson Burr surveys about 270 examples of this art. Of these, eighteen were the work of poets, nine of novelists, and seven of playwrights. This, as Miss Burr suggests, may seem a small proportion of men of creative imagination, who, we might suppose, are more likely than most of us to be interested in themselves, as well as in their own works. Of the rest, thirty-three were written by philosophers and men of science, nine by historians, and thirteen by statesmen. Twenty-six examples which Miss Burr groups together as the autobiographies of 'general literary workers' may be given a place about midway between these two classes. Monarchs, thirteen; great personages, twenty-one; lawyers, eight; soldiers, fourteen; rogues and impostors, five (Ashe, Bonneval, De Choisy, Ireland, Psalmanazar); police agents, four; actors, eleven; and freaks, four (Beers, Borulaski, Colburn, Viterbi)—these combine to make up Miss Burr's grand total.

Many of her authors give the reasons that persuaded them to look into themselves and write. Self-study and science were the incentives of between sixty and seventy of them. Fifteen of them set to work at the request of friends. Over fifty wrote for amusement, or, which is much the same thing, to recall the past. Forty-two had at heart their witness to religion. Twelve winningly confess that they have written their own lives because no one else was likely to do it for them. Only one gave the need of money as his reason—Galt, who apologized at the same time for being no gentleman in writing such a book at all! Another suggested pride of birth as his occasion, a third the study of insanity, a fourth the revival of his Latin. Thirty-seven volunteered no reason whatever. Twenty-six had their children and posterity chiefly in mind;

Autobiography

and De Quincey—solitary snarl of silver trumpet—hoped 'to emblazon the Power of Opium'. As we have seen, Miss Burr did not confine herself to autobiographies in English, but ranged over the civilized world and many centuries; and this grateful reference to her book can give but the feeblest notion of its scope and interest.

Among her subjects, who had their descendants in mind, are Benjamin Franklin and Charles Darwin. And it was a tragic lapse in the affairs of men that Darwin should have written the Life of the Earth Worm but never a *complete* book entitled 'Myself'. Even in the fascinating company of his potted earth-worms, our eyes continually stray towards the observer, as he experiments, red-hot poker or bassoon in hand. But this he never for a moment intended. His few pages of autobiography, a *Sketch* written for the sake of his children, are therefore invaluable, and not least for the fact that while apparently he recounts his early memories not for his own sake but only for theirs—as definite facts in the world of nature, that is, just as the various climbing devices of plants are facts—we ourselves treasure them chiefly because they are *his*. Clear and concise expression, he confesses, was always a difficulty to him. Yet, consummately simple and matter-of-fact though the prose of his recollections may be, Vaughan's radiance glints over them none the less. He turned his mind to them, he remarks, 'as if I were a dead man in another world looking back at my own life. Nor have I found this difficult, for life is nearly over with me. ...' He was born in 1809, and when he wrote these words he was sixty-seven.

Having 'emerged from the poverty and obscurity' in which he was 'born and bred' and had in much been happy, Benjamin Franklin also thought well to let his posterity share the 'conducing means' of his so doing. Such was that happiness too that, even though he were forbidden to 'change some sinister accidents and events in his life', and could have it all over again, *that* would be his choice. Hume agreed with him, but only in respect to his last illness! How many of us would reply with an emphatic No to this proposal? Apart from this impracticality, Franklin continues, 'the next thing most like living one's life over again seems to be a recollection of that life, and to make that recollection as durable as possible by putting it down in writing'. He freely confesses that

Early One Morning

in so doing he would gratify his vanity; but then he himself gave vanity 'fair quarter' wherever he met with it. Is not *praise* the sweetest kind of music? Indeed, 'it would not be altogether absurd if a man were to thank God for his vanity among the other comforts of life'.

All this is completely reassuring. But what of other memoirists? In view of reasons and justifications so many and so various for the writing of it, can we safely depend on the information concerning childhood and children derived from autobiography— judging by the specimens of it already given? Only with circumspection. The deceits of sentiment and the enchantment of the distant view may be no less misleading than psychological graphs and the illusion of the 'average'. Nevertheless with so much material available it is easy to compare similar memories one with another and these with our own, and so test if not verify them. The general practice certainly suggests that autobiographers intend the truth and nothing but the truth, even if in the attempt to elucidate they amplify. The whole truth remains beyond their scope even if it were within their design; and the reasons they offer for exposing their lives to the public gaze may indeliberately divulge on which side any bias is likely to be.

Pure interest in self (at Thoreau's divers 'levels') is one of the chief motives for self-revelation, though the degree and kind of interest sharply varies. The ramifications of egotism may affect even the chapters devoted to a writer's childhood. But since these usually betoken so peaceful and solacing a reunion it is of fondness rather than falsity we must beware. The butterfly (or death's-head moth) has returned to the cocoon; the wide and busy river to its prattling source; the hot frequented afternoon to daybreak. There is little need to excuse or explain the things of childhood; nothing to prove, no vanity to be hurt, even pride has a smiling face. Since, however, autobiography has usually been the work of those who in life have been in some degree unusually gifted, of men with genius, or of a strange or prominent or illustrious destiny, it may far from faithfully reflect humanity at large. Nevertheless the exceptional, although it excludes, may illuminate the normal*. It will reflect it at any rate a good deal more faithfully than can the common run of fiction or the newspapers. Few of us perhaps are keenly self-conscious or mind-conscious, or acutely curious concerning

Autobiography

the inner workings of the mind, senses, intellect, memory and so forth. What am I? Whence am I come? Whither am I going? What *is* this place? Are these things *real*? What is the precise relation between myself and the not-self? Was I always, shall I be for ever? *Can* I be merely of the Now? Such questions as these are perhaps brooded over more frequently than we suspect. But in general they are asked in private, and adjourned.

2. 'As traceless as a thaw of bygone snow.'

But if one sits down late in life, when the candles are burning low, to share as candidly as possible one's past with strangers, *some* deliberate attention to them is hardly avoidable. And memories of childhood tend to quicken them. Its beginning, we realize, was no less mysterious than the long day's journey now seems, and than its end promises to be.

Not that autobiography usually announces these problems. Allusion is seldom made even to what is after all one of the strangest facts in life—that most of its experiences have been shed as irrevocably as the leaves in Vallombrosa; that of the garish patchwork of childhood only a few shreds can be recovered from Memory's museum. Yet one after another these memoirists blithely profess, *My first memory* ... or, having apparently made no effort to fish a little longer, *My earliest memory* ... and even more remarkable, *The only thing I can recall up to the age of.* ... The writer may then proceed to record a complex experience in his childhood with so eager and lively a clarity that a rather dismal fact may escape our attention, namely, that what is recorded has twice suffered burial—the child referred to had become entombed in the adult who in old age held the retrospective pen which he himself, a few years afterwards, was compelled to surrender to the grave. Many memoirists too are careless in their statements and very few of them are heedful with their dates. In this William Hutton's *Life* is exemplary. It is brief, though he himself died at the age of ninety-two in 1815, and a separate section is devoted to each year of it.

He recalls four several memories relating to his second year (during which he set fire to his frock and petticoats, and crossed the Trent in a barge—the weather 'serene', the water 'clear' and 'deep'); two in the third ('I saw my mother in the pangs of labour');

165

Early One Morning

six in the fourth ('My eldest aunt . . . was taken sick, and I saw her breathe her last'); four in the fifth; two in the sixth and four in the seventh. For most of these he must have depended solely on his own memory, not on reminders from other sources. And a proof that life is not necessarily either fuller or richer in its later years than it is in its earlier, is suggested by the fact that while the entries for his fourth year occupy three whole pages of his book, those for the ten years after his thirty-third birthday average about one page each. Yet this decade includes references to the birth of his first daughter, of his two sons, the purchase of the 'paper warehouse' which founded his 'ample fortune', the death of his father, and a transit of Venus: 'She appeared a small black spot, the size of a large fly or bee, moving over the face of the sun.' If we ourselves were compelled to build up our past with bricks but no straw, memories *sans* revivers, how would the house of life we could so erect compare with his?

As to any system of recalling childhood, the general practice is to accept the already given and to range at random from that. But more is likely to be retrieved, perhaps, if instead of asking: What is my earliest memory? or: What can I recall of my third or fifth or seventh year? one enquires instead—for example: Which is *one* of the first churches I ever saw?—or sea, or island, or brook, or parrot, or widow, or fine gown, or birthday party, or set of chessmen, or fire-irons, or copper? Having recaptured a church it may revive a remote verger, or tombstones, or bells; or hymn, or anthem, or prayer, or mental rebellion against a statement from the pulpit with which—hot penny in hand for the plate—we flatly refused to concur. The merit of this method is that we thus afford memory a definite peg for her garlands. What we need, like the spider, are salient points in the past whereto we may be able to attach an inviting web, though we may have to lie in wait a long time, and our catch may be scanty.

Another curious fact is that few self-students who have written of their own lives express any particular surprise either at the nature or the quality of their early memories, or make any attempt to analyse them. Robert Southey had an unusually large repertory, but none of a kind more unusual than he himself was unusual as a poet. And he refers with amusement to St. Nicolas de Huë.

'The popular saint of the democratic cantons in Switzerland,

Autobiography

St. Nicolas de Huë (to whom I paid my respects in his own church at Saxeln), remembered his own birth, knew his mother and the midwife as soon as he was born, and never forgot the way by which he was taken to be christened, nor the faces of the persons who were present at that ceremony. But he was an extraordinary child, who, though he neither danced nor sung nor preached before he was born (all which certain other saints are said to have done), had revelations in that state, and saw the light of Heaven before he came into the light of day. . . .'

Southey is chaffing the saints, as easy an amusement as chaffing the 'scientists'. Nevertheless, if we consider the question without prejudice, what would be odd, if it were not universal, is not that St. Nicolas should have remembered his own birth, but that we should have forgotten ours. Apart from such a feat as recognizing one's mother's midwife, we cannot invoke the faintest recollection of being weaned, even though in bitterness and sorrow and mystery that experience must have resembled being exiled from Eden by an angel that until then had been our most natural joy and grace. St. Nicolas, whether we believe what is reported of him or not, is merely asserting that he actually recalls what such poets as Vaughan divined. When, says Bolingbroke, we seem to be taught, we are only put in mind of what we knew in a former state. 'As far back', says Thoreau, 'as I can remember I have unconsciously referred to the experiences of a previous state of existence.' 'Would truth dispense,' says Sir Thomas Browne, 'we could be content, with Plato, that knowledge were but remembrance, that intellectual acquisition were but reminiscential evocation, and new impressions but the colouring of old stamps which stood pale in the soul before.' Pleasant to tongue and mind are those last words after the polysyllables that precede them. And the charming metaphor (with its evocation of boyhood's treasured clear-green and crimson-lake St. Vincent's, St. Helena's, and dark, three-cornered, blue Cape of Good Hope's!) might alone convert one to Plato.

3. *'My tender years must vouch my truth.'*

And what of Henry James's glimpse of Paris when he was little more than a year old? There was no hour, says Mr. Percy Lubbock, in which he was not alive with the whole of his sensibility;

Early One Morning

he could scarcely persuade himself that he might have had time for more. If, too, in railway carriage or omnibus, we attentively watch a baby of eight months, who is wide awake and at ease, we shall find little reason for supposing that this few minutes in a cab in Paris in 1844 was the less pregnant for Henry James than any that succeeded them. Nevertheless a glimpse so early is exceedingly rare. Out of 270 autobiographers, Miss Anna Robeson Burr tells us, only three could recall any experience before the age of two, and only thirteen before the age of three*.

To take a few examples: Ruskin, Southey, Harriet Martineau, Frances Power Cobbe, Thomas Holcroft, and William Hutton flower freely; Joseph Priestley, John Stuart Mill, Lord Brougham (who talked fluently when he was about thirty-six weeks old, and showed, says his mother, a marked attention to everything he saw long before that) and Mrs. Oliphant are scanty even in buds. In our own day, Mr. John Drinkwater recalls little before he was nine years old except a highly dramatic event concerning a hated female oppressor, a starched white frock, and a pail of soapy water. Sir William Rothenstein devotes two packed pages of his *Men and Memories* to the years before he was seven—vivid glimpses of soldiers, a circus, a nurse, and the pattern of a carpet; of a black cabinet 'hand-painted' with flowers and birds; a small front garden, with a laburnum tree near the gate; and a stone 'ash-pit' where rubbish was thrown. About ten pages of *Theatre Street* suffice for Madame Karsavina's first five years—including precise recollections of her father at work on his water-colours; an early experiment in 'toddling'; the taste of tonic birch-sap that she watched jetting out into an earthenware jug; and remorse at making fun of a harmless lunatic she sometimes met when walking by a canal near the family flat in St. Petersburg. And again the familiar tribute: 'A few things were impressed so deeply on my mind that even now they stand out clear and have not lost all their magic.'

In *My World as in My Time* (1862-1906) Sir Henry Newbolt—delighted at the discovery that one of the very earliest of his memories proved to be accurate in every particular above sixty years after it had been recorded—devotes some thirty out of three hundred pages to the recollections of his first decade; recollections as endeared to him as they are endearing to his readers. As

Autobiography

with Lord Berners, Mr. Frank Kendon's first ten years brim a complete book. No record, however, of early childhood of any date or country or language is likely to transcend in abundance Serge Aksakoff's scrupulous and inexhaustible *Years of Childhood*— a volume of 340 pages, concerned solely with the first eight years of his life.

Before quoting further examples of memories of childhood, which will be most conveniently arranged in accordance with their content rather than with a view to any unusual quality they may possess, or to the age at which the experiences they relate to occurred, I will venture to give in detail one of my own. It has no particular interest but I can vouch for its accuracy. It is obviously at first hand, can be submitted to a close examination, and so may suggest what kind of quite unintentional glosses and alloys are apt to creep in. It has been recalled several times, but, so far as I am aware, without any consequent change in its appearance, and it relates to an event which occurred when I was not more than four years of age, and, perhaps, but lately three.

I do not see myself, but *am* actually walking—in a vague open place, and to the left of a nursemaid who is propelling an iron-tyred, three-wheeled perambulator. My right hand is resting on the iron support of its handle. In this perambulator, beneath an ample leather apron, reclines—though I can see nothing of her except the frill of a bonnet—an infant sister. This detail is dubious; the vehicle may have been empty; the 'frill' linen. My nurse is talking to a soldier. Not only am I aware that he is a soldier, but also that she should not be thus improving the shining hour. The day is bright, but neither sunny nor hot, and I detect no *colour*, neither the green of the grass, the blue or grey of the sky, that of the wood of the perambulator or my nurse's clothes, nor her attendant swain's artillery blue picked out either with red or yellow. For an artilleryman of some kind he almost certainly was. At this moment I am suddenly startled—alarmed and shattered would be nearer the mark— by an explosive sensation as if icy cold or scalding hot water had been dashed between my shoulderblades. I stare about me in amazement and dismay and see at some little distance men holding shining metal objects. They, I realize, were the origin of the shock. It is a brass band; and it has begun to play. I recollect nothing— and no one—else, am aware of no voices, or of any experience

Early One Morning

preceding this moment, or following it. And yet its only *once* apparently was this crash of brazen instruments, the sensation of which I attributed (since I did not recognize it as a *sound*) not to my ears but to my spinal column.

Yet even this sensation cannot have been positively new to me —apart from its volume. We can be outrageously startled by an unexpected noise even when we hear it for the hundredth time. My own wailing, my infant sister's, the tinkling of a Victorian piano, a malign cook whose favourite aria was *Her bright smile haunts me still*—such strains as these, apart from what was no doubt the habitual morning procession, including perhaps the 'sodger boy', must have been already familiar. It is unlikely even that I was then censorious for the first time! I was aware his company was forbidden, and was 'not amused'.

There is a facetious rhyme of Locker-Lampson's about 'a nurse called Ann', but it contains more than a hint of poetic licence; and Tom Hood's tragedy appears *not* to be autobiographical:

> 'I sawe a Mayd sitte on a Bank,
> Beguiled by Wooer fayne and fond;
> And whiles His flatterynge Vowes She drank,
> Her Nurselynge slipt within a Pond!'

The reader will, I hope, forgive my spending so much space on anything so trivial—a mere vignette of memory, isolated, insulated, instantaneous. But if we carefully examine any equally definite and detached early memory, it will prove, I think, to have these characteristics. It is an image of something that was focused, observed, attended to. It is now immutable (if we do not tamper with it), out of time, un-infantile, of something realized and comprehended—even if it were not fully explained; and it is momentary. It represents a minute cross-section of human experience, and of complex experience, and may draw into its orbit what was antecedent to it—an infinitely swift survey to explain it *now*. When recording early memories, however, we incline not only to locate them definitely in time and place, but also to explain, rationalize, embroider and amplify them with after-knowledge, to romanticize a little and make them more 'childish' than in origin they actually were, and so to lose the very crux that caused their retention. The words *first* and *earliest*, in any case, must be accepted with extreme caution.

4. '*I can only say, I* AM—*A phrase, a word, that hath no rhyme.*'

One of these so-called firsts, and a particularly significant one, which occasionally occurs in autobiography, is the access of self-consciousness. As an experience it must have been preceded by a host of firsts, such as 'My first sensation of my hand' or 'of light' or 'of a human shape' or 'of a chair', and so forth. And, apart from the extreme difficulty this might entail of defining the term consciousness, I know of no such first as: 'My first consciousness of consciousness. . . .' Consciousness itself, in Myers' words, is a recent, perfunctory and superficial thing; and 'our knowledge of hidden processes of mentation is still in its infancy'.

'I stood one afternoon, a very young child, at the house door,' says Jean Paul Richter, 'when all at once that inward consciousness *I am a ME*, came like a flash of lightning from Heaven, and has remained ever since.' As if in the radiance of a flash of lightning we ourselves share his recorded moment—its intense hush and the beauty of the face of the child rapt by the wonder of this discovery. Mr. Gerald Bullett has admirably analysed a similar moment of self-realization.

'I come upon a four-year-old child standing alone in a sunlit country lane . . . the summer sky arching over him. . . . The moment . . . has nothing at all of drama or poignancy . . . nor could I hope to express in words . . . the meaning it holds for me. But if I shut my eyes, and hold myself very still, I no longer see that child: I *am* that child. The chalky road is hard under my feet and brilliant to my eyes; I feel the sun on my hands and face, and the warm air on my shins. . . . Except for this aloneness, this sense of *me*, it is perhaps a purely animal or sensual experience, and it occupies, as I conjecture, the merest point in time, a fraction of a second.'

Lord Berners in his *First Childhood* adds 'hitherto' to his 'first', and recalls not only his surroundings at the time and its effect on them, but his age—three and a half years. 'I can remember', he says, 'very vividly the first time I became aware of my existence; how for the first time I realized that I was a sentient human being

Early One Morning

in a perceptible world. The conditions in which this epoch-making event in my mental career took place could not possibly have been more trivial. I was merely standing beside a table in the library at Arley, when, all at once, what had hitherto been a blurred background became distinct, just as when someone who is short-sighted puts on spectacles. Objects and individuals assumed definite shapes, grouping themselves into an ordered whole, and from that moment I understood that I formed part of it—without, of course, a full premonition of all that this exactly entailed.'

This vital crisis, by no means always alluded to or always either pure or simple, may be long deferred. Mr. Romilly John, for example, at about the age of seven—*twice* 'three and a half'—was 'still', he believes, 'un-self-conscious', even though he was then privily inserting at the end of the Lord's Prayer a sharply Them-conscious petition that his mother might be persuaded to wear 'proper clothes' and that neither of his parents should be permitted to appear at the forthcoming school sports.

To what extent, we may pause to enquire, does this early consciousness of self depend on the consciousness of others? We might assume indeed that the former must precede the latter. Until *self* is realized—this living, feeling, space-occupying, unique and isolated creature which, as Jean Paul discovered, is ME—how, one speculates, can a child conclude: '*This* is quite other than, and yet delightfully or distressingly, *like* me! It is a fellow creature.' Or is the inference from objective husk to subjective kernel?

One of my own very early, dismal, but, in the event, joyous memories, appears to have been an acute combination of awareness of self *and* of others. I am standing on a footstool at a table, spoon in hand, and a little plate of translucent but detested jelly is under my chin. The room resembles that in Blake's drawing of the solitary child. It is sombre, lamplit (I think), airless and obscure. Two silent, very gentle and faded old ladies are seated in armchairs on either side of a fireplace. They are smiling at me. I am in utter misery. The door on my right opens suddenly. A servant appears. No seraph could have been more welcome. I have been 'called for'.

Here, it is the opening door that is the fulcrum-memory. Was this then the first access of self-consciousness? Hardly so, since I can recall a little group of young faces—schoolgirls, I fancy—smiling down on me in *admiration*!—the feminine kind that never

Autobiography

fails an infant. And that can hardly but have been before I could talk. But there is no means of making certain.

These groping and tentative remarks may perhaps have entailed a needless *invention* of difficulties, the making of a mountain out of a molehill. None the less a problem is here involved; even though it is no bigger than a molehill, and whatever its solution may be. To most recorders of childhood even the molehill is invisible. Here, for example, are four asseverated *firsts*, and it would be difficult to find as many witnesses so dissimilar to whom we should listen with more interest, and follow with more attention.

First, Sir Walter Scott. 'It is at Sandy-Knowe', he tells us, 'the residence of my paternal grandfather . . . that I have the first consciousness of existence; and I recollect distinctly that my situation and appearance were a little whimsical. Among the odd remedies recurred to to aid my lameness, someone had recommended that so often as a sheep was killed for the use of the family, I should be stripped, and swathed up in the skin, warm as it was flayed from the carcase of the animal. In this Tartar-like habiliment I well remember lying upon the floor of the little parlour in the farmhouse, while my grandfather, a venerable old man with white hair, used every excitement to make me try to crawl. I also distinctly remember the late Sir George MacDougal of Makerstoun, father of the present Sir Henry Hay MacDougal, joining in this kindly attempt. He was, God knows how, a relation of ours, and I still recollect him in his old-fashioned military habit (he had been colonel of the Greys), with a small cocked hat, deeply laced, an embroidered scarlet waistcoat, and a light-coloured coat, with milk-white locks tied in a military fashion, kneeling on the ground before me, and dragging his watch along the carpet to induce me to follow it. The benevolent old soldier and the infant wrapped in his sheepskin would have afforded an odd group to uninterested spectators. This must have happened about my third year, for Sir George MacDougal and my grandfather both died shortly after that period. . . .'

It is a vivacious picture, full of colour and detail, some of which, clearly, has been added in explanation. Yet again it is the memory of a moment, its focusing-point, the shining watch, since the two old gentlemen may well have been kneeling on the floor together.

173

Early One Morning

No women are present, and it is amusing that we are not finally told if the 'excitements' were successful. The question of *self-consciousness* is left a little dubious, though Scott's recollection of his 'appearance' in the sheepskin (a remedy which I have read somewhere was put into service when King Edward VII, then Prince of Wales, had typhoid fever) seems to suggest it. So too, do Wallace's earliest recollections of himself—as 'a little boy in short frocks and with bare arms and legs, playing with his brother and sisters, or sitting in his mother's lap listening' to fairy tales.

In the next picture, a sharp contrast with the serenity of Scott's, we must *imagine* the child's clothes—about the year 1821-2. The headstrong little creature is Queen Victoria.

'My earliest recollections are connected with Kensington Palace, where I can remember crawling on a yellow carpet spread out for that purpose—and being told that if I cried and was naughty my "Uncle Sussex" would hear me and punish me, for which reason I always screamed when I saw him! I had a great horror of *Bishops* on account of their wigs and aprons, but recollect this being partially got over in the case of the then Bishop of Salisbury . . . by his kneeling down and letting me play with his badge of Chancellor of the Order of the Garter.'

What Sir Walter Scott revelled in—in life as well as fiction, Queen Victoria in due season insisted on in actuality. Her series of vignettes is a peep into a pocket looking-glass, but is a reflection also—pomp, splendour, ceremony—similar to those in the vast gilded mirror of her long and supremely central life. The alarming 'wigs and aprons' and the starry blue-ribboned badge can hardly have been afterthoughts. Besides, Samuel Johnson was but a baby when he was touched for the King's evil by Queen Anne; and he retained a confused, but somehow a sort of solemn recollection of a lady in diamonds, and a long black hood. In what follows not only the colour of the royal liveries is mentioned, but a child's *respect* for them.

'I was brought up very simply, never had a room to myself till I was nearly grown up—always slept in my Mother's room till I came to the Throne. At Claremont, and in the small houses at the bathing-places, I sat, and took my lessons in my Governess's bedroom. . . . My Aunt, the Queen of Württemberg . . . came over, in the year '26, I think, and I recollect perfectly well seeing her drive through the Park in the King's carriage with red liveries and 4 horses, in a *Cap* and evening dress. . . .'

In 1826 she visited Windsor for the first time, to see George IV.

'When we arrived at the Royal Lodge the King took me by the hand, saying: "Give me your little paw." He was large and gouty but with a wonderful dignity and charm of manner. . . .

'We went . . . to Virginia Water, and met the King in his phaeton in which he was driving the Duchess of Gloucester, and he said "Pop her in", and I was lifted in and placed between him and Aunt Gloucester who held me round the waist. (Mamma was much frightened.) I was greatly pleased, and remember that I looked with great respect at the scarlet liveries, etc. . . . .'

'The font was of silver. . . . The old Duchess of Norfolk bare the child in a Mantle of purple velvet with a long train furred with Ermine. . . . The Godfather was the lord Archbishop of Canterbury. . . . And the child was named Elizabeth': a first-hand memory of her christening by the infant mistress of *that* ceremony would make a lively companion-piece.

Victoria was seven when, to her mother's horror and her own delight, she was thus perched up in the King's phaeton. What is most striking in her dramatization of these few brightly lit moments is the emphasis on the *I*. The child herself is easily first as a conspicuous object in her own memory.

Not so Harriet Martineau: 'I was carried down a flight of steep back stairs, and Rachel (a year and half older than I) clung to the nursemaid's gown, and Elizabeth was going before (still quite a little girl), when I put down my finger ends to feel a flat velvet button on the top of Rachel's bonnet. The rapture of the sensation was really monstrous, as I remember it now. Those were our mourning bonnets for a near relation; and this marks the date, proving me to have been only two years old.' There follows a *revived* recollection:

'My first recollections are of some infantile impressions which were in abeyance for a long course of years, and then revived in an inexplicable way—as by a flash of lightning over a far horizon in the night. There is no doubt of the genuineness of the remembrance, as the facts could not have been told me by any one else. I remember standing on the threshold of a cottage, holding fast by the doorpost, and putting my foot down, in repeated attempts

Early One Morning

to reach the ground. Having accomplished the step, I toddled (I
remember the uncertain feeling) to a tree before the door, and
tried to clasp and get round it; but the rough bark hurt my hands.
At night of the same day, in bed, I was disconcerted by the coarse
feel of the sheets—so much less smooth and cold than those at
home; and I was alarmed by the creaking of the bedstead when
I moved. It was a turn-up bedstead in a cottage, or small farmhouse at Carleton, where I was sent for my health, being a delicate
child. . . .'

In the opening sentences of *A Backward Glance* Mrs. Wharton
so accentuates this objective view of herself as a child—about four
years of age—that she refers to her as 'this little girl who bore my
name'. She records not only her first onset of 'self-consciousness'
and the birth of a sense of 'identity', but this is also her first recallable memory 'of anything':—

'It was on a bright day of midwinter, in New York. The little
girl who eventually became me, but as yet was neither me nor
anybody else in particular, but merely a soft anonymous morsel of
humanity—this little girl, who bore my name, was going for a
walk with her father. . . .

'She had been put into her warmest coat, and into a new and
very pretty bonnet, which she had surveyed in the glass with considerable satisfaction.'

So precise and ravishing a description of the white satin bonnet,
the 'gossamer veil of the finest white Shetland wool' and the rest
of this small siren's attire follows that when presently in the ice-
cold and exhilarating sea air of an almost parochial New York,
father and daughter meet Cousin Henry and his small boy Daniel,
the dénouement is clearly inevitable:—

'The little boy, who was very round and rosy, looked back with
equal interest; and suddenly he put out a chubby hand, lifted the
little girl's veil, and boldly planted a kiss on her cheek. It was the
first time—and the little girl found it very pleasant.'

'I . . . date', says Mrs. Wharton, 'from that hour the birth of the
conscious and feminine *me* in the little girl's vague soul. . . . This
is my earliest definite memory of anything happening to me; and
it will be seen that I was wakened to conscious life by the two
tremendous forces of love and vanity.' And yet what a mystery
remains the darkness of the long preceding years out of which

Autobiography

this one vivid recollection emerged! For even though Sleeping Beauty was *awakened* by Prince Charming, her dreams up to that moment must at least have seemed to be real.

Vanity, effervescent, sweet and heady*, and itself by no means a simple state of mind in a child, is, as Mrs. Wharton says, as powerful an aid to self-recognition as the juice of the love-in-idleness which Ariel's second-cousin Puck, girdling the earth in forty minutes, brought back to Oberon. And shame, of a self shrouded and clouded, is, as we shall see, yet another. This first realization, *I am a ME*, then, and it is impossible to say at how early an age it may occur, cannot but be an experience, whether revocable or not, of a peculiar intensity. But however early that 'first' may be, we should still be confronted with the question, where was the Self skulking before it was perceived? Did it, like Eve, present itself to an Adam—its discoverer—complete in all its parts? In what degree moreover self-consciousness may pervade the mind after its first onset, or it affects conduct, or strengthens the will, or is a hindrance to a wise simplicity is a difficult question. Can one go through life, as Jeremy Taylor suggests of another crisis, without its occurring at all?

'. . . To feed, and sleep, and move a little, and imperfectly, is the state of an unborn childe; and when it is born, he does no more for a good while; and what is it that shall make him to be esteemed to live the life of a man? and when shall that account begin? . . .

'Neither must we think, that the life of a Man begins when he can feed himself or walk alone, when he can fight, or beget his like; for so he is contemporary with a camel, or a cow; but he is first a man when he comes to a certain, steddy use of reason, according to his proportion, and when that is, all the world of men cannot tell precisely. Some are called *at age*, at fourteen, some at one and twenty, some never; but all men, late enough; for the life of a man comes upon him slowly and insensibly. . . .'

CHAPTER XIV

CLOTHES

★

1. *'For then I'm drest all in my best*
To walk abroad with Sallie.'

Even if an attractive child is not naturally self-conscious, a doting mother or nurse may vie to make it so. The looks of an adult—however keen the temptation—are seldom referred to in polite company and, had Little Red Riding Hood been nicelier brought up, she would have retired from her granny's bedside without comment, and possibly uneaten. A young and defenceless child, on the other hand, on appearing before a motley group of its elders, who even when seated are about twice its stature, is at once the centre and topic of conversation. The darling! The pet! The love! And a round dozen of adoring eyes are focused on the dangling golden ringlets, or the miniature of Papa's roman nose.

'Upon this promise did he raise his chin,
Like a dive-dapper peering through the wave,
Who, being look'd on, ducks as quickly in.'

The cheek pales, one leg sidles over the other, that chin seeks the shoulder, and a sidelong searching eye sums up each flatterer in turn. And there are worse ordeals than admiration—cajolings, coaxings, entreaties—and worst of all, perhaps, 'methods' of circumventing a diffident temperament. As to caresses, here is Fanny Kemble confessing herself in a letter of 1841:

'Dear Harriet,
'I must tell you a droll little incident that occurred the day of our leaving Bowood. As I was crossing the great hall, holding little

Clothes

F—— by the hand, Lord Lansdowne and Moore, who were talking at the other end, came towards me, and, while the former expressed kind regrets for our departure, Moore took up the child and kissed her, and set her down again, when she clutched hold of my gown, and trotted silently out of the hall by my side. As the great red door closed behind us, on our way to my rooms, she said, in a tone that I thought indicated some stifled sense of offended dignity, "Pray, Mamma, who was that little gentleman?"

'Now, Harriet, though Moore's fame is great, his stature is little, and my belief is that my three-year-old daughter was suffering under an impression that she had been taken a liberty with by some enterprising schoolboy. Oh, Harriet! think if one of his own Irish rosebuds of sixteen had received that poet's kiss. . . . I believe if he had bestowed it upon me . . . I might have made a little circle on that cheek, and dedicated it to Tom Moore and dirt for ever. . . .' And has not Miss Eva le Gallienne recently told of a kiss bestowed on her by Sara Bernhardt and similarly treasured?

It is worse than dangerous to disagree with Fanny Kemble, but I doubt if the little gentleman's age had anything to do with the affront. Even a Tom Moore's insulting kisses however may be more endurable than being *made* amusing. In a letter to a friend in 1796 Southey declares that at the age of two his feelings were very acute: 'They used to amuse themselves by making me cry at sad songs and dismal stories'—the Death of the Lady, Billy Pringle's Pig, 'Three children sliding on the ice'. He would beg them not to proceed, he says, and adds: 'I cannot now hear a melancholy tale in silence, but I have learned to whistle.'

Flattery of the young is so usual that it is remarkable that a child with a 'fine head' manages to keep the brains in it unaddled, and that a charmer of five does not perish of flattery. And what wonder if children become vain? 'I have next to nothing to say', admits Thomas Huxley in his reminiscences, 'about my childhood'. But included in his 'next to nothing' is a recollection which almost every 'sweetly pretty' child must have shared—an early and protracted gaze into a looking-glass followed by a sigh, and, 'Oh, what a cherub am I!'

'In later years, my mother, looking at me almost reproachfully, would sometimes say: "Ah! you were such a pretty boy!" whence I had no difficulty in concluding that I had not fulfilled my early

179

Early One Morning

promise in the matter of looks. In fact, I have a distinct recollection of certain curls, of which I was vain, and of a conviction that I closely resembled that handsome courtly gentleman, Sir Herbert Oakley, who was vicar of our parish, and who was as a god to us country folk, because he was occasionally visited by the then Prince George of Cambridge.'

But however long and languishing the stare into the glass, the details of the image in it may fade out of mind. A memoirist may mention his infant petticoats and yet forget being breeched. Even the sharpest of experiences may fail to record the slightest detail of the clothes that accompanied it—though it would be an odd bride who forgot her orange-blossom. Clothes, then, though most children may revile their Sunday best, and most small boys abhor bear's grease and party gear, are not often mentioned in auto-biography. Nevertheless a child's pleasure in silks and laces, in ribbons and velvet, in colour and finery more closely resembles an appetite than a taste. And even the ridicule or worse of other children does not necessarily root it out. Heedless of all warnings, when Joseph set out for the vale of Hebron to find his brothers, he went attired in his many-coloured patchwork coat.

> 'Joy to Philip! he this day
> Has his long coats cast away,
> And (the childish season gone),
> Puts the manly breeches on. . . .
> Sashes, rocks, to those that need 'em,
> Philip's limbs have got their freedom.
> He can run, or he can ride,
> And do twenty things beside,
> Which his petticoats forbad:
> Is he not a happy lad? . . .'

When Philip Hamerton, whose mother died in his infancy, was about six years old, his father, having decided to make a man of him, ordered his tailor to design him a suit. Left to his own de-vices, and realizing that this was an occasion to put away childish things, the tailor measured, cut, and fitted; and having dressed the child up in the finished garments, proudly presented him to his father and the ladies. He was greeted with roars of laughter—a strutting squire in miniature, in 'a green cut-away coat, a yellow

Clothes

waistcoat, and green trousers, the whole adorned with gilt buttons'. The laughter over, his father forbade him ever to wear these 'beautiful clothes' again. 'Even to this day I am capable of regretting that suit.'

Louis Spohr tells us that he was rewarded by his parents for his first composition with a gala suit 'consisting of a red jacket with steel buttons, yellow breeches, and laced boots with tassels'. For this 'I had long prayed in vain'. William Cowper, in one of the truest, simplest, and loveliest poems ever written about childhood, recalls that when he was six he was drawn to school every morning 'along the public way' by a gardener named Robin, in a 'bauble coach', a velvet cap on his head, and enwrapped in a warm scarlet mantle. John Keats at the same age sallied off to Edmonton for his first day at school, tucked up in his father's gig beside his brother George, and attired in a frilled collar, a tasselled cap, and a short jacket—its buttons of mother-of-pearl and as big as half-crowns. His reception in the playground is not described. But even if he was utterly out of the mode, there showed under the cap 'a brisk, winning face', and he was already a bonny fighter.

Mundus, in the old poem, gives Dalyaunce whom he nicknames Wanton 'garments gaye' to wear. And it was not merely of tassels that William of Wykeham disapproved. His first seventy scholars at Winchester, in age between eight and twelve, were to be not only of good behaviour, apt to study, and well versed in reading, plain-song and the *Ars Minor* of old Donatus, but also staid and sober in dress and bearing—a plain gown and hood, no colours pied or striped, no shoe-peaks, no red or green garters, or knots or tassels to their hoods. And Charity, however kind, has seldom when children are concerned revelled in colour, except blue and scarlet—a preference for scarlet, according to Ruskin, being evidence of a noble nature.

Edgar Allan Poe was a handsome child, with luminous dark grey eyes, and long dark brown hair. When his devoted foster-mother, Mrs. Allan, took him 'calling' in Richmond, Virginia, he is said to have accompanied her in a peaked purple velvet cap with a gold tassel, from which his dark curls flowed down over an ample tucker descending into baggy trousers of yellow nankeen or silk pongee, and buckled shoes. He used to recite, and was rewarded with sweetened wine and water. There is a tragic picture

Early One Morning

of him in later years, when his customary wear was as funereal as Hamlet's, declaiming *The Raven* to anybody who cared to listen to him in a newspaper office.

William Hutton's 'best suit' in his fifth year was finished off with a cocked hat and a knobbed walking stick; and he resented to some purpose the snatching off of the cocked hat by a buxom young woman merely in fun. Though Robert Southey as a child was tall for his age, his aunt, Miss Tyler, 'would not suffer' him to be breeched until he was six; and then, on 'highdays and holydays', he was pranked up in a costume of nankeen trimmed with green fringe—called a *jam*. The *jam* in pyjamas, says the dictionary, is from the same Hindoo original, but Southey's 'jam'—both word and garment—became obsolete about 1793.

Fashions change—as Disraeli discovered when he made his first speech in the House of Commons—and for males young and old during the last century they changed steadily towards the drab. Most small boys in the 'eighties were doomed sooner or later—Etons, velveteens, Vandyke collars, sailor-suits apart—to the kind of clothes described by Mr. Forrest Reid in *Apostate* as his wear when he chaperoned his elder sister.

'Dressed in a dark blue jersey, with a broad white linen collar turned down outside it, and blue serge shorts (rather wide in the leg, because they had been manufactured by my mother out of somebody else's old trousers), I would accompany her proudly....'

There is safety and freedom for the young in old clothes, and the comfort of the familiar. So stubbornly attached was I in my childhood to an old 'polo' cap that I can remember one evening having it still on my head when I stepped into my bath; and once, owing no doubt to indolence rather than absent-mindedness, I was discovered in bed in my boots!

2. *'Love, naked boy, has nothing on his back.'*

Pictures of little girls of the same period, with *their* boots and sashes and stockings and flounces and manes of hair, are curiously dejecting; fifty years further back nursery fashions are not only antique but amusing. At the moment it appears to be generally agreed that the less young children have on the better they look.

182

Clothes

Maternal taste however is an unsafe arbiter in these matters. Schoolboys and schoolgirls, once broken in, soon become the willing slaves and tyrants of the queerest conventions. Yet young children of either sex may suffer for years from too singular a début. *Suffer* is, indeed, far too mild a word, though 'years' is literal enough; as is revealed by the misery caused to Alfred Russel Wallace even in his middle teens by the black calico sleeve-protectors which a thrifty mother compelled him to wear over the cuffs of his school jacket. The shame he felt, he says, at this indignity was 'perhaps the severest punishment I ever endured'. How anxious and bitter a business indeed—a gnawing fret and anxiety—shabby and scarecrow clothes may be to the lustiest of schoolboys is shown by the fact that no fewer than three of the few letters home appended to this volume are concerned with them. It must always have been so—from the days of our first aprons. Here is William Paston junior in the fifteenth century, writing from Eton, to his brother John.

'Also I beseche yow to sende me a hose clothe, one for the halydays of sum colore, and anothyr for the workying days, how corse so ever it be it makyth no matyr; and a stomechere, and ij schyrtes, and a peyer of sclyppers. And if it lyke yow that I may come with Alwedyr be watyr, and sporte me with yow in London a day or ij thys terme tyme, than ye may let all thys be tyl the tyme that I come, and than I wol telle yow when I schall be redy to come from Eton, by the grace of God, Whom have yow in Hys kepyng.'

Parents, well-meaning souls for the most part, preached at by spinsters and butts of the bachelor, are often heedless or obstinate in face of these difficulties. Having forgotten their own early woes they cannot realize that even to be too conspicuously clean may be misery to a child. There is the household budget to be taken into account, of course; but how many fond mammas realize that pretty corkscrew curls, kid gloves, home-made knickerbockers, or even a sleek top hat may temporarily condemn a beloved poppet to torture; a torture in these days less of the body maybe (as in the bad old days painted by Charles Lamb), than of the nerves and spirit. Hence perhaps in part the institution of the school uniform. 'We don't care what you look like so long as you look like Us.' Still, a novice can easily trespass over the margins of individual taste allowed even by that—and be persecuted.

183

Early One Morning

Juvenile traditions, whether rational or ridiculous, are first the curse and at last the dogmatic ritual of the young, and their influence is felt long before the appearance of the 'prison-house'. Who cannot recall the scandalized faces at a children's party over the misbehaviour of one of the guests? To flaunt apron-strings, to mope, to scratch, to snuffle, be sick! The rubrics, the rites, the initiations and the shibboleths! These are of course a happy hunting ground to the sharp and acid little creature who esteems herself a leader of nursery society and parades 'the last thing' in clothes or taboos or Nannies! Bantlings not yet halfway to their teens may be seen surveying one another with an eye as green and pitiless as Mrs. Grundy's.

As for the shame produced by self-consciousness, naked we came into the world and naked we may unabashedly appear before our fellows when we are fairly new to its odd commitments. But who would expect Adam's conviction after tasting the apple in a child only four years old brought up in the homeliest of circumstances? 'My mother,' says William Hutton, in his *Life*, 'unknown to me, came to Mountsorrel to fetch me home. The maid took me out of bed naked, except the shirt, and, having her left hand employed, could only spare the right, with which she dangled me down stairs by the arm, as a man does a new-purchased goose, her knee thumping against my back every step. I was exceedingly ashamed to appear before my mother, then a stranger, in that indecent state. . . .'

In her *Life and Letters of Robert Browning* Mrs. Sutherland Orr says, 'His sense of certain proprieties was extraordinarily keen. He told a friend that on one occasion, when the merest child, he had edged his way by the wall from one point of his bedroom to another, because he was not fully clothed, and his reflection in the glass could otherwise have been seen through the partly open door. . . .'

'Burningly it came on me all at once.' Much later in life and not clothed at all, Shelley so edged his furtive way behind a luncheon party. But there are less natural things to be ashamed of than nudity.

'To Day I pronounced a word which should never come out of a ladys lips it was that I called John a Impudent Bitch and Isabella afterwards told me that I should never say it even in a joke but she

Clothes

kindly for gave me because I said that I would not do it again I will tell you what I think made me in so bad a homour is I got 1 or 2 cups of that bad bad sina tea to Day.'

This diarist was six, but her penitence and apology were a good deal less juvenile than Samuel Pepys's on April 28th, 1667, when he was thirty-four:

'After dinner, by water, the day being mighty pleasant, and the tide serving finely, reading in Boyle's book of colours, as high as Barn Elms, and there took one turn alone, and then back to Putney Church, where I saw the girls of the schools, few of which pretty; and there I came into a pew, and met with little James Pierce, which I was much pleased at, the little rogue being very glad to see me: his master, Reader to the Church. Here was a good sermon and much company, but I sleepy, and a little out of order, at my hat falling down through a hole beneath the pulpit, which, however, after sermon, by a stick, and the help of the clerk, I got up again. . . .'

Not all children are 'kindly' forgiven their offences, even when 'bad bad sina tea' or feeling sleepy or being 'a little out of order' may have occasioned them. When they are not, the alternative punishment may resemble an earthquake in its effects even on a six-year-old. 'I got punished for lying', says Philip Hamerton, 'when my only fault was the common childish inability to explain.' I have known a child five or six years old after some hours of close confinement for saying that a servant had told a lie about him, on hearing from his remorseful parent that she had confessed to it, remark with complete composure: 'Yes, but I said so.' And here is Edmund Gosse:

'. . . It was about the date of my sixth birthday that I did something very naughty, some act of direct disobedience, for which my Father, after a solemn sermon, chastised me, sacrificially, by giving me several cuts with a cane. This action was justified, as everything he did was justified, by reference to Scripture—"Spare the rod and spoil the child." I suppose that there are some children, of a sullen and lymphatic temperament, who are smartened up and made more wide-awake by a whipping. It is largely a matter of convention, the exercise being endured (I am told) with pride by the infants of our aristocracy, but not tolerated by the lower classes. I am afraid that I proved my inherent vulgarity by being

185

Early One Morning

made, not contrite or humble, but furiously angry by this caning. I cannot account for the flame of rage which it awakened in my bosom. My dear, excellent Father had beaten me, not very severely, without ill-temper, and with the most genuine desire to improve me. But he was not well-advised, especially so far as the "dedication to the Lord's service" was concerned. This same "dedication" had ministered to my vanity, and there are some natures which are not improved by being humiliated. I have to confess with shame that I went about the house for some days with a murderous hatred of my Father locked within my bosom. He did not suspect that the chastisement had not been wholly efficacious, and he bore me no malice; so that after a while, I forgot and thus forgave him. But I do not regard physical punishment as a wise element in the education of proud and sensitive children. . . .'

Sooner or later, whether by means of cuts with a cane, or of carrot and bridle, the colt is broken down into an admirable hunter or steeplechaser or cart- or hearse-horse. The slings and arrows less affect a hardened hide. And,

'. . . how might ever sweetnesse have be knowe
To him that never tasted bitternesse?'

But there can be no misdoubting the impact on the inward recluse, even at the age of three, when he receives his first, entirely unexpected and well-merited slap administered by an irate father. The stare of enflamed consternation on his fair face and in his widened eyes is past description; not even a viceroy can have looked more incredulously and bitterly affronted. But the novelty soon wears off. One could not distinguish at sight, or even on acquaintance perhaps, a man who was slapped in his childhood from a man who never had cause to envy a cherub. It is as well none the less to have some notion what a child feels at this crisis before toleration or indifference sets in.

Samuel Johnson declared that his first headmaster was 'very severe, and wrongheadedly severe . . . for he would beat a boy equally for not knowing a thing as for neglecting to know it'. None the less Samuel admitted that he owed Mr. Hunter his Latin: 'My master whipt me very well. Without that, sir, I should have done nothing.' The rod, he was convinced, was better discipline than the exciting of emulation. By exciting emulation you

186

Clothes

make even 'brothers and sisters hate each other'. But then, he 'seemed to learn by intuition', and his schoolfellows accepted his predominance.

CHAPTER XV

CONSCIENCE

★

1. 'No meanes at all to hide
Man from himself can find.'

Even a very young child may be capable not only of affronted pride, of inane vanity, and of shame, but also of a conviction of sin against self, against others, and against God. It concerns his inmost being; in whom shall he confide? 'My most painful delusion', says William Bell Scott, 'was that I had committed the sin that could never be forgiven which I found to be the sin against the third person of the Trinity, a very indefinite definition. This perplexed me for years, and buried me many times in despair.'

That indomitable Scots divine, Robert Blair, the grandfather of the author of *The Grave*, recalls an overwhelming realization of this nature when he was seven. His father who had been 'twice spoiled at sea by pirates' because he refused to enrich himself, as his neighbours did, by 'buying their commodities', died when he was six. 'At his interring,' he writes, 'I used my bairnly endeavouring to be in the grave before him.' 'Upon a Lord's-day,' the next year afterwards, 'being left alone in the house through indisposition, the Lord caused my conscience to reflect upon me with this query, Wherefore servest thou, unprofitable creature? I not being able to answer, looking out at a window, I saw the sun brightly shining, and a cow with a full udder. I thought with myself, I know that sun was made to shine and give light to the world, and that cow was made to give milk to nourish me, and the like; but being still ignorant wherefore I was made, I went pensive up and down that gallery wherein I was: then perceiving neither young nor old upon the streets, nor hearing any noise, I did remember

Conscience

that the whole people used often to meet together, in a very large house, called the kirk, where, no doubt, they were about that errand and duty which I had not yet laid to heart. . . .'

As still and radiant a sun shines here, as in Jean Paul's fragment, and how intense is this solitude and silence. 'And it came to pass at that time . . . ere the lamp of God went out in the temple . . . and Samuel was laid down to sleep; that the Lord called Samuel: and he answered, Here am I.' Although any such experience at the pitch described by Blair may be unusual, there is no reason whatever to suppose that similarly solemn self-communions are uncommon in childhood.

And so with William Penn when he was a boy eleven years old. Overwhelmed with grief at Cromwell's arrest of his father, the royalist admiral, after the capture of Jamaica in 1655, and as wildly overjoyed at his release, he was one day 'surprised in his room, where he was alone, with an inward and sudden sense of happiness, akin to a strong religious emotion; the chamber at the same time appearing as if filled with a soft and holy light'. There came upon him 'the strongest conviction of the being of a God, and that the soul of man was capable of enjoying communication with Him'. Mystical vision and delusion are the extremes of comment on experiences like these. But, explain such moments as we may, there is no denying the profound effect they had on the children concerned in them. And we can at least be cautious. *Plus negabit unus asinus in unâ horâ quam centum philosophi probaverint in centum annis.*

'It appears to me', says William Bell Scott in his *Autobiography*, 'that the earliest remembrances we retain from childhood do not refer to the externals of life, which are altogether apart from the child . . . but that they relate to the difficulties of consciousness—difficulties which appear very quickly through the mental dawn which takes place sooner than the old people observe. Under this impression I have observed frequently on the faces of very small children wonderful expressions that defy interpretation. . . . It is not the objective world that disturbs the child—*that* stands in the sunlight; it is the subjective, the interior self separate from all that, with the darkness of life. The very same questions are presented to childhood that remain unsolved to the grown-up man, that drive him to some creed or church, and nevertheless remain to him on his deathbed. . . .'

189

Early One Morning

Soon after the experience related by Robert Blair he heard his first sermon. The preacher gave out his text: ' "But as for me . . . it is good for me to draw near to God." ' With this 'my heart was much affected'. 'And though it be now sixty-three years since that time, the countenance, carriage and voice of the speaker remain fresh upon my memory, and these words have been most sweet unto me, so that, in the very entry of my public ministry (as I had vowed before), I handled that text.'

In maturity his mind had become attuned to such memories as these. When recording his childhood, he may have selected them from others which seemed to him of little account. But that both these experiences were faithfully set down and were momentous self-realizations at this early age, what reason have we to doubt? Their urgent gravity to himself is in accord too with later memories. He refers to the 'riotings' of Yule when he was a boy. To the end, he confesses, that he 'might play the fool the more boldly', he feigned to be drunk, and lied to his mother when he came home late for supper that he had been mourning at his father's grave. This lie, he says, was easily 'digested' until he read 'Holy Augustine's Confessions'. Then he began to ponder on 'the paths of his youth'. He recalls also reasoning with himself at this age whether or not he would be justified in partaking of the sacrament after having broken his fast. In the event he decided to do so, since Christ himself had first celebrated this sacrament 'after supper'.

Samuel Johnson's father, says James Boswell, when Samuel himself was an infant of three, took him to hear Dr. Sacheverell preach, and excused himself for so doing by saying, 'it was impossible to keep him at home'. For 'young as he was, he believed he had caught the public spirit and zeal for Sacheverell, and would have stayed for ever in the church, satisfied with beholding him.' When he was still a child his schoolmistress followed him one morning on his way home—no servant having been sent to fetch him—to see that he came to no harm. Already near-sighted, he was obliged 'to stoop down on his hands and knees to take a view of the kennel,' or street gutter, before he 'ventured to step over it'. He then detected he was being watched. He ran back to her in a rage, and beat her as a punishment for this 'insult to his manliness'. His mother also relates that, while he was still in petticoats, she gave him a collect to learn by heart. Before she had reached the

ALBRECHT DURER, AT THE AGE OF THIRTEEN
From a lithograph after his own self-portrait

Conscience

second floor of the house, he came running up after her. 'What's the matter?' said she. 'I can say it,' he replied. 'The boy is the man in miniature:' and yet if in old age Dr. Johnson had chanced to misuse Dick's magic stone, he would have been treated in Grown-upland with precisely the same condescension as would any other wiseacre of his size.

2. *'Few and short were the prayers we said.'*

In a letter to a friend, Robert Burns said that had his father continued to be a gardener, he would himself have been 'marched off to be one of the little underlings about a farmhouse; but it was his dearest wish and prayer to have it in his power to keep his children under his own eye till they could discern between good and evil. . . . At those years I was by no means a favourite of any body. I was a good deal noted for a retentive memory, a stubborn, sturdy something in my disposition, and an enthusiastic idiotic piety. I say an *idiotic* piety, because I was then but a child'.

If by idiotic he meant unpondered and irrational, this appears to be a rickety conclusion. It is the kind of bland affirmation that is erected with such ease on no better base than a brick with a bias. There are serious children, there are flighty children, and in this kind probably they will grow up.

Cardinal Bellarmin, it is said, was preaching in public at the age of five or six on the sufferings of Jesus. 'I believe', says Lord Eldon, in his anecdote book, 'I have preached more sermons than any one that is not a clergyman. My father always had the Church Service read on Sunday evenings, and a sermon after it. Harry and I used to take it in turns to read the prayers or to preach: we always had a shirt put over our clothes to answer for a surplice.' And here are a few sentences from a sermon delivered by Charles Kingsley to his family circle and taken down *verbatim* by his mother when he was four years old:

'It is not right to fight. Honesty has no chance against stealing. Christ has shown us true religion. We must follow God, and not follow the Devil, for if we follow the Devil we shall go into that everlasting fire, and if we follow God, we shall go to Heaven. When the tempter came to Christ in the Wilderness, and told him to make the stones into bread, he said, Get thee behind me, Satan.

191

Early One Morning

He has given us a sign and an example how we should overcome the Devil. . . .'

Thomas Hardy, as a child, when rainy Sunday mornings kept the household indoors, delighted to enwrap himself in a table-cloth, and after the manner of the local vicar take Morning Prayer and preach a sermon. His grandmother was his chief auditor.

In Victorian days, long before the Sabbath æther became a *mêlée* of radio, these little domestic ceremonies were common and pleasing—at any rate for the lay preacher. Nursery lectures on astronomy and biology may now have superseded them. I very well remember my own début, as solemn and serious in intention as the recital of the Commination service should be. I was perhaps seven years old. A nightshirt served for a surplice, and a chair concealed by a clothes-horse draped with a sheet for a pulpit. I delivered my text, *God is Love*; paused in that bottomless vacuum which lies in wait for the unpractised public speaker, and burst into tears. And the congregation burst out laughing*. Whereupon I incontinently took refuge in the lap of the most beloved member of it.

Rousseau claims, much too boldly in face of the facts, that in knowledge of religion he was unique as a child. 'I knew as much about religion as was possible for a child of my age. . . . My childhood was not that of a child; I always felt and thought as a man. It was only when I grew up that I re-entered the class of ordinary individuals. . . . Find me Jean Jacques Rousseaus of six years old and speak to *them* of God, when they are seven. I will guarantee that you run no risk.'[1] Alexander Bain, in his *Autobiography*, declares

[1] 'A horror of insincerity makes Rousseau dread "the little saints who are forced to pass their infancy in prayer".' Neither religion nor any study, he considered, should be made tedious or melancholy, and not even prayers should be learnt by heart. This he applied in particular to girl children, his view being that they must learn religion early, since if they wait until they are capable of discussing questions so profound, the moment may never arrive! 'Ne faites pas de vos filles des théologiennes et des raisonneuses; ne leur apprenez des choses du ciel que ce qui sert à la sagesse humaine; accoutumez-les à se sentir toujours sous les yeux de Dieu, à l'avoir pour témoin de leurs actions, de leurs pensées, de leur vertu, de leurs plaisirs; à faire le bien sans ostentation, parce qu'il l'aime; à souffrir le mal sans murmure, parce qu'il les en dédommagera; à être enfin tous les jours de leur vie ce qu'elles seront bien-aises d'avoir été lorsqu'elles comparaîtront devant lui.'

But this wholly ignores certain experiences which are not the less real for

Conscience

that when he was a child he endured 'occasional fits of anguish from the fear of hell', and from the conviction of the possibility of his 'being cut off before making my peace with the Almighty. . . . I carefully concealed from my parents, and from everybody, the seriousness that I actually felt in the matter of religion, and continued the same attitude of reserve and concealment through all my early years'. He compared facts with statements, and like most children was quick to perceive contradictions in his elders, both in what they said and in what they did. Time increased this disposition, and was, in the end, he affirms, fatal to his religious conversion.

Among his books, including *The Pilgrim's Progress*, which he must have read 'many times over', was one on the Scotch martyrs. Its appendix, entitled 'God's Judgments on Persecutors' 'proved still more attractive owing to the vindictive and malevolent interest that it awakened'. In *The Hieroglyphic Bible* pictures appeared as substitutes for names:

'Of these last, the most notable was a figure of God as a naked old man in sitting posture. . . . This figure has haunted me ever since when the name of God is pronounced, if I do not forcibly exclude it from consciousness. ·. . .'

Is it possible indeed to root out the insidious influence on the imagination in childhood of certain lifeless and soulless types of 'religious' pictures?—as compared with those which a child unwittingly builds up in his own mind merely from hearing or reading the direct and noble prose of the Authorized Version.

Sir William Jones—the great orientalist, and translator from the Persian of the famous epigram:

'On parent knees a naked new-born child
Weeping thou sat'st while all around thee smiled;
So live that, sinking in thy last long sleep,
Calm thou may'st smile while all around thee weep.'

being unusual. 'Many children', says Dr. Allen Brockington, in *Mysticism and Poetry*, 'have visions easily and naturally. They do not distinguish between the visions of the mind and the visions of the eyes. They speak in the same way of both, without any special excitement. A daughter of mine informed me quite calmly that she had seen Jesus, "and He was leaning up against an apple-tree and He laughed and I asked Him to tell me a story", This vision remained with her all her life. In a sense, it was her life.'

193

Early One Morning

—on listening when a child of five to the description of the angel in the tenth chapter of the *Revelation of St. John*, was filled with such imaginative delight that he never forgot the occasion:

'And I saw another mighty angel come down from heaven, clothed with a cloud: and a rainbow was upon his head, and his face was as it were the sun, and his feet as pillars of fire: and he had in his hand a little book open: and he set his right foot upon the sea, and his left foot on the earth, and cried with a loud voice, as when a lion roareth: and when he had cried, seven thunders uttered their voices. . . .'

But other children of a marked intelligence may listen and remain unmoved. Of all the conditions in his youth, says Henry Adams in his *Education*, which puzzled him as a man, the disappearance of religion puzzled him most. Church attendance, Bible reading, religious poetry, prayer—'he went through all the forms'—but religion remained unreal. To his brothers and sisters as to himself 'even the mild discipline of the Unitarian Church was so irksome that they all threw it off at the first possible moment'. In spite of his efforts to recover it, this—in his own words, 'the most powerful emotion of man, next to the sexual'—had irrevocably vanished. He found, it seems, no solution of this puzzle. It may perhaps have been beyond memory to recover, for he acknowledges that his mother, 'the queen bee of the hive', was helpless to give her children any guidance—except in the direction they fancied.

Religion to Frances Power Cobbe as a child, she declares, had always been a secret and serious interest. 'I think I may say that I *loved* God, when I was quite a young child.' When she was seven years old—though the reading of it was intended for her brothers and not for the child seated apart with her slate doing sums—she listened enthralled to *The Pilgrim's Progress*, realizing through its poetry that 'life is a progress to Heaven'. But later—and every detail of the experience was engraved on her memory—she found herself questioning the miracle of the loaves and the fishes. Four years of doubt and inward conflict followed. She became an agnostic; and out of this wreckage grew the conviction: 'Can I not rise once more, conquer my faults, and live up to my own idea of what is right and good? Even though there be no life after death, I may yet deserve my own respect here and now, and, if there be a

194

Conscience

God, He must approve me.' She became at last an ardent Theist—a term denounced contemptuously by her family as 'a word in a dictionary, not a religion'. She was related, she adds, to no fewer than five archbishops and one bishop—evangelical Christians. 'I was the first heretic ever known amongst us.'

On Sundays Alfred Russel Wallace as a boy went either to church or to the Friends' Meeting House or to chapel; but chapel, with its extemporary prayers, singing and preaching, he liked best. 'As, however, there was no sufficient basis of intelligible fact or connected reasoning to satisfy my intellect, this feeling'—of fervour—'soon left me and has never returned.'

'When the existence of the Deity was first taught me', says William Bell Scott, 'I have no remembrance; it must have made no immediate impression.' But when we consider how few early and emphatic impressions of childhood do remain in memory, this hardly follows. Is, he goes on—is the existence of a supreme being ever 'self-suggested' in the childish mind, 'or is it only planted there as a tenet—a necessary one, but planted there by the paternal instructor, and received gladly, it may be, yet with difficulty'? The evidence suggests that, quite apart from the mind willing to receive and accept it, with most children this instruction comes usually from a mother; and may be accepted as candidly and as kindly as a bowl of bread and milk.

To a teacher with shining eyes, when he was six years old, Mr. Romilly John attributes his 'religious conversion'. It was 'a revelation'. At seven (like Edmund Gosse) he was rapt into metaphysics and magic, began pondering on the limits of infinity, and on a universe that was nothing but a sizeless point, whose everything might come to an end if by chance someone made with a pencil a certain *mark*—which he himself could not specify—on a piece of paper. He believed that his pony Topsy was a fairy in disguise. Yet at the same age he was gabbling a purely nonsensical secret gibberish with his brother that afforded them both infinite amusement and made them the envy of their friends.

Even when he was sixty William Morris could remember his resentment at being punished and called naughty and wicked for doing things he could not help doing, such as falling down and breaking his knees, or staining his own and his sister's faces with the pollen from tiger-lilies. That 'he has a strong sense of justice' is

Early One Morning

a tribute frequently paid to the black man, but it is no less true of the white child. William became aware of paternal bias in other respects than broken knees. His parents were Evangelical and taught him that Unitarians were very bad, and Dissenters not respectable. He used to be taken to a dull church, the parson of which had written a book called *Bible Reading Simplified*, or some such title. This he afterwards 'picked up and found to be as difficult to read as the Bible was easy'. Later he discovered Robert Nelson's *Companion for the Festivals and Fasts of the Church of England* (in its thirty-sixth edition in 1824); and he became a Puseyite.

3. 'O silly souls! O subtle Satan that deceived them!'

For most children of the Victorian era there stood always a grim enemy straddling the path—Apollyon. Satan, Beelzebub, the Devil—to what level of disrepute he has nowadays sunk in most young minds I cannot say. Like many of the captains and the kings of the Great War he has been debased, has lost caste, meaning, status and imaginative reality. The trap-door of the Unconscious has descended over his head; though the self, if goodness and evil mean anything, is not the more easily defended even if, under this *alias*, there he remain. That being so, to a modern child, hardly deserving perhaps even to be described as advanced, Milton's hero in *Paradise Lost* is mere romance. That the devil, actual or otherwise, was a foully affrighting agent of anguish and horror to the young in other days, needs no witness. When a child imagines, he can not only see and hear horror but can smell and taste it. Its presence surrounds him like the stench of a bog. He may, then, very well hate and fear him, since Satan is the name he accepts as that of the destroyer of his own innocence and peace and courage, who brings to ashes all beauty. A child's intuition of evil, as of good, is beyond that of many men, of those at any rate who have temporized, and thus destroyed their faculty of conceiving both it and a tempter of a power and pride worthy to represent it.

Charles Babbage as a child stoutly challenged his powers. At the age of ten he was sent to a school in Devonshire, and being delicate was given little bookwork. 'Perhaps great idleness may have led

Conscience

to some of my childish reasonings.' He played a ghost trick on a playfellow, and seeing its effect began to speculate if 'ghost or devil ever really existed'. Having noted the forms in which the Prince of Darkness is recorded to have appeared—owl, black cat, cloven foot—he went all alone one evening about dusk into a garret, cut his finger, and with his blood drew a circle on the floor. He then said or read the Lord's Prayer backwards and awaited what might follow. He waited in vain. There came no response. A deep and dismal silence prevailed. At last he ventured out of his magic circle, stealthily opened the door, gently closed it, 'descended the stairs, at first slowly, and by degrees much more quickly'. In bed that night he found he had forgotten a sentence in the Lord's Prayer, and could not continue it. He then resolved, after long meditation, to settle the question whether an all-merciful God could punish a poor little boy with eternal torments because he had tried to verify the truth of the religion he had been taught. 'I resolved that at a certain hour of a certain day I would go to a certain room in the house, and that if I found the door open, I would believe the Bible; but that if it were closed, I should conclude that it was not true. I remember well that the observation was made, but I have no recollection as to the state of the door. I presume it was found open from the circumstance that, for many years after, I was no longer troubled with doubts, and indeed went through the usual religious forms with very little thought about their origin.' But could there be a more curious kink in memory than that he should have forgotten 'the state of the door'?

We might discard all this as a 'childish ignorance', if there were not sexagenarians still among us who are the victims of sortileges at least as absurd. The voice of the palmist is loud in the land, the charmer continues to charm, and the soothsayer to prefer the dark. Dr. Johnson being a wise and sagacious man did not explain even to Boswell such human habits as collecting orange-peel, or counting palings, or refusing to tread on the cracks between paving stones. More recently, observing this last little trick in a friend still in her teens, who was pensively yet sportively tripping beside him, a famous philosopher amiably announced: 'Ah! I see you have a complex!' It would be both ignorant and irreverent to suspect him of a simplex.

CHAPTER XVI

SIN

★

1. *'Liars have short wings.'*

There is a voice within, too, in early childhood, that may convict not self but the Others of sin, those spiritual pastors and masters, those betters, whom we had supposed innocent even of the liability to error. When talking about children to a young French lady whom I met recently in an English school, she told me that she could recall not only a wilful deception of her mother—the pretence that she herself was looking for wild birds' feathers in the orchard when she was actually in search of green apples (and this, after they had already taught her their lesson!) but also her uncontrollable grief at detecting a grown-up in a lie. She was then four years old. 'The second of my nursery-governesses, Miss Daly,' says Frances Cobbe, 'who was known as "the Daily Nuisance", was succeeded by a Miss W. And Miss W. was detected in a trick which appeared to me as one of unparalleled turpitude!' While her charge one night lay as if asleep, Miss W. abstracted the key of her writing desk, opened it and read a copy-book, which the child herself had hidden there. Censorious Miss W.! It contained only solemn religious 'reflections'. 'But it was long before I could sleep for sheer horror.' Lucy Snowe was herself a governess when she had a similar experience, and so lustrous is the flame of Madame Beck's candle in the story that even in memory it dazzles the inward eye.

It was as though, he says, his soul had suffered an avalanche when Edmund Gosse, in his sixth year, detected that omniscient moralist, his father, not in an untruth, but in merely having failed to detect a little escapade of his own in connection with a home-

198

made rockery and a pretty little artificial fountain—'a silvery parasol of water'—fed by a leaden pipe. First, he confesses that he was not ashamed at having by keeping silence deceived his parents. That had provided 'a providential escape' from a whipping. Nor was he most impressed by the fact that his father, once a deity, had fallen to a human level—as his conception of the Almighty also fell when in the solitude of an upper room he ('ridiculous act') 'committed idolatry' and prayed to a chair.

'Of all the thoughts which rushed upon my savage and undeveloped little brain at this crisis, the most curious was that I had found a companion and a confidant in *myself*. There was a secret in this world and it belonged to me and to a somebody who lived in the same body with me. There were two of us, and we could talk with one another. It is difficult to define impressions so rudimentary, but it is certain that it was in this dual form that the sense of my individuality now suddenly descended upon me, and it is equally certain that it was a great solace to me to find a sympathizer in my own breast. . . .

But this strange confidant and sympathizer, this other self, may make its entry upon the stage of childhood long before the age of six. The following letter from a friend, which he has very kindly permitted me to print, refers to his daughter, Elizabeth.

'. . . She has always been of a very happy, philosophical temperament, though very far from being merely placid, and during her second and third years she used often to lie awake in the dark apparently enjoying something tremendously. The first sign was a quiet chuckle, which grew intermittently until presently she was roaring with laughter, but there was never the least external indication of any cause of amusement.' Presumably emotion recollected in tranquillity? Or——?'

Four years afterwards, and again two years after that, these self-communings—now less amusing than baffling—were openly confided to her father.

'At the age of seven and a half she turned to me one evening in a sudden burst of confidence, after a few minutes of silence, and said: "You know, John, sometimes I think about things. I think t-h-u-m-b spells thumb and t-h-i-n-g spells thing, and *why* should they spell thumb and thing? Why shouldn't they spell something else? And then I think two from six leaves four, and two from

Early One Morning

eight leaves six, and why shouldn't they leave three or something else? And when I think like this I get all puzzled."

'At the age of nine and a few months she fell down a flight of stairs at school and returned in the full glory of iodine and bandages, rather proud of herself. At the time she made little comment, but some weeks afterwards she said to me, again quite suddenly after a few minutes' silence: "When I fell down the steps and hurt myself did it just happen or did they know it was going to happen?" I said: "I am not quite sure what you mean. Can you tell me in different words?" And after some little discussion it emerged quite definitely, as I had expected (though I am certain that I did not contribute), that what she meant by her question was whether the fall was pure accident or part of a predestined scheme of the universe! I am afraid I hedged and left her with the problem, which will no doubt reappear before long. Who "they" were could not be elucidated. . . .

Since however this concerns the mind of a child—a mind that is, we know, habitually thronged with images—her 'they' was probably at least as clear a conjuration as the 'they' who haunt with such devastating effect the miscellaneous old men in Lear's limericks. Nor are problems of this kind momentary will-o'-the-wisps. They may be pondered over—'Some *weeks* afterwards she said to me. . . .'

2. *'Our mortal Nature Did tremble like a guilty thing surprised.'*

But here was no concern of Conscience. A child may be miserably haunted by the remembrance of a misdeed—weighing lighter in St. Peter's scales than his own shadow—which if confessed would at once be comforted away.

When William Hutton was six, and his mother was out, he had the care of his two brothers, himself and his father; and 'began housekeeping'. 'My father had borrowed two Newspapers. I was sent to return them. I lost both. The price of each was only three halfpence, but I was as much harassed as if I had committed a crime of magnitude.'

'. . . But Rebecca recollected
She was taught deceit to shun;
200

Sin

And the moment she reflected,
Told her mother what was done;

'Who commended her behaviour,
Loved her better, and forgave her.'

Unshared, these thoughts are heavy as lead in the mind for days together. Rebecca had broken a handsome china basin, and that basin was on a shelf—an enormity! But what of such a misdemeanour as telling a shopman that change for a sixpence was needed not for his small customer's private purposes but her mother's? For weeks this deception gave her tender heart no peace! Moral rhymes for children usually indict graver deeds than this— but even they are chiefly concerned with those that give the adult most inconvenience: 'But when she was bad she was horrid.'

'. . . Cruel children, crying babies,
All grow up as geese and gabies,
Hated, as their age increases,
By their nephews and their nieces.'

That is amusing for all parties. But Isaac Watts, having painted one of the most seductive gardens in English verse—the Sluggard's —*meant* his warning against its stagnant owner:

'Said I then to my heart, "Here's a lesson for me;
That man's but a picture of what I might be. . . ." '

'There, but for the grace of God. . . .' And Charles and Mary Lamb were serenely in earnest in:

'Anger in its time and place
May assume a kind of grace.
It must have some reason in it,
And not last beyond a minute.
If to further lengths it go,
It does into malice grow. . . .'

At what age, then, may *this* kind of self-communion, the un-instilled, become active? 'I do not know what to say about X,' wrote Margaret Fuller to her mother; 'he changes so much, has so many characters. He is like me in that. . . . A very gay, impetuous, ardent but sweet-tempered child.' There follows a full and spark-

201

Early One Morning

ling description of his gestures, emotions, accomplishments, amusements, tricks, activities and charms; and X, whose name was Angelino, and who with his mother and father was wrecked on the coast of New York, though his body alone was found, was not five or six years old, as we might have assumed, but fifteen months. Even a child as young as this, then, according to his mother, is 'known by its doings'. No less so if his doings are misdoings?

On one occasion Augustus Hare refused to say his grace*, and suggested instead, ' "Mama thanks God for Baby's good dinner".' He finally consented to the solo provided only that he was allowed to kneel down under the table. This struggle 'lasted perhaps half an hour'. Late in life he could recall not only being whipped at this age—three—but also conversations about the Fathers and Tract XC, of which he managed to get a glimmer of understanding though no one supposed him to be listening. It is chiefly when children are not intended to hear that they listen most heedfully. When he was four years old, Augustus was denying that when he was alone both God and Jesus Christ could see him, and even arguing about it. At four also he enquired, 'May I ask Jesus Christ to take away the naughtiness out of Satan? then (colouring he said it, and whispering) perhaps He will take him out of hell.' I remember in my own early years making a similar prayer, with some little unction, and—while in actual inward view of Satan stepping up out of his own place in joy and gratitude at my intervention— speculating whether this was right or wrong.

'There are children', and these the most difficult of all, said Fénelon, 'who are born polite, close, unconcerned, but drawing everything secretly to their own ends; they deceive their parents, whose tenderness makes them credulous; they pretend to love them. . . . Their real temper, long dissembled, does not entirely display itself until the opportunity of reforming it is past and gone.' After their bitter controversy over Quietism, Pope Innocent declared finally that Fénelon erred by loving God too much, and Bossuet by loving his neighbour too little. There was no love at all lost between the author of *Traité de l'Education des Filles* and Lord Chesterfield—as his reader, that is; and him, in turn, John Wesley dismissed, after reading his letters to his son: 'And what did I learn?—That he was a man of much wit, middling sense, and

Sin

some learning; but as absolutely void of virtue, as any Jew, Turk, or Heathen, that ever lived. . . . If he is rewarded according to his desert, his name will stink to all generations.'

We hear of naughty, difficult, obstreperous children, of bad boys, of unmanageable urchins of eight confronting a magistrate, and, later, of juvenile delinquents, of confirmed reprobates. I remember an ample and voluble washerwoman declaring to my mother after a tactful enquiry concerning her boy—a child of about my own age—who had been 'tiresome': 'He's a *good* boy, m'm; he's a *honest* boy; and there ain't *no* fault to be found with him; but he's *incorrigible!*' A maternal summary to that effect. I wonder what became of him.

There are scarcely perceptible gradations between self-will, unruliness, deliberate rebellion, sin, evil—at any age. And the law has no concern with any of them until they edge over not necessarily into what is worse from a moral or spiritual point of view, but what is definitely *against* the law. And a few minutes' close observation of a child when the 'Black Dog' is mounted on his back or of one's self in similar circumstances—anger, hatred, jealousy, passion—will shed a clearer beam of light on the iciest of malefactors, at any age, than can all the narcotic treacle of the *Newgate Calendar.*

Every miserable poisoner who has perished on the scaffold or lived on in terror of it was once a child of five. That is a platitude which in such a context as this resembles the decoration of a Christmas tree with midget gibbets, skulls and crossbones. But it is equally true, though not less truistic, concerning that poisoner's judge and jury, and every patriot, man of genius, martyr and saint —of mankind in general. The realization of this will come upon us sharply if also a little sentimentally if, on glancing at the grown-up's hands, we imagine them as they were when he himself was a child only five years old.

3. *'The blasted tree that yet still green is withering at the roots.'*

At what age do the roads definitely fork, the broad and the narrow? At what age are connecting byways between them unlikely to occur? It is a question that was by no means disposed of in Chapter I. The scenery may be deceptive, the compass may jam,

203

Early One Morning

the metaphor breaks down. 'No man', says Jeremy Taylor, 'is discerned to be vitious so soon as he is so, and vices have their infancy and their childe-hood and it cannot be expected that in a child's age should be the vice of a man; that were monstrous as if he wore a beard in his cradle; and we do not believe that a serpents sting does just then grow when he stricks us in a vital part: The venome and the little spear was there, when it first began to creep from his little shell: And little boldnesses and looser words and wranglings for nuts, and lying for trifles, are of the same proportion to the malice of a childe, as impudence and duels and injurious law-suits, and false witnesse in judgement and perjuries are in men.' When writing this, he may have had the Confessions in mind. 'For these same sins,' says St. Augustine, recalling his own, (gluttonous pilfering from cellar and table) 'as we grow older, are transferred from . . . nuts, and balls, and sparrows . . . to gold and land and slaves, just as the rod is succeeded by more severe chastisements.'

The editor of *The Chronicles of Crime* frequently points a moral, but in doing so, it must be confessed, seldom adorns his tale. 'Mankind is never corrupted at once,' said Eugene Aram, a self-taught scholar and linguist, who left behind him materials for a comparative lexicon of five languages, including Celtic and Hebrew. The old aphorism is taken from a speech which he made in his own defence, about fifteen years after the murder was done which brought the two 'stern-faced men' to Lynn. 'Villainy', he went on, 'is always progressive, and declines from right, step by step, till every regard of probity is lost, and every sense of all moral obligation totally perishes.' How then, was his argument, could so harmless a past as his have landed him in this appalling quagmire?

'My Lord,' began John Thurtell, in his last harangue from the dock—a murderer so scrupulous that he had refused to allow cards to be played in his house on the Sunday after the sordid crime he had committed, because it would set a bad example to the children: 'My Lord, and Gentlemen of the Jury. Under greater difficulties than ever man encountered, I now rise to vindicate my character and defend my life. . . . I have been held forth to the world as a depraved, heartless, remorseless, prayerless villain, who had seduced my friend into a sequestered path, merely in order to dispatch him with the greater security—as a snake who had crept into his bosom only to strike a sure blow—as a monster. . . . The hor-

Sin

rible guilt which has been attributed to me is such as could not have resulted from custom, but must have been the innate principle of my infant mind, and must have grown with my growth, and strengthened with my strength. . . . Beware then, gentlemen, of an anticipated verdict. . . . Do not believe that a few short years can have reversed the course of nature, and converted the good feelings which I possessed, into that spirit of malignant cruelty, to which only demons can attain. A kind, affectionate, and a religious mother, directed the steps of my infancy in the paths of piety and virtue. My rising youth was guided in "the way it should go", by a father whose piety was universally known and believed. . . .'

But all in vain. At the end, he was fast asleep when he was awakened. He said: 'I am quite satisfied. I forgive the world; I die in peace and charity with all mankind.' Manacled, in mourning, and wearing black gloves, he bowed to a friend from the scaffold, and begged the hangman to 'give him fall enough'. How then of his 'must have been', and his 'infant mind'? William Palmer, the Rugeley poisoner, we are told, was 'a very regular and earnest churchgoer', a tribute which is followed by the less weighty information that he had lived with his father in a large red-brick house 'with a carriage drive and grounds overlooked by a couple of churches'. 'The carriage and liveried coachmen . . . were familiar local objects.' What kind of child looked out of *that* window?

Of Nicol Brown, convicted of murder, we read that he was decently educated and apprenticed to a butcher; and of 'William Andrew Horne, Esq.' convicted of incest and the murder of an infant three days old, that he was the heir of a gentleman of fortune who had striven in vain 'to instil into the mind of his son any of those principles of rectitude without which man cannot be considered to be humanized'. He was hanged when he was seventy-four, thirty-five years after his crime!

John Bunyan before he found Salvation for his soul was twice saved from drowning. But this crucial experience four times repeated in less than nine years failed to save William Page, 'a lad of promising parts', from being hanged for highway robbery.

Even the atrocious Landru, bald and black-bearded, who went womaning, one might say, as a poacher goes rabbiting, had had 'the usual education', was a chorister in his childhood and became a server in his parish church. Charles Peace, on the other hand,

Early One Morning

who seems to have inherited his love of music and of animals from his father, a tamer of wild beasts in a menagerie, was 'always brutal and unruly'. At an early age he was employed in a mill. There, owing to an accident, he maimed his left hand (hence the hook), and became permanently lame. 'He never did any more honest work', says Lord Birkenhead in *Famous Trials*. His gift for disguise, his choice of the grave scene from *Hamlet* for a declamation to schoolboys, his genuine delight in music (he 'collected' fiddles and other musical instruments)—suggest a tinge of genius, and there also remained in him to the end a trace of the childlike. Before he was hanged he sent his wife a funeral card: 'In Memory of Charles Peace, who was executed in Armley Prison, Tuesday, February 25th, 1879. Aged 47. *For that I don but never intended.*' And his last words to a group of reporters expressed the hope 'that no one would taunt or jeer at his wife and children on his account "but will have mercy upon them".'

'A most respectable family', a 'superior education', the exertions of her parents 'to implant in her breast sentiments of piety and virtue'—nothing of this dissuaded Mary Blandy at last from wilfully murdering her father. After conviction, however, she behaved with 'the utmost decency and penitence'. 'Habited in a black bombasin dress, her arms being bound with black ribands . . . she begged she might not be hanged high, "for the sake of decency".'

There must be scores of unctuous statements such as these in *The Chronicles of Crime*; they deepen the mystery of human affairs but give little insight into children. The editor refers frequently to early circumstances, now and then to nurture, but to early nature, so far as I can remember, not at all. Cruelty, malicious lying, and a kind of brutal indecency and malignity make a louring human sunrise. But what was the sun like, before it came up?

4. 'Heaven in her eye and in her hand her Keys.'

There is little nature either—except her own—but there is the clearest nurture in the following letter written in 1732, by Susanna Wesley to her son John. In this, at his desire, she gives the principal rules she observed in the management of her children. And she was the mother not only of a large and lively family, as the account of the peculiar antics of the *follet* or *poltergeist* that

Sin

haunted the Rectory at Epworth in the winter of 1716-7 attests, but so spirited a helpmeet to her husband Samuel that he deserted her for a year or more because, being a good Jacobite, she refused to say 'Amen' to his prayers for 'the king'!

'Dear son,' she begins crisply:

'The children were always put into a regular method of living, in such things as they were capable of, from their birth. . . . When turned a year old (and some before) they were taught to fear the rod and to cry softly, by which means they escaped abundance of correction which they might otherwise have had, and that most odious noise of the crying of children was rarely heard in the house, but the family usually lived in as much quietness as if there had not been a child among them. . . . There was no such thing allowed of in our house as sitting by a child till it fell asleep.

'They were so constantly used to eat and drink what was given them that when any of them was ill there was no difficulty in making them take the most unpleasant medicine; for they durst not refuse it, though some of them would presently throw it up. . . Our children were taught as soon as they could speak the Lord's prayer. . . . They were very early made to distinguish the Sabbath from other days, before they could well speak or go. They were as soon taught to be still at family prayers, and to ask a blessing immediately after, which they used to do by signs, before they could kneel or speak.

'They were quickly made to understand they might have nothing they cried for, and instructed to speak handsomely for what they wanted. . . .

'Taking God's name in vain, cursing and swearing, profanity, obscenity, rude ill-bred names, were never heard among them. . . .

'There was no such thing as loud playing or talking allowed of, but everyone was kept close to business for the six hours of school. And it is almost incredible what may be taught a child in a quarter of a year by a vigorous application if it have but a tolerable capacity and good health. . . .'

And with what zest, may be the comment, the children who were subjected to so grisly a code must have discarded it at the first gleam of liberty! That is one way of regarding it. Alternatively, is it conceivable that any child thus brought up could come to a bad end? *Were* then these children utterly cowed and suppressed,

207

Early One Morning

sucked dry of will and initiative? If their heredity is given its due weight a plain answer to this question at any rate will be found in the *Dictionary of National Biography*. Charles Wesley wrote over 6000 hymns; his brother John preached 40,000 sermons. That hardly suggests a lack either of will or initiative.

In reproof, says Roger North, concerning his mother, she was 'fluent and pungent', but 'debonair, familiar, and very liberall of her discours to entertein all'. She guarded against the contraction of all ill habits, and especially lying, which she 'hardly forgave'. 'We had, as I sayd, stubborne spirits, and would often set up for ourselves, and try the experiment, but she would reduce us to termes by the smart of correction'; after which the delinquent would be forced to leave crying and condescend to the abject pitch of thanking 'the Good Rail'—kissing the rod. She taught her children religion and to read, used to tell them tales—with morals, and on Sundays relate scriptural history.

North insists above all on the dangers of that 'gangreen', idleness and aversion to Industry in the young—'any vacancy or idle time'. The more idleness there is, 'the more profligate and debauch't the age prooves. And I wish the present were not a sad example of it'.

What would be his censure of to-day? But vigilant mothers cannot be always with their children; and the debauched may be young themselves. Here is an experience of Miss Ethel Mannin's:

'I was so agonisingly shy and timid that I was fair game for the older children's teasing. A group of the older girls would amuse themselves by tormenting me until I would say a funny little obscene word. But I would think of God listening, and of Jesus who had died for sinners, and keep silent, and then they would twist my wrists and goad me, "Go on, say it! Say it!" until at last, unable to bear the torment any longer I would sob out the required word, trusting that God would understand how it had been forced out of me, and hoping He would not see it as a sin., . . . And then I would remember that Jesus had had nails driven through His hands, and I could not stand a little pinching and wrist-twisting, and would be terribly ashamed. . . .'

When then we share or recall the inward and hidden life of early childhood—its complexity and intensity—we shall not be merely amused at Joseph Priestley's parable of the pin. As a man he came, he says, 'to embrace what is called the heterodox side of

Sin

every question'; he was laughed at as a believer abroad, branded as an atheist at home. 'Once,' he says of his infancy, 'when I was playing with a pin, my mother asked me where I got it; and on telling her that I found it at my uncle's, who lived very near to my father, and where I had been playing with my cousins, she made me carry it back again—no doubt to impress my mind, as it could not fail to do, with a clear idea of the distinction of property, and of the importance of attending to it.'

Ann Taylor preached a different kind of sermon on the same text:

' "Dear me! what signifies a pin,
    Wedged in a rotten board?
I'm certain that I won't begin,
    At ten years old, to hoard;
I never will be called a miser,
    That I'm determined," said Eliza. . . .'

And I can myself remember surveying a casual pin and being reminded by it of more than the difference merely between *mine* and *thine*. And now? Well, this very book chiefly consists of spoliations from the dead!

At the other extreme is Alexander Bain's earliest memory of going to school to an old dame, 'who taught only reading (with spelling), and that wholly from the Bible'. He was then not much above three. On Saturday of every week this old woman set her scholars a short psalm to be memorized for the following Sunday. He found this oppressive, learned two psalms by heart, and repeated them on alternate Saturdays. And, 'as the old woman's memory was too short to detect the manœuvre, it lasted me out my attendance with her.'

Thomas Holcroft, when his parents were reduced to beggary, went with them to hawk pedlary in the villages. He himself begged from house to house, 'and on this day my little inventive faculties shone forth with much brilliancy'. But when he shared these 'false tales' with his father, it was determined that he should 'never go on such errands again', lest he should turn into 'a confirmed vagrant'. This same father, none the less, 'used to beat me, pull my hair up by the roots, and drag me by the ears along the ground, till they ran with blood. . . .'

209

Early One Morning

5. 'Tom never from his word departed.'

Even Darwin—devoted to truth and avid for facts—confesses that as a child he was much given to falsehoods, solely for the sake of the excitement they caused. He assured a small friend of his that he could produce new and charming varieties of primroses by watering them with coloured fluids. About fifty years afterwards he wrote a book entitled *Variations of Animals and Plants under Domestication*! Having concealed a hoard of fruit from his father's orchard, he announced to the family's consternation his discovery of it as if it had been stolen. None the less, he continues, 'I must have been a very simple little fellow.'

A boy named Garnett persuaded him that it was quite an easy matter to get cakes free of charge if, when he went into the shop to ask for them, he moved the old hat his counsellor was wearing in a privy and particular manner. After exhibiting this mystery in a baker's where he himself had a credit account, this friend lent the hat to Charles for a similar purpose—and Charles had to run for dear life. Similarly, entirely un-Darwinian company-promoters have had to run for dear life. I can myself recall a remarkable small boy who, when I was perhaps eight, assured me, though he never produced it, that he had invented an acorn-trap. Given the art, I could paint too from memory the portrait of an immense, empurpled and very kindly dairyman at the moment when he archly shook his head at me after I had ventured, on a friend's behalf, to ask him to oblige me with half a pint of pigeon's milk. Yet this child, at the age of three and a half, having stolen an egg, stoutly denied that he had, until it broke in his pocket and refuted him. Then he blamed it all on to 'Satan'!

Birds rather than eggs or apples were the wiles that waylaid Lord Berners. He became, he says, a bird bore. One of his early delights was a screen in the drawing-room of his grandmother's house, its panels pasted over with brightly coloured pictures.

'Here you could see "Doves of Siam, Lima mice and legless Birds of Paradise" and countless other things as well. Views of Italian lakes and towns were framed in sprays of orchids. Against a background of Swiss mountains, chamois and chalets, glittering humming-birds thrust their rapier-like beaks into the calyxes of tropical flowers. . . . The whole thing was without rhyme or

Sin

reason, but it conjured up a magical vision of some fantastic fairy paradise. . . .'

This is what the recently defamed 'magic' in poetry does to the world, but not without rhyme. Many years later Lord Berners chanced on this screen again in a lumber room, and was astonished to find 'that it was composed for the most part of political caricatures and sporting scenes', and that the 'exotic birds and tropical flowers' formed only a small part, and were all at the top of it. It was birds of the swallow tribe that were his particular quarry, and he was so keenly disappointed that no sand-martins built their nests in a sandy cliff near the house where he lived with his mother that he was reduced to burrowing holes himself 'in the face of the cliff and pointing them out to people as the genuine article'.

Lord Eldon, the nursery preacher, was, as a child, he declares, and apparently with some pride, a sturdy liar; and for the time being even the birch proved ineffectual in instilling a love of truth. It is easy to assume, apart from any 'hardening', that the birch may instil a wholesome avoidance of what brings it into action; less so that it can instil a love—of anything.

And Shelley: 'On one occasion,' said his sister Hellen, who was seven years younger than himself—'he gave the most minute details of a visit he had paid to some ladies with whom he was acquainted at our village. He described their reception of him, their occupations, and the wandering in their pretty garden, where there was a well-remembered filbert-walk and an undulating turf-bank, the delight of our morning visit. . . . The boy had never been to the house. . . . It was not considered as a falsehood to be punished; but I imagine his conduct must have been . . . unlike that of the generality of children.' Not, evidently, so much unlike as she supposed.

A little wit may spice the wickedness, as in this reminiscence confided to me by a friend, less than twenty years as yet from the event.

'I was about four and a half, and can vividly remember a most discreditable incident. We were staying with a great aunt and one day she said to me that the love of money was the root of all evil. I knew the saying, but deliberately misunderstanding her, burst into floods of tears. I ran into the dining-room and hid under the

Early One Morning

table and howled. When made by my mother to explain the matter, I told them that "old auntie" had said that Mummy was the root of all evil.'

Even white lies are not permitted in childhood, whatever may be the example set. Other kinds, as we have seen, may be told for the sake of the excitement they cause, out of sheer love of invention, from an inability to distinguish between fact and fancy, or be inspired by fear, covetousness, greed and the Evil One. Alexander Carlyle recalls a schoolfellow who explained his being flush (on stolen money) by confiding to him that the ghost of his grandfather had divulged a secret cache hidden between the floor and ceiling of his mother's house. There is no mistaking the motive of that. But what of this? When I was about six years old, I had for schoolfellow a child of blameless repute whose name was Herbert Naughty. He had the misfortune in class one morning to be sick. We surveyed him with sorrow and repugnance; and I enjoyed to the full my mother's reception of this dramatic piece of news. Next day when I returned from school she enquired after my little friend—and not perhaps without that cadence in her voice which suggests that bad news would be better than none. The truth about Herbert Naughty at that moment must have seemed intolerably dull. I hardened my heart and said he was worse. And as the days went by, worse and worse he became; until at last, and to my relief, he was in sober fancy dead and buried. I hoped—with some misgiving—that I had finally disposed of him. But evil birds come home to roost. A week or two afterwards I was haled out of bed and in terror carried downstairs to confront the scandalized dame whose favourite little pupil I had consigned to the tomb. Her blue and frozen eye haunts me still, and I wailed out my penitence. Yet I cannot remember apologizing to Herbert Naughty for this lapse or any extreme grief for it.

Lord Herbert of Cherbury was infinitely more sensitive:

'I remember in that time I was corrected sometimes for going to cuffs with two schoolfellows, being both elder than myself, but never for telling a lie, or any other fault; my natural disposition and inclination being so contrary to all falsehood, that being demanded whether I had committed any fault whereof I might be justly suspected, I did use ever to confess it freely, and thereupon choosing rather to suffer correction than to stain my mind with

Sin

telling a lie, which I did judge then, no time could ever deface; and I can affirm to all the world truly, that from my first infancy to this hour I told not willingly any thing that was false, my soul naturally having an antipathy to lying and deceit. . . .'

The tone—with that naïve 'being both elder than myself'—is a trifle self-righteous. And even on earth there is more joy and not less edification over a sinner, however young, that repenteth than over a paragon self-convicted of intellectual pride.

Belated remorse for a deliberate unkindness or act of cruelty in childhood may survive until the end, as is revealed in an early memory that was magnanimously confided to me by Thomas Hardy a few years ago, his face smiling yet earnest, for of his self-reproach there could be no question. He said that one winter's morning, when he was a child at the village school, he had mischievously pushed another child on to the hot stove behind her in the schoolroom, and she had burned her hand. He was then an old man in his eighties, but the time, the place and the child herself were still vividly present in his mind. He afterwards showed me not only her grave but also the manuscript of a poem in which he mentions her and, if poetry can, makes her ever lovable.

And from cruelty it is but a step or two to wilful murder, even in infancy! When she was eighteen months old Elizabeth Grant so keenly resented the appearance of her brother William in this world that the failure of a spoonful of gin (administered by his Highland nurse before he was first washed) to be the death of him was 'a great sorrow', and on being left alone with him one day she seized his clothes and tried to throw the complete bundle on to the flaming peats, exclaiming 'with all the spite of a baby . . . "Dere! burn! nassy sing!" ' But this was hearsay, not one of her many early memories. Among these, when she was about three, were some 'West Indian seeds, pretty, red and shiny, with black spots on them', some sweet-smelling beans and a variety of small shells; beating a boy in a red jacket who was playing with her; shutting up another in a cupboard while she enjoyed his drum; an old woman with a wooden leg; climbing a pair of steps in her father's study, in terror not of a fall, but of being punished; a foxtail for dusting; and the dark place in the wall where the peats were kept. It is an amusing catalogue and its contents consist chiefly of the naughty.

Early One Morning

6. ' "How canst thou be such a hypocrite?" said I even audibly.'

That a child is capable of rank deceit does not preclude its being credulous; and its being credulous, and therefore teachable, need not imply that it has no reasoning faculty or that its elders are always richly blest in this respect. Its problems and riddles, and the most profound are unshared, may amuse the adult, but then, in Olympus Man himself is a standing joke. Not many of us would get full marks for a paper on bacilli, and glands, and electrons, and genes, and invisible exports, and inferiority complexes, and expanding universes—but how much less sprightly would parlour talk be without them. With a narrow range of knowledge and of room for experiment a young and enterprising child faces a severe handicap. But he may face it open-eyed; and will find reasons though he may fail to find right ones. After visiting a bald grandfather a child aged twenty months renamed a doll whose wig had come off *Grandpa*. A child of between two and three roguishly informed her Nannie: 'If they cut *me* open, brains would come out; if they cut you open, it would be mutton, Nannie'; and on being reproached for pinching that beloved Nannie's nose, remarked: 'But it's a very *pretty* nose!'

If pleasure comes of it, a child may prefer to be deluded, or pretend to be. It may receive without accepting. Otherwise the folk tales of Faerie and magic it delights in would rival green apples in their effects. In the realm of the imagination all things except the unimaginable are possible. I yearned to believe in my young friend's acorn-trap. After all, it was no more fascinating a marvel than an acorn itself. As for pigeon's milk, it is a fluid easier to swallow than, let us say, the fact that the sea-shouldering whale is a mammal. And it is not necessarily a stupid child who can sit, in fancy, sharing with the prophet Jonah the accommodation of that mammal, and may to the end of his life remain amused at the unfortunates who can believe in neither. There are nursery problems that hinge on much more troublesome dilemmas—questions which, as William Bell Scott said, remain beyond human solution.

Charles Waterton, the naturalist, the boldest of infants, who on some occasion as a child had shown his distaste for a thrashing by biting his schoolmaster's calf clean through its worsted stocking,

Sin

was one day innocently tickling the big black school-cat's bushy
tail when it whipped round and did exactly the same to him.
'This I kept a profound secret; but I was quite sure I should go
mad every day for many months afterwards.'

There are other fears that silly tongues implant. 'A certain Lord
Boringdon,' says Charlotte Yonge, 'son of Lord Morley, was
killed by a beard of barley getting into his throat. I was told of this
as a warning when I was biting bits of grass, and for many years
really thought my uvula was such a bit of grass and would be the
death of me.' How many children too have been racked with foreboding after swallowing the minutest scrap of sponge or cork or
sewing-cotton, in the belief that it will expand in the stomach, or
twine and twist and tangle about the throbbing heart until the
undertaker is compelled to intervene? That fond parent, the ear-
wig, too, with its habitual craving to set out to explore any convenient youthful brain! Old Boney (still a menace in the 'eighties),
the Black Dog, the Blue Monkey, the all-fortunate and friendly
Sweep, the Gypsies, Bobbie Peeler—such bugbears as these *may*
excite contempt; they may also make life a burden. In either case
the images of them in the adult mind bear very little resemblance
to those in the child's.

A child's own private little animisms are more attractive—the
common one referred to by Mrs. Hodgson Burnett, for example.
As a young child she would sometimes pick up a stone, carry it on
in her flower-basket, and put it down again. She was giving it the
opportunity of seeing a little life. Some children kick the stone on
into a new and better life and leave it with a word of advice. Nor
need a credulous child remain content with what it is told.
The least doubt may work as quickly as leaven in a lump of dough.
When Alfred Russel Wallace was about four years old, the device
of the thirsty fox in the fable 'puzzled him greatly'. It suggested
positive magic. Not content to leave it at that, he experimented
with a bucket, a mug, some water, pebbles and sand. Instead however of the water rising in his bucket as he emptied in the sand, it
merely turned into mud. Tired out and disappointed at last, he
gave the experiment up, having concluded that anything of this
kind related in story-books is not to be believed!

If the heart in small matters find itself in conflict with the head,
the odds are at least even that the head will win. A child speechless

Early One Morning

with rage and grief may weep her heart out watching the dismemberment or execution of one of her favourite dolls, and mourn for days over the death of a pet bird or mouse. She may none the less consent to play chief mourner at the doll's funeral, and a week or so afterwards proceed to dig up the mouse's remains to 'make sure'. Some years ago a child of six was playing in the kitchen of a country cottage, in which she was spending her summer holidays, when a shot hare was brought in out of the heat of the harvest fields. At sight of it she broke into a passionate fit of weeping, and nothing would comfort her. The heart having lulled at last, the head became active; and at noon she sidled up to her mother with the half-whispered request, 'Mummie, please may I go and see the hare skinned?'

In the ordinary affairs of life a child is far less often at sea than is commonly supposed. It may be observed listening closely to the idle talk of its elders and may then chirp a question which suggests that the conversation was not so much above its head as beside or beneath it; 'What *can* be so amusing if it amuse not *me*!' Lowered voices, knowing little nods, a pregnant shrug of the shoulders, a word or two in dubious French—such devices as these at once attract attention. They advertise to the pitcher what they are intended to hush up. When forbidden topics are in debate very young eyes can see a good way in, and may no less easily see through. It is the deceiver found-out that feeds the knowing child. Its judgement is less likely to be at fault than its knowledge; it can comprehend beyond its experience and has antennæ of its own.

No grace or beauty, no honeyed condescension, no 'charm', or bribe even, will necessarily cajole a child or win even its bare approval. The most exquisite old lady, anod with silvery curls, her voice as dulcet as milk and roses, can be an object of the utmost suspicion to a vigilant creature of four whom she supposes herself to be managing with a twist of the little finger. 'Grey iniquity' may not be within the infant vocabulary, but there is ample room for it in the youthful mind. At no time in life—since charity suffereth long and is kind—do we necessarily respect even those whom we dearly love. One of Charles Darwin's sons when he was four years old tried to bribe his father with sixpence to come and play in working hours—hours which he knew well were kept rigidly sacred.

Sin

And now and then, the shattering explanation of a momentary problem is expressed. A friend was travelling some years ago from Spain to Switzerland with a young party, of whom her Spanish goddaughter, aged three and three-quarter years was one. When the nurse was unpacking in Paris she promised to show the boys from one of the bridges l'Ile de Paris, whereupon her goddaughter piped up: 'Y yo? Y yo?' 'And with each repetition the heartbreak grew.' Away they went, the four-year-old dancing (as I have seen a child of the same age dancing at a lavish sunset) and shouting: 'Paris es una isla!'

'When we reached the one spot on the bridge from which you can see, the parapet was too high, so I lifted the mite and sat her on top. She had no hat and a crown of tight golden curls was lit up by the sun. Presently a man stopped in front of us, swept his hat off and said: "Quel beau petit bouton vous avez là, Madame!" I said: "C'est une fillette, monsieur." Then he made Lucy a long speech, wishing her long life and the happiness her beauty deserved. I said: "Bien aimable", or something like that. When he had gone Lucy said: "Conosces aquel hombre?" *Dost thou know that man?* I said no, but that he had wished her long life and happiness. She still looked puzzled. Suddenly her brow cleared: "Sin duda es un borracho," she said. *Without doubt he was a drunk man.*' Lucy, it seems, disapproved of enthusiastic strangers as much as I did of amorous soldiers; but a child can enjoy a joke, in season, and even a practical one.

CHAPTER XVII

DOLLS, TOYS, & PLAY

★

1. *'Angels alone that soar above Enjoy such liberty.'*

Dolls and their houses, their clothes, furniture—beds, tables, chairs, pots, pans and all the rest of their domestic utensils, are to a motherly child pretty much what a walnut or a ball of wool is to a kitten—a compound of real and earnest, of a make-believe that is also a pantomime of coming events. Their owner is as earnest in this make-believe as a fine novelist is serious over his characters; and *they* may be nearer if not dearer to him than his own flesh and blood. 'My great world', says Charlotte Yonge, the creator of a hero, Sir Guy Morville, adopted as an ideal by the Burne-Jones group at Oxford in the 'fifties, and a writer of prodigious industry—'my great world was indoors with my dolls, who were my children and my sisters; out of doors with an imaginary family of ten boys and eleven girls who lived in an arbour. My chief doll, a big wooden one, Miss Eliza by name, was a prize for hemming my first handkerchief. . . .'

Her two burning desires in childhood—never fulfilled—were for a *large* wax doll and a *china* doll's tea-service. That she crossed the bridge from dolls to children her books for children demonstrate—*The Daisy Chain,* for but one example, winning her a multitude of young readers. The annual sales of dolls—English, Dutch, French, Japanese, Uglies and the rest—would make a more amusing piece of statistics than most. They do not appear to have fallen off; since all the world's children tend to be little conservatives. And after carefully watching the facial expressions and gestures of an engrossed three-year-old preparing her wax or wooden, rag or sawdust progeny for the night, there will be little

218

Dolls, Toys, and Play

doubt left in the observer that if practice can make perfect, the family is still fairly safe. As for a real live baby—a child even of three, with this burden on her knees, will sit gazing down upon it with a faint far-away smile on her countenance that she must have inherited from Eve, and will remain motionlessly lost in a Madonna-like rapture and wonderment.

We cannot, and yet how often we do, disparage love because its object may seem to us a poor one, and particularly when a child is concerned. Yet her doll is to her a *living* thing, and may (like William Hutton) be only the more endearing for its ugliness. Besides, does a mother never 'play with' her baby? I recall an almost life-size handsome doll that was presented to my children many years ago and had come all the way from Madrid. Its presence became so real even to my hardened fancy that when alone in its company I grew positively uneasy at its concentrated stare. A child would know a good deal more about that. It is as well to be circumspect, then, when the 'maternal instinct' comes 'into play', even if, as in the rat, it may depend on (or rather be in association with) 'a chemical in the pituitary gland'.

In the dedication to Henry Vaughan's first collection of poems, which was published when he was twenty-four, is the following sentence: *You have here a* Flame, *bright only in its owne* Innocence, *that kindles nothing but a generous* Thought; *which though it may warme the Bloud, the fire at highest is but* Platonick, *and the* Commotion, *within these limits, excludes* Danger. . . .' It might easily have been written after he had seen just an ordinary child playing with her dolls.

'On one of my birthdays,' says Lady Horner in *Time Remembered*, 'my father, who loved practical jokes, sent me a large official paper saying:

"Frances Jane Graham,
 "I send thee a little sister in token of my Royal love.
                              "Victoria Regina."

'The paper had the Royal Arms and two great seals on it, and, to complete the illusion, he made my mother stay in bed to breakfast and have the enormous doll, to which the letter referred, in a cradle beside her, and I was brought in to kiss it! I think I was eight years old then.'

Early One Morning

A boy may amuse himself (if only in tepid pretence) with his sisters' dolls; his own stuffed bears, monkeys and other animals being creatures of a different and masculine species. But it is improbable that any feeling of paternity is entailed. Even to confess to having played with dolls as a child requires some courage in the grown-up of his sex. Francis Thompson had that courage. Dolls are included in the delightful photograph of himself with his sisters. But, he says, 'I dramatised them, I fell in love with them; I did not father them'. To the most beautiful of them he gave the name Eugénie, 'after the Empress of the French'. 'There is a sense', he writes, 'in which I have always been and even now remain a child. But in another sense I never was a child, never shared children's thoughts, ways, tastes, manner of life, and outlook of life. I played, but my sport was solitary sport, even when I played with my sisters; from the time I began to read (about my sixth year) the game often (I think) meant one thing to me and another (quite another) to them—my side of the game was part of a dream-scheme invisible to them. And from boys, with their hard practical objectivity of play, I was tenfold wider apart than from girls with their partial capacity and habit of make-believe.'

Aksakoff also had his 'dream-schemes' but he *could* share them; and here, it is into his sister's imagination that one would welcome a clearer glimpse:—

'Every day', says Aksakoff, in *Years of Childhood*, 'I gave my little sister a reading-lesson; this was a complete failure, as she had not mastered even the alphabet. . . .' Every day he made her listen while he read to her, until from sheer want of understanding rather than ingratitude she sometimes fell asleep.

'. . . She had a number of dolls, all of which she called her daughters or nieces; this gave rise to many conversations and entertainments in complete imitation of grown-up people. I remember how I gave full play to my imagination and described many surprising adventures that had befallen me. . . . Thus, for example, I described a burning house, and how I jumped down from the window with two children—the children being two dolls which I was holding in my arms; another scene was an attack by robbers, all of whom I put to flight; my final effort was a dragon, which lived in a cave in the garden, with seven heads, which I intended to hack off.' But it is easier to share his make-believe than hers.

FRANCIS THOMPSON, AGED ELEVEN, WITH HIS SISTERS
*From a photograph in the possession of Mr. Wilfred Meynell
and with his kind permission*

Dolls, Toys, and Play

There are so many grains of a rather dubious sugar in Oscar Wilde's touching story of his toy bear and his beloved brother that a grain or two of salt may be advisable in accepting it. 'I had a toy bear', he says, 'of which I was very fond indeed, so fond that I used to take it to bed with me, and I thought that nothing could make me more unhappy than to lose my bear. Well, one day Willy [his brother] asked me for it; and I was so fond of Willy that I gave it to him, I remember, without a pang. Afterwards, however, the enormity of the sacrifice I had made impressed itself upon me. I considered that such an act merited the greatest gratitude and love in return, and whenever Willy crossed me in any way I used to say: "Willy, you don't deserve my bear. Give me back my bear." And for years afterwards, after we had grown up, whenever we had a slight quarrel, I used to say the same: "Willy, you don't deserve my bear. You must give me back my bear." '

'Penny bloods' are rather literature than toys, but this reminds me of an episode of a different dye. My brother and I in our early days made independent collections of these romances, which, after puncturing them with a red-hot meat-skewer, we tied together with a piece of string. Beset one day with doubts of their moral value, I burned *his*!

2. '*Cupid and my Campaspe played.*'

There are toys *and* toys, at all times of life. The most expensive are the most ardently coveted, but they are apt to wear out the quickest, both themselves and in the affections. The home-made are the most serviceable and the most endearing.

> 'And what does he lack to make him blessed?
> Some oyster-shells, or a sparrow's nest,
> A candle end and a gutter. . . .'

With but a penny a week for pocket money, until he was ten years old or more, luxuries were out of Alfred Russel Wallace's reach. The consequence was that, like Robinson Crusoe, he and his brother made for themselves whatever play-gear they coveted most—fireworks for instance; miniature cannon (out of keys); pop-guns of elderwood; spring-pistols of carved mahogany or walnut with goose-quills for barrel; leather-covered balls for cricket;

cherry-ring necklets and bread seals. The pages in his *My Life* that describe these engines should be treasure-trove to any child of any skill with his hands.

But there are methods of dealing with toys other than either making or playing with them. 'From my earliest years,' says Charles Babbage, in *Passages from the Life of a Philosopher*, 'I had a great desire to enquire into the causes of all those little things and events which astonish the childish mind.' 'My invariable question on receiving any new toy was: "Mamma, what is inside of it?" ' If he remained unenlightened, he broke it open to find out. The donor of the toy may have disapproved of this practice, the surgeon would sympathize. But Babbage kept to the inanimate. His Calculating Machine was far in advance of its predecessors, from Pascal's onwards. He spent twenty years on it. And now, all that remains is an exquisitely ingenious fragment. Leibnitz's machine for astronomical calculations, which cost him £3600, had a similar fate. Both machines were supernal toys, whatever their cost and practical purpose may have been.

Babbage describes also two pieces of mechanism that may well have been the germ, if not of his analytical engine, at least of the chess-playing automaton which he devised but never constructed owing to the conviction that Tom Thumb, then in his heyday, would be likely to continue a more popular form of public entertainment. During his boyhood he went to see some 'machinery' made by a man called Merlin, in Hanover Square. He showed so keen an interest in it that Merlin invited him up into his workshop, an attic. Imagine if we can the rapture of such a boy when his eyes alighted on:—'two uncovered female figures of silver, about twelve inches high. One of these walked or rather glided along a space of about four feet, when she turned round and went back to her original place. She used an eye-glass occasionally, and bowed frequently, as if recognizing her acquaintances. The motions of her limbs were singularly graceful.

'The other silver figure was an admirable *danseuse*, with a bird on the forefinger of her right hand, which wagged its tail, flapped its wings, and opened its beak. This lady attitudinized in a most fascinating manner. Her eyes were full of imagination, and irresistible. . . .'

But of toys that can at once and for good irradiate and enrich a

Dolls, Toys, and Play

child's mind, few can excel a toy theatre. The realists who deplore even fairy-tales may deem it too romantic. The scope, none the less, that it offers an imaginative child is boundless. It has the charms of the miniature, of the make-believe, of the dramatic, of an audience and of something in the dark. Few things more signally exhibit the chasm between what may be a chronic state of mind in the usual grown-up and one that is not at all unusual in a child. All in a row on their chairs sit the adults, smiling (among themselves) but presently yawning, their eyes glazed with staring beneath the tiny gaudy proscenium at the erratic cardboard figures sliding in and out, their throats (at least in days that are past) parched with the suffocating fumes* of little tin colza lamps or guttering candles. The puppet-master, meanwhile, alike manager, producer, possibly author, and the whole vocal cast, though fretted with mechanical cares and clumsy fingers, is in the seventh heaven of delight. Not even one of the old true-blue Victorian pantomimes complete with luscious Transformation Scene and Harlequinade—sausages, red-hot poker, and magic lath—could surpass it in rapture.

Goethe's toy theatre is as famous as Drury Lane. He had a celestial grandmother who one Christmas evening 'crowned all her good deeds' by producing a puppet show. 'And so a new world was created in the old home,' and there was kindled a fire in that young imagination whose flames have not yet been put out. Where now, I wonder, is the lumber-roomed Punch and Judy Show with which Mrs. Ruskin prevented her son John from becoming a second Shakespeare?

When Charles Lever was eight, his father thought 'to make him an architect'. But 'during his schooldays', we are told in his *Life*, 'he had a theatre of his own at the back of the house'. Here 'he produced stock pieces—*Bombastes Furioso* was one of his favourites, and improvised dramas'. It was no less excellent practice because in later life he kept his puppets to the little theatre of the mind.

When, again, Ibsen was eight years old, he took to a paint-box—copying pictures out of books. Then, as monkeys and other 'uglies', he would caricature his brother and sister when he was angry with them. Later, he cut his paintings out, pasted them on cardboard, and with little wooden blocks for base paraded them as

223

characters for a kind of doll theatre. He hated anybody touching it; it was his solitary joy. There could hardly be a more condensed epitome of his life's work.

From a toy theatre to parlour acting is no journey. Fine feathers make fine birds, and children delight in borrowing them. There may be better reasons for this too than vanity, since 'dressing up', as any charade or masque or pageant will prove, is one of the easiest human ways of escaping from self-boundedness into freedom and fantasy. Up to the age of thirteen or thereabouts acting to many children, with this for one of its gayest rewards, is little short of a more natural thing than simply remaining themselves. And merely to recall a few recent cinema films suffices to suggest that the genius for this is as likely to fade away as that of the calculating boy, whose odd talents, according to Mr. H. G. Wells, are put to such excellent purpose in the Moon.

Children delight beyond measure in *Let's pretend* and the dramatic, and will take an infinitude of pains in preparing for it. The headmistress of a school in the Midlands told me recently that a child of twelve had appeared before her during the previous term to ask permission to 'produce' *The Pilgrim's Progress*. With some misgiving she agreed to this, but only on the understanding that no school hours were to be squandered in its preparation and that no help would be forthcoming from the mistresses. And what, she added, for *coup de grâce*, are you going to do about the cast and the dresses? Have you thought of *that*? Whereupon from under the jumper a detailed list of the complete cast was produced, together with a description of the clothes required by each character, and their approximate cost. There was just one last request. Might a girl from another form be borrowed to take the part of Apollyon?

3. 'That little Jackdaw came hopping about.'

The firstfruits of collecting are yet another kind of toy, and the onset of a habit that may prove to be the joy of a long lifetime. 'Mania' it may be, but few prizes for sanity can match its reward. At his first day-school Charles Darwin had already become a passionate collector—of shells, seals, franks, coins and minerals. This passion, he observes, was 'clearly innate', being unshared

Dolls, Toys, and Play

by his sisters or brother. His uncle Charles, none the less, at a 'very early age' collected specimens of all kinds—until, at least, at sixteen, the 'vigour of his mind languished in the pursuit of classical elegance' at Christ Church, Oxford. His Uncle Erasmus, when a boy, collected information; and in pursuit of it counted not only the houses in Lichfield, but as many also as he could of their inhabitants. The hours of vigilant bliss this must have entailed! He watched to good purpose, moreover, since an official census soon afterwards approximately confirmed his estimate. Even the remembering of facts is a kind of automatic collecting, and Charles's father, Dr. Darwin, had so extraordinary a tenacity for dates that it became a positive annoyance. He could never forget the name even of a patient he had lost.

Whether the craze for collecting is due merely to a passing fashion or to jackdaw instincts, the schoolboy who collects nothing at all (except good or bad marks, or 'colours', or certificates), must be an odd fish. In his childhood, Mr. Forrest Reid tells us, he was an insatiable collector, generally with, and sometimes against the grain. His treasures on the one hand included matches, nibs, puzzles, stamps, wallpapers, posters, butterflies and moths; and on the other, anatomical specimens, to secure which he buried a dead rat and a sizable fish, and, 'stomach-turning task', 'dug them up a great deal too soon'. One wet afternoon, after aimlessly prowling through the house, and at last abandoning the piano, he ascended into a lumber room. There—and across the intervening years its 'dry and slightly bitter smell' wafted itself to his nostrils again—he discovered an old dress suit once his father's. He arrayed himself in it and postured in front of a cracked and foggy mirror. In doing so, he dislodged a stack of magazines, and his eye fell upon a woodcut. Fell and stayed: 'There and then, under the sunless pallor of the skylight, I sat down and looked for other drawings. There were plenty. . . .' Scissors, candlelight and musty murk —that afternoon a craving sprang up in his heart; and for proof of its ravages there is his packed and absorbing *Illustrators of the Sixties*.

What need to find excuses for any pursuit so natural and so full of zest? He prayeth best who loveth best, says the poet, all things both great and small. And we have reason to know that it was not the moral of the *Ancient Mariner* that gave Coleridge the most

225

comfort in the writing of it. Collecting is a short cut to all kinds of knowledge and learning; to systematic habits of the mind and discriminating habits of the senses. It trains the eye, practises taste and judgement and is a godsend in an untidy world. In proof of which we have only to appeal to the antiquary, the bibliophile, the statistician and the archæologist. Dryasdusts these learned and laborious savants may appear, but within their bosom burns—one could safely offer very long odds on it—a lamp that was first kindled in early childhood.

> '. . . A box of counters and a red-veined stone,
> A piece of glass abraded by the beach . . .
> And Thou rememberest of what toys
> We made our joys. . . .'

All this indicates, as Miss Fleming has pointed out, that, with but few exceptions, boys have more hobbies than girls. Even in early childhood this is true. It is due in part perhaps to imitation, in part to promptings of the innate. Sisters may share in them, and ravenously too, since sex is not as simple a pervasion as all that; but childhood none the less is a working model of life in maturity; and, as for sex, a gilded Amazon is as antique a piece of femininity as a Titaness in shorts is a modern. William Morris, a manufacturer and lover of objects all his life long, could in his sixties recall, with at least the ghost of his old delight in them, a toy lamb that squeaked, a model of London Bridge, a suit of armour in which he rode on his pony, and the puppetry of Twelfth Night and Christmas—St. George and the rest—accompanied by 'delicious rum punch'.

4. 'On a bank, as I sat a-fishing.'

Needless to say, perhaps, he was not 'interested in locomotives'. One of his chief ambitions as a child was 'to shoot a woodpigeon with a bow and arrow'—both of which incidentally can be made out of the ribs of an old umbrella, though toy *harps* are less practicable now that elastic-sided boots have gone out of fashion. Fishing too—and before he became a pupil at the Misses Arundel's Academy for Young Gentlemen—was another passion. 'There was a pond in Walthamstow' where he lived as a child, and what the word pond really *means* to a child only a child could say—if he

226

Dolls, Toys, and Play

could find the words to say it with. A visit any summer evening to the bawling host of urchins, with their galley pots, encircling the Round Pond will testify to that. While earth breeds tadpoles and sticklebacks, there is not the faintest danger of the art of angling being forgotten. It is the sport of the philosopher.

Herbert Spencer tells us that as a child he loved fishing, but not, alas, what he thought about when gloating over his float. As for Aksakoff, not to have read *his* pages on the sport is to have failed in one's duty to Izaak Walton.

Of Dryden's childhood hardly anything is known *except* that he loved to fish—in the lovely Teme, a sister river of the Severn, and renowned, it is said, for its grayling. Of Swift it is related that in his early youth he not only lost a fish at the crucial moment, but that 'the disappointment vexed him ever afterwards'.

Fishing is not merely a sport either—when the angler is a child. Apart from the tackle and the bait and the sweet south wind and the excitement of the preparations; apart from the water-rats and the kingfishers and the stony lullaby; there is the leafy peace and quiet and magic, when the mind resolves itself into a looking-glass, wherein nature, sitting like a mermaid over a rocky pool, is reflected in her utmost secrecy.

Although very little is known about John Keats in his early years, there is no question that he also was an out-of-doors child, and loved to rove the wooded country round about Enfield with its 'Goldfinches, Tomtits, Minnows, Mice, Ticklebacks, Dace, Cock Salmons and the whole tribe of the Bushes and Brooks'. 'But verily,' he adds, 'they are better in the Trees and water.' The list comes from a letter written to his sister Fanny many years later, to ask her what she would like for a present: 'Anything but livestock. . . .' So far as I can remember there is no reference in the poems either to the Goldfinches—and what can compare with a bevy of six or seven of them busy in a tuft of seeding Michaelmas daisies?—or to the gay, nimble and omnivorous Tomtit. If this be so, it hints that poets may know a little more about birds (as distinct from the Bird) than their naturalistic critics are led to assume.

Since up to the age of five Alfred Russel Wallace lived beside the beautiful Usk, he was as little likely not to fish as not to breathe. Minnows and sticklebacks, dace and roach were less his quarry than lampreys: a fact which sadly conflicts with what I

227

Early One Morning

have been told of these peculiar and historical fish—that they can only be caught on the seashore at full moon and flood spring-tide. Charles Darwin also as a child loved fishing, but being a merciful one, first killed his worms with salt. He was so remorseful at having once beaten a puppy that in old age he could recall the exact spot where the beating occurred. He delighted in birds but adored shooting—soothing his conscience with an argument which proved to his own satisfaction that it must be an intellectual pursuit. John Clare—who at a very early age went off to find the horizon, and who grew so fond of being alone at last that his mother endeavoured to force him into company—was less punctilious. 'Of a Sunday morning', he says, 'I have been out before the sun delving for worms in some old weed-blanketed dunghill and steering off across the wet grain . . . till I came to the flood-washed meadow stream. . . .'

Incident to the fish is the water they inhabit, and that, whether in pail, puddle, brook, lagoon or ocean, is pure sorcery to the youthful soul; though, like fire, it may also have its horror. No less magical in its effects on the mind is ice—water, as a child defined it, that has fallen asleep in the cold. Mr. Romilly John in *The Seventh Child* recalls the beauty of a frozen pool. 'Beneath the surface of the ice an extraordinary landscape revealed itself with exquisite lucidity to my gaze; the stillness of it was almost supernatural, like something you might expect to find on the face of some infinitely remote planet.' In fantasy he saw himself a minute denizen of the lovely, sinister and motionless world beneath the glassy surface. And let us remind ourselves yet again that he is not 'making this up', but attempting to recapture the very experience itself this was to him as a child.

And last there is a pond referred to in *Theatre Street*, a pond whose water was never cold to any human hand and never fished in, but was the more vivid to Tamara Karsavina as a child for its being an 'image' whose origin she could never trace or explain.

'I, a child, and a woman that seemed to be my mother, stepped out of a carriage. She held my hand and we walked round the pond towards a large house with a somewhat flat façade and many windows.

'I moved with some difficulty; the path was gravel, and my high heels made me unsteady. My dress was voluminous, heavy and stiff. . . . I felt timid. . . . There the image stopped abruptly. . . .'

228

CHAPTER XVIII

FOOD

★

1. *'For he on honey-dew hath fed,*
And drunk the milk of Paradise.'

Mention has been made of a 'delicious rum punch'—
William Morris's. What then, by and large, of eating and drinking in childhood? Children are reputed to be greedy. Is this reputation deserved?
In appetite they may rival the robin that will devour its own
weight in twenty-four hours. And song, figure, looks, ways,
feather and habits, he pays well for every crumb. But to eat for
eating's sake is an art wholly remote from eating because one must.
A rampageous fire is burning in a child's body, and it needs plenty
of fuel. Children then may be inclined to gourmandism but are
seldom gourmets, even if they are easily tempted to become dainty.
To a child in good fettle every meal is in the nature of a feast; its
'enough' is the difficulty. The *what* is at any rate less important
than the how much. Tommie Tucker having sung for his supper
was rewarded with *white* bread and butter. Payment in kind is the
pleasantest fee of any. What Baudelaire said of Proudhon in
one of his letters, Mr. Henry Savage applies to Richard Middleton, and it can be applied even more aptly to a child:

'J'observai que ce polémiste mangeait énormément. . . . *Pour un
homme de lettres, lui dis-je, vous mangez étonnement.—C'est que
j'ai de grandes choses à faire,* me répondit-il, avec une telle simplicité
que je ne pus diviner s'il parlait sérieusement ou s'il voulait
bouffonner.'

Seeing that nature is the mentor in these matters, it is very
doubtful if a child, given the run of the larder, would overeat himself—not at any rate very often. Envy or regret at the loss of a

229

Early One Morning

young healthy appetite, and the adult's conviction that his own
flesh is weak, may account to a great extent for the pertinacity
with which nursery moralists have insisted on childish gluttony.

'But the unkind and the unruly,
And the sort who eat unduly. . . .

To think that Stevenson, who habitually watched his words,
should have bracketed such a trio as this, even if the rhyme for the
first line suggested the subject for the second! 'I must not throw
upon the floor, The crust I cannot eat'; 'Take your meals, my
little man, Always like a gentleman'; 'O take the nasty soup away!'
'And there [Dick] cast his greedy eyes Round on the jellies and the
pies'; 'With rich plum cake and macaroon I ne'er knew joy like
this again'—so runs the tale. If however food means so much more
to a child than it ought *o—and many a temperate adult would
agree that it remains even to the last sip and suppet one of the few
sure rewards of being alive—is it odd that comparatively little
mention of it is made in early autcbiography? Perhaps not; even
though a child of seven must have enjoyed, or otherwise, some
eight thousand several meals. Still, there are such casual bounties
as brandy balls, pink sherbet, roast sparrow, 'boot laces', sop-in-
the-pan, toast- and sandwich-crusts; and these too for the most
part have been left unsung.

One such recollection was compounded of sugarplums, tragedy
and bitter disappointment. Among the earliest memories of Alexander ('Jupiter') Carlyle, 'the grandest demigod' Walter Scott
'ever saw', was jealousy of a cousin. He was born in 1722, and
wrote his autobiography when he was seventy-nine: it would be,
he said, 'a faithful picture'. A later memory did even less justice to
an infant heart. A youth of eighteen, named Bell, he tells us, a
friend of the family's and entrusted with a commission by Alexander and his brother, set out for Dumfries on a clear frosty night
in December, missed the road, fell into a 'peat pot', and was
drowned. 'He was impatiently expected at night, and next morning. My brother and I had got some halfpence to give him to
purchase some sugarplums for us, so that we were not the least
impatient of the family. What was our disappointment, when,
about eleven o'clock, information came that he had been drowned
and our comfits lost! This I mention merely to note at what an

Food

early age interesting events make an impression on children's memories, for I was then only two years and ten months old, and to this day I remember it as well as any event of my life. . . .'

What a child eats depends far less on himself than on his betters. Roger North tells us that he had a grave and decorous father, who after giving him his blessing if he had been a good boy, would follow it up with a 'petit Régale' in his closet—'a reward of obedience and vertue'. He could drink as much small beer (the little Wesleys' drink also) as he pleased—'there was alwais a stone-botle kept going in our quarters', to which his mother added slices of rhubarb and other medicaments, so that even his physic was never 'extream odious' to him. 'It was stole upon us.'

'Our dyet was very plaine, and rather short than plentyfull, but often. Never indulged with bitts and curiositys. I have seen some so treated with seeming dayntys, as the medullas, braines and the like, that nothing ordinary would doune with 'em. This tends to deprave not onely the appetite, but the fancy, and makes children grow meer fopps in eating. We must be contented with what was assigned us or fast, and consequently never were tormented with vaine expectations of Dayntys. . . . Wee saw what was to be had and knew there was no more.'

'My nursery', says Miss Yonge, 'would frighten a modern mother. It was like a little passage room, at the back of the house, with a birch tree just before the window, a wooden crib for me, and a turn-up press bed for my nurse; and it also answered the purpose of workroom for the maids. But I did not live much in it. I was one of the family breakfast party, and dined at luncheon so early that I cannot remember when I began, and never ate in the nursery except my supper. Breakfast and supper were alike dry bread and milk. I so much disliked the hot bowl of boiled milk and cubes of bread that I was allowed to have mine separately, but butter was thought unwholesome, and I believe it would have been so, for I never had been able to eat it regularly. As to eggs, ham, jam, and all the rest, no one dreamt of giving them to children. Indeed my mother made a great point of never letting me think that it was any hardship to see other people eating of what I did not partake, and I have been grateful for the habits she gave me ever since.'

When Elizabeth Grant's family were living in a queer old house at Twyford—with its turrets, observatory, odd closets, yew hedges,

Early One Morning

vast garden and orchard, and everywhere populous with bats—an ogre named Mrs. Millar came into Elizabeth's childhood, an ogre with a strict régime. The nursery breakfast consisted of dry bread and cold milk all the year round, with the exception of the three winter months, when Scotch porridge took its place, boiled by English maids in any but Highland fashion. 'A large, long tub stood in the kitchen court, the ice on the top of which had often to be broken before our horrid plunge into it; we were brought down from the very top of the house, four pairs of stairs, with only a cotton cloak over our night-gowns, just to chill us completely before the dreadful shock. How I screamed, begged, prayed, entreated to be saved!...' Cotton frocks with short sleeves and low necks and no flannel underneath followed the immersion, and then an hour on a low sofa, books in hand, and away from the fireplace, while the stone cold breakfast was prepared. Milk Elizabeth's digestion could not endure. 'From being a bright, merry, though slight, child, I became thin, pale and peaky, and woefully changed in disposition'—sly as well as violent. Her dearly loved father, however, upheld Mrs. Millar's authority. Attired in his dressing-gown he would stand over his small daughter, answering every beseeching look over her disgusting mugful of milk with a sharp cut of his whip. Her sister Jane had not a milk, but a spinach aversion—and the cold green mess that she had refused when it was hot would appear at meal after meal until she was starved into eating it. Even Mary, three years old, would be sat down on the lowest step of a back staircase 'at naughty times', and forbidden to move until she was permitted to do so. On one occasion her father found her there, asleep, at midnight.

But all this is only the dark side of the picture. At dinner these three sisters with their brother would appear with the second course—in full dress like the footmen—and would seat themselves in a row on four chairs against the wall, seeing, smelling, hearing, but neither tasting nor speaking. With dessert came release, and after that 'romps' with their father. 'We looked forward to this happy hour as to a glimpse of heaven; milk, cabbage, fat, rhubarb', whippings all forgotten. 'We dreaded hearing of his absence, as all our joy went with him; we hailed his return as our chief blessing.' 'How very odd,' she adds later, 'how very odd and how individualized, were the people of those old days.'

Food

'I was bro't up in such a perfect inattention to [victuals] as to be quite indifferent what kind of food was set before me,' says Benjamin Franklin, 'and so unobservant of it, that to this day, if I am asked, I can scarce tell a few hours after dinner what I dined upon' —that day being in 1771, in which year he began his *Autobiography* at the country house of the Bishop of St. Asaph. He none the less in his salad days turned vegetarian, and fell away from the most innocent of all *isms* only on snuffing the unexpected and admirable odour of *fried* cod. 'I balanced some time between principle and inclination, till I recollected that, when the fish were opened, I saw smaller fish taken out of their stomachs; then thought I "If you eat one another, I don't see why we mayn't eat you." So I din'd upon cod very heartily. . . .' His moral is no less savoury than, it appears, was the fried cod; for he adds, 'So convenient a thing it is to be a *reasonable creature*, since it enables one to find or make a reason for everything one has a mind to do.' The tone is as suave as Jacob's (and Robinson Crusoe's), but the hands are Esau's.

Roger North also moralized over his dainties, but (since he had never been a 'fopp in eating') with him these were apples. He had 'a most insatiable helluo' for them. 'There was seldom a night when I did not eat a pennyworth of apples (and no small one) in bed before I slept, but this was in the time of ripe apples, for green fruit I never could like.' When he was ten or eleven years old he went to the Free School at Thetford. 'Here it was that I began to have a sense of myself'; and 'here I first knew what debt was, for this ingordigiousness of fruit having exhausted our stock, being good customers we found credit, and once was upon the score 2s. 6d., which was a burden so heavy to a little man of honour, that he declined ever after to be in like circumstances, and having cleared this by an expedient of old clothes, was firmly resolved in the matter.'

Wallace returned thanks for frugal habits, and so did Augustus Hare—with reservations. In one thing, however, in connection with eating, Charlotte Yonge was unique. Rousseau (who at the age of six was not only 'a chatterbox . . . and sometimes a liar but also a glutton'—'I would have stolen fruits, bonbons or eatables'— and as an apprentice stole apples and asparagus), declared that his false charge against 'poor Marion'—that of stealing a piece of old

rose and silver ribbon—was 'the only offence' he had ever committed, and that his unhappiness in his last days together with forty
years of honourable and upright conduct in difficult circumstances
assured him of its expiation. What then would have been his
comment on Charlotte Yonge's 'I wonder' in the following?

'I remember my indignation when a good-natured housemaid,
who thought me cruelly treated, brought up a plateful of slices
with the buttered side turned downwards. With conscious pride
and honour, I denounced the deceit. I wonder whether the strict
obedience edified her, or whether she thought me a horrid little
ungrateful tell-tale. . . .'

2. 'Cato seemed to dote upon Cabbage.'

With all due respect to man's friend the 'pretty cow'—whether aided or otherwise by this tell-tale's dry bread—
there is no doubt that in childhood milk may prove both an
affliction by day and a horror by night; in part perhaps because
a cow's main diet consists of 'greens', and in part perhaps because
the animal too often refuses to take Jane Taylor's advice:

'Do not chew the hemlock rank,
Growing on the weedy bank;
But the yellow cowslip eat,
That will make it very sweet.'

Elizabeth Grant's impassioned lament is still ringing in our ears,
and Harriet Martineau is no less doleful.

'The long years of indigestion by day and night-mare terrors
are mournful to think of now. Milk has radically disagreed with
me, all my life: but when I was a child, it was a thing unheard of
for children not to be fed on milk: so, till I was old enough to have
tea at breakfast, I went on having a horrid lump at my throat for
hours of every morning, and the most terrific oppressions in the
night. Sometimes the dim light of the windows in the night
seemed to advance till it pressed upon my eyeballs, and then the
windows would seem to recede to an infinite distance. If I laid my
hand under my head on the pillow, the hand seemed to vanish
almost to a point, while the head grew as big as a mountain. . . .'

Like strong drink, then, the wrong food can affect the mind of

Food

a child as well as its body—and that is a very old and yet still an obscure story. 'A more evident example', says Robert Burton, 'that the minds are altered by milk cannot be given, than that of Dion, which he relates of Caligula's cruelty; it could neither be imputed to father nor mother, but to his cruel nurse alone, that anointed her paps with blood still when he sucked, which made him such a murderer, and to express her cruelty to a hair: and that of Tiberius, who was a common drunkard, because his nurse was such a one. . . .' And this when the fountain of Hippocrene was full in flow!

Jane Carlyle, alas, burnt the account she had written of her early life, but even if it had seen print it is not certain it would have contained a reference to a dinner at the *Black Bull* in Edinburgh when she was four. A solemn waiter enquired, says Thomas: ' "And what will little Missie eat?" ' ' "A roasted bumm[ble] bee," ' said 'Missie'. At three she had sipped a drop of Mamma's wine. 'Mamma, wine makes cosy', was her verdict. Another Jane, Jennie Wren, had also tasted wine; but then hers was currant 'wine', and *she* merely moralized.

Even when remembered impressions of nursery days are only 'fleeting', as in Lady Horner's experience, an appetizing morsel may have been safely embalmed. She recalls 'how the baby's food, a tough sort of baked cereal, was always boiled by the nurse in a pudding cloth on the nursery fire, and how we elder children were allowed bits off the outside which were very succulent; and how we used to be given the inside scraps of cheese from the nursery-maid's supper, and were once or twice allowed to sit up in our dressing-gowns, when nurse was in a good temper, and enjoy them by the nursery fire.'

The west a flame of colour, a Sabbath evening and solitude, except for a squalling rose-and-grey parrot and a kind-hearted servant, in a strange land—this and a slice of forbidden bread and dripping is a memory of mine which no fine Banquet will ever equal and none could excel. Was it mere bread and *butter* that fed Teufelsdroeckh's rapture as he sat lost in wonder at the sunset on the garden wall? Because perhaps Ruskin was allowed no luxuries as a child, he could recall, when an old man, the three raisins which his mother gave him out of her store cabinet, one 'fore-noon', when he was two or three years old, and could place his first taste of custard—'in our lodgings in Norfolk Street'. The custard was a remnant of his father's dinner (he sat eating in a front room), and his mother secretly bestowed it on John in a back. That he so frequently mentions dainties denied him—the red and white currants, for example, that dangled like bunches of garnets and opals from the bushes in the sun in the garden at Herne Hill— suggests how much he pined for them. With what effect?

William Morris had the run of 'a splendid garden at Woodford with as much fruit' in it, including peaches, as he could eat, and had vivid recollections of the eleven o'clock lunches he enjoyed as a child, cake and cheese and a glass of small ale brewed at home—the cake nicer than anything of the kind in later life. Bread and cake and ale and cheese, who could doubt their efficacy in filling out for future service that figure of heroic energy and indomitable vigour? And is not all cake in childhood (except seed) nicer, richer with selfhood, than any in later life, even if too little of it is likely to be of better service than too much? In view of the infant Caligula, might not an occasional sugar-stick, or spoonful of honey, or of rum-punch have sweetened the austerities of *Modern Painters*?

Henry Adams, who flatly refers to himself in his infancy as 'ten pounds of unconscious babyhood', and to having survived up to the age of three years 'like other babies, unconsciously, as a vegetable', begins then and there, in reference to himself, with, 'he knew only the color of yellow. He first found himself sitting on a yellow kitchen floor in strong sunlight. He was three years old when he took this earliest step in education; a lesson of color. The second soon followed; a lesson of taste'. 'On December 3, 1841, he developed scarlet fever. For several days he was as good as dead.' He retained no recollection of this illness except only that of seeing his aunt come into the sick-room 'bearing in her hand a saucer with a baked apple'.

3. *'Seeking the food he eats,*
And pleased with what he gets.'

It is the out-of-the-common, the surreptitious, the 'tastes', the overings, the pickings and pilferings, that are the most memorable ticklers of a child's palate. Or such joys of out-of-doors as

Food

Mr. Herbert Read's: 'We gathered wild gooseberries and stewed them in a tin over a fire of twigs. We ate the tender shoots of sweet-briar, sorrel and pig-nuts.'

Jam for tea, an outrageous stickjaw between whiles, a massive ice-pudding in June, oyster patties at a Christmas party, and such a pie as is called veal-and-ham but is compounded solely of un-forgettable bliss—did Selkirk ever muse on such ironies revived from childhood? Occasionally the chance luxury is a disaster. As a child Charles Babbage went for a walk one day in the Mont-pelier Gardens in Walworth, and there coveted, gathered, and swallowed some black-currant-like berries. On his return home his father put him between his knees and gave him a glass of castor oil*. He remembers his being seated 'on the right-hand side of the chimneypiece in the breakfast-room, under a fine picture of our Saviour taken down from the cross. On the opposite wall was a still-celebrated "Interior of Antwerp Cathedral".'

The dryest and mouldiest of crusts is manna when hunger is the sauce. But *no* sauce (except that of fancy) can avail to lubricate a meal, fit otherwise for all the little gods and goddesses, when in infancy the stomach pines and there is no zest left. Sick-room slops, large and lucent beads of suet in half-cooked 'duff', semi-gelatinous tapioca, sago, British cabbage stewed in its juice, frigid mutton fat—an occasional burst of indignation greets recollections such as these. Sharply silhouetted against the dark of my past is the face of an usher, naturally sanguine in complexion but now of a sallow salmon pink, as he protests, yet again, after attempting to prove it, that a half-raw cod's eye is not only edible but a titbit. It is odd that recollections of this kind should be so few; for anyone who has watched a child's face when it is glued to a pastrycook's window, or its dreamlike absorption when jelly comes to table, will realize how many mute inglorious Beetons in this hungry world must have been nipped in the bud by sheer lack of oppor-tunity.

Women, it is said, have better memories for detail than men, and to judge by autobiography this is especially true in regard to childhood. But here Mrs. Oliphant was an exception. 'I have not', she says, 'the clear memory of what I saw in my youth that many people retain.' One of her few early recollections is of a 'wintry road', along which her favourite brother Frank 'came home on

237

Early One Morning

Saturday nights to spend Sunday at home, walking out from Edinburgh (about six miles) to walk in again on Monday in the dark winter mornings. I recollect nothing about the summer mornings when he set out on that walk, but remember vividly like a picture the Monday mornings in winter; the fire burning cheerfully and candles on the breakfast table. . . . I can see myself, a small creature seated on a stool by the fire, toasting a cake of dough which was brought for me by the baker with the prematurely early rolls, which were for Frank. . . . And my mother, who never seemed to sit down in the strange, little, warm, bright picture, but to hover about the table pouring out tea, supplying everything he wanted to her boy.'

Whether the dough or Frank or the consciousness of self or the morning candles were the fulcrum of this recollection, it is all in Memory's capricious fashion. All those few full overwelling summers of childhood vanished clean out of the mind; and yet this one clear glimpse of winter!

CHAPTER XIX
PEOPLE

★

1. *'When thy father first did see,*
   Such a boy by him and me.'

My mother, who never seemed to sit down'—few tokens of so narrow a range as this warrant so wide an application; and if paternity educed in all men such qualities as motherhood is likely to evoke in most women, then the world would be none the worse off. Not that autobiography confines itself to mother-worship. We meet in it mothers who have been ardently loved, idolized, tenderly revered; or merely respected, or feared, or tolerated, or pitied and explained, or even despised, with little attempt either at understanding or sympathy.

'Some nurses', says sage old Robert Burton, 'are much to be preferred to some mothers. For why may not the mother be naught, a peevish drunken flirt, a waspish choleric slut, a crazed piece, a fool (as many mothers are). . . . There is more choice of nurses than mothers; and therefore except the mother be most virtuous, staid, a woman of excellent good parts, and of sound complexion, I would have all children in such cases committed to discreet strangers. . . .'

Such was Augustus Hare's lot in his infancy. His mother handed him over to his godmother, who was also an aunt, more perfunctorily than if he had been the least promising of a litter of pedigree puppies. 'The knowledge that my mother had died early', says Philip Hamerton, 'cast a certain melancholy over my childhood; I found that people looked at me with some tenderness and pity for her sake'. William Hutton was at birth, as we know, so 'very ordinary (a softer word for ugly)' that his mother was

Early One Morning

afraid that she should never love him. 'But,' he continues, 'whatever were her parental affections then, I had no cause to complain during the nine remaining years of her life. Perhaps she might not consider that very fear indicated the strength of her love.' In his tenth year on coming home from the mill he was accosted by one of her friends, Nanny Ease: ' "Your mother's gone." I burst into tears. "Don't cry, you will soon go yourself." This remark did not add to my comfort.'

Elizabeth Grant apologizes for, but disliked her mother. Roger North's mother he thought no less 'kind and happy' to him because she was strict and brisk in discipline, and we have seen John Ruskin's tribute to his. 'Perdita's' mother makes a rather hazy appearance, and the haze is not a flattering one. But in general love is easily a child's usual way of dealing with its mother; and little mention of her may well imply a deep and secure affection taken for granted. A young child may be also not only a hostage of tenderness and comfort between father and mother, but with a subtle intuition *act* as one.

Love indeed in a young child for its mother, triumphing over every obstacle or disaster, surviving undreamed-of hurts and hindrances, is looked upon rather as a duty than a rarity. Duty or otherwise (and trying *may* help), early memories abound with it, and the exceptions rather lead one to suppose that responsibility for the lack of it is usually not the child's. A child may be fastidious or otherwise in its affections, and the safest generalization would be to say merely that it knows what it likes. But after that, the prospect is boundless. And in all their affections children (of any account) keep their hearts free from cant. Their 'Let's pretend' seldom enters here.

Augustus Hare was still at the breast, and he had been 'a most unwelcome addition to the population of this troublesome world' when his aunt who had been recently widowed petitioned to adopt him. His mother's answer was brief: 'My dear Maria, how very kind of you! Yes, certainly the baby shall be sent as soon as it is weaned; and, if any one else would like one, would you kindly recollect that we have others.' He was despatched to England with a little green carpet-bag containing two white night-shirts and a red coral necklace—his 'whole trousseau and patrimony'. Long afterwards he came to know his mother well, though he 'never in

240

any way regarded her as such'. His father on the other hand remained little more than a polite stranger. When Augustus was four it chanced that they were both of them staying in the same house. A friend took the liberty of informing his father of this happy circumstance. He 'called me to him and patted my head, saying, "Good little Wolf: good little Wolf!" It was the only notice he ever took of me.'

His foster-mother however took the most vigilant notice of him. 'On Tuesday, August 26, 1835'—he was then a baby of seventeen months—she wrote in her Journal: 'My little Augustus came to me. It was about four o'clock when I heard a cry from upstairs and ran up. There was the dear child seated on Mary's knee. . . . He smiled most sweetly and with a peculiar archness of expression as I went up to him, and there was no shyness. When dressed, I brought him down into the drawing-room: he looked with great delight at the pictures, the busts, and especially the bronze wolf—pointed at them, then looked round at Jule and me. When set down, he strutted along the passage, went into every room, surveyed all things in it with an air of admiration and importance, and nothing seemed to escape observation. . . .'

He delighted in flowers; stooping, obediently, only to smell those in the garden, but gathering the wild ones in the fields. *Numbers* of things, whether apples, or acorns, had an especial charm for him. When thwarted, he would fall into a violent fit of passion, a fit usually soon over, and followed by laughter. If continued, it might last for half an hour together.

At the age of nineteen months he was astonished to find himself in a new house. 'The first evening [there] he kissed me over and over again, as if to comfort and assure me of his affection.' He became more obedient and ready to share his playthings, and was overjoyed at sight of the moon, calling 'Moon, moon', as if he could not help himself, and next day running to the window to look for it. He was always 'merriest and most amiable when without playthings', and took great pleasure in the flowers painted on the china, and in all kinds of pictures.

In one of his tantrums his foster-mother said, 'It makes Mama very sorry to see Baby so naughty.' 'He instantly stopped, threw his arms round my neck, and sobbed out—"Baby lub Mama—good."' A little after he was two years old he knew the name of

Early One Morning

every flower both in garden and field, and never forgot any he
had once seen. 'When he sees me hold my hand to my head, he
says, "Mama tired—head bad—Baby play self." ' When dipped
into the sea at Eastbourne he was always frightened at first, and
then, 'in the midst of his sobs from the shock, would sing "Little
Bo Peep".'

Augustus will presently be speaking for himself, but *not* concerning days as early as these. I have referred to them here only as
an indication of the vicissitudes not only of life but of feeling,
thought and impulse in a child so young, and in part as a contrast
to Elizabeth Grant's indictment of Mrs. Millar. If only we could
also reverse the situations—hear Mrs. Millar on Elizabeth Grant,
and Augustus at this age on his beloved 'Mama'.

2. *'He said, I'll teach my children as a father oughter.'*

The *father* in early autobiography is usually a more nebulous
figure, though his early appearances within the nursery orbit
—and especially when he is a Rhadamanthus in reserve—may be
both grim and abject. Here again there are degrees of filial emotion, from indifference down to fear and hatred, and up to devotion and adoration. The easiest and closest and happiest of com-
panionships is another blissful alternative. Charles Darwin paid
his father a matchless tribute—that he was the wisest man he ever
knew. Elizabeth Grant's attitude to her father, and vividly real she
makes him, passed through nearly every one of these stages in
turn.

It was he who gave her, when she was five years old, her first
recallable notion of the appearances of humans. 'I see my father',
she says, 'in his study at a table writing; a little sallow man without
any remarkable feature, his hair all drawn back over his head,
powdered and tied in a queue with a great bow of black ribbon.
He has on drab-coloured stocking pantaloons and little boots up
to the knee, from the two-pointed front of which dangles a
tassel.' Even the voice of this little sallow man was to his small
daughter, she tells us, the herald of joy.

But the most brutal of fathers does not necessarily erase every
vestige of affection in his child's heart, which may have an inexhaustible grace of forgiveness even when not the faintest chance

People

is afforded it to forget. Thomas Holcroft's portrait of his father is bleakly realistic yet not vindictive. Not until he was twenty-four did William Hutton receive his first kiss from his father—and then he was 'elevated with liquor'! 'My dear father!—I now think of him', says William Bell Scott, 'with much veneration: veneration and respect, with a smile underlying these virtuous feelings. He lost much money and time over his new ideas. . . .'

On the familiar epitaph,

> 'Here lies good master duck,
>   Whom Samuel Johnson trod on;
> If it had lived, it had been *good luck*,
>   For then we'd had an *odd one*.'

Miss Seward based a little sermon respecting 'infant numbers', 'the seeds of propensities', 'poetic talent' and even 'superstitious bias', since she herself believed that Samuel Johnson as a child of three had dictated it to his mother. Boswell's comment is hardly less amusing: 'There is surely internal evidence, that this little composition combines in it what no child of three years old could produce, without an extension of its faculties by immediate inspiration'! We shall come to this question later. Dr. Johnson, alas, confessed that both 'inspiration' and rhyme were his father's. He added: 'My father was a foolish old man; that is to say, foolish in talking of his children.' How many children, one speculates, have shared this view? It is embarrassing enough to a child to overhear himself being talked about—unless flatteringly. On the other hand, these fathers who are being thus talked about by their children, it must be remembered, are far beyond being able to answer back.

There is a tragic and vivid portrait of John Hamerton, as seen through a child's eye, in his son's autobiography. The painfulness of telling the truth deferred the writing of it for years:—

'He was extremely severe at times. . . . When inflamed with brandy he became positively dangerous. . . . My existence . . . was one of extreme dulness varied by dread. Every meal was a *tête-à-tête* with my father . . . he was now like a black cloud always hanging over me and ready, as it seemed, to be my destruction in some way or other not yet clearly defined. . . . Even now everything about Ivy Cottage is as clear as if the forty years were only as many

Early One Morning

days, and the writing of these chapters brings everything before me most vividly, not only the faces of the people and the habits and motions of the animals, but even the furniture, of which I remember every detail, down to the colouring of the services in the bedrooms, and the paint on my father's rocking-chair. . . .

'I awoke one bleak winter's morning about five o'clock, and heard the strangest cries proceeding from his room. His man-servant had been awakened before me and had gone to the room already, where he was engaged in a sort of wrestling match with my father who, in the belief that the house was full of enemies, was endeavouring to throw himself out of the window. Other men had been called for, who speedily arrived, and they over-powered him, though even the remnant of his mighty strength was such that it took six men to hold him on his bed. The attack lasted a whole week, and the house would have been a perfect hell, had not a certain event turned it for me into a Paradise.

'I had been able somehow to get to sleep late at night for a short time, when a light in the room awoke me. The horrible life I had been leading for many a day and night had produced a great im-pressionability, and I was particularly afraid of my father in the night-time, so I started up in bed with the idea that he was come to beat me, when lo! instead of his terrible face, I saw what for me was the sweetest and dearest face in the whole world! It was his sister Mary, she who had taken my mother's place, and whom I loved. . . . For the suddenness of revulsion from horror to happi-ness, there has never been a minute in my existence comparable to the minute when I realized the idea that she had come. . . .

'I was not in the room when he died, but my aunt took me to see him immediately after, and then I received an impression which has lasted to the present day. The corpse was lying on its side amidst disordered bedclothes, and to this day I can never go into a bedroom where the bed has not been made without feeling as if there were a corpse in it. . . .'

Even advanced age, and paternity itself, may fail to effect a reconciliation. Samuel Butler, who died a bachelor, says of his father that he could remember 'no feeling during his childhood except fear and shrinking'. 'He never liked me, nor I him.' Canon and Mrs. Butler had a little book of precepts, including 'Break your child's will early, or he will break yours later on'. In this case

244

People

there seems to have been a failure on both sides. Cellini's father appears to have been less concerned with his son's will than his memory. And would that other fathers—perhaps with milder methods—had realized what pleasures they were thus preserving for the future of their offspring!

'When I was about five years of age, my father happened to be in a little room in which they had been washing, and where there was a good oak fire burning: with a fiddle in his hand he sang and played near the fire, the weather being exceedingly cold. Looking into the fire, he saw a little animal resembling a lizard, which lived and enjoyed itself in the hottest flames. Instantly perceiving what it was, he called for my sister, and after he had shown us the creature, he gave me a box on the ear: I fell a-crying, while he, soothing me with his caresses, said, "My dear child, I don't give you that blow for any fault you have committed, but that you may remember that the little lizard which you see in the fire is a salamander, a creature which no one that I have heard of ever beheld before." So saying, he embraced me, and gave me some money. . . .'

'I cost my mother her life,' says Jean-Jacques Rousseau, 'and my birth was the first of my misfortunes.' To his father, who had been sweethearts with that mother when they were children, Jean-Jacques became a source of bitter regret and of tender remembrance. 'Jean-Jacques,' he would say, 'let us talk of your mother,' and 'I used to answer: "Well, then, my father, we will weep!"' He felt, he says, before he began to think, but 'I do not know what I did until I was five or six years old'. At that age he sometimes spent whole nights with his father over one of his mother's romances, each reading in turn, until the swallows began to twitter at daybreak, and his father, ashamed of this debauch, would say: 'Let us go to bed. I am more of a child than yourself.'

Envy and jealousy of a newcomer in childhood have not as we have seen always fallen short of murderous intent, or indeed of more than intent. The relations of brother to brother may be those between David and Jonathan, a state of mere neutrality, or a bitter rivalry or dislike. One of the most blessed of any such kinships is that between a younger brother and a beloved elder sister, such, for example, as Galton's with his sister Adele. Sir Egerton Brydges also refers to the precious influence of a sister fourteen and a half

Early One Morning

years older than himself, who 'could almost repeat the chief English poets by heart', and was herself an easy writer of verse.

Whether children in the close contact between themselves that family life imposes really understand the workings of the child mind *in one another*, is a question difficult indeed to decide. Most of them have the requisite insight probably, and leave it at that. There is none the less usually an open alliance between them, if not an *entente cordiale*, when the grown-up declares war. And they often in private share difficulties usually unconfided to their elders; though one father's inward ear is still ringing with the accents of a shrill and indignant voice expostulating from an upper room into the silence of the universe: 'Daddy, *can* you cuddle God?'

It is hardly an exaggeration to say that young children are a nation and people apart, with their own observances, customs and laws, unwritten and otherwise. As with the grown-ups, secrets remain secrets between themselves; though now and then the adult can return from a visit to their Jericho, otherwise secure against his trumpet-blasts, burdened with milk and honey and a handsome cluster of grapes. One of such secrets, and one kept as close as possible from forbidden or forbidding eyes, is that of falling in love.

> 3. '*Silly boy, 'tis full moon yet,*
> *Thy night as day shines clearly.*'

For most happy victims it is an event and a condition that, without any question at all, can be as real as it is earnest. My sweetheart when a *toy*, then, refers to a much later period in life. Nevertheless nothing provokes so shallow and easy an amusement in most adults than the suggestion that such and such a child is 'in love', an amusement that may not fall short of a deadly snigger. It is an attitude which not only implies a complete forgetfulness of our feelings—deep as first love, and wild with all regret—when they were as genuine as they were intense, but may also be a devastating commentary on their present state.

Romanticism and sentiment are common enough in childhood, but neither is alien to a genuine and passionate devotion at any time in life. And what devotion touched with passion, even in a child of seven, is wholly of the mind? *Annabel Lee* is a poem as densely scented with sentimentality as *The Raven* is coloured with

People

what is called the morbid, though neither fact need preclude an unfailing delight in both of them. Both poems at any rate are faithfully characteristic of their author, and there is a far smaller share of 'fudge' in either, or in *To One in Paradise*, than there is of genius. In any case the statement,

'But our love it was stronger by far than the love
Of those who were older than we,
Of many far wiser than we. . . .'

if we look into our own hearts and criticize, is merely the plain truth.

'I loved a Love once, fairest among women'—even *that* 'once' might be childhood, since time and age have little concern with love. When Thomas Hardy was nine or ten years old, his feeling for the lady of the manor at Bockhampton was, says Mrs. Hardy, 'almost that of a lover'. He so much longed to see her that he jumped at an offer from a young woman of the village to take him to a harvest-supper at which he knew she would be present. She greeted him with 'O Tommy, how is this? I thought you had deserted me!' In anguish he assured her that he had not, and never would. He danced with a small niece of hers, and then was left stranded until three o'clock in the morning, famished and utterly tired out.

There is nothing wanting in seriousness in Wordsworth's poems about Lucy, nor, apart from a tinge of fondness, is there anything wanting in naturalness and freedom from patronage in William Motherwell's *Jeanie Morrison*:

. . . 'Twas then we luvit ilk ither weel,
'Twas then we twa did part;
Sweet time—sad time! twa bairns at schule,
Twa bairns, and but ae heart!
'Twas then we sat on ae laigh bink,
To leir ilk ither lear;
And tones, and looks, and smiles were shed,
Remembered evermair.

'I wonder, Jeanie, aften yet,
When sitting on that bink,
Cheek touchin' cheek, loof locked in loof,

247

Early One Morning

What our wee heads could think!
When baith bent doun owre ae braid page,
    Wi' ae buik on our knee,
Thy lips were on thy lesson, but
    My lesson was in thee. . . .'

Yet, although early love in childhood, lacking few of the less
dismal pangs incident to love itself in later life, has been, one might
surmise, the common lot of those who occasionally or habitually
fall in love at all, the English poets have said little about it, and
some of that little has been a little silly. But there are exceptions.

In his *Life of Francis Thompson* Everard Meynell refers to the
fact that his poem *Dream Tryst* had been alluded to as erotic. It was
in fact, said Francis Thompson himself, a poem 'addressed to a
child. Nay, hardly that—to the memory only of a child known but
once when I was eleven years old'. Her name was Lucidé, and she
was entirely unaware of his admiration.

At his first school Crabbe wrote his first tale in verse. It was
addressed to a damsel who shared their evening classes with the
boys, and whose vanity had been dazzled by a bunch of blue ribbons on her new straw bonnet. It cannot have been at a very far
remove from *Tales of the Hall*, and was at least in the same *genre* as
'Proud Maisie is in the wood, Walking so early. . . .' and

'Sweet, be not proud of those two eyes,
Which, star-like, sparkle in their skies;
Nor be you proud that you can see
All hearts your captives, yours yet free. . . .'

"Mr. Craigie and I walked to Craigiehall hand in hand in innocence and meditation, sweetly thinking of the kind love which
flows in the tender-hearted mind we seem to share—a mind over-
flowing indeed with a majestic pleasure. No one was ever so
polite to me in the whole course of my existence.'

Should we, taking that on its face value, be completely incredulous if it were attributed to a discovered diary of Jane Austen's? It
is actually an extract from the Journal of a six-year-old, although
there it appears in slightly different terms:—

'. . . Mr Crakey and I walked to Crakyhall hand in hand in
Innocence and matitation sweet thinking on the kind love which

flows in our tender hearted mind which is overflowing with majestick pleasure. No body was ever so polite to me in the hole state of my existence. . . .'

In similar spelling the love letters of Héloïse would be merely amusing. Or try, 'But if the wile I think of thee deer frend. . . .'

Destiny, nowadays, I suppose, seldom in childhood brings together those whom no man may long years afterwards put asunder; but Dr. Newton, the famous dean of St. Paul's, we are told, had known his wife from the time when she was 'a little girl in a white frock'. And the following statement by William Hutton concerning the eighth year of his life is a very endearing rarity: 'March the eleventh, was born, quite unknown to me, at Aston upon Trent, six miles east of Derby, a female child, who, twenty-four years after, was to become my wife; be my faithful and dear companion, and love me better than herself. I was to possess this inestimable treasure forty years, then to lose it, and mourn its loss every future day of my life. . . .'

There is in Browning's diary, says Mrs. Sutherland Orr, a summary entry on a Sunday in the seventh or eighth year of his age: 'Married two wives this morning.' She hastens to explain that it refers only to 'a vague imaginary appropriation of two girls whom he had just seen in church'. Imaginary appropriations of this kind were the theme of many of his poems (those about Porphyria, for instance, the 'light woman', and the lady with the piano), and had the entry occurred in a journal kept in his childhood by Brigham Young, it might have been otherwise interpreted. One can never be sure of the machinations of the interloper who disports himself in *Daphnis & Chloe*—'a certain young boy, very disdainfull, very fair; one that had wings at his shoulders, wore a bowe, and little darts'.

4. *'The wanton, Cupid, scoffs at odds.'*

During school hours . . .' says Philip Hamerton, 'I managed to fall in love with a girl about a year older than myself, who was a very nice girl indeed, though she squinted to an unfortunate degree.' He accepted his 'fall' as an argument in favour of co-education. Nor indeed is only a man child capable of overlooking life's little handicaps:

Early One Morning

... I made no friends at that dreadful little school [says Miss Ethel Mannin], but I fell in love with a boy about two years older than myself who had wetted himself standing on the "dunce's stool", and burst into tears when he was finally released to go and do what he had already done. I felt his suffering terribly and loved him from that day on. I wanted to tell him not to cry, that it wasn't his fault, that I understood, that he needn't be ashamed. Actually I never spoke to him all the time I was there, but I would lie in bed at night and think of him, and a warm new sensation, exciting and a little frightening, yet pleasurable, would sweep over me. He got so much into my imagination that for weeks I would look forward to going to bed so that I could snuggle down into the warmth and dark and secrecy of the bed and indulge the voluptuous pleasure which invariably came with the thought of him. I was six years old and affected by a personality for the first time. I remember that the boy's name was Maurice, that I thought him beautiful with his riot of waving brown hair, and loved him with an aching compassionate love. . . .

That first sweethearts are seldom referred to in early memories is less likely to be an indication of how much an autobiographer inadvertently leaves out than of what he prefers not to put in. In his last years in the asylum at Northampton John Clare was haunted by the lovely phantom of a young girl, named Mary Joyce, with whom, on seeing her for the first time, he instantly fell in love. He was then, however, not a child but in his sixteenth year.

> . . . I met her in the greenest dells
> Where dewdrops pearl the wood blue bells
> The lost breeze kissed her bright blue eye,
> The bee kissed and went singing by,
> A sunbeam found a passage there,
> A gold chain round her neck so fair;
> As secret as the wild bee's song
> She lay there all the summer long. . . .

Byron—come to his senses, and five years before he began *Don Juan*—is astonished at the fervour of what he calls his childish amour with Mary Duff, when he was about nine years old. There is the oddest medley of stark worldliness and naïvety in his

BYRON, AT THE AGE OF SEVEN
From a miniature in the Vaughan Library at Harrow

People

account of it, written in his twenty-fifth year. It is as though a cuckoo had chanced to discover a forsaken nest not only of her own building, but with a half-hatched egg in it, a meadow pipit's. But that he cannot 'explain' his feelings—who can?—does not detract from their genuineness or from his own realization of 'the lovely Peri existing in her' referred to in the last sentence of what follows.

'I have been thinking lately a good deal of Mary Duff. How very odd that I should have been so utterly, devotedly fond of that girl, at an age when I could neither feel passion, nor know the meaning of the word. And the effect! My mother used always to rally me about this childish amour; and, at last, many years after, when I was sixteen she told me one day, "Oh, Byron, I have had a letter from Edinburgh, from Miss Abercromby, and your old sweetheart Mary Duff is married to a Mr. Coe." And what was my answer? I really cannot explain or account for my feelings at that moment, but they nearly threw me into convulsions, and alarmed my mother so much, that after I grew better, she generally avoided the subject—to *me*—and contented herself with telling it to all her acquaintance. Now, what could this be? I had never seen her since her mother's *faux pas* at Aberdeen had been the cause of her removal to her grandmother's at Banff; we were both the merest children. I had and have been attached fifty times since that period; yet I recollect all we said to each other, all our caresses, her features, my restlessness, sleeplessness, my tormenting my mother's maid to write for me to her, which she at last did, to quiet me. Poor Nancy thought I was wild, and, as I could not write for myself, became my secretary. I remember, too, our walks, and the happiness of sitting by Mary, in the children's apartments, at their house not far from the Plain-stones at Aberdeen, while her lesser sister Helen played with the doll, and we sat gravely making love, in our way. . . .

'How very pretty is the perfect image of her in my memory— her brown, dark hair, and hazel eyes; her very dress! I should be quite grieved to see *her now*; the reality, however beautiful, would destroy, or at least confuse, the features of the lovely Peri which then existed in her, and still lives in my imagination, at the distance of more than sixteen years. I am now twenty-five and odd months. . . .'

Early One Morning

Early friendship is more seldom referred to than early love, but it may be no less ardent. Wallace speaks of a lifelong friend, whom fate itself, as it seemed, repeatedly persuaded into his company. After the arrival of his family in Hertford, where he lived for eight or nine years, he remembered that a strange boy of about his own age looked over a wall in the garden and enquired, 'Hullo! who are you?' 'Thus began the friendship of George Silk and Alfred Wallace, which, with long intervals of absence at various periods, has continued to this day.' Again and again the two families moved, and again and again found themselves in close proximity to one another. Wordsworth in *The Prelude* speaks, between joy and sorrow, of 'a Friend, Then passionately loved'—in his boyhood—John Fleming. Edmund Burke had a beloved friend in childhood, Richard Shackleton; and William Cowper another, Walter Bagot.

Galton too found a friend and hero at his first school, Matthew P. Watt Boulton. 'I owe much to his influence,' he says. In retrospect even the cause of a deep infatuation may elude remembrance. This was not so with Shelley. His old schoolfellow, at Eton, Captain Gronow, relates in his *Reminiscences* that he chanced on Shelley, in 1822, seated on the seashore enjoying a meal of bread and fruit. They talked of old days, and of Spires's, the tuckshop; and Shelley burst out wildly: 'Gronow, do you remember the beautiful Martha, the Hebe of Spires's? She was the loveliest girl I ever saw, and I loved her to distraction.' This was a year before his death. Among his papers after his death, says Mr. Roger Ingpen in his *Shelley in England*, was found a fragment in his handwriting which was intended as a dedication to an essay: 'I once had a friend whom an inextricable multitude of circumstances has forced me to treat with apparent neglect. . . . The nature of love and friendship is very little understood and the relation between them ill established.' He was 'a boy about my own age . . . generous, brave and gentle. . . . There was a delicacy and a simplicity in his manners inexpressibly attractive. . . . His . . . every word pierced into my heart; and their pathos was so deep, that in listening to him the tears have involuntarily gushed from my eyes. . . . I remember in my simplicity writing to my mother a long account of his admirable qualities and my own devoted attachment. I suppose she thought me out of my wits, for she returned no answer to my letter'. Shelley was then eleven years old.

Almost the reverse situation presented itself to Southey. 'I have seen many instances', he remarks, 'wherein the promise of the boy has not been fulfilled by the man, but never so striking a case of blight' as that of a schoolfellow whose appearance and manners prepossessed everyone he met. Mrs. Southey was so much taken by his charms that she entreated Robert to become intimate with him; but in vain. At five-and-twenty, Southey continues (not without a tinge of complacency), this Adonis had become 'an insignificant withered *homunculus*, with a white face shrivelled into an expression of effeminate peevishness'.

It is also possible to fall into hatred. Lord Berners's mother was most anxious that he should be fond of sport, and chiefly of riding, which he disliked. For this reason she encouraged him to be friendly with a girl called Nesta, a tomboy much given to boasting of her skill in riding. One day, when he was feeling particularly resentful of her 'taunts and overbearing patronage', he pushed her off the top of a haystack. She fell on the shaft of a cart and cut her leg. Lord Berners and the two boys with him were 'beset by that same primeval panic that brings about mass hysteria, pogroms or stampedes'. All three jumped down, tore away her clothes, and smacked her. It was the last time he had to play with her.

'I was ashamed of myself. I was suffering from a guilty conscience. None the less I now hated Nesta more than ever, after what had happened. I hated her for having caused me to behave like a cad.'

CHAPTER XX

PLACES

★

1. 'Feed apace those greedy eyes
   On the wonder you behold!'

Thesefew pages are far too superficial a reference to incidents so vital in a child's life, but a superabundance
of early memories in autobiography reflects them and
they may have an indelible influence. The remoter
planets in a child's solar system may also make their appearance—
aunts, uncles, cousins, neighbours and friends, observed, marked
and completely digested. An admirable study of a grandfather,
for example, appears in *The Small Years*—consisting in all essen-
tials chiefly of childhood memories. Taught to be unheard, and
therefore frequently unseen or unnoticed, a young and intelligent
child has ample opportunities for watching, comparing and
listening to his elders—and he has an eye between his shoulderblades, a faculty resembling the second sight.

How then of scene and place and streets and buildings?

Glimpses of an earth rarefied and transmuted in a young
imagination have been already referred to. They seem to be the
outcome of a moment spent in an unusual solitude, and may bestow a happiness beyond words to describe, or as extreme a
despair—then

'when the melancholy fit shall fall
Sudden from heaven like a weeping cloud
That fosters the droop-headed flowers all
And hides the green hill in an April shroud. . . .

When Thomas Hardy was a child of three or four, the old airs
his father used to play on the fiddle, to which he himself used to

dance, always moved him to tears, however much he tried to hide them. In later life he used to say that like Calantha in Ford's *Broken Heart* 'he danced on to conceal his weeping'. It was about this time that he was lying alone one day on his back in the sun—his face concealed by a straw hat. Its lining being gone, the sunbeams came crinkling through the twisted straw upon his face. And suddenly there fell upon him the conviction that he had no wish to grow up. The wellspring had ceased to flow. He afterwards confided this to his mother, and always regretted how much he had grieved her in so doing, since she had nearly died in giving him birth.

It is the strange collusion such as this between sunshine, solitude and the mind within—as in the incident described by Blair—which, if we could fully share it, would be a revelation indeed of childhood. It confronts us again a little more intelligibly in connection with the daily tryst that Thomas Hardy used to keep on the staircase of his home at Bockhampton, the walls of which had been coloured by his father a Venetian red. Sitting alone there, he would await the radiant effects on them of the evening sun at the window, and would recite to himself 'with great fervency' Dr. Watts's hymn, 'And now another day is gone', 'perhaps not for any religious reason, but from a sense that the scene suited the lines'.

Mrs. Oliphant again could remember 'with the most vivid clearness' lying on her back in the grass among the speedwells one warm summer day in her childhood, and looking up into the sky: 'the depths of it, the blueness of it. . . . I feel the giddiness in my brain still, and the happiness, as if I had been the first discoverer of that wonderful sky'. All my little recollections are like pictures, she adds, 'to which the meaning, naturally, is put long afterwards. . . .' Not that it had no meaning then. 'When Edward Calvert', writes Mr. Laurence Binyon, 'was six years old, as he sat in a garden at Honiton, the evening light transformed the grass and flowers into a Paradise of miraculous splendour and serenity; the child was overcome with a sense of the glory of earth; he had a sense "as of a living spirit taking up his abode within him, and seating himself beside his own soul".'

These are experiences, rifts in Time, irretrievable visions, wherein mood, feeling and scene are interfused. The merely

Early One Morning

observant eye is not concerned with them. The following is of quite another kind. Walter Scott when he was about six years old visited Bath, as lovely a city as his own Edinburgh. The circumstances, he says, a little sedately, 'which I recollect of my residence [there] are but trifling, yet I never recall them without a feeling of pleasure. The beauties of the parade (which of them I know not), with the River Avon winding around it, and the lowing of the cattle from the opposite hills, are warm in my recollection, and are only rivalled by the splendours of a toy-shop somewhere near the Orange Grove. I had acquired, I know not by what means, a kind of superstitious terror for statuary of all kinds. No ancient Iconoclast or modern Calvinist could have looked on the outside of the Abbey church (if I mistake not, the principal church at Bath is so called) with more horror than the image of Jacob's Ladder, with all its angels, presented to my infant eye. . . .'

Only as intent an observer as himself could have interpreted the expression on that young face transfixed by the horrifying ladder and its angels—for most children one of the clearest and happiest visionary scenes in the Old Testament.

Walter Scott's recollection is of looking *up* at a sacred edifice, Samuel Butler recalled looking down on one. When he was seven years old he was taken to the top of St. Peter's in Rome, and surveyed the wonders beneath him. A year afterwards the words of a Signora Capocci profoundly impressed him. She told the children of a dear young friend of hers who had had a great misfortune: ' "Povero disgraziato!" she exclaimed, "Ha ammazzato il suo zio e la sua zia" (Poor unfortunate fellow! he has murdered his uncle and his aunt).' This double meaning of *disgraziato*, he tells us, remained as ineffaceable in his mind as did the love of Italy in his heart.

In his fourth year Herbert Spencer's aunt took him to Bath and thence by sea to London. A quarter of a century later he again visited the Tower of London and Westminster Abbey, and was astonished to find how accurate his recollections 'of these celebrated places' had been: 'I have ever since trusted more implicitly to my juvenile reminiscences.'

When he was about six or seven years old Robert Southey, having left his first day-school, went to live with his aunt, Miss Tyler, at Bedminster, and was happy. 'If I possessed the skill,' he

Places

says, 'I should delight in tracing' a bird's-eye view of the house and garden. 'My memory would accurately serve'.

'. . . The furniture consisted of a clock, a large oval oak table with two flaps (over which two or three fowling-pieces had their place), a round tea-table of cherry wood, Windsor chairs of the same, and two large armed ones of that easy make (of all makes the easiest), in one of which my grandmother always sat. On one side of the fireplace the china was displayed in a buffet—that is, a cupboard with glass doors; on the other were closets for articles less ornamental, but more in use. The room was wainscoted and ornamented with some old maps, and with a long looking-glass over the chimney-piece, and a tall one between the windows, both in white frames. The windows opened into the forecourt, and were as cheerful and fragrant in the season of flowers as roses and jessamine, which grew luxuriantly without, could make them. . . .'

Alfred Russel Wallace, who wrote *My Life* when he was in his sixties, remarks on the fact that in looking back to his early childhood he entirely failed to recall any peculiarities of feature, form, dress or habits in his family at this time, and that similar limitations both in observation and memory continued to manifest themselves throughout his life. But concerning place and scene he has quite a different tale to tell. He could recall vividly the house in which he lived beside the Usk, its very shape and colour, and even the pattern of the wallpaper of the room in which he slept. He remembered, too, an elder brother demonstrating to the family that the reflection in the flowing water of the hills beyond it was sometimes visible and sometimes not, however calm and clear the mirroring river. He listened intently to the explanation of this phenomenon, but failed to follow it. He could revive in detail the lovely babbling river, which must also have been the delight of Henry Vaughan—its old bridge with three arches, a quarry, a ruinous mediæval castle, and he associated these surroundings with the poems he read as a child. And when many years afterwards he returned again to these scenes, everything was as his memory had declared it to be. In 'modern psychology', he continues, he could find nothing that would satisfactorily explain these facts. But he succeeded in doing so when he made a phrenological examination of the shape of his head. In this the 'bumps' of form and individuality were less developed than those of locality, ideality, colour and comparison.

Other children, apparently, may exult in an outfit of *both* kinds of 'bumps'. ('Mummie,' a small boy was heard to enquire a few years ago on emerging in the train into view of the lovely Malvern Hills, 'Mummie, what's them 'eaps?') A recollection of Alexander Carlyle's—place, setting *and dramatis personæ*—resembling a gay conversation piece by Zoffany, was connected with the Lady Grange. This was the lady whose funeral was in 1732 publicly celebrated by her husband, James Erskine (appointed lord justice clerk in 1710), when in fact he had marooned her on St. Kilda, the remotest of the little islands of the Outer Hebrides, from which she never returned alive. She appeared to me, says Carlyle, who met her about this time, when he was ten years old, 'to be the lady with whom all well-educated children were acquainted, the Great Scarlet Whore of Babylon'. She had found him wandering on the banks of the Red Burn, had thrust him into her coach and taken him home. Her two young daughters and her son John were in the coach. They invited him to drink tea with them the following Saturday.

'The young ladies had a fine closet, charmingly furnished, with chairs, a table, a set of china and everything belonging to it. The misses set about making tea, for they had a fire in the room, and a maid came to help them, till at length we heard a shrill voice screaming, "Mary Erskine, my angel Mary Erskine!" . . . The girls seemed frightened out of their wits, and so did the maid. The clamour ceased; but the girls ordered John and me to stand sentry in our turns, with vigilant ear, and give them notice whenever the storm began again. We had sweet-cake and almonds and raisins, of which a small paper bag was given me for my brother. . . . I had no great enjoyment, notwithstanding the good things and the kisses given, for I had by contagion caught a mighty fear of my lady from them. But I was soon relieved, for my father's man came for me at seven o'clock. The moment I was out of sight of the house, I took out my paper bag and ate up its contents, bribing the servant with a few. . . .'

How curiously *small* and bright the picture is, resembling the glimpse of the garish Linton drawing-room seen at night through a window by the children Cathie and Heathcliff in *Wuthering Heights.*

258

Places

2. *'O Mother-My-Love, if you'll give me your hand*
And go where I ask you to wander . . .'

William Morris, equally late in life, could recollect being taken by his father when he was eight years old to see Canterbury Cathedral, his 'first large church', and the Minster in Thanet. Of the Minster he could distinctly recall the long nave and other details. The Blackgang Chine in the Isle of Wight had keenly interested him, but not merely as 'scenery'—he was told that it had been the resort of pirates.

A poem of George Crabbe's, concerned with his childhood, is full of the sea and sailors and of tales of the sea:

> 'I to the ocean gave
> My mind, and thoughts as restless as the wave.
> Where crowds assembled I was sure to run,
> Hear what was said, and muse on what was done. . . .
> I loved to walk where none had walk'd before,
> About the rocks that ran along the shore;
> Or far beyond the sight of men to stray,
> And take my pleasure when I lost my way. . . .
> Here had I favourite stations, where I stood,
> And heard the murmurs of the ocean-flood,
> With not a sound beside, except when flew
> Aloft the lapwing, or the grey curlew. . . .
> When I no more my fancy could employ—
> I left in haste what I could not enjoy,
> And was my gentle mother's welcome boy.'

His first pleasure-trip on the ocean-flood which began after a serene sunrise in the company of a number of merrymakers ended in disenchantment:

> 'As the sun declined,
> The good found early I no more could find.
> The men drank much to whet the appetite,
> And, growing heavy, drank to make them light.
> Then drank to relish joy, then further to excite
> Till on the colder water faintly shone
> The sloping light—the cheerful day was gone. . . .'

259

Early One Morning

'What will that *thing* ever be good for?' was Mr. Crabbe's summary of his son's clumsiness in a boat. Still, he was a favourite with the old dames of Aldeburgh, and, unlike Keats, was once let off a street fight when he was a boy on account of his 'larning'. Verse, as these few lines prove, may be the most translucent amber wherein to enshrine memories of childhood. In his *Elegy* Robert Bridges tells how with a telescope he used to watch the sea and its ships from 'the Summerhouse on the Mound' when he was a child ten years old. This brought 'a circle of the sea Enlarged to swiftness' so near that it seemed he could hear the dashing waves, the canvas and tackle; and he began to wonder if the sailors might not become aware of his gaze on them and resent his prying and spying! He recalls a particular Sunday, since it was two years after the death of the Iron Duke, whom he had grieved for even then, 'And whose white hairs in this my earliest scene Had scarce more honoured than accustom'd been'.

'. . . One noon in March upon that anchoring ground
Came Napier's fleet into the Baltic bound:
Cloudless the sky and calm and blue the sea,
As round Saint Margaret's cliff mysteriously,
Those murderous queens walking in Sabbath sleep
Glided in line upon the windless deep:
For in those days was first seen low and black
Beside the full-rigg'd mast the strange smoke-stack,
And neath their stern revolv'd the twisted fan.
Many I knew as soon as I might scan,
The heavy *Royal George,* the *Acre* bright,
The *Hogue* and *Ajax,* and could name aright
Others that I remember now no more;
But chief, her blue flag flying at the fore,
With fighting guns a hundred thirty and one,
The Admiral ship the *Duke of Wellington.* . . .'

Mrs. Hardy relates that when Thomas Hardy was aged eight or nine he came up to London with his mother, and that they stayed at the *Cross Keys,* Clerkenwell, where Shelley and Mary Godwin used to meet. In old age he could recall some of its streets as he had seen them then, the Pantheon, Cumberland Gate into Hyde Park, 'which then could boast of no Marble Arch', and

Places

'the pandemonium of Smithfield with its mud, curses, and cries of ill-treated animals'. At what is now called Swiss Cottage the two of them stopped and 'looked back at the *outside* of London creeping towards them across green fields. . . .'

No less vivid was his recollection of being taken a little later by a village girl to a harvest home, and of the young women in their light gowns seated on a bench against the wall in the barn, lolling one against another as they warbled the Dorset version of the ballad, 'May Colvine'.

> 'Lie there, lie there, thou false-hearted man,
>   Lie there instead o' me;
> For six pretty maidens thou hast a-drown'd here,
>   But the seventh hath drown-ed thee!
>
> .   .   .   .   .
>
> 'O tell no more, my pretty par-rot,
>   Lay not the blame on me;
> And your cage shall be made o' the glittering gold,
>   Wi' a door o' the white ivo-rie!'

Another meat market, Farringdon, makes its appearance in Richard Middleton's recollections of his childhood. He loathed his morning journey through it to school, though he was 'no nut-eater'.

'Æsthetic butchers made the market hideous with mosaics of the intestines of animals, as if the horrors of suety pavements and bloody sawdust did not suffice. . . . I saw the greasy, red-faced men with their hands and aprons stained with blood. . . . the masses of entrails, the heaps of repulsive hides; but most clearly of all I saw an ugly sad little boy with a satchel of books on his back set down in the midst of an enormous and hostile world.'

But how are we to lay down the law in matters even as mundane as these? All depends on the mood and momentary outlook in a child. I must have been a good deal younger than Richard Middleton when, with a creeping loathing but also with a calm curiosity, I stood examining a mass of entrails—the entrails of a horse, which had been deposited for manure, I suppose, in a meadow. In a like cold and afflicted absorption I find myself standing as a child at an upper window in distant view of a miserable rib-raked

261

Early One Morning

horse that was in the act of being pole-axed—the hollow temples, the sagging forelegs, the discoloured hide.

Here was much the same recognition as that referred to by W. B. Scott when he lifted a stone and disclosed nature's awful world of the minimal writhing beneath it. *This is this!* At about the age of thirteen I witnessed a fight between two butchers in the Smithfield market. The greasy, furious, blue and bloodstained ring, shafted with sunlight, is etched as sharply on memory as a Callot engraving is cut on its copper. In the midst of the pandemonium that followed when one of the principals of this bout was knocked out, their seconds set to! I was breathlessly engrossed in this spectacle when sharp raps on the shin from a schoolmaster's malacca cane restored me to decency again, though not perhaps to a sense of it.

Thomas De Quincey when he wrote his *Confessions* remembered that he remembered remembering—a very unusual trophy. He tells how he ran away from school to escape from a confinement that had induced a chronic disorder of the liver. He came to Altrincham. There he put up for the night at an inn in the market square, and next morning threw open his window to view the gay and lively scene below. It recalled instantly another morning of just as 'superb' and 'dazzling' a day in July when he was a child only three years old, suffering from 'the hooping-cough'. He had wakened earlier than his nurse approved of—a common and excruciating dilemma for nurses—and it was he who prevailed. 'After putting me through my morning's drill of ablutions and the Lord's-prayer, no sooner had she fully arranged my petticoats, than she lifted me up in her arms, threw open the window, and let me suddenly look down upon the gayest scene I had ever beheld'—fruit, flowers, stalls, butchers, bonny young women in cap and apron. All this 'rose up like a fountain to the open window', and 'left so profound an impression upon me that I never lost it'.

From the birth of her sister Mary in 1803 when she herself was six years old, Elizabeth Grant dated all her 'perfect recollections'. 'All that happened stands clearly before me now at the end of a long life as if that one event had wakened up a sleeping intellect'. A strange fact. She mothered this new marvel, preferring her infinitely to the company of her dolls. It was at this time that her

Places

memory first recorded her family's annual return to the Highlands, *via* Scarborough, Houghton, Edinburgh, Perth, and so at
length home to Rothiemurchus, 'the magnet to which all our
purest, warmest, earliest, and latest affections were steadily
drawn'. Her mother was ill and secluded. She lay comfortably in a
large four-horsed *berline*—its two postillions in green jackets and
jockey caps. This was followed by a heavy post-chariot containing William, the baby, two nurses and a footman. They travelled
as the snail crawls, some thirty miles a day, starting late in the
morning, stopping early, and greeted with unbounded satisfaction by every inn-keeper on the road. Even from Perth onwards
this journey took three whole long summer days.

Few young English travellers, moreover, can have seen so much
so well of their own beautiful country as did John Ruskin when
a child. His father, that 'entirely honest' wine merchant, would
start off from London every summer with Mrs. Ruskin for a two
months' round of visits to his country customers. They went, at a
jog-trot pace, by postchaise and pair; and John, aged four or five,
perched on a little bracket especially designed for him, would sit
for hours surveying the view from its four windows. Thus 'I saw
all the high-roads, and most of the cross ones, of England and
Wales, and great part of lowland Scotland'. *Saw*, and not, a word
we have had to invent, 'glimpsed'. Nowadays, little Johns, if a
paternal Jehu gives them the opportunity, glean so little so rapidly
that, for Memory's purposes, they might as well have kept their
eyes shut.

Public events may leave no less indelible an impression. Goethe
could not only recall his exploration of Frankfort when he was a
child—'Thus was a certain liking for the antique implanted in the
boy'—but describes the effect on him of the great earthquake at
Lisbon when he was six, and a great storm when he was seven.

Oliver Wendell Holmes, again, after describing the low room
in the old house where he was born—'the little patch called the
front yard—somewhat larger than the Turkish rug beneath my
rocking-chair—the back yard with its wood-house, its carriage-
house, its barn, and, let me not forget, its pig-sty', relates that his
earliest memory, when he was aged six: 'goes back to the Declara-
tion of Peace, signalized to me by the illumination of the College
in 1815. I remember well coming from the Dame School, throw-

263

ing up my "jocky", as the other boys did, and shouting "Hooraw for Ameriky", looking at the blazing College windows, and revelling in the thought that I had permission to sit up as long as I wanted to. . . .'

Memories like these even in early childhood should not surprise us—though at first sight they may—if we return ourselves to our infancy. A friend tells me that she can distinctly recall the coronation procession of the King. Seated on a dusty window-sill, she looked down on it, watching its slow progress; and she was then less than four years old. An engraved portrait of the Empress Eugénie at the time of the death of the Prince Imperial is as clearly depicted in my own memory, not to mention a most romantic Christmas picture, 'Through my Heart First'. Also a packed and surging Fleet Street festively illuminated for the first Jubilee of Queen Victoria. I see again the trim beard and irradiated blue eye in these coloured lights of the headmaster whose arm I was clutching at the time—and with no particular desire (at that moment) to be detached from his company. But I was then in my fourteenth year, and already an elderly 'child'. Entertained with recollections such as these it is not merely that we *remember*, however: we re-become. And the most engaging effort is to look about in this revived experience—just as Keats would watch a sparrow pecking in the gravel—to see what other little treasures we can retrieve.

3. *'O Yes! O Yes! has any lost*
A heart which many a sigh hath cost?'

As for the apprehension of crowds and of being lost, childish fantasy by day and night is full of it. One might assume the actual adventure to be uncommon. But no fewer than three of our autobiographers were not only lost in childhood, but 'cried for', an experience which at its zenith one would suppose must be a particularly painful one. When, however, private dismay is tinged with public glory, the heart rebounds. Herbert Spencer refers to this adventure. Frances Power Cobbe mentions it as a 'trivial incident', but since the Town Crier cried for her after she had run away—a pungently different crisis from being lost—it is little wonder that the experience left 'a charm' in her memory.

Places

Charles Babbage was aged five when he found himself all alone on London Bridge. He made his way to Tooley Street, sat down on the doorstep of a linen-draper's shop and presently heard a gold-laced crier proclaiming that he had vanished. 'But I was too much occupied with eating some pears'—given to him by the draper—'to attend to what he was saying.' Long afterwards as he passed by this very spot, a slate of the largest size, called a Duchess (as distinguished from Countesses and Ladies—the smallest), came skimming from the roof of a house and penetrated into the earth at his feet. He recommends this episode to those who delight in coincidences.

Children eating are usually engrossed. But occasionally they lift singularly intent eyes from the platter to their surroundings; and the ears may be shut when the eyes are wide open. If only, then, one could share the musings of *this* particular child, a very unusual one, as over his pear he watched from the draper's doorstep the hive of London!

Walter Scott's pleasantest recollection of Bath followed the arrival of an uncle who introduced him to 'all the little amusements which suited my age, and, above all, to the theatre'. His first play was *As You Like It,* 'and the witchery of the whole scene is alive in my mind at this moment'. It was so much alive in his mind as he sat watching it that he was utterly scandalized at the quarrel between Orlando and his brother, and 'screamed out: "A'n't they brothers?" ' Until then he had lived, an only child, in the house of his grandfather. When he went home he realized that a fraternal quarrel is 'a very natural event'.

Elizabeth Grant tells us that she and her sisters not only learned Shakespeare by heart, 'thus filling our heads with wisdom, our fancy with the most lovely imagery, and warming our hearts . . . but [at Covent Garden] we fixed . . . all these impressions'. A little oddly perhaps, she accepts this fact as a vindication, or at any rate as an excuse for the statues and pictures in 'the churches of *infant* times.'

Robert Southey's aunt, Miss Tyler, was a fervid playgoer and brought him up in the way she had gone. He learned to his cost however one Sabbath morning that it is unseemly to apply to a church a phrase reserved for the theatre. He had returned from the morning service with the joyous news that there had been 'a

265

Early One Morning

very *full house*. 'I had seen more plays before I was seven years old', he asseverates, 'than I have ever seen since I was twenty. . . . When I was taken to the theatre for the first time, I can perfectly well remember my surprise at not finding the pit literally a deep hole, into which I had often puzzled myself to think how or why any persons could possibly go. You may judge by this how very young I must have been. I recollect nothing more of the first visit, except that the play was *The Fathers*, a comedy of Fielding's . . . and the farce was *Coxheath Camp*. This recollection . . . fixes the date to 1778, when I was four years old. . . .'

Whether or not then we accept Plato's view that children should not be taken to the theatre because the drama encourages false sentiment—and Plato had views equally austere and 'rational' concerning poets and poetry—there can be no question of their delight in what comes of it. Of all the poets, as we shall see, the name of the greatest recurs most frequently in early memories, and chiefly because he was also a dramatist.

As an amusement Southey was allowed to play with his aunt's collection of old play-bills:

'I was encouraged to prick them with a pin; letter by letter; and for want of anything better, became as fond of this employment as women sometimes are of netting. . . . I learnt to do it with great precision, pricking the larger types by their outline, so that when they were held up to the window they were bordered with spots of light. The object was to illuminate the whole bill in this manner. I have done it to hundreds; and yet I can well remember the sort of dissatisfied and damping feeling which the sight of one of these bills would give me, a day or two after it had been finished and laid by. It was like an illumination when half the lamps are gone out. . . .'

Titus Andronicus was his favourite play, *because* of 'its horror'; whereas Robert Burns when a boy was, contrariwise, so much shocked by this particular play that he threatened to burn it if his schoolmaster, who had purchased a copy as a legacy for his scholars, left it behind him. It needs a strong digestion, as do certain actualities in life itself.

Much depends on use and custom. Pig killing, poultry killing, the birth of cattle, 'even the lewdness of a half-witted labourer'— the continuous 'life' of a farmyard, a good deal of its very *raison*

266

Places

d'être being the end of it—all this was witnessed, says Mr. Herbert Read, by himself and his brothers 'with complete passivity—just as I have seen children of the same age watching a bull-fight in Spain quite unmoved by its horrors'. A child of a vigorous imagination may not only digest but indulge in horrors which may overwhelm with helpless misery an equally imaginative but more sensitive one. The early pages of autobiography are eloquent of both extremes.

Some years ago, one cloudless summer morning, my eye was attracted—as I was exploring the market-place of an English town —by a group of absorbed children aged from four or five to twelve, hanging over the hurdles of a pen among the sheep. Curious to see what gave them such pleasure, I drew near and discovered that a boy of fourteen or fifteen was cutting a sheep's throat with a penknife. No doubt he was obeying orders. In any case—it is a grievous confession—my stomach so much revolted at the spectacle that I hastened away and made no enquiries! These young children one and all were soberly intent, but not a single face among them suggested horror. Children will haunt a slaughter-house—an empty knot-hole in the wood of the fence making of it a lurid peepshow. The emotions—fear, revulsion, loathing or contrariwise a sharp intellectual curiosity—seem to depend on the *kind* of onset, whether, that is, the object appeals to the seeker after knowledge, the student of actuality, or the novice with a tender heart. And all three of these may be *aliases* of the same child.

For this reason incidents in a rhyme or a story may bring tears and pangs, torments of grief and fear far more acute than those of an actual experience of the same kind. Even here, one child may be sobbing within at the twentieth repetition of 'Dilly-dilly, dilly-dilly, come and be killed', while another can digest the worst that the brothers Grimm (who have been unjustly accused of inventing tales for *children*, whereas they merely collected them from the folk) can put before him. He will turn not a single hair as he watches the spiked barrel containing the wicked queen rolling down the rocky hillside towards its final precipitous leap into the deep blue sea. And for this assertion I am myself trusting to an early recollection!

CHAPTER XXI

WOES

★

1. *'Well—tell! Where should I fly to,*
   Where go to sleep in the dark wood or dell?'

Harriet Martineau's 'terrific oppressions in the night',
however, would alone refute any notion that children are incapable of a sheer glut of spiritual misery,
howsoever induced, such as in later life, we may well
thank Heaven, seldom recurs at such a pitch. Our worst experiences in this kind are such as we have to confront in secret, and
cannot share, or dread to. For a tumble, a graze, a bruise, or a
black eye—a mother's kiss, a confectionery plum, or a sprinkle
of 'fragrant waters' may be all but salve enough. The shock and
sobbing over, the infant stoic parades the black eye, the pigeon-
egg bump on his forehead, the bandaged knee or thumb. If he is
not by nature a fainter he may pore over the blood, and secrete
a little of it with which to sign his name on some privy docu-
ment. As a mere trick to awaken admiration or horror in a
passing stranger, he may smite the back of his hand with the
bristles of a stiff hairbrush, and whirl that stricken hand at arm's
length over his head until it spurts minute trickles of gore in every
direction. But pangs and griefs of the mind, unforeseen and vile
affronts of the self within, the persecutions of other children, or of
a nurse, the fear of a father, physical shame, the dread of strangers
—these, and the list might be extended, may be beyond the power
of expression in childhood. Or, rather, an inscrutable instinct
forbids the attempt. A frightful fiend may be in pursuit of him
every night a child creeps upstairs to bed. He may pine, grow pale
and nerve-wracked, but mum's the usual countersign.
    What may even a delicate and sensitive child not endure, and

yet survive to enjoy telling about it! Augustus Hare vividly remembered hating when he was only four years old his step-
grandmother and her daughter. For defending himself against the
attacks of a bellicose cousin, he was shut up for two days, on bread
and water—to break his spirit. For 'executions' his uncle, Julius
Hare, was called in—with his riding whip—from the Rectory
near by. He was the joint author of *Guesses at Truth* and wholly
author of *The Mission of the Comforter*. In anticipation of the whipping Augustus used to scream 'dreadfully', but bore the lash itself
without a groan or a tear. On one occasion when told to go upstairs and 'prepare', after emitting three appalling shrieks at the
head of the staircase, he fled for his life and hid under a bed behind
a large black travelling trunk. 'I turn cold still when I remember
the agony of fright with which I heard Uncle Julius enter the nursery, and then, with which, through a chink, I could see his large
feet moving about the very room in which I was.'

As a punishment for sucking a lollipop his aunt (Mrs. Julius)
administered a large dose of rhubarb and soda 'with a forcing
spoon'. For two years, every morning and evening, and between
the ages of five and seven, he was compelled by this martinet,
whom with his foster-mother he visited every day, to swallow a
similar dose; and if he were more fretful than usual, semi-jellied
senna tea accompanied the rhubarb. Roast mutton and rice pudding were his only dinner dishes. All dainties were strictly forbidden. When he was six, even his devoted foster-mother, inspired
we must suspect by his aunt, would deliberately (and Pavlov-
wise) talk to him about delicious puddings, having arranged at the
ripe moment for some such pudding to be put on the table beneath
his nose—for savour and inspection. Whereupon he would be told
'to get up and carry [it] off to some poor person in the village'.
And though he cared little for the puddings, he was made acutely
conscious of the cook's wrath at their fate.

This is one drastic method. There is another. 'I have known',
says Jeremy Taylor in *Holy Living*, 'some wise persons have ad-
vised to cure the passions and longings of their children by letting
them taste of everything they passionately fancied: for they should
be sure to find less in it then they looked for, and the impatience of
their being denied would be loosed and made slack.' Precisely the
reverse of this was Augustus's fate; and it may have been to the ex-

Early One Morning

tremes of woe and happiness which he experienced in childhood that the rich detail of the earlier chapters in *The Story of My Life* is partly due. In any case his childhood was one of the utmost economy and therefore intensity in pleasure; a new book, a new flower were conspicuous events in it, blossoming perhaps twice a year. In some restrictions his elders had to share. There were then, about 1840, no steel pens, for example, no wax matches, no night-lights, and only a footpan or bidet for bath.

At the age of six he was remarking how dreadful it must have been for Noah to see all the dead bodies when he came out of the ark; and, after further thought, added later, ' "How much ground there will be when we all die!" "Why so?" "Because we shall all be turned to dust." ' When he was eleven, his detested Aunt Esther, intent on utterly subduing him, regardless of his constitutional delicacy and of the chilblains which were often open wounds on his feet and fingers, put him into an uncarpeted north room, with no fireplace, looking out on to a damp courtyard, a well and a howling dog. 'My only bed was a rough deal trestle, my only bedding a straw palliasse, with a single coarse blanket.' The water in his basin was often frozen in winter, and he had to break the ice with a brass candlestick, or, that taken away, with his chilblained hands.

When at times he was almost speechless with sickness and misery, he was accused of bad temper and given 'saur-kraut' to eat, because the very smell of it made him sick. A favourite torment was to revile all his relations to his face, including his sister. And though she knew that he was agonized at the very thought, this tyrant—who, he declares, was unboundedly kind, generous and considerate to those who submitted to her—insisted on robbing him of his cat, called Selma. Nor did his mother intercede. He was compelled to carry the cat in a basket to his uncle Julius's hated Rectory, and for a while was comforted a little by being allowed to visit it. But there soon came a day when Selma was missing. His Aunt Esther had ordered it to be 'hung'. Sadistic is a word which was then not yet in almost alarmingly common use; and no doubt this martinet believed—she seems even to have convinced his adoring foster-mother—that these torments were all for Augustus's 'good'.

Woes

2. 'I heard him shriek and call aloud for help.'

But even if a child is anxiously sheltered from every avoidable shock and alarm—not merely because the dark is the dark, and Nature is an austere nurse—no vigilance can secure it from the promptings of its own nerves or the fears engendered by its own fantasies. And perhaps to safeguard it too anxiously from all that can trouble mind and heart, or stir its darker emotions, will result in leaving it an easy prey to horrors which it may some day have to face alone. Is any inward mastery of instinctive dreads and forebodings attainable, even though their ravages in childhood may be past our conceiving, without payment of a heavy price for it? Many of Man's noblest achievements, and many as fool-hardy as they are irresistibly endearing, have been clutched at under the cold gaze of the goddess, Danger. There is the old dilemma: whether courage is the priceless armour of a soul that has triumphed over fear, or the weapon of one that has never learnt so much as the meaning of the word?

The worst that can happen out of one's own nature in childhood may have an unforeseen value as experience; and even if we could delete the scar of a wound of this kind which time has healed, how many of us would hasten to consult the plastic surgeon? The psychoanalyst indeed reveals to his patient a wound that he himself has forgotten, in order to prevent further suppuration. The wholly fearless, the ever-bold, the never-shy or timid escape many pangs, but in so doing may miss certain zests and flavours in the feast of life. And who has tasted the full sweetness of the peace and safety of daybreak that never shared a solitary hour with a demon in the dark? Moderation in all things. There is plenty of evidence in this book that a child delicate in body and sensitive in mind may win through to self-security. We cannot estimate how many have failed to do so, or at what atrocious expense.

Man-imposed miseries are quite another matter. The toughest-fibred martinet would hardly *invent* terrors for the nurseling. Nor would any Society for the Production of Genius be likely to choose the old tombstoned parsonage at Haworth as an earthly paradise for the next Brontë brood to grow up in; although grow *up* the Brontës emphatically did. One does not invest even a penny in a packet of heartsease seed to sow it in gravel, yet it may flourish

Early One Morning

there. To ignore, none the less, or ridicule a child's fears and terrors, when we become aware of them, for no better reason than that we may have forgotten our own, is as stupid as it may be disastrous. Isabella's parable of the beetle in *Measure for Measure* remains no less apt if for 'beetle' we substitute infant. 'The sense of death is most in apprehension'; so also is the sense of some viewless Horror worse than death whose shuffling footstep never so much as stirs the dust, and the tap of whose ominous knuckle is felt, rather than heard, as it pauses at the nursery door.

We hear a good deal of this visitor in childhood's memories, and he takes many shapes and disguises. A few children—and unexpected ones—may confess, as it seems, even to welcoming him. At a venture for example one might assume that Shelley in his childhood would have awaited any such onset in terror. If so, it must have been in very early childhood. When, at dessert, the children came down to the dining-room at Field Place, he would tell his small sisters stories so wisely and so well that he came to believe in his own inventions—of a vast Tortoise that haunted the lake; of a hoary alchemist, with his crucible and furnace, turning lead into silver and gold, in a garret over their heads. Far from shunning the spectral he would keep watch for ghosts. Like Francis Bacon, who as a mere child left his play to visit in secret a vault in St. James's Fields, in the hope, not to raise spectres, but to discover the cause of a singular echo, Shelley on spectres *bent* tried to get the keys to the vaults of Warnham Church; and once, at midnight, it is said, a skull tucked under his elbow, stole out at Eton across the fields to a brook which he straddled, and there, after repeating an incantation, sipped thrice from the skull. Satan refrained; the brook still softly babbles; but Shelley is gone.

Robert Burns, who in his own words (which the dusky astonishing scrap of humanity in a daub representing his son does little to deny) was 'the most ungainly awkward boy in the parish', returns thanks for the influence of the supernatural on his young imagination but is silent as to its effect on his nerves.

'In my infant and boyish days I owed much to an old woman who resided in the family, remarkable for her ignorance, credulity, and superstition. She had, I suppose, the largest collection in the country of tales and songs concerning devils, ghosts, fairies, brownies, witches, warlocks, spunkies, kelpies, elf-candles, dead-

272

Woes

lights, wraiths, apparitions, cantraips, giants, enchanted towers, dragons, and other trumpery. This cultivated the latent seeds of poetry; but had so strong an effect on my imagination, that to this hour, in my nocturnal rambles, I sometimes keep a sharp look-out in suspicious places: and though nobody can be more sceptical than I am in such matters, yet it often takes an effort of philosophy to shake off these idle terrors. . . .'

Unsavoury additions to this list—things terrible, pernicious, grievous, violent, noisome, hideous, fearful, detestable, including the Spoorn and the Puckle—will be found in *The Discoverie of Witchcraft* and in *The Anatomy of Melancholy*. There are country children too who are threatened with Clap-cans, Church-grim, Jack-in-Irons and Old Bendy, and may lie awake listening for the Shriker, or Gally-trot, the Phooka, the Neugle, or the Gabble Raches. Oliver Goldsmith had his share of them. As a child he went to a village school kept by an old retired quartermaster on half-pay who professed to teach nothing but the three R's, but had an inexhaustible fund of stories about ghosts, banshees and fairies, and about the great rapparee chiefs, Baldearg O'Donnell and Galloping Hogan. In the *Anatomy* too, is a brief account of the effects of a 'ramble', and one not in the dark, on nerves more sensitive than those of the author of *Tam o' Shanter* appear to have been. And how natural a simplicity steals into Burton's fascinating prose the moment a child comes into view!

'At Basil many little children in the spring-time went to gather flowers in a meadow at the town's end, where a malefactor hung in gibbets; all gazing at it, one by chance flung a stone, and made it stir, by which accident, the children affrighted ran away; one slower than the rest, looking back, and seeing the stirred carcase wag towards her, cried out it came after, and was so terribly affrighted, that for many days she could not rest, eat, or sleep, she could not be pacified, but melancholy, died. In the same town another child, beyond the Rhine, saw a grave opened, and upon the sight of a carcase, was so troubled in mind that she could not be comforted, but a little after departed, and was buried by it. . . .'

Burns looked back on the 'idle terrors' of his childhood much as Byron, through his fifty intervening amours, surveyed his child-like devotion to Mary Duff. They had become a little sceptical of love- and fear-affairs; and with that, the secret virtue had de-

273

parted out of female and fairy and reduced them to 'trumpery'.

Of all states of the self, that of fear and especially of fear in childhood, is one of the most difficult to revive; not less difficult than that of extreme pain or grief. We may remember but cannot realize. Terror too has pronounced physical symptoms; suppress them, said William James, and the terror ceases. How then recall its full effects when the mouth is shut, the scalp supple, one's breathing slow and even, and the heart beats on as soberly as a grandfather's clock?

Not indeed that fear of the supernatural is confined to children. We fear what we cannot explain, and what we cannot explain is less any particular phenomenon than its influence upon us. To a child a hanging dress in a dark closet, a door ajar into the vacancy of a lightless house, a vagrant moth, a wailing as of the wind, the shriek of a night-bird, is a decoy, a spell, an invocation; and it is what is invoked that troubles his entrails and chills the blood. The adult has whittled down the invocations: but *if* there is no wind to account for the sigh in the dark, or only the faint *whirr* and tapping *as of* a moth, if the pendent dress stir, swell, remove itself from the hook and come forward, what kind of hero is he then? Dr. Montagu James selects hoary ecclesiastics, Uncle Henries, the hardened and mature, for his admirable ghosts to play upon, and with; not children. Not assuredly for the reason that æolian harps strung with their nerves are stubborn in response, but too sensitive. On the other hand, and rightly enough, it is not the children in *The Turn of the Screw* who are appalled at the onset of Miss Jessel and Peter Quint—they know them only too well and of old—but their governess. For when, again, a child is *not* a phantast it can be the starkest of actualists. The *ménage* is of the Box and Cox order.

Thomas Love Peacock as a child was 'a very pretty little fellow', with handsome dark blue eyes, a fresh colour, and a fine head adorned with masses of Samsonian flaxen curls which hung below his waist. Moved by their splendour, Queen Charlotte once stopped her carriage to give him a kiss. He had a friend called Charles who lived not far away in the Abbey House; and on visiting Charles one day he found him in disgrace. 'I found him in his chamber, sitting by the fire, with a pile of ghostly tales, and an accumulation of lead, which he was casting into dumps in a mould. . . . His position was sufficiently melancholy. His chamber was at the end of a long corridor. He was determined not to make any submission, and his captivity was likely to last till the end of his holidays. . . .' Such is the association of ideas that when the author of *Nightmare Abbey* first read in Lord Byron's *Don Juan*, the couplet, 'I pass my evenings in long galleries solely, And that's the reason I'm so melancholy,' the lines immediately conjured up the image of poor Charles in the midst of his dumps and spectres at the end of his long empty gallery.

Use and habit, as the old Latin proverb says, is second nature. On the night of November 27, 1758—a night of whistling wind and beating rain, in 'a dismal and singular' chamber 'over the mouldering Gothic arches of the ruinous monastery of St. Augustine in Bristol'—a chamber whose casement windows opened on the Minster and shed a dim, midday gloom—Mary Robinson first opened her eyes 'to this world of duplicity and sorrow'. Her *Memoirs* are pitched in this lugubrious key, and even recollections of childhood when thus inhearsed lose their bloom and naturalness. In her nursery could be heard morning and evening the deep tones of the Minster organ and the chanting of the choristers. She recalls with what pleasure she listened, and would sit 'on the winding steps which led from the aisle to the cloisters', and, when an old sexton whom she called Black John was in a good humour, even under the brazen eagle of the lectern. As soon as she had learned to read, her delight was in epitaphs and monumental inscriptions, and before she was seven years old she could repeat Pope's 'Elegy to the Memory of an Unfortunate Lady' and Mason's on the Countess of Coventry. Her father gave her a harpsichord, but the only melodies she cared for were also 'mournful and touching', and she would regale her mother with ' 'Twas when the sea was roaring' and 'The Heavy Hours'. That George, says Thackeray, 'was the handsomest prince in the whole world was agreed by men and alas! by many women'. Had he perhaps been a little 'handsomer' in other respects, Perdita *might* have remembered enjoying *Old King Cole*.

Even the most hardened sceptic would agree with Edgar Allan Poe 'that the most horrible thing he could imagine . . . was to feel an ice-cold hand laid upon his face in a pitch-dark room when alone at night, or to waken in semi-darkness and see an evil face

Early One Morning

gazing close into his own'. 'These fancies had so haunted him as a boy that he would often keep his head under the bed-covering until nearly suffocated'. It was Andrew Lang, I think, who suggested that 'ghosts' are sometimes perceptible solely by the light they themselves emanate.

One might easily read into Poe's midnight fears the rudiments of 'Ligeia' and 'The Black Cat' *if* his 'nearly suffocated' were an unusual experience in childhood. On the contrary; stable and stolid-*looking* adults who scoff at all such excesses may well have been hag-ridden infants—adults wholly incapable too of Poe's icy rationality. I can recall the very odour of the breath-damped blanket! The most trivial of objects may become a bugbear. A black-painted funeral escutcheon fixed to the outside walls of a house near the Usk was the cause of a recurrent nightmare in Alfred Russel Wallace's childhood—a dream of vast wings approaching in the silence of night, wherein he would lament to himself, The hatchment is coming; the hatchment is coming; and I *hope* it will not get in! A harmless but immense hairy trunk on the staircase on his way to bed induced a nightly agony of fear in Elizabeth Grant's brother, William. As is the way with children, they kept this ordeal secret, until William's peaked pale face divulged how much had gone wrong. Calling for lights, his wise but severe father showed the child the object of his dread. 'He was led gently to it, to look at it, feel it, sit on it, see it opened', and not only when night was come, but again in the morning. Familiarity breeds contempt. That is why perhaps the far-seeing in times past kept ready their shrouds in a press and their coffins under their beds.

3. *'But nought distinct they see.'*

In much then the most anxious and intuitive of grown-ups who would save a child from every ill and affliction of the mind that vigilance can, is helpless. How exorcize a horror which has no detectable cause, or of which only the vaguest account in the frailest of terms can be given? I remember, years ago, lying tranquilly in the small radiance given by a night-light in a basin, in order to be company to and to soothe a restless child beside me in her cot. And suddenly, without the least apparent cause or warn-

276

ing, a deadly terror swept over me as of some appalling presence that had entered and now infected the room. A nightmare too may be *merely* a nightmare, but there's little comfort in the statement when we first emerge from one, panting and sweating between the sheets. The bear—with flaming eyes in a head that is crouched watching on shaggy paws under a child's bed—is of course the purest illusion. And when the sobs follow one another at longer and longer intervals, and, with the sweetest reasonableness, the victim is assured that the departed beast cannot by any possibility have been a *real* bear, he may only begin to weep afresh for that very reason. For how can bolts and bars or the most loving of parents keep out a bear that isn't real?

Once for minutes together, as a child, I lay in terror listening to the pulsations of what I supposed was a death-watch in the dark. The moment I sat up, its knockings ceased. I lay down and they at once began again. What then was the cause of this silly terror? It was the rail of my bedstead, responding to the throbbing of my heart.

'Sometimes', says Harriet Martineau, 'I was panic struck at the head of the stairs, and was sure I could never get down; and I could never cross the yard to the garden without flying and panting and fearing to look behind, because a wild beast was after me. The starlight sky was the worst; it was always coming down, to stifle and crush me, and rest upon my head.'

Any human company would probably have sufficed to keep the wild beast at bay, but what hand can keep the starlight sky from descending on a child's head? Besides in childhood we may be terrified by something that 'destroyeth in the noonday', which we can actually trace, and see, and even realize is harmless. The assault in this case is not on the reason but on the spinal column, and who can guess what primeval echoes it may not be awakening, what pre-natal complex?

'It now occurs to me,' says Harriet Martineau, 'and it may be worth while to note it, what the extremest terror of all was about. We were often sent to walk on the Castle Hill at Norwich. In the wide area below, the residents were wont to expose their feather-beds, and to beat them with a stick. That sound—a dull shock—used to make my heart stand still; and it was no use my standing at the rails above, and seeing the process. The striking of the blow

Early One Morning

and the arrival of the sound did not correspond, and this made matters worse. I hated that walk; and I believe for that reason. My parents knew nothing of all this. . . .'

Nowadays the term pathological would be used for her condition—but though we thus classify its cause we do not explain the horror. Obviously as a child she was exceptional. It is borne out by the evidence that she became an exceptional woman. Within twenty years of this ordeal she was publishing a book entitled *Devotional Exercises for Young Persons*, and afterwards wrote stories with less austere titles that were the delight of a host of children. Blue her stockings may have been, and extreme her views, but she said of herself, for a posthumous summary: 'None of her novels or tales have or ever had in the eyes of good judges or in her own any character of permanence.'

Nor had her terror at the thumping of the featherbed-beaters; though she herself ascribed her taste for study and reading to her feeble health as a child. Nettle and dock, as if kindly Nature herself had decreed it, seldom grow far apart.

The most curious contrasts may occur. What alarms one child may enrapture another. Among the ornaments in my mother's small drawing-room of old were two glass candlesticks hung about with dangling prisms, which used to quiver gently at the least disturbance. When the sunbeams traversing the room lit up the marble chimney-shelf on which they stood, I was captivated by the effect; and sometimes took one of the pieces of glass off its hook, and holding it up to my eyes would gaze in rapture at a world of fascinating angles and abysses decked in all the colours of the rainbow. It was a transport familiar to Alice and similar to that produced by peering out through the strips of hideous blue and red and yellow glass with which (in Mr. Forrest Reid's and my own early days) the Victorians delighted to glaze their garden or balcony doors, though not apparently for this purpose.

One morning, I remember, though this was strictly forbidden, I pocketed one of these glass pendants, set out (to show off with it) for my dame school very early, and arrived to find no one there— not even my reanimated friend Herbert Naughty. So I sat alone for a while in the small sunny basement room, practising my magic colours on the map-hung, whitewashed walls; the lovely silent butterflies of light zigzagging from floor to ceiling; and I can now

Woes

recall perhaps just a fraction of their wizardry. In so many words, they enchanted me, as they would, it might be assumed, any such imp. What then of Harriet Martineau's similar experience?—

'One summer morning, I went into the drawing-room, which was not much used in those days, and saw a sight which made me hide my face in a chair, and scream with terror. The drops of the lustres on the mantelpiece, on which the sun was shining, were somehow set in motion, and the prismatic colours danced vehemently on the walls. I thought they were alive—imps of some sort; and I never dared go into that room alone in the morning, from that time forward.'

It may be said that every child is exceptional in some respect, and that no child is exceedingly so except in degree. Pick out twenty-six of them at random, and in temperament, character and so forth they may appear to be as unlike one another as are the letters of the alphabet. Still, all the letters *belong* to the alphabet, and each child will have more in common with the other twenty-five than he has of difference from any one of them. In that case Harriet Martineau as a child (and as a woman) was one of the less familiar letters—a Q or X or Z. When she was just three years old, in the summer of 1805, her father transported his family to Yarmouth. On arrival there he 'took me along the old jetty—little knowing what terror I suffered. I remember the strong grasp of his large hand being some comfort; but there were holes in the planking of the jetty quite big enough to let my foot through; and they disclosed the horrible sight of waves flowing and receding below, and great tufts of green weeds swaying to and fro. I remember the sitting-room at our lodgings, and my mother's dress as she sat picking shrimps, and letting me try to help her'.

That 'large hand' is a detail that it would be well to keep in mind when in such circumstances it is our own that is needed. This odd dread in childhood of falling through a hole or crevice not big enough to admit the passage of a bumblebee is far from unusual. In later life the catastrophe itself may actually occur—if only in a dream! It was in a dream that I once saw my own small daughter one brisk and bright summer morning suddenly vanish through a minute cranny between the planks of a seaside jetty. I paused, lost between horror at the catastrophe and terror of the deep, and awoke at the moment in my dream when, having dived

Early One Morning

over the railing, I was in mid-flight between the pier itself and full fathom five of salt water—inexpressibly relieved at this noble action, in spite of the fact that on reaching it I should infallibly have sunk like a stone! But what does this inability alike of child and dreamer to realize physical magnitude imply? It *suggests* at any rate a tenant of the body that is not yet wholly familiar with earthly conditions.

4. *'The poor fellow trembled so that I scarce knew what to do with him.'*

The loveliest summer evening in a lifetime's experience, a pool of water—Mein water, the company of a dearly beloved father, and, yet again, the sensation of fear—all this made up one of Thomas Carlyle's earliest recollections. 'My memory dawns', he says, '(or grows light)' [and this is a metaphor used also by Southey: 'The twilight of my recollection does not begin till the third year of my age']—'my memory dawns at the first aspect of the stream, of the pool spanned by a wooden bow, without railing, and a single plank broad. He lifted me against his thigh with his right hand, and walked careless along till we were over. My face was turned rather downwards. I looked into the deep clear water, and its reflected skies, with terror yet with confidence that he could save me. Directly after I, light of heart, asked of him what these "little black things" were that I seemed sometimes to *create* by rubbing the palms of my hands together, and can at this moment (the mind having been doubtless excited by the past peril) remember that I described them in these words: "like penny-rows but far less." He explained it wholly to me: "my hands were not *clean*." He was very kind, and I loved him. All around this is Dusk, or Night, before and after.'

Carlyle was an old man when he wrote this—but how complete a recollection it appears to be. It is as tenderly related as it is precisely explored—the attitude, the water, the reflection of the sky and, above all, the state of mind. The ordeal over, he breathed not a syllable concerning it to his father, but to free *himself* of it, at once change the subject! As for the penny rolls, I can recall no other reference to them, but what child can have failed to observe the phenomenon? They bring back to me the very shape and size of my own grubby glistening palms of more than half a century ago.

Mute too was Aksakoff when as a child he crossed in anguish the frozen Volga and watched its tumultuous waters coursing beneath the ice. And one scents an understatement when Alfred Russel Wallace describes the crossing in childhood of the Severn in an open ferry boat as 'a little awful to me'. On the other hand there was no *fear* in William Hutton's heart when in a barge he crossed the Trent at the age of two (after having already distinguished himself by swallowing a large hollow brass drop from a chest of drawers). 'A pleasure boat in view, with the people in it, seemed gradually to sink under water, and rise up alternately. This shews how very delusive is the sight of an infant of two years old. The weather was serene, the water clear, and, though deep, the pebbles at the bottom were visible.' Byron on the other hand, gives *a* reason for a similar experience, though it need not have been the only reason:—

'The Brig of Don, near the "auld town" of Aberdeen, with its one arch and its black deep salmon stream, is in my memory as yesterday. I still remember, though perhaps I may misquote the awful proverb which made me pause to cross it, and yet lean over it with a childish delight, being an only son, at least by my mother's side. The saying, as recollected by me, was this, but I have never heard or seen it since I was nine years of age:

'   "Brig of Balgownie, *black*'s your wa',
      Wi' a wife's *ae son*, and a mear's ae foal,
      Down ye shall fa'." '

A child may be made mortally afraid in a manner that in itself suggests reminiscence. The imagination supplies from its own obscure recesses what the terrifying object only hints at:—

'In returning from the coast of France,' says Leigh Hunt of his early childhood, 'we stopped at Deal, and I found myself, one evening, standing with an elder brother on the beach, looking at a shoal of porpoises, creatures of which he had given me some tremendous, mysterious notion. I remember, as if it were yesterday, feeling the shades of evening, and the solemnity of the spectacle, with an awful intensity. There they were, tumbling along in the foam, what exactly I knew not, but fearful creatures of some sort. My brother spoke to me of them in an under tone of voice, and I held my breath as I looked. The very word "porpoise" had an awful, mouthfilling sound.'

The scene, as it was recorded by a child's eyes, has the solemn ominousness of a drawing by William Blake.

When Charles Lamb was a child he chanced on an illustration in Foxe's *Book of Martyrs* which after one horrified scrutiny, he refused ever even to glance at again. Leigh Hunt was similarly terrified by the picture of a fabulous beast called the Mantichora. In shape and appearance this monster suggests a hybrid between a dog and a lion; the tail is tasselled with spikes, the head is that of a bearded man (resembling John Donne!) grinning with wide-open jaws that are lined with catlike teeth:—

'In vain my brother played me repeated tricks with this frightful anomaly. I was always ready to be frightened again. At one time he would grin like the Mantichora; then he would roar like him; then call about him in the dark. I remember his asking me to come up to him one night at the top of the house. I ascended, and found the door shut, Suddenly a voice came through the key-hole, saying, in its hollowest tones, "The Mantichora's coming". Down I rushed to the parlour, fancying the terror at my heels. . . .'

He would 'call about him in the dark' has the very ring of the verbal devices by whose means that master of 'otherness', Sheridan Le Fanu, decoys his reader into the state of nerves and mind he needs for his own sinister purposes. It was Hazlitt, I fancy, who descanted on the terror of a child confronted by some ingenious grown-up in a frightful mask which, on its removal, disclosed an even worse one beneath it!

What children may *not* be frightened at is the problem. Queen Victoria when she was three or four years old screamed at the sight of apron and gaiters; Herbert Spencer was terrified at the jangling of bells from a Derby steeple; Goëthe at the hollow thunder of skittles in a bowling-alley; William Bell Scott on turning over a turf in an orchard, quaked at the swarm of 'annulose and centipedral creatures'—an 'antagonistic creation'—that were hidden beneath it. And though some fifty years have gone by since we met, I can still exchange gaze for gaze with a straddling, hairy, and, as it seemed to me, vilely sagacious spider—its luminous pale yellow little eyes fixed on me from the refuge to which it had scuttled

HARTLEY COLERIDGE, AT THE AGE OF TEN
From an engraving by Holl after a sketch by Sir David Wilkie

Woes

behind the leg of a chair. That same evening I was reduced to such terror on observing that my younger sister, in spite of all my anguished entreaties, appeared to have fallen asleep, that I pushed up one of her eyelids—only to disclose the white unpupilled sightless ball beneath it!

On the other hand Benvenuto Cellini when he was a child of three discovered a scorpion one morning under a wooden conduit, and dangling it in his hand—its tail on one side, its two darting mouths on the other—ran overjoyed to his grandfather, exclaiming, 'Grandfather, look at my pretty little crab!' The old gentleman was 'ready to drop down dead', but his father, snatching up a pair of scissors, caressed and played with Benvenuto until he had contrived to cut off the scorpion's mouths and tail. He then accepted the event as a happy omen.

'Crabs' are common in childhood. I recall a three-year-old seated—as round and solid as a full stop—at play with his mudpies, who merely lifted his eyes as if in polite reprimand of the heavens at a clap of thunder sudden and loud enough to waken the dead. On being missed one day in his infancy during a furious thunderstorm, Walter Scott, too, was discovered lying on his back enraptured at the brilliance of the 'bonny' lightning.

Mary Lamb's poem about little Henry who shared his morning bowl of bread and milk with a wily snake that he spoke of as 'a fine *grey bird*' and called Grey Pate, and tapped on the head with his spoon if it was greedy, may or may not have been founded on fact. In either case, W. H. Hudson who delighted in serpents hardly less than in birds would have given him his blessing. Most children perhaps are *taught* to be afraid of the dangerous; and fear increases the danger. When Mr. Romilly John was five years old he was fascinated at the appearance of an adder or viper which he found one day in a wood. He gently stroked and caressed the creature's flat, beaded head, and carried it home with him. Even in this wicked world the child and the cockatrice *can* be at peace together. Of Thomas Hardy's infancy, 'nothing has been handed down save the curious fact that on his mother's returning from out-of-doors one hot afternoon, to him asleep in his cradle, she found a large snake curled up upon his breast, comfortably asleep like himself. It had crept into the house from the heath hard by, where there were many.'

Early One Morning

There is another kind of wiliness familiar to the young. When Coleridge was under the age of three his eyes were bound by the doctor preparatory to his being 'inoculated'; 'at which I manifested so much obstinate indignation, that at last they removed the bandage, and unaffrighted I looked at the lancet, and suffered the scratch.'

Even London policemen—the admiration of the civilized world —have been known to faint dead off at the mere threat of this ordeal. Samuel Smiles as a child was also of sterner stuff. When, he says, a Dr. John Welsh came to bleed his elder brother during an attack of inflammation of the lungs, 'I remember seeing three full cups of blood taken from his arm, lying on the table, waiting for the doctor's next visit. Though the boy was only seven years old, the bleeding at once cured him.'

That sounds matter-of-fact enough; but not all children are indulgent of the 'little black bag', in spite of its persuasive owner's paregoric. Some of them endure pain and illness with a silent, curious, ruminating, clear-eyed patience. 'At the hospital of La Charité,' says John Evelyn in his *Diary*, 'I saw the operation of cutting for the stone. A child of eight or nine years old underwent the operation with most extraordinary patience, and expressing great joy when he saw the stone was drawn. The use I made of it was, to give Almighty God hearty thanks that I had not been subject to this deplorable infirmity. . . .'

Others rage and roar at the mere mention of castor oil or a black draught—though I once had a friend who enjoyed the former on bread and butter—and in every spoonful of untimely jam suspect a powder. 'Two spectres', said Oliver Wendell Holmes, 'haunted my earliest years, the dread of midnight visitors, and the visits of the doctor.' That could hardly be less complimentary.

CHAPTER XXII

NIGHT-FEARS

★

1. 'It's wearisome lying in bed.'

It is both the second and the third word of what follows from
Charlotte Yonge that require an emphasis:
'My only real trouble was terrors just like what other solitary
or imaginative children have—horrors of darkness, fancies of
wolves, one most gratuitous alarm recurring every night of being
smothered like the Princes in the Tower, or blown up with gunpowder. In the daylight I knew it was nonsense, I would have
spoken of it to no one, but the fears at night always came back.'

The fears . . . always came back, there's the rub: fears of the known
and unknown, fears stifling, irrational, inexplicable, and for the
most part unmentioned, kept secret. To what end or purpose?
An epic thrice the length of *The City of Dreadful Night* would fail
to exhaust the grisly paraphernalia. Summer, with her hot, languid, interminable hours of evening, when sleep refuses its boon
to squinting eyes and fretted body, may be a torment. A year
before his death William Morris remarked that whenever he
smelt a may tree he was reminded of going to bed by daylight—
when he was five. But what of winter? The daylight ebbs away,
the blinds descend, the curtains are drawn, the clock strikes: it is
bed time; and Childe Roland pale, hollow-eyed, speechless, sets
off to keep his nightly tryst in the Dark Tower.

It was when his old and beloved nurse, Emma, had left him that
these appalling assignations began for Mr. Forrest Reid when he
was a child. Till then he could call, sure of an all-comforting
answer. But now:—
'Alone, in a room near the top of this not very friendly house, I

Early One Morning

seemed to be miles and miles from any human being. There were shut doors, there were many flights of stairs, to deaden effectually any sound I might make. Unless I went out on to the landing and screamed I could not possibly be heard.

'The effect of this new state of things upon the darkness was immediate and startling. It was no longer a soft dim curtain hung before the gate of sleep: on the contrary, it drove all my drowsiness away. It had become like a vast rotting body swarming with obscene life. I could hear stealthy movements; I dared not open my eyes, because I knew hideous things were there, waiting, gloating, eager to display before me their half shapeless horror. From what Limbo did they flock to me, like vampires who have marked their prey from afar? These were no dreams, no creations of a child's imagination. . . .

'It was all for one's good, I had been assured: I must learn to conquer this senseless, superstitious cowardice. And an easy way to conquer it was to remember God was with me in the dark. He wasn't; he never had been—unless he was a tall smiling figure with long, pointed, yellow teeth, that I saw one night standing at the foot of my bed. This, at least, was no dream. At all events, I was not asleep. If I had the requisite skill I could draw that face now, as I still half believe I could have photographed it then.

'It is true I did not talk about these nocturnal terrors; on the other hand, they were much too painful for me to conceal them. Everybody knew about them, and I had not only to bear what was really a form of torture, but the reproach, as well, of being an arrant little coward. Nor was the disgraceful secret confined to my own family. I guessed this at once when I began to hear from visitors accounts of "manly" little boys, who, so far from being afraid of it, seemed positively to prefer darkness to daylight. I detested these small heroes, and with a crimson face would vow I wasn't afraid either, which was "naughty", being a lie. . . .'

'It was my firm though vague belief', says Mr. Frank Kendon, 'that some unmentionable and fabulous Thing lived in the hall cupboard. Not a real Thing, you must understand, who would do anything so definite as to attack or eat you, nothing that you could be sure you had seen or heard, certainly nothing to describe, nothing to fear for what it might do, but a formless terror, just as fearful to think of safely shut in behind the door as if it were mov-

286

ing abroad and breathing the chill and sunless air of the hall and
passage. Moreover the Presence polluted all this end of the house,
and it required resolution to go there alone. . . . [It] could be felt
like a vapour as you descended the front stairs; and nowadays
(unless it was indeed some evil memory belonging to the house)
I think I know what it was. The haunted parts of the house were
the sunless parts. . . .' Only that and nothing more; yet I could
name a rocky creek on the west coast wherein not even the local
geologist cares to remain for longer than his hammer needs.

2. 'And the eyes of the sleepers waxed deadly and chill.'

The saving grace of ordeals such as these, if grace there be, is
that even in childhood—like the absurdly exaggerated
troubles and anxieties which if we lie awake may in later
life pester the small hours, and vanish with the morning—
they are usually confined to the night-time, and are not 'all
in the day's *work*'. Even William Blake makes no mention in
'The Chimney Sweeper' of the dread and terror of the morrow
that must have haunted even the blackest nightmares of little Tom
Dacre—and 'Dick, Joe, Ned and Jack'. And in the days of child
labour in the mills and mines such experiences as those recorded
by William and Samuel Hutton must have been common enough
for innumerable children, and some of them younger than themselves.

At the age of seven William was sent to work in a silk mill—so
stunted a child that he had to wear high pattens on his feet to
enable him to reach the machines. The Christmas holidays, he
relates, three months after his eighth birthday, were 'attended with
snow, followed by a sharp frost. A thaw came on, in the afternoon
of the 27th, but in the night the ground was again caught by a
frost, which glazed the streets. I did not awake, the next morning
till daylight seemed to appear. I rose in tears, for fear of punishment, and went to my father's bedside, to ask what was o'clock?
"He believed six"; I darted out in agonies, and, from the bottom
of Full street, to the top of Silkmill lane, not 200 yards, I fell nine
times! Observing no lights in the mill, I knew it was an early hour,
and that the reflection of the snow had deceived me. Returning,
it struck two. As I now went with care, I fell but twice.'

Early One Morning

'Agonies'—it is as hard to share his meaning of the word as it is to restore to a penny the value it had for us when we were six. Self with self, he actually counted how many times he fell headlong in the snow. To his brother's experience of the same kind was added a visitor from another world:—

'At seven years of age I was set to work in the silk mills, where I toiled from five o'clock in the morning till seven at night for the weekly sum of one shilling. This paid for my board and lodging, and rendered me independent of my father, except for the clothes I wore.

'There a remarkable circumstance occurred to me. Afraid of being past my hour in the morning, and deceived by a clouded moon, I frequently rose in the night mistaking it for day. At one of these times, I found all was silent in the mill, and I knew that I was too early. As I stood leaning pensively on the parapet of the bridge, I heard the clattering of horses' feet; and, without turning my head, I asked what it was o'clock. No answer being given I turned to look, and I distinctly saw the appearance of a man, riding one horse and leading another, on the mill-wheel. The clock then struck four, and the apparition vanished. . . .'

He adds that when, at the time, he spoke of this, it was suggested that the apparition was nothing more than the wreckage of a dream from which he had been awakened by the striking of the clock. This he flatly denies: 'I am not afraid of ghosts. On the contrary, the certainty of having seen one has made me desirous of meeting with others, and I have sought them at midnight in churchyards, and on fields of unburied dead.' And he too, like Shelley, sought in vain.

There is evidence that children at a very early age, like domestic animals, may be aware of what is assumed to be preternatural— and that without alarm. A friend tells me that a few years ago she was sitting alone with a child a little over two years old in a house that was reputed to be haunted. Suddenly he gave a cry, the colour ebbed out of his face, she feared a sudden illness; when he exclaimed, gazing over her shoulder, 'Look! O, mother, mother! Tell that old man to go away!' She herself was anxious at the time concerning her father who was not in the house, and that day he died. Could communication between mind and mind—mother and child—account for this?

Night-Fears

The paidologist has compiled a complete list of the 'stimuli' of fear in childhood, and in it the terms psychosis and primeval make their appearance—such 'stimuli' as certain vermin, darkness, strange animals, persons (and children) of unfriendly mien, solitude, thunderstorms, and 'probably loud or sudden noises with certain peculiar qualities'—such as the feigned howling of the fabulous Mantichora, the distant thumping of a feather-bed, and even the morning postman's sudden harmless jangling tug at the doorbell—a dread of Mr. Frank Kendon's. It is also noted that any 'combination' of these stimuli may intensify the fear, and a catalogue follows of thirty-one different responses to them! Comfort, we are told, may soothe them away, good habits may evade their onset, adult example help to inhibit them, appeal be made to reason, and a trust in God give courage and assurance. On the other hand, it may be the conviction that God is not concerned with night-fears which will darken the very dark.

But superannuated, seasoned, reasonable and god-fearing grown-ups may themselves become victims of the stimuli mentioned. I used to know a music-loving old gentleman who at threat of the dreaded thunder-stone would retire quaking into a gloomy corner and cover his face and silvery head with a large white handkerchief; and I can recall the awful omens conjured up in the minds of two matter-of-fact adults who were tending a sick child merely by the faint clickings and whinings of a hair-comb that had been temporarily electrified. Even the tuneful 'little owl' prowling in the small hours may alarm listeners a good deal bigger than Tom Thumb.

Few of us moreover would be other than chary of watching the night out in a vacant and sinister house; and any prolonged solitude which begins to hint at the intangible will speedily drive us into human company again. Yet all this by no means precludes a heedless or impatient attitude to children who stubbornly refuse to go to sleep because they are in fact oppressed by 'fancies' that may out-Dante the *Inferno* in horror, and at which even Gustave Doré's brush might blanch. The moment we revive in memory what Mr. Reid reminds us of, we are bound to realize that in comparison with its *effects* any mere stimulus to fear in childhood may resemble that of a speck or two of strychnine (from the bitter silky seed of the Koochla tree), a word which made its memorable

289

Early One Morning

entry into my vocabulary when I was about five years old. Standing at my mother's side, my head hardly up to her elbow, I overheard: 'He thought he was being continually followed. . . . His body was arched up on the bed—like this'. It may be very difficult to exorcize a child's nocturnal visitants, but if we can clearly recall even the faintest of their shadows we shall at least listen carefully to any such appeal as,

> 'Father, O Father! What do we here,
> In this land of unbelief and fear?'

3. 'A wind blew out of a cloud.'

There is yet another fear that may darken the mind in childhood and haunt the day—the dread and fear of death. Here again contraries may almost co-exist in the same mind. A child in play and in talk refers to 'killing' with relish and without concern. He may remark casually at the age of five—after passing by sad relicts in the garden: 'I always look at dead mice, Mummie, because if it's just the body with nothing in it, I know Benjie killed it. But if it's just dead, I know it died.' In this respect he resembles his elders, but is less evasive. Mutton, he knows, is dead sheep; and then, suddenly, the bare fact wings in unawares, and he may stubbornly and violently refuse to taste the horrid stuff—until next time. The departure of a nurse to be married may cause a sturdy boy of four years old who abominates a dancing-class and exults in 'soccer' to mourn bitterly for her for three whole days; another, whatever the reason, may of his own accord never so much as mention her name again.

So too, that a friend or neighbour is dead may cause acute curiosity, some meditation, but no tears. The mystery is reflected from the grown-ups' outlandish customs and conversation. It is one of the many arresting things that *happen*. Nevertheless, within is a self that may confront the spectre of Death in his horror as unexpectedly as a strange dog may be met at a turn of the street. And then it is as if the light of life itself had gone out. Or a carking dread and anxiety may gnaw at a child's mind that some loved one is in danger of dying; and the sight of a corpse congeal the heart with icy horror. Such impressions are at least sharply defined. I remember—in the company of a few other boys about ten or eleven years of age—seeing the body of a woman who, poor hapless soul, had been drowned in the Thames. We hung over the granite parapet of the Embankment, the morning light reflected from the water beating up into our faces, and stared. The body had been secured to the stern of a police boat, and the bloated head and shoulders lolled gently in the clucking tide as the boat edged gently to and fro. There was horror on this occasion, but at least as much calm curiosity, and, I think, compassion.

Francis Galton, who seems to have been an alert and matter-of-fact child, had a similar but more protracted experience a good deal later in his boyhood—at the age of sixteen. He went then, in 1838, as an indoor pupil, to the Birmingham General Hospital. Some little time before this he witnessed his first post-mortem examination. ' "Would I like to come?" Oh, the mixture of revulsion, wonder, interest, and excitement!' He trod softly up the back stairs to the cold garret where the poor girl lay—a housemaid. 'I can easily reproduce in imagination all the ghastly horror of the scene and could describe it in detail. . . . Death "with a little pin, bores through the castle wall, and—farewell, King!" ' She had died of peritonitis. And the dissector himself all but followed her soon afterwards in consequence of pricking his finger. 'I returned home, chilled, awed and sobered, and seemed for the time to have left boyhood behind me.' A younger boy might perhaps have been less affected.

'I was a mere boy,' says Thomas Huxley, 'I think between thirteen and fourteen years of age—when I was taken by some older student friends of mine to the first post-mortem examination I ever attended. All my life I have been most unfortunately sensitive to the disagreeables which attend anatomical pursuits; but on this occasion, my curiosity over-powered all other feelings, and I spent two or three hours in gratifying it.' Though he makes no mention of having fingered the instruments, this experience resulted in some sort of blood-poisoning, followed by complete apathy, and he attributed his lifelong hypochondriacal dyspepsia to this particular illness.

At sixteen, again, Alexander Carlyle was persuaded by two Irish friends to think of surgery as a profession:—

'I drew up with them, and they had almost induced me to be a doctor, had not the dissection of a child, which they bought of a poor tailor for 6s., disgusted me completely. The man had asked 6s. 6d., but they beat him down the 6d. by asserting that the bargain was to him worth more than 12s., as it saved him all the expense of burial. The hearing of this bargain, together with that of the dialogue in which they carried it on, were not less grating to my feelings than the dissection itself.'

When Edward Gibbon's mother died he was nearly eleven years old and at school. His 'poor father', he says, 'was inconsolable . . . the transport of grief seemed to threaten his life or his reason. I can never forget the scene of our first interview, some weeks after the fatal event; the awful silence, the room hung with black, the midday tapers, his sighs and tears; his praises of my mother, a saint in heaven; his solemn adjuration that I would cherish her memory and imitate her virtues; and the fervour with which he kissed and blessed me as the sole surviving pledge of their loves. . . .'

'I was too young', he declares, 'to feel the importance of my loss.' In his childhood he was the prey of many illnesses, and in part for this reason, perhaps, repudiates the common notion that childhood is a happy state: 'That happiness I have never known, that time I have never regretted'. 'My own recollection is dark; nor do I wish to expatiate on so disgusting a topic'. Of the death of his father he said that it was 'the only event that saved me from a life of hopeless obscurity and indigence'; and said also that the death of his five brothers in infancy was similarly fortunate. He was not only a great historian, but a philosopher.

Lord Berners suggests that an 'exuberant vitality' in childhood is apt to be mistaken for happiness. 'For true happiness . . . there must be a certain degree of experience'. But 'experience' begins very early. 'All sunny to her', says Carlyle of Jane Welsh Carlyle's childhood. But that too had its poignant moments. As a child she would occasionally visit a barber's shop near her home to watch the old barber at his work. There came in a customer one morning who, 'in a pause of the razor', asked the old man, 'How is John So-and-so now?' 'He's deid', replied the barber hollowly, and resumed his work. She herself burst into tears and hurried out.

Sir Henry Newbolt tells us that when he was nearly four years old his father died: 'I was too young to have any feeling of my own about death'. About the same time he was enraptured by what was probably his first glimpse of soldiers in uniform—troopers in scarlet crossing a wooden bridge. He noticed that his nurse, 'his own old Emma', paid them no attention. When he asked her why she had refrained from looking at them, she replied that it was because 'they are dressed like that to go to their death'. The words, although they awakened no sense of grief or fear in his mind, affected him strongly. They intimated mysteries, strange, afflicting, transmuting. Death then, he continues, may affect a child of four with something like a rudimentary sense of tragedy: but grief depends upon long and deep association. Two years afterwards he was bitterly grieved at his grandmother's death, and told a playfellow that a promised game of marbles must be deferred—'I can't play to-day,' he explained, 'my grandmamma has died'. At his reply of an equal simplicity, 'Has she? What a pity!' the commonplace remark revolted him to such a degree that he went back into the house and never played with this boy again.

'The first sense of sorrow I ever knew,' wrote Richard Steele, 'was upon the death of my father, at which time I was not quite five years of age; but was rather amazed at what all the house meant than possessed with a real understanding why nobody was willing to play with me. I remember I went into the room where his body lay, and my mother sat weeping alone by it. I had my battledore in my hand, and fell a-beating the coffin, and calling, papa; for, I know not how, I had some slight idea that he was locked up there. My mother catched me in her arms, and transported beyond all patience of the silent grief she was before in, she almost smothered me in her embraces; and told me in a flood of tears, "Papa could not hear me, and would play with me no more, for they were going to put him under ground, whence he could never come to us again." '

Somewhere in memory—in that densely packed yet impenetrable darkness—must lie concealed the record of my own experience when my father died in my fifth year. I can recall two sharp and meaningful glimpses of him, one of them perhaps that of bidding him goodbye; but of his death and of what immediately followed it there remains recallable not a shadow. On the other hand a sorrow was not less real because it has been forgotten; and

Early One Morning

to an observer a child may seem indifferent only because his one desire is to hide his true feelings.

One of Crabbe's earliest memories—he was born on Christmas Eve in 1754—was the death of a sister in infancy. And among his unpublished papers these lines were found:

'But it was misery stung me in the day
Death of an infant sister made his prey;
For then first met and moved my early fears
A father's terrors and a mother's tears.
Though greater anguish I have since endured,
Some heal'd in part, some never to be cured,
Yet was there something in that first-born ill
So new, so strange, that memory feels it still.'

The father he mentions resembled, he tells us, Howard the philanthropist, but his face was 'stamped with the trace of passions which that illustrious man either knew not or had subdued'.

A little before the death of Joseph Priestley's mother, she dreamed, he relates, that she was in a delightful place, which she described in detail, and believed to be heaven. Her last words were, 'Let me go to that fine place.' A day before his own death in America, when he was seventy-one, he asked that his grandchildren should stay after evening prayers in order that he might speak to each one of them in turn. ' "And you, little thing," he said to Eliza, "remember the hymn you learned; 'Birds in their little nests agree'. . . . I am going to sleep as well as you: for death is only a good long sound sleep in the grave, and we shall meet again." '

What *thought* the 'little thing' of that? Did it remain one of her early memories? Severe illness in childhood—the distortions of fever, its lassitude and helplessness, the fleeting hallucinations, the abject physical misery, the ghastly limbo—all this may lie all but beyond recall in later life. The fact that he could recollect being scalded in early childhood, but no consequent pain, suggested to Wallace the view that since pain is a physical warning of danger, and infants cannot unaided escape from such danger, the sensation of pain by a provision of nature is faint in early childhood and does not reach its maximum until much later in life. 'This', he says, 'is rather a comforting conclusion in view of the sufferings

Night-Fears

of so many infants needlessly massacred through the terrible defects of our vicious social system'. But is the recollection of *pain*—and even of days of grave and acute illness—at *any* time in life more than the mere vacant shell of the reality?—and this, even though one's observation at such times may have been abnormally alert, however inaccurate? Aksakoff is exceptional in this respect.

The actual journey of a child into the valley of the shadow *no* words can ever describe, although, if another personal recollection may be condoned, I remember having ventured so far on it when I was a child that—as I learnt afterwards—the doctor had decided not to come to see me again. I am lying in my mother's arms and realize how desperately anxious she is about me. There are shadowy but unrecognizable human figures in the background and I am gazing up at the ceiling, which seems suddenly to evaporate or become transparent. What showed beyond it I cannot recollect, though I do remember that it was nothing that could be described as angelic. And presently I began, half involuntarily, to whistle softly, and can recall not only my mother's incredulous, 'Oh, thank God! He's whistling!' but also my own unuttered ruminations to the effect: How silly of me! Now they know I am better, and they won't be anxious about me any more!

CHAPTER XXIII

HORROR

★

1. 'O little did my mother ken . . .'

But there are more outrageous things a child may suddenly be confronted with than a poor suicide's body or that of someone dearly loved. Nowadays, scenes of battle, murder and sudden death are, for the young at any rate, chiefly confined to the Picture Palace—to moving (not always in a metaphorical sense) pictures. Tens of thousands of children can, and do, take their weekly draught of these. Some such luxuries, specified as 'A'—usually a kind of Los Angeles absinth or home-made Gorgonzola—are forbidden them; and, when shared, are usually dismissed (though probably after a close attention to them) as silly and soppy. They make their choice—the gangster, the impulsive cowboy, the bloody pirate on the one hand; the can-can, the drug-fiend, 'sex appeal' on the other. With what result?

When we reconsider for a moment the admirable table delicacies which most children, in spite of all incitements and penalties, stubbornly refuse to relish or continue to abhor—burnt porridge, parboiled suet duff, crusts, greens, gristle, fat oleaginous or chilled; and contrariwise, those wild and wanton snares of the Evil One which they welcome as ardently as green grass welcomes the spring —honey, unripe apples, cherries, butter, new bread, plum cake, ice-cream, pink sugar-biscuits, strawberry jam, jellies smoother than the creamy curd and lucent syrops tinct with cinnamon, we can hardly avoid speculating why Mother Nature goes so far astray. This is not at the moment a question of moral discipline, of breaking in the infant stomach and accustoming it to the plain and frugal; but of whether or not a child instinctively wants and pines

296

Horror

for what is good for it rather than the reverse. Do lambs, or lion cubs, or infant gorillas?

In later life most of us eat not what the dietician prescribes but what (if we have the means) we prefer; and, to some extent, we survive. If only we could recover our youthful digestions, what doubt have we that they would wait assiduously on appetite, and that then little harm would follow. *Is* the child, then, in this respect as in others, a child of wrath, however hearty its grace?

Similarly—with regard to the diet of the mind. Is childhood's astonishing penchant for and apparent assimilation of horrors—as distinct from night-terrors—morbid and injurious, and disastrous in effect? To what extent can it secrete and supply its own antidote or antiseptic?

Now among the scenes of horror witnessed and recorded even within the limited range of autobiography referred to in these pages, there are no fewer than nine public executions, actualities solely of human origin. They were thronged about with a mob of men and women, whose foulness and bestiality even Dickens's vocabulary failed to exhaust. As many as twenty such sightseers were once trodden to death at one such spectacle. At Burke's execution, 'The crowd which had assembled to witness his final exit from the scene of life was tremendous; and seats commanding a view of the gallows were let at a large price. Upon his coming forth upon the platform, he was assailed by the hideous yells of public execration, with a species of ferocious exultation. The concluding moments of his existence must have caused him the most acute suffering, for, stung to madness by the horrible shrieks with which he was greeted, he appeared anxious to hurry the executioner in the performance of his duty, as if desirous to escape from that life which he had spent so ill. . . . A struggle took place among the officials present for scraps of the rope with which he had been hanged, shavings of his coffin, and other relics of a similar character.'

Alexander Bain, who was destined to be a philosopher, was not only thrilled at the age of ten at reading of this 'wretch', but used to test his courage by passing the Surgeons' Hall in Edinburgh at night; since, as he supposed, this risked his having a plaster clapped over his mouth prior to his being murdered and bagged for dissection. Thomas Holcroft as a child nine years old was accus-

297

Early One Morning

tomed to the life of a vagrant, to bad food and every conceivable hardship—he one day at this age 'travelled on foot thirty miles'. But, having witnessed an execution in Nottingham, he vowed never again to witness another. William Hutton in his old age describes how on August 18, 1732, a month before he was ten years old, he saw a woman, Eleanor Beare, ascend 'the hated machine'— a pillory—which 'overlooked an enraged multitude'.

'All the apples, eggs, and turnips that could be bought, begged, and stolen, were directed at her devoted head. The stagnant kennels were robbed of their contents, and became the cleanest part of the street. The pillory, being out of repair, was unable to hold a woman in her prime, whose powers were augmented by necessity, she released herself, and, jumping among the crowd, with the resolution and agility of an Amazon, ran down the Morlege, being pelted all the way; new kennels produced new ammunition, and she appeared a moving heap of filth. With difficulty they re-mounted her. . . . A human being in distress excites commiseration whatever is the cause. Her punishment exceeded death. By the time they had fixed her the hour expired, and she was carried to prison, an object which none cared to touch. The next Friday she appeared again, not as a young woman, but as an old one, ill, swelled, and decrepit—she seemed to have advanced thirty years in one week. The keeper, suspecting some *finesse* from the bulk of her head, took off ten or twelve coverings, among which was a pewter plate, fitted to the head, as a guard against the future storm. He tossed it among the crowd, and left no covering but the hair. The pillory being made stronger, and herself being weaker, she was fixed for the hour, where she received the severe peltings of the mob, and they her groans and her prayers.'

The date 1732 may suggest the ages of barbarism; but in the year before my father's birth, 1810, 'four detestable miscreants' (as *News From The Past* relates), were put in the pillory at the head of the Old Bailey—to be greeted with the garbage and filth that had been collected by an 'immense concourse' in preparation for the event. And in that year it took a jury two hours to find Leigh Hunt not guilty of a libel which consisted of a discussion on the propriety of abolishing flogging in the army; he had cited many cases in which a thousand lashes had been inflicted.

A child's attitude to the atrocious spectacle described by Hutton

Horror

is *suggested* in his own words, 'a human being in distress excites commiseration, whatever is the cause'. He had already witnessed the execution of this woman's accomplices. 'I could not get over the steps at the brook, and the crowd was more inclined to push me in than assist me. My father accidentally came, handed me over, and moralized upon the melancholy subject.' He himself withholds the moralizings and adds no comment. His brother Samuel arrived in London on the same day in August, fourteen years afterwards. He was thirteen.

'On my arrival in London I was not a little surprised to see that the immense population of this great city was all moving the same way. Thousands were in motion before and behind me; but I scarcely met a human being. Whatever their business might be, it could not interrupt mine, and I made one of the throng, till we joined a multitude already assembled on Tower Hill. . . .

'I had heard much of the rebels at Nottingham. I believed a rebel to be the blackest of all bloody-minded villains, and I was delighted with the opportunity of seeing two rebel chiefs, as I understood these lords to be, punished as they deserved. I had very nearly paid for this gratification with my life; for on the bustle which preceded the entrance of the first lord, the pressure of the crowd became so great that I thought I should be suffocated; and this would probably have been the case, had not some one cried out, "The lad will be killed!" when a tall, strong fellow, whose humanity equalled his strength, made a violent effort, and seated me on his shoulder. Here I sat at my ease during the whole time, and perhaps saw the sight better than any other person present.

'I must acknowledge that I did not find the beheading of a rebel so entertaining as I expected; and the generality of the crowd seemed to be of the same opinion. We, somehow, forgot that he was a rebel, and could not help feeling for him as a man. . . .'

Alexander Carlyle (who could well remember his scorn and distaste as a child at the jests and fun and buffoonery with which his father and a fellow minister lightened a long journey by coach) witnessed in Dumfries the execution of a young man named Jock Johnstone, who had been convicted of robbery. He was 'a great ringleader'. Apprehensive of an attempt to rescue him, the magistrates erected the gallows before the door of the prison rather than on the moor outside the city, and armed a

Early One Morning

hundred of their stoutest burgesses to guard the scaffold. Alexander, with other boys, sat at a window directly opposite it overlooking the mob. As soon as the hangman laid hands on the condemned man he became like a furious wild beast. He seized the rope round his neck and wrenched off the pinions binding his arms in spite of the six burgesses who were endeavouring to overpower him. The strongest man in Dumfries, a master mason, was summoned to their aid. He bound him hand and foot in a few minutes, laid him quietly down on his face near the edge of the scaffold, and retired.

'This dreadful scene', said Carlyle, 'cost me many nights' sleep.' He was then eleven years old. Three years afterwards he was not only present in kirk when another convict under sentence of death for abstracting his own goods from the Customs House made good his escape, but also witnessed the execution of his accomplice, and the Porteous Riots that followed it. Captain Porteous, himself condemned to death on this account, was reprieved, but while lying in gaol was carried off by friends of his victims.

'This happened on the 7th of September 1736; and so prepossessed were the minds of every person that something extraordinary would take place that day, that I, at Prestonpans, nine miles from Edinburgh, dreamt that I saw Captain Porteous hanged in the Grassmarket. I got up betwixt six and seven, and went to my father's servant, who was thrashing in the barn which lay on the roadside leading to Aberlady and North Berwick, who said that several men on horseback had passed about five in the morning, whom having asked for news, they replied there was none, but that Captain Porteous had been dragged out of prison, and hanged on a dyer's tree at two o'clock that morning. . . .'

Thomas Hardy was four years older when 'One summer morning at Bockhampton, just before he sat down to breakfast, he remembered that a man was to be hanged at eight o'clock at Dorchester. He took up the big brass telescope that had been handed on in the family, and hastened to a hill on the heath a quarter of a mile from the house, whence he looked towards the town. The sun behind his back shone straight on the white stone façade of the gaol, the gallows upon it, and the form of the murderer in white fustian, the executioner and officials in dark clothing and the crowd below being invisible at this distance of nearly three miles. At the moment of his placing the glass to his eye the

300

white figure dropped downwards, and the faint note of the town clock struck eight.

'The whole thing had been so sudden that the glass nearly fell from Hardy's hands. He seemed alone on the heath with the hanged man, and crept homeward wishing he had not been so curious.' It was the second and last execution he witnessed, the first having been that of an 'ill-used woman', Martha Brown, when 'he stood close to the gallows'—a schoolboy about twelve years of age. He could remember in detail his grandmother's account of the burning of a woman for poisoning her husband, Mary Channing. This took place in the Roman amphitheatre at Dorchester about the year 1800.

Edward Calamy was not yet nine years old when in 1679 he was 'much affected' by seeing Ireland, Pickering, Grove and other Catholic victims of the 'Popish Plot' pass on their way to be executed at Tyburn. At fourteen he saw that 'foul-mouthed' wretch Titus Oates whipped at the cart-tail—and marvelled at his invincible courage. Two years before this he had been so close to Alderman Cornish at his execution for his alleged complicity in the Ryehouse Plot that he could hear very distinctly 'a great many passages of what in his agony he said on the gibbet'.

Even Vidocq, at the close of a career which must have left him at the least far from squeamish, recalls that when in his boyhood (and he was already a notorious bully and a thief), he witnessed the prolonged miseries of an old man on the guillotine—to the accompaniment of a fanfare of trumpets—he reached home afterwards 'almost as lifeless as the victim himself'.*

2. '. . . And hang on a gallows-tree.'

These children and 'young persons' had little in common, but in one thing their accounts agree. Surrounded by a yelling mob of their elders who knew well what they had come out to see, they were horror-stricken and had compassion on the sufferer. At what age then does the mobschild turn into a mobsman? How did the hangmen who were following their dreadful trade on these occasions respond to similar experience in *their* early years? Had they too proceeded little by little, from a weeping sister's favourite mammet, to a mouse in a trap, and thence to the kitchen cat? Or

Early One Morning

were they always, boy and man, no worse at heart than the slave
who brought Socrates his hemlock—an executioner of whom
Lady Jane Grey was reading a few years before she herself faced
the scaffold, when Ascham came to say goodbye?—

'"I know that I shall not find you unreasonable like other men,
Socrates. They are angry with me and curse me when I bid them
drink the poison because the Archons make me do it. But I have
found you all along the noblest, gentlest, and best man that has
ever come here; and now I am sure you will not be angry with
me. And so farewell, and try to bear what must be as lightly as
you can; you know why I have come." With that he turned away
weeping and went out. . . .'

Is it possible that spectacles even of cruelty and human vileness,
while leaving an indelible impression on a sensitive spirit, may yet
have a cathartic effect? Can we judge of the mind by the operations of the body? Children, we are told, can take relatively large
doses of belladonna without any consequent symptoms of poisoning, but are extremely susceptible to opium. So too a young child
may watch the fatuous antics of a drunkard with precisely the same
urbane disapproval as it will confer on a cat being sick. William
Hutton, again, who was breeched when he was four years old, not
only recalls 'insults' at this age from his relatives, but describes at
length a journey across the fields at evening with an aunt who was
so drunk that she fell repeatedly as they went on together. He
sharply observed her symptoms and every detail that had led up to
them, but, as he says, had to wait to determine the cause of them.
A child sees but cannot explain. Similarly, there are problems in
science and metaphysics of which Man has the data but not yet
the all-elucidating key.

To-day, there are other gratuitous horrors than public hangings.
Our streets and alleys supply them in abundance. Death on the
highway to-day laughs at Dick Turpin. Worse perhaps, there is a
sordid and continuous dinginess in the black spots where life has
still to be lived. Here is a glimpse of Chicago, from *Al Capone*:

'. . . The girl bride of 1913—now a woman of thirty-one—had
seen it [the shooting of "Diamond Joe Esposito"]. She had been
hearing whisperings. She was keeping vigil at a front window,
with the three children—Joseph, thirteen; Jeanette, nine; and
Charles, three. She ran to the sidewalk.

Horror

' "Oh, is it you, Giuseppe?" she wailed, and saw that it was he. 'There he lay, on his back, the diamonds that had gained him his nickname glittering in the moonlight—the $5000 solitaire ring on his right hand; the belt buckle, with the initials J.E. patterned in diamonds; the tie-pin and the shirt studs. . . .'

The three children were also watching through the moonlight. It was Jeanette who in part, and Charles who wholly had to wait 'to determine the cause' of this event. Children, as young as they, are themselves, of course, by no means incapable of violence and malice and cold cruelty; though they may often give pain in mere curiosity or astonishment at the sight of how some small living creature 'works'. A child will weep bitterly at the fast-sealed eyes, the dangling head and the cold claws of a sparrow which he has found dead in a brick-trap of his own setting, or a less lucky captive that has pined away in a cage. The sorrowful love for the wild bird is no less genuine than the craving to capture and tame it. He may fail to *imagine* pain in his victim. Did not Izaak Walton counsel the devotee to truss up his live frog-bait for fishing 'an if he loved it'?

One of my earliest recollections indeed, at the age of three, is of a minute frog, or was it perhaps an infant crab? It had been condemned by the children I was playing with to the lowest dungeon in a sand castle on the beach at Ventnor; and I grieved at its evil fate. A later memory, however, is of massacring, like a juvenile Caligula, not merely an arrogant array of purple-turbaned thistles with a kitchen knife, but all the domestic flies within reach with a kitchen duster: 'I say, Beware! If yet another of ye settle on my hand! . . .' Of this kind of challenge ultimatums are made; and flies, unlike grouse or partridges, are not even marketable.

Very few adults however think as amiably of these pests as either Thomas Hardy or William Oldys wrote about them:

'Thine's a summer: mine's no more,
Though repeated to three-score:
Three-score summers, when they're gone
Will appear as short as one. . . .'

Indeed I once heard a stoical old lady of more than *four*-score summers declare that she would gladly dismantle the horrid vermin leg by leg and wing from wing. Even a child can do no more!

CHAPTER XXIV

A GLANCE BACK

★

'But what passes for stupidity is much oftener a want of interest.'

The memories borrowed from many souices in the last few chapters relate to the childhood of all sorts and conditions of childien—class, surroundings, nature and nurture. They are a selection from a multitude of others that were themselves isolated relics retrieved from a past of which complete drifts had vanished beyond recall—momentary glimpses of the pattern in life's swiftly twisted kaleidoscope. Some of them may have been but copies of copies of memories; very few may wear the lively colours, the atmosphere, the primal novelty of their originals. If the present resembles a room in the glare of an electric lamp, memories of childhood have for illuminant nothing more powerful than a single candle or the crescent moon. They stand out clear and small, share a pronounced family likeness, and disclose again and again what the subtlest intuition and the closest communion with a child may fail to perceive or to interpret. They suggest too, that, although every child is a child unique, childhood itself in retrospect is an elusive state of being, unlike any other in life, and exceedingly difficult to recapture, but not *so* difficult, perhaps, and for other reasons, as that of early youth. The one we view as it were from within, the other from without; though this may vary with individuals.

Generalizations widely differ. To Edward Gibbon, the historian of an adult and decadent Empire, and even to Mary Coleridge— 'We were young, we were merry, we were very, very wise'—the loss of childhood seemed little but gain. By no means according always to the cage will be the song of the bird. To some adults the

304

A Glance Back

state of childhood, however beguiling it may be in recollection, seems to have been of as little intrinsic value and interest as its sloughed skin to a serpent—though once it was their only livery; its affairs appear to be petty, its range narrow, its faculties feeble, and its existence insipid. If the comparison is merely of worldly with nursery affairs, and we imagine *ourselves* in childish surroundings again, this is true. It resembles making a choice between the delicacies prescribed for children in an old Victorian *Cook's Guide* —rice-water, barley-water, *eau sucrée*, sago, tapioca and gruel, and what were then the latest drams and stingoes for their elders from across the Atlantic—gin-sling, brandysmash, ching-ching, locomotive and floster. Children themselves would readily return the compliment. They may be eager to grow up, but not, necessarily, like *us*. Owing chiefly perhaps to the appearance of grown-ups, I remember vowing to myself as a child that I would never survive the age of forty—not a day beyond that! Twenty years have passed by since that vow was broken; and yet, I still struggle on.

The fact is that even nice children, and not merely the dour and the saturnine, may not care very much for the adult—not as a *class*. If given the choice between a tea-party even of 'distinguished' grown-ups and a solitary visit (whether or not provided with buns) to the Zoological Gardens, there is little doubt they will prefer the animals. They may be of the politest parentage and yet have a rather plebeian taste in humanity. Duke and belted earl are to them but pawns by comparison with anything in the nature of a Robinson Crusoe or the morning sweep.

But other ages, other outlooks. We must accept the situation with what grace and philosophy we can; with Mr. Wilfrid Gibson's for example—

'Fools of the jest which God
Plays ever and again,
We, who thought old men odd,
Are now the odd old men.'

The paradox is that children so often appear to be more elderly than their elders. They may play at being pirates, Red Indians, dustmen, horses, mothers-and-fathers-and-infants, schoolmaster-and-scholar, even bankers and medicine-men; but they very seldom play at being children. The recurrent difficulty is to be sure of our

305

Early One Morning

whereabouts in their half-forgotten country. We may dissent from Henry Vaughan's statement that 'all that age doth teach is ill', though it would be as well to consider it first; and yet agree that, even by way of the imagination, we cannot really 'reach' childhood. The interwoven theme of the 'Ode on the Intimations of Immortality' is Wordsworth's grief that he cannot regain the glory and the freshness of a dream that haunted him in infancy, the splendour in the grass, the glory in the flower. He repeats the word again and again. And he comforts himself as it were with the sorrow that has revealed and augmented his love for nature and humanity but yet has not charmed back the vision that is gone.

This poem and many others reveal his delight in children, his insight, and his devotion to them, but, unlike William Blake, he cannot all but share their inward being. Indeed Blake himself idealizes children, and alike to their innocence, happiness and grief gives the beauty and youth of immortality. Stevenson plays at being a child, and Carroll, again, carries off his sedate little Victorian Alice into a dreamlike, antic and deathless world of the fantastic and there (though an infant of a peculiar impermanence comes her way), she meets nothing even faintly resembling a child.

The glass of time, then, through which even the most eager memoirist looks back upon his childhood may be transparent; but in much is impenetrable. Nevertheless there appears to be no break in the continuity of temperament and personality. One's character changes with age; but whether stunted and mildewed, or green and flourishing, it stays throughout life the same tree. However far back the self may be that we attempt to invoke, it is the self within us *now* that answers the summons, and a self little affected by physical conditions. The Me that Richter speaks of may wear on occasion a strange and estranging and forbidding mask (in extreme illness, for example). But, from first to last, it has always been with us, and will never abandon us, as we confidently believe, this side the grave. In childhood indeed that Self, however secret, seems to be more signal and complete. Innocence is not only a passive but an active thing, both sword and shield; and there is an innocence of the mind of a like character. Nor do we acquire energy of mind, or more than keep sensibility of heart; these are innate.

A Glance Back

By the 'childish things'—the sole use of this adjective in the Bible—that St. Paul declares he put away when he became a man —the speech, the understanding or apprehension, and the reasoning—he cannot have intended that which alone is the key to the kingdom of heaven. In the former we may progress as age advances; he is referring in parable to what must be 'done away' before what is perfect is come.

As with childhood, so with its experiences. These may be as austere as Edmund Gosse's, as meagre as William Hutton's, ample as Roger North's or Frances Power Cobbe's, tragic as Hamerton's, as variegated, romantic and extreme as Aksakoff's. Yet is it extravagant to say that, because they were alike in being *children*, there is a marked resemblance in the effect on us of what happened to them? Every slice of life contains life's essential ingredients, though its plums and spices may differ both in quantity and quality in every specimen. So also with life from our very infancy onwards. If mortal existence confronts humanity with experiences more salient, urgent, moving, woeful or ecstatic—according to our compass—than those inadequately transcribed above, then it is the memoirists themselves who are grossly deceiving us. A burden must be judged by the back that bears it. In any case, it is the earlier chapters in autobiography that are usually the most limpid and animated. Time, place and circumstance are comparatively immaterial; and even though children themselves need be no more at ease one with another than their elders may be, in the contemplation of childhood humanity has a common bond—

'This fond attachment to the well-known place,
Whence first we started into life's long race,
Maintains its hold with such unfailing sway,
We feel it even in age, and at our latest day.'

CHAPTER XXV

LEARNING

★

1. 'By good example, was his bisiness.'

Whether actively or passively, consciously or sub-consciously, by intuition or laborious observation, beyond all things else childhood is the age of learning. Certain faculties both physical and mental may lie latent awhile, but they are legacies awaiting fruition and will fall due. Otherwise—its body as an entity brand-new and yet of an architecture compared with which that of Stonehenge is brief as a fairy ring—a child from its first wild moment in this world, from its first curiously low-pitched squall, like the murmur of a distant rookery, continues to learn—even the simplest act of recognition being of this order. And by far the greater and maybe the more profoundly effective part of this learning is dependent on self-teaching, however richly the process may be eased by example and instruction.

What a child learns depends equally on itself and its opportunities, but it cannot possibly evade the process. As with honey or 'sina tea', a sip of currant wine or a gulp of the waters of Acheron, the supreme question is, has it vitally nourished the child? Unless a minute Barkis is willin', unless he finds what he receives acceptable, he will remain more or less ill-nourished or will learn by rote. The latter method has its convenience, but since to learn life by rote appears to entail a gradual desiccation of the mind, if not degeneration of the heart, it cannot be the best.

Passing over the irksome accomplishments already referred to which are usually surmountable, as we are told by the expert, by a child of five, e.g. those concerning the nose, the bowels, the

308

Learning

comb, the button, the spoon and the soap, the first of what may be called its artificial sciences is that of speech. And this, clearly, is chiefly self-taught. For speech is not the outcome of an instinct, as walking is; and the self-teaching of it is not the less the result of effort for seeming all but automatic.

'Babies', says the author of *Modernism in Language Teaching*, 'babies cry for the same reason that lambs cry: because they want their mothers.' The crying is an instinct. Not so speech: speech is a faculty that has to be acquired. None the less, he goes on, 'the child . . . with its passionate craving for communication . . . is born a *language-learning* animal'. Lord Brougham, exceptional other-wise for the poverty of his early memories, began to talk freely, as we know, when he was a little short of nine months old. Less rash or more contemplative infants than Brougham, though back-ward is the usual term for them, may prefer to resist for thrice as many months even the temptation to 'answer back'. Sooner or later only the deaf refrain, and even they may learn to communi-cate at last by touch *and* by speech.

The normal infant (if it will forgive so dead-alive a phrase), listens, and transmutes one by one the speech-sounds it hears into the noises it makes—each one of them involving the most rapid and complex adjustments of the vocal organs. Days and weeks go by; little by little, it persists. Even a two-year-old who can already manage small sentences may show a voracious appetite for words new to him. He will repeat the last one or two words of any sentence said to him in talk by an adult, who in turn may no less spontaneously find himself doing likewise. He may again and again cockneyfy his o-sound, and at once at a frown from his mother rap out a sonorous oratorical correction.

Indeed, 'infants', as Fénelon says, 'before they can speak plain, may be prepared for instruction. . . . Let us only consider what a child does before it can speak. It learns a language which it will shortly speak with more accuracy than scholars can the dead languages they have so painfully studied in riper years'.

Practice in this art from the cradle is so perpetual and so gradual that it needs a very attentive ear to detect its continual progress. In later life we may find it impossible to master even to our own satisfaction the French *u* or *n* sound, the Dutch gutturals or the Zulu click, or to imitate any dialect or peculiarity of speech.

Early One Morning

Between thirty and forty different ways have been recorded of pronouncing, in the dialects, such common standard English words as *close, cold, daughter, father, cucumber, hold* and *whole*; and over forty for *earth, old* and *home*. It is by no means easy for the novice in such matters to explain, let alone exhibit, even vaguely, how he manages to pronounce, let us say, his *k*'s or his *l*'s or his *g*'s. Few mothers make any such precise attempt in decoying their infants on, though patient incitement now and then may woo away a passing difficulty. In three or four years, none the less, a child, chiefly by listening and mimicry may not only have taught himself most of the vocal elements in his mother tongue—and there are some 270 of these in English—but also the very use of self-acquired words and sentences, and is perpetually babbling a workaday vocabulary. A magician secreted between ear and vocal apparatus has somehow effected this astonishing feat.

Individual difficulties of course over, say, *f* or *r* or *y*, may continue to be obstructive. Here is 'Johnny', for example, being tutored in his aspirate on modern (American) lines:—

'But about this sound which Johnny calls "a pant". Here are the letters which stand for it, "breath letters", h—H. When you make these scales, breathe out in this way, h—H. Breathe very gently. Notice, too, that both teeth and lips are open. Now why is not this a voice letter?'

'Oh!' said Johnny, 'because we just breathe out its sound.'

'Yes, that is just the reason. . . .'

And here he is not only enquiring about his *d*'s, but using them for that purpose:

'There are pigeons at the barn, mama. What letter stands for the sound they make?'

'This one: d—D. It is a sound made by young pigeons. You may outline these pigeons and sound as you print each d.'

'This sound presses the tongue up, near its point, a little harder than *n*. Try the two together, *n, d, n, d.*'

'I can scarcely hear that sound when you make it.'

'No, you can not. It is, besides, a hard sound to make, but I think it sounds like the young pigeon's cry. . . .'

Adults 'drop' their h's much less than once they did; we may be unable to pronounce our r's; and in old age the aspirate will perhaps once more become precarious, or too conscientious—as

Learning

may other letters when the dentist or a touch of aphasia intervenes. Few complete personal sets, so to speak, of pronounced English speech-elements are free from obvious blemishes; and an American imitation of a *refined* English voice is not less amusing than a refined English voice's imitation of an American's—of which there are as many varieties as there are of nations in the collect for Good Friday.

There is a spoken English which Professor H. C. Wyld describes as the Received Standard. It is an English, he says, neither provincial nor vulgar; one that most people would willingly speak if they could, and desire to speak if they do not. Its chief merit is a sonorous quality in the vowels and a clear distinction between them. In Professor Wyld's view 'it is most consistently heard at its best . . . among Officers of the British regular army'. Children can manage the sonorous with ease! Many also have a particularly pleasing, small, sweet and delicate way with their tongues. There is no reason why the army should commandeer them all.

One child I have in mind on nearing the age of three chattered freely in a lingo all but innocent of any consonants which only a brother two years older could easily follow. Having at length mastered most of them, in her fourth year she became a little sensitive over her missing r's. What wonder then if—blushing and falling mute at being detected by this brother in calling the family bulldog (Jerry) *Jellie*—she blushed again with delight when her mother in a moment of inspiration referred to the animal as Jinks.

She is by nature a punctilious child, usually refusing aid with her buttons; and once sent her brother into spasms of resentment when on being asked her favourite colour she replied, 'My *favourite* colour is red, but I like blue best.' 'If your favourite colour is red,' he protested vehemently, 'you *can't* like blue best.' 'But I do.' A few days afterwards he enquired with a sly glance, pointing to a bowl full of lilac, 'Which do you like best of *those*, the white or the mauve?' But the bait was too obvious. She scented it at once, and replied, 'I like them both best, because, you see, they are either mauvy white or whity mauve.'

There are many fine shades of speech—a new and odious nasal *i*-sound having recently spread over the kingdom like an imported weed; and though many children speak a genteel English, few

Early One Morning

have been persuaded into speaking a wholly delightful English. When Ellen Terry was a few years old, a child was wanted in a pantomime to represent the Spirit of the Mustard-pot. And no doubt because she was of an ardent nature the choice fell upon her. Alas, 'when they tried to put me into the mustard-pot, I yelled lustily and showed more lung-power than aptitude for the stage!' Her début was at the age of eight, in the part of Mamillius—and there may be happy nonagenarians who are still enjoying the recollection of that exquisite event. Her sister Kate was two years younger at *her* first appearance, in 1850. My father, says Ellen Terry, had never ceased teaching me 'to be useful, alert and quick. Sometimes he hastened my perceptive powers with a slipper, and always he corrected me if I pronounced any word in a slipshod fashion. He himself was a beautiful elocutionist, and if I now speak my language well it is in no small degree due to my early training. . . .'

Never, said Roger North, should parent or 'curator' descend to a child's capacity in his converse. Let the contrary be the rule. If, he says, 'the child speaks broken, the nurse will too'—to be on equal terms; and 'this is only to establish defects'. 'Baby talk' can certainly be of the most miminy-piminy silliness. But his name would be Grim who forbade *gee-gee, baa-lamb, cockadoodle* and *moo-moo*; or *'mo-mo'* either, as a child recently christened a bulky family car. On the other hand, if we allowed children to *invent* words for us, how much enriched our daily English would soon be.

An accent once acquired is prodigiously difficult to eradicate. Country children for example speak with one voice in school and in quite another in the playground, just as well-meaning lecturers both simplify their vocabulary and change their tone at the breakfast-table. Speech acquired, though the acquisition of numbers of words as aural symbols had long preceded it, learning in general is infinitely facilitated; just as walking, running, hopping, skipping, jumping and balancing on stilts follow on from toddling, standing, crawling, sitting, and lunging spasmodically a pair of Raphaelesque legs in a cradle. And at last, pirouetting on her 'points', may appear a rival to Pavlova—or a female orator. The female orator, like the *prima donna*—who has spent at least as many years in producing her colorature and cadenzas—may be forgiven a little vanity. A chatterbox, with a prattle sweet as brook-water and gay

Learning

as a chimney swallow's, witless of whence the melody came, is contented unapplauded to continue to chatter.

So far from learning to speak being a simple operation, then, it might, if it were not almost universal, impress us as one little short of the miraculous. Even our earliest memories seldom surrender a glimpse of it, and none that I can recall in autobiography makes any attempt to reveal the method or to descant on the difficulty.

2. *'I took the little book out of the angel's hand, and ate it up; and it was in my mouth sweet as honey.'*

Learning to read, on the other hand, is usually referred to and frequently enlarged upon. But before consulting our memoirists again, we might first glance at the usual methods. In former times a child's first lesson-book was a printed primer—a minute prayer-book, simple but profound. It was succeeded by the wooden or metal or ivory horn-book, or 'Christ's-Crosse-Rowe', which was hung by its handle round its toddling owner's neck and contained the alphabet, the nine numerals and the Lord's Prayer. It is described by Shenstone, and by Cowper:

'Neatly secured from being soiled or torn
Beneath a pane of thin translucent horn,
A book (to please us at a tender age
'Tis called a book, though but a single page). . . .
Presents the prayer the Saviour deigned to teach,
Which children use, and parsons—when they preach.'

About two centuries ago the alphabet stamped out in seductive gingerbread came into use:

'And that the child may learn the better,
As he can name, he eats the letter.'

How long a Dunce, Dunce, Double Dee might have to eke out his stale relics one can only guess. Then Dr. Bell invented his sand-tray, for tracing the letters, and the 'Battledore' came into use. And John Locke mentions a happy man who pasted the letters on the sides of four dice 'whereby his eldest son in coats has played himself into spelling'; a phrase which once again recalls Henry Vaughan—also Froebel and Madame Montessori.

313

Early One Morning

We have long ago transcended such simplicities as these. 'The methods of learning to read', says Dr. Huey, 'that are in common use today (1912) may be classed as alphabet, phonic, phonetic, word, sentence'—and combinations of them. He criticizes them individually, some of them severely, and no less severely three-quarters of the primers in use in America—he is not concerned with ours—which, he declares, are chiefly attempts to get down to the child's 'level'. 'The child avoids adults who try to play with him or talk with him in this manner, and down in his child heart he scorns such reading-matter'. There are other systems, including the imitative method. 'In the Orient, children bawl in concert over a book, imitating their fellows or their teacher till they come to know what the page says and to read it for themselves.'

The bawling *may* be due to modern manners. As Ernest Renan expresses it in *The Life of Jesus*, 'He learned to read and to write, doubtless, according to the Eastern method, which consisted in putting in the hands of the child a book, which he repeated in cadence with his little comrades, until he knew it by heart.'

Every method has its advantages and defects; but 'willing effort is what makes a child learn to read fast'. 'One can pick out the children', says Professor Dewey, 'who learned to read at home. They read naturally. One cannot read naturally when he reads for reading's sake.' He is convinced that valuable time in childhood is wasted in merely learning to read as a mechanical tool, and that young children may suffer from this enforcement, since their minds are not adapted to it.

First store the mind and the imagination with the riches of the outer world; the spoken words for them will soon become a highway to the treasure-house of memory—instant evocations of the images in the mind, of eye and ear and the other senses. It was indeed John Milton's view that the knowledge of words is best obtained in union with the knowledge of things. Language, he wrote, is but the instrument conveying to us *things* useful to be known; and he maintained that all true methods of learning must begin from the objects of sense. From life and nature to words, from words to life and nature again. It is chiefly because we so poorly see, observe and distinguish, that our words are wanting or feeble in a personal content. How many adults could name all the parts of a chair, of a church, all the flowers in a meadow, all

Learning

the bones in a human arm? A quick child hungers for the names of things, though often in vain, and once he acquires them, they become all but indelible. He may then play himself into reading as he played himself into naming. By merely hanging up plain or, better, coloured pictures in the bedroom or nursery, of birds, of flowers, of anything that will attract his eye and his attention; by printing or scrawling in large letters the names for them underneath, and by always explaining any written or printed word he asks the meaning of, he will teach himself to read as he taught himself to talk.

But, says Professor Dewey, if he does not, there is no good reason to force books upon him, or that he should be compelled into book-reading before his eighth or ninth year. In the schools of the future, Dr. Huey confidently predicts, books will be but little used before the child's eighth or ninth year. Not that active-minded enterprising children are likely to wait to read until that age. By hook or by crook they will have found out a way. Nor of course is this a new discovery. The *Lady's Magazine* of the 1750's included a series of chapters translated from the French of Fénelon, whose presence among the children he sees in his mind as he writes, is so courteous, wise, and gentle that one might suppose Titania had mingled 'euphrasie and rue' in his 'well of life'.

'I have seen several children learn to read in diverting themselves; one need only relate some pleasant stories out of a book in their presence, to teach them to know the letters insensibly. . . . Endeavour to choose a child a book' [preferably 'handsomely bound', with gilded edges, pretty figures and a good type], 'that shall contain a number of stories, short and surprising; this done, fear not but he will learn to read. Neither tease him to do it exactly well; let him pronounce in his natural way, as he please. . . .

'Nothing so confounds a dull and faint-hearted child as harshness. . . . Bend all your care to teach him with ease and pleasure . . . and every task you desire he should perform. . . .' If he fails, or falters, let perhaps an inferior, or another child, 'irritate him by some degree of contempt', and so egg him on. And again: 'If they pass judgment upon anything without thoroughly understanding it, embarrass them by some new question, which may show them their fault, without roughly confounding them. . . . Show you take a pleasure in their questions, and by this means you will in-

315

sensibly teach them.' 'Suffer a child . . . to have his play, and mingle instruction with it, that wisdom may not show herself to him but at intervals, and ever with a smiling countenance.'

Sir Thomas Elyot, the familiar friend of Sir Thomas More, considered also that children should be 'sweetly allured' to learn 'with praise and such pretty gifts as they delight in'; that their alphabet should be painted in gay colours, that their nurses should learn Latin so that it shall come pure and early. But he misliked baby-talk and disapproved of lengthy holidays.

Reminding ourselves then that any new learning in childhood is only the coatinuation of a habit; that no learning from books or any other source is of its utmost efficacy unless life itself continually shines in upon it like the sun of morning through a window; and also that Moses, Samuel and Joseph, Sophocles and Socrates, Horace and Cicero, when they were children, used to think and talk and play and quarrel in their mother tongues, let us now return to our memoirists and see how they were 'grounded' in their rudiments. Namely, in reading, which may be one of life's inexhaustible pleasures and blessings, but may also become a mere habit, an escape from thinking, or a drug; in writing, which is first a very useful wherewithal and resource, and may eventuate even in childhood, as we shall see, into the medium of an art; and last, in arithmetic, which, in spite of all the tears and headaches of the past, for most of us remains rather primitive in kind and extent, and which, I gather, is not held in extreme estimation by the mathematician.

Whatever their import may be, recollections of this kind of nursery learning canter along in the merriest fashion and are astonishing in their variety. What follows is arranged roughly according to age, and neither in reference to the recorder's special gifts, which must of course be taken into account, nor to the accomplishments of the instructor who helped him on his way, since these are not often referred to.

3. *'That pretty person, your strangely hopeful boy.'*

But first, the prodigies; of whom there must have been many, though but few are famous. Their records show how much childhood in mere *learning* is capable of, and may cast a searching

316

Learning

beam of light nor merely into our own *childhood*. We may find ourselves, on the other hand, less astonished at the taught than at the assiduity (or possibly the vanity) of the teacher.

'I have no remembrance of the time', says John Stuart Mill, 'when I began to learn Greek. I have been told that it was when I was three years old.' As he began, so he continued; and at fourteen, 'already possessed the intellectual acquirements of a well-educated man'. Even his daily walks with his father were spent in a kind of Sandford-and-Merton catechism, a continuation class of two. In Mill's own words, 'I never was a boy', and by boy he meant perhaps also child. Nevertheless there seems to have been nothing wanting of childhood in John Evelyn's 'dear son' Richard, who died on January 27, 1657-8, 'five years and three days old only'.

The diarist confesses that he himself was 'not initiated into any rudiments until near four years of age', and knew no Latin until he was eight. Richard, said his father, was 'a prodigy for wit and understanding; for beauty of body, a very angel; for endowment of mind, of incredible and rare hopes.' At half this age 'he could perfectly read any of the English, Latin, French, or Gothic letters, pronouncing the three first languages exactly. . . . When, seeing a Plautus in one's hand, he asked what book it was, and, being told it was comedy, and too difficult for him, he wept for sorrow'. He had by heart many propositions of Euclid that were read to him in play. Having read thus far, the ignoramus may hope for the worst; but in vain; for Richard Evelyn appears to have been a charming and natural child—'all life, all prettiness, far from morose, sullen, or childish in anything he said or did'.

Two other wonders of childhood are mentioned in the *Diary*. One of these was William Wotton, who as a boy of eleven, declared his father, knew all that he himself knew, and could 'both read and perfectly understand Hebrew, Greek, Latin, Arabic, Syriac and most of the modern languages', and was also 'dexterous' in chronology, antiquity and mathematics. The other was the son of Dr. Andrew Clench, who was afterwards strangled in a hackney coach by a stranger who had brought him away from his house on the pretence of visiting a patient. This child, not yet twelve, was examined by Evelyn and Pepys, and apart from his languages and vast learning was not only beautiful of countenance but 'full of play, of a lively, sprightly temper, always smiling, and exceeding

317

Early One Morning

pleasant'. He too was 'perfect in arithmetic', but would spend in playing among other boys four or five hours every day, and was 'as earnest at his play as at his study'.

Jean-Philippe Baratier's languages at the age of five were Latin, Greek and French. Four years afterwards, to catch up, he was compiling a Hebrew dictionary. He died, aged nineteen, in 1740. Christian Heinecken was not only an infant linguist, but at fourteen months was conversant with the history of the Old and New Testaments. His *Life*—1721 to 1725—was written by his tutor— who was evidently of the same mind as the father of Robert Boyle. *He* had a 'perfect aversion' for such parents as 'breed their children so nice and tenderly that a hot sun or a good shower of rain as much endangers them as if they were made of butter or sugar'. For this reason he sent his son Robert from home to be nursed, and 'he was taught very young to *speak* both Latin and French'. In later life he pressed on to Greek and Hebrew, not chiefly to acquire these languages for their own sake but in order to read the Scriptures in the original, since he hated 'verbal studies' and chemistry was his chosen occupation. We might have guessed, unaided, that Isaac Watts was no butter and sugar child. When he was only four years old he was taught 'the learned languages'. Yet that he probably wrote his wholly English hymns and songs for children—plain songs but always neighbouring poetry—in his early twenties is an even more impressive fact. Thought, lesson, feeling, rhythm and rhyme are so easy and natural in them that the art eludes us:

> '. . . Yet to read the shameful story
> How the Jews abused their King,
> How they served the Lord of Glory,
> Makes me angry while I sing. . . .'

A childhood without the busy bee and the sluggard would resemble a hymnal without '*O God, our help in ages past. . . .*'

4. '*She saw he was a goodly child.*'

The modern parent is likely to be as much shocked as impressed by prodigies such as these. There is no reason to assume, however, that a polyglot of four need be less enlivening

318

company than a dunce of fifty or a wiseacre of seventy-five. We are apt to judge children by ourselves, falter at the very word Hebrew, and may dismiss any juvenile exponent of it whom we may read about (we are less likely to meet one nowadays), as a tiresome, pygmy, brazen highbrow. But precocity, as we have seen and might have assumed, is usual rather than otherwise in those who, like King Saul among the tribes of Israel, are destined in intellectual stature to stand head and shoulders above their fellows. According to its effect on a child we must judge of his learning; and perhaps the wisest summary on this subject is John Locke's:

'Under whose care soever a child is put to be taught during the tender and flexible years of his life, this is certain, it should be one who thinks Latin and languages the least part of education; one who, knowing how much virtue and a well-tempered soul is to be preferred to any sort of learning or language, makes it his chief business to form the mind of his scholars, and give that a right disposition; which, if once got, though all the rest should be neglected, would in due time produce all the rest; and which, if it be not got, and settled so as to keep out ill and vicious habits—languages and sciences, and all the other accomplishments of education, will be to no purpose, but to make the worse and more dangerous man.'

Progress even in the precocious may be curiously intermittent. Alexander Pope, 'the little nightingale', for example, in spite of his crooked body and ill health as a child, although he was founded in Latin and Greek when he was eight years old, learned nothing at his first two schools. That he was flogged at the earlier of them for composing a lampoon upon his headmaster, suggests a lesson, it is true, but it hardly taught him to refrain from lampooning!

So with learning of a kind other than letters. Christopher Wren, that youth, in Aubrey's words, 'of prodigious inventive wit', 'that miracle of a youth', in Evelyn's, had been a small and weakly child, and was educated at home by his father and a private tutor, until he went to Westminster School, under the wing of Dr. Busby. In 1645, his fourteenth year, he invented a new astronomical instrument. This he dedicated to his father, in an address in Latin prose and eighteen hexameter verses; and followed it up with a pneumatic engine, and a device for use in gnomonics.

Early One Morning

Before he was twenty-five, the age at which William Pitt became Prime Minister, he had a European reputation as a man of science.

Thomas Lawrence's father (apart from having begotten such a child) deserved well of mankind—he kept an inn, the White Lion of Bristol, and loved poetry. At four years old his son, a 'very beautiful and charming' child, would, like little Ann Taylor in the baker's shop, spout poetry for the entertainment of his customers —Addison's 'Nymphs of Solyma' at five, 'Lycidas' at seven. At this age, it is said, he had taught himself to draw and to make portraits commended by their sitters! At eight he was contributing verses to the magazines; and at nine had become a skilful and rapid draughtsman and painted his picture on the subject of Peter denying Christ. Apart from a few lessons in French and Latin, he had had only two years' schooling.

Robert Browning, to use his own words, was as a child 'unluckily precocious'. He was taken away from a dame school because the *parents* of the other children attending it became jealous of his prowess. He delighted in music, at the age of two was a 'young wonder at drawing', and soon afterwards took to caricature. He was a voracious reader of what the shallow-witted, who take good care to avoid them, call 'deep books'; and he recalled them in his verse. To Nathaniel Wanley's *Wonders of the Little World* he and his father not only owed their Pied Piper poems, but Robert many (possibly obscure) references, from *Pauline* to *Asolando*. Gerard de Lairesse's *The Art of Painting in All Its Branches* was a book, he said himself, which he had read and re-read as a child 'with greater delight' than any other; but his 'pet book' was the *Emblems* of Francis Quarles; a poet, incidentally, who in his twenty-first year became cup-bearer to the princess Elizabeth, afterwards Queen of Bohemia, and known as the Queen of Hearts.

> '. . . If all those glittering Monarchs, that command
>   The servile quarters of this earthly ball,
> Should tender in exchange their shares of land,
>   I would not change my fortunes for them all:
>   Their wealth is but a counter to my coin:
> The world's but theirs; but my Beloved's mine.'

Learning

It appears then that a child with a quick intelligence and a gift for words, if he is allowed like a subterranean stream to wander unheeded and at liberty upon his course, will learn anything within—and even outside of—reason that comes his way and takes his fancy. Nor need such learning be skin deep if it lie in his mind fallow for a season. In apt proportion this seems to be true of all children. To restrain and keep a child back is less just than with judgement to encourage him; though on occasion an ingenious but not insuperable dam to the headlong waters may add depth and energy to his character. Even milk teeth are excellent teeth and are meant for mastication. Is it then, again, our present practice to expect too little of children? Have they rich enough opportunities to teach themselves when very young? Let a willing and witful child but hear the voice of the charmer, he is bound to follow. And to an observant and appreciative eye early promise declares itself as lustrously as Sirius among the night stars of October.

'That', said Chatham one day, of his son William, 'is the most extraordinary boy I ever knew.' 'This child waiting at table,' Cardinal Morton would say of Thomas More, who was then fourteen, 'whosoever shall live to see it, will prove a marvellous man.' A like prediction was made by his father concerning Robert Burns in his early childhood: 'Whoever may live to see it, something extraordinary will come from that boy!' And Mr. Wicks, his schoolmaster, announced of Thomas Love Peacock, when he was a child of six, that he would prove one of the most remarkable men of his day.

There may have been similar predictions that failed to come true, since such ventures into the future are easily forgotten; and others may have been the outcome of the wisdom that follows the event. But hardly so when the child is observed not merely in the revelation of an impulse to learn, but in the discovery, as if it were simplicity itself, of the one sovereign method. The Duke of Argyll in 1718 found a copy of Newton's *Principia* lying on the grass in his garden, and summoned his gardener's son to take it back to the house. This young man, Edmund Stone, then eighteen, claimed the book as his own. ' "Yours!" replied the Duke; "do you understand geometry, Latin, and Newton?" ' At his answer the Duke sat down on a bank and asked him how this had come about. The young man, who was afterwards the compiler of the

Early One Morning

New Mathematical Dictionary, told him that when he was eight years old a servant had taught him to read.

'The masons were then at work upon your house. I approached them one day, and observed that the architect used a rule and compasses, and that he made calculations. I inquired what might be the meaning and the use of these things, and I was informed that there was a science called arithmetic. I purchased a book of arithmetic, and I learned it. I was told there was another science called geometry; I bought the necessary books, and I learned geometry. By reading, I found that there were good books of these two sciences in Latin; I bought a dictionary, and I learned Latin. I understood also that there were good books of the same kind in French; I bought a dictionary, and I learned French. And this, my Lord, is what I have done: it seems to me that we may learn everything when we know the twenty-four letters of the alphabet.'

And that (even if by counting *i* and *j*, and *u* and *v*, as four letters we make it 26), is a deduction lamentable enough to one who sits in contemplation of a wasted past. 'You have waked me too *late*,' an inward voice may fretfully retort, 'I must slumber again.' But it is a truism for all that. And Richard Porson, who as a child had so retentive a memory that he could, it is said, repeat a lesson which he had learnt one or two years before and not seen meanwhile, would have agreed. ' "Gracious heavens, papa!" exclaimed the fair-haired little Ebenezer to his father, after eyeing for a while the enormous whale now freely disporting its huge bulk in the deep: "Do you really *mean* that this prodigious mammal flourishes solely on shoals of the pelagic?" '

322

CHAPTER XXVI

LESSONS

★

1. '*Schooled only by his mother's tender eye.*'

Even a child's method of learning may have been originated, though recollection of that method may have been lost. Coleridge declares that when he was three years and two months old he could read a whole chapter in the Bible without, as he surmised, his having been taught to do so. He had probably taught himself. But since we can recall only moments or chains of moments and not prolonged processes, perhaps no more than a glimpse of a primer, or of a teacher, or of the page whereon a 'hard word' was first seen and mastered, may be retrievable from years of effort. And here is Charlotte Yonge:

'I have a hazy remembrance of a green spelling-book, and the room where I read a bit of it to some unaccustomed person. It must have been while I was very young, for I could read to myself at four years old, and I perfectly recollect the pleasure of finding I could do so, kneeling by a chair on which was spread a beautiful quarto edition of *Robinson Crusoe*, whose pictures I was looking at while Grandmamma read the newspaper aloud to my mother. I know the page, in the midst of the shipwreck narrative, where to my joy I found myself making out the sense.

'Otherwise I can hardly date my earlier recollections. Mine was too happy and too uneventful a childhood to have many epochs, and it has only one sharp line of era in it, namely my brother's birth when I was six and a half. I can remember best by what happened before, and what happened after. . . .'

English spelling has for many years been the butt of the phoneticians. They would rather disrupt the habits of a complete genera-

323

tion of readers than allow its anomalies and absurdities to continue; and, in defence of this, they lament the woes of the children who have to submit to so irrational a persecution. Yet there seem to be very few enraged or indignant early memories on this score. However, there are other methods of learning to spell than by ear. Was not Ann Taylor, with her insurmountable t-h-y=*thy*, whipped for not realizing this? An illiterate child of five may finish a jigsaw puzzle in half the space of time required by a grown-up aunt and uncle, about six times his age. He has divined his own method.

Carlyle could vaguely recall learning to read, but not, even vaguely, learning his alphabet—an accomplishment very seldom revivable, however many laborious hours may have been spent on it. What appeared to him to be a remote glimpse of fat black letters declaring, *This is a Cat*, was all of this prolonged process that returned to his mind. Macaulay appears to have surpassed Coleridge: 'From the time that he was three years old he read incessantly'—prone on his stomach, a wholesome posture, in front of the fire, his book on the hearth-rug, and a piece of bread and butter in his hand! And Macaulay, in his turn, seems to have been surpassed by Cecco Oliphant. He was, says his mother, in her *Autobiography*, 'always so original even in his babyhood, learning to read in Mademoiselle's wonderful way in a fortnight without a tear'. When she wrote these words, she tells us, he, the last left of her family of five, was 'lying in his coffin in the room next to me'.

When Southey was three years old—'quite capable of learning the alphabet, far too young to be put to it as a task'—he went to school to a Ma'am Powell. She had a forbidding face. In a flood of tears he told her this, and in a second flood related that he had done so when he returned home. As soon as he could read 'which was very early', he was presented with a set of Francis Newbery's sixpenny books for children, 'splendidly bound in the flowered and gilt Dutch paper of former days'. This was when—from two to six—he was living with his 'injudicious' but captivating aunt, Miss Tyler. At six years of age he planned to remove to an island graced with one mountain of gingerbread and another of sugar-candy. He had a lively desire to be a soldier, once slept with a sword in his bed, and out of a reverie remarked earnestly to an aunt, 'Auntee Polly, I should like to have all the weapons of war,

Lessons

the gun and the sword, and the halbert, and the pistol, and all the weapons of war.'

Of Samuel Butler's early days there is little in the *Memoir* until he is ten, and at school at Allesley. But the childhood of Ernest Pontifex in *The Way of all Flesh*, says Festing Jones, was drawn by Butler as faithfully as he could draw it from his own: 'Before he could well crawl he was taught to kneel; before he could well speak he was taught to lisp the Lord's prayer, and the general confession. . . . Before he was three years old he could read and, after a fashion, write. Before he was four he was learning Latin and could do rule-of-three sums'.

When Augustus Hare was only one year older than this, besides English reading, writing, spelling, history, arithmetic, and geography, he had to do German reading and *writing*, a little Latin, botany and drawing. 'I never recall the moment of [indoor] childhood', he says, 'in which I was not undergoing education of some kind, and generally of an unwelcome kind.'

Francis Galton was 'a shy and naughty child', though he was once 'quite subdued by the charm of Elizabeth Fry', and looked back eighty years to the joy of it. He began his *Memories of My Life* when he was eighty-six, which at that time, he remarks, was the average age of himself, his mother, his two sisters and his two brothers. Here he handsomely acknowledges his debt to his progenitors (Galtons, Darwins and Barclays), including a few little shortcomings—hay-fever, for example, which he inherited when he was nearly eighty! He refers in all gratitude and with a moving tenderness to his beloved sister Adèle, twelve years his senior, and a sufferer from spinal curvature. She was gifted with an astonishing energy of mind and beauty of character. To her he owed the Bible (as a 'verbally inspired book'), his Latin rudiments, and a great deal of English verse. In the last he was a little family prodigy, spouting at any excuse Pope's *Odyssey*, Scott and Milton: but he was *not* a prig—'a nice little child'.

Lucy Hutchinson, who was born in 1620, little more than two hundred years before Galton, relates that her parents were 'pious and vertuous', and careful instructors of her youth, not only by precept but example; and she reflects with deep humiliation on the small improvement she had made of so rich a stock. She adds (and I have ventured on italics): '*Whoever considers England will find itt*

Early One Morning

no small favour of God to have bene made one of its natives'. By the time, she says, 'I was foure yeares old I read English perfectly, and having a greate memory, I was carried to sermons; and while I was very young could remember and repeate them exactly, and being caress'd, the love of praise tickled me, and made me attend more heedfully. When I was about 7 yeares of age, I remember I had att one time 8 tutors in severall quallities, languages, musick, dancing, writing, and needlework; but my genius was quite averse from all but my booke . . . and every moment I could steale from my play . . . I would steale into some hole or other to read. . . . I was so apt that [in Latin] I outstripped my brothers who were at schoole. . . . As for my needle I absolutely hated it. . . . Play among other children I despis'd . . . I tir'd them with more grave instructions than their mothers, and pluckt all their babies to pieces'.

But a single governess, it seems, may prove more indigestible even than '8 tutors'. Elizabeth Grant describes herself as 'a tall, pale, slight, fair child to look at', though she 'seldom ailed anything'. Against one of her (transitory) governesses, a Miss Gardiner, stark rebellion set in. She sat down one day to make her report to Elizabeth's absent mother. 'She took a small packet of very small pens from a box near her, and a sheet of very shiny paper, and after some moments of reflection she began. I observed her accurately. "What do you call those pretty little pens?" said I. "Crow quills, my dear," said she, for she was very kind in her manner to us. "William," said I in a low aside, "I don't think we need mind her any more, nor learn any more lessons, for she can't really teach us. She is a fool, *I* shan't mind her any more." "Very well," said William, "nor I, nor I shan't learn my lessons." He never yet had learned one. . . .' At Miss Gardiner's next appearance with her pygmy quills and satiny paper the two children secretly tied her up by her dress and her feet to the legs of her chair and the table.

Merciless little asps, one's compassion goes out to the governess, as to other masters and mistresses whose ill fate, whether they deserve it or not, it is to be continually 'ragged'. However, she married happily later, and 'had a fine set of children of her own'.

Charlotte Yonge, in her early days, had but one tutor, her mother, 'who never once spoke angrily or harshly to me in all her life'. When she was seven years old, she came to Geography and

326

Lessons

to Mrs. Trimmer's Histories, *Sacred* and *Profane,* 'with their smudgy woodcuts (at ten shillings apiece),' and she quickly learned to write. Whereupon she drew on the gravel walk this 'deeply touching' sentence: 'Lessons! Thou tyrant of the mind!' She envied the peacock who could sit all day in the sun and was never expected to learn anything. And here is a statistical maternal memorandum concerning her daily industry—after her breakfasts of dry bread and milk—when she was between five and six years old.

'January 7, 1828—Charlotte began Fabulous Histories (i.e. Mrs. Trimmer's *Robin, Dicky, Flapsy, and Pecksy.* I loved them, though the book is one of the former generation—pale type, long s's, *ct* joined together. I have it still). . . .

'Aug. 3.—Ch. began *Sandford & Merton.* (This means for lessons.) . . .

Dec. 19.—C. began Rollin's *Ancient History.* (It lasted me *years,* but it was excellent for me; I am very glad I read so real a book.) . . .

March 20.—It is noted that C. has done since the 1st of August 1016 lessons, 537 very well, 442 well, 37 badly. Reading, spelling, poetry, one hour every day; geography, arithmetic, grammar, twice a week; history and catechism, once.'

With four successive governesses Frances Cobbe entered into a *concordat* that when lessons were ended at noon she was free to do as she pleased, their authority being confined to the house. 'I was so uniformly happy that I was (what I suppose few children are) quite conscious of my own happiness.' She wondered indeed if other children could be as happy. 'I can recall walking along the grass walks of that beautiful garden and feeling as if everything in the world was perfect, and my life complete bliss for which I could never thank God enough.' At twelve came 'Kubla Khan', *The Curse of Kehama, The Cid,* early Scott, and astronomy as a hobby. She pinned peacock eyes on the sloping roof of the two garrets that she took possession of, and began (as we shall see) to write verse. With her fourth and last governess she read not only Rollin, but Plutarch, Gibbon and the French and English poets; and she learned harmony and thorough bass. She had now become so much of an astronomer on her own account that she searched for and detected the comet of 1835 a night before she convinced her family of this feat. 'Few events in my long life have caused me such delightful excitement.'

Early One Morning

Fanny Burney, who began her Diary when she was sixteen, has already been referred to. As a child she was short, and short-sighted; demure, shy, silent and backward. Even at eight years old she had not yet learnt to read, and her brother James—who had been to school to Eugene Aram, and afterwards twice sailed round the world with Captain Cook—would for amusement give her a book upside down 'in order to see what she would make of it'; a typically fraternal sense of humour. She was known as 'the little dunce' and as 'the Old Lady'. But she took notice quietly and acutely; in her play showed humour and inventiveness; and when overnight she had sat in Mrs. Garrick's box at Drury Lane, was quite capable next day not only of mimicking the actors, but of making up their speeches. In short, she was a child whose first flowers are far from showy, but she had a sound and flourishing tap-root. She was afterwards a voracious reader of novels good and bad, including *Rasselas* and the *Sentimental Journey*, and also Plutarch, Homer, Cicero and so forth.

Jane Welsh Carlyle, when one day—'the old horse and the old fly'—she was jogging along round and round Hyde Park with her friend Mrs. Oliphant, told the story of *her* childhood, and of how her tutor, Edward Irving, when she was six years old and he twenty, used to set her up on a table and teach her Latin. After bestowing on her friend the charming garland that she was very dark, mordant and captivating, Mrs. Oliphant plucked a primrose for herself. She claimed one gift—that of 'making people talk, at least of making some people talk'. It is a gift, if one puts the right gloss on her word 'making', that will assuredly be no less precious in the nursery at times than in the drawing-room. For it is easier to make even a misanthrope talk than a stubborn or es-tranged or oysterlike child.

It may be *impossible* on the other hand to make a child, who has neither the ear nor the voice, *sing*. 'Mr. Griffiths, a brother-officer of my father', says Charlotte Yonge, 'used to carry me on his shoulder to gather laburnum and lilacs; and another, Captain Bentham, tried to teach me to sing:

' "I've been roaming, I've been roaming,
    Where the meadow dew is sweet,
    I'm returning, I'm returning
    With its pearls upon my feet. . . ."

328

Lessons

'He signally failed, as did every one else who tried to impart any music to me.' Whereas Elizabeth Grant, at about the same age, on hearing the 'sweet and tuneful' voice of a beggar-woman singing 'Over the Mountains', caught up the air there and then, and continued to pipe it out in her own shrill treble.

Alexander Carlyle was taught to read English—accent and pronunciation—long after he had been taught to read Scots, but succeeded so well in this that at the age of six, he tells us, he read a large portion of the Bible to a score of old women who had been unable to get into church, and were sitting about outside the door. They stood him up on a tombstone, and he read them the Song of Solomon. It was in church too at this age that he saw the famous gambler, Colonel Charteris, who he had heard was a wizard. 'I never took my eyes off him during the whole service, believing that I should be a dead man the moment I did.'

Thomas Holcroft's father was a shoemaker who specialized in shoes for London chair-men. His mother, he believed, sold greens and oysters—an odd but somehow harmonious match. When he himself was about six years old his family moved into Berkshire, and here his father began to teach him to read. 'The task at first I found difficult.' Then he too discovered the secret befitting his mind:—'The idea one day suddenly seized me of catching all the sounds I had been taught from the arrangement of the letters; and my joy at this amazing discovery was so great, that the recollection of it has never been effaced.' His father was so proud of this son that to encourage him he set him to learn eleven chapters a day of the Old Testament. We have heard already how Ruskin as a child also insisted on taking his own way.

'For myself,' says William Bell Scott, 'I confess to have been very backward . . . at learning what others of the same age found easy. It was long before I could tell the hour of the day by the eight-day clock; [an] amiable uncle winding it up every Saturday night used to try to teach me in vain'. And I can recall another and a most lovable child who had failed even with 'the little hand' when she was a good deal older than Scott. At her first school she was sometimes sent to see the time by a clock upstairs. There she would pause for a moment, guess the answer, descend, and, quaking with dread, hope for the best.

Guessing indeed may at times be a godsend. When William

Early One Morning

Hutton was four years old and was standing one evening by the fire 'at the hob, eighteen inches high', in his aunt's kitchen, his supper-spoon in his *left* hand, his uncle (to teach him manners) asked him which was his right. He guessed, 'This'; and, as it chanced, guessed right. For many years afterwards, when this question had again to be decided, he would imagine himself, with his porridge-spoon, back again beside the hob and the kitchen fire. A hard-won scrap of 'learning' of this kind, in which teacher and taught share the honours, may masquerade at last as 'instinctive'. But how explain the *process* of recognition?

Bret Harte, whose father was a soldier, also described himself as a precocious child. He was reading Shakespeare at the age of six and continued with Fielding, Goldsmith and others 'through the great masters of the English language'. It is said of Madame de Warens that at the age of nine she had read every book in the house where she lived as a child at Le Basset. In this she resembled Charles Lamb's 'Bridget', who 'was tumbled early, by accident or design, into a spacious closet of good old English reading, without much selection or prohibition, and browsed at will upon that fair and wholesome pasturage. Had I twenty girls. . . .' 'Turn her loose into your library,' was Dr. Johnson's advice to Mrs. Sheridan in regard to her daughter's reading. 'If she is well inclined she will choose only nutritious food, if otherwise all your precautions will avail nothing to prevent her following the natural bent of her inclinations.'

Reference has been made already to Rousseau's midnight readings with his father—turn and turn about—of the romances that his mother had bequeathed to them. These exhausted, they turned to history, and to Ovid, Molière, Fontenelle and Plutarch. When he was about seven years old Plutarch became his favourite author. Later he announces that—thanks in much to his books and still more to his father's example, to that of 'his virtuous and pious aunts', and of other prudent people—'if ever a child received a sensible and sound education, it was myself'. Indeed he lived to preach on this text to an attentive and spellbound Europe.

Lessons

2. *'For noble youth there is no thing so meete*
   As learning is, to know the good from ill.'

N or need even chronic illness in childhood entail a desperate
handicap—given the aptitude. 'I remember', says Lord Herbert of Cherbury, 'the defluxion at my ears . . . continued in that
violence, that my friends did not think fit to teach me so much as my
alphabet, till I was seven years old, at which time my defluxion
ceased, and left me free of the disease my ancestors were subject
onto, being the epilepsy. My schoolmaster, in the house of my
said lady grandmother, then began to teach me the alphabet, and
afterwards grammar, and other books commonly read in schools,
in which I profited so much, that upon this theme —*Audaces fortuna
juvat*, I made an oration of a sheet of paper, and fifty or sixty
verses, in the space of one day.' Armed with the Greek tongue and
logic he went up to Oxford at the age of twelve and was married
at fifteen.

During a severe illness in his boyhood, owing to the rupture of a
blood vessel, when he was not allowed to speak or move, and
chess was the only alternative, Walter Scott was plunged, he says,
into 'an ocean of reading without compass or pilot', and became 'a
glutton of books'. Rather less than a century after this the novels
of this 'glutton' were forbidden a child whom I can vouch must
have been unusually sensitive in heart and conscience. But his
fascinations were irresistible. One by one she furtively borrowed
some of the *Waverleys* and, sitting on the floor beside the open
bookcase so that she could at once slip them back on to the shelf
at sound of a footstep, she read them to the end.

It is difficult to estimate the effects on mind and inward self of
any illness, and particularly of an illness in early childhood. I know
of one child who so suffered, and who is now—many years afterwards—less by some inches in height than her sister and brothers,
but she is certainly not wanting in energy and independence. To
the effects of a severe attack of scarlet fever when he was three
years old, Henry Adams on the other hand attached 'greater and
greater importance . . . the longer he lived'. Not merely because
he fell behind his brothers two or three inches in height and pro-
portionally in bone and weight, but that 'his character and processes of mind seemed to share in this fining-down'. His timidity,

331

his delicate nerves, his hesitancy in decision and in action, his dislike of responsibility and distrust in his own judgment, his æsthetic sensibility, horror of ennui, and craving for companionship and aversion from society—all this he thinks was due in part at any rate to this illness, although, after recovering from it, he grew up in excellent health.

Herbert Spencer, another delicate child, was first prompted to read of his own accord by *Sandford & Merton*, but not before he was seven. After that he strode on like a giant refreshed with wine, and at the age of twelve was devouring novels—tabooed by both his parents—in secret in bed; although 'reason rather than authority was the supreme court of appeal' in his home life.

Like Spencer and Edmund Burke, Edward Gibbon was also delicate as a child. When he was nine years old he went to a boarding-school but made little progress owing to ill-health. None the less he was very young when he learned to write and to cipher—and how vividly the mere words pot-hook and hanger (which I never associated either with pot or sooty chimney until I was thus reminded of them!) may revive in memory the phantasm of an early, ink-blotted copy-book. 'As soon', he declares, 'as the use of speech had prepared my infant reason for the admission of knowledge, I was taught the arts of reading, writing, and arithmetic. So remote is the date, so vague is the memory of their origin in myself, that, were not the error corrected by analogy, I should be tempted to conceive them as innate. In my childhood I was praised for the readiness with which I could multiply and divide, by memory alone, two sums of several figures: such praise encouraged my growing talent; and had I persevered in this line of application, I might have acquired some fame in mathematical studies. . . .'

The phrase 'by memory alone' seems to imply that he did his sums 'in his head', by means of visual images—*one* of the methods, perhaps, of all 'calculating boys'; of Zerah Colburn, for example, who at six could in twenty seconds give the correct answer to any such question as, 'How many seconds were there in the year 1811?' But Jerediah Buxton, a native of Derbyshire, was an even more extravagant oddity. Despite the fact that his father was a schoolmaster, Jerediah was taught neither to read nor to write. As a child he could manage in his head such sums as, How many barleycorns

Lessons

would reach eight miles? in a minute and a half; although his method appears to have been rather primitive. If he merely strode over a field, indeed 'a whole lordship', he could calculate its measurements accurately, even to a square 'hair-breadth', computing about forty-eight hair-breadths to the lineal inch. And when he was taken to see *The Tragedy of King Richard III* at Drury Lane, neither the splendour of the theatre nor the genius of the players nor the charms of the poetry appeared to move him one iota. He merely counted the words uttered by David Garrick in the chief part—a talent rather tedious to check. He had several children, and died in 1775 at the age of seventy.

A thick duodecimo *Paradise Lost*, with cuts, was Leigh Hunt's earliest remembered home-book, and with this *The Pilgrim's Progress, The Seven Champions of Christendom, Fairy Tales* and a *Hamlet* in one volume. It is a queer medley; but there is no reason to suppose that what was pertinent in them to him influenced his mature work any less than Thomas Hardy's home-books when he was eight years old influenced his. At this age Hardy excelled in arithmetic and geography. His mother 'gave him Dryden's *Virgil,* Johnson's *Rasselas*, and *Paul and Virginia*. He also found in a closet *A History of the Wars*—a periodical dealing with the war with Napoleon, which his grandfather had subscribed to at the time, having been himself a volunteer. The torn pages of these contemporary numbers with their melodramatic prints of serried ranks, crossed bayonets, huge knapsacks, and dead bodies, were the first to set him on the train of ideas that led to *The Trumpet Major* and *The Dynasts.*' I wonder if the Doctor's Prince of Abyssinia ever enticed a *younger* reader into his train. Sir Egerton Brydges just *may* have been such a one, since *Rasselas* appeared three years before he was born—in 1762.

'The intense delight', he tells us, 'with which I read romances and fairy tales from the earliest age, is indescribable. My mother had a trunk full of them, and I almost got them by heart; not one of them did I omit to read over many times. My grandmother . . . first taught me to read before I was four years old; but at that age I was a refractory scholar. At six I began to delight in books.'

John Stuart Mill, on the other hand, though of children's books and playthings he had 'scarcely any', delighted in Anson and Hawkesworth—*Voyages*; and *Robinson Crusoe* was pre-eminent.

Early One Morning

Soon after Man Friday came science: 'I never remember being so wrapt up in any book, as I was in Joyce's Scientific Dialogues'. 'I was not born in Arcadia,' says Mr. Henry Nevinson of his childhood. 'We lived in proud and quiet seclusion. . . . No doubt the town and country were dull, and so were we. There was a theatre, but we never went to it, well knowing it to stand upon the road to hell. There were dances in winter, but we never learnt to dance, for the devil lurked even in quadrilles. . . . Our secular reading was almost limited to ancient volumes of the *Penny Magazine*, and the current number of the *Sunday at Home*. . . . The "Arabian Nights" were banned. . . . Fairy stories were banned because they were untrue.'

When, as a boy, he bought a Shakespeare in one volume, his mother was so horrified that he hid it away. ' "It is a great immoral book," she said to me, in one of her rare outbursts of feeling; "I know some people put it next the Bible, but that is mere wickedness." ' His father on the other hand, who had a great tenderness for children and was a man of many sympathies and enthusiasms, angrily forbade him to buy a Latin copy of the *Imitatio Christi*. 'The book was Papish'.

In lieu of this forbidden reading there was an edifying volume containing twelve (Protestant) death-bed scenes, and entitled *The Family Sepulchre*. And there was the Bible—it was his daily diet, his daily lesson.

Later, says Mr. Nevinson, a curate came into his life. He thrashed Latin grammar into him, opened his eyes to the beauty of Virgil, and lent him a huge volume, containing the complete novels of Walter Scott—'a ponderous nugget of gold'. 'I thank him both for his sense of beauty [in literature] and for his violence. In comparison with him, no human being has ever seemed to me terrific.'

Notwithstanding these restrictions, 'my childhood', says Mr. Nevinson, 'was far from dull, far from unhappy.' He had a passion for 'what is called Nature'—for 'any gleam of wildness. . . . From the earliest years I was possessed by a passionate longing, not so much for solitude as for the wilderness. . . . My mother used to say, "I know you'll be a hermit and live among the rocks." '

How tenacious is the self within of childhood's habits—and appetites! My own prescribed Sunday reading as a child was *The Day of Rest*—interlarded now and then in private with a *Bow Bells*

Lessons

Novelette. It contained a serial story, accepted by its editor possibly by virtue solely of its title—*God and the Man.* This was a melodramatic romance of love, icebergs, jealousy and shipwreck, and as if it were yesterday, I can recall its noble hero and hapless villain (a violent hunchback armed with an axe), and at least one of its rugged pictures. A romance entitled *The Schoolboy Baronet* touched me to the quick! And what of Solomon Eagle and old St. Paul's?—the molten lava continues to creep, the flames to roar, the trapped and raving human rats live on. Yet Paley's 'Evidences' were handy!

Like Mr. Nevinson, I was taught to revere the Bible, apart even from its contents, I mean, which I at least *heard* read, whether listening or not—at least five times over. I still, rather furtively, I fear, kiss its covers if it has the mischance to fall on the floor, and I feel uneasy at the sight of any book resting on top of it. I shared too his devotion to Newman's line, 'O'er moor and fen, o'er crag and torrent'; but while he, as his *Changes & Chances* relates, must have defied a greater number of such perils than any other Englishman now living, all but *my* only 'fen', alas, has been an inkpot.

'One of the gravest rebukes', says Coventry Patmore, 'which I can remember to have received from my father was for my disrespect, when I was about twelve years old, in taking from the bookshelves a thick old Bible in order to enable me to sit more conveniently at my dinner. . . .'

Ruskin's tribute is characteristic. He knew his Bible through and through. There were whole chapters which his mother in his infancy compelled him to learn by heart. 'And having always a way of thinking with myself what words meant, it was not possible for me, even in the foolishest times of youth, to write entirely superficial or formal English'.

To William Bell Scott as a child the book was, he tells us, 'an inexhaustible treasure, inspiring equally awe and delight'—particularly the Song of Songs and the Revelation. The mystery indeed of the Revelation, he confesses, 'gave its portentous scenery an absolutely dangerous power over' his young mind. He adds a tribute to the Shorter Catechism. A Scotchman, he says, who learns this well in his childhood 'will know that religion has nothing to do with physics; that nature is a fatalist and an atheist;

Early One Morning

that religion has only an existence in the soul, in the conscious kernel of us; and that morality even has little to do with it, except as an act of obedience allied to self-preservation'. So much meaning is seldom confined within so few words.

After what Elizabeth Grant describes as 'a season of all blank'—a common but curious phenomenon—which succeeded her third year, her eyes open again at the age of five on a gloomy house in London. There she was taught to sew by her mother's maid, and she shaped and cut out and stitched up her dolls' clothes from very early days. Though she could recall neither when she was taught to read, nor the aunts who taught her (and she could not only read 'well' at the age of three but could count 'miraculously'), she remembers her books—'gaudy paper backs, red, and green, and all manner of colours, with dashes of gold dabbled on'—midget books, their contents enchanting: 'Puss in Boots', 'Cinderella' and the like. In a pygmy history of Rome one print so shocked her—Tullia in her car riding over the body of her father—that she would never 'open that classic page again'. Apart from this, 'I have no recollection', she says, 'of learning anything from anybody', except when she was shown by her mother the spot where brave King Harold fell. None the less she 'was a little wonder'. Once—a few years afterwards—when she was sitting up with her mother to help her *toilette* on some grand occasion—a rout at the Duchess of Gordon's—she chanced on the letters of Lady Hertford and Lady Pomfret, and sat on in the candlelight, reading them with avidity, absorbed*. In this solitude she was discovered by her father. Having scolded her well for wasting the candles, he took the hint and presented her with a volume of Lady Mary Wortley Montagu's letters. 'I somehow', she says, 'mix up the transactions of these three years'—eight to ten. And no wonder—in an existence as crammed with events as a soap-bubble is with reflections.

When Philip Hamerton's father saw him as a child in his ninth year flitting from one book to another he would say, 'Take one of those books and read it steadily, don't potter and play with half-a-dozen'.

3. *'I love contemplating.'*

William Morris, too, could not remember learning to read, but could fondly recall a little book with cuts on yellow paper entitled *Ladder to Learning*. By the time he was nine he had exhausted the Waverley Novels, and Marryat's *Peter Simple, Mr. Midshipman Easy* and the rest. He was taught to write at ten, and wrote well in two months. His spelling, however, lagged a little, for he could remember being stood on a chair with his shoes off, because he had made so many mistakes. He was no nibbler of books; he devoured them even when he was a child—because he was that kind of child.

And not books only. When he was 'left till called for' at his father's office near Abchurch Lane, he would stand at the window and watch the tea-dealers opposite. As Ruskin watched the man with the water-cart; as John Aubrey, in his 'eremiticall solitude' at Eston, used with the greatest delight to haunt the company of 'the Artificers that came there, *e.g.* joyners, carpenters, cowpers, masons', and so learned to understand their trades; as Charles I— who according to his nurse, an old Scottish lady, was 'of a very evil nature in his infancy . . . beyond measure wilful and unthankful', used to 'discourse freely' with any artist or good mechanic, traveller, or scholar who came his way—and in consequence 'often gave light to them in their own art or knowledge'. Benjamin Franklin's father, too, who when his son was twelve thought of making him a cutler, would take him to 'walk with him, and see joiners, bricklayers, turners, braziers, etc., at their work'. 'It has ever since been a pleasure to me to see good workmen handle their tools.' Thus Benjamin himself became a ready job-man in the house and learnt to construct 'little machines' for his experiments. Roger North, too, 'got acquainted with artificers, and learnt to turn'.

It is indeed these steady infantine *watchings* indoors and out (eyes intent, motionless bodies, devouring minds; even the watcher's hands hanging beside him, forgotten) of objects animate and otherwise, including cooks, gardeners, knife-grinders, lamplighters, butchers, bakers, plumbers, house-painters, glaziers, paviours, dustmen and sweeps—it is these that etch in life's superbly vivid commentary to a child's first books. When a water-cart is not available, even a tutor may serve; as is shown by John Ruskin's letter to his friend Mrs. Monro when he was aged ten:

'Well, papa seeing how fond I was of the Doctor, and knowing him to be an excellent Latin scholar, got him for me as a tutor; and every lesson I get I like him better and better, for he makes me

Early One Morning

laugh "almost, if not quite," to use one of his own expressions, the whole time. He is so funny, comparing Neptune's lifting up the wrecked ships of Æneas with his trident to my lifting up a potato with a fork, or taking a piece of bread out of a bowl of milk with a spoon! And as he is always saying [things] of that kind, or relating some droll anecdote, or explaining the part of Virgil (the book which I am in) very nicely, I am always delighted when Mondays, Wednesdays and Fridays are come.'

Could any tribute to a Latin scholar be more indulgent, or any comment on his methods more illuminating than this 'always delighted'? Who had taught John Ruskin at so early an age to become so entirely himself is another question altogether!

CHAPTER XXVII

SCHOOL

★

1. *'The Master's word Enrapturèd the young man heard.'*

But the mention of a tutor introduces a matter less laughable than potatoes, namely, schools and schooling. About fifty years ago I was standing with a lifelong friend and more than friend, who was then in 16th century attire—bands, skirts, buckled girdle and yellow stockings. We were engrossed in the proceedings of a middle-aged, ginger-haired hodman or bricklayer who was cooking his morning rasher of bacon, enwrapped in grease paper, in a heap of quicklime. 'Pre-eminence in cookery', said the most learned of chefs, 'is never to be obtained under the age of thirty.' *Our* expert, who looked at least ten years older than that, glanced up at last and—I can see his clear lightlashed eyes—quizzed round at us. 'Well, old cock!' was his genial enquiry, 'and what might they *larn* you at that school?'

I fancy no reply to his question was expected. Was there a tinge of irony in its tone? Besides, it was an intrusion; we were intent on the bacon, we were 'watching', and were filled with that mute admiration which to this day never fails to reduce me to silence—the admiration of a man who can do *things*. Nevertheless that word 'larn', and possibly also in Mr. Punch's sense of it, has continued to resound in memory. What do 'they', did they, should they, and in the future will they learn the younglings of the human species?

For sooner or later dawns the day when, satchel on back and with shining morning face, every English child creeps for the first time to school. The aspiration which King Alfred conjured his bishops to follow, 'that all the youth of England may be grounded

339

Early One Morning

in letters', is now actualized, and by compulsion. Nor do we stay at his 'more especially those who are of a gentle kind'. ' "When I took the kingdom, very few on this side of the Humber, and not one that I could recollect south of the Thames, could understand their prayers in English or could translate a letter from Latin into English".' In spite of our advantages, there is even nowadays a double-edged barb in these words. Still, to the gentle or otherwise, to the bright and the dull, to the quick and the stagnant, a 'grounding' is given, for whatever fair edifice may be reared upon it.

The process, largely by way of books, has been described as a preparation for *life*. In its effects it is also in the nature of a life-sentence, since in later years it may prove exceedingly difficult to escape from them, whether they are good or bad. For the vast majority of the youth of England it occupies not less than nine or ten years. For those who are bound for college or university the ten may expand into sixteen or seventeen years, a period that is rather more than a third of the total number of years which, on coming of age, one can nowadays expect to spend in this world.

The rich man has a wide choice of schools for his children, and if for any reason he disapprove of a school education or of a particular school that fails to please him, he is at liberty to find an alternative. Only with the utmost difficulty can a poor man exercise this privilege.

In former times the term of probation was far less prolonged. Henry Peacham, the author of *The Compleat Gentleman* of 1622, after describing the barbarities of the ignorant and incompetent schoolmasters of his day, and no less severely the mean-spirited ignorance of 'some of its domestic tutors', blames parents for sending to Oxford or Cambridge 'young things of twelve, thirteen or fourteen, that have . . . no further thought of study than to trim up their studies with pictures, and to place the fairest books in open view, which, poor lads, they scarce ever open, or understand not'.

Yet in spite of the time that is spent on education, what it is best to teach, and by what method, are still hotly debated questions, and are likely to remain so, since human beings, at any age, in their teachableness, in their desire to learn, and in the means whereby they can learn best, widely differ. The accepted ideal is a similar—it cannot be an equal—opportunity for all children, in the hope that

School

this will eventually entail the greatest happiness and utility of the greatest number.

But whether a child sets out from home on this first and fateful morning like a snail or like an eager cherub, it means for him, as melancholy Jaques declared, the taking up of a new part on the stage of the world; and the novice himself usually suffers a change at least no less perceptible than any which he is likely to exhibit afterwards. If, as with many children nowadays, he is then of so tender an age as to be penned among the Infants, he will almost at once become a slightly different kind of infant. If he is five, six or seven years old, and still to all appearance no more than a little tiny boy, the change will be more explicit. He will be transformed into a schoolboy. If his destination is a boarding-school, the stamp may rapidly make a deeper impression. There may be a perceptible change in mien, in talk, in attitude and manners.

'We find', says Mr. Kurt Hahn, 'the boy and girl of six hardly ever bored by empty hours. We find them forever dreaming, planning, building, discovering, asking, singing, and making-believe. Then suddenly all that stops together. The child home for the holidays does not know what to do with himself. Why?'

There may be many reasons for so striking a change. Mr. Hahn considers that it is due to organized games having begun too early. It will vary of course with individuals. But the more childlike the child, and that is equivalent to saying the more manlike the man, the sharper may be the immediate contrast. The spirit of childhood has been challenged. And that spirit, in those in whom its flame burns brightest, is a clear and essential spirit, and may be little dependent either on the age or the usage of the lamp. Nurture and culture trim the wick. It may accept the challenge and burn the brighter; it may falter and languish, perhaps go out.

To one child school may prove a happy hunting-ground, fresh woods and pastures new, to another a prison-house. The social and sociable child delights in companionship, the ambitious exults in rivalry, the natural solitary pines. A child goes whither he is sent; there is little grading of schools according to the temperament or constitution of their inmates, or to their gifts and aptitudes. The wolf lies down with the lamb, and the wolf is the better pleased. Whether it is desirable to be happy or unhappy in our early years, to be free or captive, to be diffident or self-confident, whether a

341

Early One Morning

prolonged period of purgatory then will ensure a paradisal reward later, whether forced labour and compulsory play are 'good' for a child; all these are easy questions to ask and less easy to answer. But are they in respect to schools and a national system of education practical ones? 'Better build schoolrooms for "the boy",' cried Eliza Cook, 'Than cells and gibbets for "the man".' 'The Schoolmaster is abroad!' announced Lord Brougham in the House of Commons on January 29, 1828. 'And I trust to him, armed with his primer, against the soldier, in full military array.' Assuredly; and yet this problem of 'education' still towers into the heavens over the vast amphitheatre like a prodigious thundercloud.

The aim, crudely, of schooling is that a child shall learn that he is merely one among many and thus shall find his own level, shall submit to a certain discipline of body and brains, and be taught for the most part such knowledge as his contemporaries shall share. It is safer, more convenient, and comfortable, to know what one's own kind knows; though for incentive and delight what can excel the by-ways of knowledge that are usually trodden alone?

There are many views and voices on this problem, past as well as present. 'Public schools', said Fielding, 'are the nurseries of all vice and immorality'; and Pope, 'Some are bewildered in the maze of schools, And some made coxcombs nature meant but fools'; and Swift, 'Oh, how our neighbour lifts his nose, To tell what every schoolboy knows.'

One thing certain is that a broth, whatever its ingredients may be, which is intended to nourish millions of young creatures should be good and serviceable for its purpose, if only for the sake of the cooks whose arduous obligation it is to concoct, decoct and serve it up. Memory, mind, manners, morals, imagination, together with the body whereby they manifest themselves—all in varying degree are made subject to this *must*; and the only aspiration worthy of them is to persuade them to 'work' as effectively, but much more flexibly, variously and humanly than can a mere machine. Stuffing may be good for a goose, but not for a live goose; and there is a method conceivable by man alone of preparing *foie gras*. To persuade a human being to continue teaching himself, and aid him to that end is a benefit beyond all price; and, apart from nature and intention, it may be the outcome of a moment's insight, of a moment's profound *rapport* between teacher and

342

School

scholar. Happy both, who achieve it! Could we not most of us name the friend or master, or friend *and* master, who kindled in our young minds, let us say, an inkling into geometry, or pushed the window a little wider open that looks out upon the world of poetry?

2. 'O Father! I am young and very happy.'

The notion however that 'education', whether good, bad or indifferent—a word which did not acquire its current meaning until the disastrous year 1616—begins at school is preposterous. It would be as absurd to say that de-ducation begins there. A multitude of early memories recorded in these pages flatly refutes it. A child has been actively, eagerly, perpetually learning from its swaddling onwards; urged on by the mere momentum of being alive. And when a boy's best friend *is* his mother, that mother is also as patient and eager a teacher as he will ever get.

A candid and circumspect schoolmaster could state with ease what any particular pupil on bidding him farewell has been offered in the way of knowledge. But how much of this knowledge, apart from the learnt-by-rote, his young friend has positively mastered and made his own would need deeper reflection and less paper. He may have won many blessings; but was his progress in proportion to the promise of his past? In the nature of things, *could* it be?

To attempt on the other hand to set down what an as-yet-unschooled and intelligent child of seven in propitious circumstances has, first, been offered, and, secondly, made his own, would strain, and might finally baffle the efforts of a committee consisting even of such experts as Drs. Busby, Boyer, Wooll, Udall and Keate, with Miss Beale as secretary and William of Wykeham in the chair. Apart from close study in the vast, various and termless book of life, he may be perfectly *capable*, as we have seen, of bringing a spoken Latin and French and a little Greek with him to school, but in any case he will bring English. The subsoil of any grounding in letters is the ability to understand and to use words and languages. And could it not be said at a venture that few of the children already mentioned would at the age of seven have faltered at more than a few words in *The Ancient Mariner*, or at a great many even in the Authorized Version of the Bible?

343

Early One Morning

They may themselves have their own private and triumphant methods with the difficult. A child, less than seven years old, was recently asked how he managed with the outlandish names of the Greek heroes in the book he was eagerly reading. Oh, he said, I call them all Jack. And as Jacks, one and all, he distinguished them. Southey 'went through' Beaumont & Fletcher before he was eight. 'Circumstances enable me to recollect the time . . . accurately. . . . What harm, indeed, could they do me at that age? I read them merely for the interest which the stories afforded, and understood the worse parts as little as I did the better'. If 'went through' is to be taken literally, this child of seven read fifty-two plays and there is nothing to suggest that it was their long words that were insurmountable.

This return to Southey, who will reappear presently, is only to exemplify the enterprise and assiduity of which a child at this age is capable; allured on as he was through reams of sweet but often dull verse chiefly for the sake of their story. There is an irresistible pining of the mind, whether in love-work or task-work, for the experience, sensuous, imaginative and intellectual, which reading gives—that wellspring of knowledge. It is the thirst for this wellspring when its waters are made compulsory that is in danger of failing. For it can hardly be denied that schoolboys in general *tend* to become passive resisters to the very goddess they have been sent to school to serve—Learning. This depends, of course, on many factors. With some the experience resembles the effects of an overdose of morphia: 'a stage of excitement precedes the stage of irresistible sleepiness, which passes into a third stage of profound narcosis'. In others it sets burning a torch which only death can extinguish.

In any case, exile into a foreign country, of which one knows neither the people, the patois, the customs nor the laws, is a mild ordeal, whether pleasant or otherwise, compared with a child's initiation into a boarding-school of some hundreds of strange boys, or even of fifty. And the boy of rare gifts, which cannot but be accompanied by an unusual nature, will need the most fortitude. Genius, it has been said, has the secret of an enduring childhood. And that is as remote from mere childishness as womanhood is from girlishness. Many of our present difficulties and dangers seem to be due, in part at least, not to the fact that too many adults have refrained from leaving their childhood behind them, with its natural energy, enterprise, intuition and seriousness, but are overgrown schoolboys, chiefly mere working models of themselves, with habits, appetites, traditions and fixed ideas for internal clockwork. Autobiography has already shown that a child is seldom that, at any rate of its own choice. Every plant has its own virtue and habit, yet we cannot accuse it of being stereotyped.

We few of us seek new disciplines—man-made and man-managed—in later life, though they may be thrust on us. Urged on by self or by circumstances, we may work our fingers to the bone; but even if the pleasantest of our national gaols should invite us in, few of us would hasten to profit by a mere six-months' hard labour. Should we welcome a year or two's schooling? When Mr. Bultitude (a never tedious friend, whatever we might think of him as an acquaintance), was compelled to face blackboard and playground again, he thoroughly misenjoyed himself. Many human beings were, or at any rate believed that they were, blissfully happy at school. And yet if in gentle sleep to-night all we adults now over forty years of age should find ourselves small boys back at school again, how many of us to-morrow morning would describe our experiences as a delicious dream, and how many, as a nightmare?

Four very various and mutually enlightening aspects of school life present themselves in what follows. 'My sensitiveness from childhood', says Egerton Brydges, 'was the source of the most morbid sufferings, as well as of the most intense pleasures. It unfitted me for concourse with other boys, and took away all self-possession in society.' Extreme opinions of him were the consequence of this; 'some thinking well of my faculties, others deeming me little above an idiot. In my first schoolboy years I never enjoyed a moment of ease or cheerfulness. But I was perfect in my lessons'.

Next, is an advertisement quoted in *News of the Past*, from the *Times* of February 16, 1864:—

'Boarding Schools Wanted, in London, for a boy, nine years, and two girls, six and seven years old, requiring firm discipline, having become wild and unruly, through neglect occasioned by family misfortunes. No holyday could be given, as holydays destroy any good effected at school. The father, quite a gentleman,

Early One Morning

can only pay 20 guineas each. This advertisement is only intended for schools of pre-eminent efficiency for such cases, and prosperous enough to be able and willing to accept such terms, and undertake the needed task of reformation for the sake of the school's own additional credit of success.' And next:—

' "I prithee tell me, for God's sake," said Anselm centuries ago to a pious abbot who was also a martinet, "wherfor ye are so set against them. Are they not human [he was referring to children], sharing in the same nature as yourselves? Would ye wish to be so handled as ye handle them?" ' He then ventured on a parable— and he had been a schoolmaster himself—concerning a goldsmith and the cunning and delicate fashion in which he shapes his gold; gently, discreetly, caressingly, and not by blows alone.

And last, this little episode:—The dominant topic of Henry Adams's autobiography is Education. One fine morning, he tells us, when he was a child six years old he refused to go to school. All efforts of his mother to persuade or to compel him to do so were in vain. His battle all but won—they were standing at the foot of the staircase, and the President, his grandfather, must not be disturbed—the door above them of the President's library gently opened, and the old man slowly emerged. It was a hot summer's morning, the school was a mile distant, the road to it was un-shaded. Hand in hand with his grandfather, who was close on eighty, Henry traversed the mile, yearning and burning for an opportunity to escape. But in vain. He was vanquished. What, however, most impressed and astonished him afterwards was not his defeat; but first, that the incident had had not the slightest effect on his affection for his grandfather; and next, that this tyrant had shown neither temper, irritation, personal feeling nor any display of force. 'Above all, he had held his tongue.' He loved the old gentleman no less, and now to love for him had been added respect.

Nevertheless, whatever may be the necessity and advantages of a school discipline, 'a boy's will', says Henry Adams, 'is his life, and he dies when it is broken, as the colt dies in harness, taking a new nature in becoming tame'.

No doubt the fortunate, the hardy and the docile neophyte may flourish at school, the less fortunate fails to flourish, or postpones this happy state awhile. But even the veriest molly learns early the

346

School

unwritten law that his feelings are best kept to himself, and the axiom, *Never tell!* The famous Dr. Boyer condensed both into a single·sentence when, on the first day after the holidays, he encountered Coleridge, crying in the cloisters in Newgate Street. 'Boy!' he said, 'the school is your father! Boy! the school is your mother! Boy! the school is your brother! the school is your sister! the school is your first cousin, and your second cousin, and all the rest of your relations! Let's have no more crying!' How far as a humorist he meant this waggish counsel, how far Coleridge who, with Lamb, was to be the most radiant of the fixed stars in the annals of that school, was consoled or strengthened by this condensation of kinship is another matter.

But there is a star in the heavens of literature more radiant even than these. What welcome had that when it rose above the horizon?

3. *'I have heard that Mr. Shakespeare was a natural wit, without any art at all':* '*Was there ever such stuff as a great part of Skakespeare. . . . What? What?'*

If William Shakespeare ever attended the grammar school at Stratford on Avon, he went as a day-boy, home was at hand, and there was no need to discard his relatives in Boyer's summary fashion. This is the accepted assumption. But, as Mr. Dover Wilson says, 'there is not a tittle of evidence to prove he went there, and an ardent Catholic might well seek other means for the education of his son than instruction at the hands of a Protestant schoolmaster who was also a clergyman'. His plays and poems are his autobiography, but one of the imagination, not of his daily life. We can infer, deduce, divine, but concerning that actual sovereign childhood there are very few facts. And being so few, they are well worth recalling.

His father was an active and ambitious man, and, in 1564, still a prosperous wool-merchant. His mother was the daughter of a well-to-do farmer, 'himself probably connected with . . . gentle folk of the county of Warwickshire'. Since, when her signature was needed, she made her mark, though she may have taught her children to read, and much else, she cannot have taught them to write. There is no reason to doubt that the Shakespeares must have

347

Early One Morning

known well the chief worthies of Stratford, then a busy market town, though only of some two thousand inhabitants. For immediate neighbours they had John Whelar, a yeoman; George Badger, a draper; Adrian Quyny, a mercer and afterwards the grandfather-in-law of the poet's daughter, Judith; and William Smith, a haberdasher and 'probably' his godfather. Inns and hostelries abounded: the *Swan*, the *Bear*, the *Angel*, the *Peacock*. Into this rural scene came William Shakespeare as a child.

'A child in Adam's field I dreamed away
My one eternity and hourless day,
Ere from my wrist Time's bird had learned to fly,
Or I had robbed the tree of which I die. . . .'

The eldest *son* of a family of ten children, five of whom died in infancy, he was baptized by the Vicar of Stratford, John Bretchgirdle, on April 26, 1564. It was the year of a grievous visitation of the plague in his birthplace. The next thing, after a break of eighteen years, we hear about him is his marriage, in 1582. And about the time of his twenty-ninth birthday there was published by a Stratford friend of his, of his own age, Richard Field, a poem that he himself describes as 'the first heir of my invention' *Venus and Adonis*. What does it suggest concerning his past?

It is a poem radiant with light, in which every visible object is lovely and 'good' according to its kind, and as virginal to the senses as if the creation of Man had but just taken place, not in Eden, but in the Gardens of the Hesperides, and *their* divinities were his seraphim. The poem, bewitching like the wanton mermaids's songs, is utterly devoid of mysticism. To think of it in relation to Wordsworth is to change worlds. Herrick's by comparison is an exquisite puppet-show—and not one of Herrick's puppets is naked. Shelley has rarefied the poem's very element. Keats strays within its borders. But Shakespeare *himself* remains all but outside them—though the light and music are his, and every flower and living creature is the offspring of his commerce with the world of nature, England's. The poem does for sensuous youth —a youth scarcely conceivable nowadays in precisely these terms —what Blake does for childhood, imagining its innocence. It irradiates the spirit of youth with a kind of immortal guilelessness. For Adonis is its chief marvel. He, too, one might, Methuselah-

348

HENRY JAMES, AGED ELEVEN, WITH HIS FATHER
From a daguerreotype taken in 1854

School

wise, almost say, is a little boy in peril of being lost, and he is as remote from Iachimo as a bowl of love apples is from the craters of the moon. We can at least assume then that the child this poet once was had at least *this* poet's senses. Can we imagine that child's personal appearance?

Of Mozart at the age of six, the cocked hat under his left arm suggesting a bottle of ethereal champagne, there is an animating portrait at Salzburg—wide, welcoming face, dark eyes, apple cheeks, powdered hair, gold-braided flowered 'lily-white' coat, waistcoat and knee-breeches. For background he has the folds of a green curtain, a tassel dangling from it suggesting distant bells; and he is posing by a clavichord or a spinet. And this *is* Mozart. A glance, again, at the photograph of Henry James and his father (the hand of the small boy, with the vigilant yet contemplative gaze, resting gently on the massive paternal shoulder) bids us penetrate both into the past of the one and into the future of the other. Nevertheless this *is* Henry James.

But how extract the looks of a lively child from the moon-faced Droeshout painting, or from the brisk yet stolid Stratford bust, the quill pen in which appears to be engaged in automatic writing? All that they both assure us of, and the Chandos portrait suggests a far 'prettier' infancy, is a high-crowned head, a straight nose, and a full, well-cut mouth. In *Shakespeare the Boy*, by Dr. William Rolfe, a cut of this child has been put; but it is a creation rather of the fancy, than of the imagination. On the other hand, was it within the power even of a Holbein or a Rembrandt or a Velasquez to portray in one human countenance the author, or authors, rather, of *Twelfth Night*, *The Tempest* and *Macbeth*— and at the age of seven? It has been said of Charles Waterton that his 'saint-like and love-inspiring smile will be preserved only in the mind of those that knew him'. Such precious things as these indeed *can* only be so preserved.

Stratford on Avon, beside its placid river, in the 'heart of England', lies amid some of her pleasantest scenery. When Shakespeare was a child—its streets assailing both nose and hose—it consisted of some five hundred houses. Its population (that of London did not much exceed 150,000) was strictly regulated, as ours continues to be, by statutes and by-laws; relating to the muzzling of dogs, drinking hours, bowling, brewing, dressing, the enter-

349

tainment of strangers and so forth. That they spoke good racy Warwickshire is suggested by the numerous dialect words in the plays; words, as Mrs. Wright points out, that Francis Bacon can never have prattled in when *he* was a child. Kenilworth, Warwick, Coventry—then the third largest city in England, which Shakespeare and his company visited eight times, Oxford itself faring no better—were all within reach of a small boy.

There might come a pageant to marvel at, and travelling shows to watch. Fairs, every child's El Dorado, were in full swing at Stratford itself for twenty-seven days in the year. There were feast days and festivals, there was May Day and morris-dancing, Midsummer Day, Christmas, and the complete diurnal country round from seed time to harvest—its dark and tedious winter, its utterly enravishing spring; besides all manner of sports, from hunting and hawking to bear-baiting and cock-fighting. All this was well within the range of a child, and this particular child cannot but have been no less continually eager of eye than he was active and questing in mind. There can be no two opinions on his mental digestion.

As for children's games, indoors and out, they are as old as the Ark and as immutable as the laws of the Medes and Persians. Recollections of them at need seem to have been within instant call of that compacted memory, as was all but every flower that blows in England, and every bird that sings. Nor are cards, shovelboard, dice, backgammon and chess latterday inventions.

Apart from the discomfort and bareness of the houses in Stratford in those days, what perhaps, after a pause, would most sharply impress a visitant from our own would be the absence of books and of 'reading matter'. Beyond all fancy are an Elizabethan's reactions to what we now light our fires with. Of 'divers pleasant' books, *The Book of Riddles* and the *Hundred Merry Tales* were household words. Painter's *Palace of Pleasure,* the *Gesta Romanorum* and the *Chronicle* may early have come Shakespeare's way, not to mention one of Leonard Digges's calendars such as Bully Bottom called for to look up moonshine.

What stories were *told*, on the other hand, can have been no less simple and racy than any that Burton or Burns listened to in their childhood. And here it is not difficult to trace Shakespeare's footprints in other men's snow. For manners and morals there

School

were *The Schoole of Virtue* and *The Booke of Nurture*—primers of conduct that might well be modernized (a little) and reprinted.

In his *Grammar Schoole* of 1612 John Brinsley states that the time of entrance for children into the country schools of his day was 'commonly about seven or eight years old; six is very soon. If any begin so early they are rather sent to the school to keep them from troubling the house at home, and from danger, and shrewd turns, than for any great hope and desire their friends have that they should learn anything in effect'—a comment not yet pointless. Like Richard Mulcaster (in his *Elementarie* of 1582) Brinsley was an eager advocate for the teaching of English.

At the Stratford grammar school a new boy was not admitted until he could read, but in his ten-hours' schoolday, exclusive of 'intermissions', he learnt no English except by way of Latin—the only language, it used to be affirmed, 'understanded of devils'. In his later life Shakespeare 'understood Latin pretty well', French as much, Greek a little. He 'could read and brood', it is said, 'over his beloved Ovid in the original'.

What, or what else, any mortal schoolmaster taught him is all but pure guesswork. What by motherwit, and watching, by thinking, dreaming and imagining, he learnt at large concerning his own mind, heart and nature, his world, man and the universe, his Plays disclose. It was with feathers such as these this upstart little crow beautified himself. Since, as John Keats said out of the abundance of his heart, 'he could do easily man's utmost', is it not also likely that as a child he could do easily child's utmost? And his superbly original, supple, delicate, vigorous and enchanting English, which he owed solely to the energy of his mind and the subtlety of his senses—since his words are all but always the very spit and match of his objects—was not the least of his masteries. It is, above all, one that must have begun very early. To think of him as an accident in man's history is tantamount to asserting that the universe is irrational. His brothers Gilbert, Richard and Edmund shared his surroundings at Stratford, but that is no reason why they should have shared his genius. When he was seven his sister Anne, who died when she was eight, was born; Gilbert was then five. They must all three have been constantly at play together. Gilbert is said to have seen his brother act in *As You Like It*. He would then have been in his early thirties. Alas, poor soul, his memory was failing when in old age he told of it. All that he could recall, or could manage to convey, was that William in the part of Adam ('venerable burden'), had worn a long beard— presumably over his own.

4. 'But to go to school in a Summer morn—Oh, it drives all joy away!'

WHEN they meet with a 'hard-witted scholar', said Roger Ascham, of certain schoolmasters, 'they rather break him than bend him, rather mar than mend him'. But Shakespeare can never have been hard-witted, and there is nothing to suggest that Simon Hunt, the master at Stratford from 1571 to 1577, was a tyrant of this vintage. On the other hand, it is by no means the least amiable of schoolmasters whom schoolboys may most delight in mocking and baiting, and if he ever had the opportunity of seeing *Love's Labour's Lost* or *The Merry Wives*, he might easily have been much amused. There is no venom in either skit. He might none the less have breathed a sigh that their author should have confined his waggeries to the rudiments of his school Accidence and to Lily's grammar.[1]

Shakespeare's own 'views'—to use a word flagrantly out of keeping with his company and his practice—on what he himself was taught between the ages of eight and thirteen can only be distilled from the plays. And though common courtesy forbids that a dramatist should be saddled with the sentiments of his characters, inferences are admissible: such as, for example, that he can never have had any violent bias against daffodils, or sweethearts,

---

[1] In *The Two Noble Kinsmen*—the authorship of which has been an apple of discord between critics and poets alike—appears a schoolmaster followed by some of his pupils, 'boyes' and 'wenches'; and this is the beginning of his first speech: 'Fy, fy, what tediosity, & disensanity is here among ye? have my Rudiments bin labourd so long with ye? milkd unto ye, and by a figure even the very plumbroth & marrow of my understanding laid upon ye? and do you still cry: where, and how, & wherfore? you most course freeze capacities, ye jane Judgements, have I saide: thus let be, and there let be, and then let be, and no man understand mee? *Proh deum, medius fidius,* ye are all dunces! . . .' Whose memories was he invoking, Shakespeare's or Fletcher's—who went up to Oxford in 1597, when he was twelve years old?

School

or moonshine, or melodrama. Even then though we might be tempted to assume that a child so unusual can hardly have failed to learn everything of real value that he was taught, it would be but squinting to deny that all but every reference to schools and school-boys in the Plays falls short of enthusiasm. 'I am no breeching scholar in the schools', says Bianca, eager for her lesson in Ovid, less eager for that in the gamut. 'I'll not be tied to hours nor 'pointed times, But learn my lessons as I please myself'. That perhaps is only a touch of the Old Eve, and from hearsay; but hardly, 'His bed shall seem a school'; 'As willingly as ere I came from school'; 'toward school with heavy looks'; 'to sigh like a school-boy that has lost his ABC'; 'school-boys' tears'; 'like a school broke up Each hurries towards his home'. These suggest an amiable amusement, but they hardly flatter. Must we discount such indirect evidence because Shakespeare was a poet?

Englands Parnassus, that appeared in his heyday in 1600, contains *no* excerpts on the theme either of schools or of schoolmasters. There are eight on Knowledge, six on Learning, five on Languages, inclusive of four references to the Tower of Babel, and one on Arithmetic. There are over forty on Nature, Flowers, Trees and Birds; fifteen on Pleasure; and about thirty on Love. But then, while there are eighteen on Youth, there are only five on Children*.

As for our own day, while the 1924 edition of Mr. Gurney Benham's *Book of Quotations* contains upwards of 150 extracts from the literatures of the world on the subject of Children and Childhood, there are—though quotations apt for Speech Days must be often in demand—only 36 on Schools, Schoolboys and Schoolmasters. Three of these may be said to be polite to their theme, four or five are neutral, and the rest adverse. These figures mean little perhaps, but they do vaguely hint at a certain bias—not only in those who had been grounded in letters, but were themselves men of letters.

If Shakespeare attended the grammar school at Stratford, he left it when he was thirteen. And a glance at other boys who afterwards 'made good' when they were of the same age, may not be amiss.

Early One Morning

**5. *'Twelve yere were they subjecte to kynge Kedorlaomar,
and in the xiii yere rebelled.'***

R embrandt who was the son of a miller and a baker's daughter
and was born ten years before the poet died was at thirteen
already working in the studio of a painter, Van Swanenburch.

Isaac Newton (the posthumous son of a farmer, and so minute
an infant at birth that a quart pot could have contained him) was
in 1655—when he too was thirteen—at the Grantham Grammar
School, and so inattentive at his studies that he then 'stood very
low'. But soon, with the aid of little saws, hammers, hatchets and
other tools during his play-hours he was busy contriving mechanical models—a windmill, a water-clock, a carriage. In later
life meek, sedate and humble, and so intent on his world within
that he sometimes forgot the meal prepared for him, he too, as a
boy, was a watcher; a 'sober, silent and thinking lad', neglectful of
play, and continually 'knocking and hammering in his lodging
room'. He is said to have introduced kite-flying, and on dark
nights to have flown his own with a 'crimpled paper lantern' tied
to its tail.

> '. . . Unfading recollections! at this hour
> The heart is almost mine with which I felt,
> From some hill-top on sunny afternoons,
> The paper kite high among fleecy clouds
> Pull at her rein like an impetuous courser. . . .'

Sir William Hamilton, another great mathematician, at the age
of thirteen (in 1818) had with the aid of a tutor acquired 'a good
knowledge of as many languages', and was also well on his way to
his life's work.

And what of Francis Bacon, Queen Elizabeth's 'young Lord
Keeper'? 'At thirteen he was entered at Trinity College, Cambridge, which he left after a residence of three years, "carrying
with him", says Macaulay, "a profound contempt for the course
of study pursued there, a fixed conviction that the system of
academic education in England was radically vicious",' and the
seeds of its reform.

Other boys other destinies. At thirteen Captain Cook went to
sea. At thirteen, Nelson, who as a child was weakened by the ague,

School

was on board his Uncle Maurice's ship, the *Raisonnable*. He had been to two schools, one of them at North Walsham. Here one night by means of knotted sheets he descended from his dormitory to steal pears from an orchard. He refused his share of the spoil, his only incentive being that every other boy had funked making the attempt. Frederick Marryat was a year older when he became a midshipman. He soon took part in many actions. ' "Here's a young cock who has done crowing". . .' cried an officer who found him lying among the wounded. ' "Cheated the gallows!" ' ' "You're a liar",' retorted the corpse. 'And wives still pray to Juno', as the poet says, ' For boys with hearts as bold.'

Joan of Arc was taught as a child to sew and spin, but not to read or write. When she was thirteen years old she was working one day in her father's garden, and became conscious of a great light in the direction of the church in the village of Domrémy, and of a voice crying 'from heaven'. She was afraid, but soon lost her fears, and accepting her inspiration began to live a life apart in the reality of her own mind. Three years afterwards, after the coronation of the Dauphin, having obeyed that inspiration, she besought the Archbishop of Rheims, to let her return home again: 'Would it were God's pleasure that I might go and keep sheep once more with my sister and my brothers; they would be so glad to see me again.'

At the age of thirteen, Faraday who was the son of a blacksmith was apprenticed to a bookbinder. Chemistry and electricity even then however were the sirens enticing him on. Robert Bloomfield, an orphan, was at the same age working as a farm-boy; William Gifford, also an orphan, penniless and homeless, began as a ploughboy, went on to cabin-boy, then to cobbler's apprentice—all on his way to the tartarly *Quarterly*; and Thomas Hood, yet another orphan, who had been born 'with ink in his blood', left his third and last school, his second having been kept by two maiden ladies of the name, immortalized by Charles Lamb, of Hogsflesh.

Richard Garnett, the son of the philologist, it will be remembered, was pondering over King Theodore and the state of Abyssinia at the age of five. Sixty-seven years afterwards, his son Edward Garnett wrote to John Galsworthy: 'David is very well and happy'. It was his thirteenth birthday. 'He reminds me extraordinarily of what I was at 13—his expression and gait and every-

355

Early One Morning

thing bring back my boyhood to me. He is interested in *everything*, and never *does* anything! Long may he be able to keep that programme up!' But, as Joseph Conrad three years before had confided to him, when sending him the tales of Fenimore Cooper which he himself had delighted in as a child: 'Time spares no one. Even you shall grow old some day. But I have great confidence in you. . . .'

So expands and, even in spite of the weather, breaks into flower a gifted mind. There is a natural instinct to preen the wings and choose the food and water; as will a goldfinch in its solitary waste, converting into song and beauty and energy the seed of a thistle.

CHAPTER XXVIII

BULLIES

★

1. *'What if I beat the wanton boy With many a rod?'*

To return to the memoirists. There is little reason to suppose that they have been deliberately false or unfair in recounting the memories of their schooldays. Indeed we might assume that they would tell of them as gladly and go back to them as sweetly as an old hunter to his stable. We might expect too, if not perpetual praises of master, lessons and diet, a good-natured tolerance at least for their young companions; such tolerance for example as Pall Mall clubmen have one for another. However that may be, we may believe what we are told.

A certain allowance perhaps must be made for the fact that the experiences referred to in the next few pages were those of boys in varying degree out of the common run. But they seem to keep the general balance true. The merits or defects of one school are weighed against another's; praise or sufferance for this, contempt for that. Reflection and worldly experience may have given weight to such judgements, and also made light of joys and miseries, afflictions long past, but that does not affect their general veracity.

Southey's youth was copious in schoolmasters. At the age of six, he tells us, he went to the only school where he was ever treated with severity. 'Lessons . . . were frightened out of my head.' But his worst dread was the sermon, in winter, on Sunday evenings. Then, cold and inert, his eyelids heavy as lead, he was kept awake by fear alone. In this school he saw 'much more of the evil side of human nature than I should ever have learned in the course of

357

Early One Morning

domestic education'. It was broken up; he went to live with his aunt at Bedminster, and was happy. He records incidentally the 'devilish cruelty' of the boys at Charterhouse to a schoolfellow of 'weak understanding', who none the less lived to take orders. Long before he ever heard the word physiognomy he had detected in the eye of this boy's father 'a wild unquiet look, a sort of inward emanating light, as if all were not as it ought to be within'. Years afterwards he was under the impression of having been told that this boy himself and one of his sisters died insane.

Of his three hundred contemporaries at Westminster, where an uncle was headmaster and whence he himself was expelled for protesting in the School magazine against the bullying that was rampant, he could call to mind only one 'of moral and intellectual excellence'—an excellence expressed also in his features. Few 'bore the stamp of reprobation'. The great majority were 'clay in the potter's hand, more or less fine; and as it is fitting that such subjects should be conformed to the world's fashion and the world's uses, a public school was best for them'. Earlier in his memories he remarks: 'I would gladly send a son to a good school by day; but rather than board him at the best, I would, at whatever inconvenience, educate him myself'. By comparison with his three hundred schoolfellows he was himself of course in some respects 'different'; he practically says so; but not *so* different as many other men of unusual ability and of genius have been. His 'talent was pedestrian', wrote Mr. Arthur Symons—in a summary resembling the operation of a Sphex wasp with its egg and a grasshopper— 'and it was his misfortune that he tried to fly, with wings made to order, and on his own pattern, and a misfit'. This in respect to his most ambitious poems; but of the man—he was, says Coleridge, 'as son, brother, husband, father, master, friend . . . alike unostentatious, alike exemplary'. That being so, Southey's comment on the potter's clay and the evil side of human nature is the more impressive. To an ineffectual angel or an archangel ruined we should pay a different kind of attention.

Roger North is more precise and less indulgent in his list of 'characters'; 'honest boys' being given the last place:—

'This gives me occasion to note the benefit of public schools to youth, beyond private teaching by parents or tutors. For there they learn the pratique of the world according to their capacities.

358

Bullies

For there are several ages and conditions, as poor boys and rich, and amongst them all the characters which can be found among men, as liars, cowards, fighters, dunces, wits, debauchees, honest boys, and the rest, and the vanity of folly and false dealing, and indeed the mischiefs of immorality in general may be observed there.' He does not say how the liars, debauchees and cowards became so, nor what the effect of their example may be. And he continues:—

'Besides, the boys enter into friendships, combinations, factions, and a world of intrigues, which though of small moment, yet in quality and instruction the same as among men. And further, boys certainly league with equals, which gives them a manage and confidence in dealing; teaches them to look before they leap; being often cuffed and put to cuff again; laugh at others' follies and are laughed at themselves. . . . Whereas in private teaching, their company is either superiors, inferiors, and if equals, but a few, without the liberty and variety of pratique as in a populous school. If superiors, the youth is overawed and sneaks, if inferiors he grows insolent, being taught by the freedom of abusing such companions to insult all the days of his life, and in either of these ways of breeding, never gets a true weighed habit of converse, and besides, wants the spur which is raised by emulation, upon others' performances, than which nothing conduceth more to make a youth sedulous and industrious. But, after all, fondness of parents will prevail, and against the greatest reason in the world with respect to private good, and policy with respect to the public, parents [keep] their children near them, or rather near their ruin.'

Ben Jonson had similar views, but he omits mention of the dunces, wits, debauchees and the rest. Children, he says in *Discoveries*, 'should not be affrighted, or deterred in their entry, but drawn on with exercise and emulation. A youth should not be made to hate study, before he know the causes to love it, or taste the bitterness before the sweet; but called on, and allured, entreated, and praised: yea, when he deserves it not. For which cause I wish them sent to the best school, and a public; which I think the best. . . . To breed them at home is to breed them in a shade where in a school they have the light and heat of the sun. They are used and accustomed to things and men. . . . I would send them where their industry should be daily increased by praise, and that

Early One Morning

kindled by emulation. It is a good thing to inflame the mind. . . .
And from the rod or ferule I would have them free, as from the
menace of them; for it is both deformed and servile.'

If worldly wisdom is for sale at one of the booths in Vanity
Fair, then North must have visited it early. At his first school,
the Free School at Bury, although he was then 'very young and
small', he had already detected that in this world there are 'two
great articles of happiness—liberty and the use of money'. And he
at once put the latter discovery to account. He fell ill; and in spite
of his 'Garagantua stomach', was starved for a cure. As a solace, he
extorted money from every one of his visitors; and was afterwards
deluded into buying a calf. To this desperate illness he later as-
cribes a certain 'imperfect command of thought' in maturity, 'an
aptness to oversee', and an equivalent weakness of body which
made him less salacious than others of his family and so eased him
of infinite cares. A diet mostly of bread and cheese and good air
finally restored him to health. When he was ten or eleven he went
to the Free School of Thetford, where his 'agreeable master' was
scholar enough, 'mild and discreet'. 'He had no fault but too much
addicted to drinking company, which at last made him a sot and
ended his days'. Though himself, he confesses, below 'the prime
of his rank', as a schoolboy, North was 'not contemptible', but
lazy, and he borrowed verses from books which he gave in to his
tutor as his own. He passed whole days naked with his schoolfellows by the riverside, and once got drunk, but was instantly
sobered by the cold water again.

Under the tutorship of his brother John, a fellow of Jesus College, and to study Common Law, he went up to Cambridge
in 1667, when he was fourteen, but stayed there only a year. He
followed his own appetite in study; natural philosophy, 'which
they call physics', and particularly Descartes, 'whose works I dare
say I read over three times before I understood him'. If, his brother
told him, he was not pleased with mathematics, it meant merely
that he did not understand them. With that, he went back to his
Euclid, fell in love with the forty-seventh proposition, and then
'devoured the science with great greediness'. 'At the last I was sent
home with a fever ague . . . and returned no more.'

William Cowper agrees with neither North nor Southey on the
question of schools. Like Porson, when a child, he was so atroci-

Bullies

ously bullied at his first that he had to be removed. So had his persecutor. 'I well remember being afraid to lift my eyes upon him higher than his knees; and that I knew him better by his shoe-buckle than any part of his dress'.

> 'Lisping our syllables we scramble next
> Through moral narrative and sacred text
> Well-tutored only while we share
> A mother's lectures and a nurse's care. . . .'

We know the vivid and loving remembrances Cowper had of his mother, even though she died when he was six. In her care, he tells us, he took 'delight in the masterpieces of literature' at so early an age that at fourteen he feared he had suffered an irreparable loss in not having met before with Milton. After a wretched two years at his private school he went on to Westminster.

> 'Would you your son should be a sot or dunce,
> Lascivious, headstrong, or all these at once . . .
> Train him in public with a mob of boys. . . .'

But Cowper's couplets may be discounted by the matter-of-fact because he was not only a poet but the prey also of melancholia.

Hardly so Edward Gibbon. And he, after the passage decrying what he thought is a fallacy concerning happiness in childhood, and extolling his own progress in learning quoted above, continues: 'By the common methods of discipline, at the expense of many tears and some blood, I purchased the knowledge of the Latin syntax'.

Peering into his distant past, Anthony Trollope could recall how from very babyhood, 'I had to take my place alongside of [my father] as he shaved at six o'clock in the morning, and say my early rules from the Latin Grammar, and repeat the Greek alphabet; and was obliged at these early lessons to hold my head inclined towards him, so that in the event of guilty fault, he might be able to pull my hair without stopping his razor or dropping his shaving-brush.'

Whether hair or knuckles or elsewhere be its medium this is one example among many of early and home discipline. He was, then, definitely fortified, when in 1822 he became a day-boarder at Harrow; although he was not fortified enough:

361

Early One Morning

'I was only seven, and I think that boys at seven are now spared among their more considerate seniors. I was never spared; and was not even allowed to run to and fro between our house and the school without a daily purgatory. No doubt my appearance was against me. I remember well, when I was still the junior boy in the school, Dr. Butler, the headmaster, stopping me in the street, and asking me, with all the clouds of Jove upon his brow and all the thunder in his voice, whether it was possible that Harrow School was disgraced by so disreputably dirty a little boy as I! Oh, what I felt at that moment! But I could not look my feelings.'

From Harrow, when he was twelve years old, he was sent to Winchester. There his college bills fell into arrears, and the local tradesmen were warned not to give him credit, a crisis disquieting at any age. Boots, waistcoats, even pocket-handkerchiefs were in consequence 'closed luxuries'.

'My schoolfellows of course knew that it was so, and I became a Pariah. It is the nature of boys to be cruel. I have sometimes doubted whether among each other they do usually suffer much, one from the other's cruelty; but I suffered horribly! I could make no stand against it. I had no friend to whom I could pour out my sorrows. I was big, and awkward, and ugly, and, I have no doubt, skulked about in a most unattractive manner. Of course I was ill-dressed and dirty.'

These trials over—and it seems a little odd that a dirty boy should have been so very conspicuous and that he refrained from discontinuing to be so—at fifteen he went back to Harrow as a day-boy. It meant a three-mile walk four times every day through 'miserable' muddy lanes. 'The indignities I suffered are not to be described. . . . But, ah! how well I remember all the agonies of my young heart; how I considered whether I should always be alone; whether I could not find my way up to the top of that college tower and from thence put an end to everything. . . . When I left Harrow I was all but nineteen, and I had at first gone there at seven. During the whole of those twelve years no attempt had been made to teach me anything but Latin and Greek, and very little attempt to teach me those languages. I do not remember any lessons either in writing or arithmetic.'

Bullies

2. 'His form was of the manliest beauty.'

Queer-looking or eccentric children, of looks or ways, that is, not acceptable to their contemporaries—long noses, shock-hair, 'carrots', prominent ears, tallowy skin, the knock-kneed, the bow-legged, the splay-footed—are liable to a preliminary handicap. It is for them a school 'extra'. Oliver Goldsmith, for example, who can hardly have been a very odious child, at his Irish grammar school 'suffered from his appearance' and was jeered at for his ugliness.

Charles Lamb was in this respect, at least, an exception. He had a peculiar plantigrade walk, eyes differing in colour, and what has become the most famous stutter in literature. But he was also amiable, sensible and keenly observant, and was indulged on account of his stutter by both boys and masters. Walter Scott, too —in his own words 'a self-will'd imp', in Tibbie Hunter's 'a sweet-tempered bairn'—when at the age of eight he went to the grammar school in Edinburgh, though he 'glanced like a meteor' from one end of his class to the other—now disgusting his master by his frivolity, now placating him by flashes of intellect and talent —was very popular with his schoolfellows, in part *because* of his lameness, and in part for his gifts of story-telling, particularly in winter. 'Boys', he comments, 'are uncommonly just in their feelings, and at least equally generous'. And yet—there seems to be little of either in making lack of means a worse drawback even than lack of looks, as with Anthony Trollope.

In his *Sheridan*, a study of over eleven hundred pages, Walter Sichel devotes about a dozen lines to 'boy Dick's' first four years —from the age of ten to fourteen—at Harrow; where Mr. 'Perdita' Robinson was one of his schoolfellows. The 'little fellow' was very 'low-spirited . . . and much given to crying when alone'. This Sheridan himself attributed in great part to his father's neglect of him. He left him without money, and seldom saw him even during his holidays. But even had the boy spent the whole of his holidays in scenes of bliss it would not have much affected the fact that 'he was slighted by the masters and tormented by the boys as a poor player's son'. Ishmaels come and Ishmaels go, but *snobisme* goes on for ever. It is a human mummery of many strands and may be an inheritance, but it also resembles measles in being

363

infectious, and may be endemic in schools. To what degree such martyrdom *aided* the author of *The School for Scandal* or one of the best-beloved of the English novelists, who was also one of the most conscientious of public servants and assiduous of craftsmen, must be left to the psychoanalysts.

There may be early humiliations that not even the friendliest of witnesses would detect. Three serious and nearly fatal illnesses followed Wallace's first experiences of a grammar school, where he had at once been set upon 'that most wearisome of tasks, the Latin grammar'. Yet again we hear the contemptuous complaint against a master who punishes a stupid boy or a boy with a poor memory for an 'incapacity to learn' what he takes 'no interest in', or what may have 'no meaning for him'. He found the hours of labour and mental effort expended on Geography, then consisting chiefly of statistics, even though it proved useful to him, very painful. School History was 'very little better'; his own most valued supply having been derived from Shakespeare and fiction. These were burdens at least shared with his schoolfellows; but he had a far heavier one that was all his own. To help towards the payment of his fees, he took the younger boys of the school in the three R's, and felt acutely sensitive at this dual position, of pupil and teacher. After he left school, dreams of this unhappy experience repeatedly recurred. Since—among the boys who remained as he remembered them—he himself grew taller in his dreams, and therefore became more conspicuously out of keeping with the others, his shyness and sense of disgrace intensified. For twenty years this dream pestered his night hours! 'It shows how deeply impressionable is the mind at this period of boyhood'.

William Hutton's testimony is as brief as it is decisive. 'I now [at five years old] went to school to Mr. Thomas Meat, who often took occasion to beat my head against the wall, holding it by the hair, but never could beat any learning into it; I hated all books but those of pictures'.

3. *'From beginnings so small.'*

Thackeray's summary of his schooldays is no less condensed. He came home from India as a child of six, having seen *en route* Napoleon at St. Helena. When he was eleven years old he was

Bullies

sent to the school he afterwards disguised as Slaughterhouse, and later, as Greyfriars. He was described by his friend and school-fellow Venables, who had the honour of breaking his nose—hence the Michaelangelo of his pseudonym, Titmarsh—as a gentle and pretty boy. In his own words he was as a child 'licked into indo-lence, abused into sulkiness, bullied into despair'. Experiences wholly different but certainly not less dark and dismal in retrospect nurtured the childhood of Charles Dickens. Neither a strong nor healthy boy, he had only one year's schooling before at the age of ten the blacking-factory at Hungerford Market swallowed him up, and three or four at a private school in Hampstead after his father had come out of the Marshalsea. What, one speculates—but in vain!—would have been the effect on the genius of these two writers, who were the source of incalculable vivification, solace and happiness to their fellow-creatures, if they had exchanged their early surroundings, or had had Chaucer or More for tutor.

At about the age when William Hutton went to sit under Mr. Meat, Francis Galton was also trotted off to his first school and—'my memories become more or less continuous'. 'I think I can revive my principal feelings at that early age with fair correctness, their change during growth seeming to have been chiefly due to the increased range of mental prospect.' At the age of eight he was sent to a school at Boulogne to learn French, but in fact learnt 'a detestable patois'. He played marbles on the gravestones of an old convent, used to go bathing by the old fort, larding his breakfast bread with delicious mussels, and on these occasions boys used to compare their penal scars. Birchings were rampant and vocal. He could not imagine how it was that copies of Cæsar's *Commentaries* had remained spotlessly fresh and clean for nearly two thousand years, and recalls a schoolfellow who could outfrog the Froggies. Between finger and thumb he would dangle by its hind legs one of these amphibians into his open mouth, pause, then allow it to descend head foremost into his gullet. On being ques-tioned, he agreed that he could feel the frog not only all the way down, but in its destination. What became of this epicure is not related.

Galton hated the school and returned home to another small and private one at Kenilworth. Here he was happy for three years and 'began to develop freely'. At the age of fourteen he was sent to

Early One Morning

King Edward's School in Birmingham, but though he admired his headmaster, Dr. Jeune, afterwards Bishop of Peterborough, he learned nothing there and chafed at his limitations. What he craved for was English, mathematics and science. He was given grammar and 'dry' Latin and Greek rudiments. Some of the boys went that way to glory; to him it was abhorrent. 'I was a fool to have been recalcitrant', but none the less, 'I was very willing and eager to learn, and could have learnt much if a suitable teacher had been at hand to direct and encourage me.' Here, precisely adjusted, is a nice balance between *pro* and *con*.

As a means of educating himself Charles Darwin concluded that his school at Shrewsbury was 'simply a blank'. He had no gift for languages, but could easily learn by heart forty or fifty lines of Latin verse; which, he says, were clean forgotten in as many hours. Two years after leaving school at the age of sixteen, and when thinking of Cambridge and of becoming a clergyman, he found, 'incredible as it may appear', that he had forgotten almost everything he had learnt, even to some few of the Greek letters. On looking back to these days at the age of sixty-seven, the only promising qualities he could discern in himself were 'strong and diversified tastes, much zeal for whatever interested me, and a keen pleasure in understanding any complex subject or thing'.

At his first school, 'seeing the other boys begin to dress themselves, poor George [Crabbe], in great confusion, whispered to his bedfellow, "Master G——, can you put on your shirt?—for—for I'm afraid I cannot".' Punished with others of his schoolfellows, for playing at soldiers, by being put into a vast dog kennel called 'the black hole'—he himself being the furthest in—he was nearly suffocated. In this extremity he bit the lad next to him. 'Crabbe is dying—Crabbe is dying!' roared the bitten one. 'A minute more,' said Crabbe long afterwards, 'and I must have died.'

For a time he helped his father in his warehouse on the quay—piling up butter and cheeses, and, like John Ruskin who lamented late in life that he had refused to learn from his father how to cultivate his palate, was sorry afterwards for his fretful indignation at this drudgery. When at fourteen, 'a low-spirited, gentle lad', he set out to his first apprenticeship he made his appearance with a shaven head, the outcome of illness, and its curls had been supplanted by 'a very ill-made scratch-wig'. 'La!' mocked his

366

Bullies

master's daughters at sight of him, 'here's our new 'prentice!'
He astounded a conjuror one day by translating his Latin patter.
And this reminds me of a sad occasion when I was perhaps nine. A
conjuror at the Crystal Palace had produced from nowhere such a
white rabbit as lives only in Wonderland, and having as it appeared
deftly deposited it, ears and all, in a large paper bag, genially
enquired if any small boy in the audience would care to take it
home. Enthralled and, like Crabbe, almost suffocated, between
shyness and desire, I ventured up the alley way, and to the roars of
amusement of the surrounding host was presented with the empty
bag. Was it a telling 'lesson', or was I too young and too woebe-
gone at the moment to realize that life is full of paper bags, and
also of imagination's rabbits?

Of his chief comforts in life, Benjamin Franklin commends
above all his father, who had taught him 'what was good, just,
and prudent in the conduct' of it. A sagacious man, with a gift for
mechanics, he could 'draw prettily' and was 'skilled' a little in
music, and he died aged eighty-nine. Benjamin Franklin himself
could not remember when he was unable to read, but at the age of
eight (in 1714) he was put to 'Grammar-school', and was then
intended for the service of the Church. He did well, but was taken
away at the end of a year, and sent to a school for 'writing and
arithmetic', 'kept by a then famous man, Mr. George Brownell'.
He 'acquired fair writing pretty soon', but made no progress in
arithmetic. 'From a child I was fond of reading, and all the little
money that came into my hands was ever laid out in books'—
Bunyan*, Burton's historical collections—small chapmen's books;
Plutarch, Defoe, Dr. Mather.

At ten he went home to assist his father in his business, a 'tallow-
chandler and sope-boiler'. He cut the wicks, filled the moulds,
went errands, but disliked it all. Living near the water in Boston,
he delighted in all water craft. When he was nineteen he swam
from Chelsea to Blackfriars; and he pined to go to sea. As to
'coming events', 'when in a boat or canoe with other boys, I was
commonly allowed to govern, especially in any case of difficulty;
and upon other occasions I was generally a leader among the boys,
and sometimes led them into scrapes', including that of borrowing
stones from a new house to build themselves a 'wharff'.

At sixteen, having, as we have heard, become a vegetarian, he

Early One Morning

taught himself to cook and thus to live on one-and-sixpence a week. On coming back to Cocker's Arithmetic 'I went through the whole by myself with gre?t ease'. This odd capriciousness in arithmetic, as is already evident, recurs again and again.

Seemingly capricious or not, a child of any magnitude will follow its destined orbit. That prince of men and scholar of birds, Charles Waterton, was born on June 3, 1782. Even after his eightieth birthday he could climb an oak in his stockinged feet; but on one occasion, when using a ladder to scale a cherry tree, he fell heavily and injured his arm. It began to wither. For three weeks he endured the ministrations of a bone-setter, and, 'as a finishing off', the smashing into atoms of the bone above the elbow, an 'act of unmitigated severity', the callus cracking in the operation as if it had consisted of 'tobacco pipe shanks'. Having, he says, 'predetermined in my mind not to open my mouth, or to make any stir during the operation, I remained passive and silent whilst this fierce elbow-contest was raging'. This tree-climbing all came of his devotion to birds; and that devotion makes it first appearance in his reminiscences when he was a child exactly a tenth of this age—eight.

'I had managed to climb upon the roof of an out-house, and had got to a starling's nest under one of the slates. Had my foot slipped, I should have been in as bad a plight as was poor Ophelia in the willow-tree, when the "envious sliver broke". The ancient housekeeper . . . had cast her rambling eye upon me. Seeing the danger I was in, she went and fetched a piece of gingerbread, with which she lured me down, and then she seized me as though I had been a malefactor.'

As he began, so he proceeded. He went to school at the age of nine. 'Literature had scarcely any effect upon me, although it was duly administered in large doses by a very scientific hand. But I made vast proficiency in the art of finding birds' nests'—to extirpate which pursuit his headmaster resorted to the birch. 'Thus are bright colours in crockeryware made permanent by the action of fire', an aphorism which perhaps should have been cited on an earlier page.

According to his morning mood and temper this master wore two kinds of wig, in one of which his cat once kittened. He was a fiery, human and charitable man, and Waterton, birched or

Bullies

unbirched, was happy under him, especially when the feast of whin-flower-dyed 'Pasche eggs' came at Easter, and Nut-crack Night, and evenings ringing with song to the bagpipes, and garnished with fruit, cakes, and tea.

When a year later he went on to Stonyhurst—he was an ardent scion of an ardent Catholic family—the 'good Fathers' having discovered that they could not cure him of his passion for birds'-nesting and other joys that led to his breaking bounds, appointed him the official school rat-catcher, fox-taker, foumart-killer, and cross-bow charger at the season of the fledging of the rooks. 'I was now at the height of my ambition'.

Neither tears nor blood are referred to by Izaak Walton, in his *Lives of Donne*, Henry Wotton, Hooker and Herbert. Of John Donne's early years—he was born in 1573— he says only: 'He had his first breeding in his Father's house, where a private Tutor had the care of him, until the ninth year of his age; and, in his tenth year was sent to the University of *Oxford*, having at that time a good command both of the French and Latine Tongue. This, and some other of his remarkable Abilities, made one give this censure of him, *That this age had brought forth another Picus Mirandula*; of whom Story sayes, *That he was rather born than made wise by study. . . .*'

By rights with the prodigies, Giovanni Pico Della Mirandola, 'the Phœnix of the wits', who was born in 1463, was one of the wonders of the world. In his twenty-third year he issued a challenge at Rome and in every university in Italy, to maintain against any intellectual knight-errant who would dare to accept it nine hundred theses; 'and lest poverty should reduce the number of his antagonists' he offered to pay their travelling expenses!

A marvellous and symbolical sight, it is said, was seen before his birth—a fiery garland standing over the chamber of his mother in her travail, which suddenly vanished away. As a child, 'he was of feture and shappe semely and beauteous, of stature goodly and hyghe, of flesshe tendre and softe: his vysage lovely and fayre, his coloure white entermengled with comely ruddes, his eyen gray and quicke of loke, his teth white and even, his heere yelowe and not to piked' (carelessly arranged). 'Cupid himself', quotes Burton, 'was yellow-haired.' Under the rule and governance of his mother he was set to masters and to learning, and laboured with so ardent

Early One Morning

a mind his studies of humanity that 'within shorte whyle' he was counted among the chief Orators and Poets of his time. He was 'in lernynge mervaylously swyfte and of so redy a wyt, that the versis whiche he herde ones red he wolde agayne bothe forwarde and bakwarde to the grete wonder of the herers reherse', and more-over could keep them in sure remembrance, 'whiche in other folkes wonte comenly to happen contrary'.

But to return from this seemly and beauteous child to Walton's *Lives*. Donne, we are told, took no degree because his parents were 'of the Romish persuasion' and were 'averse to some parts of the Oath that is always tendered at those times'. Between the ages of fourteen and seventeen he was at Cambridge, 'all which time he was a most laborious Student, often changing his studies'.

Both Henry Wotton and George Herbert, Walton relates, were during their childhood taught at home by their mothers—friends and tutors 'all in one'. When he was twelve years old—in 1605—George Herbert went to Westminster 'where the beauties of his pretty behaviour and wit, shin'd and became so eminent and lovely in this his innocent age, that he seem'd to be marked out for piety, and to become the care of Heaven, and of a particular Angel to guard and guide him.' At about the age of fifteen he went up to Cambridge, having by then come 'to be perfect in the learned Languages, and especially in the Greek Tongue.'

Richard Hooker was born 'about the Year of our Redemption 1553, and of parents who were not so remarkable for their Ex-traction and Riches as for their virtue and industry, and Gods blessing upon both.' The phrase is the 'poor but honest' of our own democratic age, but now a mere gibe! 'His Complexion', Walton continues, 'was Sanguine, with a mixture of Choler; and yet, his Motion was slow even in his Youth, and so was his Speech, never expressing an Earnestness (? impetuosity) in either of them, but a Gravity suitable to the Aged.' He was an early Questionist*, quietly inquisitive ' *Why this was, and that was not, to be remembered? Why this was granted and that denied?*' But he was also of a 'remarkable modesty, a sweet serene quietness of nature and a quick apprehension.' His master and others believed him 'to have an inward blessed Divine Light'. 'For in that, Children were less pregnant, less confident, and more malleable, than in this wiser [? more learned], but not better, Age.' So shining was his promise in nature and grace, that his schoolmaster, rather than that he should be apprenticed, offered to double his diligence in instructing him, and without any reward. In short, he was 'a dutiful and dear child'. But then 'all who had care of him taught him to love and fear God, who knows the very secrets of our Souls', and to be free from all hypocrisy. At fifteen he was sent to Oxford, with the help of an uncle, and of John Jewell, the great bishop of Salisbury.

4. *'Fayre* Algebra *with fingers richly dight.'*

There could hardly be a greater contrast to Charles Waterton than the author of *The Importance of Being Ernest*. As a boy of nine, said his mother, Oscar Wilde was 'wonderful, wonderful'. Before his eighth year he had 'learnt the ways to "the shores of old romance," had seen all the apples plucked from the tree of knowledge, and had gazed with wondering eyes into "the younger day" '—which is quite pretty but uninformative. The best of his early education, it is said, was obtained at his father's dinner table and in his mother's drawing-room. When he was eleven he went to school. He disliked games, was reserved and not 'popular', clever at nicknames, always well dressed, used expensive class-books, got 'quicker into a book than any boy that ever lived', but was absolutely incapable of mathematics. His conduct was uniformly good, but he once cheeked the headmaster 'something awful'.

Henry Adams, in spite of the lesson he learned from his grandfather, detested school. His dislike of it was so strong, he says, as to be 'a positive gain. The impassioned hatred of its methods was almost a method in itself'. What he needed, he maintained, for success in the life afterwards imposed on him was 'the facile use of only four tools: Mathematics, French, German and Spanish'. He never mastered those tools. For what Latin and Greek he needed, six weeks, he maintains, in later life instead of six years in his childhood would have sufficed. 'Indeed, had his father kept the boy at home, and given him half an hour's direction every day, he would have done more for him than school ever could do for' him. He agrees that the school-taught disparage home-bred boys, and themselves exult in their own ignorance. 'But the man of sixty can generally see what he needed in life, and in Henry

Early One Morning

Adams's opinion it was not school'. Not without a hint of bias, he defines a schoolmaster as 'a man employed to tell lies to little boys'!

Alexander Bain was the grandson of a small farmer and the son of a weaver—a man 'remarkable on the moral side', and for his energy and endurance. And he alone, apparently, inherited these qualities. Of a family of nine brothers and sisters he was the only one that 'saw forty', and of the four who survived infancy he remarks with unusual candour: 'I may say that they were all failures in life: every one of them had, at some time or other, to be assisted by me.' His references to his school-days are of a stoical kind. Having survived his deceit of the old woman who taught him to read, he climbed a little higher, and remembered having his ears frequently pulled when he was a child of five and six on account of the badness of his writing, inferring from this that he must have learned arithmetic with ease. Before he was seven his mathematics had taken him by surprise. In algebra he went from strength to strength, but his Euclid up to the age of eleven he learnt merely verbatim, until the *pons asinorum* revealed this fact. 'The faculty for Algebra does not involve the comprehension of the demonstrative processes of Geometry. What I could not do at nine or ten, was found perfectly easy at fourteen, by mere brain growth.' Before he was eleven he had the rudiments of Latin 'pretty well by heart', apart, that is, from Latin composition. How many tears and groans and headaches and nightmares might be spared the young if only that comment on geometry could be kept in mind!

Though he repented of it later, Thomas Gray rejected mathematics altogether. 'Must I pore into metaphysics? Alas, I cannot see in the dark. . . . Must I pore upon mathematics? Alas, I cannot see in too much light: I am no eagle. It is very possible that two and two make four, but I would not give four farthings to demonstrate this ever so clearly; and if these be the profits of life, give me the amusements of it'.

Dryden, who enjoyed Polybius in English before he was ten years old and confessed to his 'shame' that he never read anything but for pleasure, history being his most delightful entertainment, said of 'Master Busby', then at Westminster, that he 'used to whip a boy so long till he made him a confirmed blockhead'. He respected his character and system of teaching however, and afterwards placed two of his sons under him—but after a long interval.

372

Bullies

It was Busby who said of Robert South—that vigorous and matter-of-fact divine—'I see great talents in that sulky boy, and I shall endeavour to bring them out'. He then went to work in the usual way, and South, in turn, paid Westminster a handsome tribute. What had made him, one speculates, a sulky boy? Or did sulky mean merely unseasoned?

Laurence Sterne's first schoolmaster may, it appears, have sat for the portrait of the governor that Mr. Walter Shandy rejected for his son Tristram: 'the governor I make choice of shall neither lisp, or squint, or wink, or talk loud, or look fierce, or foolish; or bite his lips, or grind his teeth, or speak through his nose.' 'He shall neither strike, or pinch, or tickle, or bite . . . his nails . . . or snift, or drum with his feet. . . .' At the Grammar School at Hipperholme, to which he went at the age of twelve, Laurence 'learned to read and write Latin with great facility', to share the minds of his authors—Horace, Pliny, Virgil, Ovid and others—and, in imagination, the griefs and joys of the phantoms he met with in them.

'Was I not as much concerned for the destruction of the *Greeks* and *Trojans* as any boy of the whole school? Had I not three strokes of a ferula given me, two on my right hand, and one on my left, for calling *Helena* a b—— for it? Did any one of you shed more tears for *Hector*? And when king *Priam* came to the camp to beg his body, and returned weeping back to *Troy* without it—you know, brother, I could not eat my dinner.'

'It grieved him to think that "poor Ovid" died in exile', and he mourned for forsaken Dido. Yet even in class he found time to idle, scribbling in an old 'dogged eared volume' such declensions as *Nickibus Nonkebus* and *rorum rarum*, memoranda such as 'I owe Samuel Thorpe one halfpenny but I will pay him to-day', and 'Labour takes panes', together with rude drawings of owls and cocks and hens, soldiers in sugar-loaf caps, guns, heads of women, a drummer and a piper, and a 'long-nosed, long-chinned face', subscribed 'This is Lorence'.

And Mr. Shandy recited Lorence's early Life: 'Five years with a bib under his chin; Four years in travelling from Christ-cross-row to Malachi; A year and a half in learning to write his own name; Seven long years and more $\tau\nu\pi\tau\omega$-ing* it, at Greek and Latin; Four years at his *probations* and his *negations*—the fine statue still

373

Early One Morning

lying in the middle of the marble block—and nothing done, but his tools sharpened. . . .' And yet this unique sinuosity of the wits.

Robert Browning went to school at Peckham, where, he says, he was taught nothing and bullied:

> 'Long constraint chained down
> My soul till it was changed. I lost myself;
> And were it not that I so loathe that time,
> I could recall how first I learned to turn
> My mind against itself; and the effects . . .'

When he was seven years old, Lord Berners began to have lessons from a curate, 'a meek and gentle young man', who seemed at first to be a 'perfect specimen of a nincompoop'. 'I remember saying to my mother, "I am sure that I could love Jesus better if He were not so dreadfully like Mr. Allen".' He proved, however, to be a born teacher. 'I even enjoyed Latin Grammar, which he encouraged me to look upon in the light of an acrostic or word game. I enjoyed it almost as much as I came to loathe it later on, when, at my preparatory school, it ceased to be a game (as did also games themselves) and was held up as a serious object in life, acquiring a definite moral value, so that a misconstruction of syntax came to be considered a more egregious offence than a misconstruction of the facts of life'.

In varying phrase, or by inference, this contrast between learning for delight in it and learning within a narrow range of enforced interest recurs repeatedly. An alternative is when schoolwork is a *dolce far niente* that may sour into boredom and monkeyishness. This wears badly in memory; even its willing victim being hostile to it in his heart, and scornful of the hand too lax to feed him.

To Charles Lamb in his first years at Christ's Hospital, however, class-play was his only joy. 'We had plenty of exercise and recreation *after* school hours; and, for myself, I must confess, that I was never happier than *in* them.' On one side of the classroom was the dreaded and redoubtable Boyer, on the other the good, easy, often-absentee Rev. Matthew Field. 'We lived a life as careless as birds. We talked and did just what we pleased, and nobody molested us. We carried an accidence, or a grammar, for form; but, for any trouble it gave us, we might take two years in getting

Bullies

through the verbs deponent, and another two in forgetting all that we had learned about them. . . .' Paper sun-dials, cat's-cradle, dry peas dancing at the end of a tin pipe, and 'a hundred other such devices' mixed 'the useful with the agreeable so beguilingly that it would have made the souls of Rousseau and John Locke chuckle to have seen us.'

As for Boyer, an odd name for his destiny, he would break out from his 'inner recess', and fixing a 'turbulent eye' would roar, 'Od's my life, sirrah, I have a great mind to whip you', retreat into it again as if all were forgiven and forgotten, to emerge once more with an expletory yell, *And I will too!* In his gentler moods he would combine his morning *Times* and chastisement—a lash at his victim between each paragraph of a parliamentary debate.

Other scenes awaited Lamb beyond the classroom walls. He was 'a poor friendless boy', a child 'barely turned of seven', when he entered this abode of 'six hundred playmates'.

'The oppressions of these young brutes [the monitors] are heart-sickening to call to recollection. I have been called out of my bed, and *waked for the purpose*, in the coldest winter nights—and this not once, but night after night—in my shirt, to receive the discipline of a leathern thong, with eleven other sufferers. . . .

'There was one H——, who, I learned, in after days, was seen expiating some maturer offence in the hulks. . . . This petty Nero actually branded a boy, who had offended him, with a red hot iron.'

On his first day at the school he saw a boy in fetters. This was part of a punishment for having twice attempted to run away. A glimpse of the dungeons followed: straw and a blanket, bread and water, the silence unbroken even by the servant who brought the culprit these dainties, and a beadle who came in to chastise him twice a week. On being detected in a third effort to escape, the victim was dressed up for the occasion like a London lamp-lighter, was publicly scourged, and derisively expelled into the universe. Lamb is referring to 1783.

One Sunday afternoon about a century after this I paid a visit to my friend at Christ's Hospital, then in Newgate Street. After a perambulation of the cloisters we mounted a stone staircase and came upon a group of four or five of his schoolfellows, the eldest fifteen or so, the youngest a pasty, blubbering, swollen-faced little

imp arraigned in his skirts and yellow stockings before this tri-
bunal. The eldest boy, observing a visitor, turned to me and said,
'Hello! Would you like to see what we do here to little milksops
of this sort?'—words to that effect; and before I could answer
either Yes or No, he had felled his victim with a blow on the side
of his head.

Every school of course has what may be called its public and
its private life; and here is a glimpse, from Evelyn's diary, of
Lamb's a hundred years *before* he entered his:

'I went this evening to see the order of the boys and children at
Christ's Hospital. There were near 800 boys and girls so decently
clad, cleanly lodged, so wholesomely fed, so admirably taught,
some the mathematics, especially the forty of the late King's
foundation, that I was delighted to see the progress some little
youths of thirteen or fourteen years of age had made. I saw them
at supper, visited their dormitories, and much admired the order,
economy, and excellent government of this most charitable seminary. Some are taught for the Universities, others designed for
seamen, all for trades and callings. The girls are instructed in all
such work as becomes their sex and may fit them for good wives,
mistresses, and to be a blessing to their generation.'

5. '. . . *And even find Some sugar in the cane.*'

That Boyer had ever been a child—and not eternal fifteen—
is no more remarkable a fact perhaps than that in his later
years Coleridge was easily just enough to pay a tribute to him as a
teacher, and that Lamb himself could lovingly and faithfully regret the old familiar faces of his '*happy*' schooldays. That is human
nature, or at least theirs. So too the lines, 'Where once my careless
childhood strayed, A stranger yet to pain', in Gray's Ode on Eton
—five stanzas of which describe the joys of boyhood and five the
woes of the adult—hardly suggest the fact that his mother in the
poet's childhood had been forced to leave a violent husband who
refused to help in his education. Contrariwise, although Thomas
Hood had an appreciative schoolmaster, his 'Ode on a Distant
Prospect of Clapham Academy' far from suggests it:

'. . . There I was birched! there I was bred!
There like a little Adam fed

Bullies

> From Learning's woful tree!
> The weary tasks I used to con!——
> The hopeless leaves I wept upon!——
> Most fruitless leaves to me! ...'

Owing, as it has been related, chiefly to difficulties with his liver and to the results of clumsy leechcraft, De Quincey ran away from his third school, Manchester Grammar School. Yet apart from his having practically no leisure he had lived there in the lap of luxury. He had a room to himself; a bottle of brandy was occasionally available, and a piano for his own private use. He had plenty of money, plenty of books. When in his own fascinating and prolix fashion he describes his sudden departure, he is at pains to prove that it was not *his* example that afterwards induced his brother to decamp also. This boy, of a 'generous and heroic temper', had been sent to a school 'governed by a brutal and savage master', a man of 'diabolical malice'. After becoming 'a pirate amongst pirates', he 'joined the English storming party at Monte Video, fought under the eye of Sir Home Popham, the commodore, and within twenty-four hours after the victory was rated as a midshipman on board the Diadem, which bore Sir Home's flag'.

In my own young days two of my schoolfellows ran away together. Footsore and exhausted, they quarrelled so bitterly on their journey that when they came to a fork in the country road they were wearily trudging, they decided to part. In England, a country road that forks into two may—like husband and wife who find they cannot live apart—decide to become one again. So it was with theirs. They met, made up their quarrel, and continued their brief and hapless expedition.

John Keats, in the company of his friend Cowden Clarke, appears to have been happy at his Enfield school, the lovely brick façade of which now adorns the South Kensington Museum. They read the *Faerie Queen* together, and at fourteen, though he had always been an orderly scholar, there awoke in him a sudden passion for learning. 'He was at work before the first school-hour began and that was at seven o'clock; almost all the intervening times of recreation were so devoted; and during the afternoon holidays, when all were at play, he would be in the school—almost the only one—at his Latin or French translation; and so

Early One Morning

unconscious and regardless was he of the consequences of so close and persevering an application, that he never would have taken the necessary exercise had he not been sometimes driven out for the purpose by one of the masters.' He must, said Clarke, in those last months, have exhausted the school library, including not only *Robinson Crusoe*, many histories, all Miss Edgeworth, and Spence's *Polymetis* but also Lemprière's Classical Dictionary, which he appeared to *learn*. As for Shakespeare, 'no one', he says himself, 'would dare to read *Macbeth* alone in a house at two o'clock in the morning'. Keats was a boy always in extremes, 'from tears to laughter'. So with his reading. Even at school supper he would sit with a folio volume of Burnet's *History of His Own Time* between himself and his plate.

CHAPTER XXIX

MISFITS

★

1. *'Only one youth and the bright life was shrouded.'*

As a child, Shelley was described by his sister Hellen, who was seven years younger than himself, as slight and beautiful, his hands models of delicacy. There was a 'fixed beauty' in his 'deep blue' eyes—eyes of an unusual brightness—and he had so unruly a mop of hair—he was fair, golden and freckled—that his sister Elizabeth, less than two years his junior, at last insisted on a barber, in hope to make him look 'like a Christian'. He was a good-tempered child, loved playing with fire, offered to cure chilblains by means of an electric battery, and once, disguised as a rustic, and carrying a truss of hay, went to visit a young lady at Horsham who had been prescribed not electricity but 'hay tea' for hers. He also applied to a local landowner in good Sussex dialect for a job as a gamekeeper's boy, and was all but given it. He talked of buying and adopting a little girl, and hesitated over a small tumbler who had shown him her tricks at the back door at Field Place. During an illness when he was fourteen his third sister Margaret remembered his coming to the window and kissing her through the glass. She could recall his face and lips pressed against the pane.

When he was ten years old he went to Syon House Academy—peopled by some fifty boys of ages ranging from eight to sixteen. Here, he enjoyed the lectures on natural science and, according to Medwin, must have intuitively acquired his knowledge of the classics, since he would sit in school-hours gazing out of the window at the clouds and the flitting swallows:

Early One Morning

'I never saw a man who looked
With such a wistful eye
Upon that little tent of blue
Which prisoners call the sky. . . .'

Or he would scrawl in his books—a habit never abandoned—drawings of the pines and cedars at Field Place, whence a sharp box on the ears would recall him to actuality. Though he was himself capable of playing a practical joke on a schoolfellow, his slender figure, girlish gestures and dislike of games had the usual result. He looked like a girl in boy's clothes, fought with open hands, and when he was flogged rolled on the floor, not to stifle the pain but 'from a sense of indignity'.

When he was treated with a decent forbearance his natural virtues shone, and it is to Syon House that the following lines refer in *The Revolt of Islam*. It records (and, as we have seen, other children have had a similar experience) what may be called a conversion of the mind. It was, he says, the actual hour 'which burst My spirit's sleep':

'. . . And from that hour did I with earnest thought
    Heap knowledge from forbidden mines of lore,
Yet nothing that my tyrants knew or taught
    I cared to learn, but from that secret store
    Wrought linkèd armour for my soul, before
It might walk forth to war among mankind;
    Thus power and hope were strengthened more and more
Within me, till there came upon my mind
A sense of loneliness, a thirst with which I pined.'

He had a tenacious memory, especially for words; delighted in a kind of 'blue books' not of the official order, but concerned with battle, murder and sudden death; and particularly in *Peter Wilkins*. How much, says Medwin, he pined 'for a winged wife and little winged cherubs of children!' At Syon House he also took to astronomy, but not to dancing. When the morning stars sang together only the clumsiest foot replied. 'Mon Dieu, Madam,' exclaimed his dancing master at a ball, '. . . Master Shelley will not learn any ting—he is so *gauche*.'

He went to Eton when he was twelve, and that cock-hatted,

380

Misfits

ruddy-faced, shag-eyebrowed, quacking, bulldog-like 'little widow-woman', Dr. Keate, then master of the lower school, was by no means his worst enemy. There was a daily Shelley-bait about twelve o'clock: 'he was known for not wearing strings to his shoes'. But he was averse to *all* school sports, and sought for peace and joy in the meadows beside the river and in his own mind. 'Sweete Themmes runne softly, till I end my Song.' There is a story that he once stabbed a bully with a fork or with a pen-knife, as he told Peacock; and, it is said, he spouted Greek before he was knocked out in a fight with Sir Thomas Styles.

'No good man', wrote Scott to Shelley, probably before he went up to Oxford—'no good man can ever be happy when he is unfit for the career of simple and commonplace duty. . . . Cultivate then, sir, your taste for poetry, and the belles-lettres, as an elegant and most interesting amusement, but combine it with studies of a more serious and solid cast, such as are most intimately connected with your prospects in future life. . . .' It was for the composition of a tract of a somewhat solid cast that Shelley was 'expelled' from Oxford. 'I never saw him so deeply shocked and so cruelly as on this occasion', said Hogg. A few years afterwards, says Peacock, he debated becoming a clergyman, in the hope and desire of doing good.

Byron had at best a chequered childhood. His mother has been described as 'at least as great a vixen' as his father was 'a rascal'. Her fortune squandered, she retired to Aberdeen on an income of £130 a year. At Aberdeen, says Byron himself, in *My Dictionary*, 'I was sent at a fee of five shillings a quarter to a school kept by a Mr. Bowers, who was called "Bodsy Bowers", by reason of his dapperness. It was a school for both sexes. I learned little except to repeat by rote the first lesson, of monosyllables ("God made man". "Let us love him"), by hearing it often repeated, without acquiring a letter. Whenever proof was made of my progress at home, I repeated these words with the most rapid fluency; but on turning over a new leaf, I continued to repeat them, so that the narrow boundaries of my first year's accomplishments were detected, my ears boxed (which they did not deserve, seeing it was by ear only that I had acquired my letters), and my intellects consigned to a new preceptor. He was a very devout, clever, little clergyman, named Ross, afterwards minister of one of the Kirks.

Early One Morning

. . . Under him I made astonishing progress; and I recollect to this day his mild manners and good-natured painstaking.'

The moment he could read, his 'grand passion' was history, and in a letter of 1821, asking for a copy of the Bible, he told John Murray that he had read the Scriptures through and through before he was eight years old. (Perhaps he was unaware that Jonathan Swift, a weakling in infancy, could read any chapter of the Bible before he was three.) The scholarly son of a shoemaker was Byron's next tutor. He then went to a grammar school, and, after yet another tutor, to a quiet boarding-school at Dulwich. Two years afterwards he was sent to Harrow. 'An irregular and turbulent scholar', he was not remarkable for his learning, but, in spite of his lameness, was a great lover of games, and preferred hockey to Horace. He seems to have exchanged black eyes with any contemporary who desired the privilege, including Rice-pudding Morgan and Moses Moore'("the clod")'. There was an altar tomb in the churchyard, looking towards Windsor and Eton, where, during Byron's last year at Harrow, Shelley was learning to 'grow heavy'. There 'I used to sit for hours and hours when a boy'. The absence in schooldays indeed of these blessed opportunities of 'doing nothing' may account in part for the paucity of poets.

2. *'What checks the fiery soul of James?'*

Swinburne (who at birth was not expected to live an hour) enjoyed when a child the privilege of a book at meals and was already deeply read when he arrived at Eton in 1849. He was then just twelve years old, 'a queer little elf', with green eyes, and an aureole of hair of three different colours, orange red, dark red and bright pure gold. He carried about with him a bowdlerized Shakespeare, 'adorned with a blue silk bookmarker with a Tunbridge-ware button at the end of it' that had been given to him by his mother when he was six. In the following year he was reading Marlowe, Ford and Webster; and was usually to be found sitting tailor-wise in a bay window of the college library—'a folio as big as himself spread open upon his knees'.

It has been falsely said, wrote Edmund Gosse, that Swinburne was bullied at Eton. Of his *happiness* there Edward Thomas in his 'critical study' expressed himself a little dubious: 'since Swinburne

SWINBURNE, AT THE AGE OF SIX
WITH HIS SISTERS ALICE AND EDITH
From the drawing by George Richmond
By permission of the National Portrait Gallery

Misfits

was neither an athlete, nor an ordinary amusing person, it is probable that he enjoyed his schooldays chiefly in retrospect'. He was a 'formidable' boy, tactful and courageous. Already a fearless rider, swimmer and climber, he could, like Shelley, 'walk for ever'. But he never cared for games, or coveted school honours. He was looked upon as odd and left alone. In the September of his first year at the school he was taken to see Wordsworth, and when the poet as they parted said a word about the child's not forgetting him, Swinburne burst into tears. Earlier in the same year, Samuel Rogers (then nearing his ninetieth year) his aged hand resting on the boy's fiery head, assured him, 'I think that *you* will be a poet too!' 'I saw Mr. Dryden', says Alexander Pope, 'when I was twelve years of age'—in 1700, that is, the last year of Dryden's life. 'I remember his face well, for I looked upon him even then with veneration, and observed him very particularly'. So, doubtless, from Homer onward, weanling poet has been blessed by or paid tribute to the vanishing master.

Shelley's and Swinburne's delight in solitude, in escaping into themselves—and during childhood, no less than in the years of maturity, the imaginative are never less alone than when alone—has been shared by many writers in their young days. Sheridan Le Fanu, a boy of uncommonly high spirits who delighted in practical jokes, seems to have been happy at school, says Mr. S. M. Ellis. But he never cared for games or field sports, and much preferred to be left in seclusion, and to his own devices. Under the roof of his father's house, he had a refuge only to be reached by a ladder which he drew up after him. There he could be alone and at ease. Mortimer Collins took no pleasure, either, in games and sports, but 'used to wander about the country in dreary loneliness'. Not unendurably dreary perhaps if, dreaming his dreams, as Mr. Ellis says, he was colloguing with his weird 'phantoms' in the fashion described in his story, *Sweet Anne Page*.

Richard Blackmore, shy, reserved and proud by nature, went as a boy to Blundell's at Tiverton. There he was so much 'bullied and maltreated that serious results continued in after life, causing attacks of epilepsy'. Even at the age of eight Aksakoff had to be taken away from school on this account and for the same reason. Blackmore was fag to Frederick Temple, whose favourite mode of correction was tapping him on the head with a brass-headed

Early One Morning

hammer. One of Temple's boys at Rugby afterwards said of his headmaster, 'He may be a beast and a brute, but he is a just beast', a generous variant of, If she vixen be to me, what care I how fair she be!

Before he went to Shrewsbury and at twelve years old, Samuel Butler 'knew every page of his Latin and Greek grammars by heart. He had read the greater part of Virgil, Horace, and Livy; he was proficient in arithmetic; knew the first four books of Euclid thoroughly; and had a fair knowledge of French'. His father had thrashed Latin and its grammar into him ('I mean physically') day after day from when he was a few months over four years old. This was the Eton Latin Grammar. At Shrewsbury he was told that he must learn Dr. Kennedy's—his headmaster's. He was not beaten, and therefore, as he says, failed to do so; with the consequence that he forgot his Eton Grammar and at seventeen or eighteen had none. Long before Shrewsbury he had already learned to observe, boldly to take advantage of having done so, and to be tactful. When a boy of about thirteen years old he met one day an elderly gentleman in a shovel hat and gaiters, waylaid his servant to discover who he was, and then begged the old gentleman to ask for a half holiday for the boys. ' "But how do you know that I am able to get you one?" I was afraid to say that I had asked Thomas and replied: "By your clothes, sir." '

His headmaster at Shrewsbury, Dr. Kennedy, appears in *The Way of All Flesh* as Dr. Skinner. One afternoon Samuel was bidden 'parse ἠδυνήθη'. He knew that it meant 'he was unable', but floundered into inventing a Greek verb, was told to look up δύναμαι and given an imposition. Some forty-five years afterwards he tracked the word down: 'At last! We were both of us very silly and very lazy; but which of us was the sillier and lazier our Father which is in heaven knoweth, but I know not'.

The first great event in his life was the visit to Italy, already mentioned, when he was not quite eight years old. The second was first hearing the music of Handel. 'All day long,' Butler recorded in 1883, 'whether I am writing or painting or walking—but always —I have his music in my head; and if I lose sight of it and of him for an hour or two, as of course I sometimes do, this is as much as I do. I believe I am not exaggerating when I say that I have never been a day since I was 13, without having Handel in my mind

384

many times over'. As to 'the others', he did not dispute their greatness, but 'he was out of sympathy with them'.

'When my father died', says Philip Hamerton, 'I was simply a child. . . .' Between two and three years after that event the child had become a boy, with a keen taste for literature, which, if it had been taken advantage of by his teachers, ought, he believed, to have made his education a more complete success than it proved. He went first to Doncaster School—of sixty to seventy boys. Its headmaster believed in the cane—an exercise which unfortunately roused him to fury. But he allowed Hamerton to keep a tawny dog, and boy and dog became deeply attached to one another. An older and private pupil, on malice bent, first (like Alcibiades, but for a different reason) cut off its tail, and then led it off into a field for a little filthy pistol-practice at a living target. A dog Hamerton had as a child fell foul of his father. He gave it a kick that sent it into the middle of the room, took no notice of it, said what he had to say, in his usual peremptory tone, and went out. 'I knelt down by the . . . dog, which was in its death agony.' And the child's agony can have been little short of it.

Hamerton gives a telling portrait of an usher, who, although he was 'no gentleman,' refrained from sparing the rod, was painstaking and honest, and had one sovereign quality—'an extreme readiness' to help a willing boy in his work by explaining away difficulties. This usher was too fat to make a really good cricketer, but fat enough to make a capital swimmer. He was a voluptuous snuff-taker, and in the heat of summer would lay a train of it, like gunpowder, on his bare arm. Once in the playground he thrashed Hamerton with an apple-switch, and on being asked the reason for this chastisement explained that a master owes no explanation to a schoolboy. Apart from the usher, Hamerton had a kindly but pompous and silly drawing master, and a French master—an Italian—whom he pitied and flourished under. He delighted in drawing, learned to play the violin, and read widely and well; but for cricket he acquired an intense aversion. Like Swinburne when he was a child he was ardently religious.

At thirteen he went to Burnley grammar school; and he approved of it. Here, however, his headmaster, though he was a good scholar and could diffuse his love for the classics, was too tender-hearted to force him on. His pupil pined for the apple-switch. At a school debate on the subject of Queen Elizabeth he spoke for an hour and a half; a youth with a cold, who followed him, being content with a single sentence: 'Id my opidiod Queen Elizabeth was to be blabed, because she was a proud wobad'.

And so, as we approach our own times, the tale—already perhaps too tedious a tale—continues. The day after his twentieth birthday Rupert Brooke wrote to a friend: 'I am now in the depths of despondency because of my age. I'm filled with an hysterical despair to think of fifty dull years more. I hate myself and everyone'. The fact that this dirge, never to be fulfilled, is followed by 'The sunset on a child's face no longer reminds me of a bucolic caesura', points to a passing mood, however genuine its gloom. On the other hand, 'I am seated on the topmost pinnacle of the Temple of Joy' is a statement in a letter written during his last year at Rugby which can be accepted as it stands.

As an apology for the 'sentiment' in a paper he afterwards read at Cambridge, he declared: 'I had been happier at Rugby than I can find words to say. As I looked back at five years, I seemed to see almost every hour golden and radiant, and always increasing in beauty as I grew more conscious; and I could not (and cannot) hope for or even quite imagine such happiness elsewhere'.

It was a happiness, says Mr. Edward Marsh, compounded of friendship, games and books: a cricket ball in one pocket, a book in another. Not many years of later life are perhaps likely to share that golden *haze* even in retrospect.

Some schools have the virtues of their defects, is Sir Henry Newbolt's not too pungent comment on his own preparatory school at Caistor; and that, intermittently, is the general judgment. Two chapters of lyrical enthusiasm follow—to celebrate his five supremely happy years at Clifton. Indeed he fell in love with Clifton at first glimpse of it.

Francis Thompson was born three years before him—in 1859. As a child, he delighted in Scott, Coleridge and Macaulay. What is more unusual, he could in later life recall the *kind* of imaginative delight this early reading had given him. At school he said goodbye to childhood. He became, he says, 'a timid, shrinking little boy . . . teased and frightened'. How easy is an amiable shrug of an elderly shoulder at that word *teasing*. To him it was a torture—the torture of a sensitive boy, who, unlike most

386

Misfits

men, has virtually no privacy. He has no doubt of Shelley's 'terrible misery' at school. 'Those who think otherwise must forget their own past. Most people, we suppose, *must* forget what they were like when they were children. . . .' And if he meant that, while being able to remember childhood, they cannot 'become' as children again, we cannot question the statement. 'The malignity of my tormentors was more heart-lacerating than the pain itself', and it was accompanied by unutterable 'distresses of the mind', which it is in the nature of childhood to conceal.

Richard Middleton's school, St. Paul's, which in the 'nineties was in the Churchyard he describes as greasy with London soot and paved with gritty asphalt.

'I hated the stuffy malodorous classrooms, with their whistling gas-jets and noise of inharmonious life. I would have hated the yellow fogs had they not sometimes shortened the hours of my bondage. That five hundred boys shared this horrible environment did not abate my sufferings a jot; for it was clear that they did not find it distasteful. . . .' Misery is apt to be short-sighted.

An illness followed. He describes his first dubious glimpse in the twilight of the new boarding school. For perhaps the first time in his life, a strange boy speaks to him kindly. Another insisted that 'it was a jolly good thing to be different'. However that may be, at the end of the term 'I had learnt more of myself in three months than I had in all my life before, and from being a nervous, hysterical boy I had arrived at a complete understanding of my emotions, which I studied with an almost adult calmness of mind. I knew that in returning to the society of my healthy, boyish brothers, I was going back to a kind of life for which I was no longer fitted. . . . I saw further still. I saw that after a month at home I would not want to come back to school, and that I should have to endure another period of despondency. I saw that my whole school life would be punctuated by these violent uprootings. . . .'

3. *'But where am I? Into what subjects have I rushed?'*

Not that a school where punishments are trivial and persecution is unknown is necessarily the abode of sweetness and light, or even a hotbed of the sciences. Its follies may be as disastrous as its fees are high. There was little of the 'proud wobad' in

387

Early One Morning

Miss Cobbe, but, instead, a spirit of quicksilver and a heart of furious energy, if not of furious fancies. And her account of her schooldays, though, again, it takes us beyond childhood, is a telling foil to the masculine ones already given, and a revelation of the difference in atmosphere and odour and aim between the educations of the two sexes, at least in her day.

Her *Life*, she declared, was to be the complete history of a woman's existence as seen from within—a woman, too, who, while being a staunch claimant upon Women's Rights, admits with the utmost geniality that she herself had never been made to feel a Woman's Wrongs. The value claimed for her book is its evidence of how 'pleasant and interesting and useful' an existence is open to anyone of her own sex even though no man may ever desire to share it, and none may appear in it whom she would wish to ask her to do so! 'She should have been a man', said Monsieur Héger of Emily Brontë, 'a great navigator'; and one of Frances Cobbe's old friends once said to her laughingly, 'You know *you* are your father's *son*.' She appeals to her cranium for proof of it. Though 'dear Mrs. Somerville's little head', she says, 'which held three times as much as mine has ever done, was below the average of that of women', her own, with 'good, sound, working brains' inside it, was $23\frac{1}{4}$ inches in circumference and was 'larger than most of her countrymen's—doctors included'.

She rejoiced in particular at being 'well born'—in every sense. The windows of her roomy nursery at Newbridge looked down on an enchanting spectacle of dogs, cats, horses, grooms, gardeners and milkmaids; stable, coachhouse, kennels, laundry, dairy, carpenter's shop, granaries and fruit-loft. A world indeed for a watcher! She was 'a merry little chick with a round, fair face and an abundance of golden hair', but subject to furious fits of anger. At the age of seven, arrayed in a beautiful new sky-blue silk pelisse, she deliberately tumbled herself into a gutter full of melted snow in Bath one morning—in order that she could resume her 'little cloth coat'. With her cousin Charley, aged five, she extracted a tuft of hair from a savage bull in the cow yard, explored the roof of the house, and discussed theology. They both of them had Power for a second name, and therefore argued that they would both of them be assured of Paradise—'The heavens and all the Powers therein'.

Misfits

After a succession of four governesses of varying efficiency; after much poetry—Coleridge, Southey, Scott; history—Plutarch and Gibbon; also harmony and astronomy she was sent at fourteen to a boarding-school at Brighton to be 'finished off'. And she very nearly was. There follows the liveliest comparison between this and her mother's school of 1790, in Queen Square, Bloomsbury, kept by a Mrs. Devis, the author of an admirable Grammar and of a Geography. The girls in her mother's school had the usual book-learning, including well-spoken French, and were taught the harpsichord. But far more important in Mrs. Devis's eyes was the conviction that manners maketh woman. 'The abrupt speaking, courtesy-neglecting, slouching, slangy young damsel who may now perhaps carry off the glories of a University degree, would have seemed to Mrs. Devis still needing to be taught the very rudiments of feminine knowledge': decorum, grace, self-possession, calm. 'Every girl was dressed in the full fashion of the day', and Frances's mother, 'when she entered the school a blooming girl of fifteen', like all her companions, wore hair-powder and rouge on her cheeks—excellent rouge too 'at five guineas a pot'. They were trained in the Art of Society; suavity, courtesy, tact. 'We seem to have lost the tradition'.

Frances's school at Brighton was at No. 32 Brunswick Terrace. The nominal annual tariff of £120 was scarcely a quarter of the charges for extras. Her own two years at this academy cost £1000. It was locally referred to as the convent; but its youthful nuns were neither contemplative nor silent. 'The din of our large double schoolrooms was something frightful . . . four pianos might be heard going at once . . . while at numerous tables scattered about the rooms there were girls reading aloud to the governesses and reciting lessons in English, French, German, and Italian. . . . This hideous clatter continued the entire day.' There was no time for recreation, the daily hour's walk being given over to verbs. On Saturday afternoons there was an ordeal known as 'Judgement Day'. Solemnly sat the five-and-twenty 'damosels', anything but 'blessed', expecting their sentences. There was a fiendish conduct-marking system called 'cards'. Their sins confessed to, the offenders, aged nine to nineteen, were then severely reprimanded, and sat in the corner for the rest of the evening. Frances had seen as many as nine of them, heiresses and offshoots of the peerage among

Early One Morning

them, obliged 'like naughty babies . . . to sit for hours in the angles of the three rooms . . . with their faces to the wall', half of them being of marriageable age, and all of them dressed in full evening attire, silk or muslin, with gloves and kid slippers. The rest meanwhile were allowed to write home—provided that the envelopes were left unlicked.

Everything was taught 'in the inverse ratio of its true importance'; music and dancing at the top, morals and religion at the bottom. A girl was detected in a lie. "Don't you know . . ." said Miss R. impressively, "don't you know we had *almost* rather find you have a P—" (the mark for Pretty Well) "in your music, than that you should tell such falsehoods?" One Ash Wednesday the salt fish was followed by roast mutton. The preceptress *hoped* they would refrain from the mutton. "It would be good for your souls and your figures."

On the piano-playing and the harping and the singing, on the dancing and the calisthenics; on the French and the German and the Italian chattered all day long—'and such French, such German and such Italian!'—and on the study of 'English' faltering far in the rear; on the Galvanism and the Optics and the Hydrostatics; on the Arithmetic and the 'Religious instruction'—on all alike Miss Cobbe pours down the vials of her wrath, pausing only to deny that though in *Rose, Blanche and Violet* G. H. Lewes accurately describes the views of the girls of her day, they themselves were not, as he makes out, snobs. 'One of our heiresses,' she assures us, and also 'the granddaughter of a duke' were 'our constant butts for their ignorance and stupidity'; which, despite 'Miss R.', suggests a callous brightness *some*where. Heiresses or not, however, all that these unfortunate young women actually learned to hope for from life was to become an 'ornament of society'.

Her last term over, tucked up inside the Brighton coach, the Red Rover, and on her way home, Frances mused within herself, 'What a delightful thing it is that I have done with study! Now I may really enjoy myself. . . . I will not trouble my head with learning anything; but read novels and amuse myself for the rest of my life'. The way in which she utterly failed to keep this resolve might bring a blush to the cheek of the most learned of dons. Samuel Smiles compiled a book on the theme and entitled it *Self-Help*.

390

Misfits

4. 'Dozing out all his idle hours, And every night at play.'

This highly Victorian but fecund faculty may also show itself very early in life, and then often in a dense disguise. Robert Clive, when being questioned before a select committee of the House of Commons, became so incensed at last at the indignities thrust on him that he exclaimed, 'By heavens, Mr. Chairman, at this moment I stand astonished at my own moderation'. That can never have been his experience as a child. At the age of seven he had a violent temper, an impregnable will, and a boldness and intrepidity that no elder could daunt. He climbed the church steeple at Market Drayton and was observed by the townsfolk straddling a stone spout near the summit. He idled on from school to school—four of them in all—and was an incorrigibly 'naughty' boy. This bud 'of Brutus' land', none the less, suddenly finally *burst* into flower.

Arthur Wellesley was another idler, spirited but shy and meditative. Lounging against a great walnut tree in his school playground at Chelsea, he would watch and criticize the bouts between his schoolfellows; but nothing—not even the assaults of a party of five or six of them which he repelled with the utmost courage—could induce him to take a share. He was 'ugly Arthur' to his mother, and the family dunce, and at Eton 'displayed little aptitude for elegant scholarship'. But somewhere he was taught to be punctual. ' "I owe all I have achieved", he modestly explained, "to being ready a quarter of an hour before it was necessary to be so; and I learned that lesson when a boy".' The other wayside lesson for which he is renowned I have never seen in print. Merely being commonsensical in the highest degree is perhaps one of *the* marks of genius—between the frenzies. Genius, says Coventry Patmore, is 'high, prompt and invincible good sense'—whatever the age of him whom it possesses.

Edmund Waller as a child was dull and slow—an exemplification of the hare-and-tortoise fable. William Bell Scott describes himself as stupid—but *that* really stupid people very seldom do. Abraham Cowley had so wretched a memory that he could not retain the ordinary rules of grammar; so 'he got the Greek and

Early One Morning

Roman languages as he had done his own, not by precept but use'. He practised them as 'a native'.

So too, when he was ten years old, John Hunter, the great surgeon, could scarcely be taught even the elements of reading and writing. Latin had to be abandoned. Like the Duke in exile in the forest of Arden he spent his time in country amusements, was apprenticed to a carpenter when he was twenty, and, the carpenter failing, joined his brother William in London. He then discovered that he was a born dissector. In his private museum he amassed over ten thousand specimens.

But for sheer joy in the subtle ways of this wanton world, what could excel the tale told of himself by Sir Joseph Banks, the famous naturalist and President of the Royal Society, who equipped the ship that carried Cook on his first voyage round the world. Active and endlessly venturesome, he was, when a boy, so immoderately fond of play that he was never seen at Eton to be reading a book in his spare time until he was fourteen. And why was he reading then?—

'One fine summer evening, he bathed in the Thames, as usual, with other boys, but having stayed a long time in the water, he found, when he came to dress himself, that all his companions were gone: he was walking leisurely along a lane, the sides of which were richly enamelled in flowers'. Flowers: he stopped to look at them, exclaiming to himself. 'How beautiful!' And in this instant of strange in-sight, yet in the most rational fashion, he began to reflect that since it was his father's command that he should learn Greek and Latin, it was his duty to do so, but that since these flowers of nature were more natural than either, he would learn about *them* for himself. So he took to botany (not poetry); and would pay sixpence for any piece of information he thought worth it from the women who 'culled simples' for the apothecaries' shops. This was in 1757. This boy, these flowers, the evening sun—is not this yet another example of what may be termed a conversion of the mind? A moment's light-filled silence may be all that is needed; though it takes a Trump to wake the dead.

'There exist moments in life', says Mr. P. D. Ouspensky of his boyhood in *A New Model of the Universe*, which are 'linked together by their inner content and by a certain singular sensation peculiar to them. Several such moments always recur to my mind together, and I feel then that it is these that have determined the chief trend of my life. . . .' He continues:

'I am a schoolboy in the second or third "class". But instead of Zeifert's Latin grammar, entirely consisting of exceptions which I sometimes see in my dreams to this day, or Evtushevsky's "Problems", with the peasant who went to town to sell hay, and the cistern to which three pipes lead, I have before me Malinin and Bourenin's "Physics". I have borrowed this book from one of the older boys and am reading it greedily and enthusiastically, overcome now by rapture, now by terror, at the mysteries which are opening before me. All round me walls are crumbling, and horizons infinitely remote and incredibly beautiful stand revealed. It is as though threads, previously unknown and unsuspected, begin to reach out and bind things together. For the first time in my life my world emerges from chaos. Everything becomes connected, forming an orderly and harmonious whole. I understand, I link together, a series of phenomena which were disconnected and appeared to have nothing in common.

'But what am I reading?

'I am reading the chapter on levers. . . .

All central events in life are events not only of moment but of a particular moment. And experiences of this nature in childhood and in boyhood must be far more frequent than may be assumed. Ebenezer Elliott, for instance, a shy and morbid boy and a dullard at four different schools, was working in his father's foundry when he was sixteen. his only promise being that of turning out 'a sad drunken dog'. While there he chanced on Sowerby's *English Botany*. The picture of a primrose led him into the fields—and thence, inestimable journey, to poetry. Even when he was only four years old John Galt 'got out of bed by break of day one morning' and hastened into the garden, after a few days' absence from it, to see the sprouting narcissuses he had left behind him. And 'Lo! they were in blossom'—sheer magic. 'From that day I became passionately fond of flowers.'

Every great man, again, was once a child: Buddha, Plato, Leonardo, Thomas Aquinas, Confucius, Goethe, Bach. Were they not then, as children compared with other children, what they were as men compared with other men? Is there any virtual and essential change in kind between a child and a man? A child recognizes,

Early One Morning

realizes, acquires, becomes articulate, grows; but the acorn is so much the oak that it can become no other *kind* of tree; and the man made rich is still the man who was once poor.

CHAPTER XXX

THE HIDDEN

★

1. *'Hame, hame, hame, hame, fain wad I be'.*

B ut even if a child were sent to school in the loveliest of the
Islands of the Blest, and in the greenest of its valleys sate
among the birds with his book, St. Francis for headmaster
and cherubim for schoolfellows, he might still be homesick. He might be homesick for a miserable hovel in a sunless slum,
and not a blade of grass or a green leaf within sight. It is a peculiar
imbecility in human nature—this passionate pining for the familiar,
for solitude, for the loved, of which even Emily Brontë nearly
died. But it appears to be incurable. It may be a spectre at one's
deathbed, and a lifelong hindrance to sharing the amenities of
'the Others' and the charms of human society.

In mute childhood it has not even the merit of measles or the
mumps, since it does not affect the temperature, is not contagious,
and can recur acutely with every departure from home, having no
remedy but exhaustion, and exciting little compassion even in a
fellow victim. The silly tears that have been shed in secret on this
score alone would fill to over-flowing

'the dim lake of Auber
In the misty mid region of Weir.'

Fear of the future, a craving for a certain state of self and spirit
and perhaps for certain company of the mind are other strands of
the malady; and few griefs in later life can be compared with it
for torment so dark and so profound. Little by little, possibly,
even poor little Erics may accustom themselves to the Busby and
the Bully; but there are fortunate-unfortunate souls who never in

Early One Morning

this world will accustom themselves even to being happy for long together in strange places, and who cannot endure having their roots disturbed.

Fielding was aged forty-seven when he set sail on his last voyage. 'On this day the most melancholy sun I had ever beheld arose, and found me awake at my house at Fordhook. By the light of the sun I was, in my own opinion, last to behold and take leave of some of those creatures on whom I doted with a mother-like fondness'. To the sickness of his body were joined these pangs of leaving home. 'She [his own nature] drew me in to suffer the company of my little ones, during eight hours; and I doubt whether in that time I did not undergo more than in all my distemper. At twelve precisely my coach was at the door. . . .'

But what young barbarian at play would suspect a *master* of this? 'But I may,' wrote William Cory to a friend, on leaving Eton in 1872, 'I may, very likely, sicken for want of work: no more scolding, no more punctual early rising. . . . I could hardly have lived through the summer half, knowing all the while it was the last, and grudging the days and wandering like a ghost in the playgrounds. . . . I break my heart every day in the partings; and I could not have gone through the summer with so much sorrow— the lonely half-holidays would have been insupportably pathetic.' But there was another side to the account: 'I am really enjoying my liberty. I was tired of that inevitable and manurious street, tired of being a "myope", exposed to the fire of 900 young scoffers, but not tired of teaching, and still, more than ever, devoted to the few boys that seek me or like me'.

Partly for shame and partly because the worst pangs are long over, partly because perhaps the crisis is taken for granted and was so often repeated, there are not many references in autobiography to the recurrent ordeal in childhood of 'going back', and of, when gone, languishing to be home again. A letter from Stevenson and another from Stopford Brooke (when he was in his seventeenth year!) at least sketch the condition.

'No letter from home'—'I am half distracted about it,' writes Stopford Brooke to his mother. Only a long one, he says, would allay his woe a little. His head is aching with disappointment. And so the letter proceeds, his spirit bandied to and fro between longing, grief, indignation and reproach. He despairs at time's 'lazy,

396

The Hidden

groaning pinions', and tortures himself with a description of the blissful fireside at home, imagining what each of his loved ones would be doing there. And the open and reiterated refrain of this lament is, 'I am *heartily* sick and weary of school', and that yet even a word from home might alleviate his sorrow.

Mother-sickness may be no less acute. The following letter from Victor Hugo was written at the age of thirteen, not from school, but from home. It is dated August 2, 1815.

'My dear Mamma,—We are very dull here since you left. We often go to see M. Foucher, as you told us to do. He proposed to us to join in the lessons his sons are taking; we thanked him and declined. Every morning we work at Latin and mathematics. A letter with a black seal, and addressed to Abel, came the evening you went away. M. Foucher will send it on to you. He was kind enough to take us to the museum. . . . Come home soon. We don't know what to say or do without you; we are quite lost. We are always thinking of you. Mamma, mamma!—Your dutiful son Victor.'

And here, from another century, is Dorothy Plumpton writing home not from school but from the household of her stepmother's mother—a kinship that in her case was not less than kind—where she had been 'placed'. She writes, says Miss Dorothy Gardiner in her *English Girlhood at School*, to beg her father 'to send for me to come home to you', or 'to send a servant of yours to my lady and to me, and shew now by your fatherly kyndnesse that I am your child, for I have sent you dyverse messuages and wryttings and I had never answere againe. Wherefore yt is thought in this parties by those persones that list better to say ill than good, that ye have litle favour unto me; the which error ye may now quench yf yt will like you to be so good and kynd father unto me. Also I besech you to send me a fine hatt and some good cloth to make me some kevercheffes. And thus I besech Jesu to have you in his blessed keeping to his pleasure and your harts desire and comforth. . . .' The very rhythm of these sentences betokens the forlornness of a loving heart.

Lord Berners too in his *First Childhood*—and he was a resolute child and critical of his home life—describes his first night at school when he was nine:

Early One Morning

'Misery descended upon me with the darkness. For a long time I lay awake. So apparently did most of the other occupants of the dormitory, for the air was full of the sound of muffled sobbing.

'Through a chink in the blinds I could see that there was bright moonlight outside, and through the half-open window I could hear the nocturnal sounds of the country, the lowing of cattle in a neighbouring field, the cry of a night-bird, the whistle of a distant train (wending its way northwards perhaps, in the direction of Althrey), and from the garden below there came up a faint scent of lilac. Now that the turmoil of human contact had died away, all these things reminded me poignantly of my far-off home. . . .

'I remembered the four volumes of *British Birds* in my locker. These seemed now to constitute the only link with home life.'

'The only link'! My early and daily walk at school was along the Thames Embankment, and bound for the dark granite of the austere Waterloo Bridge. Low tide or brimming, winter or summer, how grossly I often wasted 'the beauty of the morning', since I can recall envying beyond words the butcher boys—reins between finger and thumb—lolling back on their bowling cart-fulls of raw meat. Carefree, blissful Jehus, they were driving *home*!

'Most wretched men', wrote Shelley when he was twenty-five,

'Are cradled into poetry by wrong:
They learn in suffering what they teach in song.'

And many of them *from* the cradle. Yet this *per se* wholly fails to explain why poets are so few, or to deny that in Utopia one might well go to school only to happiness and, having done so, teach in a different kind of song. There is on the other hand no question that experience not merely of unhappiness but of what might appear to be deadly misery feeds the imagination, and, salved and pacified at last, may in time produce the unlikeliest fruit.

'I think Affliction', says Perdita, 'may subdue the Cheeke, but not take in the Mind.' So may it be with unhappy children—but in the long run. And there are two chief kinds of children of promise, each complementary to the other. 'Build up the imagination of the boy of action', says Mr. Kurt Hahn; and 'make the sensitive dreamer work for and love the common cause.'

The Hidden

2. 'But truth is truth, and muste be tolde, Though danger keepe the doore.'

All knowledge is childhood's province, even if, like Coleridge's 'beauteous boy' in the wilderness, encinctured only by a twine of leaves, a child is fated to stray along sad and narrow paths in search of it. And the instilling of the knowledge of sex—with how enigmatic a smile must Nature greet any such statement!—is *still*, four thousand years after the Flood, one of the thorniest problems for parent and pedagogue. Is it even possible to be serenely wise on behalf of the young in this matter, when our own minds for the most part are in so squalid a confusion? Crime and sex are the staple mainstays of modern fiction, the one treated usually with a sublime amorality and objectiveness; the other, which, whatever it may owe to the science of dreams, is probably the bastard offspring of the Victorian love-story, in a very different fashion.

To imagine that a few simple, dewy and veracious sentences in reply to a child's forthright enquiries on the subject, enquiries which may have welled up from many solitary ponderings none the less, and may begin at the age of two, will immediately and finally still and placate the secret stirrings of its own physical and mental consciousness, resembles assuring some young terrified creature just come out of the dark, 'But look! darling! Here is a *taper!*' Still, in this as in much else the right mother is probably 'worth a hundred schoolmasters'—and abysmally aware the latter may be of it. And a nursery phalanx of brothers and sisters may cancel out, say, seven sexologists. That nursery has its own fixed frontiers. Passports for adults are cautiously issued, even if adult regulations may be as welcome as they are effective.

Whatever simplifications, too, scientific knowledge may dictate, even the man of science, like most of his fellow-creatures, is likely to remain an overgrown child in these matters. He also has been to school. His simplifications are concerned with what remains a mystery, and is itself a trinity-in-unity pervading body, mind and spirit. Every love-poem flowers from this antediluvian soil, as does every obscene scrawl in a privy. No work of the imagination is devoid of its influence, nor even perhaps any profound personal judgement. The mere attempt to marshal the kinds of humour

Early One Morning

'Sex' is nowadays productive of—witty or tolerant or vindictive or tired-out or smirking or putrid; and to observe its gradations from burning-sun-colour or verdigris green to tropical black, gives a hint of its range. And I am conscious of prejudice; for without sex and its activities, the very subject of this book would have been denied to its author!

The majority of young children, and even those seething with 'polymorphous perversities', appear to accept life's physical routine as naturally as they welcome life itself. As to their 'reasons' for things, they live chiefly from hand to mouth, but may be quick to detect the false and the faked. Even young children within their measure can be straightforwardly animal, and in their humour, at times, *sextodecimo* editions of Rabelais. Some are by nature of a coarse fibre, and remain so; some catch or are taught depravity, and, by example or precept, may become intentionally lewd and poisonous. But the word *wrath* in 'a Catechism' signifies, as I understand it, God's 'righteous indignation' at the Old Adam and Eve, not with the unchristened. If a child once acquire a bleared or distorted or a fatuously cramped or finical view of its bodily functions, its influence may skulk in the mind for years like a rat in a garbage heap, its furtive and sinister rustlings never stilled.

Most English autobiographers keep both the rat and the rat-fanciers, if they encountered them, to themselves. 'There was lewd company among us', 'debauchees', says Roger North, 'but I was not forward enough to be taken into their gang though I, like others, was very desirous to come up to the state of manhood most shewed, as I thought, by the conversation of women.' Edward Calamy refers to 'several childish sallies of corruption', on which he was still reflecting with shame and concern; but he refrains from specifying them. Even at the age of six, it will be remembered, Southey had seen 'much more of the evil side of human nature' in his first school 'than I should ever have learned in the course of domestic education'. There are more or less veiled allusions elsewhere. And to some of those memoirists who have made no faintest mention of it one can guess what a hideous woe lewd company at its first onset must have been. Football, flogging, dulness, logarithms, *Goody Two Shoes* and newspapers appear in the index to John Timb's *School-Days of Eminent Men*, but neither bullies nor morals nor vice. Our fathers and grandfathers,

400

The Hidden

worldly-wise or otherwise, seem to have concluded that at any
rate in print, 'The potent poyson quite ore-crowes my spirit. . . .
The rest is silence'.

Henry James, the theologian, and the father of William and
Henry, had pronounced views on this question. He said in reference to Emerson, 'He took a downright literal view of the reality
of men's moral differences, and I have even heard him tell with
infinite gusto of some virtuous youth in college with him, who had
such a gross faculty of moral effusion as actually to suppress all
naughty conversation among his companions by his bare presence
—which made me wonder what a pitch of spiritual idiocy this
moral peacock, if left to himself, would be sure eventually to
attain to. Only we are none of us left to ourselves, nor can be,
fortunately.'

A chapter in Mr. Forrest Reid's *Apostate*, however, casts a beam
of light on these dark places. A young philatelist from a public
school had come to see him, at home. This visitor had dark, rather
sad, rather dull eyes, and thick clumsy short-nailed fingers. And
he presently stole over and locked the door. His aim was an initiation into the mysteries of sex. He discovered he had a stubborn
and wary pupil. In a husky, uneven bass he at last offered a free
choice from all his rarities. 'And then I knew he was frightened'.
Those eyes and fingers recall to me a memoried portrait of well
over fifty years ago; and if I had the skill of an artist I could paint
from memory a certain boy who one afternoon confided to me a
shred of perfectly harmless information on the subject of obstet-
rics, straight from Priapus's mouth—a god whose sacrifices included asses and perhaps the foals of asses. I recollect the very
expression on his flushed mock-innocent face, and the actual
asphalted City spot of the occasion; which suggests how indelible
these impressions may be. He found me ignorant of this very
rudimentary fact, but informable, and left me confused. In *his*
recollection of that little secret talk it may be *he* was the novitiate!
The mystery is that out of the foundered past—including how
many congested hours spent on the Greek irregular verbs!—this
petty if not sordid episode should remain as distinctly fixed in my
mind as a minute knot in an oak plank. But such is *human* nature.

It is certainly not less odd that in spite of my prudish confusion, and unless memory deceives me, I can recall no relevant

passage in the Old Testament whose meaning to me when a child
—and I sometimes heedfully pondered certain passages—seemed
not in essence to be as it were innate. Is this the indictment of a
'knowing' child? *Mens mala, malus animus.* 'The secrets of the farm
and field,' says Sir Henry Newbolt, 'are a necessary part of knowledge, but one that few find it possible to teach.' It is a summary
echoed in a fragment already borrowed from *The Innocent Eye*.

3. *'Little may an old horse do if he may not neye.'*

B ut this is to range beyond childhood; and in these last few
pages many kinds of children have been observed casting off
yet another skin and transforming themselves into 'young persons'. From the pangs of nostalgia and 'sex' let us turn home again
to those first and early memories with which we are chiefly
concerned. Even from what has been so flagrantly torn from its
context and forced into comparison with similar extracts, one conclusion at least conspicuously emerges: namely, that life may be as
inexhaustible at the age of seven as it may happily prove to be at
the age of seventy.

What, with few exceptions, these recollections of childhood
have had in common, and however dismal at times their burden
may have been, is an eager, sharp-cut zest, with joy and animation in the telling, and this even though the most garish of autobiographies is but as a play of shadows compared with the brilliant
and ardent sunshine of life, or, reveals, rather, but instantaneous
gleams of that sunshine, through peepholes into oblivion. And
even an hour's quiet observation of a young and busy child will
suffice to suggest what that oblivion conceals.

Every remembrance of childhood too consists of highly complicated parts. Its apparent unity is but a shell. It may hide in itself a
life and virtue we cannot now retrieve. So the most trivial of
objects will at times take to itself a momentary luminous beauty
and meaningfulness. The beauty, the apparent 'meaning' fade
away; the object remains, but the magic is past recapture. Its
moment was the revelation of an inward treasury. 'Each new year
is a surprise to us,' says Thoreau. 'We find that we had virtually
forgotten the note of each bird, and when we hear it again it is

remembered like a dream, reminding us of a previous state of existence': but only reminding us.

Such memories in every scanty hoard have none the less a pronounced likeness. The squirrel within stores up common nuts and acorns, but once they are safe in his larder they become his. Like bats in a mute and dusty belfry, memories may remain asleep, not only for a winter but for years; yet if furtive touch or ray of lantern arouse them they will prove to be *our* bats. It is astonishing, too, how amiably and naturally an old man may hobnob with his infancy. Even St. Augustine's bitter remorse at his wanton boyhood is less on account of a dead self than over an intensely alive truant come safely home.

In the telling of what *is* told a harmless vanity may show itself— as if no one else, apart from the memoirist, had ever been young, as if his memories were not mere spectral relics of the dead and gone but resurrected Eurekas; as to him indeed they are.

In general the recalled misdeeds, stupidities and failures of childhood are as easily forgiven as others must have been forgotten. 'I have lingered by the past,' says Sidney Dobell,

'As by a death-bed, with unwonted love,
And such forgiveness as we bring to those
Who can offend no more.'

It is none the less true that we may owe to ourselves when we were children some of the worst handicaps we labour under in our later life. And we extend this charity—or tolerance—to others.

Some outstanding tyrant or tormentor, sneak or bully or worse, may remain as repellent in recollection as he was in fact. But this is unusual. The old helpless fear and hatred, the rankling injuries, the greenhorn grudges, slights, humiliations, rebuffs die away out of the mind. Those we loved in childhood remain in memory to bless us; its foes are for the most part become shadows.

On the whole indeed it is the adults who spoil children, the affected 'child-lovers', the anxiously well-meaning, the patronizers, the mock-juveniles who in recollection suffer most. Hardship wears better in memory than pampering; inevitable pain than fumbling over the administration of it. Children who are neither merely sharp nor clever may be quick to detect incompetence, the sham, conceited stupidity, favouritism, injustice, malice, bribes.

and wily palaver. As if by a sixth sense, they know whom they like, including perhaps the gruff and grim; they enjoy the outspoken and downright, appreciate the matter-of-fact, respect a reasonable selfishness, and adore the queerest of heroes. They can be passionately grateful for the smallest of mercies; patient as Griselda with those whom they love and indulge; and incarnate icebergs to the unapproved of.

Unusual sensibility, of course, is hard to cope with, if only for one reason out of many—that it is secretive. There are 'sad and sepulchral pitchers that have no joyful voices', and we must incline our hearts as well as our ears to listen to them. The smart, sly and clever promise more than they perform—may just stay clever; and the stupid may soon tire trouble out. But seeming stupidity may be due to a highly individualised way of mentalizing things, and to what is a scarcely conscious determination in the self within to pursue its own ends in its own fashion. 'We must be right by nature', says Goethe, 'that good thoughts may come before us like children of God, and cry "Here we are".'

All young children perpetually delude us by their stature. His 'exterior semblance' cannot but belie *any* 'six years darling of a pygmy size'. There could be no more disarming mask of what is within than his own young, stolid, absent, grimacing, scowling, shy or heedless face. His silence is embarrassing enough. But his very accents deceive us—that piping voice, politely exchanging sentiments befitting the no-man's-land that all but always lies between the adult and the child; while his chief aim and hope may be that he shall be left at peace—and especially from anxious, fumbling and edifying enquirers.

The more unusual the child, the more likely he is to want his own way and quietly to ensure that he gets it. Like an unquestioning faith in God, or an all-hospitable love of humanity, a rarely gifted mind in childhood is its own reward. It is self-sufficing; and its revelations come chiefly in solitude. It may realise its own good fortune and yet be unaware how unusual it is; though experience will soon expose the danger of manifesting an extreme originality. It learns caution and then may flourish unperceived. But even if this were not so, if in lieu of the ducal strawberry mark an infinitesimal fleur-de-lis branded, between his shining eyes, the brows of every child of genius, would that child, in respect not

The Hidden

merely to its own true welfare but to its future work in the world, be greatly the better off? In Utopia, yes; but here and now?

In the case of a richly promising child, God proposes, and too often man disposes. However that may be, a conscientious school-master, I should imagine, would far prefer a wholly worthy and manageable class of well-nourished goslings to the sole charge of a cygnet of Avon—if only for the reason that he might feel bound to attempt to teach this *rara avis* to teach itself to fly.

There are many methods, ancient and modern, of 'bringing up' children, and one of them is that of the Old Woman who lived in a Shoe. And what more obvious symbol than a shoe could there be for the journey that never ends? She had, it will be remembered, '*so* many', not *too* many children. She gave them some broth (a 'decoction', says the Dictionary, especially that in which meat is boiled—the English word itself being connected with *brew*!) 'Without any bread': doubtless because what she had in the pan was either too new, or was stale. She then whipped them, not just by ones or twos, but *all* round, share and share alike, in view no doubt of the wintry weather. Then she sent them to bed—where they could listen to stories of their own making or remembering, and talk and daydream until the 'gentle sleep from Heaven' should slide into their souls and fill their morning buckets with dew!

PART III

EARLY WRITINGS

CHAPTER XXXI

JOURNALS

*

1. *'The Wren with little quill.'*

To turn from recollections of childhood to the writings of children is less to change the subject than the point of view. The former resemble detached glimpses of a wide, familiar, but remote landscape, seen by a balloonist through the rifts of a cloudy sky. The engrossed occupant cannot descend. From a multitude of such glimpses we can piece together a fragmentary chart which we can compare with early memories of our own and with direct and heedful observations of children. They will represent, as we have seen, what range and what kind of experience children possess to write *about*. But to ponder a moment on the accounts given by Leigh Hunt of his childhood solitude, by William Hutton of the mob and the pillory, by Blair of that moment of 'inwit' in the morning sunshine, by Edmund Gosse, in his infancy, of the purloining of the leg of mutton, is to realize that though one and all of them may be both true and accurate, none could have been related precisely *like that* by the children involved in them.

Not that any detail so recorded was absent in early consciousness, only that the child concerned could not precisely thus have seen himself or expressed himself in words. He had neither the telescope nor the vocabulary. But that seems all that we need to allow for in such accounts. What, however, for their complete meaning's sake should be added—childhood's senses and sensibility, childhood's full and peculiar consciousness—is perhaps beyond us, as in large measure it was beyond even the memoirists themselves.

With a child's writings a different caution is desirable. We must

Early One Morning

avoid reading too much of the adult into them, and at the same time endeavour to discover all that his words actually meant to *him*. Their range of reference will be far less ample than our own. Those that express his feelings may conceal more than we suspect —that cry of 'Mother, mother!' for example, at the conclusion of Victor Hugo's letter, as sharp with forlorn longing as an old folk-song of the Hebrides. As for his imagination, a child can flit as swiftly from real to fantasy as Ariel himself. Unless at any rate the children now living are more imaginative than their elders appear to be, then heaven's lights are going out, and the future is dark indeed.

We must beware too of imitation, the second-hand, and of lip-service; also, if need be, of external aid and supervision. A great many letters for example written in childhood are duty-letters, though affection or vanity or the loving wish to please may have been jam to their powder. And the shadow of parent or aunt or pedagogue may have darkened the paper. What more fantastic irony has life to offer than the old-fashioned, set letter home from school?

Above all, we must keep in mind a child's difficulties. He may be able to talk with the utmost freedom. When, too, he begins to dictate some shapeless and vehement 'story', pausing only, like one child I could name, to stand on his head, not as an old wives' cure for the colic, but in an instinctive effort to enliven his ideas, it is his amanuensis who may tire first. Children who can neither read nor scrawl their ABC may be able to extemporize at ease. But writing of any kind, as so many masters of the art have confessed, is a very different matter.

Walter Scott tells of a schoolfellow who was always at the top of the class they shared. He noticed that whenever this paragon was calling upon his memory, he twiddled one of the buttons on his waistcoat. His rival seized an opportunity to snip this off. Next morning, the victim, his button gone, fumbled, faltered, failed, and down he went. The adult author may suffer in a contrary fashion. Feverishly eager, luminous with ideas, ardent to gratify his publisher, he may sit down at his table, and the very touch of finger on pen may at once coagulate his vocabulary. Even Rousseau confesses that the abundance of his ideas and the impetuosity of his feelings often made composition impossible. The

Journals

very sight of ink and paper dumbed his mind. 'Many of my periods have been turned and turned again five or six nights in my head before they were fit to be set down on paper'. Even a letter on the most trifling subject cost him hours of fatigue.

But for a young child, not only may any chance of privacy be rare, the sheer labour involved in the use of a pen is also prodigious. His briefest scrap of writing, then, while it may be little short of an insult to his actual wits, can be a telling tribute to his character. We shall sometimes have to guess at his target merely by observing his aim.

All this allowed for, is there any reason why we should trust what he does manage to put on paper less fully and confidently than we trust the writings of his elders? A child is less able than they to conceal himself of set intent. He may in some degree conceal himself *to* himself; and this we may detect. It need not be, then, because a child has little to express that what he succeeds in communicating is likely to be bare, broken, jejune, seldom very near his heart, and, at any stretch, tedious. In fact, he may have far too much. Nor of course are his attempts of any intrinsic or literary value *because* of his age. Something of his own life may be in them that is beyond price in spite of that age; but for the most part they are worth study far less for their own sake, than for his and childhood's. It is therefore advisable to enjoy them (if we can) in small doses—as perhaps would the angel Gabriel even the *Paradise Lost*.

The specimens, apparently genuine and spontaneous, that follow, have, with few exceptions, already appeared in print, and are mainly the work of children who lived to be famous. That is their chief interest. They also have the advantage of being less impeded than usual by the lack of any gift for words. There is no great abundance of them to choose from; for such things, even if they are treasured and hoarded for a while, are apt to vanish like snow in April. There must be many others of a similar kind that have evaded a random net. As for the sea of the present, it simply swarms with similar fry. The quantity of ink consumed every day by the children of England in the composition of letters and exercises, essays, rhymes and fiction would suffice a myriad Bacons for their complete life's work. Much of it may be welcomed work. Otherwise, the tears alone refrained from or spent on its account would suffice for a complete summer daybreak's dew.

Early One Morning

My borrowings here then have been very slender. And since a diary or journal is one of the most personal and private of all kinds of writing, and published examples of them written by children are rare, I will begin with these.

> 2. *'Why did I write? what sin to me unknown*
> *Dipt me in ink, my parents', or my own?'*

Although an English diary is apt to prefer facts to confessions, we still hope somewhere in its pages to meet its author face to face. The following extract from a diary of 1842, for example, is clearly the work of a cultivated mind—one too of a certain bent, and as anxious to be informed as to record information. What precise kind of fellow creature does it reflect?

'Near Rhydland is Penwarn, the seat of Lord Mostyn; the house is small and unpretending, the grounds are beautiful. There is a very handsome dog-kennel, in which are kept forty-four couple of fine fox-hounds ready for work, besides old ones in one kennel, and young ones in another: the dogs all in such good order and kennels so perfectly clean. In one field were sixteen hunters without shoes. . . . About eight miles from Rhyl is Trelacre, the seat of Sir Pyers Mostyn, a very excellent modern building; the grounds are laid out with most luxuriant taste, nothing is wanting to give effect to it as a whole. In the woods opposite the house is a rich but rather formal distribution of flower-beds, everything appeared to be in blossom. On an elevation is placed the most ingeniously contrived Grotto, at every turn there is a device of another character to the last, here a lion couchant, there the head of Momus, a wild boar's head, a heron, a skeleton, &c., &c. . . .

'The church at Dyserth has an east window which is considered the greatest antiquity in Wales, many figures of the saints are represented in coloured glass, the lead betwixt the panes is the breadth of two fingers. The yard has several old trees—two very fine yews, and certainly the largest birch for miles round.'

Would any word of this surprise us if we learned that the diarist was aged eighty? He was, in fact, eight. It is Philip Hamerton, evidently a 'little pitcher', writing 'to please his father', but still 'very observant' on his own account. This was absolutely the last year in his life, he says, in which he could live 'in happy ignorance

Journals

of evil'. The delight that his diary reveals in beautiful materials, he tells us, was wholly his own, and never left him. But 'I had acquired a way of talking about things as older people talk . . . and the reader will remember that I had been learning Latin for more than two years'. But had he written in words of one syllable, with spelling to match, the aim and interest behind them would have been the same. It is the quantity and quality of the *meaning* in any sentence that alone counts—whatever the age of its writer. The extract from a *Household Gazette* of 1883 that follows suggests a seasoned, easy-going traveller, with an ironic eye. It is Gilbert Sheldon, then twelve years old.

'On Wednesday April 11th Miss Lilian Sheldon drove to Eastnor and back by the Kilbury Camp in the invalid carriage together with Mr. Gilbert Sheldon. This gentleman has been so kind as to give us a detailed account of this "jaunt" which I subjoin:—

'Last summer it was an almost daily occurence for me to drive out in the invalid carriage, sometimes to a great distance. Of late however riding has been more in vogue than driving and consequently the donkey had got rather unused to being driven. When therefore it was decided that a grand drive was to be taken serious fears were expressed as to whether the donkey's pace would be of the most rapid. At length at 9.15 on the morning of April 11th our stately equipage drove up to the door and having been packed up and put comfortable we set forth on our journey. Up to the top of "Gardener's" the road is not very interesting, though the view is lovely, to those who are driving. It is nearly all downhill to Eastnor Park gates which are reached in fifty minutes. There we have a notice given us asking us to confine ourselves to the paths. As we can't very well do anything else, even if we'd liked, the temptation is not very strong. There is quite a change of scene now that we are on the Ridgeway. Before we have had a glorious view and the horizon was almost unbounded, now the sides of the roads are flanked by trees and shrubs which as the Guide Books say, are of most luxuriant growth. And among these trees lurk squirrels, some of which we now and again caught sight of, and once we see a cock pheasant hard by. But we don't stay long for soon the gate of the Deer Park looms in front and through it we drive. No fear of a big buck attacking us today, for the deer are shy and get out of our way in a great hurry. Our charger evidently thinks that the deer are young donkeys and wants to go and speak to them. But soon we join the highroad and leaving deer and Deer Park behind us jog on towards Ledbury. Then the Sómers Arms, which looks a very suitable place for a "Blue Pig" [the generic family name for the sign of a pub where one could bait man and beast] comes in sight and then a pleasant old farmhouse, which we learn from the map is called The White House. Near this latter place we sit down and have lunch, wondering meanwhile whether a lane which turns off at this point and saving a great corner is practicable or no. But a carter coming up at this juncture informs in very broad Herefordshire, that we should do better if we stuck to the highway. This advice we accordingly follow and are soon on the highroad to Malvern again. After an arduous pull, on the donkey's part, up Chance's Pitch and the last, but not the least, hill outside the Winnings we get home again, having gone the round in 4½ hours.'

'This gentleman', it may be added, was one of those children whom a physical handicap appears to make only the more eager and intent to reach a definite goal. The handicap becomes an incentive. The chart indeed depicting Gilbert Sheldon's later English travels—coloured inks denoting the vehicle used, whether bicycle, dog-cart or motor car—resembles in its webbings that which must have been kept unfathomably secret by the Old Man of the Mountain concerning the routes and itineraries of his 'Assassins'.

Emily Shore was born at Potton near Biggleswade on Christmas Day, 1819, and kept a journal regularly for eight years—from the age of eleven and a half to within a few weeks of her death, from consumption of the lungs—when she was nearly twenty. 'I need not say', says its editor in his introduction, 'that she went to no High School, no College, no Lectures, passed no Examination, and competed with no rivals; her teaching was that of Nature and of Love'—'though much, very much was done by herself. She made her whole existence a happy schoolroom'—the word school, after all, being derived from a Greek word meaning *leisure*.

No trace of any other hand—though omissions have been made—appears in its pages. There is nothing affected, if there are faint tinges of the prim. There are a few self-communings but very few careless raptures. There is little self-consciousness but a serene self-confidence, together with a humour and wit and irony not the less effective for being quiet. In all she does, and in all she says, a constant care is evident. Her intense and heedful delight in nature, reading, and solitude shine out as spontaneously as does her love for those she loved. 'Our Court shall be a little Achademe'.

Three years before her *Journal* was begun she produced (in paper covers) her first *opus*, entitled:—

'NATURAL HISTORY, by Emily Shore, being an Account of Reptiles, Birds, and Quadrupeds, *Potton, Biggleswade, Brook House, 1828, June 15. Price 1 shilling.*'

Reptiles and all occupied sixteen pages of pencilled writing in 'a clear childish hand', and with very few mis-spellings. Here is a brief extract:

'Towards the end of spring, in the month of May, the rose and currant trees are greatly infested by an insect called the green fly. These insects are little more than a quarter of a quarter of an inch in length. They have six legs, each about the length of their bodies. These legs are thinner than a hair. They have three tails, each of which are black.' Thus the *aphis* is explored, and a footnote adds: 'The tails of these insects are very curious. One tail, which is green all over, sticks out horizontally behind; the two others, which are black, stick out higher up, and rather perpendicularly. . . . They have two feelers placed on the top of their heads. Their legs have one joint. Here is a drawing of this little insect. . . .'

For comparison with this piece of minute observation, which few rose-growers will stay to check, here is Edmund Gosse at the age of nine (her own at this time) on a similar subject. Emily by the way gives both the Latin *and* English names to her flowers.

'My dearest Papa, The Idotea is dead in the large tank and we think 1 astrina gibbeossa to. My catterpiller has changed its skin, it looks beautiful, it has changed the colour of its toes from black to pink, it is now sitting on the edge of the top of a primula leaf which I find it eats as well as dandelion, and I hope it will soon begin to eat . . . all the seeds which you sowed my side of the garden are up, Convolvolus minor looks best, Convolvolus major is coming up in my salt-cellar in-doors. I have put away 259 of my shells, 22 of which I wish to question you about as I do not know what they are. . . .'

Two hundred and fifty-nine! Before Emily Shore was eleven

years old her *Natural History* was followed by a *History of the Jews*. It contained an Introduction, an Index, 'a beautiful map, and twelve illustrations, composed out of her own head, and two of them coloured'. She was clearly a born craftsman; and constantly busy with her pencil. A year or so afterwards came a translation of seven chapters of Xenophon's *Anabasis*, 'literally and faithfully done . . . very skilfully printed'.

All this, of course, with the three other histories, the fantasy, the novels and the verse that followed during the next three years, was play- or leisure-work. Her stockings were no bluer than her eyes; and she was often out at daybreak in the woods, telescope for the birds under her arm. Indeed, the chief concern of her *Journal* is first, her own *life*, next, that of her happy family and her father's pupils, and again and in particular, Nature's—flowers, trees, insects and birds—for which she had a passion. It is written with a clear and candid ease and freshness, the outcome of fine senses, a lucid mind and a quiet imagination.

In her eleventh year she sees a printing-press and exactly describes it; glass-blowing, and exactly decribes that; the Ramsgate packet and makes a model of it; an exhibition of paintings and engravings, and her choice is Gainsborough and Morland. At twelve she has listened to *Julius Cæsar*: 'I like it extremely' is her tribute, 'the characters are remarkably well-drawn'. She is delighted with Spenser's *Fowre Hymnes* on Heavenly Love and Beauty; is observing ants; follows up her discoveries with 'a nice game of play when we dirtied ourselves terribly'; a lively story about a lady and a bull; and a witty skit on an impulsive, erratic, topsy-turvyish, beloved and charming friend, concluding: 'Dinner is announced. She laughs herself into the parlour, and makes a hearty meal. She concludes the day with gossip and screaming to the sound of the harp'.

To call her a prodigy would be absurd; she is possessed by a gentle *jinnee* and follows her bent. In July 1835, when Fabre was twelve years old, Lubbock fifteen months, she begins an entry:

'For two or three days I have observed a species of wasp come frequently into my room, and enter the keyhole of my dressing-table drawer, where it stayed a considerable time. This morning I found two green caterpillars in the lock, each rolled up in a particular position, and both alive.

Journals

'It did not occur to me that there was any connection between their appearance and the visits of the wasp, and I was much puzzled to account for their being there. Soon after the wasp returned, bearing, to my surprise, one of these caterpillars amongst its feet; it carried it into the interior of the lock, and there spent some time in rolling it up into a ball, so that, though still alive, it had not the power of moving. I then discovered that it was the *Odynerus mucarius*, or mason-wasp, which always hoards up caterpillars in its nest for its progeny to eat; and I was greatly pleased at the opportunity of watching its curious habits.'

More than a century away we see her, this eager child, alone in her Georgian bedroom, eagerly in watch of, and pencilling down her careful notes on the busy maternal *Odynerus*. For about two hours (following her *own* 'curious habits'), she continued to observe the creature's sinister proceedings. She recorded the precise time of each of its thirteen visits to the keyhole, what it did there, and how long it stayed. Its usual burden, she says, was a pellet 'about the size of a gooseberry seed. She dropped one by accident. I picked it up; it was not broken. I found it to consist entirely of moistened sand'. Unlike Southey who at the age of eight took a great dislike to the ants in his garden, and 'discovered that they make their way into the cockchafer through an aperture in the breast, and eat out its inside while it is yet alive', she is not shocked at the insect's larder—whereas even Bluebeard's wives were at least at rest!

And so her *Journal* placidly proceeds, rilling with excitement here and there, now at the science of which she is in pursuit, and now at the poetry which is seldom far away from it; and to read its pages is to share her very self.

3. *'First lullaby my youthful years,*
   It is now time to go to bed.'

Child for child, there could be no sharper contrast to Emily Shore than Marjory Fleming, her love-names being Madgie, Maidie, Muffy and Muff. 'One of the most charming' of the characters in the *Dictionary of National Biography*, her life is 'probably its shortest'. Her Works have recently been republished both in handsome facsimile and in an edition copiously annotated by

Early One Morning

Mr. Frank Sidgwick, which should finally lift any fog of sentimentality that may have blurred her clear-cut image. Since, as we have seen, so many unusual men were no less unusual in a childhood of which we know so much less than hers, she is almost too famous. Her childish sun obscures their stars. But to omit all mention of her writings in a chapter on other children's would be to leave out its liveliest hue from the rainbow.

She was born at Kirkcaldy on January 15, 1803, and died after a brief illness—the only one that ever kept her an hour in bed—when she was a month under nine years old. She came of good Scotch stock on both sides of her family, a family endowed with brains as well as character. Her elder brother William, when he was nineteen months old, was presented with a cap and feathers by the officers of a Militia regiment quartered in Kirkcaldy, for a resolute recitation of his Shorter Catechism, beginning, *Wha made ye, my bonnie man?* And (in spite of all menaces from his Scotch nurse) for 'dust' in his fifth answer he invariably substituted *dirt*.

Her portraits—and as she confesses she was not 'of the fair but of the deficent . . . in looks'—faintly recall Jane Austen as a child. If a single word could describe that young, resolute, challenging face, it might well be redoubtable. One of her own favourite words was *majestick*.

Her eyes, set wide apart, were deep and dark, her mouth was proud and sensitive; her hair, lint-white when she was an infant, darkened to a deep brown. As for her mind, apart from her 'little mathematics and music' it is hard to say what she had not. She loved (naturally) 9 times 9; hated 8 times 8 and 7 times 7. In this unfaltering and impulsive fashion she dealt with her small universe. In her fifth year she met for the first time her cousin Isabella Keith, then still 'a girl', not older than seventeen. For Marjory this was love at first sight, a devotion without a trace of pose or silliness. One of the two book-markers left in her Bible was in the second Book of Samuel: 'Very pleasant hast thou been unto me: thy love to me was wonderful, passing the love of women.' She went to stay in Edinburgh, and Isa became her guide, guardian and (now and then perhaps, exacting) tutor. 'By love', says Traherne, 'may He be gotten and holden, but by thought never'; and this, infinite measure for measure, is true also of a child. From

418

MARJORY FLEMING
From a water-colour drawing by Isabella Keith

Journals

Edinburgh she sent a letter to her sister—in a bold handwriting ten words or so to the page, befitting its onset:

'My dear Isa
'I now sit down on my botom to answer all your kind and beloved letters which you was so good as to write to me. This is the first time I ever wrote a letter in my Life.

'There are a great many Girls in the Square and they cry just like a pig when we are under the painfull necessity of putting it to Death.

'Miss Potune a Lady of my acquaintance praises me dreadfully. I repeated something out of Deen Sweft and she said I was fit for the Stage. . . .'

A month or two after her seventh birthday she began her first Journal—one of three. It was Isa's heaven-sent idea; to aid her mind, heart and spelling; and contains her first poem:

'Beautious Isabella say
How long at breahead will you stay
O for a week or not so long
Then weel desart the busy throng. . . .'

The first Journal opens, 'Many people are hanged for Highway robbery Housebreking Murder &c &c'; the second, 'The Day of my existence here has been delightful & enchantinting'; the third (four pages are missing), '[We should] not be happy at the death of our fellow creatures, for they love life like us'.

As even these brief extracts hint, it is probable that more or less faultless spelling in the Journals implies copying. What is closest to her is of course what we want most. Here then are a few others, in order of date—and chiefly about animals and birds.

'. . . A Mirtal is a beautifull plant & so is a Geramem & nettel Geramem. . . . I have been washing my dools cloths today & like it very much. . . . There is a dog that yels continualy & I pity him to the bottom of my heart indeed I do. . . . Yesterday the thunder roared & now and then flashes of lightning was seen but today their is no such thing & far from it, for it is very warm sunny & mild.—The Monkey gets as many visitors as I or my cousins. . . .

'The days are very long and very light just now which is very pleasant to me & I darsay to every body. . . . Ravelston is a fine

Early One Morning

place because I got balm wine and many other dainties and extremely pleasant to me by the company of swine geese cocks &c and they are the delight of my heart. . . . Yesterday the thunder bolts roled Mightiy oer the hils it was very Majestick, but to Day there has been no thunder, but I will speak about another thing. . . .

'Yesterday I am very glad to say a young Cocker came to our house to stay, it is very beautifull & it is named Crakey it was Isabella that named him & white & black is its coualer but all the white will come of is not that wonderfull. . . . Mrs. Craford has a dog & I believe it is as beautifull as any in good Old England, I am sure; & she had 5 pups but they are all drowned but 1; Now am I quite happy. for I am going tomorrow to a delightfull place, Breahead by name, belonging to Mrs. Crraford, where their is ducks cocks hens bublyjocks 2 dogs 2 cats swine. & which is delightful; I think it is shoking to think that the dog & cat should bear them & they are drowned after I would rather have a man dog then a women dog because they do not bear like women dogs, it is a hard case it is shoking. . . .

'Every Morn I awake before Isa & Oh I wish to be up & out with the turkies but I must take care of Isa who when aslipe is as beautifull as Viness & Jupiter in the skies. . . . I got a young bird & I have tamed it & it hopes on my finger. Alas I have promised it to Miss Bonner & the cage is here & little Dickey is in it. . . . here there is planty of goosberys which makes my teath watter. . . . I have seen the Wild Beasts & they are excelent particularly the Lion & hunting Tiger the Elaphant Bolted and unbolted a door & such like wonders but of all the birds I admired the Pelecan of the Wilderness.

'My Aunts birds grow every day more healthy. . . . The weather is very cold & frosty & plenty of ice on the ground and on the watter Love your enemy as your friend and not as your foe this is a very windy stormy day and looks as if it was going to snow or rain but it is only my opinion which is not always corect. . . . The hedges are spruting like chicks from the eggs when they are newly hatched or as the vulgar says clacked.—I pretended to write to a lord Yesterday named Lord Roseberry about killing crows & rooks that inhabit his castle or estate but we should excuse my Lord for his foolishness for as people think I think Too for people think he is a little derangeed. . . . Wallflor grows very well I think

Journals

so at least. . . . The Casawary is an curious bird & so is the Gigan-
tick Crane & the Pelican of the Wilderness whose mouth holds a
bucket of fish & water. . . .' 'I am monarch of all I survey.'

4. 'Pleasure it is to hear, I wis, the birdës sing.'

It is as if one stood peering through its bottle-glass window-
panes into a brightly lit toyshop—and these are the contents of
but one of its shelves! Criminals and sweethearts, Satan and Ana-
baptists, bonnets, pineapples, fighting, females, aerolites and the
Genius Demedicus (? Venus de Medici)—all is fry that swims into
Marjory Fleming's net. And the books she mentions, ranging from
the Elegy to King John, from Mother Goose to the Newgate Calendar,
fill more than two columns in Mr. Sidgwick's Index.

'I have still', says Herbert Spencer of his childhood, 'vivid recollections of the delight of rambling among the gorse bushes, which
at that early age towered above my head. There was a certain
charm of adventure in exploring the narrow turf-covered tracks
running hither and thither into all their nooks, and now and then
coming out in unexpected places, or being stopped by a deep
sandy chasm made by carts going to the sand-pits. Then there were
the blue-bells to be picked from among the prickly branches,
which were here and there flecked with fragments of wool left
by passing sheep.'

In reading this we should add perhaps a little warmth to that
rather frigid phrase, 'a certain charm of adventure', must catch if
we can the peculiar magic, to a child's eyes, of the dew-sheened
fragments of wool, and at the same time endeavour to see this
remarkable philosopher in his 1826 clothes as a child of six among
the gorse bushes—towering above his head. Only then can we take
advantage of his own warning: 'In adult life it requires an effort
to recall even faintly that more imposing aspect which the world
has to children, caused by the relative largeness of objects and the
greater proximity of the eyes to things on the ground.' Having
made that effort, we can remind ourselves what ideas this philosopher was pondering when in his infancy his father asked him what
he was laughing at—and that will be 'the end to size'.

Early One Morning

And so with Marjory Fleming. It is only by intently watching her, as if she were one of our own children, pen in hand—the stooping head, the protruded tongue-tip, the clutching inky fingers, the spluttering nib, the blots, the fatted loops and quaking upper strokes—that we shall be able to estimate even the physical toil entailed in the writing of her Journal. But the physical toil was a reflection of her earnestness; she gave way to Isa because she loved her; she had the *strength* of character to resist herself. 'I hope I will be religious again but as for reganing my charecter I despare for it'. In spite of all difficulty, in spite of its crudities, the style is the child herself.

The mysterious self within—firm as a rock in the drifting tides —comes straight out at us from these laborious syllables. Even the badness of her spelling—as capricious as her wicked fits of passion and remorse, which repeatedly impel her to 'turn over a new life' —is her own badness, and with that we see her wrestling as Jacob wrestled with the angel. The spelling is only a surface thing, too, though amusing, like Charles Lamb's stutter; and to be fair to her mind we should correct it as we read.

She hated drudgery, she was in continuous rebellion against her Isa whom she loved so dearly, still more against her better and worser self. She is defiant, disdainful, humble, penitent, shocked, shocking, satirical—all in a morning. The moment after in her abasement she has trodden upon herself, like a daisy she is fronting the noonday sun. And nothing escapes the appraisal of her own small judgement—even when she repeats what she has borrowed, hoping for the best. In positive life lived, the contents of her minute valise need fear no comparison with that of any adult's more cumbersome travelling trunk. Nor would it perhaps if she had unpacked it before our eyes when she was not six years old but three.

'Human, humorous, genial, hospitable, emotional, sentimental, impulsive . . . egoistic, wayward, credulous, lovable and pathetic' —in these words Mr. Harold Nicolson has described not this seven-year-old Scotch wee bit lassikin but Lord Curzon when he was Minister for Foreign Affairs. Only one epithet has been omitted from his list—'childish'. That would not apply to Marjorie Fleming. She was child*like*. One of her last letters to her Isa begins:

Journals

'My Dear little Mama
    I was truly happy to hear that you are all well. . . . We are sur-
rounded with measles at present on every side for the Herons got
it and Isabella Heron was near deaths door and one night her father
lifted her out of bed And she fell down as they thought lifeless
Mr Heron said that lassie is dead now she said I'm no dead yet she
then threw up a big worm nine inches and a half long. . . .'

'Near deaths door'; what image had this child of that? Within
three months she was writing:

> 'O Isa pain did visit me
> I was at the last extremity
> How often did I think of you
> I wished your graceful form to view
> To clasp you in my weak embrace
> Indeed I thought Id run my race. . . .'

When she had finished these rhymes she lay down in bed and
was silent, and three days afterwards, after continual pain in her
head, with a whispered 'Oh, mother, mother!' she died: on
December 19, 1811. She had been desperately anxious to be 'let
out' at the New Year; as she wanted to buy a gift for Isa with a
sixpence her mother had given her 'for being patient in the
measles'.
    If she had lived, what would she have become? Our only cer-
tainty is that she would have remained a *character*.

5. *'Hearke how he crassheth these grystals bytwene his tethe.'*

Shakespeare, Milton, Hooker and Locke were Elizabeth Barrett's reading in her childhood, but, apparently, no Newgate
Calendar. At the age of ten—having learned Greek and Latin, as
they themselves once did—she could browse 'with delight inexpressible' on Homer and Virgil. 'Such early fruites are quickly in
their prime.' Four years afterwards she set to work on an epic entitled *The Battle of Marathon*, and wrote *My Own Life*; and, since
children have neither diffidence nor misgivings concerning such
feats of the mind as they set themselves, epics in early life (as we
shall see) are less unusual than autobiography. What views of early

childhood at this age—fourteen—should we expect from Miss Moulton Barrett of Wimpole Street? These are what we get:

' I was always of a determined and if thwarted violent disposition. My actions and temper were infinitely more inflexible at three years old than now at fourteen. At that early age I can perfectly remember reigning in the Nursery and being renowned amongst the servants for self love and excessive passion.— When reproved I always considered myself as an injured martyr and bitter have been the tears I have shed over my supposed wrongs. At four and a half my great delight was poring over fairy phenomenons and the actions of necromancers—and The Seven Champions of Christendom in "Popular tales" has beguiled many a weary hour. At five I supposed myself a heroine and in my day dreams of bliss I constantly imaged to myself a forlorn damsel in distress rescued by some noble knight and often have I laid awake hours in darkness, "THINKING," as I expressed myself, but which was no more than musing on these fairy castles in the air!

'I perfectly remember the delight I felt when I attained my sixth birthday; I enjoyed my triumph to a great degree over the inhabitants of the nursery [who had followed one another at intervals of about a year] there being no UPSTART to dispute my authority. . . .'

It is the portrait of a termagant, and one which should perhaps be sweetened a little by some lines she wrote much later in *The Pet Name*:

> '. . . I hear the birthday's noisy bliss
> My sisters' woodland glee,
> My father's praise I did not miss
> When stooping down, he cared to kiss
> The poet at his knee. . . .'

CHAPTER XXXII

LETTERS

★

1. *'A letter timely writ is a rivet in the chain of affection.'*

A journal or diary, whether by intention or not, is bound to disclose at least two selves, and these perhaps in many moods and phases. The more of them the merrier, unless our desire is for peace with plenty. Emily Shore by comparison with Marjory Fleming is serenest aquatint to a sketch by Hogarth. A letter *may* be as many faceted; but it will also reflect the human being to whom it is addressed. The less it does so the more self-centred, settled, earnest, or stereotyped the writer of it. This is equally true of letters written by children. But since a sensitive child tends to conceal—until the dam breaks down—what is closest to his heart, any expression of his feelings may have meant to him much more than we can ourselves distil from his words— a freshness, a life, a beauty, a woe, a craving, a hope, which in this intensity may be no longer, or very seldom ours.

'Darling Mother,—I hope you had a nice journey. I woke up about half-past three this morning, and I could not get to sleep again. At last I got out of bed, and went slowly into Dimpling's room, she was asleep, I stayed there a little while, and then went back to my own bed. But soon I got out again and went once more into Dimpling's room; she was still asleep. At last I came out and went slowly downstairs. At last I stopped at Father's door, I waited there till it struck four, and then I knocked gently at the door (no answer). I knocked again, Father came and opened the door, and then I got in his bed and stayed there for the rest of the morning. I hope you found the key of your portmanteau. Send

Early One Morning

my love to Mr. and Mrs. Patmore. Dear, Sweet, Love, Goodbye. Viola.'

Up to its last five words this letter from Miss Viola Meynell, written when she was about eleven years old, is a bare statement of facts. We must do our best to divine the feeling beneath it—the small hours, the solitude, the self-dramatization in that 'slowly', and the sleepless longing. On the other hand, a complete, almost Jovian comprehension, vast as the dome of St. Paul's, seems to canopy another letter to Alice Meynell written during her absence from home; its writer being about thirteen:

'My own girl,—I hope you had a nice journey and warm feet and a better head. You're a lovely woman. Tell Mr. Patmore he's a brick for loving you so much, and that I appreciate him awfully. Viola's in perfect spirits now. Miss Swain says I've been an *eccelentissima figlia*! Your girl, Monnie.'

In some respects a child's words—though there are likely to be very few *dead* ones—may mean less than they intimate. How is it possible indeed to realize the difference in concept between the same words as used even by two adults of a wholly different outlook? A scholarly and pious recluse's concepts, for example, of such specialities as night club, make-up, film-star, gangster, gag, crime, third degree, with those of the Hollywood magnate or of a 'cop' in Chicago; or contrariwise, of modesty, private life, publicity, taste, sin, money, happiness?

A like difficulty and one hardly more extreme confronts us in reading the poems written by Miss Helen Keller, who lost her sight and hearing when she was a child less than two years old. How can we share her world of a colourless dark, that voiceless silence? We think at once, indeed, of what in our own world of the mind may or must be absent from hers. Can we conceive what of hers is absent from ours? So with the astronomer's or the poet's moon, as compared with a young child's—which is all pure sensuousness and wholly innocent of 'knowledge'. How far precisely again were Marjory Fleming's concepts in her sentence 'All the King Jamess died mesirable deaths one of griefe, another murdered, but Lord Darnlys was the most cruel' *our* concepts of these terms? Less in some respects but more in others.

Letters

The child may write, as at times we may all of us write, only what is expected of him, and may rapidly acquire the requisite artifice. So be it, but even if his letter be a model of tact, or a serpent in subterfuge, it will remain also a little looking-glass reflecting his face. And he is of course no more taught all this than a minx is taught to simper or a duckling to swim; not much more taught at any rate than was a child of twenty-eight months who, wearied of tactful and winning allusions to a brand-new infant brother, mimicked bitingly, 'Darling baby! darling Nannie! darling Mummy! *darling* apples! DARLING grapes! . . .' and retired.

The letters that follow are in no particular order, and their best commentary is themselves. Let us keep our eye on the man-to-be in the child, and play eavesdropper to the occasional cajoleries between the lines. An abrupt sentence oddly out of kind for instance with its context is the one beginning 'I suppose' in our first example, which is dated February 4, 1785, and was written by Coleridge from Christ's Hospital when he was a few months over twelve. But even the plumb cake is Coleridgean.

'Dear Mother,—I received your letter with pleasure on the second instant, and should have had it sooner, but that we had not a holiday before last Tuesday, when my brother delivered it me. I also with gratitude received the two handkerchiefs and the half-a-crown from Mr. Badcock, to whom I would be glad if you would give my thanks. I shall be more careful of the somme, as I now consider that were it not for my kind friends I should be as destitute of many little necessaries as some of my schoolfellows are; and Thank God and my relations for them! My brother Luke saw Mr. James Sorrel, who gave my brother a half-a-crown from Mrs. Smerdon, but mentioned not a word of the plumb cake, and said he would call again. Return my most respectful thanks to Mrs. Smerdon for her kind favour. My aunt was so kind as to accommodate me with a box. I suppose my sister Anna's beauty has many admirers. My brother Luke says that Burke's Art of Speaking would be of great use to me. If Master Sam and Harry Badcock are not gone out of (Ottery), give my kindest love to them. Give my compliments to Mr. Blake and Miss Atkinson, Mr. and Mrs. Smerden, Mr. and Mrs. Clapp, and all other friends in the country.

Early One Morning

My uncle, aunt, and cousins join with myself and brother in love to my sisters, and hope they are well, as I, your dutiful son,

'S. Coleridge, am at present.
'P.S. Give my kind love to Molly.'

The next letter was written from 'Spring Grove School' when Stevenson was thirteen. All appears to be bliss—the magnificent 'gatteaux', the fireworks, the ragamuffins—and then, suddenly, after a relapse into Anglo-Saxon, the anguished, 'You told me. . . .' *This* papa hearkened; and home he went.

'Ma chere Maman,—Jai recu votre lettre Aujourdhui et comme le jour prochaine est mon jour de naisance je vous écrit ce lettre. Ma grande gatteaux est arrivé il leve 12 livres and demi le prix etait 17 shillings. Sur la soirée de Monseigneur Faux il y etait quelques belles feux d'artifice. Mais les polissons entrent dans notre champ et nos feux d'artifice et handkerchiefs disappeared quickly, but we charged them out of the field. Je suis presque driven mad par une bruit terrible tous les garcons kik up comme grand un bruit qu'il est possible. I hope you will find your house at Mentone nice. I have been obliged to stop from writing by the want of a pen, but now I have one, so will continue.

'My dear papa, you told me to tell you whenever I was miserable. I do not feel well, and I wish to get home. Do take me with you.

'R. Stevenson.'

The last words echo, as have similar forlorn appeals, the earliest extant letter written by a child—that on papyrus in the second or third century A.D. and now in the Bodleian Library:—

'Theon to his father Theon, greeting. Thank you for not taking me to town with you. If you won't take me with you to Alexandria I won't write you a letter or speak to you or say goodbye to you; and if you go to Alexandria I won't take your hand nor greet you again. That is what will happen if you won't take me. Mother said to Archelaus, "He drives me crazy: take him." Thank you for sending me presents. . . . Send for me, *please*. If you don't I won't eat, I won't drink; there now!'

The challenging vivacity is obviously nothing but a veil to con-

Letters

ceal the poignancy of the feelings beneath? Only Marjory Fleming's Journals, again, and her devotion to her Isa can fully illuminate the longing in six-year-old Charles Kingsley's letter from
Barnack to his Miss Dade.

'My dear Miss Dade,—
    'I hope you are well is fanny well? The house is completely
changed since you went. I think it is nearly 3 months since you
went. Mamma sends her love to you and sally browne Herbert and
geraled [his brothers] but I must stop here, because I have more
letters of consequence to write & here I must pause.
                            'Believe me always,
                                'Your sincere friend,
                                    'Charles Kingsley.'

   His sermon at the age of four on a previous page will be a useful
commentary on his remarks to his mother, when he was twelve,
about reading his Bible. Sententiousness there may be; but not an
iota of cant:—
    'I am now quite settled and very happy. I read my Bible every
night, and try to profit by what I read, and I am sure I do. I am more
happy now than I have been for a long time; but I do not like to
talk about it, but to prove it by my conduct.
    'I am keeping a journal of my actions and thoughts, and I hope it
will be useful to me.'
   A child of four (I was told by a friend recently), having bidden
his father goodbye before he went to France during the War, was
discovered after his departure standing on his head in an armchair.
This was not in hope of becoming a tumbler; nor was he intending
by this means to revive his ideas. He explained that he wanted to
burst a blood-vessel, and die. At the last moment of farewell he
had entreated his father to write to him the very instant he reached
the trenches, and not on any account to fail to tell him in his letter
the colours of the cream in the two chocolates that had been his
own parting present. How ineffably childish! one might comment; and add, after a flicker of reflection, how supremely human!
Could any private piece of information more swiftly link the
parted ones together again? It would be for impeccable evidence
such as this that we might pine if we supposed ourselves to be in
communication with a friend who is dead.

429

Early One Morning

In their behaviour children often appear to be silly and witless when, all else forgotten, like lamb, puppy, kid and kitten they are merely indulging their animal spirits. This makes it easy to overlook their no less natural gravity of mind and spirit. No dignity of self-expression, not even the grand manner, could be in excess of that gravity. A steady look at the Infanta in Velasquez's well-known picture, at Dürer in the drawing he made of himself when he was fourteen, or at Emerson on his mother's knee, is all that is needed. Indeed the habitual expression of an intelligent suckling is that of gravity.

Young children may be imps of mischief, owls in stupidity, slaves of the giggles, half tipsy with utter nonsense. But in the presence of anything he himself regards as serious a child will bitterly resent grown-up flippancy and frivolity. The candour of his silent rebuke is shattering. He may consent to be amusing, never, against his will, to be amused. Like pools of motionless water, young eyes at rest reflect the sky, and will refuse even a cat's-paw at the behest of a mere parlour breeze. A child may be forced into compliance, and it is early in life that the *inward* compromises begin. Even Coleridge's genial remarks on an old pair of breeches in a letter to his elder brother George had probably been extorted from him after a good deal of anxiety on that account.

'Dear Brother,—You will excuse me for reminding you that, as our holidays commence next week, and I shall go out a good deal, a good pair of breeches will be no inconsiderable accession to my appearance. For though my present pair are excellent for the purpose of drawing mathematical figures on them, and though a walking thought, sonnet or epigram would appear in them in very *splendid* type, yet they are not altogether so well adapted for a female eye—not to mention that I should have the charge of vanity brought against me for wearing a looking-glass. I hope you have got rid of your cold—and I am
'Your affectionate brother,
'Samuel Taylor Coleridge.

'P.S. Can you let me have them time enough for re-adaptation before Whitsuntide? I mean that they may be made up for me before that time.'

EMERSON, WITH HIS MOTHER
From a daguerreotype in the Fogg Museum at Harvard University
By kind permission of The R. W. Emerson Association

Letters

There is an inward detachment and a candid guilelessness in a letter from Lewis Carroll written to his sisters from his first boarding-school when he was twelve. The picture it gives of the game in the churchyard has the lively qualities of a Bewick woodcut. It is followed for contrast by a few sentences from a report sent about this time by his headmaster to Mr. Dodgson. He was not apparently a witness of the initiation at the tombstone!

'My dear Fanny and Memy,—I hope you are all getting on well, as also the sweet twins, the boys I think that I like the best, are Harry Austin, and all the Tates of which there are 7 besides a little girl who came down to dinner the first day, but not since, and I also like Edmund Tremlet, and William and Edward Swire, Tremlet is a sharp little fellow about 7 years old, the youngest in the school, I also like Kemp and Mawley. The rest of the boys that I know are Bertram, Harry and Dick Wilson, the two Robinsons, I will tell you all about them when I return. The boys have played two tricks upon me which were these—they first proposed to play at "King of the Cobblers" and asked if I would be King, to which I agreed. Then they made me sit down and sat (on the ground) in a circle round me, and told me to say "Go to work" which I said, and they immediately began kicking me and knocking me on all sides. The next game they proposed was "Peter, the red lion," and they made a mark on a tombstone (for we were playing in the churchyard) and one of the boys walked with his eyes shut, holding out his finger, trying to touch the mark; then a little boy came forward to lead the rest and led a good many very near the mark; at last it was my turn; they told me to shut my eyes well, and the next minute I had my finger in the mouth of one of the boys, who had stood (I believe) before the tombstone with his mouth open. For 2 nights I slept alone, and for the rest of the time with Ned Swire. The boys play me no tricks now. The only fault (tell Mama) that there has been was coming in one day to dinner just after grace. On Sunday we went to church in the morning, and sat in a large pew with Mr. Fielding, the church we went to is close by Mr. Tate's house, we did not go in the afternoon but Mr. Tate read a discourse to the boys on the 5th commandment. We went to church again in the evening. Papa wished me to tell him all the texts I had heard preached upon, please to tell him that I could not

Early One Morning

hear it in the morning nor hardly one sentence of the sermon, but the one in the evening was 1 Cor. i. 23. I believe it was a farewell sermon, but I am not sure. Mrs. Tate has looked through my clothes and left in the trunk a great many that will not be wanted. I have had 3 misfortunes in my clothes etc. 1st I cannot find my tooth-brush, so that I have not brushed my teeth for 3 or 4 days, 2nd I cannot find my blotting paper, and 3rd I have no shoe-horn. The chief games are, football, wrestling, leap frog and fighting. Excuse bad writing.

'Yr. affec^t brother Charles.'

'Gentle and cheerful [so runs the report], in his intercourse with others, playful and ready in conversation, he is capable of acquirements and knowledge far beyond his years, while his reason is so clear and so jealous of error, that he will not rest satisfied without a most exact solution of whatever appears to him obscure. He has passed an excellent examination just now in mathematics, exhibiting at times an illustration of that love of precise argument, which seems to him natural.

'I must not omit to set off against these great advantages one or two faults, of which the removal as soon as possible is desirable, tho' I am prepared to find it a work of time. As you are well aware, our young friend, while jealous of error, as I said above, where important faith or principles are concerned, is exceedingly lenient towards lesser frailties—and, whether in reading aloud or metrical compositions, frequently sets at nought the notions of Virgil or Ovid as to syllabic quantity. He is moreover marvellously ingenious in replacing the ordinary inflexions of nouns and verbs, as detailed in our grammars, by more exact analogies or convenient forms of his own devising. This source of fault will in due time exhaust itself, though flowing freely at present. . . . You may fairly anticipate for him a bright career. . . .'

'Capable of acquirements and knowledge far beyond his years', yes: but, apart from that, the report exactly as it stands might be a synopsis of Dodgson's complete 'career', except—but what an exception!—its connection with Looking-Glass-land.

Letters

2. *Their cheeks are like the rose in May,*
Their lips are of the dove.'

Augustus Hare's letter, the next example, written at the age of nine, is also from his first boarding-school—and that also was within easy reach of a churchyard. With an imaginative effort we can share his 'dark'; but the sentence, as usual, that tells most, is that which conceals most—its first.

'Darling Mama,—I like it rather better than I expected. They have killed a large snake by stoning it, and Gumbleton has skinned it, such nasty work, and peged it on a board covered with butter and pepper, and layed it out in the sun to dry. It is going to be stuffed. Do you know I have been in the vault under the church. It is so dark. There are great big coffins there. The boy's chief game is robbers. Give love and 8 thousand kisses to Lea [his nurse] and love to the Grannies. Good-bye darling Mama.

'Frederick Leuis has been very ill of crop. Do you know what that is? I have been to the school-feast at Mr. Clutterbuck's. It was so beautiful. All the girls were seated round little round tables, amongst beds of geraniums, heltrope, verbenas, and balm of Gilead. We carried the tea and were called in to grapes and gooseberries, and we played at thread-the-needle and went in a swing, and in a flying boat. God-bye Mamma.'

And here is another no less sensitive and loving juvenile Achilles among the ladies—Edmund Gosse, also round about nine years old.

'June 3, 1858.

'My extremely precious Papa,—
'I am quite longing for the month to end (but still it is shorter than I thought it would be) and it is so lonely sometimes without you—Bolcera egis auratus has fatally burst. This morning a lerianthus Lyodii came (oh! such a monster) but I fear it is dead. I enjoyed myself very much at Miss Willses yesterday among the young ladies we played at Lotto, and Bell & Hammer and solitaire and I saw the gymtastics and held them too. We have not had such a brilliant day for a couple of months—how is it with you?
'I remain your
'afectionat Son
'E. Wm. Gosse.'

Early One Morning

In an earlier letter he had speculated—'W. Guy is such a young Turk, I wonder if Helena Guy will be one too?'—which recalls a song familiar to me in my infancy, 'And the captain with his whiskers took a sly glance at me'.

No less clear than the resemblances are the dissimilarities between these three children in temperament and character. A child teaches itself to speak and possibly to read, and it is helped to write. But it cannot, as has been said already, be helped to portray itself in writing. Yet each of these children has somehow mastered this mystery; and though the mystery itself is as plain as a map before our eyes, how difficult it is to detect in the choice of words and the tone and rhythm and cadence of the sentences how the result is attained.

3. *'In Pope I cannot read a line,*
But with a sigh I wish it mine.'

We turn to a letter written in 1788, from Wem, by William Hazlitt at the age of ten to a younger brother, and an utterly different human being presents himself. He moralizes. He who only two years before was confessing that he could not 'sifer any at all' is now teaching arithmetic to a boy nearly twice his age. The sagacity, the thirst for knowledge, the range of interest, the unfaltering summary of his schoolfellows, the curtness and incisiveness are pure Hazlitt and Hazlitt only.

'Dear Brother,—I received your letter this morning. We were all glad to hear that you were well, and that you have so much business to do. We cannot be happy without being employed. . . . You want to know what I do. I am a busybody, and do many silly things: I drew eyes and noses till about a fortnight ago. I have drawn a little boy since, a man's face, and a little boy's front face, taken from a bust. Next Monday I shall begin to read Ovid's Metamorphoses and Eutropius.

'I shall like to know all the Latin and Greek I can. I want to learn how to measure the stars. I shall not I suppose paint the worse for knowing everything else. I begun to cypher a fortnight after Christmas, and shall go into the rule of three next week. I can teach a boy of sixteen already who was cyphering eight months

434

before me; is he not a great dunce? I shall go through the whole cyphering book this summer, and then I am to learn Euclid.

'We go to school at nine every morning. Three boys begin with reading the Bible. Then I and two others show our exercises. We then read the [Enfield's] Speaker. Then we all set about our lessons, and those who are first ready say first. At eleven we write and cypher. In the afternoon we stand for places at spelling, and I am almost always first. We also read, and do a great deal of business besides. I can say no more about the boys here: some are so sulky they won't play; others are quarrelsome because they cannot learn, and are only fit for fighting like stupid dogs and cats. I can jump four yards at a running jump, and two at a standing jump. I intend to try you at this when you come down. We are not all well, for poor Peggy has a great cold. Write soon again. I wish I could see all those paintings that you see, and that Peggy had a good prize. I don't want your old clothes. I shall go dancing this month. This is all I can say. I am your affectionate brother,

'William Hazlitt.'

In sublime self-confidence, surely, and in zest for mastery of what life provides not even Leonardo da Vinci's famous memorandum addressed to Lodovico Sforza transcends this screed from boy to boy.

In early letters however we may occasionally confront a child that we might never without further information have suspected the man himself of having been. We should not, I think, associate, for example, the poet of 'Dora' and 'The May Queen' with the superb assurance and judgment exhibited in the following acute and learned epistle to his Aunt Marianne from Alfred Tennyson in his thirteenth year! To enjoy the full flavour of it perhaps we must attempt to see the writer of it with that aunt's eyes. But, yet again, should we be incredulous if it were presented to us as the work not of a boy of twelve, but of a patriarch of 120? The one Alfred is evidently practising his brains, his craft, his wit, and his vocabulary, and at the same time tactfully 'playing up to' an endearing and promising relative. Alfred Senior would be able to plead none of these excuses; but we should condone his copious informativeness and even his condescending 'When I inform him' by the time we reach his 'volatile and fickle'.

435

Early One Morning

'My dear Aunt Marianne,

'When I was at Louth you used to tell me that you should be obliged to me if I would write to you and give you my remarks on works and authors. I shall now fulfil the promise which I made at that time. Going into the library this morning, I picked up *Sampson Agonistes*, on which (as I think it is a play you like) I shall send you my remarks. The first scene is the lamentation of Sampson, which possesses much pathos and sublimity. This passage,

> Restless thoughts, that like a deadly swarm
> Of hornets arm'd, no sooner found alone,
> But rush upon me thronging, and present
> Times past, what once I was, and what am now,

puts me in mind of that in Dante, which Lord Byron has prefixed to his "Corsair," "Nessun maggior dolore, Che ricordarsi del tempo felice, Nella miseria." His complaint of his blindness is particularly beautiful,

> O loss of sight, of thee I most complain. . . .

I think this [passage] is beautiful, particularly

> O dark, dark, dark, amid the blaze of noon.

'After a long lamentation of Sampson the Chorus enters, saying these words:

> This, this is he: Softly awhile;
> Let us not break in upon him:
> O change beyond report, thought, or belief!
> See how he lies at random, carelessly *diffused*.

If you look into Bp. Newton's notes you will find that he informs you that "this beautiful application of the word 'diffused' is borrowed from the Latin." It has the same meaning as "temere" in one of the Odes of Horace, Book the second,

> Sic temere, et rosâ
> Canos odorati capillos,

of which this is a free translation, "Why lie we not at random, under the shade of the plantain (sub platano), having our hoary head perfumed with rose water?" To an English reader the metre

436

of the Chorus may seem unusual, but the difficulty will vanish, when I inform him that it is taken from the Greek. In line 133 there is this expression, "Chalybean tempered steel." The Chalybes were a nation among the ancients very famous for the making of steel, hence the expression "Chalybean," or peculiar to the Chalybes: in line 147 "the Gates of Azzar"; this probably, as Bp. Newton observes, was to avoid too great an alliteration, which the "Gates of Gaza" would have caused, though (in my opinion) it would have rendered it more beautiful: and (though I do not affirm it as a fact) perhaps Milton gave it that name for the sake of novelty, as all the world knows he was a great pedant. I have not, at present, time to write any more: perhaps I may continue my remarks in another letter to you: but (as I am very volatile and fickle) you must not depend upon me, for I think you do not know any one who is so fickle as

'Your affectionate nephew,
'A. Tennyson.

'P.S. Frederick informed me that grandmamma was quite growing dissipated going out to parties every night. . . .'

The surprising 'plantain' is an old name for the plane tree. The only feature in common between this letter to an aunt and the following to his 'incomparable Dulcinea' is its mastery of expression. After receiving it, Dulcinea could never at least have fallen into the vulgar error of believing that poets are unable to write respectable prose. The sentences have a rhythm, poise and balance, which not even a Gibbon could disdain. Mimicry to some extent this may be—but the competence of its writer to invent and enjoy his own fluent and transparent palaver is beyond question. Less than twelve years before this he could not even talk.

'My dear Dulcinea,
'Pursuant to your request and the honour of knight-errantry, and in conformity to my bump of conscientiousness (which has grown so enormous since my visit to you that I can scarce put on my helmet), I now intend, as far as lies in my power, to fulfil that promise which the lustre of your charms extorted from me. Know then, most adorable mistress of my heart, that the manuscripts which your angelic goodness and perfection were pleased to commend are not with me. If however my memory, assisted by the

Early One Morning

peerless radiance of your divine favour, avail me aught, I will endeavour to illume the darkness of my imagination with the recollection of your glorious excellence, till I produce a species of artificial memory unequalled by the *Memoria Technica* of Mr. Gray. Who would not remember when thus requested? It would cause a dead idiot to start afresh to life and intellect. Accept then, soul of my soul, these effusions, in which no Ossianic, Miltonic, Byronic, Milmanic, Moorish, Crabbic, Coleridgic etc. fire is contained.

'The first is a review of death:

> Why should we weep for those who die? etc.

'The second is a comparison:

> Je fais naître la lumière
> Du sein de l'obscurité.
>
> (Rousseau)
> How gaily sinks the gorgeous sun, etc.

'And now farewell, my incomparable Dulcinea. In the truest spirit of knight-errantry,

> 'Yours ever, Don Quixote.'

4. *'Do you see any green in my eye?'*

The letters from Macaulay that follow were written from his private school at Shelford in 1813—before he was twelve and a half years old. As a child he had 'advanced' with the utmost rapidity, but seems also to have come into the world a trifle elderly. Both letters simmer with a sagacious cheerfulness. Nature, aided perhaps by Fénelon's Dialogues, smiles, a little wistfully, at the window, and Macaulay was seldom other than '*employed*' in reading. His tolerant glimpse of the amusing dean reminds us of Ruskin and his tutor, and his 'tolerably cheerful', 'takes my part' and 'quite a friend' in the one letter, and the 'want home' in the other, hint at a good deal more than they say out. He sits 'like a king', but a king, none the less, in exile.

'My dear Papa—

'As this is a whole holiday, I cannot find a better time for answering your letter. With respect to my health, I am very well, and tolerably cheerful; a Blundell, the best and most clever of all

438

the scholars, is very kind, and talks to me, and takes my part. He is quite a friend of Mr. Preston's. . . .

'My room is a delightful snug little chamber, which nobody can enter, as there is a trick about opening the door. I sit like a king, with my writing desk before me; for (would you believe it?) there is a writing desk in my chest of drawers; my books on one side, my box of papers on the other, with my arm-chair and my candle; for every boy has a candlestick, snuffers, and extinguisher of his own. Being pressed for room, I will conclude what I have to say to-morrow, and ever remain,

'Your affectionate son,
'Thomas B. Macaulay.'

'My dear Mama,—
'Pursuant to my promise I resume my pen to write to you with the greatest pleasure. Since I wrote to you yesterday, I have enjoyed myself more than I have ever done since I came to Shelford. Mr. Hodson called about twelve o'clock yesterday morning with a pony for me and took me with him to Cambridge. How surprised and delighted was I to learn that I was to take a bed at Queen's College in Dean Milner's apartments! Wilberforce arrived soon after, and I spent the day very agreeably, the Dean amusing me with the greatest kindness. I slept there, and came home on horseback to-day just in time for dinner. . . . The books which I am at present employed in reading to myself are, in English, Plutarch's Lives, and Milner's Ecclesiastical History; in French Fénelon's Dialogues of the Dead. I shall send you back the volumes of Madame de Genlis's *petits romans* as soon as possible, and I should be very much obliged for one or two more of them. Everything now seems to feel the influence of spring. The trees are all out. The lilacs are in bloom. The days are long, and I feel that I should be happy were it not that I want home. . . .'

After an interval of almost exactly a year his Mamma received the next letter; and what a change is here. No faintest trace of childhood remains. It is as if the gently budding aloe (entirely of its own volition and never to blush unseen) had burst into full bloom. The substance, the assurance, the aplomb!—'How can his ambitious mind support it?' We can accept too his 'ten minutes' as it stands. Indeed when any stranger mounts the school platform, it is the lynx that of all the animals is best represented in his audience. As for the second paragraph, it rings like a Gatling gun.

'My dear Mamma,—The news is glorious indeed. Peace! peace with a Bourbon, with a descendant of Henri Quatre, with a prince who is bound to us by all the ties of gratitude! I have some hopes that it will be a lasting peace, for the troubles of the last twenty years will make kings and nations wiser. I cannot conceive a greater punishment to Buonaparte than that which the allies have inflicted on him. How can his ambitious mind support it? All his great projects and schemes, which once made every throne in Europe tremble are buried in the solitude of an Italian isle. How miraculously everything has been conducted! We almost seem to hear the Almighty saying to the fallen tyrant, "For this cause have I raised thee up that I might show in thee My power."

'As I am in very great haste with this letter I shall have but little time to write. I am sorry to hear that some nameless friend of Papa's denounced my voice as remarkably loud. I have accordingly resolved to speak in a moderate key except on the undermentioned special occasions. Imprimis, when I am speaking at the same time with three others. Secondly, when I am praising the "Christian Observer." Thirdly, when I am praising Mr. Preston or his sisters. I may be allowed to speak in my loudest voice, that they may hear me.

'I saw to-day the greatest of churchmen, that pillar of Orthodoxy, that true friend to the Liturgy, that mortal enemy to the Bible Society,—Herbert Marsh, D.D., Professor of Divinity on Lady Margaret's foundation. I stood looking at him for about ten minutes, and shall always continue to maintain that he is a very ill-favoured gentleman as far as outward appearance is concerned. I am going this week to spend a day or two at Dean Milner's, where I hope, nothing unforeseen preventing, to see you in about two months' time.

'Ever your affectionate Son,
'T. B. Macaulay.'

The next letter, all rhythmical high spirits—from Shelley—is dated July 18, 1803, a few days before his eleventh birthday. Dante Gabriel Rossetti's which follows it—caustic, critical and matter-of-fact, and showing clearly both scent and gusto in his choice of books at the time—was written from Chalfont St. Giles when he was fourteen.

'Dear Kate,—We have proposed a day at the pond next Wednesday; and, if you will come to-morrow morning, I would be obliged to you; and if you could anyhow bring Tom over to stay all night, I would thank you. We are to have a cold dinner over at the pond, and come home to eat a bit of roast chicken and peas at about nine o'clock. Mama depends upon your bringing Tom over to-morrow, and if you don't we shall be very much disappointed. Tell the bearer not to forget to bring me a fairing—which is some ginger-bread, sweetmeat, hunting-nuts, and a pocket-book. Now I end.—I am not, Your obedient servant,

'P. B. Shelley.'

'My dear Mamma,

'We arrived safely at Chalfont at 12 o'clock yesterday. The village is larger than I expected. The first thing we did on our arrival was to demolish bread and butter, of which I at least was much in want. We then, with considerable difficulty, opened Uncle Henry's trunks, and after depositing a portion of their contents in a chest of drawers, sallied forth to reconnoitre. I saw Milton's house, which is unquestionably the ugliest and dirtiest building in the whole village. It is now occupied by a tailor. . . .

'Yesterday I commenced reading "The Infidel's Doom," by Dr. Birch, which work forms part and parcel of Uncle Henry's library. However, I have abandoned the task in despair. I then began "The Castle of Otranto," which shared the same fate, and am now engaged on Defoe's "History of the Plague." This morning we deposited Uncle Henry's books in a closet in Uncle Henry's bedroom, which, in common with all the other closets in this house, possesses a lock but no key.

'I do not think that I shall go to church on Sunday for in the first place I do not know where I can sit, and in the second place I find we are so stared at wherever we go that I do not much relish the idea of sitting for two hours the loadstone of attraction in the very centre of the aborigines, on whose minds curiosity seems to have taken strong hold. . . . I "in longing expectation wait" the appearance of my dinner; for which, however, I need not yet look, since it is now nearly three o'clock, which is the nominal dinner hour, but, the fire having gone out, Uncle Henry prophesies that it will not come till four.'

Nine years before this—at the age of five—Rossetti had favoured his Aunt Eliza with a letter. Its 'with no white' and 'for my amusement' are particularly interesting. Perhaps Christina's 'hook' —that 'fisherman of men'—was magnetized.

'Dear Aunt Eliza,
'We went to a fancy fair in the Regent's Park where I bought a box of paints, Maria, an album, and Christina, two fishes and a hook. The fair was for the benefit of a Charity School. I have been reading Shakespeare's Richard the 3rd for my amusement, and like it exceedingly. I, Maria, and William know several scenes by heart. I have bought a picture of Richard and Richmond fighting and I gilded it after which I cut it out with no white. My Aunt came yesterday and gave Maria a pretty little basket it was worked in flowers of green card.
'I remain, my dear Aunt,
'Your affectionate Nephew
'Gabriel C. D. Rossetti.'

So much impressed was Thomas Love Peacock's schoolmaster by the following 'entirely unassisted' letter written 'without orders' at the age of seven, that he sent it on to Mrs. Peacock:—

'Honoured Mother, I wish you would write to Caperny Cray to send me my poney, and my books; and I wish that you would come and see me as soon as possible, and bring me some candied lemon, and figs, and cakes, and write to my Father to tell him to send home some Sweet meats, for your dutyful son, Thomas Love Peacock.'

Four years afterwards Thomas is still begging, but concludes with an aphorism which no urbane publisher ever neglects:—
'Placeat tibi recordari promissum tuum, et dare mihi unum solidum, mercedem, pro epistolâ Latinâ quam nunc tibi scribo. . . . Pecuniâ mihi semper opus est, sed nullo tempore magis, quam praesenti.'
And at the same age—but with the aid of a voluble writing-master—he improved the shining hour with,

Letters

'Dear Sir. . . . The French, now inflamed by victory, in their turn deny us peace; not only that, but they are making vast preparations to invade us. . . . Shall we, like cowards, when the existence of our country is at stake, when every thing that is dear to us is devoted, shrink back at their approach, and basely seek to preserve by dastard inactivity or concealment, leaving all for which life is worth preserving, parents, wives, sisters, or children to be cruelly slaughtered or their honors violated by merciless Frenchmen? Forbid it Heaven!'

Byron, who was born on January 22, 1788, was about the same age as Thomas, the Latinist, when he wrote the following letter from Newstead Abbey, dated November 8, 1798, to an aunt, Mrs. Parker. That being so, its postscript is the most surprising part of it.

'Dear Madam,
'My Mamma being unable to write herself desires I will let you know that the potatoes are now ready and you are welcome to them whenever you please.
'She begs you will ask Mrs. Parkyns if she would wish the poney to go round by Nottingham or to go home the nearest way as it is now quite well but too small to carry me.
'I have sent a young Rabbit which I beg Miss Frances will accept off and which I promised to send before. My Mama desires her best compliments to you all in which I join.
'I am, Dear Aunt, your sincerely,
'Byron.
'I hope you will excuse all blunders as it is the first letter I ever wrote.'

The next letter is from Byron to his Egeria, Elizabeth Pigot, and is dated August 29, 1804. He was sixteen. She had recently met him for the first time, and two years later was to enkindle in him an ambition to print 'a small volume for private circulation'. She describes him as 'a fat, bashful boy, with his hair combed straight over his forehead'. He continued 'shy and formal' until—they had been talking of Gabriel Lackbrain, a character in a play—she said, 'Goodbye, Gaby'; at which 'his handsome mouth displayed a broad grin and all shyness vanished never to return'.

Early One Morning

At sixteen Byron was hardly a *child*, but his handwriting is described as still 'childish' none the less, even though this was eight years after his childlike devotion to Mary Duff.

'August 29 1804

'To Miss Pigot.

'I received the arms, my dear Miss Pigot, and am very much obliged to you for the trouble you have taken. It is impossible I should have any fault to find with them. The sight of the drawings gives me great pleasure for a double reason—in the first place, they will ornament my books; in the next, they convince me that *you* have not entirely *forgot* me. I am, however, sorry you do not return sooner—you have already been gone an *age*. I perhaps may have taken my departure for London before you come back; but, however, I will hope not. Do not overlook my watch-riband and purse, as I wish to carry them with me. Your note was given me by Harry, at the play, whither I attended Miss L—— and Dr. S——; and now I have sat down to answer it before I go to bed. If I am at Southwell when you return,—and I sincerely hope you will soon, for I very much regret your absence,—I shall be happy to hear you sing my favourite, "The Maid of Lodi." ["My heart with love is beating, Transported by those eyes . . ."] My mother, together with myself, desires to be affectionately remembered to Mrs. Pigot, and, believe me, my dear Miss Pigot, I remain your affectionate friend,

'Byron.

'P.S. If you think proper to send me any answer to this, I shall be extremely happy to receive it. Adieu.

'P.S. 2. As you say you are a novice in the art of knitting, I hope it don't give you too much trouble. Go on *slowly*, but surely. Once more, adieu.'

The sentiment in this letter is as wistful as the fragrance of faded woodruff, and when we compare it and the earlier one with Hazlitt's or Tennyson's or Rossetti's, and do so with Byron's amazing career in mind, how odd a problem presents itself! No other man of genius, surely, ever swept through so swift a metamorphosis.

There is nothing even remotely childlike in Henry Brougham's letter to the Principal of Edinburgh University, written in January 1792 when he was nearly fourteen—a 'boy of the World'.

Letters

'Dear Sir, ...

'You will perhaps remember that you allowed me to translate either Livy or Florus. I pitched upon the latter—not that his style appeared to me any way superior to that of the other; but as I had read, partly at Edinburgh and partly here, almost the whole of the first five books of Livy (a copy of which was the only part of his works I had), it naturally occurred that there would be less field for exertion in translating an author with whose works I was acquainted, than in trying one whose works were quite new to me. Besides, I was confirmed in my choice when I recollected that *you* seemed to give the preference to Florus. . . .

'I am sorry, dear sir, that I can give you no news, as affairs in the country commonly wear a very uniform aspect. As for my studies, I have read about four books of Virgil's Æneid, beginning at the VI; one of Livy; have got through above three parts of Adam's Roman Antiquities; and am employed in the Greek verbs. When business is over I amuse myself with reading, skaiting, or walking. If you can find leisure to write me a few lines, I shall think myself particularly honoured by it. As I fear I have already tried your patience, wishing many happy new years to yourself and Mrs. R., the college family—Russells and Brydons—in which I am joined by all this family, I beg leave to subscribe myself, dear sir, yours with the greatest respect and esteem,

'Henry Brougham.'

Nor might we expect in a boy of fourteen the amenity, the plangent sense of the days that are no more, and the pensive elegance of gesture in the following letter from Horace Walpole to his friend Charles Lyttelton. They might be old cronies discussing a talk at the Athenaeum:

'My dearest Charles,

'The pleasure that the interview, tho' so very short, that I had with you the night before you left town, gave me, has I think made your absence seem still more insupportable. That little snatch of conversation was so agreeable, that I am continually thinking how happy we should be in a much longer. I can reflect with great joy on the moments we passed together at Eton, and long to talk 'em over, as I think we could recollect a thousand passages, which were something above the common rate of schoolboy's diversions. I can

Early One Morning

remember with no small satisfaction that we did not pass our time in gloriously beating great clowns, who would patiently bear children's thumps for the collections, which I think some of our contemporaries were so wise as to make for them afterwards. We had other amusements which I long to call to mind with you: when shall I be so happy? Let me know, my dear Charles, how far you are from Ragley; I have some thoughts of going down thither this summer, and if it is not too far, I will spend a day with you in Worcestershire. You may assure yourself I am mightily put to it for news, when for want of that, I send you some trifling verses [apparently not preserved] of my own, which have nothing to recommend 'em but the subject. I know you will excuse 'em, when you consider they come from

'My dearest Charles
'Yr sincere Friend and Servant
'Hor: Walpole.'

The writer of the next letter was about a year younger than Horace Walpole at this time. Is it pure fancy that even at 'my uncle called on me twice', we remain in little doubt of her sex—and are amply justified? It is Mary Mitford. Three years before this, on her tenth birthday, and in the company of her 'dear papa', she chose the lottery ticket that won her £20,000. Hence the expensive school.

'My dear Papa,
'I sit down in order to return you thanks for the parcels I received. My uncle called on me twice while he stayed in London, but he went away in five minutes both times. He said that he only went to fetch my aunt, and would certainly take me out when he returned. I hope that I may be wrong in my opinion of my aunt; but I again repeat, I think she has the most hypocritical drawl that I ever heard. Pray, my dearest papa, come soon to see me. I am quite miserable without you, and have a thousand things to say to you. I suppose that you will pass almost all your time at Odiam this season, as it is a very good country for sporting; and that family is so agreeable, that it would be very pleasant for mamma to stay there with you.
'Remember me to all the family, particularly to Grandpapa and William.

Letters

'Feb. 23, 1801

'I really think that my dearly-beloved mother had better have the jackasses than the cart-horses. The former will at least have the recommendation of singularity, which the other has not; as I am convinced that more than half the smart carriages in the neighbourhood of Reading are drawn by the horses which work in the team.'

A vivid, eager, breathless and no less feminine desire to share scene and clothes sparkles in a letter from Charlotte Yonge, that industrious writer of over a hundred books in some fifty years. It was sent in 1834 from Otterbourne, and at the age of eleven, to a cousin, after a visit to Oxford.

'My dear Anne—Have you seen any more of Charles's owl? The shells got home quite safe. I send you a *carrier Trochus* and Charles a *waved welk*, Duke a fresh-water *mussel*, and Jane a *cypraea*. I went to the theatre whilst I was at Oxford; it is a great large place shaped like a horse shoe; at the flat end sat all the musicians and singers on a stand raised on pillars; in the middle was a great round place called the area, in which all the gentlemen squeezed in if they could; at the tip-top of all the college people all round under them were all the ladies and doctors; there were two great sticking-out boxes like pulpits, at the end of each was an axe tied up in what was meant to look like the Roman lictors' bundles of rods. The Duke of Wellington sat on a most beautiful velvet cushion on a carved chair. The Duke of Cumberland on a velvet and gold chair. His uniform was very funny; first he wore a red coat, then fastened on his shoulder a blue coat trimmed with fur; tied to his sword was a sort of pocket called a sabre-dash. The Duke of Wellington wore robes of black and gold. One day when he came to Exeter C. he kissed Julian and shook hands with me. There were a great many people besides doctors; they all wore red robes. We went to New College and Magdalen; the windows of the first were painted all manner of colours, but the other was brown.—I am your affectionate

'Charlotte Mary Yonge.'

Early One Morning

5. *'A mighty monarch must whilest greening youth doth flowe,*
Make one or two or three proofes of his peerles power'.

What is clearest in the next two letters, written in the 'green-ing youth' of Queen Victoria is not 'power' but a tender impulsive heart: the first was written from Kensington Palace when she was nine years old, the second from Tunbridge Wells only two years and nine months before she came to the throne. They have in common the same cadences, the characteristic 'pretty', the impulsive 'very's, and the same intense affectionate-ness:

'My dearest Uncle,—I wish you many happy returns of your birthday; I very often think of you, and I hope to see you soon again, for I am very fond of you. I see my Aunt Sophia often, who looks very well, and is very well. I use every day your pretty soup-basin. Is it very warm in Italy? It is so mild here, that I go out every day. Mama is tolerable well and am quite well. Your affectionate Niece,

'Victoria

'P.S.—I am very angry with you, Uncle, for you have never written to me once since you went, and that is a long while.'

'My dearest Uncle,—Allow me to write you a few words, to express how thankful I am for the very kind letter you wrote me. It made me, though, very sad to think that all our hopes of seeing you, which we cherished so long, this year, were over. I had so hoped and wished to have seen you again, my *beloved* Uncle, and to have made dearest aunt Louisa's acquaintance. I am delighted to hear that dear Aunt has benefited from the sea air and bathing. We had a very pretty party to Hever Castle yesterday, which per-haps you remember, where Anne Boleyn used to live, *before she lost her head.* We drove there, and rode home. It was a most beauti-ful day. We have very good accounts from dear Feodore [her half-sister], who will, by this time, be at Langenburg.

'Believe me always, my dearest Uncle, your very affectionate and dutiful Niece,

'Victoria.'

In tone and temper there could hardly be a sharper contrast

between this pair of letters—from one great and masterful queen in her childhood—and the two that follow from yet another, Elizabeth. The first was written in her seventh year to her stepmother Anne of Cleves. It may have been 'helped', but if so the helper exhibited the acutest foresight; for what follows it closely resembles it and is no less characteristic of its writer than the famous 'Proud Prelate' letter of Elizabeth's maturity: 'Proud Prelate,—You know what you were before I made you what you are now. If you do not immediately comply with my request, I will unfrock you, by G——!'

'Madame,
    'I am struggling between two contending wishes; one is, my impatient desire to see your majesty, the other that of rendering the obedience I owe to the commands of the king my father, which prevents me from leaving my house till he has given me full permission to do so. But I hope that I shall be able shortly to gratify both these desires. In the mean time, I entreat your majesty to permit me to show, by this billet, the zeal with which I devote my respect to you as my queen, and my entire obedience to you as to my mother. I am too young and feeble to have power to do more than to felicitate you with all my heart in this commencement of your marriage. I hope that your majesty will have as much goodwill for me, as I have zeal for your service.'

    The other letter, dated February 27, 1547, was addressed to the Lord Admiral Seymour when she was fourteen—three months before he was secretly married to Queen Catherine, and became Elizabeth's brutal guardian. Henry VIII died on January 28, 1547.

'My Lord Admiral,
    'The letter you have written to me is the most obliging, and, at the same time, the most eloquent in the world. And as I do not feel myself competent to reply to so many courteous expressions, I shall content myself with unfolding to you, in a few words, my real sentiments. I confess to you that your letter, all eloquent as it is, has very much surprised me; for, besides that neither my age nor my inclination allows me to think of marriage, I never could have believed that any one would have spoken to me of nuptials at a time when I ought to think of nothing but sorrow for the death

of my father. And to him I owe so much, that I must have two years at least to mourn for his loss. And how can I make up my mind to become a wife before I shall have enjoyed for some years my virgin state, and arrived at years of discretion. . . . Let your highness be well persuaded that though I decline the happiness of becoming your wife I shall never cease to interest myself in all that can crown your merit with glory, and shall ever feel the greatest pleasure in being your servant and good friend.

'Elizabeth.'

There is no mistaking in this masterly letter the iron hand beneath the velvet glove, minute though both may be. The 'never could have believed' can hardly have flattered its recipient, and after so suave and disarming an onset! With what skill, too, the period of 'two years at least' expands into 'some years', and so into a vague future and the chilly prospect of the standard reply (in all guides to polite letter-writing) to an unwelcome suitor. A woman of forty could be no more supple and downright.

In view of some of the preceding letters it is not easy to decide to what precise extent, if at all, the following from Henry Duke of Richmond, the natural son of Henry VIII, to his godfather, Cardinal Wolsey, was of his own composition. Since Wolsey had established a Household for him when he was six years old, the reference in it to an advancement in honour suggests that the writer may not have been much older. He died—poisoned perhaps by Anne Boleyn and her brother—when he was seventeen. The complete letter may have been dictated, but it has a personal ring; and Henry VIII's children were from their earliest years tutored in a classical culture—a prayer book of Elizabeth's still extant manifesting how deeply.

'Pleas yt your Grace to bee advertised that at thys tyme I do write unto the same not oonly to make a demonstracion off thys my proceding in writinge, but also in my right humble and lowly wise to beseche youre Grace off youre dayly blissynge and pardone, for that I have soo longe tyme delayed and forborne to write unto your Grace, to whos favoure and goodnes no creature living ys more bounde thene I am. And like as it hathe pleased almightie God and the Kings Highnes, moche parte by the meanes and good favoure off youre Grace, to preferre and advance me in honor, so shal I (God willinge) endevor my selffe and applie my tyme for th'attaynyng and encreas off lernynge, vertue, and cunninge, correspondente to the same, wherby I may be more able to do unto the Kingis highnes suche service hereafter as shal consiste with his mooste gracious pleasure, wiche off all thyng under God, is and shalbe my oonly myende, entent, and purpoos; as maister Magnus thys berer, Director off my Counsaill shall make relacion unto your grace, whome Almightie God evermore have in his mooste hoolie and blissid tuycion and governance. At Shireff Hutton the fourthe daye off Marche by youre moste humble Godsonne

'H. Rychemond.'

Nothing but pure childhood, limpid, loving and self-oblivious beams out of the next two scraps, one from the Princess Elizabeth, the other from her brother Charles, then Duke of York (the children of James I), to their elder brother Henry, Prince of Wales, who died when he was eighteen. Elizabeth was between nine and fourteen, and Charles was little over five, too illiterate at any rate to be able to write more than his own signature.

'My most worthy and dearest Brother: I geve you a million of thanks for the servant you sent mee, but more of your kind Letter, takyng few thinges so joyfully as to hear of your health, and though I cannot requite you with so pleasant a token, yet are these few lines a testymony of the affection of her whome you shall ever constantly finde

'Yo^r most loving sister
'Elizabeth.'

'Sweet sweet brother

'I thank yow for your Letter. I will keep it better than all my graith: and I will send my pistolles by Maister Newton. I will give anie thing that I have to yow; both my horses, and my books, and my pieces, and my cross bowes, or anie thing that yow would haive. Good Brother loove me, and I shall ever loove and serve yow.

'Your looving brother to be
'commanded
'York'

Early One Morning

Even the presents offered by Charles to that most promising of princes his elder brother were of aforethought, for he was already a renowned young horseman, and his suit of armour, made for him when he was a boy and now in Windsor Castle, is said to be one of the most beautiful specimens in the world.

CHAPTER XXXIII

STORIES

★

1. *'And I made a rural pen*
And I stained the water clear.'

Aletter even from a seven-year-old—in its discreet management, for example, of the fellow creature to whom it is
addressed—may clearly, then, be a work of genuine
artifice. So too a piece of fiction, however poor a thing
it is in itself, and whatever the age of its author, cannot but be in
the nature of a work of art. The writer of it has escaped out of one
world into another that is at least in part of his own making. And
we read what he writes in pursuit of a livelier, happier, less ham-
pered or profounder self. To a child with the requisite gift, indeed,
the spinning of stories is a far more spontaneous affair than the
concocting of letters. For the simple reason, no doubt, that he now
need only please himself. Fantasies flower in the silence of his
mind as naturally as may dreams when he is asleep. The habit is its
own delight, and may be a secret delight, though when listeners
are willing to listen, a new zest will enter into it.

Walter Scott is by no means the only schoolboy who has sunned
himself into the favour which this facility may win. Mrs. J. H.
Riddell, who, besides being the author of 156 books, was an exceedingly popular novelist in her own day, and at the age of eight
had digested the Koran, could 'never remember the time' when
she did not compose. 'Before I was old enough to hold a pen I
used to get my mother to write down my childish ideas'. In this
respect, as we have seen, she was one of a multitude.

'I cannot remember the time', says Mrs. Wharton in *A Backward Glance*, 'when I did not want to "make up" stories. But it
was in Paris [probably at the age of five] that I found the necessary

453

Early One Morning

formula. Oddly enough, I had no desire to write my stories down (even had I known how to write, and I couldn't yet form a letter); but from the first I had to have a book in my hand to "make up" with, and from the first it had to be a certain sort of book. The page had to be closely printed, with rather heavy black type, and not much margin'. Washington Irving's *Alhambra* proved to be best for this purpose. 'I had only to open it for the Pierian fount to flow . . . the "Alhambra" once in hand, making up was ecstasy'. At the age of eleven the ecstasy resulted in a novel beginning, ' "Oh, how do you do, Mrs. Brown?" said Mrs. Tompkins'.

We can all of us—with varying degrees of imaginative success and quite unconscious of the complex *process*—convert the words of a story into our own mental images, follow its thread, give life to what we make of its characters, enjoy its unfolding scenes and scenery, and bestow on it some kind of completeness. To make one up for ourselves is a similar feat but one needing rarer faculties. For although both processes are a kind of multiple self-dramatization, the latter entails a gift for words, invention, an eye for character, the faculty of arrangement, of ensuring sequence and attaining a goal.

For fiction of any merit, too, not only is a certain native impulse indispensable, but an accumulation of earthly experience; and although that is a stuff, as Sir Edward Elgar said of music, which is all around us and of which we can take as much as we need, it seems to require for its chief virtues as fiction a prolonged slumber in the mind. Whatever its vintage, it should be left long in the wood if it is to be excellent in the bottle. And since early experience sinks deepest into the mind, its choicest harvest appears to be that of childhood—its first twelve years. To decant it too early risks, apparently, our wasting not only what we have but failing to make the most of what we may acquire. Here then the metaphor fails, for the butt of malmsey that makes fiction is throughout life continually added to; even though it may derive its bouquet and even its body from these first years of one's existence. There comes a day however when what we have will alone suffice for a lifetime. I have been told that towards the end of his life Henry James had in reserve the nucleus of some sixteen unwritten novels.

The writing of tales is another method of dressing up, and to watch infants all but whose only 'country' is dingy pavement,

454

Stories

bricks and mortar dramatize some old story or rhyme which is imaged with flower and tree and star and wood and water is a revelation of this priceless faculty. The area of experience a child can of its own invention 'illuminate' may be as narrow as his taper is minute. It is none the less impossible to say at how early an age a child may begin not only collecting but rearranging and even making use of this stuff—just as a longtailed tit will accumulate hosts of tiny feathers for its exquisite nest, with a birdlike 'joy in the making' perhaps, but also (perhaps) without any foresight of its purpose.

Sir Henry Newbolt, who was an ardent bird's-nester as a child, tells of a linnet that had lined its nest entirely with the flaxen hair of his three-year-old daughter. It is with just such magical gold as this that the masters of fiction lined their nests when they were young. But always, first, the gift. One child of three I have in mind will begin at need (in order perhaps to change an awkward subject, such as plate-scraps or physic) with 'I *think* Mr. Punch is coming'. This announcement is followed by a kind of incantation, beginning *A-gie! A-gie!* and then, in the tones of a mænad, a jumble of doggerel, in which she herself, fired by these furious fancies, cheeks heightened, eyes suffused, seems to retire a league beyond the wide world's end, while her elder brother, entirely incapable of such a dæmonic crisis, exhausts himself with amusement.

We frequently read in memoirs of this story-telling habit in childhood. Shakespeare, with his usual wizardry, in thirty lines of verse presents us with the complete data of the case—the child, his mind, his outlook, his status and even a fragment of his story. As for the requisite 'experience', Mamillius confesses that he has chosen his playfellow from among the ladies not because her eyebrows have been plucked and she herself made up, but because he has observed women's faces and knows that she will not kiss him 'hard' and speak to him as if he 'were a baby still'. And what princeling of blood or beauty has not suffered in both respects? Both the ladies who talk to him are at least candid, if a trifle Mrs. Gampish, about the coming sister; but otherwise this serious child, who might well have been bosom friend with Salathiel Pavy, is toyed with, mocked at, incited to jealousy, and treated as a little fool. After giving his mother her choice for a tale—merry or sad

Early One Morning

—he chooses a sad one, a Winter's Tale, and begins, too softly even for the crickets to hear him (though his listeners could hear *them*) not with, 'There was a child', or a princess, or an ogre, or a fairy, but 'There was a *man* . . . Dwelt by a Church-yard'. And even Sheridan Le Fanû never set-to better than that.

Stories written in their childhood even by famous novelists of the past which are to be found in print seem to be rare, though a close search might be well rewarded. Like Marjory Fleming, Emily Shore went first to history for her themes. But at the age of fourteen she wrote an account of an imaginary region in the heart of Australia, not only making for it her own pictures, but with its own geography, fauna and flora; manners, religion, science, and even language of its people all complete. Alas, that has vanished. *Her* father would certainly not have thought of publishing such juvenilia. Nowadays juvenilia—and even infantilia—in print are not uncommon; and the child-artist vies with the child-author. Is this publicity bad for them? To appear in person in public, as may youthful fiddlers or dancers or acrobats or actors or bell-boys has its dangers—as well for their art as for their artlessness. But the publicizing of things of the mind—like music, or pictures, or self-expression in words—risks leaving the child responsible for them insecurely private. All authors perhaps should be heard rather than seen. What pearls they cast before their public thrive no worse if in general they themselves keep close in shell. The danger begins when a child is thus made over-self-conscious, and is tempted to imitate what he has done, or to scribble his tales not out of a genuine impulse, and not to please himself but his elders. And so the promise, if delicate, may fail to fulfil itself: 'But now my fountain stopt, it runs no more'.

Juvenile fiction (even up to the age of twenty or over) seems seldom at any rate to be of much intrinsic value. It may none the less be rich with promise. Here are three episodes which I have been privileged to borrow from a complete story, many thousands of words long, entitled *A Scrap of Paper*, by Simon Asquith. It was written with immense labour when he was in his eighth and ninth years.

PODO

'Bang! goes the loud crack of a gun, and a perfectly fit mongrel puppy at the height of health falls dead. Podo! dear Podo. At that

456

moment Keith's most faithful friend, a dog that had stood by him for the past year, through all his troubles and so far miserable life. This dog had endured much for his beloved master's sake. His history dated back to when, a miserable, starving, turned-out waif, Keith found him roaming about the streets. Keith and his mother had done their best to keep him alive, and, wonder of wonders, he had thrived, but at the end of a year of hardship and fright he was dead.

'Many dogs die each day, many dogs are born each day. Many people die and many are born each day. But the world, life and existence rolls on through sadness and grief, through merriment and happiness and delight and laughter. But for Podo this was the end.'

THE CRICKET MATCH

'They did not know who should toss, for it was a local ground, so they said they would toss for tossing, but who should toss for tossing? "Why," said one of the females, "We will toss for which side is to toss for tossing." Who was to do that? So one of the umpires tossed, and the ladies won the toss, and went in, and scored three runs, all scored by the lanky lass. Rain then came on and the match was abandoned. The ladies wept copiously, and the mischievous males laughed. And that was the end. I do not know why I have told you the story of the village cricket match. Perhaps just for a little mental relief!'

MURDER

'Then suddenly his fiery temper burst, and streaming out curses he caught hold of his wife, and lifting her higher and higher above his head, using every atom of his powerful strength, till his arm muscles were bulging like so many balloons. He swung his arms slightly backwards and hurled Keith's mother across the room. She went hurtling through the air, crashed against the decaying wall and fell to the ground with a great thud. . . . Keith rushed to his mother's side. A gash in her forehead was bleeding. A fearful cut marked her neck. She sat up smiling.

' "It hasn't killed me this time, Keith dear," she said. "But I tell you one thing. . . soon it will." '

Here and there we can of course trace this author's highly original, minute and sanguinary footsteps in grown-ups' snow.

Early One Morning

But he is well *behind* his narrative, so to speak; and if the blood-boltered realism of the last section in one so young should shock the sensitive reader, let him turn to a lyric by the same author on a later page not so much as an antidote, but as a reminder that the author of *Titus Andronicus* wrote also, 'Hark, hark! the lark.' Indeed it is no more unchildlike that both rhyme and story should have flowered out of the same mind than that the evening primrose and the deadly nightshade should exult in the same square yard or two of soil. Lyric and melodrama in fact are closer akin to one another than to a hard, incisive intellectuality. It is sharpness, hardness, smartness and wit in childhood that, like white waters on a reef, may betoken perils ahead.

Jane Austen finished her 'education' at the age of nine, having spent little more than a year at a school in Reading, kept by a Mrs. Latournelle, who afterwards welcomed Mrs. Sherwood, Mary Mitford and Fanny Kemble among her pupils. Mrs. Latournelle, who hadn't 'a word of French', was a housekeeper-like person of the old school, 'a stout woman, hardly under seventy, but very active although she had a cork leg'. Her garden was an Eden as well as old-fashioned. Here her pupils were allowed to wander at ease and unseen. Not that little Jane went to the Abbey School to 'profit much by her instruction'. It was chiefly to be in the company of her beloved sister Cassandra; indeed, as her mother said, 'if Cassandra were going to have her head cut off, Jane would insist on sharing her fate'. After the age of nine her culture, with the aid of her family, must have been purely self-culture; Richardson, Johnson, Cowper and Crabbe being among her favourite authors.

In 1933 was printed and published a note-book of 92 leaves, entitled *Volume the First*, acquired by the Friends of the Bodleian. In this she had copied out—in a handwriting 'large and not completely formed', but maturing towards the end of the book—scraps of fiction, one at least of which cannot have been written later than 1791, when she was in her sixteenth year. It seems likely that some of its contents—*Love and Freindship* in the Second Volume is dated June 13, 1790—were written a few years before this.

'It will always be disputed', says Mr. R. W. Chapman in his Preface, 'whether such effusions as these ought to be published'. It is a delicate 'ought'; but in any case the Ayes in this dispute will be

JANE AUSTEN
From a portrait by Zoffany

Stories

unfeignedly grateful, and the Noes can refrain from reading. The truly sagacious author, meanwhile, may take warning, and whether out of vanity or in reverence of the Muses, obliterate his infant tracks.

Jane Austen's early prose, apart from occasional picturesquenesses like '2 elegant young women leaning on each other's arm', is not much more precise and prosaic than the *Song* and *Epitaph* which adorn her *Frederic and Elfrida*:

> 'That Damon was in love with me
> I once thought and beleiv'd
> But now that he is not I see
> I fear I was deceiv'd.'

The epitaph recalls the Sand-seller's sweetheart: 'And down to the bottom of the dirty Thames Sank the pretty little Ratcatcher's darter':—

> 'Here lies our friend who having promis-ed
> That unto two she would be marri-ed
> Threw her sweet Body and her lovely face
> Into the Stream that runs thro' Portland Place.'

In the stories it is by no means easy to see very far into the mind of the writer; the refraction is extreme. Intended to amuse her 'dearest brother Charles',[1] they appear to have been written at that pitch of sanity when the young mind becomes conscious that the sober and genteel world of the adult is mad. This juvenile Jane Austen is indulging in a solemn mockery on the verge of a peal of hilarious laughter. In a few years she will be transmuting into her quiet and reticent comedy what she is now guying as the purest nonsense, a nonsense too (like the 'tossing' in Simon Asquith's cricket match), of her own discovery. The characters are not only

[1] Apart from Charles who lived to be an admiral (and died of cholera on the Irawaddy at the age of seventy-two) there were James, Edward, Henry and Francis—who died an Admiral of the Fleet and G.C.B. at ninety-one. Jane then, and Cassandra had plenty of company in their childhood, for they were all educated at home. They loved hunting, and it was Francis, a year her senior, who at the age of seven bought on his own account a pony, a bright chestnut which he called Squirrel but his brothers nicknamed Scug, for £1. 11s. 6d. This two years afterwards he sold at a guinea profit. His 'pink' consisted of a jacket and trousers that his mother made for him out of an old scarlet riding-habit.

Early One Morning

faintly reminiscent of Mr. Rochester's unspeakable female friends in *Jane Eyre*, but are still more markedly grown-up. There is even a flavour of Swift in the 'greazy tresses' and the 'swelling Back', and yet nothing suggestive of *The Young Visiters*.

'Agreeable to such a determination, they went that very evening to pay their respects to Mrs. Fitzroy and her two Daughters. On being shewn into an elegant dressing room, ornamented with festoons of artificial flowers, they were struck with the engaging Exterior & beautifull outside of Jezalinda the eldest of the young Ladies; but e'er they had been many minutes seated, the Wit & Charms which shone resplendent in the conversation of the amiable Rebecca, enchanted them so much that they all with one accord jumped up and exclaimed:

' "Lovely & too charming Fair one, notwithstanding your forbidding Squint, your greazy tresses & your swelling Back, which are more frightfull than imagination can paint or pen describe, I cannot refrain from expressing my raptures, at the engaging Qualities of your Mind, which so amply atone for the Horror, with which your first appearance must ever inspire the unwary visitor.

' "Your sentiments so nobly expressed on the different excellencies of Indian and English Muslins, & the judicious preference you give the former, have excited in me an admiration of which I can alone give an adequate idea, by assuring you it is nearly equal to what I feel for myself."

'Then making a profound Curtesy to the amiable & abashed Rebecca, they left the room & hurried home. . . .'

And again:

'Madam, When the sweet Captain Roger first addressed the amiable Rebecca, you alone objected to their union on account of the tender years of the Parties. That plea can be no more, seven days being now expired, together with the lovely Charlotte, since the Captain first spoke to you on the subject.

'Consent then Madam to their union & as a reward, this smelling Bottle which I enclose in my right hand, shall be yours & yours forever; I never will claim it again. But if you refuse to join their hands in 3 days time, this dagger which I enclose in my left shall be steeped in your hearts blood.

'Speak then Madam & decide their fate and yours.'

460

Stories

Miss Austen's stories, says Coventry Patmore, 'are photographed experiences, and these of the most ordinary sort'. If then we compare her early scraps of fiction with her best, we shall see with what pains she polished her lens. She 'is as small', he continues, 'as she is perfect; but in reading her we never think of the smallness, but only of her . . . perfection'.

Having described herself in her Autobiography as 'a fat, little, commonplace woman, rather tongue-tied', Mrs. Oliphant remarks, not without a confessed tinge of jealousy, that George Eliot 'must have been a dull woman with a great genius distinct from herself'. Jane Austen appears to have been precisely the reverse of this. She cannot have been for a single moment a dull woman; but had she any great genius *distinct from* herself?

2. *'The boy he had an auger to bore holes two at twice.'*

That children may have pretty shrewd notions of the perils entailed in authorship is made clear by a letter to Mrs. Meynell from her daughter Monica. 'Our parents', says Miss Viola Meynell in her *Memoir*, 'had a glamour for us that is perhaps lost by parents who occupy themselves more with their children's affairs.' This did not preclude frankness; and the rebuke that follows was one of a series of letters which were hand-delivered nearly every day.

'Dear Mother,—I hope you will in time give up your absurd thoughts about litreture. It makes my mind get quite feverish when I think of the exhaltation your undergoing. I'm getting quite frightened about calling you "dear Mother" because you will begin to take it quite seriously. Just because Mr. Henley and those sort of unsencere men say you write well simply because they know if they don't flatter they'll never get anything for their paper. Now mother take my advise and don't be quite so estatic, you'll get on just as well in the world and much better because you'll be respected. Now just you see. Monnie.'

None the less, these clear wits, that had another outlet in the family paper that was 'edited under the table', could be at least as encouraging as the unsencere:—

'There are few real writers alive now. Mrs. Meynell is certainly one of these few that are in existance. She has produced two books which the world ought to respect and venerate. They are perfect masterpieces. Her thought is a thought which very few writers got. It is mystical, but excucite. She is a little obscure to readers who are not up in litruture suficciently to understand mystical touches. . . . Her works are like her. Hers is a very docile temprement and thoroughly simpithetic. When she is singing a synpethitic song you can tell that she must have some excellent powers in her head.'

Once again the form disguises the substance. Edited for Stevenson's 'Golly-what-a-paper!', then flourishing as the *Athenaeum*, it might run:—

'Writers in touch with reality, and themselves real, are few nowadays. Mrs. Meynell assuredly is one of these. She has published two books that are worthy of the world's veneration and respect. They are masterpieces. Her thought is profoundly original, tinged with mysticism, exquisitely expressed. That mysticism, needless to say, may lie beyond the appreciation of any but the elect. . . but in many of her lyrics, none the less, even wayfaring Everyman (and for that matter, Everywoman!) may discern eminent powers of mind and heart.'

The tinge of a style may show so early that it would not need as acute a critic as was this one under the table to detect the author of *Sense and Sensibility* in *Frederic and Elfrida*. What precise idea of its writer, then—age, office, standing, character—does the following extract from a tale entitled *Memnon, or Human Wisdom* invoke in the reader's mind?

'. . . Memnon having thus in the morning abjured women, the excesses of the table, play, quarrels, and, above all, the court, had been, before night, duped and pigeoned by a fine lady, filled drunk, rooked at play, drawn into a quarrel, robbed of an eye; and had been at court, where he found himself laughed at. Petrified with astonishment, and overpowered with grief, he moves homeward, death-sick at heart. He finds his house surrounded by bailiffs, in the act of gutting it on the part of his creditors. He stops half dead under a plane-tree; he here meets the fair lady of the morning, walking with her dear uncle. She burst out a laughing at seeing Memnon with his plaister. The night came on; Memnon laid himself down on some straw near the walls of his house. A fever seized him; he fell asleep in the crisis of the disorder, and a celestial spirit appeared to him in a dream. It was clothed in resplendent light; it had six fine wings—but neither feet, nor head, nor tail, nor resemblance to anything earthly.

' "What art thou?" said Memnon. "Thy good genius," replied the being. "Restore me, then," said Memnon, "my eye, my health, my money, my wisdom." He then related how he had, in one day's time, lost all these. "These are adventures for you," said the spirit, "which we never meet with in our world." "And where may your world be?" said the man of woe. "My country," said the spirit, "is five hundred millions of leagues from the sun, in a little star near Sirius; as you see here."

' "Dear, what a nice country!" said Memnon: "so you have no sluts who dupe a poor man; no particular friends who win his money and knock out his eye; no bankrupts; no satraps who laugh at you because they refuse you justice." "No," said the native of the star, "none of these things at all. We are never cozened by women, for we have no women. We never commit excess at table, for we never feed. We have no bankrupts, for with us there is neither silver nor gold. We can't have our eyes closed up, because we have not bodies made like yours; and satraps never do us injustice, because in our little star all the world is on a footing."

'Memnon then addressed him: "My good master, wifeless and dinnerless? how do you contrive to pass your time?" "In watching over the other world intrusted to our care," said he, "and I am come here just now to console thee." "Alackaday!" replied Memnon, "why didn't you come last night to prevent me from committing so many follies?" "I was with thy eldest brother Haspar,' said the celestial being. "He is more to be pitied than thou. His gracious Majesty the King of the Indians, at whose court he has the honour of belonging, hath caused put out both his eyes for some petty indiscretion; and he is at this moment in a dungeon with his hands and feet in irons." "It's very hard," said Memnon, "when one has a good genius in the family, that one brother should be blind in one eye, the other in both—one lying on straw, the other in prison." "Thy lot shall change," replied the animal of the star. "It is true thou shalt always be half blind; but then, this excepted, thou shalt be happy enough, provided always thou shalt not form the foolish project of being perfectly wise." "That, then, is out of the question?" said Memnon, with a sigh.

Early One Morning

' "As impossible," said the other, "as to think of being perfectly clever, strong, powerful, or happy. Even we ourselves are far from it. There is, indeed, one globe where all that may be had; but in the hundred thousand millions of others which are sprinkled over space, everything is got by degrees. One feels less pleasanter in the second than in the first; still less in the third than the second; and so on, down to the last, where every mother's son is an absolute fool." "I greatly fear," said Memnon, "that our little terraqueous globe is precisely the little habitation of the universe about which you are doing me the honour to speak." "Not altogether," said the spirit, "but nearly so; everything must have its place."

' "But stay," said Memnon; "some poets and philosophers, then, are in the wrong to say that everything is for the best?" "They are quite right," said the philosopher of the upper regions, "if we consider the arrangement of the whole universe." "Ah!" replied poor Memnon, "I shall never be able to see that, till I've got back my other eye." '

Lord Brougham was in his thirteenth year when in 1791 he wrote this derisive satire on human life, of which these are the concluding pages. Whatever its metallic gibes may owe to Lucian and Voltaire (*Candide* had been published about thirty years previously), and the 'celestial spirit' may be a memory of the Apocalypse, there is little trace in it of the undigested. It is hard and scintillant as a scrap of quartz. We might expect these 'sluts', this 'death-sick dupe', this wit and cynicism from an emaciated man of the world, possessing a remarkable vocabulary for the purpose; hardly from a superannuated boy of twelve, to whom an amiable aunt might recently have presented a copy of the newly published *Songs of Innocence*.

Childhood, says William Bell Scott, who was a poet as well as a painter, 'has the credit of being a Garden of Eden, but it is rather an enchanted island full of strange noises, and haunted by a Caliban'. Caliban and very strange noises indeed haunt *Memnon*, but of 'sweet aires and drowsie voices' not the faintest echo.

Children, like their elders, write of course according to their kind—even if they may desist in view of a censor. They can be as keenly observant of the actual as of the mock earnest; and to the wide-awake among them the world of the grown-up resembles the stage of a theatre, of which they themselves are the secret,

464

amused, critical and more or less unbiased spectators. But other
children who may be equally clear of eye and keen of understanding live not only a private and a public life, but also in a secret and
visionary reality of their own. And that too—though seldom in
fiction perhaps—they may attempt to describe.

3. 'My speech shall distil as dew.'

In *Apostate* Mr. Forrest Reid recounts a dream of his early
childhood: the dream of a *place*—the fringes of an unexplored
world, that was of an unspeakable loveliness and life and mystery.
This dream haunted his waking hours with its strange beauty and
peace and filled his heart with a pining to return to it. It recurred
at intervals, the boy in it—of about his own age—who was the
secret sharer of its solitude, growing older as he himself grew
older. 'What hands in what mysterious clock in nature have on
these occasions been reversed I cannot say, but I have literally gone
back to those last days of the true dreaming; my thoughts, my
emotions, my *understanding* even, have been precisely what they
were then.'

At length there came a day, he was sixteen, when, with this
repeated *experience* for theme, he set to work on a story, deter-
mining, its first chapter done, to read not a word of it over until
it was finished. 'I wrote simply to express'—*not* such things
as excited the minds of Jane Austen or Brougham in their childhood—but 'the other, secret self', and 'without thought of anything else'. Looking back, he realizes, 'I wrote badly, with a positive, not a negative, badness; for I had every fault except insincerity'. Throughout his story his 'aim remained unaltered. . . . It
was that this book should reflect all the beauty I had found both in
the real world and in my dream world. I saw this beauty as a river,
flowing, flowing endlessly by me, while I stood lost in its dreamy
enchantment, upon the bank. . . .' It was to contain 'everything I
had ever loved'.

Having at length come to the end, he turned back to the beginning again, read it steadily through—and faced the icy revelation:
'My fairy-gold was trash. This was the story I had written, but it
was not the story I had tried to write. . . . I was intelligent enough
to see that what I had done was hopeless, that I couldn't write at

Early One Morning

all'. And what in essence is that strange and memorable novel, *Uncle Stephen*, but an attempt to recapture this early dream?

Not that Mr. Reid was by any means a docile or what we call a 'nice little' boy. 'I very seldom felt good. I very seldom *was* good, though I loved goodness in other people.' And his *Apostate* exposes an eye which was as keen as a kestrel's both for the grown-ups and the children whom he encountered in his early years: whether they were sham, silly, vicious, or sentimental; or unaffected, odd, highly natural and endearing. He was a rebel.

'This was the story I had written, but it was not the story I had tried to write'. They are words that might be applied by a true artist to his imaginative work of any kind. But should we expect them from a boy—this shattering candour? Every word, every sentence, every brush-stroke, every crotchet, every chisel-mark in a work of art is an attempt, by little and little, to represent once and for all some fragment of the inextricably complex instantaneous stuff of mind and heart—'mind-and-body'. Its translation into *any* medium, of enduring beauty though that may be, cannot but be inadequate. The nucleus too of Mr. Reid's story was not an invention of the waking mind; it was a dream. And all imaginations, all really creative ideas, are something akin to dreams.

As does the fecundated seed of a plant or an animal or a child, they contain a potential all, and are of a hidden growth. We can aid that growth, tend and safeguard it, and when the seeds have fully or in part revealed what they are the seeds *of*, we can endeavour to express their likeness in any way we choose. Absolute failure confronts us, of course, if we have no skill in the method chosen. But even fifty years' hard practice in any art may far from ensure success even with a seed that (like Mr. Forrest Reid's) may have lain awaiting its clarion in the dreaming mind since early childhood.

The notion then that a child 'makes things up' *purely* out of impulse, that its trifles are 'unconsidered', may be far from the truth. A child, L.E., not yet six years old, while hopping birdlike and restlessly in and out of her perambulator when she was taking the air one morning, explained *her* notion of this process to her mother. The stories she is referring to were as yet in her head; and her babbled monologue was taken down immediately after mother and daughter had returned home, 'as nearly word for word as

466

may be'. She may in some degree have been 'making up' 'as she went along'; but she was in any case trying to put into words rapid and momentary ideas and images.

'I often take out my stories and look at them when I'm in bed before I go to sleep. You can see all the pictures. I open the little door with my key, and take out the story book. You have to take them out sometimes, or else they get dead, and don't work. You see, they can't live without having air.

'There are little bubbles in your head that come down and gently press your tongue, and that makes the words come. If they don't get aired, for one thing, the little bubbles get stuck together, and then the words come out all wrong. If four bubbles come down stuck together there are four words missing. I've got heaps of seeds of stories in my head, and they take a long time to sprout. *They get little shoots on them.* If you tell a story it makes another seed, like when a flower grows, and then dies, it drops some more seeds down.'

Most writers of fiction, of a stuff lying any deeper than the wits, would agree, perhaps, that 'ideas' (nucleuses, germs, focal points) for stories unless they are revived occasionally in the fresh air of the life of the mind may 'get dead' and then refuse to 'work', and that such ideas may themselves seed; for which reason they are apt to appear in clusters—and these 'get little shoots on them'.

CHAPTER XXXIV

VERSE

★

1. 'They are like grasshoppers, sing they must.'

From prose let us now turn to verse, from fiction (which defies definitions, or needs none), to poetry of which there are so many. These differ widely in detail, but agree for the most part in the assurance that poetry gives delight. Three states are involved; first the seed, the conception, the imagery, the thought, the emotion in the mind of the maker of the poem; next, the words into which, as best he can, and according to a certain pattern, he translates all this; and last, the complete effect of those words when they in turn have been transmuted by the reader of them into his own thought, imagery, feeling.

The poem in words is permanent, and through them may be divined in part the infinitely complex process that went to its conceiving and making. Few readers concern themselves with this process. To like or not to like, is the usual standpoint. However that may be, the effect of any particular poem in words must vary with every individual reader, and to some degree perhaps with every renewed reading of it.

'Over that Art', says Polixenes to Perdita concerning the flowers she is presenting to him—'over that art (which you say addes to Nature) is an Art That Nature makes. . . . The Art itselfe, is Nature.' That is truth itself concerning poetry. We can examine and analyse the words of a poem and their effects on mind and senses to our hearts' content, and, possibly, to our brains' confusion; but any attempt, *thus and thus*, not to take to pieces, but consciously and deliberately fragment by fragment to build up what is within the mind and then to transmute it into words is clearly doomed to failure. Human 'nature' and the self within, in the closest and swiftest, and in an all but inscrutable collaboration, are responsible for the one; and as to the other, even the art of revealing it in words, whether spontaneously or by deliberation, is also largely of nature: 'the Art itself, is Nature'. In other words, a poet is born, he is not even self-made—though with him alone rests the proof of his own gifts.

Words are not merely fixed symbols with an absolute meaning and innumerable personal connotations; they consist also of sounds; and of sounds made by the most complex and direct of all instruments—the human voice. Which of the two is the more natural, speech or singing, I cannot say; but the one can be of at least as delicate, supple and mutable a melody and charm as the other. A poem that is a delight to hear is a delight also to utter—even if it is Bully Bottom who is reciting it to Mustardseed. In lieu of a badly needed specific term, we may call the delighting verbal sounds of a poem music. There is no one word for describing the effects of the *utterance* of that music on the mind and senses of the *speaker*. Part too of the pleasure in listening to 'ravishing accents' or even to a fiddle seems to consist in translating the sounds heard into sounds inwardly mimicked—by the vocal organs. So with words. If, for example, we repeat heedfully and intently, *O what can ail thee Knight-at-arms, Alone and palely loitering,* and alliteration is almost solely a *speech*-pleasure, we become at once cognizant of a rare rhythmical music, both in the making and in the hearing of it. If not, so far as words are concerned we are either poetry-dumb, poetry-deaf, or both.

Nevertheless this verbal music remains in much a secret. It is as direct and instantaneous as our delight in colour, or in dancing, or in the proportion of one thing with another. Having in his *Three Lectures on Aesthetic* said of music itself that it is 'the least representative' of the arts, since its 'rhythms and combinations' are 'direct resemblances of emotions', Bernard Bosanquet continues: Poetry, 'like the other arts, has a physical or at least a sensuous medium, and this medium is sound . . . significant sound. . . . Poetry no more keeps its meaning when turned into corresponding prose, than a picture or a sonata keeps its meaning in the little analyses they print in the catalogues or programmes'. Again, Poetry, says Myers in his *Essay on Virgil*, has 'that mysterious power by which

Early One Morning

... mere arrangement of sound'—'like some exquisite soft harmony' in Mr. Aldous Huxley's words, 'apprehended by another sense'—'can convey an emotion which no one could have predicted beforehand, and which no known laws can explain'. And Edgar Allan Poe: 'Music when combined with a pleasurable idea is poetry; music without the idea is simply music; the idea without the music, is prose, from its very definiteness'. And it was he who had the excellent fortune to be translated into French prose by no less a master of this verbal music than Stéphane Mallarmé; for prose of course has its own music as well as verse.

A strange feature in regard to this verbal 'music' is that although it may give us a profound and inexplicable delight, we may yet be incapable of achieving it ourselves. But this is a commonplace, true of all the arts. For one artist that can well and truly 'make' there are scores of his fellow-creatures that can, as well and truly, only appreciate.

2. 'Now from a lattice-window high.'

It is on the effect of its sounds alone of course that the music of a poem depends. But a poem in words depends also for its effect on the *mind* upon what its verbal music conveys—imagery, thought, feeling. When, then, Mr. Bernard Shaw said of Keats, in the year of his centenary, that he was 'the sort of youth who calls a window a casement ... (on paper)' his arrow went clean to the mark, though, since he uses the word literary, one may be a little less certain of his aim. Keats has many casements: 'Magic casements opening on the foam Of perilous seas, in faery lands forlorn'; 'A bright porch, and a casement ope at night To let the warm Love in!'; 'Full on the casement shone the wintry moon'. Nevertheless, in 'The Eve of St. Mark'—and in spite of the 'rich antiquity' of its Minster-square—we have, 'Bertha arose, and read awhile, With forehead 'gainst the window-pane'.

All this was not a mere choice between synonyms, nor even due to the fact that the two objects referred to (apart from their purpose, that of giving air and light) are not the same in construction. In associations they are leagues apart, as far apart as 'Give me to drink' and 'Give me a drink'; and though, as Mr. Shaw says, Keats's effect is 'magical', this, I think, was not his real intention.

Verse

The word casement in these several contexts, both in sense and in *sound*, was the only word available to convey his meaning and serve his purpose. And this is equally true of 'window' in the last quotation. Here casement would be ruinous. It was not what he *meant*.

As Marjory Fleming said in her 'Sonnet'—not on Keats: 'The beauties of his mind do shine And every bit is shaped so fine'. And she too has her casement:

> 'I love the morning sun to see
> That makes me from the house to flee
> I love the morning sun to spy
> Glittering through the casements eye.'

Incidentally, the word came into its present usage in 1556 and occurs only once in the Authorized Version: 'At the window of my house I looked through my casement, and beheld among the simple ones, I discerned ... a young man void of understanding'— as mere imitators of Keats are likely to be. And again, 'So many greedy looks of young and old Through casements darted their desiring eyes'. Would they dart quite so desirously and greedily through 'windows'?

These verbal minutiæ are no less essential in imaginative prose. 'I realise,' says Mr. Wells in his Autobiography, 'I realise that Being is surrounded, east, south, north and west, above and below, by wonder. Within that frame, like a little house in strange, cold, vast and beautiful scenery, is life upon this planet.' This statement, pure and unique, comes from the region in the mind called the imagination. Transpose the order even of the compass points 'east' and 'west' or of the group of adjectives, and something, minute it may be, but none the less vital, flickers out. The prose too is of the stuff of poetry. And yet, if it be transformed into free verse, half its magic evaporates.

> 'I realise that Being is surrounded,
> East, south, north and west,
> Above and below,
> By wonder.
> Within that frame, like a little house
> In strange, cold, vast and beautiful scenery,
> Is life upon this planet.'

471

Early One Morning

So, even with a witticism. A character in *Man and Superman*, unmindful of Byron and Mary Duff, facetiously declares that 'First love is only a little foolishness and a lot of curiosity', *not* 'a lot of inquisitiveness'. For even if the two words were precisely synonymous, the reiteration of *ness* and the absence in the substitute of the assonance *lot* and *os* would sadly dull the barb. William Blake supplies a characteristic variant of this comment on early love—calf-love as it is called by the stall-fed: 'Then she bore Pale desire, father of Curiosity, a Virgin ever young'.

It is difficult to tell to what degree Blake elaborate his own poems. His own statements differ. But in his Annotations to Lavater's *Aphorisms of Man* he added the words 'Most Excellent' to, 'The poet, who composes not before the moment of inspiration, and as that leaves him ceases—composes, and he alone, for all men, all classes, all ages'. Concerning another aphorism, 'The infinitely little constitutes the infinite difference in works of art, and in the degrees of morals and religion; the greater the rapidity, precision, acuteness, with which this is observed and determined, the more authentic, the greater the observer', he remarked, 'Uneasy'. By this 'uneasy'—to judge from another entry, 'Uneasy, but I hope to mend'—he meant apparently not that he deemed it untrue, but that he could not with assurance apply it to his own practice. That the aphorism is true of *poetry* can be easily proved. All that is necessary is to alter even by so much as a syllable what we accept as fine poetry, and then to observe the difference in the effect of the alteration on the mind, the imagination and the feelings. That decided, we can then enquire: Whatever the 'meaning' (its effects on us) may now be, has any *poetry* escaped; has any poetry been added?

Consider but a moment, for example, the following emedations, out of how many unrecorded, made by Coleridge in *The Rime of the Ancient Mariner*. For the second line in

> 'Her beams bemocked the sultry main
> Like morning frosts yspread'

he substituted, 'Like April hoar-frost spread'. For that in

> 'Alone, alone, all, all alone,
> Alone on the wide wide sea'

Verse

he substituted, 'Alone on a wide wide sea'. And for that in

'The horned Moon with one bright Star
Almost atween the tips'

he substituted, first, 'Within its nether tip'; and last, 'Within the nether tip'.

It was out of such infinitesimals as these that his creative mind built up what became at last the complete texture of his unique poem. We can explain in *part* the various causes of the difference in effect of each such verbal change on the images within our mind; we can but very superficially explain the process; nor can we explore the complete and involved area and ramifications of those images. Fine wit and humour are no less dependent on fine verbal shades; but the language of poetry, which, to some minds, is far more rare and precious than either of these, is the most sensitive, and appeals to far profounder sensibilities.

Needless to say we may value poetry more for its ideas, its philosophy, its message, its edification than for the delight which the mere music of its language may bestow. But that music absent, poetry, in the generally accepted meaning of the word, is absent, whatever else may remain. Like all immediate appeals to our senses, mind and being, it is a secret language, but one with scores of dialects. Poets may differ one from another as much as Dante from Verlaine, Marlowe from Crabbe, Sophocles from Clare; this power of invocation however they have in common. It haunts every language, as beauty may haunt a waterfall. A village Milton, then, may be a Milton of purest ray serene in the secrecy of his own mind, but if he is unpossessed of this secret, then mute and inglorious, or vocal and even more inglorious, he must remain. Thus, as Gray himself declares, he may be spared many temptations, including—

'The struggling pangs of conscious truth to hide,
To quench the blushes of ingenuous shame,
Or heap the shrine of Luxury and Pride
With incense kindled at the Muse's flame. . . .'

Early One Morning

3. '*And he shewed me a pure river of water of life*'

That a child is capable of delighting in poetry and its music the early memories of reading in childhood already quoted amply attest. Nursery rhymes, compact of rhythmical chiming and rhyming, are the joy of the merest weanling—'A troop of Echoes whose sweet duty Is but to sing'. A child too may share the very 'aura' of poetry. Of *A Midsummer-Night's Dream* Francis Thompson says, 'I did indeed, as I read the last words of Puck, feel as if I were waking from a dream and rub my mental eyes. . . .' So with *Macbeth, The Tempest, Lear*: 'Never again have I sensed so exquisitely, so virginally, the *aura* of the plays as I sensed it then. . . . But never, in any individual passage, did I sense the poetry of the poetry, the poetry as poetry. . . . I was over young to have awakened to the poetry of words . . . the sense of magic in diction. . . . It is the opening of the eyes to that wonder which signalizes the puberty of poetry. I was, in fact, as a child, where most men remain all their lives'.

Later, we may be inclined to doubt if this statement referring to 'the sense of magic in diction', despite its being Francis Thompson's, is true of all children. That, in addition to such an 'awakening', a child should be capable of using and of originating this half-secret language would seem to pass belief. Nevertheless he may have gone a good way towards acquiring not only a vocabulary as a means of expression, but also those inflexions and intonations and emphases which are essential to the feeling to be conveyed in words, and to their very sense. When he says, Oh mother, how I love you! or, Honey for tea! he is not likely to sing either out in the wrong tune. And he may even have taken in his stride the sweet uses of *will* and *shall*. The evidence available at least suggests that unless at a comparatively early age the secret *has* been revealed to him, poet he will never be, even though he be as wise and become as learned as Solomon and should outlive Melchisedec.

Indeed there is ample proof, as we shall see, that poets begin to rhyme early*. The 'prentice hand in this rare craft is not only his own master but takes a very small glove. Lucky little bards, they know as yet nothing of the malice and pedantry of literary cliques, nor have surveyed 'the cold blank bookseller's rhyme-freezing face'!

Verse

Isaac Watts as a child of eight was writing 'devotional pieces' to ease his heart and to please his mother. At five Dante Gabriel Rossetti (his own name a lyric in eight syllables), set to work on a 'bombastic drama in blank verse' entitled *The Slave*, which was 'astonishingly correct', we are told, in its spelling and versification. For second string to his Cupid's bow he had a legendary poem, *Sir Hugh the Heron*. And when he was tired of rhyming he could draw. The family milkman, amazed one day at discovering him engaged in making a sketch of his rocking-horse, announced that he had seen 'a baby making a picture!' Like a child with her dolls he was only practising two instinctive crafts. A conflict between romance and realism is characteristic of his work both as a painter and as a poet; and the two arts occasionally converge one into the other: his pictures become literary, his poems pictorial.

The wind blows where it lists, the seed germinates where it can. When he was eight years old, Thomas Hardy, as we know, chanced one day in a closet on *A History of the Wars*; his grandfather at that time having been a volunteer. It was 'illustrated' with melodramatic prints. So *may* have chanced a score of children. But here the seed fell upon good ground (as *The Trumpet Major* alone would prove), and more than fifty years afterwards it towered into that monarch of the forest, his Epic-Drama, *The Dynasts*.

So backward at the age of ten that she could neither read nor write, Lady Caroline Lamb—'Such a wicked-looking cat I never saw!'—was none the less making verses. So, at the same age was a greater poet, William Wordsworth; and not only that. During the next four or five years he spent his days, as he had determined, in heedful observation of the world around him, but in keeping a resolution to note down 'any natural appearances, hitherto unnoticed' in the poets he had read.

As for 'the little nightingale', Alexander Pope, whose body alone was denied beauty by the Graces, he was in countenance a pretty little boy, clear-eyed and rosy-cheeked. He taught himself to write, in the manner of print, and began versifying, in his own words, 'farther back than I can well remember'. At the age of twelve he wrote a play, borrowing his theme from Ogilby's translation of the *Iliad*—which was acted by his schoolfellows in the garden at Hyde Park Corner; Mr. Dean, the gardener himself, taking the part of Ajax. His Ode on Solitude—revised, but not

Early One Morning

necessarily improved later—was of the same order, its final stanza being of a verbal delicacy that even Herrick could not excel:

> 'Thus let me live, unseen, unknown;
> Thus unlamented let me die;
> Steal from the world, and not a stone
> Tell where I lie.'

Needless to say, he had an exquisitely sensitive ear—'The Rape of the Lock' resembling a web of glistening gossamer in the suns of October—and even in these early days he not only, as Miss Edith Sitwell tells us, sorted his poets according to the texture of their verse, but in his epic, *Alcandar Prince of Rhodes*, of which in two years he finished four books of about a thousand verses each, mimicked the beauty in the styles of many poets—Milton, Spenser, Ovid and Virgil, for example. If his epic had been the deadest dullest doggerel, which it assuredly was not, the sheer diligence entailed by such a feat at that age is amazing. Moreover his satirical work—the outcome chiefly of an ineffable dexterity of the wits— is of a kind which practice perfects. He was 'born to refine our numbers', and he set to his duties without delay.

When she was four years old, Elizabeth Barrett Browning, in her own words, 'first mounted Pegasus'. Two years afterwards she sent the following 'carefully indited lines' to her father—a father whom in her letters she addressed as 'dearest Puppy' and must have loved dearly. Alfred Tennyson was, I think, rewarded for his first verses with a golden sovereign; Mr. Barrett presented Elizabeth with half that sum in paper.

> 'Oh! thou! whom Fortune led to stray
> In all the gloom of Vice's way,
> Return poor man! to Virtue's path,
> The sweetest sweet, on this round Earth;
> Thou slumber of the peaceful mind.
> Be loving, grateful, good, and kind;
> Oh! beauteous virtue, prythee smile,
> For you the heaviest hours beguile.'

Are these mere words, we may ask. Can this child of six have *seen* her 'poor man' in the same fashion as Bunyan saw his Christian; could this tyrant of the nursery realize the graces in her sixth

Verse

line? In view of what has gone before is there any reason to doubt it?—though this does not of course better, as such, the verses. The words themselves were acquired; their cadences, even if borrowed, are of her own contriving; and to which of the Elizabethans might we have attributed her fifth line? That at the age of eight she set aside a complete quarto volume for her rhymes hints at dangers ahead.

Children as richly gifted are doubtless rare as 'nuts' in May; but there are infinite gradations of intelligence and enterprise; yet I have heard a well-meaning teacher complacently addressing an aerial class—'thousands of little boys and girls'—with a condescension that even a guineapig might resent.

4. 'Says the mother to the daughter,
"Why do you thus lament?" '

'Perdita' first went to school to the five Misses More, one of whom was Hannah. Her earliest remembered play was *King Lear*. In this William Powell, once Garrick's understudy and then 'proceeding rapidly towards the highest paths of fame', though death was soon to 'drop the oblivious curtain'—he died when she was eleven—took the part of the King. His wife played Cordelia, 'but not with sufficient *éclat* to render the profession an object for her future exertions'. She mentions other names 'to prove that memory does not deceive me'. 'The comforts', she tells us, 'and even the luxuries of life distinguished our habitation'; 'The bed in which I slept was of the richest crimson damask'. She played Juliet at Drury Lane in pink satin and silver, with a head-dress of feathers white as snow.

At the age of ten—'so tall and formed in [her] person' that she might have passed for thirteen—she became a boarder in Mrs. Meribah Lorrington's Seminary. This lady 'was the most extensively accomplished female that I ever remember to have met with . . . and a mistress of the Latin, French, and Italian languages'. She was said to be 'a perfect arithmetician and astronomer, and possessed the art of painting on silk to a degree of exquisite perfection.'

Unfortunately she drank; and according to Southey's 'perfect

recollection' was so little of a purist in English that she would remark, 'Her went to school to we'. To the Misses More, then,
Perdita must have owed the rudiments of her style, which drapes
at least as much as it conceals an aching heart, since *that* can hardly
have been self-taught.

She shared Mrs. Lorrington's bedchamber, and the widow confessed to the child that intoxication was her only 'refuge from the
pang of prevailing sorrow'. The phrase resembles a pall over an
empty coffin. Nevertheless mistress and pupil were good friends.
Like Rousseau and his father, they read to one another, and at the
age of ten Perdita began to versify. When she was in her twelfth
year a captain in the British Navy, 'deluded by her appearance',
proposed marriage, but alas, 'this amiable gallant officer perished'
at sea a few months afterwards. From her sixteenth year onwards
she was besieged by suitors, married and single, who were incited
for the most part by 'diabolical stratagems for the enthralment of
my honour'. And Mr. Robinson appears to have been a feeble
stronghold.

George IV was eighteen years old when he first saw her—in *A
Winter's Tale*, she being twenty-one. And *his* career in the world at
large resembled that of his childhood in the Old Palace at Kew,
where, says Miss Burney, he was to be seen 'running about from
one end of the house to the other, without precaution or care.' His
brother William, on the other hand, who put in over ten years'
hard service at sea and had Nelson for a friend, loved playing with
toy ships as a child, and once boasted, 'If ever I shall become a
king, I will have a house full of ships, and no other king shall dare
to take them from me!' As for their father, George III, so pleased
were his people to see him that at the first anniversary of his birth
he was waited on by a troop of sixty soldiers, all of them under
twelve years of age. He himself was in a uniform surmounted by a
feathered hat.

But to return to poetry and Perdita. A sheaf of her early verses
appeared in print shortly before her marriage, when she was sixteen—the age at which Felicia Hemans published *her* first poems.
Perdita's beauty has been immortalized by Reynolds, Romney,
Gainsborough, Hoppner and other painters, but she was a poor
poetess, said Southey, though she had 'a finer feeling for metre, and
command of it, than any of her contemporaries'. What merits her

Verse

earliest work may have had it is impossible to say. The several poems are not dated, and they all seem to be 'much-what in like manner'!

At the age of twelve Benjamin Franklin was apprenticed to his brother James, a printer by trade, who had returned to Boston from England. He would borrow a book in the evening, and sit up in his bedroom 'reading the greatest part of the night' in order to be able to return it next morning. 'I now took a fancy to poetry, and made some little pieces'—'The Lighthouse Tragedy' and a sailor's song on the capture of Blackbeard the Pirate. 'The first sold wonderfully', he tells us, but his father discouraged him with the assurance that 'verse-makers were generally beggars. So I escaped being a poet, most probably a very bad one.' About this time too he met with an odd volume of the *Spectator*. To this—and afterwards to Defoe—he played the sedulous ape. He re-wrote from memory some of the papers in the volume, and turned some of its tales into verse. Later, when he had forgotten the originals, he paraphrased his verse into prose again, and turned back for comparison to the *Spectator*. He was thus encouraged to think, 'I might possibly in time come to be a tolerable English writer, of which I was extream ambitious'.

These little scattered particulars are but a small glass but how vividly they reflect this tranquil, sagacious, public-spirited giant, with a genius for common sense, as Miss Anna Burr describes him, —this 'large embodiment of somewhat small virtues' and 'perhaps the most typically American of all our great men'. But since a genius for poetry by no means precludes a forte for common sense, we must await a glimpse of *The Lighthouse Tragedy* before accepting his 'probably'.

If Southey's reading between the ages of twelve and thirteen was prodigious—it included the whole of Josephus, in seventy sixpenny numbers, apart from Tasso, Shakespeare and the *Arcadia* —the bulk of his writing in the same two years almost passes belief. Apart from translations of Ovid, Virgil, and Horace, a satirical description of English manners, verses on mortality, heroic epistles in rhyme (one 'from Octavia to Mark Anthony'), he wrote the story of the Trojan War in dramatic form, 'the scene being laid in Elysium'! Three books of this poem were finished before at the age of fourteen he went to Westminster. By the time he was twenty he had burned or had lost ten thousand verses, and

Early One Morning

had preserved as many more, apart from fifteen thousand that were worthless. 'No systematic education', Southey maintains, 'could have fitted me for my present course of life as well as the circumstances which allowed me . . . to feel and follow my own impulses.'

Leigh Hunt tells us that when he was twelve years old he wrote several hundred lines of a poem entitled the *Fairy Ring*—in rivalry of Edmund Spenser. It was followed by sixty lines 'in capricious Latin metre' which sounded to his ear 'like English Pindarics'. 'I remember also an elegy on the death of a good old aunt, who used to encourage me to keep my nails pared and to write fine letters, and whom, in lamenting her loss, I called *a nymph*'. His earliest piece however was an ode lauding the Duke of York's victory at the siege of Dunkirk (in 1793). After finishing his ode he was deeply mortified to discover that the vaunted victory had been a defeat.

At this age also he was brandishing a boyish pen on the subject of Macbeth—his mind's eye none the less 'on the object':

> 'What struggling passions rule the soul;
> What passions strong that spurn controul,
>   The human bosom fire!
> The potent warrior cas'd in steel,
> The king, the beggar, all can feel,
>   The power of fierce desire!
>
> 'The tempest howl'd; the forky light
> Gilt with pale ray the shades of night,
>   The pealing thunder crash'd!
> From murder'd Duncan came Macbeth,
> And to the ground, still warm with death,
>   The bloody dagger dash'd! . . .'

But it is rather milk and honey, often pleasant, sometimes over-sweet, than blood and thunder, which we associate with him. And some time during the next four years he wrote the following lines to a friend of his boyhood at Christ's Hospital, revealing a genuine sentiment, but touched with that prettiness, poeticism and languor, the influence of which in his later years was to prove for a while so perilous to Keats:

Verse

'O how delightful was it once to sit
And talk away the hours, my friend belov'd,
Beneath the lamp's dull flame, that palely shed
Its feeble light along the cloister'd walks,
Where oft we'd ramble! o'er our youthful heads
The gloomy arch, that favour'd converse sweet
Of whisper'd vows of friendship, heav'd on high
Its massy vault, along whose time-worn roof
Soft murmurs ran of breathing constancy.
While on my shoulder hung thy easy hand,
Beyond thy bosom, not a single thought
That flutter'd from my breast, unheeding stray'd:
Fix'd, and for ever, was my soul in thee! . . .'

'From eight years old,' says Egerton Brydges, 'I was passionately fond of reading, and had always a propensity to poetry, at least from the age of fourteen. . . . I am convinced' that a literary bent 'entirely arises from the inborn structure' of the mind. To write poetry well 'is another affair'. 'What does the author do', he asks later, 'who is the creature of labour and mechanical skill? He works his words into polish and point, but he borrows his ideas and his sentiments; he has no fountain within to draw from . . . I can perceive nothing different from my feelings, opinions, and powers of sixteen, except that I write with more fearlessness.'

Robert Browning at the age of twelve had composed enough poems to fill a volume. In these, 'the Byronic influence was predominant'. They shared the fate of Pope's epic and were destroyed. When it was decided that he should adopt literature as a profession, he 'qualified himself for it'—as Walter Pater counselled the literary novice—'by reading and digesting the whole of Johnson's Dictionary'; and at the age of twenty-one he sent the Rev. W. J. Fox the manuscript of *Pauline*, with this faintly Johnsonian, highly parenthetical and unchildlike letter—

'Dear Sir,—Perhaps by the aid of the subjoined initials and a little reflection, you may recollect an oddish sort of boy, who had the honour of being introduced to you at Hackney some years back—at that time a sayer of verse and a doer of it, and whose doings you had a little previously commended after a fashion—(whether in earnest or not God knows): that individual it is who takes the

481

liberty of addressing one whose slight commendation then, was more thought of than all the gun, drum and trumpet of praise would be now. . . .'

Mr. Laurence Binyon who in his boyhood, he tells us, nourished a fervent admiration for the writer of this letter, refers in a paper on *The Case of Christopher Smart* to 'Kit's' childhood. 'Born prematurely, he was a delicate child and debarred from the normal activities of boyhood. At the age of four, according to his biographer, he produced "an extraordinary effusion". This has not been preserved; but at thirteen he wrote some verses, "To Ethelinda, on her doing my verses the honour of wearing them in her bosom"; verses of a precociously amorous strain'. There came perhaps still earlier, he adds, a brief 'Ode to Idleness'—which delivers in its third line the complete tribe of poets into the enemy's hand:

> 'Sister of Peace and Indolence,
> Bring, Muse, bring numbers soft and slow
> Elaborately void of sense,
> And sweetly thoughtless let them flow.'

The majority of the children whose rhyming feats have been here referred to became at length poets of credit and renown. Failure to do so however does not necessarily mean all wasted labour. Joseph Priestley and several other writers refer to the benefit of writing *verse* in early years if only as an aid to ease and flexibility in the writing of prose. He himself proved 'nothing of a poet', but since Mrs. Barbauld ('one of the best poets', in his view, that England could then boast of), confessed that she had owed her first attempts in poetry to his example, this for him was grace enough.

CHAPTER XXXV

PRELUDINGS

★

1. *'It looked and listened far away*
    As if for what can not have been.'

Such evidence as this, quite apart from what follows, is proof that the impulse for verse and rhyme is apt to manifest itself very early in life, and that a child, in response to some inward need, will take infinite pains to practise his mind in the skill of words. And not only on paper, of course. Far earlier the habit may have set in of fitting words to what is seen and felt, of recording experience, so to speak, in the silence of the mind. Genius is defiant of weariness. It toils on in its cocoon even when its host is fast asleep. It is more than probable then that a list of the English poets who have *not* lisped in numbers would be very brief. And what of the countless many who never succeeded beyond a lisp? A poet may do worse, on behalf of the Muses, than die young. He may break his faint promises and desert even the foot-hills of Parnassus. Beamish nephews—their Snark actually proves to be a Boojum, and they are never heard of again.

When we examine rhymes written in childhood, mere common sense will of course make the amplest allowances; and we shall expect nothing of much intrinsic value. However fair and informative promises may be, only achievement counts, whether a poet is aged eight, or as in the case of the writers of 'Crossing the Bar' and of 'The soul's dark cottage . . .' over eighty. We must remind ourselves again none the less that when a gifted child with a full heart and pent-up mind makes use of such everyday words as flower, bird, home, mother, longing; hate, afraid, magic, dark, Time; sweet, mysterious, and so forth, they may be symbols for him of objects or thoughts or feelings from the intensity of which

Early One Morning

life and habit may for us have taken off the edge. Scores of early memories have been proof enough of this: Harriet Martineau's prismatic colours, Mr. Frank Kendon's succory flower, Mr. Forrest Reid's dream, Thomas Hardy's first love and the sunset colours on the staircase, Leigh Hunt's porpoises. The mere words for such experiences are poverty-stricken to convey the states of the mind and imagination that may have been not merely of the earthly moment, but related to the experiences of the mystic.

For yet one further example; De Quincey, the dreamer, returns even to his infancy in self-defence; and his choice of the word 'stings' for remembrances so covetable and unusual at such an age is characteristic. 'The earliest incidents in my life', he tells us, 'which left stings in my memory so as to be remembered at this day were two, and both before I could have completed my second year; namely, first, a remarkable dream of terrific grandeur about a favourite nurse, which is interesting to myself for this reason— that it demonstrates my dreaming tendencies to have been constitutional, and not dependent upon laudanum; and secondly, the fact of having connected a profound sense of pathos with the reappearance, very early in the spring, of some crocuses. This I mention as inexplicable; for such annual resurrections of plants and flowers affect us only as memorials, or suggestions of some higher change, and therefore in connection with the idea of death; yet of death I could, at that time, have had no experience whatever. . . .' There may be pathos for a child, I think, even in his first glimpse of things so lovely in colour, shape and mystery; and this without hint of death. If we find pure memories so early and of this kind difficult to accept, shall we also refuse credence to the following attested scrap of doggerel which was suddenly ejected in war time by Michael Abercrombie when he was four years old?—

> 'Nell
> Fired a shell
> Out of hell.
> It reacht heaven
> Punctually at seven.'

May he not also have been confronted with the ineffable, which these words are only the nakedest attempt to express?—whereas two-year-old De Quincey would have found *any* description of

484

Preludings

his supreme dream or of his grieved delight in the crocuses wholly beyond his tongue.

That children will freely use runes of the meaning of which only the merest glimmer remains, is proved by their ancient game rhymes—and by much else. A younger sister of Sir Henry Newbolt's, when they were children together, would sometimes be called upon to say the family grace—'For these, the Lord's mercies, the Lord's holy name be praised'. A listener rather more attentive than usual asked her one day to repeat it slowly, and this was the response, 'Nees nors nurses, nors nose nays nays'. There must of course remain a good many norses, noses and nayses in a young child's mind, even when most of his words are letter-perfect; while yet his grace solely consisting of them is by no means necessarily a grace without meaning.

And what of his elders? Are we scrupulously vigilant in respect to graces, texts, hymns? There is a line, for example, in 'The voice that breathed o'er Eden' that I had wholly failed to excogitate until the occasion came for choosing a wedding hymn: 'Be present, awful Father, to give away the bride'! Are we ever too old to be satisfied with not exactly pregnant concepts of everyday terms, such as electricity, or anticyclone, or inferiority complex, or the Heaviside layer? Scorning encyclopædias, we may originate self-satisfying explanations very far from the real meaning of terms we do not understand. So also may children—though it does not follow that theirs are superficial. I must have been older than eight when (clearly because I never *read* the words), I supposed the first sentence of the Lord's Prayer to be, 'Our Father, we chant in Heaven'. The last three words none the less continued to perplex me, until one day in church I explained to myself that since, when we are praying to God, we cannot be wholly on earth, and were then *intoning* the sentences, we were literally chanting in Heaven! My own mother too once told me that when she was a little girl she furiously disapproved of the collect asking God to 'illuminate the best shops'. It was the dark little shops, like the Old Sheep's in *Through the Looking Glass*, and not the flaring gas-lit London emporiums, which in her loving kindness *she* had most closely at heart.

All this admitted, we are entitled to criticise a child's verses by any standards and as severely as we please, for unlike most things

Early One Morning

that are endued with life, a poem will survive even the most finical dissection.

To begin with, here is the rhyme referred to on a previous page. It was written by Simon Asquith at the age of six and a half, and is called a Song:

'The lark that sings with outstretched wings
On Earth is glory above most things.

'He flies such a height
Right out of sight
Oh! it is such a wonderful flight!

'I hear the lark singing
I hear its song ringing
Music and joy to the earth it is bringing.

'The lark that sings with outstretched wings
On Earth is glory above most things.'

Scalpel and forceps would at once pause at 'right' and at 'such'. Having tried to improve on these and to experiment perhaps with *a glory* or *glorious* in another line, modesty may prevail and we may decide to accept the rhyme as it stands. Indeed, far more clearly than the words of which it is composed, its rhythmical pattern conveys its writer's delight in the bird of which it sings.

This comment is no less true of the following scrap of writing by 'L.E.', which she dictated to her mother when she was three months under five years old. It lies on the almost imperceptible borderline between verse and prose.

'Where does she lie?
Does she lie in the cool green leaves
    in the shadow of the woods
The woods so still and cool?
Her love has made it beautiful.

'And she shall have a horse,
A milk white steed to mount and gallop
    away, over the hills and dells.
She is beautiful indeed, a princess she
    is as well.

Preludings

I may not even see her,
But still, but still, her steed will arrive soon,
I could kiss her feet, as she stands
    among the leaves, her loveliness and her
    long hair——
The world is perfect because she's there.
What would I do without her? I could sob,
    and if she died I would die too.'

Whatever their origin, the fourth and eleventh lines are not only true but express a truth also more clearly realized than that which put 'princess' *after* 'beauty'. No one could miss the serenity and the dovelike colour of the poem, or the unobtrusive alliteration tying the sense and music together as may the instruments in an orchestra their theme. And behold, here is *first*, horse (window) and next, steed (casement). Substitute one for the other and how fatal is the effect. Naturally, this is not to suggest that this child thought such things *out*. Whatever Pope meant by the phrase, her numbers came.

Charles Kingsley, as his sermon on an earlier page suggests, was also a solemn-minded child—not that the solemn are never merry. He preached the sermon when he was four years old; eight months afterwards he wrote the following scraps of verse. The first piece is entitled 'Song Upon Life'.

'Life is, and soon will pass;
As life is gone, death will come.
We—we rise again——
In Heaven we must abide.
Time passes quickly;
He flies on wings as light as silk.
We must die.
It is not false that we must rise again;
Death has its fatal sting,
It brings us to the grave.
Time and Death is and must be.'

The other is 'Night'.

'When the dark forest glides along,
When midnight's gloom makes everybody still,

Early One Morning

The owl flies out,
And the bat stretches his wing;
The lion roars;
The wolf and the tiger prowl about,
And the hyena cries.'

How far these things were purely spontaneous, who can say? They at least *suggest* great care and pains—of which of course a child is easily capable. I treasure for example two manuscripts. One a rhyme written by a child of about six years old which chiefly consists of scribbled out variants; the other a scrap made up solely of numerals. The compiler of this began with the units and wrote on steadily into the thirteen thousands—continuing his labours even after he had gone to bed. Perhaps he was in pursuit of what a five-year-old was recently very anxious to discover—'the name of the last number of all'. His 9's and 7's, and some of the other digits are occasionally the wrong way round, many of the figures are upside down, and the lines run from right to left!

But to return to Charles Kingsley. The chief problem in reading his verses is to conceive what precise mental images the words 'death', 'Heaven', 'time', 'rise', 'glides'—and even 'hyena'—can have invoked in his mind. Not necessarily less at any rate in anything *essential* than may ours. His hyena we can be certain did not fall short in ferocity. The rhythm here and there stumbles, with the sense; and both were in part no doubt borrowed. But if, solely out of memory, we attempt by piecing together a few sentences from Blake or from the Bible to attain as delicate a pattern and as tranquil a reflection of thought and feeling, we shall better realize the difficulties he had to face.

Technically, too, these lines are by no means mere chopped-up prose. 'Night' not only has an unusual stanza-form, but the pervasive chiming of the *i* sound (little though its writer may have realized it) is bound up with its meaning and effect. Compare with the original,

'The lion roars;
The wolf and the panther skulk about,
And the fierce jackal barks.'

Moreover Kingsley continued to be partial to sequent *i* sounds. Twenty-five years afterwards he wrote:

488

Preludings

'Watchman what of the night?'
    'The stars are out in the sky;
'And the merry round moon will be rising soon
    'For us to go sailing by.'

'Watchman what of the night?'
    'The tide flows in from the sea. . . .'

Fifty years afterwards—and in the 'Ode to the North-East Wind'
there are six successive *i rhymes*—he is cantering away with:

'. . . I would sing about the blossoms, and the sunshine and the sky,
    And the tiny wife I mean to have in such a cosy nest;
And if some one came and shot me dead, why then I could but die,
    With my tiny life and tiny song just ended at their best.'

He was, as we are told, little more than 'out of his coats' when
he wrote 'Night' and his 'Song Upon Life'. They are a child's
gropings; but if we ask ourselves which of these four examples has
the deeper origin, which are the most 'juvenile', which come closest to the secrets of the mind, is there much doubt about the
answer?

At the age of seven Marjory Fleming, 'little young devil' as she
then confessed herself to be, is bemoaning her 'wasted talents'.
And this was how the talents were being wasted:

'The lofty trees their heads do shake
When the wind blows, a noise they make
When they are cut a crash you hear
That fills your very soul with fear
Tis like the thunders loudest roar
You would not like to hear much more
It makes the earth begin to quake
And all its mity pillers shake
The viabration of the sound . . .
It makes the mountains to resound.'

And at eight (when she was fined twopence for biting her nails),
she finished an 'epic' of nearly two hundred lines on her 'Beautiful
and Angelick' Mary Queen of Scots, beginning,

'Poor Mary Queen of Scots was born
With all the graces which adorn

Early One Morning

Her birthday is so very late
That I do now forget the date
Her education was in france
There she did learn to sing and dance
There she was married to the dauphin
But soon he was laid in a coffin. . .'

and ending

'There is a thing that I must tell
Elisbeth went to fire and hell
Him who will teach her to be cevel
It must be her great friend the divel.'

Five months before her death, pining for her Isa, imagining they
are together again, she sends her a rhymed letter:

'. . . . You are the darling of my heart
With you I cannot bear to part
The watter falls we go to see
I am as happy as can be
In pastures sweet we go & stray
I could walk there quite well all day
At night my head on turf could lay
There quite well could I sleep all night
The moon would give its tranciant light
I have no more of poetry
O Isa do remember me
And try to love your
                    Marjory'

An imploring impulsive music rills through the heedless sentences. Two centuries before this, an old writer, comparing with
sack all the ales—from China ale to mum—concluded—'pure,
racy, sparkling, brisk, rich, generous, neat, choice, odorous, delicious, heart-reviving Canary!' Put *Marjory* for 'Canary'—and if
by neat is meant undiluted—the list will still hold good. Nevertheless, if she had triumphed over measles, how easily might all her
scribblings have been destroyed. That is the common fate of most
early efforts—even those of the greatest of writers. And burned
manuscripts tell no tales.

Preludings

That imaginative children can reveal in verse their differences one from another—body, mind and spirit—needs no other proof than a comparison of these rhymes with these further examples by 'L.E.' (also the author of:

> 'There was a young person called Grace
> Who had a peculiar face,
>   She wore upon that
>   A peculiar hat
> In a very peculiar place.')

In her sixth year came 'The Evening':

> 'The evening shines on the ground,
> And the moon shows her beam,
> The night is coming, and the day is ended,
> And the river is quite still.'

in her seventh:

> 'On the river bank I sit,
>   Sad, sad am I.
> I think of all the lovely things
> I did when I was young.
>   Old am I,
>   Old and tired.'

and when she was eight and a half, 'The Bird':

> 'In the willow tree
>   I saw a little bird,
> He sang the sweetest song
>   I ever heard.
> He pointed his head
>   Up towards the sky,
> There never was a bird
>   With such a sweet cry.'

One can watch (as if in a series of photographs) both experience and skill on their way.

Early One Morning

The author of the following sprightly and worldly-wise defence of a cat, with its sudden final abandonment of technique for the sake of an immediate crisis, was also about eight years old when it was written.

'A cat in distress,
Nothing more, nor less,
Good folks, I must faithfully tell ye,
As I am a sinner,
It waits for some dinner
To stuff out its own little belly.

'You would not easily guess
All the modes of distress
Which torture the tenants of earth;
And the various evils,
Which, like so many devils,
Attend the poor souls from their birth.

'Some a living require,
And others desire
An old fellow out of the way;
And which is the best
I leave to be guessed,
For I cannot pretend to say.

'One wants society,
Another variety,
Others a tranquil life;
Some want food,
Others, as good,
Only want a wife.

'But this poor little cat
Only wanted a rat,
To stuff out its own little maw;
And it were as good
Some people had such food,
To make them *hold their jaw!*'

SHELLEY, AT THE AGE OF THIRTEEN
From a portrait by Hoppner

Preludings

Whatever may be said of this as doggerel, its sentiments are not exactly what we expect of Shelley. One of his yet earlier experiments in verse was a satire on a French governess. He also collaborated with his sister in a play, which was returned by Matthews as 'unsuitable for acting'. Eleven years after scribbling his discourse on the cat in distress he is writing to his father, 'You well know that a train of reasoning and not any great profligacy has induced me to disbelieve the scriptures. . . . How then were we treated? not as our fair, open, candid conduct might demand, no argument was publickly brought forward to disprove our reasoning. . . . I hope it will alleviate your sorrow to know that for *myself* I am perfectly indifferent to the late tyrannical violent proceedings. . . .' On which sentiments Timothy Shelley's only written comment at the moment was, 'Infamous'. 'I could not descend to common life', was Shelley's explanation to Godwin of his career at Oxford. But if before he confronted the Master and Fellows of University College he had himself chanced again on this rhyme of his childhood, is it extravagant to suppose that he might have found it a little easier so to descend? It *might* in some degree have placated the Master.

John Ruskin as a child 'turned everything he observed into verse'. A month before his seventh birthday he wrote in couplets of eight syllables *The Needless Alarm*, a tale about a mouse and strikingly correct in 'rhyme, rhythm and reason'. At the same age he concluded another poem with,

> 'The pole-star guides thee on thy way,
>   When in dark nights thou art lost;
> Therefore look up at the starry day
>   Look at the stars about thee tost.'

Here the rhyme—a not uncommon event in verse—gets a little the better of the reason. At the age of nine he finished the first book of an epic poem entitled *Eudosia*, containing 220 lines; and he had ventured into 76 lines of the second:

> 'When first the wrath of heaven o'erwhelmed the world,
> And o'er the rocks, and hills and mountains, hurl'd
> The waters' gathering mass; and sea o'er shore,—
> Then mountains fell, and vales, unknown before,
> Lay where they were. Far different was the Earth

Early One Morning

When first the flood came down, than at its second birth.
Now for its produce!—Queen of flowers, O rose,
From whose fair coloured leaves such odour flows,
Thou must now be before thy subjects named,
Both for thy beauty and thy sweetness famed.
Thou art the flower of England, and the flow'r
Of Beauty too—of Venus' odrous bower.
And thou wilt often shed sweet odours round,
And often stooping, hide thy head on ground.
And then the lily, towering up so proud,
And raising its gay head among the various crowd,
There the black spots upon a scarlet ground,
And there the taper-pointed leaves are found. . . .'

The lines are observant, knowledgable, and if we take a glance at the description of himself on page 103 their vocabulary may surprise us. We may feel none the less that a child of Ruskin's ability and upbringing might have continued in this strain as long as diligence admitted. There is little inward impulse; the metre jolts; the sound *ou* that interweaves itself in the verses, unlike Kingsley's *i*'s in 'Night', is merely monotonous. The secret rhythmical music is wanting; and though Ruskin became a master of rhythmical and musical prose, this, of verse, he never acquired.

Four months after his ninth birthday Peacock despatched from school—'in a neat and careful hand'—a letter to his mother. And he himself gleams out of it like a scarlet berry in a cluster of leaves.

'Dear Mòther, I attèmpt to write you a letter
In verse—tho' in prose, I could do it much better:
The Muse, this cold weather sleeps up at Parnassus,
And leaves us, poor poets, as stupid as asses.
She'll tarry still longer, if she has a warm chamber,
A store of old Massic, Ambrosia, and Amber.
Dear Mother, don't laugh, you may think she is tipsy,
And I, if a poet, must drink like a gipsy. . . .
All the boys at our school, are well, tho', yet, many
Are suffer'd at home, to suck eggs with their Granny.
"To-morrow", says daddy, "you must go my dear Billy,
To Englefield House; do not cry, you are silly."
Says the Mother, all drèss'd in silk, and in sattin;

494

Preludings

"Don't cram the poor boy, with your Greek, and your Latin;
I'll have him a little longer, before mine own eyes;
To nurse him, and feed him, with tarts, and minc'd pies;
We'll send him to school, when the weather is warmer:
Come, kiss me, my pretty, my sweet little charmer."

'But now I must banish all fun, and all folly;
So doleful's the news, I am going to tell ye:
Poor Wade! my schoolfellow, lies low in the gravel;
One month ere fifteen, put an end to his travel:
Harmless, and mild, and remark'd for goodnature:
The cause of his death, was his overgrown stature:
His èpitaph I wrote, as inserted below;
What tribute more friendly, could I on him bestow.
The bard craves one shilling, of his own dear Mother;
And if you think proper, add to it another.'

EPITAPH

'Here lies interr'd, in silent shade,
The frail remains of Hamlet Wade;
A youth more prom'sing, ne'er took breath;
But ere fifteen, laid cold in death!
Ye young! ye old! and ye of middle age!
Act well your part, for quit the stage
Of mortal life one day you must;
And like him moulder into dust.'

About half a dozen lines in this headlong effusion jolt when they should canter. The best way to discover why is to try to improve on them. For the fifteenth, for example, we might try, *A few days I'll kèep him befòre mine own èyes.* This removes the jolt, but omits the 'little', and somehow blurs the indulgent mother! The bold bad rhymes are excellent for their purpose, especially 'asses'; and what an ingenious eel-like contrivance in words is 'All the bòys at our schòol, are wèll, tho', yet, many. . . .' The change not only of metre but of pitch, tone and key (with its *d*'s and recurrent *a* sounds) at the epitaph is little short of masterly.

Happy-go-lucky doggerel the rhyme may be, but here *is* the intuitive music, and it is no less his own than are the glimpses both outward and inward of Daddy and Billy, of his fond mother, and of Thomas Love's six-years' senior, poor dead and gravelled

Early One Morning

Hamlet Wade. All his life long Peacock thus mischievously amused himself with his fellow-creatures; but never more merrily. It is a sad thing he wrote so little verse.

Elizabeth Barrett, again, was a year younger than Peacock when, also with the family purse in view, she sent a very romantic and religious story, entitled 'Sebastian', to her mother with this business-like note:

'Madam,—

'I request you to accept this little story for three shillings, and to write copies to be sold to the public.

'I am, Madam,
'Your most ob't Humble Servant
'Elizabeth Barrett.

'Nursery Row.
'N.B. You owe me 8d. for other things.'

Five years after despatching his letter in rhyme, Peacock won a consolation prize of five shillings from the *Monthly Preceptor* for an essay in couplets on the question, 'Is History or Biography the more improving Study?' In this strain:

'With bright examples the young mind to fire,
And Emulation's gen'rous flame inspire. . . .'

The couplet might have been written with a ferule, and if it was the outcome of schooling, Thomas needed the consolation. Mere ageing of course may have been to blame; but in any case, the young poet has become a parrot, or at best a cockatoo, and we must weep for the mocking-bird.

3. '*To him no author was unknown,
Yet what he wrote was all his own.*'

When Abraham Cowley began to read, and to take pleasure in reading, he tells us that,
'There was wont to lye in my Mother's Parlour (I know not by what accident, for she her self never in her Life read any book but of Devotion) but there was wont to lye *Spencer's* Works. This I happen'd to fall upon, and was infinitely delighted with the Stories of the Knights, and Giants, and Monsters, and brave Honses,

Preludings

which I found every where there: (Tho' my Understanding had little to do with all this) and by degrees with the Tinkling of the Rhyme and Dance of the Numbers, so that I think I had read him all over before I was twelve Years old, and was thus made a Poet as irremediably as a Child is made an Eunuch.'

The Tragicall Historie of Piramus and Thisbe, which was published in 1633, his fifteenth year, was *written* at the age of ten, *Constantia and Philetus* at twelve. The former, in the words of Edmund Gosse, resembles the 'poem of a little boy (of unparalleled precocity)'; the latter, 'the correct and tedious work of some man that never can be famous.'

The *Historie* contains both a love-song, beginning

> 'Come Love, why stayest thou? The night
> Will vanish, e're wee taste delight. . .'

and an 'Epitaph':

> 'Underneath this Marble stone,
> Lie two Beauties joyn'd in one.
>
> 'Two whose Loves, Death could not sever,
> For both liv'd, both dy'd together.
>
> 'Two whose Soules, being too divine
> For earth, in their own Spheare now shine.
>
> 'Who have left their loves to Fame,
> And their earth to earth againe:'

which we should hardly resent as Sir Philip Sidney's if we found it in *Astrophel & Stella*.

In the story itself, all allowances having been made for a child of ten, one hardly knows which to marvel at most—its management, its vocabulary, the supple style, the 'ideas', or the verbal melody. Three stanzas follow out of the thirty-five:

> 'Like as a bird which in a net is taine,
> By strugling more entangles in the ginne,
> So they who in Love's Laborinth remaine,
> With striving never can a freedome gaine:
> The way to enter's broad; but being in,
> No art, no labour can an *exit* win. . . .

497

Early One Morning

'While shee thus musing sate, ranne from the wood
An angry Lyon to the cristal Springs,
Near to that place; who coming from his food,
His chaps were all besmear'd with crimson bloud:
    Swifter then thought, Sweet Thisbe straight begins
    To flye from him: feare gave her Swallowes' wings....

'With hast she let her looser Mantle fall:
Which when th' enragèd Lion did espie,
With bloody teeth he tore't, in peices small,
Whilst Thisbe ran and look'd not backe at all.
    For could the sencelesse beast her face descrie,
    It had not done her such an injury. . . .'

'O! where am I? quoth she, in earth or heaven,
Or in the ocean drench'd, or in the fire?
What hour is this? or morn or weary even?
Do I delight to die, or life desire?
    But now I liv'd, and life was death's annoy;
    But now I died, and death was lively joy. . . .'

The fourth and last-quoted stanza is from Shakespeare's *Venus and Adonis*—for comparison.

Later in life, Cowley attempted to preen and prune these 'poetical blossomes'—and, again and again, as Alexander Grosart points out in his edition of the Complete Works, not merely failed to do so, but ruined his original. Three out of many examples will suffice. As a child he wrote:

'So that it seemes Aurora wept to heare,
    For the verdant grasse was dew'd with many a teare.'

This he 'improved' into:

'It mov'd Aurora, and she wept to hear,
    Dewing the verdant Grass into many a Tear.'

For

'Assist me, this sad story to rehearse
    You Gods, and be propitious to my verse:'

he substituted,

Preludings

'Aid me, ye Gods, this Story to rehearse
This mournful Tale, and favour every Verse.'

He has thinned out the sibilants, but the 'Tale' is redundant and the melody has gone flat. And last, for

'Soone as the morne peep'd from her rosie bed,
And all Heaven's smaller lights expulsèd were;
She by her friends and neere acquaintance led
Like other Maids, oft walkt to take the ayre;
Aurora blusht at such a sight unknowne,
To behold cheekes were redder then her owne:'

he substituted,

'Soon as the Morning left her rosie Bed,
And all Heaven's smaller lights were driven away:
She by her Friends and her Acquaintants led,
Like other Maids would walk at Break of Day:
Aurora blush'd to see a Sight unknown,
To behold Cheeks more beauteous than her own.'

This, apart, perhaps, from 'driven away' is 'a successful evaporation', as Grosart says, 'of all the poetry in the stanza, especially the informing thought of the twofold "redness"!'

4. ' *"I'll burn my books! O Mephistophilis!"* '

When he was eighteen Charles Lamb's 'very dear' Cowley wrote, 'I should not bee angrie to see any one burne my *Pyramus & Thisbe*'; and later, 'Even so far backward there remain yet some traces of me in the little footsteps of a child'—many of which, however, and how often is this the fate of amending poets, he himself did his best to obliterate.

Other poets have followed his example, and some have attempted to destroy as far as possible too headlong a venture into print. This, however, is a danger that no child can run into unaided by the adult. Fortunate then is the child with any such gift who has either chosen wise parents, or has the sagacity to keep his light under a bushel. No folly perhaps will quench the genuine flair, but the fate of Romney Robinson, whose career was re-

499

Early One Morning

counted by Mr. Forrest Reid some years ago, is warning enough. He was a versifying prodigy, and a fond father and the *literati* of Belfast did their genial utmost to convert him into a self-conscious and morbid little prig.

The names of the subscribers to his *Poems*, which was published in 1806, when he was thirteen, fill twenty-seven two-columned pages, and include that of Bishop Percy of the *Reliques* and the Lord Lieutenant. It is, says Mr. Reid, a charming little volume with an engaging portrait of its author—rosetted slippers . . . nice white trousers and cambric ruffles.

Romney Robinson could rhyme at large on anything at any moment—a faculty that astounds those who cannot rhyme at all. When he was only two years old he would weep to see his father affected to tears by *The Hermit of Wirkworth*—as might most sensitive infants—but then his father wept on purpose. Four years afterwards he addressed a poem to a doctor who had cured him of a fever:

> 'Again on Fancy's wings I fly;
>   Again I strike the trembling lyre!
> Thousands are born and thousands die,
>   Yet few can feel poetic fire.'

Quenched by the sun of flattery perhaps, his own small blaze went out early. Guiltless of any other improvisations he tried some time afterwards to suppress his *Poems*, survived them seventy-six years, and died, full of honours, aged eighty-seven. Notoriety is *Fame's* ugly sister; and, in regard to the young, yet again, it is the word 'dangerous' that must be emphasized in this self-oblivious sentence in a letter from Gerald Hopkins to Canon Dixon: 'I say it deliberately and before God, I would have . . . all true poets remember that fame . . . though in itself one of the most dangerous things to man, is nevertheless the true and appointed air, element and setting of genius and its works.'

Christina Rossetti was also home-taught. When she was four months over eleven years old, in April 1842, she gave her mother 'On the Anniversary of her Birth', a nosegay of flowers. It was accompanied by this greeting—its tiny courtesy condensing how much pains and how much adoration.

Preludings

'To-day's your natal day;
    Sweet flowers I bring:
Mother, accept I pray
    My offering.

'And may you happy live,
    And long us bless;
Receiving as you give
    Great happiness.'

'Charity' was written two years afterwards, and the second of its
first two stanzas, however great may be their debt to George
Herbert, might be recognized anywhere as of her making. In how
few too of her lyrics has she forborne not merely the intimated but
the expressed 'lesson'.

'I praised the myrtle and the rose,
    At sunrise in their beauty lying;
I passed them at the short day's close,
    And both were dying.

'The summer sun his rays was throwing
    Brightly: yet ere I sought my rest
His last cold ray, more deeply glowing
    Died in the west.

'After this bleak world's stormy weather,
    All, all, save Love alone, shall die;
For Faith and Hope shall merge together
    In Charity.'

Not less characteristic, though far more seldom indulged, is the
brisk realism, at about the same age, of:

'Come, cheer up, my lads, 'tis to glory we steer,
    As the soldier remarked whose post lay in the rear'

and the tart finality of:

'The roses lingered in her cheeks
    When fair Albina fainted;
O gentle reader, could it be
    That fair Albina painted?'

Early One Morning

After yet another two years every vital quality of her nature, body and spirit, is revealed in 'The Dream' and in 'Repining'.

The lines on Albina and the rouge were written in her fourteenth year. They are as little likely to be the work of a child of *seven* as Shelley's cat-rhyme was to be the work of Shelley at Oxford. These poems show, that is, how as the years of childhood melt away the direction of the minds' attention may change in its view over an enlarging experience—as a weather-vane veers with the wind. Its faculties alter their pattern, as it were, like the revolving coloured slides once so entrancing to childhood in the little old Magic Lanterns. But it is the same lantern.

When Frances Cobbe was thirteen—two years before she left her 'finishing' school—she wrote a story in verse, having for its hero the last and best

'Of a race of kings who once held sway
From far Fingal to dark Lough Neagh. . . .'

When, in her poem, the moon has risen—'a lamp of gold', O'Nial sails out to sea—'Like arrow from an Indian bow Shot o'er the waves the glancing prow'. Disaster follows, and then, as,

'. . . when Adam rose from the dust of earth
And felt the joy of his glorious birth,
And where'er he gazed, and where'er he trod,
He felt the presence and smile of God,—
Like the breath of morning to him who long
Has ceased to hear the warbler's song,
And who, in the chamber of death hath lain
With a sickening heart and a burning brain;
So rushed the joy through O'Nial's mind
When the waters dark above him joined,
And he felt that Heaven had made him be
A spirit of light and eternity.

'He gazed around, but his dazzled sight
Saw not the spot from whence he fell,
For beside him rose a spire so bright

'No mortal tongue could its splendours tell
Nor human eye endure its light.
And he looked and saw that pillars of gold

Preludings

The crystal column did proudly hold;
And he turned and walked in the light blue sea
Upon a silver balcony,
Which rolled around the spire of light
And laid on the golden pillars bright. . . .'

The last stanza, even though it may have been but a poor copy
of what was in this earnest child's imagination, is full of a visionary light and colour. 'Laid' is a little shibboleth which Frances's
elders have not always surmounted, and so is 'hath' in her seventh
line, but a happier one. '*Hath* ceased' entangles the tongue; in '*has*
lain' there is less of death.

Later in life Miss Cobbe became an enthusiast in many causes.[1]
As Mr. Shaw, with his eye on the stanzas in 'Isabella' beginning,
'With her two brothers this fair lady dwells', predicted of Keats
if he had lived, she found her 'destiny as a propagandist'. But
would Keats have done so? Could any word either in sense or
flavour be less in accord with his native wisdom and insight, and
with the trend of his genius? A month or so before, in his twenty-
third year, he began this poem, he wrote to his friend Reynolds:

'Perhaps the honours paid by man to man are trifles in comparison to the benefit done by great works to the "Spirit and pulse" of
good by their mere passive existence. . . . Now it appears to me
that almost any man may, like the spider, spin from his own in-
wards his own airy citadel. The points of leaves and twigs on which
the spider begins her work are few, and she fills the air with a
beautiful circuiting. Man should be content with as few points to

---

1 And she feared no adversary. Charles Darwin's *Descent of Man* filled her
with alarm. A letter, enclosing a volume by Kant, drew from him a reply concluding, 'I fully feel how presumptuous it sounds to put myself even for a
moment in the same bracket with Kant, the one man a great philosopher looking exclusively into his own mind, the other a degraded wretch looking from
outside through apes and savages at the moral sense of mankind.' She sent him
an article she had written on the Consciousness of Dogs. He complimented her,
agreeing that, in respect to a canine moral sense, an 'honourable dog' that has
been guilty of a trespass against his master may certainly seem 'ashamed', if not
positively afraid, to meet that master. He cited his beloved Polly, and added,
'When I was a very little boy, I had committed some offence, so that my conscience troubled me, and when I met my father, I lavished so much affection on
him that he at once asked me what I had done, and told me to confess.' Charles
had been dumbfounded by this divination.

Early One Morning

tip with the fine web of his Soul. . . . But the minds of mortals are so different and bent on such diverse journeys that it may at first appear impossible for any common taste and fellowship to exist between two or three under these suppositions. It is, however, quite the contrary. Minds would leave each other in contrary directions, traverse each other in numberless points, and at last greet each other at the journey's end. An old man and a child would talk together, and the old man be led on his path and the child left thinking. Man should not dispute or assert, but whisper results to his neighbour. . . .'

He is following his own counsel too, and is himself 'left thinking'. In 1849, Frances Cobbe, already intent on propaganda—a word which may, it seems, sink into meaning camouflaged advertising of dubious doctrine aimed at the ignorant, and then die of exposure—published a volume entitled *Criminals, Idiots, Women and Minors, Is the Classification Sound?* 'Minors', not *children*, be it noted; how woefully and truthlessly the latter word would have flattened the irony.

5. *'Yet the lark's shrill fife may come*
At the daybreak from the fallow.'

Walter Scott, in Mrs. Cockburn's words, was 'the most extraordinary genius of a boy I ever saw. He was reading a poem to his mother when I went in. I made him read on: it was the description of a shipwreck. His passion rose with the storm. He lifted his eyes and hands—"There's the mast gone!" says he, "crash it goes!—they will all perish!" After his agitation, he turns to me, "That's too melancholy," says he, "I had better read you something more amusing." I preferred a little chat, and asked him his opinion of Milton and other books he was reading, which he gave me wonderfully.'

His mother preserved a scrap of translation from Horace or Virgil written in a 'weak boyish scrawl', within pencil marks, *My Walter's first lines, 1782.* He was then eleven. The first of the two following stanzas which came later is clearly derivative, but it is not a translation. He is describing the wanderings of the Hebrews in 'Arabia's crimsoned sands'.

Preludings

'. . . There rose the choral hymn of praise,
    And trump and timbrel answered keen;
And Zion's daughters poured their lays,
    With priest's and warrior's voice between.
No portents now our foes amaze,
    Forsaken Israel wanders lone;
Our fathers would not know Thy ways,
    And Thou hast left them to their own. . . .'

The next is entitled, 'On the Setting Sun'.

'Those evening clouds, that setting ray,
And beauteous tints serve to display
    Their great Creator's praise:
Then let the short-lived thing called man,
Whose life's comprised within a span,
    To him his homage raise.
We often praise the evening clouds,
    And tints so gay and bold,
But seldom think upon our God,
    Who tinged these clouds with gold.'

There are resemblances between these two pieces—the rather mechanical jogtrot metre; the lesson; even the rhyme-sounds—the internal *in* and *a* rhymes in the second of them being particularly interesting. We may hesitate at 'beauteous tints' and at 'so gay and bold', also at 'wanders lone' and 'voice between'. A more inward test is an attempt to share the state of consciousness of the writer by attending slowly not only to the meaning of his words, but to their effect on us as we repeat them. That being so, which of the two stanzas gives the clearest reflection of the mind responsible for it? Which carries the greater conviction? Neither is comparable with 'County Guy', 'Proud Maisie' or 'Bonny Dundee'; but the first is taken from the 'Hymn of the Hebrew Maid' in *Ivanhoe*. 'On the Setting Sun' was written in July, 1783, when its author was twelve. Early memories have suggested again and again that if only even a child of seven had the requisite language, his writings would be of an extraordinary interest. So too does Mrs. Cockburn's glimpse of Walter Scott as a boy engrossed in his shipwreck. Once a poet, always a poet, but the coal from the

505

Early One Morning

golden altar may languish; and then it is rather habit than the energy of love and delight that endeavours to fan it into flame.

About the age of ten, perhaps, and not later than twelve, Colin Francis was responsible for 'Tony O!':

> 'Over the bleak and barren snow
> A voice there came a-calling;
> "Where are you going to, Tony O!
> Where are you going this morning?"

> ' "I am going where there are rivers of wine,
> The mountains bread and honey;
> There Kings and Queens do mind the swine,
> And the poor have all the money." '

If the bleak and barren snow be taken as a symbol of the capitalistic State, this would seem to be a Karl-Marxian Eden in a nutshell, wherein

> 'Sceptre and Crown
> Must tumble down
> And in the dust be equal made.'

And what elegant company for the prodigal sons!

Thomas Chatterton was a posthumous child, 'dull and dreamy' to all appearance until his seventh year. He then learned to read from a black-letter Bible and—like other children with their picture-books—fell under the spell of the illuminations in an old folio of music. At the age of twelve he contrived to deceive an undermaster at Colston Bluecoat Hospital—where he spent seven years—with his first 'antique'. Four years after this, he hoaxed the City of Bristol with a poem which he had dated 1248—though, in fact, as Walter Skeat declared, the *language* of his Rowley poems is never more than a superficial and faulty imitation of early English. When he was two months over ten years old (in 1762) *The Bristol Journal* printed his poem, 'On the Last Epiphany, or Christ coming to Judgment':—

> 'Behold! just coming from above,
> The judge, with majesty and love!
> The sky divides, and rolls away,
> T'admit Him through the realms of day!

Preludings

The sun, astonished, hides its face,
The moon and stars with wonder gaze
At Jesu's bright superior rays!
Dread lightnings flash, and thunders roar,
And shake the earth and briny shore;
The trumpet sounds at heaven's command,
And pierceth through the sea and land;
The dead in each now hears the voice,
The sinners fear and saints rejoice;
For now the awful hour is come,
When every tenant of the tomb
Must rise, and take his everlasting doom.'

Six years afterwards, on December 21, 1768, he wrote to 'James Dodsley of Pall Mall':

'Sir—I take this method to acquaint you that I can procure copys of several Ancient Poems: and an interlude, perhaps the oldest dramatic piece extant, wrote by one Rowley, a priest in Bristol, who lived in the reigns of Henry VIth and Edward IVth. If these pieces will be of service to you, at your command copys will be sent to you by

'Yr most obedient servt,
D.B.'

The letter came to nothing. At last, after toiling like a slave in a galley for two months in London, at a wage, for his verses, of a farthing to twopence a line, and when his efforts to save himself from starvation had failed, 'too proud to accept the meal his landlady had offered him', he took arsenic (not ignorant, either, we may assume, of its hideous effects), and was buried in the paupers' pit of the Shoe Lane Workhouse.

Chatterton was indeed 'a prodigy of genius', but a genius more of the conscious mind than of the imagination. The most conspicuous feature in the 'Last Epiphany', this work of a boy eleven years old, is the unfaltering energy of its rhetoric. Its sharp-cut phrases resemble an inscription in brass. So did his life. Words could hardly mean more than these say, but what, in profound feeling and conviction did they represent in the imagination of the child that wrote them?

One is apt to forget that a piece of imaginative writing, of any

507

profound bearing, may be a salient and intense *experience*. In the experience of the actual, even at its extremes of tragedy and disaster, the self within need be no more than an intent but aloof spectator. In the experience of the ideal—of an emotion fully remembered—it is wholly *engaged*. At an easy reading we may accept, for example, 'The Dream of Eugene Aram', as a sort of idyllic melodrama in rhyme. Its lyrical beauty, and the presence of that 'gentle boy', while enhancing the contrast, none the less conceals the spiritual truth it tells—as the colours of sunset may gild a stagnant pool. It is only when we positively 'live into' such lines as:

'All night I lay in agony,
In anguish dark and deep,
My fevered eyes I dared not close,
But stared aghast at Sleep:
For Sin had rendered unto her
The keys of hell to keep. . . .'

that we realize the utmost horror of imagination entailed in the writing of the poem. To a man, moreover, who, genius apart, was a faithful 'friend to the suffering, the careworn and the needy ... generous, kind and true', and of whose work even Wainewright declared that it was 'a living proof how close lie the founts of laughter and tears'. So close indeed that Hood was destined to make his living chiefly by making jokes.

'The point of the æsthetic attitude', says Bernard Bosanquet, 'lies in the adequate fusion of body and soul, where the soul is a feeling, and the body its expression, without residue on either side'. The body of a poem is its words, its soul is its poetry, whatever the age of the writer of it may be and whatever his intention. That being so—as with many of our Hymns Ancient and Modern —Chatterton's poem, as it seems to me, is more eloquent than real; and this is seldom true of the work of a *child*. It is less promising than Cowley's *Piramus and Thisbe*, less passionate and original than Marjory Fleming's rhymes to her Isa, and has less poetry in it than Kingsley's lines on life. What on the other hand is completely absent from it is anything in the nature of the 'infantine, naive and artless'.

Preludings

6. 'Sugarplum words, which fall sweet from the lips.'

Contrariwise, there is little else but the infantine, naive and artless in eleven-year-old Jane Taylor's farewell rhyme to another Jane, who was leaving England. And yet how surely the tenderness and fidelity of a loving heart shine out of the awkward stanzas—like a pining wild bird in a clumsy cage:

> 'Alas! it must be,
>   My ever dear Jane,
> You must part with me:
>   We must not meet again.
>
> 'Accept then, my dear,
>   These verses from me;
> Although I do fear
>   Far too mean they be.
>
> 'I love you, believe,
>   My Jane and my friend;
> How much should I grieve
>   If our friendship should end.
>
> 'But this cannot be,
>   Believe me sincere,
> Though th' Atlantic sea
>   Should part us, my dear.
>
> 'Remember your Jane,
>   When alone in the grove:
> Forget not her name;—
>   She will ever you love.
>
> 'You soon sure will find
>   A friend that is new:
> Don't push Jane behind,
>   But remember her too.
>
> 'Adieu then, my friend;
>   The thought gives me pain;
> My love shall not end;
>   So remember your Jane.'

509

Early One Morning

Ann Taylor's first impulse towards writing was due to the dread that haunted her as a child of the sudden death of those around her, particularly her mother. When she was between eight and ten years old, she bought out of her small pocket money a sheet of foolscap and filled it with verses after Dr. Watts's pattern. The only lines she could recall in after years were:

'Dark and dismal was the weather,
Winter into horror grew,
Rain and snow came down together,
Everything was lost to view'—

which would at once be taken to be an echo of 'Lucy Gray', if Wordsworth's poem had not been written seven years later. Both sisters were home-bred and home-taught. Their father did not believe in imparting to his children 'those shreds of information, which serve for little except to deck out ignorance with the show of knowledge'. He taught them to learn, to want to learn, and to want to learn the best.

There is no doubt about the echo in the following political squib written by Gilbert Sheldon at the age of twelve. The date is 1882, its chief 'reform' being Suffrage. Four years later votes were again denied to women.

'Oh, Reforms are in my eye
Said the Grand Old Man,
Oh, Reforms are in my eye
Said the Grand Old Man:
Reforms are in my eye,
I will pass them bye and bye:
Let the Tories weep and sigh,
Said the Grand Old Man.

'What will the country do?
Said the Grand Old Man;
What will the country do?
Said the Grand Old Man;
What will the country do?
Surely not choose a few
Wasteful Tories in lieu
Of the Grand Old Man.

510

Preludings

'What watchword shall we form?
    Said the Grand Old Man;
What watchword shall we form?
    Said the Grand Old Man;
What watchword can we form?
Peace, Retrenchment and Reform?
("Peace" disturbed by many a storm)
    Said the Grand Old Man.

'What, after all is o'er?
    Said the Grand Old Man;
What, after all is o'er?
    Said the Grand Old Man;
Well, after all is o'er,
There'll be clamouring for more,
Worse than there was before,
    Said the Grand Old Man.'

Mary Coleridge, 'all poet, and three quarters saint', even though she did not 'awake to life' until childhood had fallen away from her, was 'always the same from childhood onwards'—gay, ardent, romantic, delighting in fantasy, and not only lovable but gifted with 'the power to love'. When she was about twelve years old, the shape of the Hebrew letters attracted her, as did the *looks* of logarithms Lewis Carroll when he was a child—and with similar results. At thirteen she became a pupil of William Cory's, and soon his devoted scholar. It was at this age she wrote 'A Ballade of Autumn'.

'Life is passing slowly,
    Death is drawing near,
Life and Death are holy,
    What have we to fear?

'Faded leaves are falling,
    Birds are on the wing,
All that dies in Autumn
    Lives again in Spring.'

Many years afterwards, in recollection of her girlhood—the iris and the cyclamen being Cory's favourite flowers—she wrote 'On

Early One Morning

Such a Day', as lovely a thing in its birdlike poise and balance and in the vista of human life it surrenders as it is in the reflection of the nature from which it sprang.

'Some hang above the tombs,
Some weep in empty rooms,
I, when the iris blooms,
Remember.

'I, when the cyclamen
Opens her buds again,
Rejoice a moment—then
Remember.'

Both poems are as 'simple' as they are utterly sincere; they share the same theme, and the earlier one is as finished in its making as some tiny sampler of a child's laborious needlework. It is neither the kind nor the depth but the width of experience that distinguishes one from the other—and a more delicate insight into the use of words. It has been said of Mary Coleridge that she was like 'the tail of the comet S.T.C.'—a pretty compliment to both of them. Still, there is a lesser *star* encircling Antares which gives the greater—as we watch their changing fires—a colour all its own*.

In his fifteenth year, and possibly earlier, S.T.C. himself began at Christ's Hospital simply cascading verse, for the most part all 'declamation' and 'Apostrophes':

'Hail! festal Easter that dost bring
Approach of sweetly smiling spring,
When nature's clad in green. . . .'

At the other extreme there are such jocularities as the 'Monody on a Tea-Kettle' and 'To the Lord Mayor's Nose'.

Of his *Dura Navis*'—a poem of eight octets on the perils of the deep, including cannibalism, 'Lo! Hunger drives thee to th' inhuman feast'—he himself modestly declared that it did not contain a line that any clever schoolboy might not have written. It was, he said, a '*Putting of Thought into Verse*'. None the less, such '*strivings* of mind and struggles after the Intense and Vivid are a fair Promise of better things'. He then went on: 'I well remember old Jemmy Bowyer, the plagose Orbilius of Christ's Hospital, but

Preludings

an admirable educer . . . of the Intellect, bade me leave out as many epithets as would turn' the poem's ten- into eight-syllable lines. Precisely the opposite and far more perilous device, I have read somewhere, was followed by Gray when he worked over the 'Elegy', a poem which Alice Meynell steadfastly maintained just fails to attain the mark of genius. Bowyer's was good counsel, even though the best line in '*Dura Navis*', 'Loud on his troubled bed huge Ocean roars', would have been ruined had Coleridge taken it.

In the following year came 'To the Autumnal Moon', also innocent neither of declamation nor apostrophe. But here at least four of the lines hint at the seeing eye of 'Christabel'; and the last just fails to effect in words what he himself declared to be one of the crucial proofs of the poetic imagination:

'Mild Splendour of the various-vested Night!
Mother of wildly-working visions! hail!
I watch thy gliding, while with watery light
Thy weak eye glimmers through a fleecy veil;
And when thou lovest thy pale orb to shroud
Behind the gather'd blackness lost on high;
And when thou dartest from the wind-rent cloud
Thy placid lightning o'er the awaken'd sky.

'Ah such is Hope! as changeful and as fair!
Now dimly peering on the wistful sight;
Now hid behind the dragon-wing'd Despair:
But soon emerging in her radiant might
She o'er the sorrow-clouded breast of Care
Sails, like a meteor kindling in its flight.'

To compare with this metaphor, we have 'Look! how a bright star shooteth from the sky. So glides he in the night from Venus' eye!' and Mr. William Davies's:

'And how we saw afar
A falling star:
It was a tear of pure delight
Ran down the face of Heaven this happy night.'

That a poet's 'struggles after the intense and vivid' do not neces-

sarily cease with youth many of Coleridge's later poems themselves suggest. In these the muse of 'Christabel' is asleep, or, as in
'The Nightingale', her face is the lovelier because she is between
dreaming and waking. Nor does this description apply to the
poems written by young children which have been already
quoted. Coleridge was speaking of school verse, which even when
it is purely voluntary, is usually aimed at an adult target. It may
be good practice—especially if the imposed language is Latin or
Greek—though it is doubtful if any set theme that calls upon a
child's imagination and feelings is desirable. Better perhaps let
these sleep until the desire to express them awaken of itself and the
outcome is purely a labour of love.

7. 'A litel scole of Christen folk there stood. . . .'

The next three examples—still warm from the oven—were
wholly spontaneous, and were written at an age—thirteen—
when presumably that goose-quilled aery of little eyases, the children of Paules, referred to in *Hamlet*, began to 'berattle the common stages'. They were contributed in the space of a year to a
school magazine for which I have a particular affection, a school
only forty boys strong but, as England used to be, a nest of singing
birds. The first of them by J.K.O'N.E. follows a difficult model—
the Petrarchan sonnet. It keeps all the rules, its rhymes are flawless, and the slight jar of 'taking' after 'took' is easily redeemed
by the admirable management of its penultimate line. Better yet,
it is tinged, I think, with that mysterious thing we call poetry.
Here is the sonnet:

> 'The day had dwindled into moonlit night
> In peaceful slumber lay the little vale;
> Across the sky the peeping bats did sail,
> And with a ghostly hoot an owl took flight,

---

[1] A mystery that, like the bloom on a wild fruit, is present even in Dorothy
Wordsworth's notes in her Journal about the weather: 'The moonlight lay upon
the hills like snow'; 'A very clear afternoon. We lay sidelong upon the turf,
and gazed on the landscape till it melted into more than natural loveliness.'
'Papered William's rooms. About eight o'clock it gathered for rain, and I had
the scatterings of a shower'; 'A very fine warm sunny morning. . . . One beautiful
ash tree sheltered, with yellow leaves, one low one quite green.'

Preludings

While here and there a rabbit, taking fright,
Ran through the meadows on the homeward trail.
The great moon made the dew o'er hill and dale
To shine like diamonds, from her glitt'ring height.
And then a rumbling sound could be discerned,
Which quickly more distinct and nearer grew;
Then, with a roar like thunder, came the train,
Whose steamy siren shrieked and shrieked again,
Awaking every echo. On it flew
Till all the peace and quiet of night returned.'

The quatrain by R.A.K.C. (also æt. 13)—which after being read over once or twice becomes so familiar that I almost hesitated to include it!—is as compact as a wren's egg, and as brief as its inmate's song will be.

'The cloud I see is like a rose
    With morning sun behind it:
I gaze, as it before me blows,
    And beautiful I find it.'

L. W. Y.'s lament is entitled 'A Criminal's Repentance'. A crisscross drift of twenty years spreads dismally out before us between the sullen thuds of its refrain, and it would have won an ardent admirer in Marjory Fleming. Every word tells. We *see* the dingily lit shop windows in the Union Road, and that abject bedroom, and yet can conjecture why the Home Secretary tempered justice with mercy:

'O unkind fate! I am so frail,
For twenty years I've been in gaol.
The court would not allow me bail—
    So here I am.

'One day, 'bout twenty years ago,
I 'lowed I'd lay Tom Jones right low,
And to his house I then did go—
    So here I am.

'For after leaving my abode
I bought a knife in Union Road,

515

Early One Morning

And then some murderous thoughts I showed—
So here I am.

'Then, late that night, Tom Jones lay dead,
His head all bloody on the bed,
And to the prison I was led—
So here I am.'

At about the same age—a month before her fourteenth birthday, and about two years after she had completed her *History of the*
Jews—Emily Shore wrote a poem called 'Autumn' which includes
the following lines:

'. . . Look around.
A gloomy pall has changed the woods to grey;
Heavy and stagnant is the air; no breeze
Rises to waft the veil, the traveller's breath
Oppressing. Look again. The luminous orb
Has melted all; it passes slow away,
And welters every wreath of foliage green,
And tangled wood and fence and upland knoll,
And every mossy tuft and silken grass,
In thickest dew. . . .'

Her 'luminous orb' has melted not merely the sullen mists of
the morning, but the literary influences of the eighteenth century.
Like the following stanza from an 'Epitaph on a Tame Jackdaw
Frozen to Death', which she wrote three years afterwards,

'. . . . Beneath his jetty brows peered forth
Two serious eyes of dull pale grey,
Which cast, whene'er he mused, to earth,
Gazed many a silent hour away. . . .'

the lines are full of a delicate observation. The seventh breaks into
poetry. Of this *kind* there is real promise in Emily Shore's verse—
a promise that was never to be fulfilled.

CHAPTER XXXVI

EMBARCATION

*

1. ' *The eldest skarsly fyf yer was of age.*'

Any generalization on early poems so few and so dissimilar as these is bound to be precarious. Since, moreover, by comparison with the vast quantities of verse that must have been written in childhood, they are like a nosegay compared with the meadows of spring, can we fairly assume that they are representative? If, following Coleridge, we separate them into two classes, the subjective and the objective, we find that we have also sifted them roughly according to the sex of their writers. That being so, there is little question that the boys bear away the bell. Despite the fact that Peacock's rhyme is a letter home to his mother, with a handsome reward full in his mind's eye, and tellingly reveals what kind of child he was, it is otherwise almost as impersonal as Flaubert said good fiction ought to be; whereas the verses by Marjory Fleming, Jane Taylor, Christina Rossetti, Mary Coleridge and 'L.E.' are for the most part expressions of personal feeling. And even though the examples by Frances Cobbe and Emily Shore are not concerned with themselves, they bring us closely into their company. This subjectiveness appears to depend not only on the sex but also on the age of the writers. At fourteen, the age at which according to the law of the land 'children' become 'young persons', the mind in boyhood also tends to turn inward.

The themes are those usual in poetry: friendship, love, flowers, birds, nature, the sea; solitude, Time, the fleetingness of life, death, dream, fantasy, horror—the lyrical, the epic, the narrative, satire,

517

epigram, parody. Even the critic who classified poetry according to the dignity, depth and majesty of its subject and therefore gave precedence to that concerned with God and theology, could not disdain these children.

We find in these poems, then, what we should expect to find—namely, that the world of the imagination in childhood, although the two orbits do not coincide, closely resembles that of man. There is a remarkable freedom from the merely 'childish'. Some of the rhymes are merry or mischievous, some are covertly or openly aimed at the grown-up. There is little appearance of self-consciousness, or even of word-consciousness, or of striving after effect. They are neither affected nor mock-solemn; mere cleverness is as unusual as the sugary-sentimental; and since an intelligent child's desire is to be intelligible, there is nothing obscure. How much indeed may he not have refrained from trying to express for fear of being so? The chief lack in such rhymes is the purely intellectual, but *not* fundamental brainwork. What incited these children to take such extreme and solitary pains? Did they toil on like the Israelites with or without straw, or await the enkindling moment—glancing up first to see if the Muse was at the window? An all-embracing answer to many such questions would be, Life.

'But in these so little bodies', says Philemon Holland, though he is not speaking of human bodies, 'how can one comprehend the reason, the power, and the inexplicable perfection that nature hath therein shewed? How hath she bestowed all the five senses in a gnat!' There is nothing at any rate to suggest, as perhaps aunt or godparent may have apprehended, that the habit led to evil courses in childhood! And since William Morris as a boy used to enjoy a suppet of Christmas punch, some of these green novices may have been enlivened by an occasional noggin of small beer. Otherwise, we can leave out of account the ravages of cowslip wine and Gregory powder.

Another thing; the work even of the youngest of them is so serious in outlook, so grave in intention, that little of it would have much chance of entry into many of the rhyme-books aimed at children nowadays. Any child with an innate delight in rhyme and rhythm will devour the old nursery jingles, sweet, merry and heady with the ancient music that no poetry is without. He loves them, as we do, *because* they are nonsense. But if he himself is a

Embarcation

poet he is likely to stalk bigger game.[1] What then can be said of the trash so freely supplied for young children even nowadays—that which is as silly as it is ill written? At a time when we need all the understanding, judgement and imagination of which humanity is capable, when every gleam of Blake's sword is like the shining of dew in the wilderness, they are treated in this respect as if they were fatuous little nincompoops, incapable even of common sense.

But in what degree are these child-writers akin to all children? No more and no less presumably than any artist is to his fellow-creatures. 'Genius does what it must, and talent does what it can'—that is true of humanity at any age. The one indispensable distinction between the born writer and the rest of mankind is a gift for expression. He is inflicted or blessed with a passion to share his all in words, or at least as much of his heart and mind as he can make significant and veracious. But he is not necessarily wiser, more human and humane, more intelligent or virtuous or cultured or faithful than those who have been denied this faculty. His range of experience too may be less essential, abundant and valuable than theirs.

The greatest writers are universal in their nature and sympathies. *Everyman*, that is, can drink and be refreshed at their fountain, even though of the precious salts that are in solution in its waters, the rarest may pass unheeded. For one devotee of Shakespeare as a poet, or as a diviner of mankind, or as a supremely versatile artist, there must be many who delight solely in the dramatist—or the melodramatist; or who read him, as did Southey when a child, for his stories or his horrors. We can enjoy Bunyan's pungent summaries of his wicked neighbours and skip the texts they were intended to exemplify. We can rejoice to see his

[1] This is no less true of an intelligent child's reading. A famous book for children, Arnaud Berquin's *l'Ami des Enfants*, of 1782, an imitation in some degree of *Der Kinderfreund*, was published in England with charming cuts by John Bewick ten years afterwards, and was crowned by the French Academy in 1874. It consists of lessons in manners, thankfulness, good sense and good nature, and its grown-ups are as natural and delightful company as its children. But as with other admirable books of this intention, its tales are a means not so much of instilling moral novelties, as of ratifying and renovating what is already in young minds and hearts. Indeed, a child in his reading, concerning his estimate of the children he is reading *about*, is unlikely to be less critical and appreciative than we are ourselves of the characters in the novels that we indulge in.

Early One Morning

Christian safely home, yet ignore every echo of the trumpets of salvation. The first half of *Gulliver's Travels* may delight alike a child and an optimist, both of whom will reject Laputa and the Yahoos, in which Swift had precisely the same corrosive end in view. And who shares his island with Robinson Crusoe for the sake of Daniel Defoe's 'heavenly meaning'?

A work of genius of an isolated order, on the other hand, essential and undiluted, has a far narrower range. And yet how widespread and inexhaustible its influence may be when those who can assimilate it have circulated it in tincture, as it were, 'by their mere passive existence'.

Like man, like child—these early rhymes represent childhood no less faithfully than the poems of maturity represent the mature. Since their frames are often narrow and their colours faint, to some tastes they will be as mawkish as are the strains of an æolian harp compared with those of a grand piano, the onset of calf-love compared with a *drame passionnel*. And criticism even of their best and brightest may suggest not merely a waste of time, but the testing of seed pearls with a sledge-hammer.

> 'Satire or sense, alas! can Sporus feel?
> Who breaks a butterfly upon a wheel?'

Or worse, a chrysalis?

2. *'With this Cargo I put to sea.'*

Sooner or later, however, a poet must issue his challenge, enter the lists, declare himself. From tentative flutterings he must take to his wings and fly. If we rule out childhood, at what age is this likely to occur? At what age are we entitled to assume—to borrow a word from the Catechism—that he should be fully 'competent', and to refuse to make allowances on this or any other count? Not, at least, before he has had time to master his mother tongue. This appears to be the sole proviso.

That being so, we might expect to find not only a radical difference between the content of a poet's earlier and his later work, but an even more marked difference in its form and technique. But is this so in fact? A true poet may cease to write in verse, or fail at length to write well, because he has been unable to acquire an adequate new technique that alone could express him. In general, however, it is the close resemblance between his first work at any age and his last that appears to be more conspicuous than any dissimilarities. The later work *may*, in certain cases, while still being characteristic, even fall short in some degree of the earlier. Evidence of this will lead us well beyond a poet's childhood, but it will reflect back upon that childhood, and the digression may perhaps be excused for this reason.

Much that is characteristic, for example, of Tennyson as a poet is clear in 'Claribel'.

> 'At eve the beetle boometh
> Athwart the thicket lone:
> At noon the wild bee hummeth
> About the moss'd headstone:
> At midnight the moon cometh,
> And looketh down alone. . . .'

The *'eths* are unfortunate, and seven others follow these three—for which his mother tongue is in part to blame; but this particular outlook on Nature and its representation in words is at least so far 'Tennysonian' as to be less any other poet's in the language. This was work of his early twenties; and, so far, seems to have been an example of what has been suggested. But Tennyson had begun versifying long before 'Claribel'. After reading Pope's Homer at the age of ten he composed—it is his own statement—hundreds of lines on this model. And when he was only four years older he wrote the first draft of *The Devil and the Lady*—a play which might easily be the work of some young intimate of Marlowe's and Ben Jonson's born two centuries late! It has obvious flaws and weaknesses in construction and invention. The sheer wonder is that its characters are wholly adult, that the verse appears to be a natural language, and that it pours on in an unflagging spate of words—'Methinks my tongue runs twenty knots an hour', as one of its characters remarks. Its racy, sardonic, even ribald humour, chiefly that of the Devil, its leading personage, is perhaps its least expected feature. Here is a speech of this Devil's to Amoret—a character faintly suggestive of Alice Arden herself—whom her doting husband Magus has left in his charge:

Early One Morning

'Get thee to bed—yet stay—but one word more——
Let there be no somnambulations,
No colloquy of soft-tongued whisperings
Like the low hum of the delighted bee
I' th' calyx of a lily—no kerchief-waving!
No footfalls i' th' still night! Lie quietly,
Without the movement of one naughty muscle,
Still as a kernel in its stone, and lifeless
As the dull yoke within its parent shell,
Ere yet the *punctum saliens* vivify it.
I know ye are perverse, and ever wish,
Maugre my wholesome admonitions,
To run obliquely like the bishop at chess,
But I'll cry "check" to ye, I warrant ye
I'll prove a "stalemate" to ye.'

To which Amoret replies '(half aside)': 'In all conscience my mate
is stale enough.'

So much for its wit and its dramatic attitude. Apart from this,
the verse every now and again, as easily as a seal into the water,
slips into the serenely imaginative; and then we not only share its
author's own young eyes—in such lines for example as:

'Then came a band of melancholy sprites,
White as their shrouds and motionlessly pale
Like some young Ashwood when the argent Moon
Looks in upon its many silver stems.'

but also his own boyish and immediate thought:

'We follow thro' a night of crime and care
The voice of soft Temptation, still it calls,
And still we follow onwards, till we find
She is a Phantom and—we follow still.
When couched in Boyhood's passionless tranquillity,
The natural mind of man is warm and yielding,
Fit to receive the best impressions,
But raise it to the atmosphere of manhood
And the rude breath of dissipation
Will harden it to stone. . . .'

The best and profoundest lines in Tennyson's Newdigate poem,

Embarcation

'Timbuctoo', were borrowed from a poem, also written about this time, entitled 'Armageddon'. They begin 'I look'd but not Upon his face', and refer to a highly unusual state of the consciousness. At the age of fourteen he wrote also 'The Coach of Death' of more than thirty stanzas. These are the first two:

> 'Far off in the dun, dark Occident,
>   Behind the burning Sun:
> Where his gilding ray is never sent,
>   And his hot steeds never run:
>
> 'There lies a land of chilling storms,
>   A region void of light,
> A land of thin faces and shadowy forms,
>   Of vapours, and mist, and night. . . .'

In coherence, in rhythmical subtlety, in its remoteness from normal experience, and in its flavour of the macabre, it excels, I think, 'The Vision of Sin', which is on a similar subject and may have shared with it the same germinal dream.

Tennyson's early poems, then, are astonishing not only in their variety, range and quality. They show also an energy of genius, the full promise of which even *his* later work incompletely fulfilled. Progress at any rate (even in experience) continued into later life at the pace of his, between the ages of ten and fourteen, is utterly inconceivable.

Browning who was an unwearying *watcher* as a child, and also an omnivorous reader, never ceased to borrow from the pages of *The Wonders of the Little World*, which came his way very early in in life. His first recorded lines were:

> 'Good people all who wish to see
> A boy take physic look at me';

and we find its sublimated echo seventy years afterwards in 'One who never turned his back but marched breast forward'! But open his autobiographical *Pauline* and compare the lines beginning,

> 'I had been spared this shame if I had sat
> By thee for ever from the first. . . .'

with the final stanzas of 'Reverie' in *Asolando*—the volume pub-

lished on the day of his death. Neither, to say the least of it, could
be more un-Tennysonian.

Compare Thomas Hardy's lines of 1865:

> 'I marked her ruined hues,
> Her custom-straitened views,
> And asked, "Can there indwell
> My Amabel?" . . .'

with the first stanza from the last poem in *Winter Words*:

> 'O my soul, keep the rest unknown!
> It is too like a sound of moan
> When the charnel-eyed
> Pale Horse has nighed:
> Yea, none shall gather what I hide! . . .'

The attitude of mind revealed in these widely severed fragments, the sense of time and mortality, the emotional and intellectual outlook, the challenging imaginative realism, and *this* use
of words—no other English poet has all these characteristics; and
they were Thomas Hardy's as a poet throughout his life.

Keats's earliest extant poem, his 'Imitation of Spenser', was
written in 1813—when he was eighteen; two years afterwards
came the completely mature Sonnet on Chapman's Homer. The
'Imitation' begins:

> 'Now Morning from her orient chamber came,
> And her first footsteps touch'd a verdant hill;
> Crowning its lawny crest with amber flame,
> Silv'ring the untainted gushes of its rill;
> Which, pure from mossy beds, did down distill,
> And after parting beds of simple flowers,
> By many streams a little lake did fill,
> Which round its marge reflected woven bowers,
> And, in its middle space, a sky that never lowers.

> 'There the king-fisher saw his plumage bright
> Vieing with fish of brilliant dye below;
> Whose silken fins, and golden scales' light
> Cast upward, through the waves, a ruby glow:
> There saw the swan his neck of archèd snow,

Embarcation

And oar'd himself along with majesty;
Sparkled his jetty eyes; his feet did show
Beneath the waves like Afric's ebony,
And on his back a fay reclined voluptuously. . . .

Here two musics intermingle; but could any ear familiar with
Spenser's mistake *this* for the *Faerie Queene's*, or fail to overhear
in it the voice in 'Lamia' and in the 'Ode to Psyche'? The pace is
Keats's, the rich loading of the subject, the precision, the solidity.
This stream, the flowers, these fish, the swan, its waters, have been
seen too by *his* eyes, and his speech bewrays him—lawny, simple,
untainted, woven, dye, ruby, bowers, jetty, Afric; and last, *voluptuously*. This, of a *fay*!—and in imitation of Spenser!

And here is Spenser himself—in an 'Epigram' from *A Theatre*,
his first 'imprinted' volume of 1569, when he was about seventeen
years old:

> 'Within this wood, out of the rocke did rise
> A Spring of water mildely romblyng downe,
> Whereto approchèd not in any wise
> The homely Shepherde, nor the ruder cloune,
> But many Muses, and the Nymphes withall,
> That sweetely in accorde did tune their voice
> Unto the gentle sounding of the waters fall.
> The sight whereof dyd make my heart rejoyce.
> But while I toke herein my chiefe delight,
> I sawe (alas) the gaping earth devoure
> The Spring, the place, and all cleane out of sight.
> Which yet agreves my heart even to this houre.'

Could this drowsy music possibly be mistaken for Keats's or for
any other writer's in English than Spenser himself? And even
though it is actually a rendering from Petrarch, would it in the
least surprise us if we found it in the *Faerie Queene,* following, let
us say:

> 'It was a chosen plot of fertile land
> Emongst wide waves set, like a little nest,
> As if it had by Nature's cunning hand
> Bene closely pickèd out from all the rest. . . .

So easily and fluently rills on its rhythmical melody that one might

525

Early One Morning

suppose Spenser had imbibed his vocabulary with his mother's milk.

No less consistent with each poet's after-work, and no less different in texture—thought, feeling, words—are these stanzas from two poems entitled 'To Hope', the one by Hood when he was twenty-two, the other by Keats, again, when he was two years younger. Hood bids the 'young seraph' take his harp and play and sing 'as thou wert wont to do', and continues:

> 'Perchance the strings will sound less clear,
>   That long have lain neglected by
> In sorrow's misty atmosphere;
>   It ne'er may speak as it hath spoken
>   Such joyous notes so brisk and high;
> But are its golden chords all broken?
> Are there not some, though weak and low,
> To play a lullaby to woe? . . .'

and Keats:

> 'And as, in sparkling majesty, a star
>   Gilds the bright summit of some gloomy cloud;
> Brightening the half veil'd face of heaven afar:
>   So, when dark thoughts my boding spirit shroud,
>   Sweet Hope, celestial influence round me shed,
>   Waving thy silver pinions o'er my head!'

The two minds here manifested differ no less than the two harmonies, the one a little thin, nebulous, wistful; the other rich and ample.

There is an amusing story that a Mrs. Grafty, an old lady of Finsbury, on meeting George Keats one day enquired, 'And what is John doing?' He replied that John intended to be a poet; whereupon the old lady called to mind that when years before she had occasionally questioned John as a child, he would answer her by rhyming on her last syllable. 'I for one,' says Amy Lowell, 'do not believe a word of this.' But would it not be less remarkable for such a child so to rhyme than for this old lady of Finsbury so to mis-remember? So far indeed Romney Robinson bade fair to be a Keats!

'Queen Mab' was privately printed in 1813, when Shelley was

Embarcation

in his twenty-first year, but part of it may have been written two years earlier. In 1815 he re-wrote about an eighth of the poem. The following is a fragment from the opening stanzas of the first draft:

> 'How wonderful is Death,
> Death and his brother Sleep!
> One, pale as yonder waning moon
> With lips of lurid blue;
> The other, rosy as the morn
> When throned on ocean's wave
> It blushes o'er the world:
> Yet both so passing wonderful!
>
> 'Hath then the gloomy Power
> Whose reign is in the tainted sepulchres
> Seized on her sinless soul?
> Must then that peerless form
> Which love and admiration cannot view
> Without a beating heart, those azure veins
> Which steal like streams along a field of snow
> That lovely outline, which is fair
> As breathing marble, perish? . . .'

This again—and not only in its verbal music, halting and rhymeless though here it is—seems to me to be as declarative of Shelley's imagination throughout his life as the petals of the blackthorn are of an English spring. The nightingale in early summer may be heard repeating its song in undertones, but however low and sweet the whisper, it is still the song of the nightingale. So here with Shelley and his theme—sleep, moon, water, death, and this aspect of the human body. It is at one with the character of his mind. 'When throned on ocean's wave' is in his very signature. Later indeed that waning moon with those Shelleyan lips is compared not with Death but with the dying—'a dying lady, lean and pale'. And this is his amended version of 1815:

> 'How wonderful is Death,
> Death and his brother Sleep!
> One pale as yonder wan and hornèd moon
> With lips of lurid blue;

Early One Morning

The other glowing like the vital morn,
    When throned on ocean's wave
    It breathes over the world:
Yet both so passing strange and wonderful!

'Hath then the iron-sceptred Skeleton,
    Whose reign is in the tainted sepulchres,
    To the hell dogs that couch beneath his throne
Cast that fair prey? Must that divinest form,
Which love and admiration cannot view
Without a beating heart, whose azure veins
Steal like dark streams along a field of snow,
Whose outline is as fair as marble clothed
In light of some sublimest mind, decay? . . .'

And here, surely, his sense of technique, now critical and rational rather than creative, has faltered. It is almost as if Godwin had been supervising the neophyte. The revisions, chiefly rhetorical, are all for the worse; they elaborate the images, but in so doing weaken them—the *vital* morn, for example; 'breathes' for 'blushes'; 'iron-sceptred Skeleton' for 'gloomy power'. 'Wan and horned', even though it particularizes the image in the original third line, obscures it; and, apart from the confusion caused by the second 'whose', and by the needless 'dark', what a sovereign loss is 'breathing marble'. As with Cowley's *Piramus and Thisbe*, the *earlier* impulse was the purer.

While Crabbe—between the ages of fourteen and seventeen—was still a 'prentice, delivering medicines, and sharing a bed with his master's ploughboy, he wrote, his son tells us, verses enough to fill a drawer. His first printed and published poem was entitled *Inebriety*—the delayed issue perhaps of an experience in childhood already referred to—as his 'first-born joy'—

'For children ever feel delighted when
They take their portion and enjoy with men'—

when he was one of a marine pleasure party at Aldborough that began with the song of the linnet and ended in a drunken brawl.

'Every man, gentle reader,' runs his preface, 'has a world of his own, and whether it consists of half a score or half a thousand friends, 't is his, and he loves to boast of it. Into my world, there-

Embarcation

fore, I commit this, my Muse's earliest labour. . . .' He was then aged twenty; he had mastered his theme; no kind or degree of toper, nicely observed, his lash neglects; and the style of the poem —in its psychology no less than in its technique—is emphatically his and his only. No less so indeed than are the hallucinations of the insane Sir Eustace Grey in his poem of that title, which was written, as Mr. Binyon has pointed out, when Crabbe himself was under the influence of opium.

> '. . . Through the sharp air a flaky torrent flies,
> Mocks the slow sight, and hides the gloomy skies;
> The fleecy clouds their chilly bosoms bare,
> And shed their substance on the floating air. . . .
>   The gentle fair on nervous tea relies,
> Whilst gay good-nature sparkles in her eyes. . . .
> Champagne the courtier drinks, the spleen to chase,
> The colonel burgundy, and port his grace. . . .
>   See Inebriety! her wand she waves,
> And lo! her pale, and lo! her purple slaves!
> Sots in embroidery, and sots in crape,
> Of every order, station, rank and shape. . . .
>   Lo! proud Flaminius at the splendid board,
> The easy chaplain of an atheist lord,
> Quaffs the bright juice, with all the gust of sense,
> And clouds his brain in torpid elegance;
> In china vases, see! the sparkling ill,
> From gay decanters view the rosy rill. . . .
> Go, wiser thou! and in thy scale of taste,
> Weigh gout and gravel against ale and rest;
> Call vulgar palates what thou judgest so;
> Say beer is heavy, windy, cold, and slow;
> Laugh at poor sots with insolent pretence,
> Yet cry, when tortured, where is Providence? . . .'

This is how Crabbe habitually oscillated between poetry and the most prosaic of all prose—that cut up into verse. The objects referred to are as vividly seen and illusively actual as if they were twinkling beyond the footlights of some remembered melodrama.

William Cowper on the other hand amused himself by deliber-

Early One Morning

ately heightening commonplace themes, when he was not, with all the grace and charm of which he was capable, making poetry of them. 'The Diverting History of John Gilpin' is itself a diversion midway between his 'Epitaph on a Hare' and his poem on his mother's picture. And at the age of seventeen we find him engaged on 'Verses Written at Bath, on finding the heel of a shoe':

'Fortune! I thank thee: gentle Goddess, thanks!
Not that my Muse, though bashful, shall deny
She would have thank'd thee rather, hadst thou cast
A treasure in her way; for neither meed
Of early breakfast, to dispel the fumes
And bowel-raking pains of emptiness,
Nor noontide feast, nor evening's cool repast,
Hopes she from this, presumptuous—though perhaps
The cobbler, leather-carving artist, might.
Nathless she thanks thee, and accepts thy boon,
Whatever, not as erst the fabled cock,
Vain-glorious fool, unknowing what he found,
Spurn'd the rich gem thou gavest him. Wherefore, ah!
Why not on me that favour, (worthier sure,)
Conferr'dst thou, Goddess? . . .'

There may be striking exceptions to this general rule. We might guess in vain, for example, which of the most beloved authors in the English language wrote at the age of fourteen these first three stanzas from 'Mille Viæ Mortis':

'What time in bands of slumber all were laid,
To Death's dark court, methought I was convey'd;
In realms it lay far hid from mortal sight,
And gloomy tapers scarce kept out the night.

'On ebon throne the King of Terrors sate;
Around him stood the ministers of Fate;
On fell destruction bent, the murth'rous band
Waited attentively his high command.

'Here pallid Fear and dark Despair were seen,
And Fever here with looks forever lean,
Swoln Dropsy, halting Gout, profuse of woes,
And Madness fierce and hopeless of repose. . .'

530

Embarcation

And what of Byron's 'Hours of Idleness'? After *Fugitive Pieces* had been burned, and Poems on Various Occasions had been privately circulated, it was published, in 1807. In Professor Saintsbury's judgment it is 'probably the worst first book ever written by a considerable poet'. Byron himself, his palate, as he confessed, 'already vitiated with the sweets of adulation', referred to its contents as 'the fruits of the lighter hours of a young man who has lately completed his nineteenth year. . . . I have hazarded my reputation and feelings in publishing this volume'—a hazard that came home to him when the author of *Memnon* anonymously ravaged it in the *Edinburgh Review*. On reading this bitter and biassed attack, Byron's face, it is said, so flamed with 'fierce defiance' that a friend asked him if he had received a challenge. Watch a young child's motionless face even after a mere sarcasm at its expense.

The opening poem, 'On the Death of a Young Lady', in his Juvenilia, was composed, Byron tells us, at the age of fourteen; and, because it was his first essay, he preferred submitting it 'to the indulgence of his friends in its present state', without 'addition or alteration'. Here are three stanzas:

> 'Hush'd are the winds, and still the evening gloom,
>   Not e'en a zephyr wanders through the grove,
> Whilst I return, to view my Margaret's tomb,
>   And scatter flowers on the dust I love.
>
> 'Within this narrow cell reclines her clay,
>   That clay where once such animation beam'd;
> The King of Terrors seized her as his prey:
>   Not worth, nor beauty, have her life redeem'd. . . .
>
> 'But wherefore weep? Her matchless spirit soars
>   Beyond where splendid shines the orb of day;
> And weeping angels lead her to those bowers
>   Where endless pleasures virtue's deeds repay. . . .

Apart from the rhythmical ease and melody of a few of these lines, there is certainly little hint of the best in *Childe Harold*; but then, though Byron's 'voice was such a voice as the devil tempted Eve with', his bosom, says Landor, 'never could hold the urn in which the muse of tragedy embalms the dead'. His lines on

Margaret, that is, are illustrative of the kind of poetry in which he succeeded least well.

Byron indeed is a paradox among the poets. His best work suggests the inescapable impulse and momentum of a mountain torrent, declaiming its own sonorous music. Yet in fact he was circumspect even in his youth. His earliest poems were thrice printed; two years elapsed before he shattered his enemies with his *English Bards and Scotch Reviewers*; and two more before he was impelled to regret having done so. Fame as a poet was his perpetual incentive, and yet his declared preference was for the 'talents of action' rather than 'the genius of poetry'. ' "To withdraw *myself* from *myself*—oh, that cursed selfishness—has ever been my sole, my entire, my sincere motive in scribbling at all." ' None the less, from first to last, he was himself his own glittering and magnificent stage—the World 'walked on'. If child he ever was, his was the epithet Temple applied to human life itself—a froward child.

We may prefer to assume that the poems we delight in and admire most came into the world in their present state of perfection. To do so is a deceit which the first draft of any such poem would unblushingly refute. Why, else, should Shakespeare's editors have insisted on his unblotted ease?[1] Even when the furnace is at white heat the ore may remain stubborn. Or again, we may take no interest in origins, fumblings and false starts, and may find technical appreciation—which is at least less subject than most to caprice—tedious and disenchanting. But however that may be, the early poems which have been quoted, no less than those written in first childhood, cannot fail to intimate how far back we may venture into the life of a poet and still find that his wellspring tastes of the river. A young poet may appear, then, to have inherited his verbal craftsmanship as undesignedly as he may have come into a fortune. But this is only seeming, since words and their sounds cannot but have been his decoy and delight almost from his birth.

[1] Ben Jonson none the less in his lines 'To the memory of my beloved, The Author Mr. William Shakespeare: And what he hath left us' does not appear to have shared this view of his friend's 'trifles', as they called the Plays. 'Thy Art, My gentle Shakespeare', he says emphatically, 'must enjoy a part' of nature's pride in them; and he presently refers to his poet's 'well torned, and true-filèd lines'.

CHAPTER XXXVII

ACHIEVEMENT

*

1. 'What nature gave me at my birth
My shaping spirit of imagination.'

B ut to return, and finally, to children, for farewell. There are, at the least, three poems in English that were written on the verge of childhood and yet need no condonation on that account. Few collections of English lyrics fail to include two of them. In music and idea, in style, outlook, idiosyncrasy, each one of them is signally individual. Each is in accord with its writer's after-work, and unconfusable with the work of any other poet.

If William Blake, in Dr. Berger's words, was an 'absolutely unique personality', so also was Edgar Allan Poe. Blake 'seems to have been subject to visions all his life'. Poe—what term should we substitute for 'visions'? When he was seven years old—he is said to have fallen in love when he was five—he came to England, and while in London went to a dame school in Chelsea kept by the Misses Dubourg, a name which, as Mr. Hervey Allen, the author of *Israfel*, remarks, occurs in *The Murders in the Rue Morgue*. Here, for books, he had Mavor's Spelling Book—which was still flourishing in 1880—Fresnoy's Geography, a Prayer Book and *The Church Catechism Explained*. Afterwards he went as a boarder to the Manor House School, Stoke Newington—from September, 1817, to January, 1820.

In what may be called domestic fiction, the autobiographical abounds. In tales of the grotesque and arabesque it is far less usual. But in *William Wilson* not only is the narrator Poe himself, but his schoolfellow in the tale is his psychic double. Completely Poesque in mood and atmosphere, it is an allegory, and one that

533

Early One Morning

in spite of its occasional theatricality pierces deeper surely into the obscurer regions of the mind than either *The Strange Case of Dr. Jekyll and Mr. Hyde* or *The Picture of Dorian Gray*. And how closely in keeping with Poe's character and temperament is his denial to others in their childhood of what he here claims for himself.

'. . . Encompassed by the massy walls of this venerable academy, I passed, yet not in tedium or disgust, the years of the third lustrum of my life. The teeming brain of childhood requires no external world of incident to occupy or amuse it. . . . Yet I must believe that my first mental development had in it much of the uncommon—even much of the *outré*. Upon mankind at large the events of very early existence rarely leave in mature age any definite impression. All is gray shadow—a weak and irregular remembrance—an indistinct regathering of feeble pleasures and phantasmagoric pains. With me this is not so. In childhood I must have felt with the energy of a man what I now find stamped upon memory in lines as vivid, as deep, and as durable as the *exergues* of the Carthaginian medals.

'Yet in fact—in the fact of the world's view—how little was there to remember! The morning's awakening, the nightly summons to bed; the connings, the recitations; the periodical half-holidays, and perambulations; the play-ground, with its broils, its pastimes, its intrigues—these, by a mental sorcery long forgotten, were made to involve a wilderness of sensation, a world of rich incident, an universe of varied emotion, of excitement the most passionate and spirit-stirring. *"Oh, le bon temps, que ce siècle de fer!"* . . .'

'Bright, clever and handsome'; 'beautiful, yet brave and manly'; 'lonely and unhappy'—all these, according to the observer, were impressions of Poe in his childhood. 'There was not a brighter, more graceful or more attractive boy in [Richmond] than Edgar Allan Poe' is countered with the comment made on him by his headmaster at Stoke Newington—that he was intelligent, wayward and wilful, and had too much pocket money. 'I grew self-willed', runs a sentence in *William Wilson*, 'addicted to the wildest caprices, and a prey to the most ungovernable passions.' Nevertheless the headmaster of his last school, from which he went up for his fatal year at the University of Virginia (and to whom on

534

Achievement

his retirement he addressed a letter in Latin verse and an English ode), testified that he 'had a very sweet disposition, he was always cheerful, brim full of mirth and a very great favourite. . . . He had a great ambition to excel'. One thing is clear; he was not easily *forgotten*.

Even in his childhood, it seems, to his fellow creatures he was what in later life he appears to have wished to be—an enigma. Neither in that life nor in his nature and destiny was there any happy medium. Concerning no man of genius, or of fudge, are the critics even of our own day more acridly at odds. It has been said of Emily Brontë—who nevertheless made her desolate moorlands blossom like the wild rose—that she was 'the Sphinx of literature'. In much the same terms, Poe is its Heathcliff. ' "I'm conscious it's night," ' says Cathie in *Wuthering Heights*, to prove that her mind is not wandering, ' "and there are two candles on the table making the black press shine like jet." ' Poe's mind is habitually on the verge of night. There is no inward radiance in his work. His candles illumine the blackness of jet—'like stars upon some gloomy grove'.

In his preface to *Tamerlane and Other Poems*, published in 1827 as 'by a Bostonian', he states that the greater part of the poems included in it were written in the years 1821-22, 'by one too young to have any knowledge of the world but from his own breast'. They were 'the crude compositions of my earliest boyhood'. Among them is one entitled 'To ——':

'The bowers whereat, in dreams, I see
    The wantonest singing birds,
Are lips—and all thy melody
    Of lip-begotten words——

'Thine eyes, in Heaven of heart enshrined
    Then desolately fall,
O God! on my funereal mind
    Like starlight on a pall——

'Thy heart—*thy* heart!—I wake and sigh,
    And sleep to dream till day
Of the truth that gold can never buy
    Of the baubles that it may.'

Early One Morning

With Truth, Poe considered—unlike Keats—that 'Song', lyrical poetry, has no direct concern. 'All that which is so indispensable in Song' ('in its various modes of metre, rhythm, and rhyme') 'is precisely all *that* with which *she* has nothing whatever to do'. The Poetry of Words is *'the rhythmical creation of Beauty'*. And, right or wrong, he might have deduced these principles from his own boyish practice. So bell-clear and insistent is the verbal music in these three stanzas to the unnamed loved one that we hardly heed the sense—or speculate what is meant in *them* by 'the truth'.

In the course of his essay on Poe, James Russell Lowell declares: 'That no certain augury can be drawn from a poet's earliest lispings there are instances enough to prove'. His instances include Collins, Kirk White, Coleridge, Byron, Wordsworth, Pope, Southey, and Shelley. Their early rhymings face the sweep of his scythe like buttercups at a haymaking. Even Cowley's first 'insipidities', 'wholly dependent on a delicate physical organization, and an unhappy memory', are not spared; and ' "the marvellous Boy" ', Chatterton, is dismissed as 'a very ingenious imitator of obscure and antiquated dullness'. A cautious exception is made of Milton's Latin verse, but not even of *Venus & Adonis*, although, as Lowell remarks very truly, this 'is hardly a case in point since it was published in Shakespeare's twenty-sixth year'.

This systematic slaughter is based on one proviso: 'An early poem is only remarkable when it displays an effort of *reason*', a statement which recalls Ruskin's equally sweeping malediction, 'no weight nor mass nor beauty of execution can outweigh one grain or fragment of thought'—wild words, says Edmund Gosse, 'that deserve an immortality of repudiation'. 'If this were true, half of the noblest poetry in the world would cease to possess any value.' Besides, the mere attempt, surely, to make a poem is an effort of reason. It divulges a plan and a design. As for any *display* of reason within the confines of its form, where is it to be found, let us say, in Herrick's 'In silks', in Shelley's 'A Widow Bird', in 'Where the bee sucks', in 'When icicles hang by the wall'? Apart from 'thought' and 'reason', what *do* they contain? How even attempt to say? The first resembles a verbal filigree as fine as it is flexible of the most delicate goldsmith's work, though it surrenders an image tenuous and isolated as the reflection of a willow in water. And what a marvel of sheer artifice is its 'liquefaction' and

Achievement

'vibration'. The second by its slow lovely music creates a scene in the nature of a dream, its symbolism enchanting even while it eludes us. 'Where the bee sucks' is all pure melody, the song of a blackcap in a breeze fragrant with flowers, its Ariel pretending to be Moth in *A Midsummer-Night's Dream*. As for 'When icicles', it was intended as a skit in the Play from which it comes, whose every detail would set its Elizabethan audience shivering at the throes of winter. For us in effect it is like a detailed Bewick wood-cut of an old English farmhouse under snow; and is as full of tingling wintry *delights* as was Mr. Pickwick sliding on the ice. Merely to bother our heads with 'reason' in connection with such 'rhymes' resembles sermonizing over May Day, and even that by no means the kind of sermonizing of which Thomas Fuller approved. For though 'Reasons', as he said, 'are the pillars of the fabrick of a Sermon; similitudes are the windows which give the best light'. Many excellent poems well over with reason, or at any rate with a sweet reasonableness, 'Rose Aylmer', for example. Some of the worst, *pace* Martin Tupper, consist of little else.

Lowell adds, however, that such early 'pieces are only valuable when they display what we can only express by the contradictory phrase of *innate experience*'. But, with no wish to be contentious, why only innate? However valuable that may be, a child, as we have seen, may have had an experience, actual and imaginative, ample enough as raw material for a host of poems.

Auguries may be deceptive; first impulses may flag; promise fail. But a promise unkept remains a promise. Lowell's one unqualified exception in his scorn of the innocents is Poe. And to justify himself he quotes 'To Helen'. This was written, we are told, when Poe was fourteen. It refers, it seems, to a first meeting with the mother of one of his schoolfellows, Jane Stanard. She was then in her late twenties. She died, insane, in her thirty-first year.

> 'Helen, thy beauty is to me
>   Like those Nicean barks of yore,
> That gently, o'er a perfumed sea,
>   The weary, way-worn wanderer bore
>   To his own native shore.
>
> 'On desperate seas long wont to roam,
>   Thy hyacinth hair, thy classic face,

Early One Morning

Thy Naiad airs have brought me home
To the glory that was Greece
And the grandeur that was Rome.

'Lo! in yon brilliant window-niche
How statue-like I see thee stand!
The agate lamp within thy hand.
Ah! Psyche, from the regions which
Are Holy Land.'

2. 'We Poets in our youth begin in gladness.'

'In Wordsworth's first preludings', says Lowell, 'there is but a dim foreboding of the creator of an era.' Before returning to Poe's 'To Helen', let us see if that is quite true.

In the first few pages of 'The Prelude', which was addressed to Coleridge, Wordsworth tells how on the wintry slopes of the mountains, when he was not yet ten years old, he would set his springes for woodcock:

> 'moon and stars
> Were shining o'er my head. I was alone,
> And seemed to be a trouble to the peace
> That dwelt among them . . .'

Sometimes, he says, he would steal away the bird 'which was the captive of another's toil', and, when the deed was done, would hear phantom footsteps in pursuit of him, 'almost as silent as the turf they trod'. In a borrowed boat—an 'act of stealth'—he dips his oars into the sparkling moonlit lake, and, conscience his only passenger, is oppressed even there by a craggy steep, 'a high peak, black and huge', towering between himself and the stars. It seems to stride after him, begetting a darkness in his mind of solitude and 'blank desertion'. Skating, fishing, kite-flying, nutting, playing cards, roving the green valleys with children of his own age, and conscious always of hidden influences on mind and heart— thus his happy, eager, and serious childhood transfigured itself away amid scenes of which he himself as we share them in his radiant verse becomes the sentient embodiment. He can scarcely contain his rapture at being a child again in the tale he is telling, and from its very beginning. 'I began my story early,' he says:

Achievement

'not misled, I trust,
By an infirmity of love for days
Disowned by memory—ere the breath of spring
Planting my snowdrops among winter snows

days that had for him the charm

'Of visionary things, those lovely forms
And sweet sensations that throw back our life,
And almost make remotest infancy
A visible scene, on which the sun is shining. . . .

How is it possible to dissever here the 'innate' from 'experience'?
Had he been able *then*, as a child, to communicate in words what
now he recalls only in piecemeal glimpses yet recalls with such
ardour and delight—what then would have been the music and
beauty of his 'numbers'? But clouds began to gather and the day to
lour.

And when he was sixteen—in 1786—he wrote this sonnet:

'Calm is all nature as a resting wheel.
The kine are couched upon the dewy grass;
The horse alone, seen dimly as I pass,
Is cropping audibly his later meal;
Dark is the ground; a slumber seems to steal
O'er vale, and mountain, and the starless sky.
Now, in this blank of things, a harmony,
Home-felt, and home-created, comes to heal
That grief for which the senses still supply
Fresh food; for only then, when memory
Is hushed, am I at rest. My Friends! restrain
Those busy cares that would allay my pain;
Oh! leave me to myself, nor let me feel
The officious touch that makes me droop again.'

Where now the springing rapture of the Prelude? Brightness
falls from the air; his good angel seems to have forsaken him. He
is driven back upon himself—in this blank of things. 'Glory and
loveliness have passed away'; melancholy has descended on him,
'sudden from heaven like a weeping cloud'. And here are the first
intimations of what was to be the theme of his famous Ode. This
boyish sonnet, then—its own music dying away in its closing lines

Early One Morning

—is as it were the threshold of his life's work. The mood and tone are his, and his alone. Its 'incidents' are chosen 'from common life'. In language, except for the melody of the opening lines, it differs little from that of 'good prose'—that magically matter-of-fact 'audibly', for example; and it is concerned with 'the image of man and nature'. Its first line is no less a revelation of an intuitive and imaginative genius than its last is pure but prosaic Wordsworth.

In every particular this poem is the very antipodes of 'To Helen'. In the one is the late twilight of country fields. In the other a curious internal darkness seems to lurk. Even its 'brilliant' gives little light. Indeed in earlier versions, first, the words *that little*, then, *that shadowy*, had the place of 'yon brilliant'; and for 'agate lamp' there was *folded scroll*! Its 'Holy Land' has little trace of any holiness that we feel sixteen-year-old Wordsworth would accept. Its decoying music is slightly metallic. Its wanderer's desperate seas—a metaphor most curiously interwoven in the development of the theme—though Rome and Greece are the havens to which they convey him, will be found (with *his* Nicæa) on no earth-bound map. Of 'common life' there is hardly an echo. Nor is there any direct sense of the writer as a human being. Nemo might be his name, his age any age, and his destiny that of the Wandering Jew. The beauty that infatuates him is less physical—far less the sensuous beauty of a woman—than an emanation of the intellect and of fantasy. Is his Psyche she herself, or the image or a phantasm compounded of both in his own mind? She *herself* is not here indeed; the statue in its window niche has supplanted her. As for the verbal form of the poem, it is as material and fragile in effect as a piece of Venetian glass, its contents almost as wastelessly fitting it as an exotic fruit its skin.

By so reading Wordsworth's sonnet as if the words were welling up out of our own consciousness, we can in part realize the mind of the boy that wrote it, and thus so to speak originate, while positively seeing, the evocatory and symbolic 'wheel' of its opening words. Any such attempt, even though we are aware of the occasion of the poem, seems to be impracticable with 'To Helen'. Poe was in age only two years younger than the Wordsworth of the sonnet when he wrote it, but how much older in both worldly and innate experience? Imagine a meeting between them. To all

Achievement

appearance it might be no more frigid than good manners would permit. In fact it would resemble that between a profoundly serene but world-vexed patriarch, and Lucifer, banished from the morning.[1]

3. '*But at the gates o' Paradise*
That birk grew fair enough.'

The *Poetical Sketches* were published when William Blake was twenty-six. The faltering and derivative 'Mad Song', the lovely 'Fresh from the dewy hill', with its 'O bless those limbs, beaming with heavenly light', no less remote from Wordsworth than from Poe; the range, colour and mastery of 'To the Muses', and the clumsy humour of 'Blind-Man's Buff', as utterly out of keeping with the rest as are Keats's jocular rhymes of 1818 with his 'Hyperion'—all these were written by Blake when he was between the ages of twelve and twenty-one. Twenty-two years afterwards —seven after he had refrained from becoming drawing master to the Royal Family—he was living in a thatched cottage at Felpham, not far from the downs and close to the sea.

As he was walking alone one day in his garden, there:
'There was great stillness among the branches and flowers, and more than common sweetness in the air; I heard a low and pleasant sound, and I knew not whence it came. At last I saw the broad leaf of a flower move, and, underneath, I saw a procession of creatures, of the size and colour of green and grey grasshoppers, bearing a body laid out on a rose leaf, which they buried with songs and then disappeared. It was a fairy funeral.'

It might be a child that is speaking. Angels, devils—'As I was walking among the fires of hell'—long-dead poets and prophets were the daily company of Blake's imagination. Their origin has been the problem of all his students. And yet perhaps it is no more of a problem than the whence of a Song which was written when he too was only fourteen years old:

'How sweet I roam'd from field to field,
And tasted all the summer's pride,

[1] Poe was born thirty-nine years after Wordsworth, and died—as did Thomas Lovell Beddoes (the author of *Death's Jest Book!*) a year before him, in 1849. Emily Brontë died in 1848.

541

Early One Morning

Till I the prince of love beheld,
　Who in the sunny beams did glide!

'He shew'd me lilies for my hair,
　And blushing roses for my brow;
He led me through his gardens fair,
　Where all his golden pleasures grow.

'With sweet May dews my wings were wet,
　And Phoebus fir'd my vocal rage;
He caught me in his silken net,
　And shut me in his golden cage.

'He loves to sit and hear me sing,
　Then, laughing, sports and plays with me;
Then stretches out my golden wing,
　And mocks my loss of liberty.'

To whom is he referring? Who precisely is this 'me'? This 'prince of love'? The visionary flowers are of a strange loveliness —lovelier indeed perhaps than any *we* may have seen of Nature's. But these fields and gardens are not hers. His 'vocal rage' may resemble an old foot-stone, thick with moss and half-buried in his gardens—mislaid by Pope or Dryden—but otherwise the words appear to have been mutely waiting to take their places here for good and all. And how untellably delicate yet indestructible are the objects to which they refer—the lilies, the silken net, the golden cage, and even the merely mentioned hair, which is of the same texture as—but utterly remote in imagination from—Donne's 'bracelet . . . about the bone'. The words at last evaporate, shed away, into their own pure music, and, like the remembered flowers of Hood's childhood, the scene they conjure up seems to be 'made of light'.

These, then, are the three poems referred to above; each one unique in its own fashion, and each as clear and defined an indication of its writer's peculiar genius as its feathers—oriole, wood lark, plover—are of a bird. There may be others as rare. And they too, each of them in its own particular degree, will irradiate childhood.

Achievement

4. *'There is but one thing under heaven to which a man should bow—genius; and but one to which a man should kneel—goodness.'*

There is a famous fragment from one of Jeremy Taylor's sermons which refuses to be forgotten when one has spent many hours in the company of young children, or in the presence rather of a childhood that has been distilled, as it were, from these early memories and poems. It is not that which concludes, 'He that loves not his wife and children, feeds a Lioness at home, and broods a nest of sorrowes', but this:—

'As when the sun approaches towards the gates of the morning he first opens a little eye of heaven, and sends away the spirits of darkness, and gives light to a cock, and calls up the lark to matins, and by and by gilds the fringes of a cloud, and peeps over the eastern hills, thrusting out his golden horns; like those which decked the brows of Moses when he was forced to wear a veil because himself had seen the face of God; and still, while a man tells the story, the sun gets up higher, till he shows a fair face and a full light, and then he shines one whole day, under a cloud often, and sometimes weeping great and little showers, and sets quickly: so is a man's reason and his life.'

Jeremy Taylor delighted in imagery of this character, at times all but losing his way awhile in contemplation of the scene or object he has conjured up, and hovering without danger on the very brink of fine writing, to alight at last on the borders of poetry and paradise. But however complex the web he spins in this aerial circuiting, its enchantment is the simplicity of his imagination, the innocence of his intellect. If this be so, should we be surprised if the concluding sentence of our quotation had run, 'So is a *child's* reason and his life'? *That* sun may appear to set almost as soon as we realize that it is risen; and whatever the new day may bring, the fields, the hills, the river, even the cock on the dunghill and the quacking ducks on the duckpond, will never be the same again. As with William Blake and Vaughan, it is the light of Jeremy Taylor's *mind* that is radiant in these words. Without that even the Sun is darkened.

But another kind of mind and character may also keep these childhood simplicities to the very end. In ways, hobbies, oddities and pursuits, Charles Waterton, the great naturalist, all his life long remained at heart what he had been as a child—wayward, impulsive, courageous, infinitely venturesome—a child of nature, as of grace. He could, and would, no more have written like Jeremy Taylor than he could have set to work on a mechanical goldfinch in precious gems and metals. 'He prayeth best who loveth best All things both great and small'; and with Waterton this meant not merely all creatures 'bright and beautiful'. He built a wall which cost him £9,000 round his estate in Yorkshire, to ensure their salvation—the brown rat, which he delighted to avow came over in the ship that brought equally-detested George I to England, being the sole outcast from his universal hospitality.

When he was a small boy, as he was walking up a lane, he met an old woman who asked him for charity. He had spent his last pocket-money and had not a halfpenny left. So he gave her a treasured knitting needle which he kept in the hem of his jacket and which was of the greatest value to him in blowing eggs. Late in life he always carried an old knife in his pocket; and if, in his daily walks, he encountered any poor soul with no shoes to his feet, he handed it over, with instructions to take it to a shoemaker's in Wakefield and exchange it for a new pair. Once having left this token at home, 'he made over his own shoes and stockings to a wayfarer with bleeding feet, and walked home bare-foot'.

What follows, and since these pages began with borrowings it may need little apology to end with one, is taken from an introduction by Norman Moore to the *Essays on Natural History*. Waterton is in his eighty-fourth year. Nevertheless, in the last sunrise he tells of, it is the sun of a lifelong childhood that is setting.

'He was well aware of his perilous condition, for he remarked to me, "This is a bad business", and later on he felt his pulse often, and said, "It is a bad case."

'He was more than self-possessed. A benignant cheerfulness beamed from his mind, and in the fits of pain he frequently looked up with a gentle smile, and made some little joke. Towards midnight he grew worse. The priest, the Reverend R. Browne, was summoned, and Waterton got ready to die. He pulled himself upright without help, sat in the middle of the sofa, and gave his blessing in turn to his grandson, Charlie, to his grand-daughter, Mary, to each of his sisters-in-law, to his niece, and to myself, and left a message for his son, who was hastening back from Rome.

Achievement

He then received the last sacraments, repeated all the responses, Saint Bernard's hymn in English, and the first two verses of the *Dies Iræ*. The end was now at hand, and he died at twenty-seven minutes past two in the morning of May 27, 1865. The window was open. The sky was beginning to grow gray, a few rooks had cawed, the swallows were twittering, the landrail was craking from the Ox-close, and a favourite cock, which he used to call his morning gun, leaped out from some hollies, and gave his accustomed crow. The ear of his master was deaf to the call. He had obeyed a sublimer summons, and had woke up to the glories of the eternal world. . . .'

NOTES

NOTES

★

'5,700,000 *children*' (p. 43).

Comparisons are odious, says the proverb; and when they take the form of statistics they are to some tastes also repulsive. Their hidden charms, I suspect, appeal chiefly to the elderly. The following particulars in varying degree all affect children. They are borrowed chiefly from that unfailing friend of the ignoramus with a hunger for information, *Whitaker's Almanack*—any blunders being the borrower's. They must of course be humanized if they are to *tell*.

Of every thousand *children* born between the years 1881 and 1890, in England and Wales, 142 died annually, on the average, before reaching the age of twelve months. In 1930, the corresponding number was 60; in 1933, 64; in 1934, 59. On the other hand, the birth-rate per thousand in 1880 was 34.2; in 1900, 28.7; in 1930, 16.3; in 1933, 14.04. At the rate of decrease shown during the last-mentioned two years, infants will altogether cease to arrive in England and Wales about 1956! However, a very slight, and perhaps temporary increase in the rate occurred in 1934. An immediate practical effect of this decline, pregnant with a host of consequences, is revealed by the fact that for every seven children in the London elementary schools twenty years ago there are now only five.

The general death rate in 1880 was 20.5; in 1930, 11.4. Private families are continuing to decline in size; the most frequently occurring family consists of three persons, the next most frequent of only two persons. Roughly, one out of every four families numbers three persons; one out of every five, two persons; usually, no doubt, husband and wife. The four-person family ranked second in frequency both in 1911 and in 1921; it now ranks third.

The average annual number of suicides to every million of the population between 1871-80 was 77; in 1933 it was 140. The total number of divorces in 1913 was 827; in 1930, 4,032. Tragic events like these, occurring in the life even of a young child, may remain for years a haunting spectre, a shadow—perhaps a grave handicap. Not to so many, a relief from gloom or unhappiness or from an incubus; or a release into freedom.

In round figures, out of every hundred births in England and Wales in 1931, four were illegitimate; the corresponding figures for France in 1922 being nine; in Germany, for 1929, twelve; in Sweden, in 1930, sixteen; and in the Netherlands, for the same year, less than two. Erasmus, Boccaccio and Cardan were love-children—an odd phrase that sets one thinking on the children born of indifference. Edmund in *King Lear* has views on this question.

In 1871, there were some 600,000 more females than males, in 1931 the preponderance was over 1,700,000—it is a prodigious waste of the maternal. On the other hand in the year ending April 1933 there were 43,000 more marriages than in the preceding year.

In the eight years from 1870 to 1877 the School Board had taken off the streets of London 8,508 'homeless and destitute and lawless' children. In that decade, of every million children under the age of fifteen, measles had annually swept away 1,038; scarlet fever, 1,908; diphtheria and croup 765; whooping cough, 1,415. The corresponding figures for 1930 were 431, 64, 340 and 211. Yet again these bare figures cannot reveal the saving in human distress, anxiety, grieving and waste of youth concealed in them. On the other hand, the present problem is not that of children homeless and destitute, but of lawless children, the devil-may-care young housebreakers, for example.

Few novelists nowadays are as prone to the pathos of describing the death of a child as were those of the last century—*Eric, Misunderstood, Uncle Tom's Cabin, Bleak House,* immediately come to mind. In actual fact death in childhood was a far commoner occurrence then than it is now. Child insurance was only one of the many removable causes that had a deadly effect on the bills on infant mortality—a phrase, again, that enables the eye to avoid the object. And a visit to any old country churchyard will tell the same tale.

Indeed, in 1872 a child at birth (if he had any respect for the laws of average), might look forward to only forty years of life. A child born in 1921 had fourteen years' advantage of him in this respect. By the age of five this advantage had sunk to nine years; at ten years old, to eight. What he can *do* with these extra years depends, naturally, not solely on himself. In Mr. Kenneth Muir's words:

> 'He has his father's brow, they say;
> his mother's mouth and eyes,

MOZART, IN GALA CLOTHES, AT THE AGE OF SIX
From a painting in the Mozart Museum at Salzburg

Notes

.

> but all his lovely mould of clay
> he wears so royally to-day
> is but a myriad legacies
> from forbears passed away.'

The newborn of 1921 have only two years more of 'childhood' before them; they have already begun spending their legacies.

'How far from easy it is . . . to remain illiterate' (p. 45).

The great majority of the Londoners who roared their applause of the Elizabethan dramatists must, I suppose, have been 'illiterate'; and Bacon in his famous essay on Studies mentions neither newspapers of any kind, nor bad fiction, nor bad science. To assert that our daily commons of 'news' is admirable food for the mind would be to stab Life itself in the back. Still, to confer a boon is not to take the responsibility for what may come of it; and it was not the *Newgate Calendar* as a literary diet that my maternal grandfather, Dr. Colin Arrott Browning, had in view when nearly a century ago and in unusual circumstances he turned school-master.

In *The Convict Ship* he gives particulars concerning the men who, sentenced to transportation, had sailed under his command on the *Earl Grey* for Van Diemen's Land on December 26th, 1842. His book reveals that he was a pious, stern, and profoundly sympathetic man, and that he took his duties very seriously. The *morals* of the prisoners were his chief concern; to give them help 'to save their souls' his one aspiration. He set about teaching them their rudiments.

At the outset, with fifteen primers to every hundred men, he divided his 264 pupils into twenty-four classes. One can picture a faint glimpse of them, their ages ranging from under twenty—thirty-five of these in all—up to sixty, seated in groups on the decks of the sailing ship. Seventy-six of them, he found, had already been 'educated', four of these in Sunday School only. Of the seventy-six, fifty-three could read and write, twenty-three could read only. The voyage took thirteen months. Twenty-eight days out from Plymouth there gathered and broke an appalling tempest of rain and lightning. The fore-royal mast was shivered to pieces by a thunderbolt; three men were struck, though not fatally; the ship seemed to be on fire and in danger of foundering. The prisoners were laid prostrate in the hulks—a dismal scene that only a Conrad could describe.

However, 261 of the 264 convicts survived and were landed at Hobart Town. In the meantime seven of them had been taught to

Early One Morning

write, and 185 had learned to read—'the Holy Scriptures'. Only one had failed to do either. Writing, naturally, was by far the more difficult feat; and the Admiralty had allowed only fifteen slates and fifty slate pencils for the voyage!

When the men had been disembarked, Sir John Franklin 'inspected and addressed them . . . and spoke in high terms of approbation in reference to their appearance and their behaviour on board the *Earl Grey*'. If a trace of vanity shows itself here, then another Franklin will condone it on another page. On a later voyage, that of the *Elphinstone*, there was the following report:

'Captain Adams, of His Majesty's 28th Regiment, who commanded the guard on board the *Elphinstone*, has assured me, that such was Dr. Browning's influence over the convicts, that during the whole voyage there was not a dispute amongst them; and there appeared to be nothing they dreaded so much as giving offence to their surgeon superintendent.' Translate the word 'convicts' into *schoolboys*, and how consolatory a tribute this passage might be, let us say, to a French master!

'*Our "intelligence-age"* ' (p. 47).

'Normal' is a word used by the expert to signify a mental status in childhood between the subnormal—the various degrees, that is, of feeble-mindedness or mental-defectiveness, ranging from that of an idiot, of an imbecile, of a moron, up to the merely backward—and the supra normal, 'ranging from the bright up to the genius'. A moron of any age is in mental ability the equal of a child of from seven to eleven years old; an imbecile, of a child between three years old and seven; and an idiot, of a child under three. Not that there is any appearance of the adult imbecile in an ordinary intelligent child who is between three years old and seven. Not only his alert young sensibilities but his potentialities must be taken into account. He is completely adequate within his own regime—as an animal is. Whereas an imbecile is not, or a moron—'a moderately feeble-minded person'—either. Their defects and deficiencies have usually been present from birth. Aments—another general term—begin to talk late, have certain special defects, are sluggish of thought, easily influenced, and have little practical imagination. They learn and form habits slowly, have a poor 'memory span', and scanty powers of attention, of reasoning and of dealing with abstractions.

Apart, we are told, from merely *retarded* or advanced development, which may be due to many extraneous causes, both subnormal and supranormal mental ability is in nine cases out of ten the outcome of

Notes

hereditary influences and endowment. Dr. Bernard Hollander states also that one out of every ten cases of imbecility in children has been due to an accident or to a blunder at birth. Special aptitudes may show themselves in children of a high, or moderate, or even of an inferior general intelligence.

But it is easier, it seems, to classify in this fashion children who are mentally defective than those of powers and faculties well above the normal—a classification that might be of very real service. We have been told, however, where to look for the latter. Having tabulated the required particulars from the lives of 977 men of eminence—men that would rank, that is, 'as one in four thousand for intellectual attainment' —Galton found that among their relatives 535 were themselves 'eminent'. This total included 89 fathers, 114 brothers, and 129 sons. Among as many men—977—of only 'average ability', but of an equal social standing, only four could claim eminent relatives. The pompous nobody with eminent relatives is thus in a sad case. A scrutiny of Royalty—as of twins, identic and otherwise—has given a similar result. What is bred in the bone will never come out of the flesh, says the old proverb. But though the State bestows anxious care on the child that is needy-minded, it has not yet set apart a special haven or forcing-house for juvenile relatives of the eminent, or even for the children who in their very early years have already proved themselves well above the median between brightness and sheer genius.

The description 'a thoroughly normal child' would be accepted by the majority of mothers as a flattering tribute to their little Nathaniel or Mary; not so the faintest hint of the 'abnormal'. And yet any unusual beauty, or grace, or skill, or fine temper, like able wits, a vigorous will, good judgement and a profound charity, may be immeasurably more valuable things than mere 'normalcy'. After his life with the Houyhnhnms Gulliver loathed even the mildest specimen of his own kind; but would he have been wholly happy in an island occupied solely by Gullivers as 'normal' as himself?

As for intelligence tests, to which so superficial a reference has been made, their name is Legion; and scores—examples only—will be found in the Report mentioned on page 38. It is perilous for the novice, we are warned, to make use of them on children. But some of them may be a lesson for him in modesty, whatever 'central fund of mental energy', whatever 'inborn general intellectual efficiency' he may possess 'which may be directed into certain channels' by his 'will and attention'. But is it a solace to be told that a positive lack of general intelligence may be an advantage for some kinds of mechanical work?

Here are a few examples of the answers to questions in an examination

Early One Morning

paper set by Alfred Russel Wallace, and referred to on a previous page. They reveal that strange growths may spring from a seed of information in the ooze of a young mind.

'The principal habitat of the elephant is the fauna, the rhinoceros, the buffalo; and the hippopotamus is the white bear.'

'The depth of the water of the Atlantic is measured by large things called ravines. The depth is 90,000,000 miles. Gold is found at the bottom.'

'Animals which lived before the Flood no longer exist except their fossilized remains. Iothoraics, Pleathorus, Mammoth, Dothorium, Adam and Eve never saw, having become extinct.'

'The cause of the long days is due to the slowness with which the moon sets, or, more correctly, the long nights, and when the moon does set it remains a long time forming the long days.'

'The ocean contains poles, insects live at the bottom of the ocean and bore holes in the poles, when the poles are reached they reach the bottom of the ocean.'

'Especially the lost from childhood' (p. 118).

Any attempt to waylay in memory what we are confident must be retrievable, and may yet for the time being elude us, is an amusing and enlightening experiment, and one that will hardly fail to reveal how much we are at the mercy of an obscure system usually beyond our conscious control. The effort may defeat itself. Even a passive and patient expectation of our prize may prove fruitless. At breakfast recently, I endeavoured, for example, to recall what I had had for dinner the previous evening—or rather I left the wicket gate of consciousness hospitably open, and a lamp in the window to lure the wanderer home. But in vain. Nothing whatever at first showed itself of the quarry I knew was *there*. The attempt was repeated at intervals through the day: and still in vain. There remained a hollow where the memoried dinner should have been.

That evening these tactics were altered. I glanced idly about, as it were, in my mind; and in a moment or two, though, alás, I cannot say how or why, the isolated image of a cream-encrusted meringue swam tranquilly into view. This was immediately followed by the phantom of a jocular remark made about it which I had failed to notice at the time. Nor had any meringue been mine. The fish followed a little later —an extremely clear visual image. Then the vegetables; first, potatoes —seen on a side table; and next, after one false guess, but, at a second, quite unmistakably, sea-kale; and last (they had proved a little tough), the tournedos.

Notes

As recollections these few particulars were isolated. The protracted and varied scene—the concurrent movements of my fellow guests, our talk and actions, my sensations, perceptions, and thoughts—had surrendered only these few scattered relics, though others perhaps might have been retrieved by steady rumination. At the moment of recovery it seemed probable that this much at least of the banquet was now secure. Far from it; since I had failed to learn it *by heart*. And when, after the lapse of a few weeks, recollection of the experiment returned, and I once more made the attempt, every single dish had vanished again.

Now, in the act of copying this account of it from a note made soon afterwards, I am only *reminded*, and this very faintly, of the details already given, and of nothing more. Everything else connected with the occasion—the date, the events of the afternoon preceding it and of the morning that followed it—is now apparently lost in the limbo of complete oblivion—that oblivion in which all but a few bright individual flowers of the years of childhood bloom unseen.

This is a very trivial but, I hope, pardonable example of ease in forgetting. Had no immediate attempt been made to recover what after all was not unpleasing in the recovery, any delayed attempt would almost certainly have been in vain. The faculty of memory differs widely of course in individuals; and this specimen may convict its producer of being little short of feeble-minded. To cast the first stone (out of the blue), however, would be rash. Is it because childhood is often so intense, eager, and *ever-present* an experience that memory even of its red letter days may soon thin rapidly into pink, and then fade out?

On the other hand, what may completely elude us for the time being may, at a waft of the wand of enchantment, swim into consciousness again with the silence and subtlety of a dream. Brooding recently on some trifling event in my childhood, I was astonished to discover that at the moment I could recall no more of the interior of the house in which it had occurred than a glimpse of a table and of the window in one of its rooms. *This* insulated recollection, however, was so intense and definite that it all but amounted to an hallucination.

I let it stay in my mind, so to speak, without stirring, in the faint hope that more would follow. And presently, as if clean out of nowhere, two wooden steps leading out of this room quietly revealed themselves; and the next moment I was able to explore other rooms in the house, upstairs and down, and so effectively that in a few moments I could recall the position of their doors, windows, and fireplaces, together with some of the furniture, the china, the pictures.

And then it was as though a ghost of the mind could draw near within the compass, as it were, of the memory itself, and *examine* the pictures—one, I remember, of cattle gathered together under the sullen and louring clouds of a thunderstorm, another of rocks and pale green trees and coursing water—and the very impress, sealed once on consciousness, was recovered in spite of the experiences massed in between —even the clear and lively colours of the china figures, and of the Chinese cups and saucers, as they were seen *then*. How strange it seems, then, that among these clear and scattered objects no living figure appears; though other memories vividly reanimate these same remote rooms again.

A far more striking but similar experience which was definitely put to the proof is recorded by Samuel Butler in his *Note-Books*. He entitles it, 'A Torn Finger-Nail'.

'Henry Hoare [a college friend], when a young man of about five-and-twenty, one day tore the quick of his finger-nail—I mean he separated the fleshy part of the finger from the nail—and this reminded him that many years previously, while quite a child, he had done the same thing. Thereon he fell to thinking of that time which was impressed upon his memory partly because there was a great disturbance in the house about a missing five-pound note and partly because it was while he had the scarlet fever.

'Following the train of thought aroused by his torn finger, he asked himself how he had torn it, and after a while it came back to him that he had been lying ill in bed as a child of seven at the house of an aunt who lived in Hertfordshire. His arms often hung out of the bed and, as his hands wandered over the wooden frame, he felt that there was a place where a nut had come out so that he could put his fingers in. One day, in trying to stuff a piece of paper into this hole, he stuffed it in so far and so tightly that he tore the quick of his nail. The whole thing came back vividly and, though he had not thought of it for nearly twenty years, he could see the room in his aunt's house and remembered how his aunt used to sit by his bedside writing at a little table from which he had got the piece of paper which he had stuffed into the hole.

'So far so good. But then there flashed upon him an idea that was not so pleasant. I mean it came upon him with irresistible force that the piece of paper he had stuffed into the hole in the bedstead was the missing five-pound note about which there had been so much disturbance.'

He immediately posted down to his aunt's house in Hertfordshire, asked, to the astonishment of his relatives, to be allowed to wash his hands in the remembered room, discovered on lifting the chintz

Notes

valance of the bed that an iron nut now filled the hole that had once beguiled his groping feverish fingers, procured, at some risk to his reputation for sanity, a bed-key, and lo, the five-pound note!

A memoried sensation then may lie latent for years until the cue it needs shall evoke it. Here it was not a question of retrieving but of ascertaining. Smells and odours have a magic power of evocation, and in yet another note of Butler's a *bouquet* is involved rather than a taste, since of savours there are, strictly, only four: acid, bitter, salt and sweet.

When he was a boy he used occasionally to sip a certain claret at his father's dinner table. Many years afterwards he tasted claret again but found it different: 'much more like weak port wine'. Many years after that, in 1883, he dined with a friend in St. James's Street, had claret after dinner, and recognized it instantly as the vintage of his childhood. 'There was no mistake about it. I asked Jason what the wine was. He said it was Château Lafite, and very fine.'

In 1900, when Butler was sixty-five, Sir Sydney Cockerell showed him a beautiful mediæval service book. But this, strangely enough, failed to awaken any interest in his mind, any vestige of recollection. Instead, his indifference called up an early experience as remote in all but one respect from missals as was Romeo's moon from green cheese. 'Give me rather', he expostulated in a Note, 'a robin or a peripatetic cat like the one whose loss the parishioners of St. Clement Danes are still deploring. When I was at school at Allesley the boy who knelt opposite me at morning prayers, with his face not more than a yard away from mine, used to blow pretty little bubbles with his saliva which he would send sailing off the top of his tongue like miniature soap bubbles; they very soon broke, but they had a career of a foot or two. I never saw any one else able to get saliva bubbles right away from him; and though I have endeavoured for some five and fifty years to acquire the art, I never yet could start the bubble off my tongue without its bursting. Now things like this really do relieve the tedium of church, but no missal that I have ever seen will do anything but increase it.'

Alfred Russel Wallace, concerning his young days, records yet another retentive trick of memory—although *the* mystery is, rather, perhaps, since we remember much, that we should forget anything. Out one day, when he was a boy, in the frozen meadows of the Ouse, he saw a young man with a double-barrelled gun, who at that moment threw it up, fired off both barrels, and—alackaday—'brought two wild swans to the ground'. He discovered that this young man's name was H. H. Higgins. It interested him, as he had a schoolfellow who was also an H.H.H.—Henry Holman Hogsflesh. Over fifty years later, when giving a lecture at Liverpool, Wallace met this Mr. H. H. Higgins again, and immediately reminded him of the frozen meadows and the swans, repeating his own very words, 'That was a good shot!' and the reply, 'Oh! you can't miss them, they are as big as a barn door'. Since Mr. Higgins's family had doubted the swans, this was a complacent moment for him, and no less pleasant a moment for the lecturer.

Both the house of my own early recollection and the house referred to by Samuel Butler were houses recalled from childhood. Houses occupied, however, much later in life *may* be difficult to explore in memory, if my own experience is a safe guide. A phantasmal orientation is necessary, since the images of rooms of different periods may become confused, and even fused in recollection. We may, too, recall the salient moment, but forget what emotion or other accompaniment gave it so sharp a character. For memory would be a capricious jade indeed if she had *no* justification for insisting on the preservation from childhood of recollections, let us say, apparently so fatuous as one small cured haddock on a slab in the little square window of a fishmonger's shop; a red-haired confectioner's wife of alarming manners; or, viewed from an upper window, a group of five harmless old ladies in mushroom hats on a green and sunny lawn, gracelessly enveloped with an unspeakable longing in the mind of the young observer never to look upon their like again!

'*The exceptional . . . may illuminate the normal*' (p. 164).

In an autobiography entitled *A Mind that Found Itself*, described by William James as a 'classic account "from within" of an insane person's psychology', Mr. Clifford Beers gives a few particulars of his childhood. The first years of his life, he tells us (he was born in 1876), 'were not unlike those of thousands of other American boys. Nothing out of the ordinary occurred'. His 'school courses' were completed with little trouble, and with 'as little distinction'.

In his eighteenth year he became the prey of delusions and of an inward dread, which were intensified by insomnia. Six years later, after a day of anguish, he attempted to do away with himself by dropping, not by throwing himself, out of an upper window. At the very instant, he tells us, his feet struck the ground his delusions vanished. All recollection of them was, as it were, at once deleted from his mind. This suggested to Mr. Beers that similar tragedies might be averted if only the needful help were available when the 'crisis impends'.

He refers to the fact that—like many seemingly commonsensical adults in their views of children—the sane are generally of opinion that the insane are unable to reason. This, judging by his own experience,

Notes

he denies. He also declares that, although, normally, his own memory was but an 'ordinary memory', when it was not noticeably poor, during the first two years of his insanity it was copious and acute. And again, when, confined a second time in an asylum, he realized that his brother had actually kept an appointment which had been arranged in a letter, a meeting craved for, but in his state of mind at the time despaired of, all illusions and delusions once more instantly left him. 'The very instant I caught sight of my letter in the hands of my brother, all was changed. . . . My old world was again mine.' There are tragic pages in this book—terror, horror, despair. Nevertheless Mr. Clifford Beers agrees with the statement made by Charles Lamb in a letter addressed to Coleridge in 1796:

'At some future time I will amuse you with an account, as full as my memory will permit, of the strange turns my frenzy took. I look back upon it at times with a gloomy kind of envy; for, while it lasted, I had many, many hours of pure happiness. Dream not, Coleridge, of having tasted all the grandeur and wildness of Fancy till you have gone mad! All now seems to me vapid, comparatively so!'

'*Before the age of three*' (p. 168).

'Observation of memory in the autobiographer', says Miss Robeson Burr, 'sustains the prevalent theory of its relation to genius. Among the cases of persistently weak memories not a single one is a mind of the first order. Though it may develop late, a strong, if selective, memory seems to be a first requisite of intellectual power.' There are memories of different kinds, she warns us. 'Some *memoiristes* omit all dates; others lay a stress on them which their value does not warrant. Rousseau never gave an accurate date, but how accurate was his memory and transcription of *feeling!*'

It is early memories, however, that we have in mind, and, in respect to specified 'firsts', only three of Miss Burr's autobiographers could recall with assurance anything of the first two years of life; thirteen were restricted to the first three years; twenty-three to the first four; eleven to five; and eleven to six years. Two of her autobiographers could retrieve nothing before their eighth birthday. Fifteen of them, out of her total number, professed that they had *weak* memories.

No reward has yet, I fancy, been offered by any enquirer for the earliest memory either on record or as yet unrecorded. Occasionally one may chance, in the last few chapters of a long Life, on a vivid reference to infancy, sheer treasure trove, that until then had escaped notice. Autobiography tends, no doubt, to fall into a routine of telling what

Early One Morning

is generally told, and to avoid such extremes as might too sharply estrange the reader: such as Brougham's. 'The *Narrative*', he announced to his executors in the manuscript of his Memoirs, 'is to be printed as *I* have written it . . . *I* alone am Responsible. . . . I desire that (it) shall be published as EXCLUSIVELY MY OWN.' A conscious egotism is for the most part kept within bounds. Indeed, no human being—whether a St. Augustine or a Rousseau or a Cardan—however frank or fervid his intentions, can have completely divulged the secret workings of his mind and heart. Not even in childhood. Still, a *nursery* trumpet, though a torment in the home, may be music in a book; and the further away one's follies and frailties are in time, the easier they are, if not to remember, at least to confess and to condone.

'*Vanity, effervescent, sweet and heady*' (p. 177)—and not confined to one sex. At times, like pride, it may have a fall. My sister, Mrs. Roger Ingpen, who, when climbing upstairs as a child in the dark, was continually haunted by the fear that an elongating arm and hand would glide up after her from nowhere in pursuit, recalls the effect of a honied little compliment that she overheard when she was not more than two and a quarter years old. In this, her earliest recollection, she was being taken for a walk by an elder sister. They met a lady who suddenly broke off her conversation to glance at her, with some such remark as, 'How sweet her hair looks peeping out from under her black bonnet!'—for even infants not so many years ago went 'into mourning'. Her hair was then of a pale gold; and she took the first opportunity on reaching home of proving if what she had heard was true. Finding herself alone in her mother's bedroom, she endeavoured to see herself in the glass, but was not tall enough. So she drew out from under the old-fashioned drapery of the dressing-table a small deed-box that she had espied there, climbed up on to it, and took a long meditative gaze at her own reflection. The vanity went unrewarded; the fair image in the looking-glass did not in the least impress her!

'*The congregation burst out laughing*' (p. 192).
John Ruskin was also among the nursery preachers. 'I arrived', he says, 'at some abstract in my own mind of the Rev. Howell's sermons; and occasionally, in imitation of him, preached a sermon at home over the red sofa cushions; this performance being always called for by my mother's dearest friends, as the great accomplishment of my childhood. The sermon was, I believe, some eleven words long; very exemplary,

it seems to me, in that respect—and I still think must have been the purest gospel, for I know it began with, "People, be good." '

Poor child, he was a paraded preacher, then. Not so Thomas Huxley —and neither of them can be said to have completely abandoned the pulpit in later life. Huxley chose for his congregation his mother's maids, and an hour when the rest of the family was at church. His surplice was a pinafore turned the wrong side forwards. He appears too to have brought his discourse off in the grand style—after the manner of the Sir Herbert Oakley referred to on page 180. 'That,' he adds, 'is the earliest indication I can call to mind of the strong clerical affinities which my friend Mr. Herbert Spencer has always ascribed to me, though I fancy they have for the most part remained in a latent state. . . .'

'His grace' (p. 202).

A child of three I know ended her evening prayer recently, after a brief pause, not with the customary petition that God would make her a good girl, but that He would make her infant brother a good boy. Such moments, surely, are seldom *heedless*, and may be no less real and earnest than the state of mind described in a recollection that Mrs. Ellis Roberts has given me permission to include here. It is 'a gleam of consciousness surrounded on both sides by oblivion' and relates to when she was less even than eighteen months old. Many similar experiences in early childhood, awakenings to a sense of sin, of the presence of God, of salvation and of eternal loss are recorded in Miss Robeson Burr's *Religious Confessions and Confessants*.

'I can check my age. . . . I see the streets of West Philadelphia (Walnut Street as I now know it to be), and myself dressed in white sitting in a perambulator, my legs covered by a white fur rug. An old woman is pushing me, very old she seems. . . . Beside the pram walks a great golden and white dog, a Saint Bernard. . . . Perhaps it was the sight of him that made me want to walk, too, and I cried to be lifted out of my "baby-coach". Soon I grew tired and cried to get back and ride. . . . Then again I wailed to be allowed to walk, and again sniffled to be put back in the pram. This went on for some time, my Nana yielding to my desires with an infinite gentle patience.

'What gives this trifling incident its slight interest is that I realized, as clearly as I might do now, that I was behaving ill and that I could stop if I wanted to hard enough. I was seeing the better and choosing the worse. Beside me was goodness and I was taking advantage of it— an ugly thing to do. . . . At that age I could hardly have had a word to clothe my thoughts . . . but my emotions were what they would be now, irritation, shame, regret. No theologian could make clearer to my adult mind the meaning of a sense of original sin than my old nurse's patience impressed it on my baby naughtiness.'

'*The suffocating fumes*' (p. 223).

In *Unfinished Adventure* Miss Evelyn Sharp relates that her first memory was of a visit to Southsea when she was five years old. The jolly Jack Tar who rowed her out in charge of her nurse to see Nelson's *Victory* and gave her a scrap of ship's biscuit, asked if he might kiss her, a liberty that was sternly refused by the nurse. Brighton came later. 'Over it all', she continues, 'was that smell of the sea—or was it only of stale fish and decaying seaweed?—which, with the smell of the magic lantern and the circus, may be ranked among the subtle smells of Victorian childhood that never failed to thrill; and with the recollection of that smell comes another of a symphony of sound, made up of nigger minstrels, and hawkers calling shrimps and lobsters "All alive-o!" and donkey boys shouting by their patient animals, and the crunching wheels of goat-chaises, in which we were never allowed to ride because the other children who had already occupied them might be recovering from measles or scarlet fever; and all of it happening in hot summer sunshine under a cloudless blue sky; for one peculiarity of the Brighton holiday, as it lives in my mind, was that it never rained there. . . .'

The sense of smell is the quickest Mercury of the senses to the region of memory. Its journey is all but instantaneous. Indeed, to have been a child whose small nose may have been unornamental, but was at least active, makes it difficult to imagine childhood without these rewards— the pinks, the wallflowers, the cowslips; moss, old man, hay, woodruff, wood smoke; not to mention kitchen riches and odours rather exciting and provocative than pleasant and soothing. Once and once only in Wordsworth's life was this dormant faculty awakened—by a bed of stocks in full bloom. He declared that 'it was like a vision of Paradise', but that it lasted only a few minutes, after which the sense remained torpid.

'*His father . . . gave him a glass of castor oil*' (p. 237).

And if any kindly father should then wish to make amends, here is Syrup of Antioch. Take a handful of daisies and a handful of bugle, and a handful of red cabbage. Of strawberry withs or creepers, and of sanicle, hemp, avens, tansey, herb-Robert, madder, take of each a handful; of comfrey or orpine (live-long) four branches; six tendrils of red briar, six crops of nettles. Put all these in a gallon of the white wine

Notes

of Italy, Vernacchia, or other good wine, and let them seethe to a pottle (two quarts), and then put thereto as much of clarified honey as thou guessest the juice cometh to, and mingle them well together, and boil it, and again skim it and boil it but a little; and keep it well, for it is full precious. And in this manner shall it be used: to three spoonfuls of syrup six spoonfuls of water. And, first and last, use it for all evils in the body.

'*Even Vidocq* . . .' (p. 301).

Little deep insight into the early consciousness of *any* kind of mind is to be gained from the *Memoirs* of the famous and notorious François Eugène Vidocq. There is some doubt of the authenticity of the book attributed to him, and its statements cannot be relied on, but Vidocq himself never disowned it. He was born, he tells us, on July 23, 1775, in a house adjoining the birthplace of Robespierre who had come into the world seventeen years before him. 'I had a most robust constitution', he tells us, and was so prodigious an infant 'that as soon as I was born they took me for a child of two years of age'! Thus budded that 'athletic figure, that colossal form' which the 'most hardened and powerful ruffians' were soon to learn to dread, and whose phantom was afterwards to haunt the pages of at least four men of genius.

When he was eight years old, having become 'the terror of all the dogs, cats and children of the neighbourhood', Vidocq began to learn his father's trade, that of a baker. Following his brother's example, he robbed the till; but was not at once detected. He 'soon joined the society of the most abandoned vagabonds of the country', and while still a boy by a heartless ruse deceived his mother into believing that his life was in danger. She was decoyed out of the house. By means of a stolen key he gutted the family money chest—and decamped.

From bad he went to worse, but was justified in refusing to practise any longer as a tumbler and acrobat in a menagerie when, disguised as a South Sea Savage, he was ordered to gnaw a live farmyard cock. He went into the army, and asserts that, in six months, while he was in a company of *chasseurs*, he killed two men and fought fifteen duels. Condemned for forgery, he succeeded in escaping from the galleys. At the age of thirty-four he turned informer against his old associates, and entered the service of the police. In this work he built up his wide reputation, though he died at last in poverty.

There are lurid and engrossing episodes in the memoirs, but it is all in the same bombastic vein as its first pages. Incidentally, Vidocq recalls at first hand no experience that occurred to him before he was eight years old.

Early One Morning

'Reading . . . with avidity, absorbed' (p. 336).

The operation seems simplicity itself. A child opens his story book, and presto, he is in another world. Nevertheless, 'we may safely conclude,' says Dr. Edmund Huey in his *Psychology and Pedagogy of Reading*, 'that meanings in reading are mainly feeling-reactions and motor attitudes attaching most intimately to or fused with the inner utterance of the words and especially of the sentences that are read. And with the utterance in which the meanings mainly inhere, we must include the movements of emphasis, of inflection, of gesture, and of expression generally.' Even the 'feelings' are obscure and confused and have been described by William James 'under the names of fringe, suffusion, psychic overtones, etc'. The holiday-maker in a hammock lazily conning his latest shocker—however little he may be aware of it—is thus engaged; and so too within his range is a child of four, as he sits on a stool by the fireside *listening* to Southey's tale of *The Three Bears*. But how explore his feelings?

A curious light is cast on the ordinary activities of the mind by experiments made under abnormal conditions. Mr. Redwood Anderson, having recovered from the effects of a dose of hashish or Cannabis Indica, set down his experiences of writing while under its influence:

'The whole sentence came quickly and clearly into my mind—much as it would under favourable normal conditions—but by the time I had written the first word (and . . . I wrote . . . quickly) the whole sentence had slipped away into a past as remote as ancient Assyria, and a thousand subsequent thoughts had followed it. It cost me a severe effort to recall what the second word of the original sentence had been in order to write it down in its turn, and when it, too, was written, I found once more that the original sentence had dived back into a still remoter past. . . .'

Mr. P. D. Ouspensky, after experiments which he does not explain but which, he declares, resulted in a change in his usual state of consciousness, attempted *in* this state, but in vain, to converse with a friend:

'When I tried having someone near me during these experiments, I found that no kind of conversation could be carried on. I began to say something, but between the first and second words of my sentence such an enormous number of ideas occurred to me and passed before me, that the two words were so widely separated as to make it impossible to find any connection between them . . . I remember for instance the beginning of a sentence: "I said yesterday". . . .

'No sooner had I pronounced the word "I" than a number of ideas began to turn in my head about the meaning of the word, in a philosophical, in a psychological and in every other sense. This was all so

Notes

important, so new and profound, that when I pronounced the word "said", I could not understand in the least what I meant by it. Tearing myself away with difficulty from the first cycle of thoughts about "I", I passed to the idea "said", and immediately found in it an infinite content. The idea of speech, the possibility of expressing thoughts in words, the past tense of the verb, each of these ideas produced an explosion of thoughts, conjectures, comparisons and associations. Thus, when I pronounced the word "yesterday" I was already quite unable to understand why I had said it. But it in its turn immediately dragged me into the depths of the problems of time, of past, present and future, and before me such possibilities of approach to these problems began to open up that my breath was taken away....'

As our own perhaps would be if we could share *all* that takes place behind the bright eyes of a five-year-old whom we have winningly challenged with, Well, and how are *you*?

'*There are only five on Children*' (page 353).

Two of these are from Sir Philip Sidney, the first of them gravely simple:

> 'Riches of children passe a princes throne,
> Which touch the fathers heart with secret joy.
> When without shame he saith, these be mine owne.'

Another is from Lodge:

> '. . . What children apprehend,
> The same they like, they followe and amend.'

None is from Shakespeare; indeed the anthology owes very much more to his two narrative poems than to his plays.

He himself had three children. His daughter, Susannah, was born in May, 1583, when he was a month beyond his nineteenth birthday. His twins, Hamnet and Judith, were born in 1585, and were christened when Susannah was a year and nine months old. At this time, it is believed, he left Stratford, and, it is assumed, saw little of his children for some eleven years. The assumption suggests either a father unusual in a fashion that one does not naturally associate with him, or very unusual circumstances, or perhaps both causes. His son Hamnet died on August 11, 1596, when Susannah was a child of thirteen. When he wrote *Cymbeline, The Winter's Tale* and *The Tempest*, his two daughters were nearing their thirties, Susannah having been married in 1607:

> 'Witty above her sexe, but that's not all,
> Wise to Salvation was good Mistress Hall. . . .'

Early One Morning

Her daughter Elizabeth was the only grandchild Shakespeare ever saw. She was then a child of four or five years old, afterwards became Lady Bernard, and died in February 1669-70, the last of his direct descendants. Judith married a few months before her father's death.

How far the children in the Plays were children of Shakespeare's actual memories there is as yet no evidence. How far they were taken from life will be seen in what follows. And there is little question but that he would have agreed with Jeremy Taylor when he says:

'No man can tell but he that loves his children, how many delicious accents make a man's heart dance in the pretty conversation of those dear pledges; their childishnesse, their stammering, their little angers, their innocence, their imperfections, their necessities are so many little emanations of joy and comfort to him that delights in their persons and society. . . .'

Here is Leontes, in *The Winter's Tale*:

> 'Looking on the lines
> Of my boy's face, methought I did recoil
> Twenty-three years, and saw myself unbreech'd,
> In my green velvet coat, my dagger muzzled,
> Lest it should bite its master, and so prove,
> As ornaments oft do, too dangerous:
> How like, methought, I then was to this kernel,
> This squash, this gentleman. . . .'

and Archidamus: '. . . You have an unspeakable comfort of your young Prince Mamillius: it is a gentleman of the greatest promise that ever came into my note.' 'I very well agree with you', replies Camillo, 'in the hopes of him. It is a gallant child; one that indeed physics the subject, makes old hearts fresh; they that went on crutches ere he was born desire yet their life to see him a man.'

And Polixenes:

> 'We were, fair queen,
> Two lads that thought there was no more behind
> But such a day to-morrow as to-day,
> And to be boy eternal . . .
> We were as twinn'd lambs that did frisk i' the sun,
> And bleat the one at the other: what we chang'd
> Was innocence for innocence; we knew not
> The doctrine of ill-doing, no nor dream'd
> That any did. Had we pursu'd that life,
> And our weak spirits ne'er been higher rear'd
> With stronger blood, we should have answer'd heaven

Notes

Boldly, "not guilty"; the imposition clear'd
Hereditary ours. . . .'
Apart from its intention in the play, and a faint tinge of rhetoric in the
last few lines, this is well within call of Traherne. And there could
hardly be a more variegated tribute to childhood than,

'If at home, sir,
He's all my exercise, my mirth, my matter,
Now my sworn friend and then mine enemy;
My parasite, my soldier, statesman, all:
He makes a July's day short as December,
And with his varying childness cures in me
Thoughts that would thick my blood . . .'

There are, again, the well-known lines in *King John*, beginning,

'If I were mad, I should forget my son,
Or madly think a babe of clouts were he . . .
For since the birth of Cain, the first male child . . .
There was not such a gracious creature born.
But now will canker-sorrow eat my bud
And chase the native beauty from his cheek,
And he will look as hollow as a ghost . . .
And so he'll die; and, rising so again,
When I shall meet him in the court of heaven
I shall not know him: therefore never, never
Must I behold my pretty Arthur more. . . .
Grief fills the room up of my absent child,
Lies in his bed, walks up and down with me,
Puts on his pretty looks, repeats his words,
Remembers me of all his gracious parts,
Stuffs out his vacant garments with his form:
Then have I reason to be fond of grief. . . .'

and those of another mother, Lady Macbeth, though we know nothing
of her children:

'I have given suck, and know
How tender 'tis to love the babe that milks me:
I would, while it was smiling in my face,
Have pluck'd my nipple from his boneless gums,
And dash'd the brains out, had I so sworn as you
Have done to this . . .'

In the same play there is the talk between Lady Macduff and her small

Early One Morning

son, consisting chiefly of questions on his part; and, at his answers, at that facing of the facts which in the adult is sometimes called cynicism, 'Now God help thee, poor monkey. . . . Poor prattler, how thou talk'st!' cries his mother. And presently the murderers enter. 'Thou liest, thou shag-hair'd villain', is his defiance of the wretch that has called his father traitor; and then: 'He has killed me, mother: run away, I pray you.'

In Scene IV of *A Yorkshire Tragedy*, after a maniacal soliloquy from the 'Husband', there enters his 'little sonne with a top and a scourge'— and wholly real he looks.

'What, aile you father? are you not well? I cannot scourge my top as long as you stand so: you take up all the roome with your wide legs. Puh, you cannot make mee afeard with this; I feare no vizards, nor bugbeares.'

'Vizards' recalls Hazlitt and the mask; but here he is defying the insane stare on his father's face, who takes him up 'by the skirts of his long coate in one hand and drawes his dagger with th' other'.

'Oh, what will you do, father?' cries the child, 'I am your white boie.' And one pauses a moment at the odd phrase, however familiar 'white man' may be, until the grim jest follows: 'Thou shalt be my red boie: take that.' And even after the father's, ''Tis charity to braine you', the child replies, 'How shall I learne now my heads broke?'

There are three references in Shakespeare's Plays to a toy top—an 'inverted conoid'; and it would be no shame to him if this 'little sonne' were of his creation. *The Duchess of Malfi* appeared about eight years after *A Yorkshire Tragedy*. The Duchess enters with her children in Act III, Scene V, and she too refers to a top:

> 'I have seen my little boy oft scourge his top,
> And compared myself to't: naught made me e'er
> Go right but Heaven's scourge-stick. . . .'

She speaks to her son, the eldest of them, bidding him farewell; but he makes no answer. There is a reference to Cariola's 'sweet armful', and to the fact that the Duchess's other children cannot prattle. Her question, 'Dost thou think we shall know one another in the other world?' reminds us of Constance, and more than by mere chance, perhaps; and one of the most tragic and affecting passages in the play is her entreaty to Cariola, before she is left alone with her 'executioners':

> 'I pray thee, look thou giv'st my little boy
> Some syrup for his cold, and let the girl
> Say her prayers ere she sleep. . . .'

Notes

Later the children are brought in solely to be strangled. But it *appears* that even if the part of Antonio's son was taken by a living child, it was a speechless one.

Marina—like Perdita—is one of the few infants mentioned in the Plays, and *Pericles* is only in part Shakespeare's. She was born during a shipwreck:—'A terrible child-bed hast thou had, my dear; No light, no fire. . . .' Later, in her helpless innocence, and in face of horror, Marina is far less lifelike than Prince Arthur; and she talks as never mortal woman talked yet, at any age, towards the end of her conversation with Boult. There is a pleasant word-portrait of a girl in the chronicle of the play, recited by *Gower*:

> 'Be't when she weav'd the sleided silk
> With fingers, long, small, white as milk,
> Or when she would with sharp neeld wound
> The cambric, which she made more sound
> By hurting it; when to the lute
> She sung, and made the night-bird mute,
> That still records with moan; or when
> She would with rich and constant pen
> Vail to her mistress Dian; still
> This Philoten contends in skill
> With absolute Marina: so
> With the dove of Paphos might the crow
> Vie feathers white. . . .'

How remote in feeling two men of intelligence can be one from another is suggested by brief extracts from two letters on Constance's theme. The first is from Jeremy Taylor to John Evelyn. It is dated July 19, 1656.

'Deare Sir, I am in some little disorder by reason of the death of a little child of mine, a boy that lately made us very glad: but now he rejoyces in his little orbe, while we thinke, and sigh, and long to be as safe as he is.'

And here is Godwin arguing petulantly with his daughter Mary: 'You must . . . allow me the privilege of a father, and a philosopher, in expostulating with you on this depression. I cannot but consider it as lowering your character in a memorable degree, and putting you quite among the commonality and mob of your sex. . . . What is it you want that you have not? You have the husband of your choice. . . . You have all the goods of fortune. . . . But you have lost a child: and all the rest of the world, all that is beautiful, and all that has a claim upon your kindness, is nothing, because a child of two years old is dead!'

Early One Morning

Elizabeth Grant gives us a glimpse, and that only, of a childless father. At Haddon Hall, when she was fifteen—'a large ugly house . . . scantily furnished'—one thing touched her: 'The duke was childless, unmarried; beside the bed on which he lay when at Haddon was a small cot in which slept the little Cavendish boy who was to be his heir.'

The boy proved to be something of a poet, but is remembered chiefly as the husband of Georgiana, his beautiful duchess.

'Bunyan' (p. 367).

The *Pilgrim's Progress*—read by Bain 'many times over' as a child—is so frequently mentioned in early memories of the past century; it has been the admiration of men of a standing in mind and outlook so diverse one from another as John Ruskin ('noble imaginative teaching'), Dr. Johnson ('great merit, both for invention, imagination, and the conduct of the story'), Macaulay ('perhaps the only book about which after the lapse of a hundred years, the educated minority has come over to the opinion of the common people'), and Coleridge ('I would not have believed beforehand that Calvinism could be painted in such exquisitely delightful colours'), that the result of an enquiry made thirty years ago by Robert Bridges is apposite here. His Essay on the book has recently been reprinted; and his own general conviction is that, though Bunyan himself would have been horrified to find that the secret of his fame is its literary excellence, yet without this excellence he would have perished long ago. Hesitating to trust his private impression that children do not attend to Bunyan's Christian theology and that it has no influence on their spiritual opinions, Bridges enquired of forty-two persons, taken by hazard, and representing 'various classes, conditions, and districts'. 'Nine had never read the *Pilgrim's Progress* at all, and one was doubtful if he had ever seen the book. Of the thirty-two there were twenty-five who had not read it since childhood; and, of the seven remaining, three knew it only from reading it to their children. Returning now to the thirty-two who had read it, twenty-one repudiated the notion that they had ever got any good from it spiritually or morally. Of the remaining eleven there were three who admitted that they might have received an impulse for good action; two were merely respectful towards it; three liked it, one for literary reasons only; and three disliked it.' Not one of them declared apparently that to his own knowledge he had taken any harm from it. What fraction of the book, I wonder, consists of texts taken from the Bible?

Robert Bridges admits 'a moderate admiration' of Bunyan: 'Had he been as unsparingly decried as he has been extolled, I might have taken the other side.'

Among anthologists for children, Kenneth Grahame is conspicuous on account of his deliberate exclusions. A child I could mention wore out two copies of *The Wind in the Willows* merely by thumbing it over, and lovers of his books for the young must be as the sand by the sea in multitude. One disagrees then at one's own peril with his views—though one may be fortified in so doing by several of the early memories of reading recorded above. In his Preface to the *Cambridge Book of Poetry for Children*, an anthology packed with bounties, he explains (a) that he has omitted dialect and the archaic, because children who are learning to spell should be spared anomalies'; (b) that he has refused to turn on 'the mournful tap of tears' by including poems concerned with death and with the dead; (c) that he has refrained from the Plays since he considers that children who ignore Shakespeare (except, of course, his Songs, of which he includes nine), until they are sixteen will be at length no losers by it; and (d) that poems written *about* children had better be reserved for the parents' primer when *they* go back to school.

Was he justified?—(a) means no Chaucer, whose flowers in the first few lines of the 'Prologue' alone are a perpetual Spring and who is ease itself as soon as one is familiar with his strange looks, and that may be very soon; no William Barnes (as near to human nature and to the nature of children as he is to all Nature); no Burns; and no Scottish ballads. Surely no 'anomalies' would baulk a child once he has tasted the 'blude-red wine' or mounted up behind, three in a row, Thomas the Rymer? As for (b), whether the 'tap of tears' is wholesome for children or for all kinds of children may be debatable. The fact that many of them delight to drink of its water, however, and seemingly take no harm from it, is beyond dispute. One has only to listen to the death-and-grave rhymes in their ancient singing games. It is as if some deeper consciousness were by inheritance frankly aware that 'such is life', and such, mortal fortune.

With regard to (c), the general evidence seems to be against Kenneth Grahame's conviction. It is said of Mary Coleridge that 'long before she was in her teens . . . she began to read Shakespeare, to read and *feel* him with a poet's instinct. Her life was changed from that moment. She learned to know men and women through him years before she knew them through life.' (d) ends in omitting by far the greater part even of Jane and Ann Taylor, and many other easy and spirited child-delighters of their time; though this is not to suggest that children who care for poetry *prefer* poetry that is about children.

Early One Morning

'*He was an early Questionist*' (p. 370).

'And the child grew, and waxed strong in spirit, filled with wisdom: and the grace of God was upon him.

'Now his parents went to Jerusalem every year at the feast of the passover. And when he was twelve years old, they went up to Jerusalem after the custom of the feast. And when they had fulfilled the days, as they returned, the child Jesus tarried behind in Jersualem; and Joseph and his mother knew not of it. But they, supposing him to have been in the company, went a day's journey; and they sought him among their kinsfolk and acquaintance. And when they found him not, they turned back again to Jerusalem, seeking him. And it came to pass, that after three days they found him in the temple, sitting in the midst of the doctors, both hearing them, and asking them questions. And all that heard him were astonished at his understanding and answers.

'And when they saw him, they were amazed: and his mother said unto him, Son, why hast thou thus dealt with us? behold, thy father and I have sought thee sorrowing. And he said unto them, How is it that ye sought me? wist ye not that I must be about my Father's business? And they understood not the saying which he spake unto them. And he went down with them, and came to Nazareth, and was subject unto them: but his mother kept all these sayings in her heart. . . .'

Nazareth, says Ernest Renan, where Jesus spent his childhood, was one of the loveliest villages in Palestine. The house in which He lived differed little probably from 'those cubes of stone', surrounded with vines and fig trees, 'which still cover the rich parts of the Lebanon', their furniture consisting of 'a mat, some cushions on the ground, one or two clay pots and a painted chest'. In Nazareth the cold is sharp in winter, but it has a wholesome climate; the gardens are fresh and green; the plateau above them is swept by perpetual breezes, and affords a wide prospect of mountain and valley, with a distant view of the sea. The women of Nazareth were of the Syrian type—of a marked grace and beauty. 'This enchanted circle, cradle of the kingdom of God, was for years His world.'

'*More* τυπτω-*ing*' (p. 373).

A prolonged and wretched personal experience is referred to, in the minutest of parentheses, by Robert Burton in the following comment on early discipline from the *Anatomy of Melancholy*. My reference to him as 'sage old Burton', while certainly not intended as an irreverence, is of course in one respect inexcusable, since he was only forty-four when the first edition of the *Anatomy* appeared.

Notes

'Parents,' he says, 'and such as have the tuition and oversight of children, offend many times in that they are too stern, always threatening, chiding, brawling, whipping, or striking; by means of which their poor children are so disheartened and cowed, that they never after have any courage, a merry hour in their lives, or take pleasure in anything. There is a great moderation to be had in such things, as matters of so great moment to the making or marring of a child. Some fright their children with beggars, bugbears, and hobgoblins, if they cry, or be otherwise unruly ... (they) are much the worse for it all their lives. ... Tyrannical, impatient, hair-brain schoolmasters ... are in this kind as bad as hangmen and executioners, they make many children endure a martyrdom all the while they are at school, with bad diet, if they board in their houses, too much severity and ill usage, they quite pervert their temperature of body and mind: still chiding, railing, frowning, lashing, tasking, keeping, that they are *fracti animis*, moped many times, weary of their lives ... and think no slavery in the world (as once I did myself) like to that of a grammar scholar. *Præceptorum ineptiis discruciantur ingenia puerorum*, saith Erasmus, they tremble at his voice, looks, coming in. St. Austin ... calls this schooling *meticulosam necessitatem*, and elsewhere a martyrdom, and confesseth of himself, how cruelly he was tortured in mind for learning Greek...

'Others again, in that opposite extreme, do as great harm by their too much remissness, they give them no bringing up, no calling to busy themselves about, or to live in, teach them no trade, or set them in any good course. ...'

'*Poets begin to rhyme early*' (p. 474).

If not merely a delight in words for their sounds' sake, for their verbal music, but promise also of the power to originate this music reveals itself in childhood, we might expect no less early in life both a delight in music itself and the revelation of some skill in composing it. This indeed is so. The psychologists specify a certain age in childhood for its manifestation, 'often before a child is six'; and many of the great composers have given abundant proof of it. It is not that they were precocious; flowers have their own seasons for coming into bloom. A few of them, it is true, were prodigies—and remained so; most of them began early, and went on. The child, then, 'that hath no music in himself, nor is not moved with concord of sweet sound', though he may not deserve Lorenzo's bitter charges, seems to be unlikely to have this joy in intensity when he becomes a man.

That glorious child, Johann Sebastian Bach, came of a musical ancestry. He lost his mother when he was nine years old, and his father a year later—in 1695. His elder brother, himself an organist, then took charge of him, and, it is said, realizing his genius, locked up in a cabinet a volume of MS. pieces for the clavier, in fear that his expressed interest in them should lead to his becoming too precocious. The child managed to abstract them, and copied them out in secret, and by moonlight. His brother discovered this, and six months' labour of love and ardour was confiscated. He became a chorister in a convent school at Lüneberg, and, when his voice broke, a violinist. When he was eighteen he was given a court appointment at Weimar.

Handel—against the wishes of his elderly and unmusical father, who intended him for the law—took to music as naturally as most children take to honey; and when he was seven or eight years old, was not only writing a weekly composition for his master Zuchau, but could himself make music on the organ, hautboy, clavier and violin. At the age of seventeen he was appointed organist at Halle Cathedral.

When he was four years old, Beethoven was discovered playing his own small music extemporaneously on the harpsichord! His father, a singer and bandsman but a thriftless drunkard, saw money in his prodigy and made a slave of him, keeping him between and after school hours strictly to 'finger exercises', until he wept for woe at the monotony. At the age of nine he was sometimes fetched out of his bed and kept practising into the small hours. An Italian named Zambona, recognizing his rare gifts, then took him in hand, and taught him French, Italian, Latin, and logic. Six weeks afterwards he was reading Cicero's letters. His grandfather, a brilliant musician, had composed as a child nine variations on a march by Dressler. These had been published when he was ten years of age in 1753. Ludwig's first composition appeared when he was thirteen. His first symphony was not produced until he was thirty-one.

Haydn revealed his musical gifts before he was eight years old, having spent the previous two years learning to play the harpsichord and the violin, and to sing. He then became a chorister and, though left to shift for himself 'in the theory of music', he refused to be discouraged. In the next five years he was scrawling compositions as fast as they presented themselves. This was between the ages of eight and thirteen. When he was twenty, his first opera, a comic opera, was performed in public. But then, although Haydn lived to be seventy-seven, he never grew up, as the 'Clock', the 'Surprise' and the 'Toy' symphonies, among the rest of his musical works, clearly prove.

And so, in varying degree of promise and performance, with other famous composers—Verdi, Berlioz, Brahms, Schubert, Chopin,

Notes

Rossini. Either in voice—and what instrument excels that of a boy, glass-clear, effortless, disembodied, like the beauty haunting a solitude, and having no other message but its own pure music—or in executancy or composition, all of them by a definite inclination revealed a natural gift. Wagner, on the other hand, is something of an exception in that he had, rather, a passionate craving for poetry. When he was thirteen years old, he translated as many books of the Odyssey; and a few years afterwards wrote a tragedy in which, since exactly six times as many characters had come to a tragic end as in *Hamlet*, he was compelled to bring in ghosts of the dead to people his stage.

Louis Spohr, after recalling in his *Autobiography* his mother's tears at saying good-bye to her parents before the household's removal to Seesen, when he was two, and also the smell of the whitewashed walls in the new house ('even now I still retain an uncommon acuteness and sensibility'), refers to his singing of duets with his mother when he was in his fourth or fifth year. His father about this time bought him a fiddle at the annual 'Fair'. Elated after his first lesson, and enraptured at the harmony he could produce, he took his fiddle into the kitchen, and to entertain his mother arpeggio'd a chord on its strings so assiduously that she was compelled to drive him out. In his seventh year he astonished his father with a composition for two violins, which he played with his teacher at their musical *soirées*—his reward being the coveted suit referred to on page 181. He soon afterwards set to work on an opera—beginning with a title-page painted 'very finely' in Indian ink. At fifteen, and on a salary of a hundred thalers bestowed on him by the Duke of Brunswick, he was living away from home and taking care of a younger brother aged seven who also showed musical promise.

As for Mozart, the very Ariel of music, at the age of six he was touring Europe professionally with his sister Marianne, who was four and a half years older than he was. I owe the following account of Mozart's childhood, and of *his* marvellous April, to the kindness of a friend, Mr. John D. Hodgkinson.

'As a human being the child Mozart was remarkable for his unaffectedness, together with a striking tenderness of heart. He would ask his friends repeatedly if they loved him and, if in joke they denied it, he was very upset and his eyes would fill with tears. On one occasion he burst into tears in a coach because he had thought of Leitgeb and Schachtner and other absent Salzburg friends. Nevertheless, as a little musician he was something of the disarming prig that Macaulay was at the same age, when in reply to the enquiries of a lady who had spilled

Early One Morning

some hot water on his bare knee, he said, "Thank you, Madam, the agony is somewhat abated".

'At the age of three he climbed to the keyboard and picked out thirds, and for a long time he could not bear the sound of a trumpet at close quarters. When his father, Leopold Mozart, with the aid of Schachtner, the Court Trumpeter, tried to break him of this terror, he almost fainted, and they had to desist. With regard, however, to his compositions at this early age, we must treat the published works with considerable distrust. The works not intended for publication, on the other hand, may be taken as being little retouched, and when he was between five and six years old he composed, and himself wrote down in the manuscript book which he shared with his sister Marianne, three minuets (K.1, K.2, and K.3) which are not only exquisite but characteristic.

'The splendid unselfconsciousness of his self-assurance is nowhere better demonstrated than in the story told by Schachtner, of how Leopold found Wolfgang very busy with a pen and a sheet of music paper. Not being much accustomed to it, he stabbed right down to the bottom of the inkwell, but was wholly unperturbed by the blotchiness of his notes. At first, Leopold and his friend were merely amused at the mess, but on examination they found that Wolfgang's "piano-concerto" was not entirely without rhyme or reason but so difficult as to defy execution. "Ah, but it must be practised", he declared. Evidently the young Mozart's ideals of virtuosity were high—and he tried to play what he had written, but could only give them the vaguest idea of what he intended. Yet who could resist so disarming a self-confidence on the part of the little composer, when joined to such diffidence as to his powers as executant?

'Mozart had the strong critical instinct of the intelligent child, and did not hesitate to use it even on the Emperor. When he had discovered the Emperor's taste in music, he insisted on asking for Wagenseil, the court composer—"*he* understands these things". At his appearance he explained, "I am going to play one of your concerti; you must turn over the pages for me."

'When he was seven years old he came to London and he still retained the same childish unaffectedness. Daines Barrington, the English musician who put him through various tests, relates that in the middle of them a favourite cat paced into the room, and Wolfgang could not be induced to come back to his musical examination for some time; and that while Barrington was talking to Leopold, he stalked round the room with a cane as hobbyhorse.

'Yet his first—and for him so independent—attempt at a piano con-

Notes

certo is characteristic of his musical achievement. In this, at any rate, Mozart the child foreshadowed the man. The keyboard was after all his first instrument, and it is significant to find that at a time when both he and Haydn were fumbling in the symphonic form, he was capable of masterpieces in the concerto form (such as the Pianoforte Concerto in E Flat—K.271), which, as Goethe said of Haydn's string quartets, can be supplemented, but cannot be surpassed. Even to the violin, the second virtuoso instrument of his childhood, he is rarely guilty—save in the "Magic Flute"—of greater unfaithfulness than that of muting it, together with the other strings, as in the second movement of his last symphony, the so-called "Jupiter".'

Even in infancy, I have read, children have been known to sing a few notes in sequence, to make a vestigial tune of them, and the mere imitation of an overheard note of music implies a complicated process. The lady who of her lovingkindness taught me to use my small singing-voice when I was young, and to gloss over a bad 'break' in it, and to whom, with much else, I owe *largo, allegro* and *legato,* had been blind from early childhood, and she too had this gift. I remember her playing over to me a setting of the *Te Deum* which she had memorized in St. George's Chapel at one hearing of it, and she once declared to me that she had been overheard wailing out the first few bars of our national anthem in her cradle!

How can we explain the above facts concerning the great composers except by assuming that the desire for music—the purest of the arts—and a delight in it, are innate, and await for their revelation only the attaining of the means and the medium. This purely spontaneous joy is the wonder. The acquisition of musical science is adult's play by comparison. Children, too, of a natural 'ear' and taste, a taste, above all, that has not been blunted or abused, a taste which though it may be refined cannot surely be instilled, will discover in childhood preferences in music that will continue until the end of their lives. Will they not prefer the best if the best is available?

To judge only from my own experience, the finest pictures may fail in so direct an entry and welcome into a young mind, and the great masters in this art seem strange and alien until later in life. But this may depend to a great extent on opportunity; for the children who love colour, and delight in pattern and form, thus love and delight early—during the first ten years, the specialist declares. I took pleasure in crude but lively cuts, and worse; but can also recall in detail several engravings of the old masters in a large volume, bound in red, which was bestowed on me in early childhood. It seems to be only in the nature of things

577

that the composers whom one delighted in most as a child should delight one most in later life.

Lord Berners tells us in *First Childhood* that listening to music held at first no charms for him. When, as a child, he was taken to a village concert he 'created a violent disturbance and had to be removed'. This reminds me of a friend who was being inspected by his Bishop, Dr. Temple, before ordination. To placate, he said, this formidable catechist, he mentioned that an aunt of his had determined at the last moment not to embark on a certain ship bound for the Antipodes. 'The ship was lost, my lord, with all souls on board. Was not that a wonderful manifestation of God's Providence?' 'I never knew your a'nt,' was the Bishop's reply. So too there are concerts and concerts. 'One day, however,' Lord Berners continues, 'I unearthed in the library at Arley an old volume of "Pieces for the Harp," compositions which seemed to consist for the most part of arpeggios, glissandos and cadenzas. My imagination was strangely moved by the sight of these black waves of notes undulating across the pages, and, having collected all the blank sheets of paper I could find, I set to work to cover them with imitation cadenzas. At first I omitted staves and clefs, for it was chiefly the notes and the heavy triple and quadruple lines of the notation that stirred my fancy with their forms almost architectural in design. In the beginning there was only a faint connection between these symbols and any idea of tone, but after a while, helped no doubt by the romantic character of the titles, they came to suggest surging waves of melody and rhythm, an ideal music of which, as yet, I had had no conscious experience. . . .'

A child of five, whose name I may not mention, painfully insisted on his thumb and little finger stretching a full octave on the piano, not merely to master the interval, but in order to complete the chords he wished to play. The transposition of simple tunes from key to key came, it seems, naturally to him. His subtlety of observation was brought to notice by his recognizing and naming one by one a large number of gramophone records, not by reading their titles, since he could not read at all, but by distinguishing the appearance of the lettering on them, the spacing, the margins, the shimmer of the light, and any other characteristics in which records differ one from another. He was discovered intently watching the changing play of the light reflected in the panels of a piano—a proceeding which his grandmother had observed in his father at about the same age.

If we can recall what ridiculous pleasure we derived as children from the veriest daub or scrap of our own handiwork, we shall the better realize what their first music must have meant to these child musicians.

Notes

Here was their life on earth—and, like intrinsic treasure trove, this revelation for its glory.

'*A colour all its own*' (p. 512).

Marked originality in habits, manners, and views is the usual equipment of a 'character', and, though it is unlikely to be conspicuous in childhood, it may, as with Coleridge, be stirring even then. When it is combined with an extreme vigilance of mind and the energy to validate its theories by enquiry and experiment, a Francis Galton is the unique result.

Firmly and picturesquely buttressed by his ancestry, he was, if not the inventor of the science of Eugenics, at least the originator of the term, and largely also the begetter of the intelligence test. He had so firm a faith in heredity that he believed a new race might be created, 'possessing on the *average* an equal degree of quality and intensity as in the exceptional case'. He was himself such a case nonpareil, but was yet so blessedly convinced of his own sanity that he did not hesitate to endanger its reputation in the eyes of the dull. The tenacity with which most of us conceal our feeble wanderings from the norm—whether downwards or even upwards—is due to little better than a conceited caution.

Egged on by the confession made to him by George Bidder, the son of the famous 'calculating boy', that he 'habitually saw numbers in his mind's eye, ranged in a peculiar form', Galton began enquiries on his own account. A preliminary catechism of the members of his club to this end invariably met with a more or less contemptuous negative. He disdained contemptuous negatives; and the result was a highly original and enlightening chapter on mental imagery in his *Enquiry into Human Faculty*.

He collected accounts of hallucinations and of phantasms—in some cases the wreckage of dreams—and concluded that the 'visionary tendency', which is usually laughed or jeered out of children into some obscure lumber-room of their minds, and with risks to *their* sanity, is much more common 'among sane people than is generally suspected'.

To 'envisage' insanity, Galton started one day on his morning's walk from Rutland Gate, imagining, as he went on his way, that by everything and everyone he was being *spied* upon. When, he tells us, he reached the cabstand at the east end of the Green Park, every horse on the stand, either with pricking ears, or with ears no less suspiciously unpricked, seemed to be watching him, and it was hours before 'this uncanny sensation wore off'. He had triumphed, and at how small a cost! To fathom the unholy power of idols, he 'made believe' with himself that 'Mr. Punch' was possessed of divine attributes. 'The effort gradually succeeded', and he long retained feelings towards that 'universal provider' of British amusement at which the orthodox would gape. 'Poor Humanity! I often feel that the tableland of sanity upon which most of us dwell, is small in area, with unfenced precipices on every side, over any one of which we may fall. . . .'

Even in his youth he had tried to substitute automatism for will; and nearly suffocated himself by taking breath only when he gave himself the order. 'I had a terrible half-hour.' He also invented spectacles for reading under water, and states that while reclining in his bath, he used to get so deeply interested in his chosen author that he sometimes *forgot* to breathe, and was in danger of drowning. This reminds me that a few years ago, during a serious illness, owing no doubt to a real difficulty in doing so, I became convinced that *only* by taking thought could I breathe at all. But for a little argument with my doctor, this conviction might well have been the end of me. One critical night I discovered, too, that I could pour water down my throat without the usual spasmodic 'swallowings'. Until, I believe, Sir Richard Burton had habituated himself to this feat, he dared not venture even in flawless disguise on his pilgrimage to Mecca!

Later in life, during the University Boat Race, and owing to the steamboat on which he had embarked colliding with the Old Battersea Bridge, Galton was flung into the Thames. He clung on to a piece of wreckage, and in this extremity firmly and flatly refused to promise a sovereign to a boatman who offered to rescue him for so modest a fee. 'I was able to resist extortion.'

Soon after he went to Birmingham General Hospital, in 1838, he began experimenting with medicines, beginning, alphabetically, to take minute doses of all that were included in the pharmacopœia. But at C, after two drops of Croton Oil, he desisted.

Charles Babbage, from childhood onwards, was yet another character, and so incessantly busy a bee that his books brim over with his own peculiar honey. Loaded with honours at last, though with one exception they came from abroad, he was convinced that straws in childhood unfailingly point to what the prevailing wind of the afterlife will be. When he was about ten years old, he discovered that *occupation of the mind is such a source of pleasure that it can relieve even the pain of a headache*—his own italics. Later he found he could forget a 'tediously wearing' toothache by reading *Robinson Crusoe*. Yet another flaming tribute to Rousseau's literary idol.

He had been only a twelvemonth at school when he planned with a friend to creep down at three o'clock in the morning, light the school-room fire, and work until half-past five. To one bigger boy he had 'the cruelty' to refuse a share in this manœuvre, and deeply regretted it ever afterwards. With another, *the* Frederick Marryat, he waged a pro-longed battle of wits to prevent his waking in time. But Marryat finally won. Interlopers began to come in; and, when fireworks superseded study, the end soon followed. Yet another bright idea was to mix a large quantity of treacle with a quart bottle of cognac, the property of a Russian parlour-boarder, which Marryat said was excellent stuff. After this orgy the boys went to prayers.

Babbage was a venturer on Newton's ocean as practical as he was original:

'One evening I was sitting in the rooms of the Analytical Society, at Cambridge, my head leaning forward on the table in a kind of dreamy mood, with a Table of logarithms lying open before me. Another member, coming into the room, and seeing me half asleep, called out, "Well, Babbage, what are you dreaming about?" to which I replied, "I am thinking that all these Tables (pointing to the logarithms) might be calculated by machinery".'

Apart from his books, he published some eighty papers and pamphlets; on such diverse subjects as the Calculus of Functions, Games of Chance, the Diving Bell, Porisms, the Moon, Neptune, Cipher Writing *et cetera* and *ad infinitum*.

Boys or children with such appetites as these, whatever in the economy of the universe they may finally represent, tend to be dismissed by their uncles, masters and schoolfellows as cranks. They may themselves not be aware what voice is enticing them on, or whither; yet still they follow. I have heard so wise an observer of the young as Dr. Phelps declare in an address (he was then Provost of Oriel, and it is the only prize-giving address I can remember), that in his view the crank is usually the most promising boy in a school. He knows what he wants to do and does it. And how is one to draw a distinction between the delights incident to a man's chosen life-work and those of a boy's 'hobby'? He, too, labours for love, and, like every fine craftsman and artist, chiefly for love. Once money begins to dictate, the imp within is apt to sulk at its bonds, and becomes a most ingenious eel in procrastination.

Some years ago I met a small boy round about nine years old who purely for his own pleasure had become an expert as an observer and critic of motor cars. On a walk one morning his father clapped a hand over his son's eyes and enquired, 'What is going on behind us?' After listening an instant, he replied, 'A Rolls-Royce is overtaking an old Ford.' Or was it vice versa? In either case, he was right. I then asked if he thought I could acquire a really sumptuous Rolls-Royce, a vehicle that not even a Maharaja could disdain, for a certain sum of money? He burst out laughing. 'Why you could get a beauty *much* cheaper than that!' Now most boys share his skill; but what of Shelley's 'stinks' and other crazes?

Of such kind are nascent cranks and hobbyists, and some of them attain at last to the rank—very much coveted, though never by mere coveting attainable—of English 'characters'.

My 'surgeon superintendent' grandfather, I cannot forbear adding, had a son, Herbert, to whose memory in my childhood I was devoted, though he had died young many years before I was born. Even before his teens, or so it seems to me, he hinted at the rudiments of a 'character'. One moonlight night of *her* childhood my mother woke to see him rising up on his bed, a tenpenny nail which he had withdrawn from under his pillow in his hand. This, with the back of a hairbrush, he proceeded to hammer into the wall. 'We *must* be *tidy*, Lucy', he explained.

Having caught a few eels, which his father much relished as a break-fast dish, he found after a while his early morning fishing for them in the Woolwich Dockyard both uncertain and wearisome. He set to work, made a lively little collection of them, and to save trouble stored them in the water cistern, out of which one presently made its way into the household supply pipe!

St. Teresa, when she was thirteen years of age, was completely mas-tered by her passion for reading sentimental and romantic books of chivalry: 'I thought I could never be happy without a new book.' About six years before, coveting the joys of Paradise, she had run away from home at daybreak one morning with her brother Rodriguez, who was four years older than herself. After secret deliberations, they had decided, begging their way thither for the love of God, to seek the country of the Moors, there to be beheaded, in martyrdom. The fugi-tives ran into the arms of an uncle on the bridge over the Adaja at Avila and were brought home. Rodriguez, Adam-wise, blamed 'la niña'; Teresa defended herself with: 'I ran away because I wanted to see God, and one cannot do that without first dying.'

My uncle Herbert as a child had far more mundane motives in a similar escapade. Early one day he decamped with his sister Lucy, armed with a half-sovereign which had been given to her by her father for a birthday present. He had promised to show her London. And he so prudently expended her present—on the Abbey, the Tower, St. Paul's, and a bun-shop or two—that when, after dark, the pair of them safely reached their consternated home again, his father, a martinet, let him off a thrashing.

Notes

Experimenting with gunpowder and a toy brass cannon, he blew off his sister's eyebrows and the top of his own thumb; whereupon to postpone facing the music for a while, he took a boat and rowed her about the dockyard. From infancy he was quick in resource. He was sorely in need of water one morning to scrub out a cupboard which had been handed over to him by his mother as a private preserve. But he was strictly forbidden to use any water from the tap. When she returned home from her morning walk—there was the cupboard, as clean as a whistle, and not yet dry. 'Where did you get the water from, Herbert?' she demanded sternly. A faint flush crept over the seraphic face. 'It was God found the water, mamma.'

If the gods are incredibly gracious, it will be a rare happiness for his aged nephew to meet some day on the remote outskirts of the Elysian Fields this extremely youthful uncle, who died when he was scarcely out of his eel-days, and, so far as literacy goes, cannot himself have been much more than demi-doctor of the Rudiments. He will long since have made himself at home there.

The whole of Dickens and a large part of the great English dramatists is a direct or oblique tribute not merely to English character but to English characters. One can hardly, even nowadays, enter a railway carriage, or sit at ease by the sad sea waves, without fixing one's eye on some fellow creature who if he (or she) is as odd or egregious or strange or sinister or formidable as he looks, could not, if he would, an extremely chequered and moving tale unfold. More especially would this be the case perhaps concerning his childhood. Obvious Hydes of the milder kind are not less arresting than probable Jekylls; and what a hard, scheming, adventurous, or open-hearted life admits to in a human face is not the less eloquent because it is mute. By no means all the failures in life have failed to stay happy and sanguine; by no means all the successful are as prosperous in the spirit as they may look in the flesh. Now and then, one may even share with a stranger a page or two concerning the past that will certainly never see print; but such chances are likely to be few. The private eccentrics appear to be more reticent even than the majority of the flawlessly conventional. A temporary insanity, also, revealing itself in no perceptible symptom, may not perhaps be rare. Whether rare or not, it will probably be endured in silence and never alluded to.

Miss Stella Benson had an amusedly discerning eye for eccentric children. In reading of early memories, again, one speculation is bound to present itself. If any of these children could have exchanged circumstances, William Hutton, let us say, with Roger North, Perdita with Miss Cobbe or Elizabeth Grant, John Ruskin with Holcroft, Emily

Early One Morning

Shore with Marjory Fleming, Edmund Gosse with Byron, what would have been the result on both sides? It is the old problem of nature and nurture.

'The children of Paules' (p. 514).

The sarcasms levelled by Hamlet at the boy actors of Shakespeare's time—the airs and graces they put on, and their shrill voices—was current coin. In the induction to Ben Jonson's *Cynthia's Revels*, acted in 1600, a boy personates a gallant. He sits down to smoke and to criticize the play, a whiff of tobacco at every pause: 'By this light, I wonder that any man is so mad to come to see these rascally tits play here. They do act like so many wrens or pismires; not the fifth part of a good face amongst them all. And then their music is abominable—able to stretch a man's ears worse than ten pillories, and their ditties most lamentable things, like the pitiful fellows that make them—Poets.' But as Mr. Percy Simpson, from whom this quotation has been borrowed, points out in *Shakespeare's England*, although some of these boy-actors were children who could not sing, or had voices 'too small' or were of 'stature too low' for women's parts, 'it is clear that they played them well', and were well paid for doing so. About a third of the actors in *A Midsummer-Night's Dream* 'must have been children'.

This innate gift in young children for acting, resembling the dramatic make-believe without which his characters cannot 'come alive' in the mind of the writer of fiction, tends, it appears, like that of the calculating boy, to wane as selfconsciousness supervenes. That it is by no means rare, and even to a degree which in an adult might be characterized as genius, is shown by the many recent films in which children have taken a dominant part. The difficulty here is to distinguish art from nature, talent from training. The swiftest means of understanding a fellow creature is by an act of sheer intuition, the transporting of oneself not only into his 'place', but into his very being, as it were. It is a faculty *allied* to that of acting and of creating characters. But whether, in this, we pretend, or *are*; create, or evoke from within, is, like so many other mysteries connected with childhood, an abstruse enquiry.

   .   .   .   .   .

One of my early memories is that of being allowed to sit up to supper one late evening in a strange house. The room is low-pitched and lit with candles. Against the wall, opposite to me, though I cannot see it, is, I know, a large glass case in which stands a dog—a stuffed Pomeranian, 'motionlessly observing the world he has left behind him'. He is a deceased pet of the family's. Between the glass case and myself, on

584

Notes

the other side of the damask tablecloth, is seated a rather sleek dark gentleman, with a steady, *looking* eye, and a neat, nut-shaped head. He intercepts my sleepy but excited stare, lifts a small fork from the table, exposes it to me full in my gaze for an instant; and the next, lo, it has vanished! He is conjuring. . . . A century of solitude with the Oxford Dictionary would fail to give me words wherewith to describe the precise rapture and amazement of that moment.

In this book, the position has been reversed. Its fork has been Childhood, and the faltering aim of its pages, long after my own childhood's evanishment, has been to bring it back again. Alas, my conjurer and I parted, and for ever, a few minutes after *his* fork disappeared; and I had no opportunity to entreat him to give me a lesson in his art.

Yet of the three of us there that night, it was the Pomeranian dog, I fancy, that was the worst off. He could neither make magic, nor marvel at it. And that, it seems, is one of the ever-present dangers of adulthood. Unlike a child, who will fall into a reverie of delight merely in drifting his heels through the thin fallen leaves of autumn, it will sit and sit in the presence of life's conjurer—all his legerdemain, even at its simplest, beyond the least fear of discovery or final explanation; and yet, never even a momentary hint of mystery or wonder may lighten the bold glassy eye. It is as if it had been stuffed. But how? And when?

'When all is done and said, in the end this shall you find,
The most of all doth bathe in bliss that hath a quiet mind.'

ACKNOWLEDGMENTS

*

My thanks are due in the first place to friends who have very kindly allowed me to include in this book contributions that have not hitherto appeared in print: to Lady Cynthia Asquith and Mr. Simon Asquith; Mrs. Aubrey de Sélincourt and 'L.E.'; Mrs. Ellis Roberts; Miss Lilian Sheldon; my sister, Mrs. Roger Ingpen; Professor Lascelles and Mr. Michael Abercrombie; Sir Sydney Cockerell, who very kindly consented to my using his notes on the early life of William Morris, and quoting an unpublished letter by Dante Gabriel Rossetti; and to Mr. John D. Hodgkinson.

For permission to reprint copyright material I am also very much indebted to the following authors and publishers: Mr. J. Redwood Anderson; Lord Berners, and Messrs. Constable & Company, Limited; Mr. Laurence Binyon; Dr. Allen Brockington and Messrs. Chapman & Hall, Limited; Mr. Gerald Bullett; Miss Anna Robeson Burr (Mrs. Charles Burr); Monsieur Emile Cammaerts and Messrs. George Routledge & Sons, Limited; Mr. W. H. Davies; Mr. A. Hugh Fisher; Miss Rachel M. Fleming and the Controller of H.M. Stationery Office; Mr. Colin Francis; Mr. Wilfrid Gibson; Dr. Bernard Hollander and Messrs. George Allen & Unwin, Limited; Lady Horner, Mr. Romilly John, Madame Tamara Karsavina and Messrs. William Heinemann, Limited; Mr. Frank Kendon and the Cambridge University Press; Miss Ethel Mannin and Messrs. Jarrold & Sons; Mr. Edwin Muir and Messrs. J. M. Dent & Sons, Limited; Mr. Kenneth Muir and the Oxford University Press; Mr. H. W. Nevinson and Messrs. James Nisbet & Company, Limited; Sir

Early One Morning

Henry Newbolt—both for contributions from *My World as in My Time* and for two poems by Mary Coleridge; Mr. Fred Pasley, Mr. Herbert Read, Sir William Rothenstein and Messrs. Faber & Faber, Limited; Miss Evelyn Sharp and Messrs. John Lane, The Bodley Head, Limited; Mrs. Edith Wharton and Messrs. D. Appleton & Company; Mr. H. G. Wells and Messrs. Victor Gollancz, Limited.

For permission to use extracts from books that are mentioned in the following list my thanks are due to Mr. J. D. Duff and the Oxford University Press (*Years of Childhood,* by Sergyei Aksakoff), Mr. R. W. Chapman (in respect to his text of *Volume the First,* by Jane Austen); The Massachusetts Historical Society and Messrs. Houghton Mifflin Company (*The Education of Henry Adams*); Messrs. Longmans, Green & Company, Limited (*A Mind that Found Itself,* by Mr. Clifford Whittingham Beers); Messrs. George Allen & Unwin, Limited (*Matter & Memory* by M. Henri Bergson and *The Story of My Life,* by Augustus Hare); Messrs. Chapman & Hall, Limited (*A Girl's Life Eighty Years Ago,* by Eliza Southgate Bowne); Mrs. Bridges and the Clarendon Press (*The Shorter Poems of Robert Bridges*); the literary executors of Rupert Brooke, and Messrs. Sidgwick & Jackson, Limited; the Bibliophile Society, Boston (*Elizabeth Barrett Browning*); Messrs. Frederick Warne & Company, Limited (*The One I Knew Best of All,* by Mrs. Hodgson Burnett); the trustees of Samuel Butler and Messrs. Jonathan Cape, Limited (*The Note-Books of Samuel Butler*); Messrs. J. M. Dent & Sons, Limited (*Reminiscences,* by Thomas Carlyle, in the 'Everyman Library'); Mr. Edmund Blunden (*John Clare, Poems*); Major Dodgson (*The Life & Letters of Lewis Carroll*); the literary executors of Frances Power Cobbe, Messrs. George Allen & Unwin, Ltd., (*Life of Frances Power Cobbe*); Mr. Bernard Darwin and Sir John Murray (*The Life and Letters of Charles Darwin*); Mr. Frank Sidgwick (*The Complete Marjory Fleming*); Messrs. Methuen & Company, Limited (*Memories of My Life,* by Frances Galton, *Letters,* by Victor Hugo, and *The State and Its Children,* by Gertrude M. Tuckwell); Dr. Philip Gosse and Messrs. William Heinemann, Limited (*Father & Son,* and *The Life & Letters of Edmund Gosse*); Sir John Murray (for extracts quoted by permission from *The Letters of Queen Victoria*; also for extracts quoted from *The Life & Letters* of Robert Browning; *Memoirs of a Highland Lady,* by Eliza-

588

Acknowledgments

beth Grant; and *Autobiography*, by Samuel Smiles); Messrs. Seeley Service & Company Limited (*Autobiography*, by Philip Hamerton); Mrs. Hardy (*The Early Life of Thomas Hardy*); Mrs. Hardy and Messrs. Macmillan & Company, Limited (*Collected Poems of Thomas Hardy*); Messrs. Macmillan & Company, Limited (*The Life & Letters of Thomas Huxley, Notes of a Son & Brother*, by Henry James, and *Charlotte Mary Yonge, Her Life & Letters*); the Houghton Mifflin Company (*Life & Letters* of Oliver Wendell Holmes); the Macmillan Company, New York (*The Psychology & Pedagogy of Reading*, by Dr. Edmund Burke Huey, and *The Psychology of Childhood*, by Drs. Naomi Norsworthy and Mary Theodora Whitley); Mrs. Dallyn (*Alice Meynell, A Memoir*); Messrs. Ernest Benn, Limited (*The Ghost Ship*, by Richard Middleton); Miss Denny Oliphant and Messrs. William Blackwood & Sons, Limited (*Autobiography* by Mrs. Oliphant); Mrs. Hall Thorpe and Messrs. Constable & Company, Limited (*Works* of Thomas Love Peacock); the Ruskin Literary Trustees and the Publishers of the only authorized editions of his works, Messrs. George Allen & Unwin, Limited; Messrs. Harper & Brothers (*Autobiographical Notes on the Life of William Bell Scott*); Messrs. George Routledge & Sons, Limited (*A New Model of the Universe*, by Mr. P. D. Ouspensky, and the *Journal* of Emily Shore); Messrs. C. A. Watts & Company, Limited, and the Trustees of Herbert Spencer (*Autobiography*, by Herbert Spencer); Mr. Lloyd Osbourne (the *Letters* of Robert Louis Stevenson); the Trustees of the late Lord Tennyson (*A Memoir, The Devil and the Lady*, and *Unpublished Early Poems*, and particularly to Mr. Charles Tennyson to whom I owe my introduction to the two last-mentioned volumes); Miss Edith Craig and Miss Christopher St. John (*Memoirs of Ellen Terry*); Mr. Wilfrid Meynell (*The Life of Francis Thompson*, by Everard Meynell); Mr. Robert Harborough Sherard and Messrs. T. Werner Laurie, Limited (*The Life of Oscar Wilde*); Mrs. Charles Burr and Messrs. Macmillan & Company, Limited (*The Journal of Alice James*); Mr. and Mrs. J. L. Hammond and Messrs. Longmans, Green & Company (*The Town Labourer 1760-1832*); Messrs. George Bell & Sons, Limited (*Dante Gabriel Rossetti*); Messrs. Chapman & Hall, Limited (*My Life*, by Alfred Russel Wallace); and to Messrs. Macmillan & Company, Limited (*The Child in the House*, by Walter Pater).

Early One Morning

For permission to use a translation of the letter on page 428 I am obliged to the Librarian of the Bodleian Library and to Mr. Strickland Gibson; and, for their information concerning certain portraits of children, to Mr. E. Glasgow, Keeper and Secretary of the National Gallery, and Mr. C. K. Adams, Assistant Director of the National Portrait Gallery.

For invaluable help and counsel in the preparation of this book, I have to thank many friends: Miss F. L. Rudston Brown; Mr. Erik Batterham; Mr. J. B. Chapman; the Rev. R. H. Couchman and certain contributors to the *Choristers' Magazine*; Mr. Anthony Crossley, Mademoiselle M. Daunser, Mrs. M. E. Dean, Miss Margot Dick, Miss Eleanor Doorly, Mrs. George Gordon, Lady Irvine (to whom I owe my introduction to the *Journal* of Emily Shore); Mr. Edward Garnett and Mr. David Garnett; Mr. R. N. Green-Armytage; Mr. John Hampden; Mr. Roger Ingpen; Mr. Geoffrey Keynes; Mr. G. E. Manwaring; Mr. E. H. W. Meyerstein; Mr. Frank Morley; Mr. C. Denis Pegge; Mr. Leonard Rice-Oxley; Miss H. K. Sheldon; Miss Melian Stawell; Mr. Anthony Thompson and Mr. Rupert Thompson.

If by inadvertence any copyright material has been included in these pages, for the use of which permission has either been unobtainable or has not been granted, or if I have failed to return thanks where thanks are due, my sincere apologies will, I hope, be accepted.

Finally and especially, I wish to thank my sister Mrs. Roger Ingpen for preparing the Index; my friend Mr. Forrest Reid, not only for many quotations from *Apostate* (Messrs. Constable & Company, Limited), but for his great kindness in reading nearly the whole of my proofs; and Miss Olive Jones, to whose patience, care, and skill the book itself owes more than can be expressed.

ACKNOWLEDGMENTS

FOR THE AMERICAN EDITION

*

For permission to use extracts from books published in the United States that are mentioned in the following list, thanks are due: Farrar & Rinehart (*First Childhood*, by Lord Berners); Charles Scribner's Sons (*A Girl's Life Eighty Years Ago*, by Eliza Southgate Bowne; *Father and Son*, by Edmund Gosse; *The One I Knew The Best OF All*, by Mrs. Hodgson Burnett; *Letters*, of Robert Louis Stevenson; and *The Life of Francis Thompson*, by Everard Meynell); Harper & Bros. (*The Life and Letters of Edmund Gosse*); Oxford University Press (*The Shorter Poems*, by Robert Bridges, and *English Girlhood at School*, by Dorothy Gardiner); E. P. Dutton & Co., Inc. (*The Note-Books of Samuel Butler; Reminiscences*, by Thomas Carlyle; *Theatre Street*, by Mme. Karsavina; and *Autobiography*, by Samuel Smiles); D. Appleton-Century Company (*The Life and Letters of Lewis Carroll; The Life and Letters of Charles Darwin; Autobiography*, by Herbert Spencer; and *A Backward Glance*, by Edith Wharton); Dodd, Mead & Company (*The Story of My Life*, by Augustus Hare; *Autobiography*, by Mrs. Oliphant, and *The Journal of Alice James*); Houghton Mifflin Company (*Letters*, by Victor Hugo, and *The Life and Letters of Robert Browning*); Aries Press (*The Ghost Ship*, by Richard Middleton); Harcourt, Brace and Company, Inc. (*Changes and Chances*, by H. W. Nevinson); Alfred A. Knopf (*A New Model for the Universe*, by P. D. Ouspensky); Longmans, Green & Co. (*The Letters of Queen Victoria*).

INDEX
OF PROPER NAMES

★

Index of Proper Names

Index of Proper Names

Index of Proper Names

Index of Proper Names

Index of Proper Names

Index of Proper Names

Index of Proper Names

Index of Proper Names

Index of Proper Names

Index of Proper Names

Index of Proper Names

Index of Proper Names

Index of Proper Names

Index of Proper Names